The Study of Islamic Origins

Judaism, Christianity, and Islam – Tension, Transmission, Transformation

Edited by Patrice Brodeur, Alexandra Cuffel, Assaad Elias Kattan, and Georges Tamer

Volume 15

The Study of Islamic Origins

New Perspectives and Contexts

Edited by Mette Bjerregaard Mortensen,
Guillaume Dye, Isaac W. Oliver, and Tommaso Tesei

DE GRUYTER

ISBN 978-3-11-125872-0
e-ISBN (PDF) 978-3-11-067549-8
e-ISBN (EPUB) 978-3-11-067556-6
ISSN 2196-405X

Library of Congress Control Number: 2021941715

Bibliographic information published by the Deutsche Nationalbibliothek
The Deutsche Nationalbibliothek lists this publication in the Deutsche Nationalbibliografie; detailed bibliographic data are available on the Internet at http://dnb.dnb.de.

This volume is text- and page-identical with the hardback published in 2021.
Typesetting: Integra Software Services Pvt. Ltd.
Printing and binding: CPI books GmbH, Leck

www.degruyter.com

Contents

III Early Islam and the Qur'ān: Social, Political, and Religious Contexts

Mette Bjerregaard Mortensen, Guillaume Dye, Isaac W. Oliver, and Tommaso Tesei

Introduction

The following volume presents select proceedings from the second and third gatherings of the Early Islamic Studies Seminar (EISS).[1] Both conferences took place in the beautiful Italian locations of Pratolino, near Florence, on June 12–16, 2017 and Gazzada (at the Villa Cagnola), near Milan, on June 16–20, 2019, respectively. They were hosted by the Enoch Seminar with the generous support of the Alessandro Nangeroni International Endowment.

The Enoch Seminar was founded by Gabriele Boccaccini in 2001 with the aim of gathering specialists of Second Temple Judaism from across the globe to share their research at conferences, which function more like small workshops, in which scholars intensively debate their ideas during several days in intimate settings that favor collegiality and dialogue. At its foundation, the Enoch Seminar sought – and still seeks – to recover both the integrity and the diversity of the intellectual traditions of the Second Temple period by breaking down the artificial and confessional barriers that have long divided its study. For too long the study of Second Temple Judaism(s) had been eclipsed by biblical studies, which naturally tends to prioritize the investigation of canonical literature. The Enoch Seminar offered ancient Jewish writings, movements, and traditions, which had hitherto been anachronistically sandwiched in between the "Old Testament" and the New Testament (and even the Mishnah), a central platform where they could be considered in their own right. Writings such as the sectarian documents discovered among the Dead Sea Scrolls or the so-called Old Testament Pseudepigrapha, received their due attention, shedding light on a period in which the Jewish Scriptures were still being composed.

Very soon, the Enoch Seminar incorporated the study of Christian origins within its scope of inquiry, since Christianity emerged from Second Temple Judaism and originally constituted but one of its many distinctive forms of expressions. This inclusion has coincided with recent trends in the scholarly investigation of

1 The proceedings of the first EISS meeting hosted by the Enoch Seminar will be published as Guillaume Dye, ed., *Early Islam: The Sectarian Milieu of Late Antiquity?*

Mette Bjerregaard Mortensen, Université libre de Bruxelles
Guillaume Dye, Université libre de Bruxelles
Isaac W. Oliver, Bradley University
Tommaso Tesei, Duke Kunshan University

https://doi.org/10.1515/9783110675498-001

Judaism and Christianity in antiquity, which sees tremendous heuristic value in studying the diverse traditions of these two entities in light of one another. Once upon a time, ancient Christianity was merely studied against a Jewish "background" (and consequently its Jewish character remained relegated to the back), while the New Testament was neglected as an important source for understanding Second Temple Judaism. The reigning assumption posited that Judaism and Christianity inevitably morphed into separate, discrete entities early on, that Jewish-Christian relations in antiquity were marked solely by antagonism and division. Studies on the New Testament/early Christianity and Second Temple Judaism were carried out in isolation from one another, with each field represented by its own academic programs, conferences, journals, specialists, jargon, and so on.

In recent decades, however, new intellectual paradigms have radically altered the historical understanding of Christian and rabbinic origins and redefined the disciplinary landscape that had hitherto reified the boundaries between Jews and Christians in antiquity. While admitting that relations between (some) Jews and (some) Christians were certainly marked by confrontation early on, many scholars now firmly situate primitive Christianity within its original Jewish environment while avoiding teleological views that reduce the complexity and diversity of early Jewish-Christian relations to inevitable fracturing and opposition. It is now more readily acknowledged that Jewish and Christian identities remained fluid, diverse, and in the making throughout Late Antiquity, with patristic and rabbinic "orthodoxies" proving formative rather than normative during this period. These newer perspectives have in turn necessitated greater collaboration between specialists from different fields, which the Enoch Seminar has readily been able to foster.

In more recent times, the Enoch Seminar has expanded its purview even further to encompass the study of Islamic origins. The genesis of this endeavor began in June 2013 in Brussels, during a meeting between Guillaume Dye and Carlos A. Segovia, who were soon joined by Emilio González Ferrín, Manfred Kropp, and Tommaso Tesei as board of directors to create the Early Islamic Studies Seminar (EISS). With the support of the Enoch Seminar, the EISS has since then organized three Nangeroni Meetings devoted to the Qur'ān and early Islam, convinced that the historical investigation of early Islam should be performed in a similar way as early Judaism and Christianity. In the inclusive spirit promoted by the Enoch Seminar, the EISS has accordingly invited to its meetings specialists in Qur'anic and Islamic studies as well as those who specialize in the Hebrew Bible, Second Temple Judaism, the New Testament, and other related fields. Indeed, the time seems ripe to appreciate the formation of the Qur'ān and early Islam in light of Jewish, Christian, and other late antique traditions (Zoroastrian, Manichean, etc.). Perhaps, this type of inquiry will yield new unexpected results about the origins of Islam that will in turn enrich our understanding of the rich religious landscape of Late Antiquity. With the publication of this volume, we hope to offer promising glimpses into this kind of undertaking.

The first part of this volume begins with two essays that address theoretical and methodological issues concerning the study of early Islam. In "The Current Status and Problems of Islamic Origins: The View from the Academic Study of Religion," Aaron W. Hughes reflects on the current state of the study of Islamic origins. For Hughes, the study of Islamic origins entails a study of Jewish and Christian origins as well, since the Arabian Peninsula and Eastern regions of the burgeoning early Islamic Empire rose from and shaped a socially porous world that extended from the period of Late Antiquity. Islam, in other words, did not merely emerge from previously established monotheisms in the area but played an active role in their self-definition. Yet institutional, epistemological, and political issues beset this kind of historical enterprise, and it is to these problems that Hughes turns with the hope of showing how the academic study of religion can promisingly illuminate Islamic origins. Throughout, Hughes argues that the academic study of Islamic origins should be reframed as a late antique problem in which Islamic origins learns from and contributes to antique and late antique social formations.

An example of such a late antique framing of the question of the origins of Islam can be found in Stephen Shoemaker's contribution to the volume where he emphasizes the importance of genre by comparing the Qur'an to its late antique predecessors. This question has long vexed scholars of the Qur'ān who have struggled to find a suitable category for what *prima facie* seems like a rather heterogeneous text. In "A New Arabic Apocryphon from Late Antiquity: The Qur'ān," Shoemaker argues that the difficulty in determining the Qur'ān's genre is not a consequence of its exceptionality but due to its amalgamation of various literary forms: oracular proclamations, hymns, instructional discourses, narrative evocations, legislative and paraenetic texts, battle exhortations, and polemical discourses. There is, however, a precedent in Late Antiquity to this type of assemblage that could shed light on the question: biblical apocrypha. Shoemaker defines biblical apocrypha broadly. They are not a genre per se but texts that maintain a solid connection with the writings of the Hebrew Bible and the New Testament (and other related writings), often focusing on persons and events from these books while occasionally expanding on them. This broad yet inviting definition allows for the inclusion of the Qur'ān in a late antique environment that makes sense. Shoemaker accordingly qualifies the Qur'ān as a biblical apocryphon written in Arabic, given its connection to biblical texts, which it originally sought to supplement rather than supplant, and inclusion of different genres.

The second part of this volume includes studies that assume some of these methodological and theoretical assumptions since they investigate the Qur'ān in light of Semitic languages, the Hebrew Bible, the New Testament, rabbinic literature, targums, Syriac Christian materials, and other ancient Near Eastern sources. This section begins with Manfred Kropp's "Body Parts Nomenclature in the Qur'anic Corpus," which provides a preliminary discussion of the vocabulary used in the Qur'ān to describe the human body and its constituent parts based on cognate languages and precedents set in biblical studies.

Ever since Abraham Geiger, a number of scholars have singled out notable affinities between the Qur'ān and extra-biblical Jewish (rabbinic and targumic) traditions. The Qur'anic retelling of Queen Sheba's visit to Solomon finely illustrates this overlap. The Qur'anic account resembles 1 Kings 10:1–13 yet differs with significant details: in contrast to the biblical story, the Qur'ān presents Solomon testing the Queen with the help of his servant *jinn* and emphasizes the Queen's conversion to proper religious practice, Solomon's magical powers and ability to speak the language of birds, and the oddities of the land of Sheba. Geiger and others accounted for these extra-biblical materials in terms of dependence by pointing to rabbinic and targumic parallels, claiming that Muḥammad relied on Jewish tradition that was used in the creation of the Qur'ān. However, in "The Queen of Shebah in the Qur'ān and Late Antique Midrash," Jillian Stinchcomb reconsiders these parallels in a way that is not limited to dependence but points to a matrix of common discourses in the seventh-century Arabian Peninsula between nebulously Islamic and Jewish groups that later came to be sharply defined against one another.

Another notable parallel between the Qur'ān and rabbinic tradition involves the depiction of Mount Sinai during the revelation of the Torah to Israel. At several points, the Qur'ān states that God seemingly raised Mount Sinai before the Israelites. This depiction finds precedent in rabbinic midrash, which posits that God actually lifted the mountain over the Israelites. Isaac W. Oliver assesses this parallel in "Standing under the Mountain: Jewish and Christian Threads to a Qur'anic Construction." In this instance, the Qur'ān does indeed seem to be indebted to rabbinic midrash. Yet the Qur'anic writer(s) did not simply "borrow" rabbinic materials. In the Qur'ān, the mountain is deployed for rhetorical effect to serve specific interests. Ultimately, Mount Sinai is raised in the Qur'ān *against* the Israelites, and by extension all Jews who do not accept the Qur'anic revelation, who are depicted in good Christian anti-Judaic fashion as rebellious sinners perpetually opposed to God's message and commissioned messengers. This image of the non-believing Jews contrasts with the Qur'ān's literary construct of the ideal believers who readily accept the new revelation granted to its Messenger.

The Qur'ān's interaction is not limited to rabbinic Jewish tradition but conversant with Christianity in many complex ways as well. In "Mapping the Sources of the Qur'anic Jesus," Guillaume Dye seeks to uncover the Qur'anic perspective(s) on Jesus. In some passages of the Qur'ān, Jesus appears as a secondary character, standing along other prophets such as Noah, Abraham, Ishmael, Moses, and John. This inclusion precludes any simplistic qualification of the Qur'ān as simply mirroring a Jewish, a Christian, or a Jewish Christian environment, since the mention of Jesus dismisses a purely Jewish background, while the rather marginal role devoted to Jesus apparently excludes Christian and Jewish Christian backgrounds. Other passages in the Qur'ān, however, highly esteem Jesus. He is not only a preeminent prophet but also miraculously born from the virgin Mary, a *wunderkind* endowed with prophetic revelation, uniquely gifted with the holy spirit, and an eschatological harbinger. The Qur'anic Jesus, therefore, embodies several paradoxes: he is a secondary and primary figure; he seems Christian and yet unchristian (at least from an "orthodox" viewpoint); he is both a figure of convergence with Christians and of cleavage with Christians and especially Jews. For Dye, this paradoxical Jesus is the result of several reworkings in the Qur'ān that reflect the confessional identity of the burgeoning movement of the *mu'minūn*. Interestingly enough though, virtually all of the main attributes of this composite Jesus can be found in Christian Scriptures, notably in Acts 2:22–24. Dye accordingly proposes that *literati* with a good command of Christian tradition used Christian texts, Acts 2:22–24 included, to subvert competing views and establish a Jesus that reflected their own convictions.

In "The Natural Theology of the Qur'ān and Its Late Antique Christian Background: A Preliminary Outline," Julien Decharneux reads the Qur'anic call to observe the divine signs in the cosmos in light of Christian late antique natural theology. Toward the beginning of the third century CE, some Christian thinkers entertained the idea that divine knowledge could be reached through the contemplation of Scripture and Nature. This theological reflection flourished especially in the fourth century among various Christian authors. Decharneux suggests that the Qur'ān's call to contemplate the universe is structurally in line with this Christian tradition of divine *theôria*. Beyond structural and thematic homologies, the Qur'ān develops specific motifs and notions within this contemplative framework – not least, the notion of "divine signs" – which could well hint at a connection with East Syrian traditions of divine contemplation.

The studies in the third and final part of this volume consider the social, political, and religious circumstances in which the Qur'ān emerged and how its founding members were active players in their immediate contexts. This section opens with a joint study by Gilles Courtieu and Carlos A. Segovia titled, "Q 2:102, 43:31, and Ctesiphon-Seleucia New Insights into the Mesopotamian Setting of the

Earliest Qur'anic Milieu," which proposes Mesopotamia as a hypothetical setting for the earliest Qur'anic milieu, detecting allusions to Ctesiphon-Seleucia in Q 43:31 and 2:102. In a similar explorative vein, Peter von Sivers situates the Qur'ān in Mesopotamia and Arabia Petraea between the Sasanid and Roman empires during 602–630 ("Prophecies Fulfilled: The Qur'anic Arabs in the Early 600s").

Wherever the Qur'ān may have originated, it seems certain that the Persian Empire wished to exert its influence upon the Arabian Peninsula. This is demonstrated by Boaz Shoshan in "The Sasanian Conquest of Ḥimyar Reconsidered: In Search of a Local Hero," who reassesses the Arab and non-Arab sources that relate the Persian conquest of the South Arabian kingdom of Ḥimyar around 570. The evidence shows that the Sasanians had clear strategic interests in controlling this region. Boaz, however, calls for a more critical approach toward the early Arabic sources treating this event, since they have aggrandized and Islamized their local hero, Sayf of the Dhū Yazan clan, in the buildup leading to the Persian conquest.

In "Contextual Readings of Religious Statements in Early Islamic Inscriptions," Marcus Milwright offers interpretations of selected early statements of religious belief in the monumental Arabic epigraphy of the seventh and first half of the eighth centuries from the Arabian Peninsula, Syria, and Palestine. He argues that their creation was meaningfully informed by past practices that can be explained by the resilience of craft traditions in the Middle East, on the one hand, but also by the need to project messages in a visual language that was comprehensible to its target audiences, on the other hand. Thus, the ways in which early Arabic inscriptions were understood by their audiences went beyond the textual content to encompass the material and aesthetic dimensions, the location, and the broader context of late antique epigraphic and oral culture. Muslim writers such as Ibn al-Kalbi and al-Hamdani indirectly support this proposition, since they propagate the idea that the profession of faith itself existed in Arabia prior to the time of the Prophet. While this may be a literary fiction, Milwright avers that statements about the oneness of God were in use among the "Abrahamic faiths" of Late Antiquity.

Archaeological work carried out in the last decades is slowly shedding light on the cultural environment of the pre-Islamic inhabitants of Arabia. Interestingly enough, newly discovered inscriptions name a number of gods, including the eight pagan deities mentioned in the Qur'ān. In "The Gods of the Qur'ān: The Rise of Ḥijāzī Henotheism during Late Antiquity," Valentina A. Grasso provides an intertextual analysis of these pre-Islamic inscriptions and the Qur'ān. She argues that stories of pre-Islamic idols have been restructured in the Qur'ān in order to emphasize Muḥammad's prophetic career within a polytheistic environment. However, Muḥammad may very well have built his career on the existing basis of a flexible henotheism and subsequently professed a strict monotheism similar to those of the surrounding scriptural communities that developed autonomously in the distinctive Arabian milieu.

The volume concludes with a social critical analysis of early Islam by Ilkka J. Lindstedt, "'One Community to the Exclusion of Other People': A Superordinate Identity in the Medinan Community." How did the early (seventh–eighth century CE) Muslims categorize and view themselves? And what did their conceptions of themselves and the others entail? Lindstedt addresses these questions utilizing theories from the field of social psychology, especially "the social identity approach." The social identity approach argues that group identification and conduct are a central component of the human experience. Lindstedt sees this social process at play both in the so-called Constitution of Medina and the Qur'ān. The Constitution of Medina, which Lindstedt views as an authentic document of the Prophet Muḥammad, recategorized the Jews and the gentile Believers of Medina under one common ingroup identity yet allowed members of both groups to retain their tribal and religious identities as subordinate ones. By contrast, the Medinan stratum of the Qur'ān articulates a sense of a community that is not very accepting of subgroup identities. Individual Jews and Christians are accepted as Believers but their identities as Jews and Christians remain suspect. Nevertheless, passages such as Q 3:110–115 contain both positive and negative depictions of the Jews and Christians. Thus it is misguided to simply posit that later Qur'anic strata repudiated Jews and Christians even if earlier Qur'anic passages seem more accepting of subgroup identities.

The second and third EISS meetings were the result of the contribution of many institutions. We would like to acknowledge in particular the contribution of the Michigan Center for Early Christian Studies and the Alessandro Nangeroni International Endowment. The partnership they have formed with the Department of Near Eastern Studies and the Frankel Center for Judaic Studies of the University of Michigan has secured the continuity of the project and the future of the Enoch Seminar for years to come.

As stated earlier, the climate of collegiality and friendship is an important component of the Enoch Seminar experience. During our stay in Florence, we visited the Monastery of Monte Senario at Bivigliano, accompanied by the President of the Associazione Biblica Italiana (ABI), Luca Mazzinghi. One of our sessions took place at the Synagogue of Florence (hosted by Rav Joseph Levi) and had lunch there. We were then invited to attend interfaith meetings at Syracuse University and the Florence School of Theology organized by local Jewish, Christian, and Muslim organizations, and a delegation of ours was received by the mayor of Florence at Palazzo Vecchio. In Gazzada we had a beautiful trip to Palazzo Borromeo,

Isola Bella on Lake Maggiore, and a guided tour of the park and interiors of Villa Cagnola.

A special thanks goes to Gabriele Boccaccini, director and founder of the Enoch Seminar, as well as Jason Zurawski, who served as the secretary. They not only took care of the logistics of the conferences but also actively contributed to the discussions, bridging the EISS group with the work of specialists in Second Temple Judaism and Christian origins and the general activities of the Enoch Seminar.

Finally, we would like to dedicate the volume to the memory of Michael Bonner, professor of Islamic Studies at the University of Michigan, who was one of the most enthusiastic members of the group and passed away just a few days before our third EISS meeting, for which he was about to present a paper. We are deeply indebted to his work and friendship.

I Early Islam and the Qur'ān: Methodological Considerations

Aaron W. Hughes

The Current Status and Problems of Islamic Origins

The View from the Academic Study of Religion

Introduction

The aim of this paper is to offer a second-order reflection on the current state of Islamic origins. It takes its cue from my colleague Herb Berg, who claimed several years ago that "to discuss Islamic origins, and as a result early Islamic history and civilization, is to discuss theory and method."[1] Theory and method, as I understand those two terms as a scholar of religion, represent those scholarly acts whereby we include and exclude, frame and marginalize, and, in the process, prioritize and arrange data we imagine to be relevant (or not). It is not just the canvas, to switch metaphors, upon which we paint our masterpieces, but also the colors, brushes, and brushstrokes that we chose to employ. In so doing, theory and method ideally attune us to the political, ideological, and genealogical agendas that inform our scholarly acts, and that reflection upon these agendas will, again ideally, prevent us from simply assuming default positions towards our data.

We also have to realize, however, that the terms "theory" and "method" are amphibolous. This is a large part of the problem. They mean different things to different people. Those who engage in questioning the veracity of traditional sources or are perceived (by others) as undermining them as anachronistic *and* those who decry such a posture as insensitive or, worse, as (neo-) Orientalist both appeal to narratives and hermeneutics that have distinct histories and entanglements. They all, in other words, make claims to being theoretically sophisticated. To avoid such simplifications or dead-ends, however, theory and method must revert to even greater "meta" levels if we are to sort profitably through these competing claims and their guiding ideologies. This is something that the following paper seeks to do in order to get at what I perceive to be some of the current problems that potentially beset the field.

1 Berg 2013, x.

Aaron W. Hughes, Department of Religion and Classics, University of Rochester, Rochester, NY

https://doi.org/10.1515/9783110675498-002

The absence of incontrovertible data, the problems associated with dating traditional sources, not to mention the often vociferous debates in modern scholarship derived therefrom would all seem to make the subject of Islamic origins a perfect subject for "theory and method" in the above sense of the term. The reconstruction of religious origins (be it Islam's or that of any other religion), after all, is ultimately about positing theories and using a variety of methodologies to support them. How we construct the origins of Islam, if it is not already obvious, is as much a modern question as it is a historical one.

Here, however, we run into a problem, one that will meander as a leitmotif through the following pages, to wit, the collision between competing epistemologies. Classically, for example, Muslims have approached their own tradition, and by extension all human knowledge, through a given set of categories (e.g., *hadīth, ta'rīkh, adab, taṣawwuf*). Some of these categories, and their frames of analysis, have translated into Western scholarship, whereas others have not. Sometimes indigenous terms are seen as translating directly (e.g., *adab* as literature, *ta'rīkh* as history). Other times, the study of such terms is brought in via analogues (e.g. the Qur'ān being studied as "scripture" or as "literature" along the model of biblical studies). Despite such translations and analogs, however, most of those involved in the contemporary study of Islam in the Western academic setting still rely on, engage with, or otherwise work in the shadow of these classically-constituted topics.[2]

From this collision emerge a set of tensions and fractures wherein we are currently stuck and upon which we would do well to reflect. Much of what will follow will focus on the faultlines of this collision, providing both egregious and more serious minded examples. It strikes me at the outset, however, that the more we make the study of Islamic origins into a late antique problem or even a Jewish or Christian problem, and less an Islamic one, the more productive we will be in our endeavors.[3] This, *at least in theory*, avoids some of the problems that have beset this topic in the larger field of Islamic studies.[4] A quick comparison of the *Cambridge History of Islam* (1970) with that of the *New Cambridge History of Islam* (2010) bears this out. The opening chapters of the latter text, unlike the former one, peel back the boundaries of the late antique

2 See the comments in Daneshgar and Hughes 2020.
3 And I think we are beginning to see the dividends of such an approach in the work of, among others, Howard-Johnston 2010; Wood 2010; Booth 2014; Penn 2014, and Fowden 2015.
4 See, for example, the comments in Griffith 2013, 54–57.

period and, in so doing, situate the rise of Islam against it, specifically Iranian and Roman rivalry in and around Arabia. This also means an explicit acknowledgement that the religions of late antiquity – Islam, Judaism, Christianity, Zoroastrianism, Manicheanism, among others – are less hermetically sealed or discrete phenomena than they are porous markers of social identity that developed both individually and interactively.[5]

Within this context, I place my own study of Islamic origins, for example, against the backdrop of the complexity of ascertaining the identity of the Jews of South Arabia and the Ḥijāz prior to the time of Muḥammad. Such an intellectual reorientation brings the fluidity of identity and the porosity of social formations that we see in the late antique period into the early Islamic one.[6] On account of this complexity and overlap, the story of Islamic origins, for me, is in part also the story of Jewish origins (and, by extension, Christian origins) as the chaotic social worlds of the Arabian Peninsula and the Eastern parts of the burgeoning early Islamic Empire created the foil to the eventual construction of orthodoxy in all of these religions.[7] It is not simply the case that Islam emerges as the sum of other, more established, monotheisms in the area, but that its appearance played an active role in their self-definition. Self-definition, in other words, works in both directions.

My goal here, however, is much more modest in scope: it is to survey and taxonomize some of the more recent trends in the study of Islamic origins, highlighting some of the problems – epistemological, institutional, and political – that currently beset the field. Though it is certainly worth mentioning within this context that much of this literature, some of which is historically very sophisticated, risks reifying religion or projecting later forms onto the period in question. Within this context, I wish to show how the academic study of religion can illumine the study of Islamic origins and vice versa.

Moving Forward, Moving Backward

We do not have to be sociologists of knowledge to admit that ancient problems have sets of overlapping and intertwined frames that stretch from the contemporaneous to the contemporary. Such frames need to be cautiously disentangled from one another, if in fact they can, and subsequently examined both for what

5 Seen also the important edited collections of Neuwirth, Sinai, and Marx 2010, and Reynolds 2010.

6 Fowden 2015, e.g., 3–5.

7 See, for example, Hughes 2017b.

they tell us about the past and what they tell us about those who created them. Even once we do this, however, there is still no guarantee that we will arrive at the so-called truth. The study of Islamic origins, like the study of so much, presents both a historical and a hermeneutical problem. While we all want to know what really happened, we have to be aware of the dark places to which such desires take us.[8]

In this regard we are consistently hamstrung by our own shortcomings. If we work centripetally, from the late antique side, Islam emerges as the sum of its preexistent parts. Without rehearsing all the arguments here, ones that I imagine are familiar to most working in this rather small field, Islam's origins have – at least since the 1970s (if not actually before) – been associated with a Jewish sect,[9] a Christian one,[10] or as arising in the Negev desert as opposed to the Ḥijāz.[11] Others have sought to make the final redaction of the Qur'ān later than tradition has it by seeing it as contemporaneous with the Sīra,[12] or as even postdating the Sīra and Ḥadīth.[13]

The other centripetal force, moving in the opposite direction, assumes, in the words of Jacob Neusner, that "the sources at hand were stenographic reports of things people really said, or a TV camera recording of things people really did."[14] It is fair to say that it is this approach that functions normatively, especially in the field of Religious Studies where I abide, where it tends to function theologically or reverentially.[15] The best most recent example of this approach may be found in *The Study Quran* (2015), which I shall examine in greater detail below.

Both of these tendencies, however, work with the assumption that there is a center – call it a momentous or revelatory event, a religious experience, or a

8 Such dark places are further exacerbated, in the words of Nicolai Sinai and Angelika Neuwirth, by the facts that "There is no critical edition of the [Qur'ān], no free access to all of the relevant manuscript evidence, no clear conception of the cultural and linguistic profile of the milieu within which it has emerged, no consensus on basic issues of methodology, a significant amount of mistrust among scholars, and – what is perhaps the single most important obstacle to scholarly progress – no adequate training of future students of the Qur'an in the non-Arabic languages and literatures and cultural traditions that have undoubtedly shaped its historical context" (Sinai and Neuwirth 2010, 1).

9 E.g., Crone and Cook 1977.

10 E.g., Luxenberg 2000.

11 E.g., Nevo and Koren 2003.

12 E.g., Wansbrough 1977.

13 E.g., Rubin 1995.

14 Qtd. in Hughes 2016, 186.

15 This is an approach of which I have been so critical over the years. See, for example, Hughes 2012 and Hughes 2015.

nascent polity – that we believe we can adumbrate with some degree of clarity. Moving temporally in both directions, these tendencies or hermeneutics bypass one another in the night and when they do periodically stop to take notice of the other, their tones are often both accusatory and recriminatory – one side charges the other as being gullible and the other retorts with the pejorative claim of "neo-Orientalism" or the more in vogue "Islamophobia."[16] In focusing on this center, however, much has been missed on the margins, places to which it seems we are beginning to turn our attentions to with some degree of regularity.

The study of Islamic origins belongs in the late antique period. That much is, I would hope, clear. What becomes more problematic is in what disciplines do we locate this study: history, archaeology, epigraphy, literary analysis, comparative religion, or some combination thereof? Yet, no one is able to master all of these fields. Relatedly and within this context, it strikes me that a not insignificant question is whence do we derive our data: archeology and inscriptions, literary analysis of the Qur'ān and its exegetical literature, or late antique cognate literature? Answers to these and related questions have a real bearing on what data are deemed significant (or not) and what theories of Islamic origins will look like. Relatedly, what is the relationship of the Qur'ān to Islamic origins? Was there, for example, an Ur-Qur'ān, was the Qur'ān a much later project, or, was it the end result of a slow process of collection and coagulation? Concomitantly, with what social groups was early Islam in dialogue: Christianity (if so, what kind? monophysitism? monotheletism?) or Judaism (rabbinic or some form of Ḥimyarite Raḥmanism), Manicheism, Zoroastrianism, or hybrid versions of all or some of these? All of these are basic, if not fundamental, questions. However, many of them have not been solved or, in some cases, even addressed with significant academic rigor.

Orientalism Redux

The study of Islamic Origins is a fraught field and not just for the reasons listed by Sinai and Neuwirth in n. 8 above. The current obsession with Islam, including the notion that one can use the Qur'ān to somehow arrive at *the* Muslim mentalité, is omnipresent. Here we must not lose sight of the fact that our work in Islamic origins is often picked up by political commentators for a host of

16 See, for example, Lumbard, whom I shall discuss below. Vernon Schubel has written a lengthy essay wherein he accuses me of this, see Schubel 2014.

nefarious reasons.[17] This means that it is incumbent upon us to pay attention to the "meta" issues that structure some of the discourses in our field. These include, but are certainly not limited to, the ideologies (whether explicit or implicit) of funding agencies, conference sponsors, academic presses, and so on.[18]

While I certainly do not want to use him as an exemplar of a scholar in our field, I think it worth mentioning Ibn Warraq, whose work shows the unhealthy triangulation of Islamophobia, scholarship, and suppressed agendas that is one of the hallmarks of a very real trajectory in the field. I mention him for two reasons. The first is that several of his edited collections (e.g., 1998, 2000) repackage the work of previous generations of Orientalists – by, e.g., Abraham Geiger (1810–1874), Arthur Jeffery (1892–1959), Charles Cutler Torrey (1863–1956) – for a new readership. With titles such as *The Origins of the Koran: Classic Essays on Islam's Holy Book* (1998), such works take traditional Orientalist scholarship, which may very well have been important, if not revolutionary, in the early part of the twentieth century, and present it as somehow new and novel, and of course, filtered through his own political agenda. Within this latter context, he provides the following as his rationale for editing the collection: "all Muslims revere the Koran with a reverence that borders on bibliolatry and superstition," for "us in studying the Koran it is necessary to distinguish the historical from the theological attitude. Here we are only concerned with those truths that are yielded by a process of rational enquiry, by scientific examination."[19]

In itself, I think we can all agree that this locution is problematic. However, it may also be worth pointing out that Ibn Warraq is also connected to the Institute for the Study of Early Islamic History and the Quran (Institut zur Erforschung der frühen Islamgeschichte und des Koran) or Inarah that was founded at the University of Saarbrücken in 2007. Its German webpage describes the Institute in the following terms, "The concern of Inarah is purely scientific and

---

17 With Islamic origins, the story is often much different from the origins of other religions (e.g., Lester 1999, 43–56; Ibn Warraq 2002; Higgins 2008; all the attention that the discovery of the "Birmingham Quran" generated). The assumption here is either that (1) understanding the origins of the Qur'ān somehow provides insights into "*the* Muslim mind," or (2) that Muslims misunderstand their scripture because, for example, they erroneously think, following Luxenberg's thesis, that Arabic virgins are nothing more than Syriac grapes.

18 The following three paragraphs rework material published in Hughes 2017a.

19 Ibn Warraq 1998, 9. This becomes even more transparent when we see who some of Ibn Warraq's bedfellows are. In his foreword to Robert Spencer's *Did Muhammad Exist?*, for example, which he calls an "impeccably researched book," Ibn Warraq continues that Spencer has "reminded us that it [is] time to get back to real scholarship unhampered by political correctness and the corruption of Saudi money." Any attempt to "get back to real scholarship unhampered by political correctness" is, of course, a political claim.

could be summarized as the establishment of an historical-critical method in Islamic Studies." I note, however, that the semantic weight put on terms like "purely scientific," are certainly meant to imply an objectivity and a disinterest that is not one of the hallmarks of scholarship on religious origins. Indeed, the page goes on to argue that, despite the fact that it does "not pursue any political or missionary goals," "if this is ultimately conducive to the emergence of an enlightenment in Islamic culture, this would only be a side effect of our research, albeit a pleasing one."[20] The connection between the secular study of Islamic origins and an attempt to reform Islam is certainly not new as witnessed by the translation of Günter Lüling's *Über den Urkoran: Ansätze zur Rekonstruktion der vorislamisch-christlichen Strophenlieder im Koran* (Erlangen, 1993; 1st ed. 1974) into English as *A Challenge to Islam for Reformation: The Rediscovery and Reliable Reconstruction of a Comprehensive Pre-Islamic Christian Hymnal Hidden in the Koran under Earliest Islamic Reinterpretations* (published in Delhi, 2003).[21]

At any rate, the Institute runs seminars and workshops devoted to Islamic origins every two years, and has published several books on the topic,[22] English translations are published by Prometheus Books in Amherst, NY, the same publisher of many of Ibn Warraq's books (not to mention new editions of those by John Wansbrough). Perhaps not surprisingly, we find the name of Ibn Warraq among the list of researchers associated with the Institute. Indeed, the Institute is in part funded by the Center for Inquiry (CFI; which, among other things, owns Prometheus Books), anonymous donors associated with CFI, and Sam Harris' Project Reason.[23]

"Money doesn't talk," to invoke the Nobel-laureate Dylan, "it swears." And, I think we need to be aware of this.

---

20 The webpage may be found at http://inarah.de (accessed May 19, 2021).

21 "Sollte dies letztendlich dem Entstehen einer Aufklärung im Islamischen Kulturkreis förderlich sein, so wäre dies nur ein Nebeneffekt unserer Forschung, wenn auch ein erfreulicher." Indeed, the translation of the German into English through an Indian press is reminiscent of the translation of Geiger's *Was hat Mohammed aus dem Judenthume aufgenommen* (Bonn, 1833) to *Judaism and Islam* (Madras, 1835) by F. M. Young, "a member of the Ladies' League in Aid of the Delhi Mission," to aid in the proselytization of Indian Muslims.

22 E.g., *The Hidden Origins of Islam: New Research into Its Early History*, eds. Karl-Heinz Ohlig and Gerd-R. Puin (Amherst, NY: Prometheus, 2010).

23 http://www.centerforinquiry.net/blogs/entry/second_inarah_conference_in_otzenhausen_germany_on_early_islamic_history_an/ (accessed May 19, 2021).

Decolonializing the Project

One extreme deserves another, albeit from the other side of the continuum. What is the alternative to such a pessimistic approach to Islamic origins, one with its implicit attempt at nudging Islam along the path of reformation? It seems that we all know at least one, to wit, that approach which parrots back what the early sources tell us. Only now we again encounter a new twist to that narrative. No longer content just to use these sources as stenography, we now see the invocation of post-colonial rhetoric to "de-colonialize" the Qur'ān, namely, to remove it from the so-called Orientalist gaze that has always defined it in Western discourse.[24] I worry that this may well be the main default position to the type of approach witnessed in the previous section. In a presentation delivered at SOAS entitled "Decolonializing Qur'anic Studies," Joseph Lumbard complains that the study of the Qur'ān in the western academic context has not taken sufficient account of, to use another *bon mot* of this hermeneutic, more "indigenous" (c.f., n.d.: 4) approaches. According to him,

> Favoring Euro-American approaches and interpretations of the Qur'an pervades the field to the extent that many of the revered studies of the Qur'an in the Western academic tradition have failed to take account of the cumulative development of knowledge that lies at the heart of the academic enterprise. Even factual evidence that would complicate contemporary theories is either explained away or willfully ignored.[25]

For Lumbard, there is an easy way out of the abyss: to engage the traditional Muslim sources. This "lack of cumulative engagement with the classical tradition leads to unnecessary methodological diffusion, delay[s] and impair[s] the methodological refinement of the field".[26] Whereas Ibn Warraq had compared the stagnant indigenous approaches to the Qur'ān with the critical and scientific approach of the West, and found the former lacking, Lumbard inverses the comparanda:

> This epistemic privileging of Euro-American approaches ensures that indigenous Muslim approaches to the text are often relegated to the meager status of 'information supply.' They are seen as efficacious when they serve the purposes of, and can be incorporated into, the Euro-American epistemological hierarchy. But in themselves, they are not permitted to generate alternative epistemic discourses, much less call into question the dogmatic foundations of those who selectively draw vittles from the larder of the classical Islamic tradition.[27]

24 See, for example, Manzoor 1987; Iqbal 2008; Lumbard.
25 Lumbard, 3.
26 Lumbard, 4.
27 Lumbard, 4.

All those engaged in Islamic origins chronologically – i.e., from late antiquity to the rise of Islam – instead of in reverse chronological order are, in the words of Lumbard, "colonialists."[28] The invocation of post-colonialism and post-modernity, not to mention grossly reified epistemes, here become the handmaiden of resistance against the types of Islamophobia discussed in the previous section.

Lumbard's complaints are certainly nothing new. Such a "decolonialized" approach would, it goes without saying, make the study of Islamic origins forbidden to many of us, at least in the politically correct contexts of Religious Studies. Again, though, reactions such as Lumbard's may well push the study of Islamic origins back into the late antique period, where it surely belongs. It may also mean that the place of critical research into Islamic origins may well, paradoxically, have very little place in the future of Islamic studies, and instead ought to be carried out within the context of Late Antique Studies.

We see this contraction in the recently published *Study Quran*, edited by Nasr, Lumbard, et al.[29] The focus of this work, as the General Introduction makes clear, is "on the Quran's reception and interpretation within the Muslim intellectual and spiritual tradition."[30] Nor does the work "limit [the Quran] to a work of merely historical, social, or linguistic interests divorced from its sacred and revealed character."[31] For this reason, as Nasr makes clear, *The Study Quran* "would have to be a *Muslim* effort and that, although the book would be contemporary in language and based on the highest level of scholarship, it would *not* be determined or guided by assertions presented by non-Muslim Western scholars and orientalists who have studied the Quran profusely as a historical, linguistic, or sociological document, or even a text of religious significance, but who do not accept it as the Word of God and an authentic revelation."[32]

This utterance is telling. Non-Muslim "assertions" are paired with those "authentic" scholars who accept the Qur'ān as the Word of God. The Qur'ān has to be studied as existing outside of "historical, linguistic, or sociological" contexts. The Qur'ān, on this reading, has no history because it exists outside of history. A look at the essays that accompany *The Study Quran*'s table of contents

---

28 Lumbard, 6.

29 This is related to the fact that, as Lumbard notes in his aforementioned article, the "composition of the editorial board [of the *The Encyclopaedia of the Qur'an*] which is composed of mostly non-Muslim scholars. Those who are Muslim or of Muslim background are thoroughly entrenched in Euro-centric epistemologies" (4n.10). *The Study Quran* is thus intended to reverse the hierarchy.

30 Nasr et al. 2015, xxiv.

31 Nasr et al. 2015, xxvi.

32 Nasr et al. 2015, xl.

is telling. There we see chapters devoted to "How to Read the Quran" (Ingrid Mattson), "The Quran in Translation" (Joseph Lumbard), "Traditions of Esoteric and Sapiential Quranic Commentaries" (Toby Mayer), "The Quran and Islamic Art" (Jean-Louis Michon), "The Quranic View of Sacred History and Other Religions" (Joseph Lumbard), and "Quranic Ethics, Human Rights, and Society" (Maria Massi Dakake). While Lumbard's second essay has the word history in it, it is modified by the adjective "sacred." Heilsgeschichte, to invoke the nemesis of this crowd, John Wansbrough, is a subgenre of literature, and the most appropriate way to analyze it is by means of form criticism, redaction criticism, and literary criticism – in much the same manner that they have been used in the study of early Christianity and Judaism.[33] Yet, not surprisingly, there is no talk of mundane history here, let alone the types of criticism that are invoked to study other religions' scripture. Then again, we should not be surprised at this when Nasr can write in his introduction that

> No sacred scripture of which we have knowledge speaks more about the cosmos and the world of nature than does the Quran, where one finds extensive teaching about cosmogenesis, cosmic history, eschatological events marking the end of the cosmic order as it now exists, and the phenomena of nature as revealing Divine Wisdom.[34]

The Qur'ān, on this reading, is sui generis, existing on a different plane of existence than other sacred scriptures. Because of this, the tools of literary criticism cannot be applied to it. This is certainly legitimate as the opinion of a religious believer, but it is anathema to a scholarly approach that asks questions such as, where do texts come from? Such a question, as Lumbard has already informed us, however, is one that is saturated in orientalism, colonialism, Islamophobia, and the silencing of the indigenous. It is unfortunate that this approach has largely become the regnant one in the North American academy, especially in Religious Studies, the field from which I write.

A brief comparison with *The Jewish Study Bible* offers interesting insights. Therein we find a whole section devoted to "Backgrounds for Reading the Bible," with essays that include: "The History of Israel in the Biblical Period" (Oded Lipschits); "The Geography of the Land of Israel" (Amitai Baruchi-Unna); "The Archeology of the Land of Israel in the Biblical Period" (Aren Maeir); "The Ancient Near Eastern Background of the Bible" (Jack Sasson); "Textual Criticism of the Bible" (Emanuel Tov), and "The Canonization of the Bible" (Marc Zvi Brettler).

Why have I spent so much time on *The Study Quran*? I do so in order to draw attention to some of the forces those of us interested in Islamic origins are

33 Wansbrough 1987, 14–15.
34 Nasr et al. 2015, xxvi.

up against. This topic is now essentially seen as "un-Islamic" or as part and parcel of the (neo)colonialist project of (neo-)Orientalism. In Religious Studies – one of the primary arenas wherein the study of Islam is located in North America – the topic is virtually non-existent. The key to changing all this, and I certainly do not think I am alone in this respect, is to begin the process of reframing the issue of Islamic origins as a late antique problem as opposed to an Islamic one. The study of Islamic origins, in other words, has to persevere in its desire to shift its traditional emphasis on working backwards from early Muslim sources to working forward from pre-Islamic ones. Islamic origins, in other words, has much to learn from and much to contribute to the conversation of antique and late antique social formations. Thankfully, this approach is slowly becoming more normative (see, for examples, the works listed in notes 2, 3, and 4 above). It means, however, that the topic of critical insights into Islamic origins will increasingly be found in other fields.

"Religion" without Religion

Despite my dissatisfaction with the way Islam is treated within some quarters of Religious Studies, there nevertheless exists a small and critical wing of that field that may well be germane to the discussion of Islamic origins.[35] Within this context, this wing reminds us that there is an overwhelming tendency to use the category "religion" in ways that either intentionally exclude or are unaware of the larger discourse of the category's utility. There is, in other words, a tendency to subscribe to a "world religions" paradigm that employs discrete and essentialized reifications: *x* is Christian, *y* is Jewish, and *z* is somehow Islamic. But if the late antique Mediterranean tells us anything it is that it is very difficult to single out with any degree of accuracy what constitutes an "Islamic," a "Jewish," or a "Christian" idea or trope.[36]

35 Parts of this section rework Hughes 2017a.

36 For example Wasserstrom, a scholar of religion, writes:

> The early Muslims did not borrow their Messiah from Judaism, nor was Jewish Messianic imagery lent by a Jew to a Muslim in the sense that a lender lends to a debtor. Rather, Muslims consciously and creatively reimagined the Messiah. These Islamic rereadings, consonant with the decentralized pluralism of the Jewish redeemer myths, never pronounced one image of the Messiah as definitive. There were, of course, no councils of Judaism or Islam to rule on the officially proper Messiah.

See Wasserstrom 1995, 57.

The very term "religion," as Brent Nongbri has recently argued, may not in fact be as universal as many have traditionally assumed.[37] He argues that we have to be cautious of assuming that people have always carved up the world – for example, a realm of the sacred and one of the profane – in the same manner that we do today. According to Nongbri,

> The real problem is that the *particular* concept of religion is absent in the ancient world. The very idea of "being religious" requires a companion notion of what it would mean to be "not religious," and this dichotomy was not part of the ancient world. To be sure, ancient people had words to describe proper reverence of the gods, but these terms were not what modern people would describe as strictly "religious." They formed part of a vocabulary of social relations more generally.[38]

I would now like to take these theoretical interventions and apply them to Fred M. Donner's *Muhammad and the Believers,* wherein he argues that "Islam began as a religious movement."[39] Donner here sets his analysis between the traditional Orientalist critique that reduces the emergence of Islam to the political *and* the rigid and exclusive interpretation provided by, among others, contemporary Salafists.[40] Interestingly, it is these Salafists that individuals like Lüling and groups like Inārah also seek to confront with the aim of encouraging some form of internal Islamic reformation. Contemporary Salafism and religious literalism, then, would seem to lurk in the background of the academic study of Islamic origins. While Donner is certainly much more sophisticated than the aforementioned, he nevertheless seeks to situate Islam, at its origins, in a highly inclusive and ecumenical environment. While intuitively such a model would seem to make sense, it nevertheless is necessary to interrogate just what terms like "religion," "belief," "monotheism," and "ecumenicism" might have meant in the context of the sixth- and seventh-century Ḥijāz.

For Donner, Islam began as an ecumenical movement of "believers" (*al-mu'minūn*) who recognized the oneness of God;[41] were concerned with the "rampant sinfulness of the world around them and wished to live by a higher standard in their own behavior";[42] and because they were "convinced that the world around them was mired in sin and corruption, they felt an urgent need

37 E.g. Nongbri 2013, 3.
38 Nongbri 2013, 4.
39 Donner 2010, xii.
40 Donner here switches the conversation from those who have also argued that the rise of Islam was an economic and social movement (e.g., Watt 1953 and 1956) or a nationalist and political movement (e.g., Crone 1987).
41 Donner 2010, 58.
42 Donner 2010, 66.

to ensure their own salvation by living in strict accordance with the revealed law, as the judgment could dawn at any moment."[43] Only gradually, Donner maintains, did these *mu'minūn* transform into *muslimūn* as theological agendas and doctrinal teaching were subsequently fleshed out. Until this happened, however, this group of believers was ecumenical and, Donner argues, would have certainly included "pious Christians and Jews."[44]

Without assessing all of Donner's arguments, many are highly speculative. While he frequently invokes the term "monotheism" or "monotheistic," for example, to describe some of the contents of religious belief, what did monotheism look like in the context of the period just before Muḥammad came on the scene? As Jack Tannous has duly noted, the term monotheism is a modern European invention and, while Greek by definition, does not appear in Greek sources before the late medieval period.[45] He, thus asks, echoing the comments of Nongbri cited above, how Christians, Jews and Muslims in the seventh century could have imagined themselves as belonging to categories derived from later centuries. While this does not deny that there were obviously many "monotheistic" elements in Muḥammad's message, it does call into question the utility of exporting later terms and concepts, and retrofitting them onto different times and places. We could say the same thing for other terms that Donner uses, such as "belief" and "piety." This may well be part of our problem, to wit, using later terms and categories to describe earlier eras and epochs. We thus need to be aware of the genealogies of such terms and categories as way to avoid potential distortions.

Another problem with Donner's model is that he wants to situate Christians and Jews into this ecumenical or interfaith community of *mu'minūn*. While this may well have been the case, we also have to entertain the idea that such groups might well have been less attached to discrete religions or religious traditions – again, the stuff of later centuries – and instead part of the same social fluidity. What, for example, were the contours or contents of Christianity or Judaism at this time and in this region? What types of "Jews" or "Christians" would have been attracted to Muḥammad's generic slogans of apocalyptic monotheism? It also ignores, as Michael Penn notes, external sources, such as Syriac and other materials, which tried precisely to mark such religio-ethnic distinctions.[46] The rise of Islam thereby helped to create "orthodoxies" in these other religions while it simultaneously developed in tandem with them.

---

43 Donner 2010, 79.
44 Donner 2010, 71.
45 Tannous 2011, 134–135.
46 Penn 2014, 180–182.

This problem, however, is not confined to Donner. Many who work on this period also work with problematic notions of religion. In his work on Ḥimyarite Jews, for example, G. W. Bowersock is convinced that they "were authentically Jewish,"[47] and that "it has become absolutely certain that the Arabs of Himyar genuinely embraced Judaism as converts."[48] But there are problems with such assessments. What does "authentically Jewish" mean in the context of the fourth century? What does an "Arab-Jew" or "Jewish Arab" mean in such a context? What does it mean to embrace Judaism as a convert, especially outside emerging tannaitic centers such as Yavneh and Usha? And, just as importantly, did more normative centers of Jewish learning embrace them as converts? The answer to the latter question would seem to be negative since neither the Mishnah nor the Talmuds make reference to them. Bowersock can also boldly claim, against the evidence, that "an entire nation of ethnic Arabs in southwestern Arabia had converted to Judaism and imposed it as the state religion."[49] Though he does not, for reasons mentioned, I think we could safely put many of the above nouns in scare quotes: "nation," "ethnic," "Arabs," "conversion," "Judaism," and "state religion."

Even the north Arabian inscriptions, as Robin notes, lack any Jewish liturgical formulae or explicit symbols.[50] Yet, for some reason, based on this lack of firm evidence, we want to make these "Jews" both pious (to use Donner's locution) and/or normative (to use Bowersock's). Robin asks: "La Première [question] est de savoir si ces juifs d'Arabie sont véritablement juifs."[51] Yet, I hope we can appreciate just how problematic such an utterance is. What do real Jews look like in the fourth century, a period prior to the codification and dissemination of the Babylonian Talmud? Why should we assume that what is going on in tannaitic and/or amoraic academies is normative and binding on all Jews at this point in time?

Rather than see "pious" Muslims and Jews – once again, as if we actually know what Judaism or Christianity looked like on the Arabian Peninsula at the time of Muḥammad, let alone what constituted pious versions of each – we need to imagine overlapping social groups: Groups with conceptual vocabularies that helped articulate what was slowly emerging as Islam *and* to which this fledgling Islam simultaneously helped to give definition. This is where and how a critical form of Religious Studies (as social theory), to which I alluded above, may offer some guidance to our collective efforts. It helps us avoid, for example, the traditional Orientalist desire to posit a stable Judaism and Christianity that

47 Bowersock 2013, 83.
48 Bowersock 2013, 84.
49 Bowersock 2013, 4.
50 Robin 2004, 842.
51 Robin 2004, 865.

gives birth to an unstable Islam. All are unstable and it is impossible to pinpoint with any degree of certainty who "owns" what. To use the suggestive language of Daniel Boyarin, what we may well have is groups of social actors, only subsequently defined as Jewish, Christian, and/or Muslim, who inhabited a shared social and intellectual space in which a wide variety of ideas – including messianism and apocalypticism in response to growing political instability, the religious contours of law, a belief in one deity, and so on – were widely distributed.[52]

Religion, on Donner's and others' reading, occupies a place in the late antique period in much the same manner that it does in modernity. It is imagined to exist as a separate sphere of existence, one that is untouched by the so-called political or other spheres. While Donner is certainly correct to posit that Islam was (and is) a movement with what we may today call a deep religious ethos, it was (and is) certainly more than just this. Islam was also a political movement, an economic movement, and even a military movement.

Conclusions

This paper has examined several recent models of Islamic origins. These models are certainly not unique or even decidedly *au courant*. Indeed, several are the products of genealogies that meander back through the centuries. They react against one another as they simultaneously seek to define themselves in the light of the others' perceived darkness. I have here tried to examine some of the theoretical and methodological assumptions behind these competing hermeneutics, while also trying to make the case that a more critical approach found in certain segments of the academic study of religion has much to offer the subject of Islamic origins. Though many in that field unfortunately tend to adopt the more traditional approach of believing all that the early Islamic sources tell us or, perhaps more recently and fashionably, of reading such sources for the insights they provide about the mentalité of early Muslims, there are some (myself included) who think the field of Religious Studies ought to attune us to think about social theory, which includes the creation and maintenance of identity as social processes. The field of critical Religious Studies, then, examines the genealogies of those terms, categories, and discourses we employ in addition to replacing discrete religions with social actors with multiple and overlapping identities.

52 See, for example, Boyarin 2014, 13–16.

Bibliography

Berg, Herbert. 2013. "Preface," ix–xi, in *Method and Theory in the Study of Islamic Origins*, ed. H. Berg. Leiden: Brill.

Berlin, Adele and Marc Zvi Brettler. 2004. *The Jewish Study Bible*. Oxford: Oxford University Press.

Booth, Phil. 2014. *Crisis of Empire: Doctrine and Dissent at the End of Late Antiquity*. Berkeley: University of California Press.

Boyarin, Daniel. 2014. *Border Lines: The Partition of Judaeo-Christianity*. Philadelphia: University of Pennsylvania Press.

Bowersock, G. W. 2013. *The Throne of Adulis: Red Sea Wars on the Eve of Islam*. New York and Oxford: Oxford University Press.

Crone, Patricia. 1987. *Meccan Trade and the Rise of Islam*. Princeton, NJ: Princeton University Press.

Crone, Patricia and Michael Cook. 1977. *Hagarism: The Making of the Islamic World*. Cambridge: Cambridge University Press.

Daneshgar, Majid and Aaron W. Hughes. 2020. "Introduction," in *Approaching Islam: Classical Categories and Modern Scholarship*, eds. Majid Daneshgar and Aaron. W. Hughes. Cambridge, MA: Harvard University Press, 1–8.

Donner, Fred M. 2010. *Muhammad and the Believers: At the Origins of Islam*. Cambridge: Harvard University Press.

Fowden, Garth. 2015. *Before and After Muhammad: The First Millennium Refocused*. Princeton: Princeton University Press.

Griffith, Sidney H. 2013. *The Bible in Arabic: The Scriptures of the "People of the Book" in the Language of Islam*. Princeton: Princeton University Press.

Higgins, Andrew. 2008. "The Lost Archive." *Wall Street Journal*. January 12, 2008. Online at http://www.wsj.com/articles/SB120008793352784631 (accessed May 19, 2021).

Howard-Johnston, James. 2010. *Witnesses to a World Crisis: Historians and Histories of the Middle East in the Seventh Century*. Oxford: Oxford University Press.

Hughes, Aaron W. 2012. *Theorizing Islam: Disciplinary Deconstruction and Reconstruction*. London and New York: Routledge.

Hughes, Aaron W. 2015. *Islam and the Tyranny of Authenticity: An Inquiry into Disciplinary Apologetics and Self-Deception*. Sheffield: Equinox.

Hughes, Aaron W. 2016. *Jacob Neusner: An American Jewish Iconoclast*. New York: New York University Press.

Hughes, Aaron W. 2017a. "Religion Without Religion: Integrating Islamic Origins into Religious Studies," *Journal of the American Academy of Religion* 85.4:867–888.

Hughes, Aaron W. 2017b. *Shared Identities: Medieval and Modern Imaginings of Judeo-Islam*. New York and Oxford: Oxford University Press.

Ibn Warraq (ed.). 1998. *The Origins of the Koran: Classic Essays on Islam's Holy Book*. Amherst, New York: Prometheus Books.

Ibn Warraq. 2002. "Virgins? What Virgins?" *The Guardian* January 11, 2002. Online at https://www.theguardian.com/books/2002/jan/12/books.guardianreview5 (accessed May 19, 2021).

Ibn Warraq. 2012. "Foreword", in *Did Muhammad Exist? An Inquiry into Islam's Obscure Origins*, by Robert Spencer. Wilmington, Delaware: Intercollegiate Studies Institute.

Iqbal, Muzaffar. 2008. "The Qur'ān, Orientalism and the *Encyclopaedia of the Qur'ān*," *Journal of Qur'anic Research and Studies* 3:5:5–45.
Lester, Toby. 1999. "What is the Koran?" *Atlantic Monthly* 283:43–56.
Lumbard, Joseph E. B. "Decolonializing Qur'anic Studies" (unpublished paper delivered at SOAS and submitted to the *Journal of Quranic Studies*).
Luxenberg, Christoph. 2000. *Die syro-aramäische Lesart des Korans: Ein Beitrag zur Entschlüsselung der Koransprache*. Berlin: Schiler.
Manzoor, Parvez. 1987. "Method Against Truth: Orientalism and Qur'anic Studies," *Muslim World Book Review* 7:33–49.
Nasr, Seyyed Hossein et al. (eds.). 2015. *The Study Quran: A New Translation and Commentary*. New York: HarperOne.
Neuwirth, Angelika. 2010. *Der Koran als Text der Spätantike: Ein europäischer Zugang*. Berlin: Verlag der Weltreligionen.
Nevo, Yehuda D. and Judith Koren. 2003. *Crossroads to Islam: The Origins of the Arab Religion and the Arab State*. Amherst, NY: Prometheus.
Nongbri, Brent. 2013. *Before Religion: a History of a Modern Concept*. New Haven, CT: Yale University Press.
Penn, Michael Philip. 2014. *Envisioning Islam: Syriac Christians and the Early Muslim World*. Philadelphia: University of Pennsylvania Press.
Reynolds, Gabriel Said (ed.). 2010. *The Qur'ān in Historical Context*. London and New York: Routledge.
Robin, Christian. 2004. "Ḥimyar et Israël," *Comptes-Rendus de l'Acadėmie des Inscriptions et Belles-Lettres*:831–908.
Rubin, Uri. 1995. *The Eye of the Beholder: The Life of Muhammad as Viewed by the Early Muslims, a Textual Analysis*. Princeton, NJ: Darwin Press.
Schubel, Vernon. 2014. "New Nostalgia for Old Orientalism: A Review Essay of Aaron Hughes' *Theorizing Islam*," *Journal of the Society for Contemporary Thought in the Islamicate World*." Online at http://sctiw.org/sctiwreviewarchives/wp-content/uploads/2014/08/006-Theorizing-Islam-Vernon-Schubel.pdf (link no longer active).
Sinai, Nicolai and Angelika Neuwirth. 2010. "Introduction," in *The Qur'ān in Context: Historical and Literary Investigations in the Qur'ānic Milieu*, eds. Angelika Neuwirth, Nicolai Sinai, and Michael Marx. Leiden: Brill.
Tannous, Jack. 2011. "Review of *Muhammad and the Believers* by Fred M. Donner," *Expositions* 5.2:126–141.
Wansbrough, John. 1977. *Quranic Studies: Sources and Methods of Scriptural Interpretation*. Oxford: Oxford University Press.
Wansbrough, John. 1987. *Res Ipsa Loquitur: History and Mimesis*. Jerusalem: The Israel Academy of Sciences and Humanities.
Wasserstrom, Steven M. 1995. *Between Muslim and Jew: The Problem of Symbiosis Under Early Islam*. Princeton: Princeton University Press.
Watt, W. Montgomery. 1953. *Muhammad at Mecca*. Oxford: Oxford University Press.
Watt, W. Montgomery. 1956. *Muhammad at Medina*. Oxford: Oxford University Press.
Wood, Philip. 2010. *"We have no King but Christ": Christian Political Thought in Greater Syria on the Eve of the Arab Conquest (c. 400–585)*. Oxford: Oxford University Press.

Stephen J. Shoemaker

A New Arabic Apocryphon from Late Antiquity: The Qur'ān

The question of the Qur'ān's literary genre has long vexed scholars, who have often struggled to find a category suitable for this frequently disjointed and disparate text. The Qur'ān's distinctive literary qualities, not to mention its regular opacity, can make it challenging to identify a fitting precursor among the vast literary remains of Mediterranean antiquity. The Islamic tradition, of course, is quite content to leave the matter of the Qur'anic genre unresolved, eagerly pointing to its exceptionalism as important evidence of its uniqueness or inimitability (*iʿjāz*). Not surprisingly, many modern scholars have willingly followed the Islamic tradition to this conclusion, an acquiescence to the Islamic tradition that is all too evident in much Qur'anic scholarship from the previous century. Accordingly, one regularly finds pronouncements to the effect that "the Qur'ān is an example of a genre of literature that has only one example."[1] Yet such a conclusion simply evades a difficult and important question: how should we conceive of the Qur'ān as a work of literature in relation to its broader literary environment? While this resolution is certainly adequate for the faithful Muslim, it should not be for the modern scholar.

Despite the inherent difficulties of attempting to classify a collection as peculiar as the Qur'ān, scholars have proposed a wide range of alternatives for how we might understand the text as a whole. For instance, several scholars have looked to Jewish and Christian liturgical collections to identify possible models, concluding that the Qur'ān should be understood as a hymnbook, or a lectionary, or a collection of psalms.[2] Not far off from these suggestions is the hypothesis that the Qur'ān represents a sort of homiletic text, akin to the metrical

---

1 Todd Lawson formulated the quotation above as being emblematic of this broader tendency within Qur'anic studies: Lawson 2017, 78. As a specific example, see Gibb 1963, 36: "As a literary monument the Koran thus stands by itself, a production unique to the Arabic literature, having neither forerunners nor successors in its own idiom."

2 E.g., respectively: Lüling 1974, translated into English as Lüling 2003; Luxenberg 2000, translated into English as Luxenberg 2007; Neuwirth 1977, and Neuwirth 2008.

Stephen J. Shoemaker, University of Oregon

https://doi.org/10.1515/9783110675498-003

homilies (*memre*) of the late ancient Syriac tradition.[3] Perhaps it is an extension of late ancient "question and answer" literature?[4] Or is it simply poetry, perhaps picking up and extending an earlier tradition of Arabic poetry in the pre-Islamic period?[5] Yet another proposal is that the Qur'ān should be understood simultaneously according to the genres of an apocalypse and an epic.[6] None of these options, however, successfully encompasses the range of materials found in the Qur'ān and their juxtaposition therein.

Such efforts to identify the Qur'ān's genre are nevertheless thwarted and undermined at nearly every turn by the sheer diversity of the Qur'ān's content. In actual fact, the Qur'ān is a document not of a single literary genre, but instead a collection of traditions that themselves evidence a wide variety of genres. It is thus not a single composition, and also most likely is not the work of a single author, despite the confidence of the Islamic tradition and modern scholarship alike in this regard. Rather than an artfully composed work of literature, the Qur'ān is, to the contrary, a late antique religious hodgepodge. Accordingly, its assemblage of textual materials holds enormous potential – still largely unrealized – for study of religious culture in the late ancient Near East, revealing a diversity and complexity of both belief and expression emerging at that time from Jewish and Christian monotheism that otherwise would be invisible from the sources of those two traditions alone. Thus, the Qur'ān is not so much a *magnus opus* as religious miscellany, whose contents witness to a breath of late ancient religious faith and practice that would otherwise be unknown.

There are, then, many genres within the Qur'ān, as other scholars have occasionally noted, and the presence of these different genres or literary forms, seemingly drawn from different sources, invites us to analyze its contents using the methods of form criticism as developed in biblical studies. This type of criticism is particularly useful for analyzing a text composed of many smaller units of tradition, of various genres, and also for investigating their *Sitz im Leben*, that is, the circumstances that gave rise to a particular unit of tradition in the first place. Only from such a perspective can we see, as Guillaume Dye helpfully elucidates, that strictly speaking, the Qur'ān is not a book, but a *corpus*, namely the gathering of texts: 1) which were not originally intended to be put together in a codex, nor composed with this goal in mind, 2) which are heterogeneous (they belong to a variety of literary genres, and sometimes express divergent

---

3 Reynolds 2010:230–58.

4 Bertaina 2014.

5 Nicholson 1930:159; Hoffmann 2007.

6 Lawson 2017.

ideas), 3) which are, in some cases, independent, and in some others, are not (there are numerous parallel passages, some Qur'anic passages rewriting, correcting and responding to other passages). The Qur'ān, therefore, appears as a text which has several layers, and which contains many parallel stories – and this implies that there is, like in the Gospels, a "synoptic problem" in the Qur'ān. In short, the Qur'ān is a text which is both *composite* and *composed*.[7]

Yet form critical analysis of the Qur'ān that would analyze its contents according to such a perspective remains, unfortunately, almost completely unattempted. For the time being, the best description of the various literary forms or genres that populate the Qur'ān is the inventory of Alfred-Louis de Prémare. According to de Prémare, the Qur'ān includes primarily oracular proclamations, hymns, instructional discourses, narrative evocations, legislative and paraenetic texts, battle exhortations, and polemical discourses.[8] For obvious reasons, it is effectively impossible to encompass a collection of such diverse textual materials within a single literary genre, as others have noted. Thus, the Qur'ān's resistance to being subsumed within a literary genre is not a consequence of its inimitability or uniqueness, but rather, it is an altogether expected result of its amalgamated nature.

The florilegia of late ancient Christianity could perhaps offer some kind of precedent for the Qur'ān's gathering of various sorts of materials within a single volume. But the Qur'ān's contents are quite different from these topical anthologies of quotations from writings of the Church Fathers. The Qur'ān's traditions are not taken from known, named authorities, as in the case of florilegia, and their themes are likewise not theological and philosophical but rather legal, eschatological, kerygmatic, liturgical, and, especially, biblical, in the sense that the Qur'ān frequently retells and alludes to traditions known otherwise in the Jewish and Christian Bible as well as other related sources. For this reason, I would propose a different category for situating the Qur'ān within the literary culture of late antiquity: the Qur'ān is best understood as a biblical apocryphon with a powerful message of eschatological urgency, repentance, and restoration. Although admittedly not every single facet of the Qur'ān is equally illuminated and explained by recognition of its apocryphal nature, the Qur'ān's location within the broader phenomenon of Jewish and Christian production of biblical apocrypha in late antiquity seems unmistakable once we begin to look at it through this lens.

---

7 Dye 2019, 785–86.

8 de Prémare 2004:35–45. A good start toward a more thorough identification of the Qur'ān's various literary forms has recently been published by Samji 2018.

Moreover, biblical apocrypha comprise a type of literature that is, as we will see, easily accommodated to the Qur'ān's assemblage of a wide range of materials and genres.

Until only rather recently, scholars tended to look upon apocryphal writings as failed scriptures – one-time rivals to the now canonical texts that were either marginalized or discarded because their teachings were considered false or unreliable by the shadowy censors of early Christian and Jewish orthodoxies. Yet such a view of this sizeable and diverse corpus of Christian and Jewish literature neither does it justice, nor does it accurately comprehend the phenomenon in question. Over the last few decades, scholarship on apocryphal literature has become increasingly nuanced as it continues to distance itself from the *sola Scriptura* mentality that originally inspired this older "scripture/rejected scripture" binary. Instead, the apocryphal landscape is now found to be not only much more vast than once thought but also more varied in terms of form, content, and function. And it is within this more nuanced and expansive understanding of apocrypha that the Qur'ān seems able to find a fitting home.

For much of the twentieth century, scholarship on apocrypha generally defined its subject as "writings which have not been received into the canon, but which by title and other statements lay claim to be of equal status (*gleichwertig*) to the writings of the canon, and which from the point of view of Form Criticism further develop and mold the literary genres (*Stilgattungen*) created and received in the NT, whilst foreign elements certainly intrude." Likewise, it was imagined that the production of apocrypha should be limited to the period before the closure of the New Testament canon, so that any "so-called" apocrypha produced after 300 CE should not be considered true apocryphal writings: only writings written with the original intent of their inclusion in the canon may be so named.[9] The result was a very narrow corpus, constricted by its delimitation according to the biblical norm. Such a framework effectively excludes acts of one of the apostles composed in the sixth century, or a gospel from the fourth, or life of the Virgin from the seventh: are these not equally apocrypha? Such a definition was obviously inadequate for the task of investigating the phenomenon of apocryphicity more broadly and separately from the question of the New Testament's canonization.

Fortunately, l'Association pour l'étude de la littérature apocryphe chrétienne (AELAC), and Éric Junod in particular, have advanced a more useful and inclusive definition of Christian apocrypha that has been widely adopted by

9 Schneemelcher 1959–64, 1:7, 17–18, 32–5; Translated into English as: Schneemelcher 1963–5, 1:28, 40–1, 60–4.

scholars since the 1980s. According to Junod's improved definition, biblical apocrypha are "anonymous or pseudepigraphical texts . . . that maintain a connection with the books of the New Testament as well as the Old Testament because they are devoted to events described or mentioned in these books, or because they are devoted to events that take place in the expansion of events described or mentioned in these books, because they focus on persons appearing in these books."[10] As a result, the canon of Christian apocryphal literature has been broadened considerably. Writings once dismissed as hagiographical or liturgical now must also be considered as apocryphal writings as well – the boundaries between these types of literature have become much blurrier than they were once imagined.[11] Likewise, this new perspective opens up the category of apocrypha to include more recent compositions, such as the *Book of Mormon* or the *Essene Gospel of Peace* – as well as the Qur'ān, for that matter.[12]

Without question, I think, the Qur'ān may be identified as a biblical apocryphon according to the terms defined by Junod: it is anonymous, it maintains a solid connection throughout to the writings of the Hebrew Bible and New Testament (as well as other related writings), focusing often on persons and events from these books while occasionally expanding on them. If such a writing is a biblical apocryphon, then certainly so also is the Qur'ān. One should not make the mistake of identifying biblical apocrypha as a genre, since the vast corpus of apocryphal writings includes many examples of numerous genres (including, one might note, paraenesis, poetry, hymns and other liturgical texts, and apocalyptic and eschatological material). Moreover, like the Qur'ān, many apocryphal writings themselves contain simultaneously materials reflecting a variety of different genres. Likewise, these diverse materials often derive from earlier, independent traditions that only come together in the compilation of the apocryphon. Finally, one should note, each of the different genres present in the Qur'ān – oracular proclamations, hymns, instructional discourses, narrative evocations, legislative and paraenetic texts, and polemical discourses – are also common elements of biblical apocryphal literature. Only exhortations to battle seem to be missing from the biblical apocrypha, and these Qur'anic materials seem to derive

---

10 Junod 1983:409–14. Junod's definition is proposed particularly within the context of the history of Christianity, for particular reasons related to the mission of AELAC. I have adjusted it slightly above through omitting specific references to Christianity to create a more inclusive – but practically identical – definition of biblical apocrypha.

11 On the complex overlap between such genres and apocryphal literature, see esp. Shoemaker 2008.

12 Regarding the production of apocrypha such as these and others up until the present moment, see esp. Piovanelli 2005, 2006.

from the particularly militant character of the religious movement and community that Muḥammad founded.

Some observations from Gabriel Reynolds are helpful in understanding the Qurʾān's relation to the biblical traditions. In proposing that the Qurʾān should be understood as a sort of homily, similar to the rhymed homilies of the Syriac tradition, Reynolds makes the important point that we must not presume, as much previous scholarship has, "that the Qurʾān was written to rival the Bible." Rather, he notes, "it would hardly be extraordinary if the Qurʾān was instead written in harmony with Biblical literature." As much seems to be indicated, Reynolds rightly observes, by the manner in which the Qurʾān presumes significant familiarity with the biblical writings on the part of its audience.[13] The Qurʾān in fact depends on the biblical traditions, in regard to which it is, in effect, supplementary, like a homily according to Reynolds, or, even more so, like a biblical apocryphon. Indeed, all of "homiletic" qualities that Reynolds identifies in the Qurʾān find a much better explanation when recognized instead as part of a biblical apocryphon.

In a recent article addressing the broader question of the Qurʾān's eschatology, Nicolai Sinai directly challenges the hypothesis that the Qurʾān should be understood as a document in the mold of the Syriac homiletic tradition. In particular, Sinai identifies a crucial difference between the Qurʾān and the Syriac homiletic tradition in the Qurʾān's self-stylization as divine speech, which is certainly not the case for the Syriac homilies.[14] There is undeniably a significant difference in how these two textual traditions relate their contents to their readers. Yet at the same time, one must recognize that with disturbing frequency it is not at all clear just who it is that is "speaking" in the Qurʾān's pronouncements and who is being addressed. Also in contrast to the Syriac homilies, the Qurʾān does not defer directly to another textual authority, as the Syriac fathers to do the Bible. Instead, it speaks with its own authority without need to refer to an external repository of truth. Yet at the same time we must bear in mind that the Qurʾān holds in the highest regard the Torah (*tawrāh*) and the gospels (*injīl*), as well as the Psalms (*zabūr*) and possibly even biblical apocalyptic literature (*ṣuḥuf*). Thus, as Reynolds and others have noted, we certainly may not presume that the Qurʾān was understood from the beginning as a new revelation intended to supersede and displace these previous dispensations.[15] When and how the Qurʾān attained this status among those who followed Muḥammad is still not entirely clear. Accordingly, we should

13 Reynolds 2010:232.

14 Sinai 2018:236, 250.

15 Sinai 2018:248–50; also Cook 2018:25–6; Ben-Shammai 2013.

remain open to the possibility that until later in the seventh century, the Qur'ān may have been understood as having a more supplementary, rather than supplanting, relation to the biblical traditions.

If we aim to bring categories and concepts from the Qur'ān's late antique religious milieu in order to gain a better understanding of its genesis, it would be best to set aside entirely the early Christian homily as a possible analogue. The Qur'ān simply does not possess the specific qualities that define a Christian homily and must instead be reckoned as something quite different. The truth of the matter is that there is very little in terms of form or content that defines the phenomenon of the early Christian homily. Indeed, the form of this type of literature is so diverse that, as Wendy Mayer observes, "all that we can claim is that a homily is something that conforms to a few essential conditions, but whose shape is elastic and changes with regional and cultural conditions and with time."[16] The emphasis on specific definitive "conditions" for a homily is paramount here. Homilies are defined by the conditions of their production for and their delivery in the context of Christian liturgical celebration. As such, their contents generally focus on moral instruction and exhortation for the congregation, particularly as related to the immediate liturgical context: the specific liturgical commemoration of the day, the biblical readings for the day, or "novel events (such as the arrival of new relics)."[17] I think it is safe to say that this is not, in fact, what the Qur'ān is: I doubt sincerely that this text or even parts of it were composed as moral elaboration of the specific liturgical themes for Eucharistic celebrations, which is what classifying it as a homily effectively entails. One should additionally note a further problem of comparison with the Syriac *memre* tradition. As Mayer notes, the formal poetic structures of this homiletic tradition demanded texts that had been carefully composed prior to oral delivery and were not spontaneous oral deliveries.[18] If, then, the Qur'ān were to be understood primarily as an extension of the *memra* tradition, we must also assume that it did not originate, at least in its present form, from spontaneous, oral teaching delivered without a script. If Muḥammad's Qur'ān were a *memra*, then it almost certainly must have been a written document from the very start. Perhaps this was indeed so, although in such case one must also consider the possibility that it was not necessarily Muḥammad who wrote it.

If the Qur'ān, then, is not a late ancient homily, it nevertheless remains that scholars have regularly described the text as possessing a strong homiletic

16 Mayer 2008:570.
17 Mayer 2008:568–9.
18 Mayer 2008:571.

character, or at least, having a great deal of homiletic content. These observations are not, it turns out, entirely incorrect: rather, they are the result of a category error and the imprecise usage of the terminology available for describing the religious literature of the late ancient Mediterranean world. The Qur'ān is not a homily, nor do I find convincing evidence for identifying any part of its contents with the phenomenon of early Christian homiletics. Rather, the so-called "homiletic" elements of the Qur'ān are simply misnamed, because while they do not share the homiletic form or "occasion," they do share with the homiletic tradition its primary mode of discourse: paraenesis, or "moral exhortation." Paraenesis was a common style of literary discourse in antiquity with its roots in Greek philosophy and Hellenistic literature (including Hellenistic Judaism). Paraenetic discourse pervades the writings of the New Testament, and its importance within this corpus has been a major focus of biblical studies almost from the very beginning. Not surprisingly, early Christian discourse is replete with examples of paraenesis, and such moral exhortation is one of the most characteristic features of early Christian homiletic literature, where it is frequently joined to exegesis of the day's appointed readings or the theme of its commemoration.[19] The Christian homiletic tradition seems to have derived this paraenetic focus from the tradition of biblical paraenesis as well as contemporary Greco-Roman oratory.[20] Thus, while no part of the Qur'ān seems to be homiletic in the proper sense of the term, there is a great deal that is paraenetic, a prominent feature that it shares not only with the Christian homiletic tradition, but with biblical apocrypha as well.

Sinai is clearly right, then, in my opinion, that the Qur'ān does not stand in the tradition of Syriac homilies, for these and other reasons. At the same time, however, the alternative solution of elevating the Qur'ān to the status of sacred scripture from the moment of its very origin also does not, it seems to me, provide the best means for understanding the complex relation between the Qur'ān and the biblical tradition. In this respect, Reynolds' remarks regarding the Qur'ān's relation to the writings of the bible remain persuasive. Yet we need a category other than homily to understand the Qur'ān's formation within the matrix of late ancient Judaism and Christianity and their scriptures. Understanding the Qur'ān as a biblical apocryphon, or in other parlance, particularly with respect to traditions from the Hebrew Bible, "rewritten Bible," can take us very far toward this goal. Looking at the Qur'ān from the perspective of late antiquity, the text becomes immediately recognizable a biblical apocryphon that participates

19 Starr and Engberg-Pedersen 2005. A helpful starting place, particularly for the importance of paraenesis in the biblical tradition, is Starr 2013.
20 Maxwell 2006: chs. 1 & 2.

in the broader phenomenon of Jewish and Christian production of apocryphal texts in this era.

To my knowledge, previous scholarship has never fully recognized the apocryphal nature of the Qur'ān and analyzed it accordingly, being content instead to identify the various traditions that it has borrowed from apocryphal literature. Nevertheless, this hunt for apocryphal parallels has always been done without full cognizance that this future sacred text should itself be seen from the vantage of the early seventh century as yet another effort to rewrite the traditions of the Bible comparable to so many earlier and contemporary Jewish and Christian apocrypha. The closest that we have seen to such an approach, in my estimation, is Sidney Griffith's study on *The Bible in Arabic*, where he persistently describes the Qur'ān in relation to the biblical traditions in terms befitting an apocryphon. Griffith concludes, for instance, that "the Qur'ān's reprise of the Bible bespeaks the opening of a new book altogether in the growing library of books on the 'interpreted Bible.' Or perhaps it bespeaks not so much a new book, as a corrected, alternate scripture, one that recalls the Tanakh and the Bible."[21] Such a work is indeed best described, from the perspective of late ancient religious culture, as an apocryphon.

Many of the very qualities that Sinai identifies to distinguish the Qur'ān from the Syriac homily tradition are in fact key characteristics of apocryphal writings.[22] Like the Qur'ān, biblical apocrypha have their basis in the biblical tradition and depend heavily on these traditions for their content, yet they do not simply regurgitate biblical material. They are not passive recipients or mere echo chambers; instead, they creatively reformulate and reshape traditions taken from the biblical writings. Very often, they speak directly on their own authority and likewise present their audience with what is frequently purported to be divine speech, a quality most obvious in revelation dialogues and apocalypses, for instance. Apocryphal writings thus implicitly if not explicitly acknowledge the traditional authority of the biblical writings that came before them and inspired them. At the same time, however, they do not defer completely to the authority of the biblical texts, and their contents offer adaptations and expansions of the biblical traditions generally aimed at supplanting or correcting the very traditions that were their original inspiration. All of this sounds a great deal like the Qur'ān, particularly in those sections that rewrite biblical traditions with authority. It is arguable, as Sinai notes, that the Qur'ān "spurns the device of pseudepigraphy." Yet

21 Griffith 2013:84.

22 Regarding the category of apocrypha and the broad phenomenon of "apocryphicity" in relation to the biblical tradition see esp. Shoemaker 2008; Piovanelli 2005, 2006; and also the various essays in Mimouni 2002.

so too do any number of apocrypha.[23] And, one should note, that while the Islamic tradition may attribute the Qur'ān to Muḥammad, it remains uncertain whether the authorship of its disparate contents is entirely his. From the historian's point of view, there is every reason to assume that the Qur'ān's author remains anonymous.

Indeed, in order to fully appreciate the apocryphal status of the Qur'ān, perhaps one must imagine how we might regard this text today if Muḥammad's followers had been soundly defeated by the Romans at Yarmuk and their movement slowly dissolved in the years thereafter as the eschaton failed to arrive as anticipated. If we further suppose that somehow the Qur'ān had come into being by this time, as the Islamic tradition effectively expects us to believe, and this text were the main remnant of Muḥammad's religious movement, what would we make of it? Almost certainly, I suspect, on the basis of its content and its relation to the biblical tradition, we would identify it as a late ancient apocryphon. Ultimately, then, the main difference between the Qur'anic apocryphon and so many other such compositions is that, like the Book of Mormon for example, a religious group eventually elevated it to a new scriptural authority. There is in fact much in common between these two apocrypha, the Qur'ān and the Book of Mormon, so much so that in late nineteenth and early twentieth century America the comparison was frequently made in order to impugn the Book of Mormon. Yet in more recent years, scholars of religious studies have studied the similarities of these texts and their histories with more learned intent, enabling the two texts to illuminate one another through comparison.[24] Like the Qur'ān, as well as the biblical writings themselves, the Book of Mormon contains "a variety of materials in different genres ranging from historical narratives, legal codes, and moral injunctions to revelations, prophecies, visions, and ecstatic poetry."[25] All three collections share the same generic diversity.

The book of Mormon, for its part, is an "intensely American book" that has often been described as "the New World scripture," and "American scripture," or an "American apocryphon."[26] As W. D. Davies notes, "Its substructure and its structures are in the Old Testament and the New Testament. But it also reinterprets

23 It is true that Junod includes "anonymous or pseudepigraphical" as qualities defining Christian apocryphal writings. Nevertheless, it is not at all clear to me why this should be a requirement. There are apocryphal texts with known authors.

24 In this regard, see especially Stark 1999 which offers an extended comparison of Muḥammad and Joseph Smith and the revelation ascribed to them. See also Underwood 2013; Green 1983.

25 Hardy 2015:136.

26 Givens 2009:125; Givens 2002:6; Vogel and Metcalfe 2002.

and accommodates or transfers ancient forms, in a very remarkable way, to an American setting and mode," so that it presents "the Jewish-Christian tradition in an American key." "The territoriality of Judaism is reinterpreted by Americanizing it," and sacred sites from the biblical narrative are relocated onto American soil.[27] The Book of Mormon is, as Laurie Maffly-Kipp describes it, "a sacred drama of the Americas that correlated with biblical accounts of early human history."[28] If we were simply to substitute Arabian for American in the quotations above, the same statements would apply equally well to the Qurʾān and early Islam. Thus, I would agree wholeheartedly with Sinai's characterization of the Qurʾān "as a properly Arabic restatement of the Biblical heritage."[29] It is, then, a properly Arabic or Arabian apocryphon much as the Book of Mormon stands, as others have noted, as a properly American apocryphon that restates the biblical heritage in a distinctively American idiom. And just like the Book of Mormon, this Arabian apocryphon would eventually come to be an Arabian scripture.

The potential payoff from recognizing the Qurʾān as a biblical apocryphon is twofold, as I see it. Firstly, understanding the Qurʾān as an apocryphon is sure to bring new perspectives on the nature and significance of both this collection and many of its constituent parts. The category of apocrypha affords a new avenue for approaching the peculiar relationship between the Qurʾān and the biblical traditions of Christianity and Judaism. As an apocryphon, we can understand now how the Qurʾān recognizes and embraces the authority of these antecedent scriptural collections while simultaneously reconfiguring and supplementing their contents. Such adaptation and modification of biblical traditions is the vital essence of apocryphal writings. Likewise, an apocryphal Qurʾān invites us to think newly about the conditions and motivations behind the production of both its individual elements and the collection itself.

No less significant, however, are the bonds that this perspective forges between the Qurʾān and the religious literature of late antiquity. Viewing the Qurʾān as a biblical apocryphon allows us to remove it from the subsequent history of the Islamic tradition and see it truly as a product of late ancient religious culture. Thus we can look at the Qurʾān with new eyes in order to investigate and better comprehend its relations to the religious traditions of its historical matrix, including late ancient Christianity and Judaism in particular, without the distracting interference of the later Islamic tradition's interpretations of this compendium of late ancient religious culture. Recognizing the Qurʾān as a biblical apocryphon anchors it to

27 Davies 1978:89. See also Maffly-Kipp 2010:xvii.
28 Smith 2009:xviii.
29 Sinai 2018:254.

the religious landscape of late antiquity and invites us to read it in new ways within this context. Such a perspective offers us the possibility of approaching the Qur'ān as if it were a text recently discovered in a cave somewhere, enabling us to interpret it completely afresh, without having so many questions already answered for us by the later Islamic tradition.[30] And given the well-known unreliability of the early Islamic historical tradition, such an approach does not seem unwarranted. Yet one thing is for sure: studying the Qur'ān in this fashion will reveal it as the product of the religious cultures of the late ancient Near East, as well as affording new perspectives on this religious milieu at the same time. Among other things, this late ancient Qur'anic apocryphon will certainly challenge us to rethink the boundaries of the scriptural canon in late antiquity, as well as conceptualizations of scripture that were in circulation at this time. It could raise questions about the nature of boundaries between the various religious communities of the late ancient Near East, and the circulation of religious culture among them. Indeed, integrating the Qur'ān more fully with the religious world of late antiquity is certain to yield many new perspectives on both.

Bibliography

Ben-Shammai, Haggai. 2013. "*Ṣuḥuf* in the Qur'ān – A Loan Translation for 'Apocalypses'." In *Exchange and Transmission across Cultural Boundaries: Philosophy, Mysticism and Science in The Mediterranean World*, edited by Haggai Ben-Shammai, Shaul Shaked and Sarah Stroumsa, 1–15. Jerusalem: Israel Academy of Sciences and Humanities.

Bertaina, David. 2014. "Rethinking Genre and the Qur'ān: Question-and-Answer Literature." *International Qur'ānic Studies Association Blog* (blog). 15 Feb. https://iqsaweb.wordpress.com/2014/05/26/rethinking-genre-and-the-quran-question-and-answer-literature (accessed May 20, 2021).

Cook, David. 2018. "The Qur'ān and Other Scriptures." In *The Routledge Handbook on Early Islam*, edited by Herbert Berg, 25–36. London: Routledge.

Davies, W. D. 1978. "Israel, the Mormons and the Land." In *Reflections on Mormonism: Judaeo-Christian Parallels*, edited by Truman G. Madsen, 79–97. Provo: Religious Studies Center, Brigham Young University.

de Prémare, Alfred-Louis. 2004. *Aux origines du Coran: questions d'hier, approches d'aujourd'hui.L'Islam en débats*. Paris: Téraèdre.

Dye, Guillaume. 2019. "Le corpus coranique: contexte, chronologie, composition, canonisation." In *Le Coran des historiens*, edited by Mohammad Ali Amir-Moezzi and Guillaume Dye, vol. 1, forthcoming. Paris: Editions du Cerf.

Gibb, H. A. R. *Arabic Literature – An Introduction*, 2d (rev.) ed. Oxford: Clarendon Press, 1963.

30 And idea also proposed in Lawson 2017:53–4.

Givens, Terryl. 2002. *By the Hand of Mormon: The American Scripture that Launched a New World Religion*. Oxford: Oxford University Press.
Givens, Terryl L. 2009. *The Book of Mormon: A Very Short Introduction*. Oxford: Oxford University Press.
Green, Arnold H. 1983. "The Muḥammad-Joseph Smith Comparison: Subjective Metaphor or a Sociology of Prophethood." In *Mormons and Muslims: Spiritual Foundations and Modern Manifestations*, edited by Spencer J. Palmer, 63–84. Provo: Religious Studies Center, Brigham Young University.
Griffith, Sidney H. 2013. *The Bible in Arabic: The Scriptures of the 'People of the Book' in the Language of Islam*. Princeton: Princeton University Press.
Hardy, Grant. 2015. "The Book of Mormon." In *The Oxford Handbook of Mormonism*, edited by Terryl Givens and Philip L. Barlow, 134–48. New York: Oxford University Press.
Hoffmann, Thomas. 2007. *The Poetic Qur'ān: Studies on Qur'ānic Poeticity*. Vol. Bd 12. Wiesbaden: Harrassowitz.
Lawson, Todd. 2017. *The Quran: Epic and Apocalypse*. London: Oneworld Academics.
Lüling, Günter. 1974. *Über den Ur-Qur'ān: Ansätze z. Rekonstruktion vorislam, christl. Strophenlieder Qur'ān*. Erlangen: Lüling.
Lüling, Günter. 2003. *A Challenge to Islam for Reformation: The Rediscovery and Reliable Reconstruction of a Comprehensive Pre-Islamic Christian Hymnal Hidden in the Koran under Earliest Islamic Reinterpretations*. Rev. ed. Delhi: Motilal Banarsidass Publishers.
Luxenberg, Christoph. 2000. *Die syro-aramäische Lesart des Koran: ein Beitrag zur Entschlüsselung der Koransprache*. Berlin: Das Arabische Buch.
Luxenberg, Christoph. 2007. *The Syro-Aramaic Reading of the Koran: A Contribution to the Decoding of the Language of the Koran*. Rev. ed. Berlin: Verlag Hans Schiler.
Maffly-Kipp, Laurie F. 2010. *American Scriptures: An Anthology of Sacred Writings*. New York: Penguin Classics.
Maxwell, Jaclyn LaRae. 2006. *Christianization and Communication in Late Antiquity: John Chrysostom and his Congregation in Antioch*. Cambridge: Cambridge University Press.
Mayer, Wendy. 2008. "Homiletics." In *The Oxford Handbook of Early Christian Studies*, edited by Susan Ashbrook Harvey and David G. Hunter, 565–83. Oxford: Oxford University Press.
Mimouni, Simon Claude, ed. 2002. *Apocryphité: histoire d'un concept transversal aux religions du Livre: en hommage à Pierre Geoltrain, Bibliothèque de l'Ecole des hautes études, Sciences religieuses 113*. Turnhout: Brepols.
Neuwirth, Angelika. 1977. "Einige Bemerkungen zum besonderen sprachlichen und literarischen Charakter des Koran." In *19. Deutscher Orientalistentag in Freiburg 1975*, edited by Wolfgang Voigt, 736–9. Wiesbaden: Steiner.
Neuwirth, Angelika. 2008. "Die Psalmen – im Koran neu gelesen (Ps 104 und 136)." In *Im vollen Licht der Geschichte. Die Wissenschaft des Judentums und die Anfänge der kritischen Koranforschung*, edited by Angelika Neuwirth, Dirk Hartwig, W. Homolka and Michael Marx, 157–91. Wurzburg: Ergon.
Nicholson, Reynold Alleyne. 1930. *A Literary History of the Arabs*. 2d ed. Cambridge: The University Press.
Piovanelli, Pierluigi. 2005. "What Is a Christian Apocryphal Text and How Does It Work? Some Observations on Apocryphal Hermeneutics." *Nederlands Theologisch Tijdschrift* 59: 31–40.
Piovanelli, Pierluigi. 2006. "Qu'est-ce qu'un 'écrit apocryphe chrétien', et comment ça marche? Quelques suggestions pour une herméneutique apocryphe." In *Pierre Geoltrain,*

ou comment «faire l'histoire» des religions. Le chantier des «origines», les méthodes du doute, et la conversation contemporaine entre disciplines, edited by Simon C. Mimouni and I. Ullern-Weité, In Bibliothèque de l'Ecole des hautes études, Sciences religieuses 128, 171–184. Turnhout: Brepols.

Reynolds, Gabriel Said. 2010. *The Qur'ān and its Biblical Subtext*. Vol. 10*Routledge Studies in the Qur'an*. Milton Park, Abingdon, Oxon; New York: Routledge.

Samji, Karim. 2018. *The Qur'ān: A Form-Critical History*. Berlin: Walter de Gruyter.

Schneemelcher, Wilhelm. 1959–64. *Neutestamentliche Apokryphen in deutscher Übersetzung*. 3rd ed. 2 vols. Tübingen: Mohr (Siebeck).

Schneemelcher, Wilhelm, ed. 1963–5. *New Testament Apocrypha*. Translated by R. McL Wilson. 2 vols. Philadelphia: Westminster Press.

Shoemaker, Stephen J. 2008. "Early Christian Apocryphal Literature." In *Oxford Handbook of Early Christian Studies* edited by Susan Ashbrook Harvey and David G. Hunter, 521–48. Oxford: Oxford University Press.

Sinai, Nicolai. 2018. "The Eschatological Kerygma of the Early Qur'ān." In *Apocalypticism and Eschatology in Late Antiquity*, edited by Hagit Amirav, Emmanouela Grypeou and Guy Stroumsa, 219–66. Leuven: Peeters.

Smith, Joseph, Jr. 2009. *The Book of Mormon.Penguin Classics*. London: Penguin.

Stark, Rodney. 1999. "A Theory of Revelations." *Journal for the Scientific Study of Religion* 38 (2):287–308. https://doi.org/10.2307/1387795. http://www.jstor.org/stable/1387795 (accessed May 20, 2021).

Starr, James. 2013. "Paraenesis." *Oxford Bibliographies: Biblical Studies*. https://doi.org/10.1093/obo/9780195393361-0143 (accessed May 16, 2019).

Starr, James M., and Troels Engberg-Pedersen. 2005. *Early Christian Paraenesis in Context*. Beihefte zur Zeitschrift fuer die Alttestamentliche Wissenschaft 125. Berlin: Walter de Gruyter.

Underwood, Grant. 2013. "The Prophetic Legacy in Islam and Mormonism: Some Comparative Observations." In *New Perspectives in Mormon studies: Creating and Crossing Boundaries*, edited by Quincy D. Newell and Eric Farrel Mason, 101–18. Norman, OK: University of Oklahoma Press.

Vogel, Dan, and Brent Lee Metcalfe. 2002. *American Apocrypha: Essays on the Book of Mormon.Essays on Mormonism Series*. Salt Lake City: Signature Books.

II Early Islam and the Qur'ān: Historical, Literary, and Cross-Comparative Analyses

Manfred Kropp

Body Parts Nomenclature in the Qur'anic Corpus*

"And say, 'He's an Ear!' Say, 'An ear for your good!'" (Q 9:61)

Introduction and Problems

In *Anthropologie des Alten Testaments,* Hans Walter Wolff applies the "synthetic conception of the body" and its allocation in the "anthropological language theory" to elaborate on the proper terminology of body and body part designations as well as other nomina for the designation of the whole human being in the Old Testament and ancient Hebrew in general.[1] This exegesis, which is close to linguistics and literary studies, has effects on the understanding of the text but especially on the practice of translation. It attempts first to clarify and describe the function and meaning of the Hebrew language formulae, apart from excessive etymologizing in the tradition of the comparative study of Semitic languages, while consciously turning away from a translation that imitates and forms the source language, without committing oneself to a translation. Thus, a gain in knowledge is already achieved, and the exegete can set aside the traditional transmissions with a general reference to these results. However, in this interlingual and intercultural comparison with the target language, it is tempting to try to determine whether synonymous translation or only a general indication of meaning is possible.

The question of functionally and lexically related somatisms, in which the key words are used in fixed phrases whose meaning is conventionally fixed, is largely excluded from this kind of linguistic analysis. Here, there are rather common subsets, because the keyword (body part designation or the like) can be seen on the word level only in the sense of metonymic and metaphoric use, which fits into the superordinate unity and meaning of somatism. In what follows, I will apply this methodology, which has been effectively used for the study of the Old Testament, to the study of body parts within the Qur'ān. Indeed, among Semitic languages, Arabic is relatively closely related to Old Hebrew, while the corpus of the Qur'ān shows more parallels with the Old Testament than the New Testament. So it seems promising to apply instruments and methods, which have led to the

1 Wolff 2010.

Manfred Kropp, Semitiic and Islamic Studies, Johannes Gutenberg-Universitäet Mainz.

https://doi.org/10.1515/9783110675498-004

clarification of the synthetic body conception in the Old Testament, to the Qur'anic text and, as far as possible and necessary, to (ancient) Arabic.[2]

Introductory Remarks on the Character and Uniqueness of the Qur'ān

A first examination and listing of the possible words and verbal roots[3] in the Qur'ān shows that a good part of its vocabulary shares identical terms with other Semitic languages. These terms, however, must be defined according to

---

2 This is an improved English version of my lecture given within the framework of the DFG project "stabilitas Dei," 17.-18. 06. 2011 at the Institute for Theology and Social Ethics, TU Darmstadt. The German version was published as Kropp 2014.

For the investigation of the Qur'ān, numerous aids are now available, including printed concordances, thematic indices, and corresponding corpora on the Internet. These include, for example, Ambros' *A Concise Dictionary of Koranic Arabic* (2004) followed by his *The Nouns of Koranic Arabic Arranged by Topics* (2006). In Arabic, the concordance of Muḥammad Fu'ād ʿAbd-al-Bāqī *al-Muʿǧam al-mufahras li-alfāẓ al-Qurʾān al-karīm* (Cairo, 1938) and many reprints are available. On the Internet there are many instruments, constantly growing in number, which allow the construction of concordances (in the original Arabic and various translations). Here are but a few examples: the *Tanzil Project* "Revelation" (http://tanzil.net); *Corpus Quran* (http://corpus.quran.com/); *Intratext* (http://www.intratext.com/); and *altafsir* "Koran Commentary" (http://www.altafsir.com/).

3 In addition to primary nouns, which at first cannot be further derived, Semitic languages have "roots," namely, two or more radical sequences of consonants and vowels on the basis of which verbs and nouns can be derived according to morphological rules, ideally belonging to a common semantic field (the "basic meaning" of the root). Such roots are in part free formations, partly secondarily formed from the radical stock of the primary nomina. Cross-pollination (partly complete uniformity, only slight differences in vocalization) leads to duplications of words, which may, however, differ semantically. Such duplications cannot be distinguished in a purely consonantal textual tradition, the chosen reading is already an interpretation, concerning which there is not necessarily unity in the tradition or in the scientific interpretation (see below the example *ʾuḏn* "Ear" – *ʾiḏn* "Permission"). That identity may have existed, but as in many cases with historical etymology, the interpretation is difficult and uncertain precisely with regard to metaphorical (here meronymy and functional metonymy) use. The communicative situation (Are speakers and listeners still aware of and able to comprehend the historical development?), which could bring decisive clarification here, often cannot be determined. Despite the extremely low decomposition rate of Semitic languages for phonemes, which leaves the phonetic word form practically unchanged over long periods of time, it can be said from experience that non-reflecting and non-linguistically trained speakers of Semitic languages are just as unaware of such historical connections as speakers of languages in which the completely changed sound form does not permit a direct insight into historical connections from the outset.

their meaning and use in Arabic and possibly be distinguished from Hebrew (phenomenon of *faux amis*). In addition, there are clear or presumable loans from the Old Testament and the New Testament or their environment.

The application of a detailed classification, such as that done by Daniel Werning with ancient Egyptian, requires knowledge of the respective communication processes available to research only in modern languages.[4] For the Qur'anic text this connection can only be grasped in rudiments. The Qur'ān is the first substantial and coherent document of Scriptural Arabic. Contemporary Arabic texts of any kind are almost completely absent, with the exception of pre-Islamic Arabic poetry. Thus, the linguistic horizon and competence of the original audience of the Qur'ān remain largely open. The same is true for the foundations and linguistic sources from which the author(s) or the editors of the Qur'ān drew. Parallels can be recognized, but often in characteristic transformation, with extra-biblical Jewish and Christian – not only biblical – texts, but here too a similar question remains: to what extent do these parallels represent innovations by the author(s) of the Qur'anic texts or attestations to pre-existent texts already in Arabic?

As noted, for the intra-Arabic comparison of Qur'anic style and expression, contemporary texts exist (apart from the "timeless" classical Arabic, which is strongly influenced by the Qur'ān) only in the form of Old Arabic poetry, which was handed down in writing only in Islamic times and whose authenticity remains controversial.[5] Although these poetic texts certainly belong to a completely different literary genus, they are meaningful nonetheless, since they offer general characteristics about the Arabic idiom and way of thinking and serve, furthermore, as a strong contrast to the corpus of the Qur'ān.

The Qur'ān contains a surprisingly large number of differentiated body and body part designations (77 in the narrower sense; more than 100 for physical processes, activities, and their products; more than 50 for physical states and idiosyncrasies as well as almost 100 for family and group designations, apart from general action verbs), for its relatively small size (approx. 60,000 words

4 Werning 2014.

5 These texts are contained in various comprehensive corpora of Arabic and Islamic literature on the Internet (e.g,. *al-Maktaba aš-šāmila*, "Universal Library": http://shamela.ws; *al-Ǧāmiʿ al-*kabīr, "Large Corpus (of Literature)"; http://www.turath.com/turath). In addition, there are special corpora for Arabic poetry. The most accessible resources are in CD format, for example, *al-Mawsūʿa aš-šiʿriyya*, "Poetic Encyclopedia," (2003). The fact that these corpora usually give only one text version or in critical editions the main text, without the variants of the apparatus, does not harm the task at hand here.

with high frequency for individual terms). This is partly due to the detailed ritual regulations that appear in the Qur'anic corpus.

The question of the synthetic conception of the body is to a large extent a problem of translation. It is evident that an adequate understanding of the texts in question cannot be achieved with literal translations, which would only be understood by the target group in the target language. What kind of misinterpretations these can lead to is illustrated by a simple example of Italian-German translation: Italian "dare una mano" simply means "to help" ("dammi una mano" = "help me"), and must be translated into German in an adequate way.[6]

In any case, a translation of an ancient text such as the Qur'ān into modern terminology is always only a partial and questionable approximation, based on many assumptions and plausible explanations rather than on empirical studies available in the investigation of modern languages and acts of communication. Finally, to be able to think in the self-definition of otherness and the past seems doubtful, even after a sustained and honest endeavor.

The detailed and investigative preoccupation with the Qur'ān was forced upon me only by biographical coincidences during the last ten years after I had deliberately avoided it as a Semitist and an Arabist in the preceding thirty years of my career, following the advice of Hans Jakob Polotsky.[7] Well, in fulfilling the task of examining the body language of the Qur'ān, I worked through context concordances (Arabic text) on the basis of a corresponding word list and came to the amazing insight and realization that this is an acceptable form of reading of this text – at least for the Occidental and non-Muslim reader. Analytical approaches and guidelines, such as the style and form analysis of "Semitic rhetoric," are of little help here. Quite often, one begins with the last short surahs and then searches, with certain questions, the way to read through the longer and composite pieces. The reception in Arabic usually takes place through recitation, and here, in my estimation, a rather aesthetic-musical reception dominates the

---

6 Cf. Gitterle 2005. In addition to the works on somatism cited in Werning's article on ancient Egyptian (Ni 2011; Siahaan 2008), the work by Kotb 2002 should also be mentioned.

7 Delivered orally during a long evening discussion on the fringes of the *6th International Conference of Ethiopian Studies* in Tel Aviv in April 1980: "Betreiben Sie Arabisch unter Ausschluß des Korans" (roughly translated as "Practice Arabic to the exclusion of the Qur'ān"). This is of course to be taken *cum grano salis*. Every text written in classical Arabic after the Qur'ān bears the influence of this text, even if only influenced by the grammar of norms later formed by the Qur'anic example. Only Jewish or Christian texts in "Middle Arabic," on the one hand, and the living Neo-Arabic languages as heirs and continuators of Old Arabic language varieties, on the other hand, can be considered as linguistic objects at a relative distance from this influence. In the case of the latter, the exact position and relationship to the classical standard language has not yet been fully clarified.

content, not to mention the special problem of the direct comprehensibility or incomprehensibility of the text even to an Arab "native speaker." Here, it should not be forgotten that the Arabic mother tongue is one of the Neo-Arabic languages, the written language as a related but quite different language is to be learned. When reading the Qur'ān in this harmonizing manner, the stereotypical and repetitive nature of many parts of the text becomes apparent, always in relation to a relatively small corpus. By drumming certain phrases with only little variation, leading ideas that were particularly dear to the author or authors become recognizable. This leads me to make another remark, unhindered: one gets the impression of an almost monotonously hammering, theologians present will excuse me, preaching style, more sharply defined by propagandists fanatically possessed by one of his ideas.[8]

The aforementioned repetitions on the syntagmic and sentence level in "parallel passages" within the Qur'ān lead to a "reduction corpus": the expressions in question are indexed only once as sigla, thereby further limiting the original text volume. This method is part of technical text compression in electronic data processing, where the high compression rates for the rather small text corpus indicates the same facts.

Incidentally, and this is a meta-remark to my remark, the atomization of the Quran'ic text into individual phrases (verses; Qur'anic *āya*, "miraculous sign") given by a context concordance corresponds first of all to the way in which the text is treated in exegesis (*Tafsir*), but above all also in practical application in Islamic law. Second, the division of the Qur'ān into verses corresponds entirely to the peculiarity of (ancient) Arabic poetry in which the verse is usually an autonomous unit, which is judged and valued as such. The poet's rank and fame are determined by the successful single verse, less by the longer poem compositions.

Among "common" high and written languages as well as in spoken languages, one should not forget that Arabic has a number of illiterate formulations of high expressiveness and brilliance, though forced by religious as well as cultural-social developments. In the Qur'anic corpus and in ancient Arabic poetry, one recognizes, besides the synthetic conception of the body, the phenomenon of a supporting word to avoid a personal pronoun or a salutation, ultimately to bypass the naming of a person or being out of respect or taboo. The choice of a supporting word is originally conditioned by a partial aspect of the body or the person or their effectiveness. But the concrete meaning fades and the supporting word becomes with the following personnel suffix or noun a conventional, fixed turn, which is understood only as a whole. This can be

8 Rodinson 1968.

observed in other Semitic languages, such as Ethiopian Semitic, to an even greater extent and higher degree of grammaticalization. Various standard forms of personal pronouns, for example, can be translated into an original "supporting word" (e.g., head) with the following possessive suffix indicating the intended grammatical person. A vivid example of this is *waǧh Allāh*, "Face of God" in Q 55:27 (see also below *waǧh*). Here, interpretation and translation must decide whether this is a respectful formula for "Your Lord," that is, a historical metonymy that speakers and listeners are no longer aware of, or a wakeful, even innovative, metonymy, possibly created by borrowing from biblical usage, which would then have to be taken into account in the translation: "the face of your Lord." In addition to the problem of appropriate translation, such questions and their clarification are of crucial importance for the assessment of the character, function, and effect of the text in its historical context, if it can be reconstructed at all. This is a problem for the historian; the theologian is able to create other solutions with reference to the immediacy of the divine word.

The same applies to other idiomatic expressions, such as the numerous expressions *per merismum* (witness and testimony = absolutely true testimony; producer and producer = procreation par excellence, etc.) in the corpus of the Qur'ān. If one tries, as Muslim exegesis has already done, to give each element its special meaning, one simply misses the intended statement.

Arabic seems to prefer abstract action nouns and in some cases uses them predominantly before the corresponding body part designations, but sometimes also in mixed or hypertrophic, redundant formulas in which the body part and its action are explicitly designated by two words:

- *samʿ*, "hearing" instead of *ʾuḏun*, "ear."
- *baṣar*, "seeing, looking, beholding" instead of *ʿayn*, "eye"; but see: *samʾ wa-baṣar wa-qalb*, "hearing, seeing, and heart" (= Understanding). ""
- *qawl*, "speech" instead of *fūh* "mouth"; but *qawl afwāhi-him*, "speech of her mouth"; *āḏān yasmaʿūna bi-hā*, "ears with which they hear."

The inclusion of the corresponding action verbs (seeing, hearing, speaking, tasting, standing, walking, etc.), even if they are not connected to the body part designation via the word root, should also be covered in a larger investigation of the topic "body part designations and their functions." However, apart from a few hints, the work presented here, which is intended to be a sketch and a program for an in-depth examination of the actual body part designations, does not include this extension.

Comment on the Qur'ān Quotation in the Title of the Essay

The excerpt from surah 9 *at-Tawba* ("the repentance") verse 61 was chosen as the title of this article because of its metaphorical use of a body part designation (see below for *uḏun*, "ear"). Additionally, the quotation offers material and the occasion to comment on the Qur'anic style with regard to the character of the text in the communicative situation portrayed as well as a hypothesis on the history of the text.

Qul ("Speak") phrases should usually be understood as theophor, instructions of the author of the revelation to his medium. Some *qul* phrases may have been added later into the Qur'anic text in order to explicitly mark the following statement as a direct divine word.

If one crosses out the phrases in the text that merely indicate the speakers, "they say," "then speak" or "then he said," signaled in modern typography with quotation marks and line changes, omitting the naming of the speakers resulting from the context, a (modern) dialogue results:

> "He is (only?) an (open? listening?) ear!"
> (Yes, but) an ear (that is open? listening?) for your best!

But such a dialogue must be integrated into a communicative situation that is conceived differently, because the medium of revelation pretends in the text not to hear directly. The author of the revelation refers to what the adversaries say and at the same time provides a *qul* action or speech instruction to his medium. Instead of carrying out this instruction analogously, that is, to speak only the revealed and ordered text, the medium passes on the instruction, which in principle is intended only for itself, completely and literally, allowing its audience to participate in the revelation dialogue in a quasi-voyeuristic manner.[9]

A variant of this textual interpretation results from the possibility given in the defective original Qur'anic orthography to read *qul* ("speak") instead as *qāl* ("he said"). This would refer then to the medium and its statement and would possibly be a premeditated protocol of the corresponding proclamation or polemical discussion situation. It was thought ahead, because the medium, the preacher, not only anticipates the objections and contradictions of his adversaries but also his answers to them.[10]

---

9 Compare my remarks on "multi-addressed religious discourse" in Kropp 2008.

10 In the style of popular and oral anticipation of conversation, consider: "[. . .] then they will say [". . ."], then you will say: [". . ."]".

In both cases, however, the *qul* phrases serve not only as memos, aide-mémoire, but also possibly as protocols of a speaker (herald, preacher). Despite all the breaks and distortions caused by changes in person and the introduction of an observant and instructing author of the (revelatory) text, such an assumption does justice to the scenic and dialogical drama of these text pieces. This would explain the nature and function of many such short pieces scattered throughout the collection of texts in the Qur'ān. This collection of notes by one or more religious propagandists, which increasingly turns into a collection of notes of political agitators and, finally, legislators, is, laboriously revised, extended, and supplemented though not sufficiently ordered in the Qur'anic corpus. Another conclusion is that these pieces were written down from the beginning.[11]

Finally, the extensive discussion and further development of the idea of aide-mémoire for a preacher can only be pointed out here – there is another reference to the scientific work of Hans Walter Wolff. In his opinion, the collection of notes mentioned above would be "sketches of appearances," as he assumes them to be for the origins and beginnings of biblical prophetic books, sketches which, in the course of tradition, were editorially supplemented, expanded, and revised.

List of Body Part Designations and Related Nomina in the Qur'anic Corpus

As a preliminary examination of the Qur'anic and to a lesser extent ancient Arabic findings, the following sketch is not a consistent and detailed categorization boasting the diachronic depth and variety of text genres that one finds in the well-known systematics of linguistics and literary studies (metaphor, metonymy, meronymy, etc.).,.[12] Preliminary and individual investigations necessary

---

11 Even Richard Bell, in his translation and commentary of the Qur'ān, assumes that such "slips of paper" were not always included in the corpus in an orderly fashion. For a more recent study on the origin and textual history of the Qur'ān, see Pohlmann 2012. As an experienced and proven researcher of Old Testament textual criticism, the author applies its methods and his research experience to selected examples in the Qur'ān (forms of God's speech, Iblis Satan text, Moses narrative, Qur'anic statements about the status of Jesus) and arrives at groundbreaking conclusions.

12 As finely presented in the work on ancient Egyptian by Werning (cited above), whose theoretical introduction (§ 0–3) contains the necessary definitions of terms and the relevant linguistic and literary literature. Ancient Egyptian also represents a stimulating category and special

for this kind of enterprise are still largely lacking, be it for the Qur'anic corpus or pre-Islamic Arabic poetry and Arabic in general.[13]

The following list, rather, is arranged with some subjective categorizations, "from head to toe." Two word lists of Arabic (alphabetical) and English (by frequency) can be found at the end of this article. The translations are taken from the sources mentioned above, in the case of longer coherent texts mostly from the translation by Rudi Paret.[14]

The ensuing comments are orientated towards the system mentioned above, but are to be evaluated as preliminary insights, still quite impressionistic, of the Qura'nic evidence. The contrasting evidence from pre-Islamic Arabic poetry, on the other hand, can be seen as an exemplary, possibly unrepresentative, selection in the first overview of the references. To what extent a Qur'anic anthropology can be determined solely from this linguistic material remains deliberately unclear, but seems for a theologian, no insoluble task.[15]

The English translations of Qur'anic passages are Pickthall's in general. The preference for this version may easily be ascribed to my limited competence in the subtilities of the English language.

digit = number of attestations

Q x(xx):x(xx) = Reference in the Qur'ān: surah, verse; in the case of several documents only one reference, or for special language use the relevant reference. Complete references can be easily determined with the aforementioned tools.

c = concrete meaning

gr = grammaticalized term

Further categorizations are explicitly indicated.

---

development for the analysis of the use and meaning of body part designations in its image-oriented writing system, which the alphabet scripts of the Semitic languages lack.

13 A first treatment of the subject covering all metaphors and comparisons in the Qur'ān can be found in Sister 1931. *Das Wörterbuch der klassischen arabischen Sprache* offers in the lemmas excellent individual studies to *ka'b, kaff, lubb, liḥya* and *lisān*. This highlights all the more the absence of a scientific reference dictionary for the other remaining letters. The wealth of material and the abundance of results and categorizations, however, is hidden in an overly reserved typographical structure and labeling, which makes its use extremely cumbersome. Studies on word fields are rare. The work by Seidensticker 1992 is an exception. For epigraphic South Arabian, there is the phraseological study of Sima 2001.

14 The preference for Paret's translation (1966 and 2007) is due to the German and idiosyncratic genesis of this paper, on the one hand, and the number of illustrative "academic" translations by Paret, on the other hand.

15 The complete scientific transliteration of the Qur'anic corpus into the Latin script according to the standards DIN 31 635 and ISO 233 by Hans Zirker (valid version: http://duepublico.uni-duisburg-essen.de/servlets/DocumentServlet?id=10802; accessed May 20, 2021) was of excellent help for preparing the text in what follows.

Body Parts List "from Head to Toe"

Full and Substitute Designations for the Body and Relatives

insān 71 *insiyy* 1 "human being"

nās 241 "people, someone, who" (filler word, grammaticalized), c, gr.

ins 18 "the human kind," c

badan 1 "body," Q 10:92, c

ǧism 2 "body," Q 2:247; 63:4, c

bašar 37 "humans" ("normal" humans, in contrast to prophets, angels, and especially God) (Q 3:79); man (meronymic, *totum pro parte*) (Q 3:47); "someone, one" (filler word or grammaticalized, indefinite pronouns) (Q 14:10); 37, c, gr. Cf. also below "skin."[16]

rağul 60 "man," 60, c (especially in hereditary)

Etymologically associated with *riğl* "foot."

nafs 292 "breath, life, soul, human being, person, someone, himself," (indefinite and reflexive pronouns;approximately 200 out of 292 attestations should be interpreted as reflexive pronouns or "person"), c, gr.

verbal root in the corpus of the Qur'ān attested: *tanaffasa* "blowing"; *nāfasa* "sniffing at each other" (?) = rivalry.

nafs as the seat of man's will and desire, but also of his understanding.

Nafs knows, recognizes, delights, longs for.

As "life" in the Qur'anic formula of the *lex talionis* (Exod 21:23–25):, *'anna n-nafsa bi-n-nafsi wa-l-ʿayna bi-l-ʿayni wa-l-'anfa bi-l-'anfi wa-l-'uḏuna bi-l-'uḏuni wa-s-sinna bi-s-sinni* "the life for the life, and the eye for the eye, and the nose for the nose, and the ear for the ear, and the tooth for the tooth" (Q 5:45).

Q 5:32: (Israelites are differentiated from Jews in the Qur'ān): *man qatala nafsan bi-ġayr nafsin aw fasādin fī l-'arḍi fa-ka-anna-mā qatala n-nās ǧamīʿan* (in Paret's incomparable translation full of explanatory brackets): "Wenn einer jemanden tötet, (und zwar) nicht (etwa zur Rache) für jemand (anderes, der von

16 The consonant root is semantically richly structured, from "announcing good news" to "man" to "skin," "being in direct contact." In addition to inner-language phonetic coincidence (homophonic roots), borrowings from related languages can also be considered for explanation.

diesem getötet worden ist) oder (zur Strafe für) Unheil (das er) auf der Erde (angerichtet hat), es so sein soll, als ob er die Menschen alle getötet hätte."[17]

Q 4:1; 6:98; 39:6: (God created all men) *min nafs wāḥida*, "from one person, one being." Here, one translator of the Qur'ān offers three different translations for the same term in the three passages: substance, soul, human being.[18]

Q 16:111: *yawma ta'tī kullu nafsin tuǧādilu ʿan nafsi-hā* "On the Day when every soul will come pleading for itself."

As an indefinite pronoun:*wa-ttaqū yawman lā taǧzī nafsun ʿan nafsin šay 'an wa-lā yuqbalu minhā ʿadlun wa-lā tanfaʿuhā šafāʿatun wa-lā hum yunṣarūna* "And guard yourselves against a day when no soul will in aught avail another, nor will intercession be accepted from it, nor will compensation be received from it, nor will they be helped"(Q 2:48). For the verb *ǧazā*, "to perform for another, to give compensation," but also "to punish," see below at *yad* "hand" and *ǧizya*. In this context (indefinite pronoun in the expression *per merismum* "absolutely none"), one may adduce as holistic designations *wālid*, "producer," *mawlūd* "product," and *walad*, "child" in Q 31:33: *yā-'ayyuhā n-nāsu ttaqū rabbakum wa-ḫšaw yawman lā yaǧzī wālidun ʿan waladihī wa-lā mawlūdun huwa ǧāzin ʿan wālidihī šay'an 'inna waʿda llāhi ḥaqqun* "O mankind! Keep your duty to your Lord and fear a Day when the parent will not be able to avail the child in aught, nor the child to avail the parent. Lo! Allah's promise is the very truth. Let not the life of the world beguile you, nor let the deceiver beguile you, in regard to Allah."

kullu nafsin ḏā 'iqatu l-mawt, "every *nafs* will taste death"; modern translation: "every human being is mortal; every (one of us) must die."

In ancient Arabic poetry, besides its pronominal use, *nafs sometimes* means "life, spirit, mood." But typical in ancient Arabic poetry, in the meaning of "person" is the use as a "second me" in the inner dialogue or self-talk: "the *nafs*, or my *nafs* speaks to me," that is, "I say to myself, I cheer myself up, I give myself the good advice," and so on.

the following expression is important: *šifā an-nafs*, "healing of the soul" = "revenge," actually, "self-healing."

---

17 Roughly translated as: "If someone kills someone, not (for revenge) for someone (someone else who has been killed by him) or (as punishment for) the evil (he has done) on earth, it should be as if he had killed all people." With less annotations: "that whoever kills a soul unless for a soul or for corruption [done] in the land, it is as if he had slain mankind entirely."

18 In German: Wesen, Seele, Mensch. The translation is to be found in Bubenheim and Elyas 2002.

The Body's Components

warīd 1 "carotid artery" (Q 50:16), c.

watīn 1 "big vein, aorta (?)" (Q 69:46) c; (word possibly invented for rhyming reasons).

ǧulūd 9 "skin, leather, fur," c (for burnt skin of the damned in hell, Q 4:56; 22:20), metonymic-functional use for an associated state or action in idioms (somatisms): crimping or smoothing the skin for fear and diminishing the fear[19] (Q 39:24); the body language involuntarily bears witness to itself against the unbelievers (Q 41:20–21), "Till, when they reach it, their ears and their eyes and their skins testify against them as to what they used to do. And they say unto their skins: Why testify ye against us? They say: Allah hath given us speech Who giveth speech to all things, and Who created you at the first, and unto Whom ye are returned." The part of the body that is treacherous in its language is still personified and addressed (in self-talk). For other treacherous and self-accusing body parts, see tongue, hands, feet (Q 24:24; 36:65).

The verbal root (four times in the Qur'ān) means "to whip."

bašar, "skin," 1, c *lawwāḥatun li-l-bašari*, "scorching the skin"; but in another interpretation: "It changes the person completely" (Q74,29). See above *bašar*, "man."

aš'ār 1 "hair" c *wa-llāhu ǧa 'ala lakum min buyūtikum sakanan wa-ǧa'ala lakum min ǧulūdi l-'an'āmi buyūtan tastaḫiffūnahā yawma ẓa'nikum wa-yawma 'iqāmatikum wa-min 'aṣwāfihā wa-'awbārihā wa-'aš'ārihā 'aṯāṯan wa-matā'an 'ilā ḥīnin* "And Allah hath given you in your houses an abode, and hath given you (also), of the hides of cattle, houses which ye find light (to carry) on the day of migration and on the day of pitching camp; and of their wool and their fur and their hair, caparison and comfort for a while" (Q 16:80). In the Qur'ān, *aš'ār* only refers to the hair of animals.

See below the unclear *šawā*, "scalp."

'aẓm 13 "bones," c (in dietary rules, or from the dead); meronymous for the whole person: *'innī wahana l-'aẓmu minnī* "my bones are weak" (Q 19:4).

laḥm 12 "meat," c *'innamā ḥarrama 'alaykumu l-maytata wa-d-dama wa-l-laḥma l-ḫinzīri wa-mā 'uhilla bihī li-ġayri llāhi fa-mani ḍṭurra ġayra bāġin wa-lā 'ādin fa-lā 'iṯma 'alayhi 'inna llāha ġafūrun raḥīmun* "He hath forbidden you only carrion, and blood, and swineflesh, and that which hath been immolated to (the name of) any other than Allah. But he who is driven by necessity, neither craving nor transgressing, it is no sin for him. Lo! Allah is Forgiving, Merciful"

---

19 See "shudder on the back, goose bumps."

(Q 2:173). It is uncertain whether the following is concrete or meronymic and metonymic functional: *'a-yuḥibbu 'aḥadukum 'an ya'kula laḥma 'aḫīhi maytan fa-karihtumūhu wa-ttaqū llāha 'inna llāha tawwābun raḥīmun* "Would one of you love to eat the flesh of his dead brother? Ye abhor that (so abhor the other)! And keep your duty (to Allah). Lo! Allah is Relenting, Merciful" (Q 49:12).[20]

dam 10 "blood" c (see above *laḥm*); meronymic: *wa-'iḏ 'aḫaḏnā mīṯāqakum lā tasfikūna dimā'akum wa-lā tuḫriǧūna 'anfusakum min diyārikum ṯumma 'aqrartum wa-'antum tašhadūna* "And when We made with you a covenant (saying): Shed not the blood of your people nor turn (a party of) your people out of your dwellings. Then ye ratified (Our covenant) and ye were witnesses (thereto)" (Q 2:84 and passim).

Head

ra 's 21 "head," 21, c,

(next to "leader," e.g., in *ra's-māl*, "head of fortune" = "capital"; then in idioms: "shake head" = "deny," "contradict,"; the following phrase in Q 21:65 is unclear: *ṯumma nukisū 'alā ru'ūsihim la-qad 'alimta mā hā'ulā'i yanṭiqūna* "And they were utterly confounded, and they said: Well thou knowest that these speak not." Other interpretations include: "Then crestfallen (they confessed): 'Truly, as you know, they cannot speak'" (Ahmad Ali); "Then their minds were turned upside down, and they said: 'You know well that they do not speak'" (Mawdudi).[21]

waǧh 72 "Face; front; reputation, honour" c, gr. (a support word for personal pronouns and with mention of persons to be respected).

Q 55:26–27: *kullun mā 'alay-hā fānin wa-yabqā waǧhu rabbi-ka ḏū l-ǧalāli wa-l-ikrām*, "Everyone that is thereon will pass away, there remaineth but the Countenance of thy Lord of Might and Glory." "Countenance," "person," and

---

20 Paret, like many other translators, opts firmly for the concrete meaning ("wie ein Aasgeier das Fleisch seines Bruders essen"; "how a vulture eats his brother's meat") and comments: "The expression *akala lahma fulānin* also appears elsewhere with the meaning 'denigrate' See J. Kraemer, Theodor Nöldeke's Belegwörterbuch zur klassischen arabischen Sprache, s. v. *akala*. In this text it is interpreted literally." At first, this seems plausible. On closer inspection, however, the metaphorical interpretation gains in importance, because the slander for a dead person (see the passage above) is definitely an intensification that is possible within the scope of the comparison and seems more realistic.

21 Interestingly enough, most of the translators and commentators gloss over this phrase without further explanation.

"face," are among the astonishingly different renderings of *wağh* in this passage, avoiding the simple and nearest solution to see it as a filling support word when mentioning persons of respect.

šawā 1 "scalp?" unclear, Q 70:16, c

ğabīn 2 "forehead," Q 37:103, c

ğibāh 1 "forehead," Q 9:35, c

nāṣiya 4 "forelock (of animals and humans)." Q 11:56: of animals; Q 96: 15–16: of humans. Meronymic (*pars pro toto*) for "whole, the whole body, the whole being" (Q 96:16), the qualities (here of the sinner) are directly transferred to it, "the lying, sinful forelock" = "the lying, sinful human being"; in somatism "to grab at the forelock" = "to have completely in control," intensified, possibly "to have completely in control." Redundant as an expression *per merismum* (Q 55:41), "grabbing at the forehead curl and at the feet" = "grabbing the whole body, completely" (see below for *qadam* "foot").

ʾuḏun 19 "ear," c (see also *iṣbaʿ* "finger";and *nafs* "life" for the Qura'nic version of the *lex talionis*). In simultaneous metonymic-functional and meronymic use, *wa-yaqūlūna huwa ʾuḏunun qul ʾuḏunu ḫayrin lakum* "and say: He is only a hearer. Say: A hearer of good for you!" (Q 9:61).[22] It becomes clear from the following that the body part stands for the whole person. The exact statement of the accusation remains unclear, but it is likely that what is meant is: one who hears what others do not hear, who believes to hear the extraordinary, but also abstruse as supernatural perception.[23]

ʿayn 59 "eye," c, ("in sight," "in the present," "under supervision, protection"), gr. ("exactly the same"; selection). The use "eye" = sight, human experience = humans in action, their action, which comes into question for a synthetic view of the body, steps back behind the abstract *baṣar* ("sight, gaze"), or stands in alternative, competing use. At the same time, it can redundantly be added to the verb *raʾā*, "to see."

ʾanf 2 "nose," c. See above *nafs* ("life") in the Qur'anic formula of the *lex talionis* (Ex 21: 23–25).

---

22 Paret's translation: " . . . and say: He listens (to everything)(?) (w. He is (all) ear)! Say: He hears for you (only) good)" and in the commentary: "The expression *huwa für* is unanimously explained by the commentators in the sense that the Prophet is accused of gullibility by his opponents. Another way of interpretation would be to accuse the Prophet of believing that he is hearing all sorts of things (and passing them on as a revelation, while in reality there is nothing tangible behind them."

23 The verbal root *aḏina* derived from the nominal root "ear" and the commonly used one for "hearing" (Arab.: *samiʿa)* go different ways. The root *aḏina*, often represented in the Qur'anic corpus with many derivatives, has the specific meaning "to hear" = "to hear, to allow, to agree."

ḫadd 1 "cheek," c in somatism (Q 31:18): *wa-lā tuṣa ''ir ḫaddaka li-n-nāsi* "Turn not thy cheek in scorn toward folk (out of contempt for people)" = "don't turn up your nose" or "don't raise your eyebrows" = "don't show contempt."[24]

fū(h) 14 "mouth,", c redundant or reinforcing in idioms: *qawlu-hum bi-afwāhi-him*, "their speeches from their own mouth"; metonymic-functional use for an associated action or product (Q 9:32; 61:8 and passim): *yurīdūna li-yuṭfiʾū nūra llāhi bi-ʾafwāhihim*, "Fain would they put out the light of Allah with their mouths" = "cover God's revealed word with their vain talk." Here two images are put together: the light of God, which cannot be blown out with the breath of the mouth = the word of God, which cannot be covered by vain talk. In both cases, however, the metonymic-functional use of the word "mouth" applies; in other context, however, only the equation "mouth = word, speech" is used in the text.[25] *Fūh*, "mouth," and *yad*, "hand": *fa-raddū ʾaydiyahum fī ʾafwāhihim*, "but they thrust their hands into their mouths" (Q 14:9);[26] see *also anāmil* and *yad.*

ḫurṭūm 1 "snout." An invective against a slanderer when used simultaneously in a metonymic-functional and meronymic sense, with degrading change of sphere from human to animal: *sa-nasimuhū ʿalā l-ḫurṭūmi* "We shall brand him on the nose" (Q 68:16). Snout = mouth of the slanderer, shameful mouth. Perhaps there was a somatism known to the contemporaries (comparable to the German "jemanden eins aufs Maul geben," "to smack someone in the mouth").[27]

šafatān 1 "both lips," c (Q 90:9)

---

24 A pearl in Paret's translation: "And don't give people the cold shoulder" (?) (literally, "don't twist your cheek towards people" ?:). If he ever dares an idiomatic translation in the target language, he has hit the wrong mark here.

25 Paret's translation: "They want to blow out the light of God (?) (want to extinguish with her mouth)," misses this fine ambiguity. In his commentary, Paret deepens the banal argument: "61.8. – In the expression *li-yuṭfiʾu yuṭfiʾu nūra bi-könnte*, the phrase *könnte qawluhum bi-llāhi* could at best have an effect in 9.30 (see the commentary on this). But probably only the purely physical process of blowing out (with air-filled cheeks) is thought of, especially since in the reference 61,8 a reminiscence of 'empty talk' (*qawluhum bi-qawluhum*) does not seem to exist."

26 In connection and in conjunction with the parallel idioms, Paret's translation seems astonishing: "Her envoys came to them with clear evidence. But then they shut their mouths (?) (literally, they put their hand in (i.e., open?) their mouth) and said: We do not believe in the message that has been given to you." The same holds true for many other of Paret's translations: "They put their hands in their mouth – and then – hands in the mouth? – answered."

27 It is noteworthy that most translations of the Qur'ān blur the clear coarseness of the formulation: Nose and mouth must stand for snout in a sacred text; a fine example of falsification by translation. This is not the only place in the Qur'anic corpus where a frustrated preacher lets his feelings run free verbally.

sinn 2 “tooth,” see *nafs* (“life”) above in the Qur’anic formula of the *lex talionis* (Exod 21:23–25).

lisān 28 “tongue; word; language,” c, the tongue is detached (from its knot) = one can speak freely and fluently.

lisān ṣidq = a true word.

“God does not send a messenger except with a message in the language (*lisān*) of his people.” The Qur’ān is in *lisān ʿarabī* “Arabic language” (?); but Muḥammad would have been offended if he had been called an Arab.

ḏiqn 3 “chin,” c in the phrase “falling on the chin” = “prostrating” (Q 17:107; 17, 109); in the sentence*ˈinnā ğa ʿalnā fī ˈa ʿnāqihim ˈaġlālan fa-hiya ˈilā l-ˈaḏqāni fa-hum muqmaḥūna* “Lo! We have put on their necks carcans reaching unto the chins, so that they are made stiff-necked” (Q 36:8). The nearest sense is that of a crude mocking and disparaging reinterpretation of the “snobbish” attitude of the unbelievers: they think that they are proud but are only camels who have to hold their heads up with a studded neck cuff and cannot drink.[28]

liḥya 1 “beard,”, c or meronymic for the whole person; at the same time, it can also appear in a double somatism (?): *qāla ya-bna-ˈumma lā taˈḫuḏ bi-liḥyatī wa-lā bi-raˈsī* “He said: O son of my mother! Clutch not my beard nor my head!” = Don’t touch my prestige and honor! Don’t humiliate me! Don’t blame me, don’t scold (and abuse) me! (Q 20:94). Both “head” and “beard” often stand for the whole person. The beard stands at the same time for the esteem and honor of the man. Numerous examples of how this esteem – through somatisms – can be lowered and humiliated appear in (old) Arabic poetry and literature.[29]

Neck

ğīd 1 “neck,” c *fī ğīdihā ḥablun min masadin*, “upon her neck a halter of palm-fibre” (Q 111:5).

---

28 Paret’s translation: “We have put chains on their necks, and they go up to their chins, so that they hold up their heads (and are inhibited in their activity).” His commentary has little to do with his translation: 34,33; 13,5, with further evidence. In 34,33 and the further references the putting on of neck cuffs belongs to punishment in the hereafter. On the other hand, in the present passage 36,8 it seems to refer to the behavior of unbelievers in this world and to be meant rather figuratively: The unbelievers throw back their heads, as if neck cuffs would push up their chins, and thus do not see what is really going on (?). Bell noticed right away: “There is here no eschatological sense. The simile is that of a spiked collar (branks) put on a camel so that it cannot let down its head to drink.”

29 Cf. WKAS (as in note XX) 2.1., 1983, 408a–417b; especially, 415b ff.

ḥanāǧir 2 (*plurale tantum*) "throat," c in the somatism *wa-balaġati l-qulūbu l-ḥanāǧira* "and hearts reached to the throats" (Q 33:10) and *iḏi l-qulūbu ladā l-ḥanāǧiri kāẓimīn* "when the hearts will be choking the throats" (Q 40:18). *Qulūb* "Hearts" stands here twice in metonymic-functional use for an associated action and its product (heartbeat, palpitations), a simple linguistic fact that most translations ignore.[30]

ḥulqūm 1 "throat,", c *iḏā balaġati l-ḥulqūma* "then, when (the soul) cometh up to the throat (of the dying)" (Q 56:83); see also below *tarāqī* "collarbone."

The traditional commentaries and most translations understand the phrase with the verb *balaġat* "reached" without an explicit subject as referring to the "soul of the dying person," even if this does require explanatory contextual additions (Q56:83; 75:26). The parallels to *balaġati l-qulūbu l-ḥanāǧira* (see above) are clear enough, especially since the situation of "fear of death and moment of death" is the same.

riqāb 3, "neck," c *ffa-ʾiḏā laqītumu llaḏīna kafarū fa-ḍarba r-riqābi* "Now when ye meet in battle those who disbelieve, then it is smiting of the necks until" (Q 47:4); metaphorical use for a sociological-functional meaning derived from a spatial concept, here "slave": *ʾinnamā ṣ-ṣadaqātu li-l-fuqarāʾi wa-l-masākīni wa-l- ʿāmilīna ʿalayhā wa-l-muʾallafati qulūbuhum wa-fī r-riqābi* "The alms are only for the poor and the needy, and those who collect them, and those whose hearts are to be reconciled, and to free the captives" (Q 9:60; similar to Q 2:177); strictly speaking, there is also a metaphor in the form of metonymic-functional use for an associated action (liberation of the slave).

raqaba 6 "neck," only in the singular and in metaphorical use for a sociological-functional meaning derived from a spatial concept, here "slave," but without the metaphor mentioned above in the explicit turns *taḥrīr raqabatin* "liberation of a slave" (Q 4:92 and passim) and *fakk raqabatin* "release of a slave" (Q 90:13).

ʿunq 9 "neck," c *fa-ḍribū fawqa l- aʿnāqi wa-ḍribū minhum kulla banānin* "Then smite the necks and smite of them each finger!" (Q 8:12); however, here also a per merismum is possible (from the largest, most important body part, the neck, up to the smallest, the fingers: "hit / tear them completely into pieces!"; often in connection with *ġill* "bondage" as "neck cuff";

in meronymic use for the whole human being and/or the whole body in connection with the metaphor "bird" = "omen and destiny": *wa-kulla ʾinsānin*

30 It is remarkable to see how some translate this idiom with forced literalism and with even more forced explanation (in brackets), even though idiomatically exact correspondence exists in German.

'alzamnāhu ṭā'irahū fī ʿunuqihī wa-nuḫriǧu lahū yawma l-qiyāmati kitāban yalqāhu manšūran "And every man's augury have We fastened to his own neck, and We shall bring forth for him on the Day of Resurrection a book which he will find wide open". (Q 17:13); hence, for instance, in corresponding German somatism: "We have written the unchangeable fate on the body of every human being."[31]

in meronymous use for the whole human being: *''in naša' nunazzil ʿalayhim mina s-samā'i 'āyatan fa-ẓallat 'aʿnāquhum lahā ḫāḍiʿīna* "If We wanted, We sent a sign from heaven to them, and their necks bowed submissively to him" = "If We will, We can send down on them from the sky a portent so that their necks would remain bowed before it." (Q 26,4).

S. a. below *yad* "hand."

warīd 1 "carotid artery," in meronymic use for the whole human being, at the same time metonymic-functional in an associated action: *wa-naḥnu aqrabu ilayhi min ḥabli l-warīdi* "We are nearer to him than his jugular vein" = "closer than he (the human being) to himself (in a vital function)" (Q 50:16).[32]

Arms

ḏirāʿ 2 "Arm; foreleg (of the animal)," c *wa-kalbuhum bāsiṭun ḏirāʿayhi bi-l-waṣīdi* "and their dog stretching out his paws on the threshold" (Q 18:18); in metaphorical use for a quantitative meaning (length measure) derived from the spatial concept: *ṯumma fī silsilatin ḏarʿuhā sabʿūna ḏirāʿan* "And then insert him in a chain whereof the length is seventy cubits."(Q 69:32).

In ancient Arabic poetry quite often in the concrete sense, but especially as a metaphor for "penis" and "man power," often used in an obscene context.

ʿaḍud 2 "(strong) upper arm" in meronymic use for the whole person, at the same time metonymic-functional for an associated action and its

31 Paret's comment on this passage includes the following quote: "For the expression *ṭā'ir* '(flying) bird' 'omen,' 'fate,' see Helmer Ringgren, Studies in Arabian Fatalism, Uppsala-Wiesbaden 1955, pp. 87–89. Ringgren comments specifically on this passage (p. 88): 'The book mentioned here obviously contains the man's good or evil deeds, for which he has to account on the day of judgment. But it is not quite clear what this has to do with his fate fastened on his neck. It may be that the ideas of a book of destiny and a book of accounts are confused, and that the passage refers to the predestination not only of man's condition of life, but also of his deeds and their consequences in the hereafter. In any case, it does show that Muhammad did not reject the word *ṭā'ir*, but used it as an adequate expression of the divine predestination of man's destiny.'"

32 In most translations, the image is translated literally and without comment even though this image is unclear and uncommon in most target languages.

product: *qāla sa-našuddu ʿaḍudaka bi-ʾaḫīka* "He said: We will strengthen thine arm with thy brother, " (Q 28:35); also: *wa-mā kuntu muttaḫiḏa l-muḍillīna aḍudan* "nor choose I misleaders for (My) helpers = strengthening and support" (Q 18:51).

marāfiq 1 "elbow," c *yā-ʾayyuhā llaḏīna ʾāmanū ʾiḏā qumtum ʾilā ṣ-ṣalāti fa-ġsilū wuǧūhakum wa-ʾaydiyakum ʾilā l-marāfiqi wa-msaḥū bi-ruʾūsikum wa-ʾarǧulakum ʾilā l-kaʿbayni* "O ye who believe! When ye rise up for prayer, wash you faces, and your hands up to the elbows, and lightly rub your heads and (wash) your feet up to the ankles" (Q 5:6).[33]

Hand, Finger

yad 120 "hand; strength, power, action"; prep. "through," 120, c, gr.

fa-raddū ʾaydiyahum fī ʾafwāhihim"but they thrust their hands into their mouths " (Q 14:9). See *fūh* "mouth" and *anāmil* "fingertips."

Q 5:64: the hand of God is not bound, as the Jews say, but open (cf. o. *ʿunq*!). In ancient Arabic poetry, among other uses, the *yad ad-dahr* "hand of fate" is a standing idiom (power of fate). This is replaced in the Qur'anic corpus and poetry influenced by it by the "hand of God."

A phrase in which *yad* "hand" = "generosity" and other body parts come together: *wa-lā taǧʿal yadaka maġlūlatan ʾilā ʿunuqika wa-lā tabsuṭhā kulla l-basṭi fa-taqʿuda malūman maḥsūran* "And let not thy hand be chained to thy neck nor open it with a complete opening, lest thou sit down rebuked, denuded" (Q 17:29); a phrase *per merismum* in the form of a sentence, as well as a proof for the grammaticalization of the verb *qaʿada* "to sit," which in Qur'anic terms often simply means "to stay," after all simply "to be." Modern translation: "Give (alms etc.) in the right measure, so you will be spared shame and ruin."

Q 9:29, which is not for nothing highly controversial for traditional Muslim exegesis and secular Islamic and studies and has accordingly caused an extensive secondary literature:

33 A controversial passage; at issue is the vocalization of the word "feet." In the version above, the accusative is read as depending on "to wash." The alternative reading vocalizes it as a genitive and second prepositional object for "to stroke over."

qātilū llaḏīna lā yu'minūna bi-llāhi wa-lā bi-l-yawmi l-'āḫiri wa-lā yuḥarrimūna mā ḥarrama llāhu wa-rasūluhū wa-lā yadīnūna dīna l-ḥaqqi mina llaḏīna 'ūtū l-kitāba ḥattā yu'ṭū l-ǧizyata 'an yadin wa-hum ṣāġirūna

"Fight against such of those who believe not in Allah nor the Last Day, and forbid not that which Allah hath forbidden by His messenger, and follow not the Religion of Truth, until they pay the tribute readily, being brought low."

The tribute is paid and at the same time implies the apparently low, inferior position of the tributary. About the meaning of the formula *'an yadin,* Muslim exegesis and scientific studies offer a whole series of explanations: from the concrete meaning "from the hand (directly into the hand of the tax collector)" to (spatial conceptual and sociological-functional meaning) "from possession, property"; "generous," "voluntary (from own power of disposal)," "submissive (renouncing his power of disposal [hand], separated from it)"; cf. finally Rubin 2006, who quotes earlier works of on this passage and other contributions. His article ends with a detailed quotation (on p. 146) from Ibn al-Qayyim al-Ǧawziyya, still today the leading figure of fundamentalist Islam, from his work on the legal status of *ḏimma*, members of non-Muslimyet tolerated religions according to a legal mindset: "*'An yadin* describes a state (*ḥāl*), i.e. they must give the *jizya* while they are humiliated and oppressed (*aḏillā' maqhūrīn*). This is the correct (*al-ṣaḥīḥ*) interpretation of the verse. Some said that the meaning is 'from hand to hand, in cash, not on credit.' Others said: 'From his hand unto the hand of the receiver, not sending it nor delegating its payment.' Others said: 'It means due to a benefaction on your part unto them by agreeing to receive payment from them.' But the accurate opinion is the first one, and the people agree on it. The most far-fetched opinion that misses God's intention is that of those who say that the meaning is: 'Out of their ability to pay it, which is why [the *jizya*] is not collected from those who can't afford it.' This rule is correct, but its application to the verse is wrong. No one of the companions of the Prophet and of the successors interpreted it in this manner nor anyone of the old masters of the *umma*. It is only the witty inference of some later scholars." From the point of view of a scholar born at a later time, nothing more would be added to this, except for the following paragraph and observation that this firm, perhaps, better, ideologically embedded conviction, – is not a characteristic of the past but continues in a series of apologetically driven (polemical) works by Muslim and non-Muslim scholars alike; As recent example concerning Q 9:29, see Haleem 2012. The tribute concerns the head tax (*ǧizya*), which is to be paid in the later Islamic state by non-Muslim subjectswho are members of a tolerated religion. This consideration alone leads to the assumption that this passage is a later editorial insertion. It does not fit with Muḥammad's time, but much better with the later Umayyad period, especially the reign of the Caliph ʿAbd-al-Malik, when the organization of the Islamic religion and state materializes. Moreover, according to recent research, the word *ǧizya* is not Arabic, thus also etymologically unrelated to the root ǦZY (see an example for this verb above under *nafs*, in the sense of compensation, stand up for, etc.). The word is documented in a Pahlavi text as *gazidak* in the sense of a head tax; the underlying verb *gazidan* "select; prefer; support" is well documented in New Persian, as is the noun *gazīd* "gift; tribute." The linguistic and historical circumstances of the loan still have to be clarified, but this seems to be a clearly different and historically plausible approach to the clarification of Q 9:29. In this context, the explanation for *ʿan yadin*, which is analogous to circumstances in the Sassanian Empire, offers itself as "according to the assets, the performance" of the taxpayer. It is thus a metonymic-functional use for an associated action and its product as a fixed, legal formula.

šimāl 8 "left hand," 8, c, gr. (location and direction)

In expressions per merismum *šimāl* – *yamīn* (right) = everywhere, in all directions.

yamīn 47 "right hand; oath," 47, c, gr. (location and direction)

mā malakat aymanu-kum "what your right hands possess" formula of legal language for legitimate possession.

kaffān 2 "the palms of both hands," 2, c

banān 2 "Finger," c see above *ʿunq*; metaphorical use for a quantitative use derived from a spatial concept (here: smallest part): *balā qādirīna ʿalā ʾan nusawwiya banānahū* "Yea, verily. We are able to restore his very fingers!" = "(from the bones of the whole human being) to its smallest parts" (Q 75:4).

iṣbaʿ 2 "fingers," c in somatism: "stuffing their fingers in their ears" a) to protect themselves against excessive noise: *yaǧʿalūna ʾaṣābiʿahum fī ʾāḏānihim mina ṣ-ṣawāʿiqi* "They thrust their fingers in their ears by reason of the thunder-claps" (Q 2:19) and b) do not want to hear in order not to have to hear: *wa- innī kullamā daʿawtuhum li-taġfira lahum ǧaʿalū aṣābiʿahum fī āḏānihim* "And lo! whenever I call unto them that Thou mayst pardon them they thrust their fingers in their ears" (Q 71:7).

anāmil 1 "Fingertips" c in somatism: *wa-ʾiḏā ḫalaw ʿaḍḍū ʿalaykumu l-ʾanāmila mina l-ġayẓ* "But when they go apart they bite their finger-tips at you, for rage" (Q 3,119);[34] an equivalent somatism see *fūh* "mouth" and *yad* "hand": *fa-raddū ʾaydiyahum fī ʾafwāhihim* "but they thrust their hands into their mouths" (Q 14:9). The twist presented here has the advantage of a sharp detailed observation.

34 Somatism, for example, well documented in Italian: "mordersi le dita / le mani dalla rabbia."

Torso

ǧawf 1 "(body-) interior", c in somatism *mā ǧaʿala llāhu li-raǧulin min qalbayni fī ǧawfihī* "Allah hath not assigned unto any man two hearts within his body" (Q 33:4); the meaning of the phrase, which certainly goes beyond the purely biological and concrete, remains unclear. It is connected with the controversial abolition of marriage obstacles for Muḥammad; if one knows the heart as the seat of understanding and wanting, then the interpretation would be possible that no person has a double, divided mind and will. But perhaps the sentence is simply a preparatory introduction to the following new legal provisions: just as one cannot contradict the simple biological fact, one can contest the new legal situation.

baṭn 17 "belly," c, in concrete terms "womb": *ḫalaqakum min nafsin wāḥidatin ṯumma ǧaʿala minhā zawǧahā wa- anzala lakum mina l-anʿāmi ṯamāniyata azwāǧin yaḫluqukum fī buṭūni ummahātikum ḫalqan min baʿdi ḫalqin fī ẓulumātin ṯalāṯin* "He created you from one being, then from that (being) He made its mate; and He hath provided for you of cattle eight kinds. He created you in the wombs of your mothers, creation after creation, in a threefold gloom" (Q 39:6; and passim); (food from the belly of animals): *wa-ʾinna lakum fī l-ʾanʿāmi la-ʿibratan nusqīkum mimmā fī buṭūnihī min bayni farṯin wa-damin labanan ḫāliṣan sāʾiġan li-š-šāribīna* "And lo! in the cattle there is a lesson for you. We give you to drink of that which is in their bellies, from betwixt the refuse and the blood, pure milk palatable to the drinkers" (Q 16:66; 69; 23:21, etc.); mostly for the description of torments of hell: *ʾinna llaḏīna yaktumūna mā ʾanzala llāhu mina l-kitābi wa-yaštarūna bihī ṯamanan qalīlan ulā ika mā ya kulūna fī buṭūnihim illā n-nāra* "Lo! those who hide aught of the Scripture which Allah hath revealed and purchase a small gain therewith, they eat into their bellies nothing else than fire" (Q 2:174; similarly: Q 4:10; 22:20; 44:45, and passim);

metaphorically for an object of comparable external form, possibly a spatial concept: *wa-huwa llaḏī kaffa ʾaydiyahum ʿankum wa-ʾaydiyakum ʿanhum bi-baṭni makkata* "And He it is Who hath withheld men's hands from you, and hath withheld your hands from them, in the valley of Mecca" (Q 48:24); see also *ḥuǧūr* "lap."

ṣulb 2 "backbone, especially lower part, loin," in a metonymic-functional sense for an associated action or product: *wa-ḥalāʾilu ʾabnāʾikumu llaḏīna min ʾaṣlābikum* "and the wives of your sons who (spring) from your own loins" (Q 4:23); see also *tarāʾib* "chest."

In ancient Arabic poetry and common language often: "hard, resistant; the core of something".

Flank, Chest, Stomach

ʿiṭf 1 "flank of the body" metonymic-functional use for an associated action in somatism *wa-mina n-nāsi man yuǧādilu fī llāhi bi-ġayri ʿilmin wa-lā hudan wa-lā kitābin munīrin* (9) *ṯāniya ʿiṭfihī li-yuḍilla ʿan sabīli llāhi* "And among mankind is he who disputeth concerning Allah without knowledge or guidance or a scripture giving light, (9) Turning away in pride to beguile (men) from the way of Allah" (Q 22:9).

ǧanāḥ 7 "flank, wing (of animals and angels)"[35] c, (clothed) body side of the person = garment slit: *wa-ḍmum yadaka ʾilā ǧanāḥika taḫruǧ bayḍāʾa min ġayri sūʾin ʾāyatan ʾuḫrā* "And thrust thy hand within thine armpit, it will come forth white without hurt. (That will be) another token." (Q 20:22; similar to 28:32); as animal wings: *wa-mā min dābbatin fī l-ʾarḍi wa-lā ṭāʾirin yaṭīru bi-ǧanāḥayhi ʾillā ʾumamun ʾamṯālukum* "There is not an animal in the earth, nor a flying creature flying on two wings, but they are peoples like unto you" (Q 6:38); of angels: *ǧāʿili l-malāʾikati rusulan ʾulī ʾaǧniḥatin*"Who appointeth the angels messengers having wings" (Q 35:1);

meronymic and metonymic-functional use for an associated action in somatism: *wa-ḫfiḍ lahumā ǧanāḥa ḏ-ḏulli mina r-raḥmati wa-qul rabbi rḥamhumā kamā rabbayānī ṣaġīran* "And lower unto them the wing of submission through mercy, and say: My Lord! Have mercy on them both as they did care for me when I was little" (Q 17:24; similar to 15:88 and 26:215) = "bow to their side (and with your protective arm) over them, take humble and merciful care of them (your two parents)."[36] One of the most moving images in the corpus.[37]

---

35 The word is a consonant homograph to *ǧunāḥ* "shame, sin"; however, the respective readings are to be carefully separated, since *ǧunāḥ* "sin" only occurs in the stereotypical phrase *fa-lā ǧunāḥ ʿalā* "and it is no sin for" in the Qur'anic corpus.

36 Paret's commentary provides the interpretation of the Muslim exegetes in addition to his own: "The expression *ḫafaḍa ǧanāḥahu* (literally 'lower its wing,' from a bird) is intended to mean that the bird in question takes its wings down, i.e. from flying to resting (Lisān al-ʿArab). From this the transferred meaning 'to be friendly,' 'to be sociable' will be derived. But perhaps the expression originally referred to another phenomenon in bird life, such as the hen's wing lowering, which takes her chicks warmly and protectively under her wing."

Both explanations leave out the closest consideration, namely, that the side (rather than a win) of the human being is meant, bending down on someone in a protective and caring way.

37 Buhl in his, according to his own words, study of "modest importance," "Über Vergleichungen und Gleichnisse im Qurʿân" (In: Acta Orientalia. 2. 1924. 1–11), dealt with this aspect of Quranic language from comprehensive knowledge of the material and sensitive understanding, from the successful and inspired comparisons and parables to the clumsy and dull.

ğanb 8 "flank (human and beast),", c, *yawma yuḥmā ʿalayhā fī nāri ğahannama fa-tukwā bihā ğibāhuhum wa-ğunūbuhum wa-ẓuhūruhum* "On the day when it will (all) be heated in the fire of hell, and their foreheads and their flanks and their backs will be branded therewith" (Q 9:35); meronymous for the whole person: *tatağāfā ğunūbuhum ʿani l-maḍāğiʿi yadʿūna rabbahum ḫawfan wa-ṭamaʿan* "Who forsake their beds to cry unto their Lord in fear and hope" = "They avoid the sleeping place, find no sleep" (Q 32:16); metaphorically for a spatial concept: *ʾan taqūla nafsun yā-ḥasratā ʿalā mā farraṭtu fī ğanbi llāhi wa-ʾin kuntu la-mina s-sāḫirīna* "Lest any soul should say: Alas, my grief that I was unmindful of Allah, and I was indeed among the scoffers!" (Q 39:56); at the same time in the expression *per merismum*: *allaḏīna yaḏkurūna llāha qiyāman wa-quʿūdan wa-ʿalā ğunūbihim*"Such as remember Allah, standing, sitting, and reclining" = "remember in every position" (Q 3:191; similar to Q 4:103; 10:12).

ğānib 9 "direction; side, flank."[38] As a body part designation, it is metonymous as a spatial concept and somatism: *wa-yaʾūsan kāna l-ʾaʿraḍaˉnibihi wa-ˉnibihi bīˉʾʾanʿamna waˉ massahu š-šarru š ʾiḏa* "When We show mercy to man, he turns away and moves away. And when evil hits him, he is very desperate" (Q 17:83; 41:51).

Dubur 18 "back"[39] metaphorical use for a spatial concept (secondary preposition): *wa-stabaqā l-bāba wa-qaddat qamīṣahū min duburin* "And they raced with one another to the door, and she tore his shirt from behind" = the back of his shirt (Q 12,25; 12,27; 12,28); with verb *ittabaʿa* "to follow behind" (Q 15:65); at the same time in an expression *per merismum* (together with wağh):*wa-law tarā iḏ yatawaffā llaḏīna kafarū l-malāʾikatu yaḍribūna wuğūhahum wa-adbārahum wa-ḏūqū ʿaḏāba l-ḥarīqi* "If thou couldst see how the angels receive those who disbelieve, smiting faces and their backs and (saying): Taste the punishment of burning!" = "to the front and to the back, to everywhere" (Q 8,50; 47,27);

metaphorical use for a time concept derived from the spatial concept: *wa-mina l-layli fa-sabbiḥhu wa-ʾadbāra s-suğūdi* "And in the night-time hymn His praise, and after the (prescribed) prostrations!" Q 50,40)

---

38 Active participle of the nominal root *ğanb* "side" with the meaning: "put aside, deter, avoid"; from this as an adjective "to be avoided, impure."

39 The lemma is a good example of the interaction of a primary body part name and root with the same radicals. The verb *adbara* (4th stem) means "turn your back, turn away," like several somatisms formed with other periphrastic verbs and the body part name. From the same consonantal framework *adbāra* can be read "in the back from = behind, after" or the infinitive of the verb cited in the accusative *idbāra with* almost the same meaning; the traditional reading decides on a reading and interpretation. In addition, a homophonic loan root *dabbara*, from Aramaic in the sense of "arrange, dispose, administer" participates.

in metonymic-functional sense for an associated action in a somatism: *lan yaḍurrūkum 'illā 'aḏan wa-'in yuqātilūkum yuwallūkumu l-'adbāra* "They will not harm you save a trifling hurt, and if they fight against you they will turn and flee" = "flee from you" (Q 3:111; similarly, *wallā al-adbār* = "turn your back on sb." = "flee" Q 8:15; 8:16; 17:46), redundantly supplemented by *nufūran* "on the run"; *yā-'ayyuhā llaḏīna 'ūtū l-kitāba 'āminū bi-mā nazzalnā muṣaddiqan li-mā ma'akum min qabli 'an naṭmisa wuǧūhan fa-naruddahā 'alā 'adbārihā* "O ye unto whom the Scripture hath been given! Believe in what We have revealed confirming that which ye possess, before We destroy countenances so as to confound them" = "before We (even high-ranking?) wipe out and bring down personalities? or: to flee?" (Q 4:47; see also above *waǧh* "face"; similarly *radda 'alā al-adbār* = "throw on your back, make fall");

yā-qawmi dḫulū l- arḍa l-muqaddasata llatī kataba llāhu lakum wa-lā tartaddū alā 'adbārikum fa-tanqalibū[40] *ḫāsirīna* "O my people! Go into the holy land which Allah hath ordained for you. Turn not in flight, for surely ye turn back as losers." (Q 5:21; the phrase *irtadda 'alā al-adbār* is the reflexive to active *radda al-adbār* s.o.; similarly, Q 47:5 and passim)

ẓahr 20 "back," c (human back) *fa-tukwā bihā ǧibāhuhum wa-ǧunūbuhum wa-ẓuhūruhum*"and their foreheads and their flanks and their backs will be branded therewith" (9:35); meronymous for an included body part (see also *ṣulb*): *wa-'iḏ 'aḫaḏa rabbuka min banī 'ādama min ẓuhūrihim ḏurriyyatahum* "And (remember) when thy Lord brought forth from the Children of Adam, from their reins, their seed" (Q 7:172); in somatism: *wa-waḍa'nā 'anka wizraka* (3) *allaḏī 'anqaḍa ẓahraka* "And eased thee of the burden (3) which weighed down thy back" = "rescued you from distress and misfortune" (Q 94:2–3; similar to Q 6:31)

c (back of animals) *wa-l-'an'āmi mā tarkabūna li-tastawū 'alā ẓuhūrihī* "and cattle whereupon ye ride" (Q 43:12–13); in dietary regulations (Q 6:138) and for taboo animals (Q 6:146);

metaphorical use for a spatial concept (preposition on): *wa-law yu'āḫiḏu llāhu n-nāsa bi-mā kasabū mā taraka alā ẓahrihā min dābbatin* "If Allah took mankind to task by that which they deserve, He would not leave a living creature on the surface of the earth" (Q 35:45); *wa-min 'āyātihi l-ǧawāri fī l-baḥri ka-l-'a'lāmi 'in yaša' yuskini r-rīḥa fa-yaẓlalna rawākida 'alā ẓahrihī* "And of His portents are the ships, like banners on the sea. (33) If He will He calmeth the wind so that they keep still upon its surface (i.e., the surface of the sea)." (Q 42:32–33); preposition or adverb

---

40 The verb can be supplemented through redundancy and as a somatism with *'aqib* "Ferse" (see above).

"behind": *wa-laysa l-birru bi- an ta'tū l-buyūta min ẓuhūrihā wa-lākinna l-birra mani ttaqā wa- 'tū l-buyūta min abwābihā* "It is not righteousness that ye go to houses by the backs thereof (as do the idolaters at certain seasons), but the righteous man is he who wardeth off (evil). So go to houses by the gates thereof" (Q 2:189); *wa-ammā man ūtiya kitābahū wara'a ẓahrihī* "But whoso is given his account behind his back" (Q 84:10);

metaphorical use for a spatial concept and as a somatism: *wa-lammā ǧā'a-hum rasūlun min 'indi llāhi muṣaddiqun li-mā ma'ahum nabaḏa farīqun mina lla-ḏīna 'ūtū l-kitāba kitāba llāhi warā'a ẓuhūrihim ka-'annahum lā ya'lamūna* "And when there cometh unto them a messenger from Allah, confirming that which they possess, a party of those who have received the Scripture fling the Scripture of Allah behind their backs as if they knew not" (Q 2:101; similar to 3:187; 6,94); *qāla yā-qawmi 'a-rahṭī 'a'azzu 'alaykum mina llāhi wa-ttaḫaḏtumūhu warā'akum ẓihriyyan* "He said: O my people! Is my family more to be honoured by you than Allah? and ye put Him behind you, neglected!" = " . . . put him back as a stop-gap, replacement?" (Q 11:92).[41] The expression is perhaps less aimed at contemptuous standing back or even throwing away than at "holding something in the backhand for an emergency out of clever calculation."

ṣadr 45 "breast, center of the body; sense, mind (seat of understanding, will and feeling)", c, gr (location: in the center, in the middle; but also: the best of, the elite, etc.).

Often synonymous with *qalb* "heart" (see below). Numerous expressions: with *ḍāqa* (to be narrow) = to be in need, in misery, but also in fear; with *šarḥa* "to live in prosperity," but also "to be joyful"; with healing = (religious) salvation; synthetic (but cf. the remark about supporting words): God knows the breast (of humans): God knows it inside and out, completely; cf. Q 22:46: *'a-fa-lam yasīrū fī l-'arḍi fa-takūna lahum qulūbun ya'qilūna bihā 'aw 'āḏānun yasma'ūna bihā fa-'innahā lā ta'mā l-'abṣāru wa-lākin ta'mā l-qulūbu llatī fī ṣ-ṣudūri* "Have they not travelled in the land, and have they hearts wherewith to feel and ears wherewith to hear? For indeed it is not the eyes that grow blind, but it is the hearts, which are within the bosoms, that grow blind."

41 Paret' s translation: "He said: Does my group (of men) impress you more than God, and have you taken him (only) as a reserve (?) behind you (instead of putting him in front of everything else)? This is based on the statement of Muslim exegetes who declare *ẓihrī* as 'unloaded camel(s) of second choice led at the end of the caravan, as a substitute for a possible failure among the other pack animals.'" The somatism from the world of the caravan trade was then directly understandable to the contemporaries with its biting sarcasm.

Modern translation: "Travel forms. But they see, but they understand nothing";

Satan whispers into the breast of the human = he deceives the human.

In ancient Arabic poetry, besides concrete meaning and "center, selection, etc.," very rarely as a seat of feeling; a stereotype and often: center of lance = lance tip; e.g. "the speech gets brilliance from what you just spread, just as the lance tip gets its brilliance from blood."

"eyes get cooling after crying, as soon as blood streams soak the lance tips"

Note the synthet (or pars pro toto?): eyes = a human, a person:

After (long crying) one comforts oneself, as soon as the lance tips (in revenge) drink blood.

The vengeance scene described here is characterized in verses other than *šifā an-nafs* "healing the soul" (see above *šifā aṣ-ṣadr* and *nafs*). Also, here there is a characteristic difference between Qur'anic and ancient poetry language.

manākib 1 "shoulders," schematic-metaphorical use of a body part for an object of comparable external or structural form: *huwa llaḏī ǧaʿala lakumu l-'arḍa ḏalūlan fa-mšū fī manākibihā* "He it is Who hath made the earth subservient unto you, so Walk in the paths thereof" (Q 67:15). Most translations miss the beautiful picture with the reproduction "surface, paths, back" that the earth must carry humans on their shoulders, a comparison, which admittedly "limps" a little, because humans do not sit quietly and are carried, but walk on the surface of the earth.

tarāqī "collar bone," 1, c as a somatism: *iḏā balaġati t-tarāqiya* "No! When the soul has reached the collar bones" (Q 75:26);[42] see above. *ḥanāǧir* and *ḥulqūm*

tarā'ib 1 "ribs, thorax," meronymic for a containing body part in connection with an expression *per merismum: ḫuliqa min mā'in dāfiqin* (7) *yaḫruǧu min bayni ṣ-ṣulbi wa-t-tarā'ibi* "He is created from a gushing fluid (7) that issued from between the loins and ribs" (Q 86:6–7). For loins, see above *ṣulb* "backbone, especially lower part." The generation of humankind from "water, drops of water" is a frequent motif in the Qur'ān. The expression *per merismum* can be simply interpreted as "body, trunk"; the second noun may have been chosen for rhythmic and rhyming purposes.[43]

42 Paret's translation: "When the soul (literally: she) (about to escape the body) comes up to the clavicle (literally (plural) up to the clavicles)." Pickthall as many others: "Nay, but when the life cometh up to the throat."

43 Traditional exegesis and in its aftermath some translations seek to give each of the two limbs its particular meaning: a human is born from the loins of a man and the breastbone (?) of a woman, even the female breast. In addition to the summing function of the two parts of

Marāḍiʿ 1 “breasts of breastfeeding people?”, 1, c or meronymic: *wa-ḥarramnā ʿalayhi l-marāḍiʿa min qablu* “And We had before forbidden foster-mothers for him (Moses)” (Q 28:12). This refers to the feeding breasts of the mother or nurse. However, the plural can also be interpreted grammatically as “nursing mothers” directly.

fuʾād 16 “Heart,” c

Seat of understanding and will, of the responsible decisions of man.

Synonymous and interchangeable with *qalb* “heart” (Classical Arabic is characterized by a wealth of (quasi-)synonyms; perhaps also because this language is a reservoir of regional and local varieties).

Frequently in mixed order (abstracta and body parts): *samʿ – baṣar – qalb / fuʾād / ṣadr* “hearing – eye – heart 1 /heart 2 / chest” (Q 6:46; 16:78; 17:36; 23:78; 45:23; 46:26; 67:23).

Q 53:11 is characteristic: *mā kaḏaba l-fuʾādu mā raʾā* “The heart lied not (in seeing) what it saw,” that is, Muḥammad. has no hallucinations or visions but a true revelation.

In ancient Arabic poetry, the grieved mind of the lover who must be comforted is frequently:

“a (grieved) heart that does not dissuade

rebuke, and an eye whose sleep is forever little”; “a (grieved) heart that cannot cheer up old wine, and a body that does not leave sickness.”

qalb 134 “heart,” c, gr. (in the center, in the middle)

seat of understanding, wanting, but also of feeling: an honest heart, a rough heart, a sick heart (in the sense of religious aberration). For the series of three “hearing – sight – heart.” see above fuʾād; for heart beats up to the neck, see above *ḥanāğir.*

Q 7:179; 22:46: *lahum qulūbun lā yafqahūna bihā wa-lahum ʾa yunun lā yubṣirūna bihā* “having hearts wherewith they understand not, and having eyes wherewith they see not”

Q 2:7; 9:87, etc.: *ḫatama llāhu ʿalā qulūbihim* “Allah hath sealed their hearing and their hearts, and on their eyes there is a covering.”

Q 41:5: *wa-qālū qulūbunā fī ʾakinnatin mimmā tadʿūnā ʾilayhi wa-fī ʾāḏāninā waqrun wa-min bayninā wa-baynika ḥiğābun* “And they say: Our hearts are protected from that unto which thou (O Muhammad) callest us, and in our ears there is a deafness, and between us and thee there is a veil.”

---

the expression, *min bayn is* also underestimated here, which is not to be translated literally as “from between”, but simply “from, from.”

Q 48:11: *yaqūlūna bi-ʾafwāhihim mā laysa fī qulūbihim* "They speak with their tongues that which is not in their hearts."

Q 39:23 (per merismum): *talīnu ǧulūduhum wa-qulubuhum ʾilā ḏikri llāhi* "so that their flesh and their hearts soften to Allah's reminder." "Skin and heart melt away" = "they melt away completely."

"To understand" is quite often rendered by a verb but not with the Arabic common word *fahima*, but rather with *ʿaqala* "to use your brain" and *faqiha* "to understand a (legal) thing" and connected with *nās* "people" or *qawm* "people": *wa-akṯaru n-nāsi lā yafqihūn* "the majority of people do not understand."

In ancient poetry there is another sphere: on the one hand, "heart of the lion, fearless heart of the hero" in contrast to the "girl's heart.";on the other, and not for nothing, many poetic verses conceive of the heart as a seat of love, mostly sad and sorrowful, but also a heart that enjoys love.

"My eye, so weep and give abundant tears, and do not tire, my heart, to consume you in sorrows";

"What is love then but to hear with the ears and a look and a delight of the heart at news and mention."

lubb 17 only in the plural *albāb* "hearts," 17.

In the Qur'ān, only in the stereotypical phrase "people of insights (understandings of the heart)." This means "people with common sense," or in legal contexts "experts." In

ancient Arabic poetry, *lubb* "heart, insight" is generally documented: "According to the judgement of reasonable people (*ḥağā*), a man's speech of insight works best if it is brief."

ḥuğūr 3 "laps," metonymic-functional use for an associated action *fī ḥuğūrikum* "in your care" (Q 4:23).

arḥām 8 "(*plurale tantum*) womb (also of animals)," c *wa-l-muṭallaqātu yatarabbaṣna bi-ʾanfusihinna ṯalāṯata qurūʾin wa-lā yaḥillu lahunna ʾan yaktumna mā ḫalaqa llāhu fī ʾarḥāmihinna ʾin kunna yuʾminna bi-llāhi wa-l-yawmi l-ʾāḫiri* "Women who are divorced shall wait, keeping themselves apart, three (monthly) courses. And it is not lawful for them that they should conceal that which Allah hath created in their wombs if they are believers in Allah and the Last Day" (Q 2:228 and passim); metaphorical use for a sociological-functional meaning derived from a spatial concept: "blood ties" = "relatives" or "relatives". *ulū al-arḥām* "the ones with blood ties": *an-nabiyyu ʾawlā bi-l-muʾminīna min ʾanfusihim wa-ʾazwāğuhū ʾummahātuhum wa-ʾulū l-ʾarḥāmi baʿḍuhum ʾawlā bi-baʿḍin fī kitābi llāhi mina l-muʾminīna wa-l-muhāğirīna* "The Prophet is closer to the believers than their selves, and his wives are (as) their mothers. And the owners of kinship are closer one to another in the ordinance of Allah than (other) believers and the fugitives (who fled from Mecca)" (Q 33:6; similar to 60:3).[44]

ǧawf 1 "(body-)interior", c (from general term for "cavity") *mā ǧaʿala llāhu li-raǧulin min qalbayni fī ǧawfihī* "Allah hath not assigned unto any man two hearts within his body" (Q 33:4)

ʾamʿāʾ 1 "bowels, viscera,", c *ka-man huwa ḫālidun fī n-nāri wa-suqū māʾan ḥamīman fa-qaṭṭaʿa ʾamʿāʾahum* "like those who are immortal in the Fire and are given boiling water to drink so that it teareth their bowels?" (Q 47:15)

Genitalia

sawʾat 8 "(in plural) genitalia, pudenda," c *fa-waswasa lahumā š-šayṭānu li-yubdiya lahumā mā wūriya ʿanhumā min sawʾātihimā* "Then Satan whispered to them that he might manifest unto them that which was hidden from them of their shame" (Q 7,20 etc.); avoidance designation, the concrete meaning "shame, abusive act, evil," even "corpse"; cf. *fa-baʿaṯa llāhu ġurāban yabḥaṯu fī l-ʾarḍi li-yuriyahū kayfa yuwārī sawʾata ʾaḫīhi* "Then Allah sent a raven scratching up the ground, to show him how to hide his brother's naked corpse." (Q 5,31).

ʿawrāt 2 "(female) genitalia, pudenda, nudity," c *awi ṭ-ṭifli llaḏīna lam yaẓharū ʿalā ʿawrāti n-nisāʾi* "or children who know naught of women's nakedness" (Q 24:31; 24"58 and passim); euphemism; the concrete meaning "nakedness, weakness" is attested: *ʾinna buyūtanā ʿawratun wa-mā hiya bi-ʿawratin ʾin yurīdūna ʾillā firāran* "Our homes lie open (to the enemy). And they lay not open. They but wished to flee" (Q 33:13).

farǧ 9 "vulva," c (euphemism; the concrete sense "slit, split" is alive Q 50:6); sociological-functional meaning metaphorically derived from spatial concept: "honour of woman to be guarded, chastity" *wa-llatī ʾaḥṣanat farǧahā fa-nafaḫnā fīhā min rūḥinā wa-ǧaʿalnāhā wa-bnahā ʾāyatan li-l-ʿālamīna* "And she who was chaste, therefore We breathed into her (something) of Our Spirit and made her and her son a token for (all) peoples" (Q 21:91 and passim).

---

44 The associated verbal root RḤM "to be merciful" with its derivatives is one of the most frequent in the Qur'ān.

Legs, Foot

riğl 15 foot; leg, c; redundant as an addition to the verb "walking"; metaphorical for spatial concept, at the same time as a filler word in an expression *per merismum: min fawqi-him wa-min taḥti arğuli-him* "above you and under your feet" = "everywhere" (Q 5:66; 6:65; 29:55); note that *min taḥti-him* "among them" would be sufficient; a similarly constructed expression, but here probably a spatial and temporal concept combined together: *wa-lā ya'tīna bi-buhtānin yaftarīnahū bayna 'aydīhinna wa-'arğulihinna* "nor produce any lie that they have devised between their hands and feet" = "standing foot, at the moment, completely improvising, anywhere and anytime"(Q 60:12);[45] for metonymic-functional use for associated state or action in idioms (somatisms), see above *ğulūd* "skin"; "tongues, hands and feet bear witness against the infidels" *yawma tašhadū ʿalayhim 'alsinatuhum wa-'aydīhim wa-'arğuluhum bi-mā kānū yaʿmalūna* "On the day when their tongues and their hands and their feet testify against them as to what they used to do" (Q 24:24), see also Q 36:65: *al-yawma naḫtimu ʿalā 'afwāhihim wa-tukallimunā 'aydīhim wa-tašhadu 'arğuluhum bi-mā kānū yaksibūna* "This day We seal up their mouths, and their hands speak out to Us and their feet bear witness as to what they used to earn."

Etymologically related to *rağul* "man"; both semantic fields flow together in *rağil* "foot soldier, infantry": *wa-stafziz mani staṭaʿta minhum bi-ṣawtika wa-'ağlib ʿalayhim bi-ḫaylika wa-rağilika wa-šārikhum fī l-'amwāli wa-l-'awlādi wa-ʿidhum wa-mā yaʿiduhumu š-šayṭānu 'illā ġurūran* "And excite any of them whom thou canst with thy voice, and urge thy horse and foot against them, and be a partner in their wealth and children, and promise them. Satan promiseth them only to deceive" (Q 17,64).

qadam 8 "foot, leg," c, meronymic in the somatism: "let the feet stand" = "give secure hold, give secure position, strengthen"; *wa-lammā barazū li-ğālūta wa-ğunūdihī qālū rabbanā 'afriġ ʿalaynā ṣabran wa-ṯabbit 'aqdāmanā wa-nṣurnā ʿalā l-qawmi l-kāfirīna* "And when they went into the field against Goliath and his hosts they said: Our Lord! Bestow on us endurance, make our foothold sure, and give us help against the disbelieving folk" (Q 2:250 and passim), but also the opposite "let your foot stumble" = "let it fall"; *wa-lā tattaḫiḏū 'aymānakum daḫalan baynakum fa-tazilla qadamun baʿda ṯubūtihā* "Make not your oaths a deceit between

---

45 The translations here vary widely, from simple, uncommented literal rendering to interpretive, such as Paret – without further explanation: . . . not to bring up any slander taken from the air by them(?). Possibly the expression is a reinforcing innovation, starting from common in front of the hands = spatially and temporally before; present etc., the nearest analog body part is added as accentuation.

you, lest a foot should slip after being firmly planted" (Q 16:94). Also "put under someone's feet"; metaphorically as a spatial concept with a sociological-functional meaning: "foot of righteousness" = "true position (with God)" *wa-bašširi llaḏīna 'āmanū 'anna lahum qadama ṣidqin inda rabbihim* "Warn mankind and bring unto those who believe the good tidings that they have a sure footing with their Lord?" (Q 10:2); in the expression *per merismum* in Q 55:41: *yuʿrafu l-muğrimūna bi-sīmāhum fa-yu'ḫaḏu bi-n-nawāṣī wa-l-'aqdāmi* "guilty will be known by their marks, and will be taken by the forelocks and the feet" = "all over their body, all grabbed."

sāq 4 "upper and lower thighs", c; metonymic-functional use for associated state or action in idioms (somatisms): *yawma yukšafu ʿan sāqin wa-yudʿawna 'ilā s-suğūdi fa-lā yastaṭīʿūna* "On the day when it befalleth in earnest, and they are ordered to prostrate themselves but are not able" (Q 68:42). The leg and thigh are exposed to heavy physical work when the upper garment is removed. Therefore "(nude) thigh, leg" in various idioms in Arabic stands for "hard, hard work; difficulty: (extreme) seriousness of situation; misfortune." In the foregoing phrase, the best interpretation is "On the day when the situation finally becomes serious (i.e. death or Last Judgement)."[46] A further somatism, in a concrete sense but unclear meaning *wa-ltaffati s-sāqi bi-s-sāqi*, "And the leg is wound about the leg; leg with leg gets caught (in the agony? in the shroud?[47])";[48] in German the best expression is perhaps: "twisting (in agony)" (Q 75:29).

kaʿbān 1 "the two ankles," c (Q 5,6) *wa-msaḥū bi-ruʾūsikum wa-ʾarğulakum ʾilă l-kaʿbayni* "and lightly rub your heads and (wash) your feet up to the ankles."

ʿaqibān, *aʿqāb* 8 "the (two) heels," c, in somatisms: "turn on your heels" *wa-mā ğaʿalnā l-qiblata llatī kunta ʿalayhā illā li-naʿlama man yattabiʿu r-rasūla mimman yanqalibu alā ʿaqibayhi* "And We appointed the qiblah which ye formerly observed only that We might know him who followeth the messenger, from him who turneth on his heels" (Q 2:143 and passim), partly redundant "turning away on the heels" (Q 8:48 and passim); transitive: "putting someone back on his heels" = "bringing him back to his former state, reneging" (Q 3, 149 and passim); "turning away on his heels" (Q 8,48 and passim); transitive: "putting

46 Paret's translation: "On the day (of judgment) "when the matter becomes hot" (literally when (the garment is unclothed and) the calf is exposed) and they (i.e. the unbelievers) are asked to prostrate (before God in worship), but are unable to do it," without further comment. The attempt to reproduce it with a German somatism does not seem entirely successful, since the German expression rather aims at self-inflicted risk.

47 Paret with amaximum of bracketed additions: 29 "and (if) it comes to extremes (?) (literally: if (in close combat?) leg gets caught with leg . . ..

48 Pickthall, interpreting more than translating: "And agony is heaped on agony."

someone back on his heels" = "bringing him back to his former state, reneging" (Q 3:149 and passim); metaphorically, a spatial concept with a sociological-functional meaning, "under his heels" = "under his descendants"; *wa-ǧaʿalahā kalimatan bāqiyatan fī ʿaqibihī laʿallahum yarǧiʿūna* "And he made it a word enduring among his seed, that haply they might return" (Q 43:28).

Concluding Remarks

The examination of the Qur'anic and Arabic usage of body part names shows that metaphorical use is widespread. But the Qur'ān and Arabic share this with practically all known languages, although the specific ascriptions for body parts and their intended functions and peculiarities in human life differ individually, especially for the different social orders and cultures. It is not for nothing that comparative somatism research in linguistics is an area that is always attractive for all language combinations and that it largely belongs to linguistic universal research. Perhaps this statement is the most serious objection to the works of Hans Walter Wolff on the specific synthetic body conception in the Old Testament and in ancient Hebrew as well as the anthropology derived from it. Some of the somatisms surveyed above give the impression of genuinely Arabic and idiomatic expressions, as if the author of the Qur'anic texts had looked intensively "at the mouth" of his people. Here, in addition to the parallels in ancient Arabic poetry, the analysis of ancient Arabic proverbs can also be productive.

The entries in the list I provided were not treated in detail. However, this preliminary research shows that a core stock of the most common words in the Qur'an, (e.g., head, tongue, hand, chest, heart) corresponds in many ways to the parallel use of words in the OT, NT, and religiously influenced speech of the religions and cultures concerned. It remains to be seen whether this is parallel polygenesis, parts of linguistic universals, or due to influence and borrowing. In this area the pictures were also for the non-Arab and non-Muslim mostly directly catchy and understandable, while a rather summary treatment seemed appropriate. The situation was different with the less frequently used "minor" pictures and comparisons. Here, pronounced peculiarities appeared that were beyond direct understanding. It was not for nothing that these passages were reproduced in many translations either only literally, without any real understanding of the specific usage of the language, or only approximately. Here the investigation brought something quite new in different places compared to previous understandings, which is expressed in longer detailed quotations with appropriate commentary.

In this context, the relatively large number of coarse and vivid somatisms in the corpus of the Qur'ān should be emphasized. This is largely a reflection of folkloristic expression and thus of deliberate eavesdropping by the "preacher and herald." In some cases, however, innovative and original twists will also be discerned, which, although they are based on a well-known stock, give it new accents and shades.

Apart from this objection in principle against an exaggerated assessment of the special position, be it of the biblical Hebrew or Old Hebrew, or here of the Qur'ān or Arabic, a precise linguistic examination of the individual documents is nevertheless worthwhile. Here a substitution test would have to be carried out for each of the individual passages as proof of a synthetic understanding of the body. If the appointment of the person as a whole or his or her action makes the intended sense, albeit in a more general, blurred form, the corresponding original body part designation shall be *pars pro toto* and the relevant part of the action or state of mind shall be the relevant part, whereby the person at the center of the statement shall be thought of as a whole. Such a survey and evaluation presupposes, however, a profound examining, probably new interpretations of individual passages, which has not yet been done in the numerous translations and commentaries of the Qur'ān that have only become more numerous in recent times. This investigation must, however, also consider the relationship between Qur'anic language use and the general metaphorical use prescribed by the Arabic language as well as between somatisms in general, before it can deal with Qur'anic idiosyncrasies. This deposition is made more difficult, in many ways perhaps impossible, by the fact that every written Arabic text after the Qur'ān is suspected of being influenced by this text. The only comparative material that remains is ancient Arabic poetry, perhaps ancient Arabic proverbs, and to a limited extent and only after the examination mentioned above, the linguistic usage of Arabic dialects.

Furthermore, the stocktaking undertaken here puts the question mentioned at the beginning of this article into sharper relief, namely, determining the adequate, idiomatically correct translation in the target language. In too many translations, even "modern" ones, the imitation of the source language is still clearly viewed as the guiding principle. This principle is often carried out in an unspoken way, caused by admiration or worship of a holy text. At times, however, it is also openly stated that the translation of the Qur'ān must serve liturgical purposes for the corresponding Muslim, non-Arab-speaking community. The latter task, however, is the duty and task of followers, adepts, and missionaries of the faith community concerned, but hardly a task for a non-Muslim academic.

Attachments

More Word Lists

A Body Part List of the English Designations Sorted by Frequency

Different categories were summed in German translation, such as human(s), heart, pubic parts, flank (side), and foot (leg), and thus received a higher frequency. However, the line items due to the different Arabic designations were left unchanged.

(342 "Man, men" insān 72, insiyy 1, ins 18, nās 241, bašar 37)
292 "Breath, soul; life; person" nafs
241 "People" nās
(167 "Heart" (fuʾād 134, qalb 17, lubb 16))
134 "Heart" qalb
120 "Hand" yad
72 (71+1) "Man" insān, insiyy
72 "Face" wağh
60 "Man" rağul
59 "Eye" ʿayn
47 "Hand, right" yamīn
45 "Chest" ṣadr
37 "Man, men" bašar
28 "Tongue" lisān
(24 "Flank, page" ğānib 9, ğanāḥ 7, ganb 8)
21 "Head, head" raʾ s
20 "Back" ẓahr
19 "Ear" ʾuḏun
18 "Back" dubur
18 "people" into the
17 "Heart(s)" lubb, only in plural albāb
17 "Belly; womb" baṭn
16 "Heart" fuʾād
15 "Foot; Leg" riğl
14 "Mouth" fū(h)
13 "Bones" ʿaẓm
12 "Meat" laḥm
10 "Blood" dam
9 (3+6) "Neck" riqāb, raqaba

9 “Vulva, pubic part, female” farǧ
9 “Page, flank” ǧānib
9 “Neck” ʿunq
9 “Skin, fur” ǧulūd
9 “Flank, side” ǧānib
9 “Fur, skin” ǧulūd
8 “Genitals, Pudenda, pubic parts” sawʾa
8 “Page, flank” ǧanb
8 “Womb” arḥām
8 “Hand, left” šimāl
8 “Foot, leg” qadam
8 “Flank, side” ǧanb
8 “Heels, the two of them” ʿaqibān
7 “Side, flank, wing” ǧanāḥ
(4 “fingers” (banān 2, iṣbaʿ2)
4 “forelock” nāṣiya
4 “Thighs, upper and lower legs” sāq
4 “Hair, forelock” nāṣiya
(3 “Body” (badan 1, ǧism 2)
3 “laps” ḥuǧūr
3 “Chin” ḏiqn
2“Fingers” banān
2 “Tooth” sense
2 “Forehead” ǧabīn
2 “Pubic parts, pudenda, genitals” ʿawrāt
2 “Backbone” ṣulb
2 “Upper arm” ʿaḍud
2 “Nose” ʾanf
2 “Lips, both” šafatān
2 “Body” ǧism
2 “Throat” (*plurale tantum*) ḥanāǧir
2 “Palms of the hand, the two of them” kaffān
2 “fingers” iṣbaʿ
2 “Arm” ḏirāʿ
1 “Body” badan
1 “Ankle, the two of them” kaʿbān
1 “throat” ḥulqūm
1 “Elbow” marāfiq
1 “cheek” ḫadd
1 “Forehead” ǧibāh

1 "Scalp ?(unclear)" šawā
1 "Shoulders" manākib
1 "Snout" ẖurṭūm
1 "Collarbone" tarāqī
1 "ribs, chest" tarāʾib
1 "Innards, viscera" ʾamʿāʾ
1 "Skin" bašar
1 "carotid artery" warīd
1 "Neck" ǧīd
1 "Hair" ašʿār (Koranic evidence given only by animals)
1 "Flank of the body" ʿiṭf
1 "Fingertips" anāmil
1 "Chest, ribs" tarāʾ ib
1 "Breasts (of breastfeeding women)" marāḍiʿ
1 "Belly, body, inside of the body" ǧawf
1 "Beard" liḥya
1 "vein, large, aorta?" watīn
1 "vein, exactly: carotid artery" warīd

List of Body Parts in the Sequence of the Arabic Alphabet (Root Sequence) of the Arabic Designations

ʾuḏun "ear"
insān insiyy "human being"
ʾanf "nose"
badan "body"
bašar "man, men"
bašar "skin"
baṭn "belly"
banān "finger"
tarāʾib "ribs, Chest"
ǧabīn "front"
ǧibāh "front"
ǧism "body"
ǧulūd "skin"
ǧanb "side, flank"
ǧānib "side, flank"
ǧanā "side, flank, wing"
ǧawf "(body-)Interior"

ǧīd “neck”
uǧūr “laps”
ulqūm “throat”
anāǧir “throat”
ḫadd “cheek”
ḫurṭūm “snout”
dubur “back”
dam “blood”
ḏirāʿ “arm”
ḏiqn “chin”
raʾs “head”
riǧl “foot”
raǧul “man”
arāḥm “womb”
marāḍiʿ “breasts (of the breast-feeding)”
marāfiq “elbows”
riqāb “neck”
tarāqī “collar bone”
sense “tooth”
sawʾat “genitals; pudenda; pubic parts”
sāq “thigh”
ašʿār “hair” (in Koranic evidence given only for animals)
šafatān “both lips”
šimāl “left hand”
šawā “(unclear) scalp?”
iṣbaʿ “finger”
ṣadr “chest, center of the body”
ṣulb “backbone”
ẓahr “back”
ʿaḍud “(strong) upper arm”
ʿiṭf “flank of the body”
ʿaẓm “bone”
ʿaqibān “the two heels”
ʿunq “neck”
ʿawrāt “genitals, pudenda”
ʿayn “eye”
fuʾād “heart”
farǧ “slit; vulva”
fū(h) “mouth”
qadam “foot, leg”

qalb "heart"
ka'bān "the two ankles"
kaffān "the two palms of the hand"
lubb, only in plural albāb "hearts; understanding, insight"
laḥm "flesh"
liḥya "beard"
lisān "tongue; word; language"
ʾamʿāʾ "bowels, intestines"
nāṣiya "curly forehead"
nafs "breath, life, soul, man, person, someone",
manākib "shoulders"
anāmil "fingertips"
nās "people; mankind"
watīn "big Vein, aorta"
wağh "face"
warīd "Carotid artery"
yad "hand"
yamīn "right hand"

Works Cited

Ambros, Arne A. 2004. *A Concise Dictionary of Koranic Arabic.* Wiesbaden: Reichert Verlag.

Ambros, Arne A., and Stephan Prochazka. 2006. *The Nouns of Koranic Arabic Arranged by Topics: A Companion Volume to the "Concise Dictionary of Koranic Arabic."* Wiesbaden: Reichert Verlag.

Bubenheim, Frank, and Nadeem Elyas. 2002. *Der edle Qurʾān und die Übersetzung seiner Bedeutungen in die deutsche Sprache.* Riyāḍ: König Fahd Komplex zum Druck vom Qurʾān.

Buhl, Frants. 1924. "Über Vergleichungen und Gleichnisse im Qurʿân." *Acta Orientalia* 2:1–11.

Gitterle, Cornelia. 2005. *Somatismen mit dem Körperteil "Hand" im Italienischen und im Deutschen. Ein grammatisch-semantischer Vergleich.* Munich: GRIN Verlag GmbH.

Haleem, M. A. S. Abdel. 2012. "The *jiyza* Verse (Q. 9:29): Tax Enforcement on Non-Muslims in the First Muslim State." *Journal of Quranic Studies* 14:72–89.

Kotb, Sigrun. 2002. *Körperbezogene Phraseologismen im Ägyptisch-Arabischen.* Wiesbaden: Reichert.

Krämer, Jörg, and Ullmann von Manfred, ed. 1970–2009. *Das Wörterbuch der klassischen arabischen Sprache. Teil I (kāf) und II (lām).* Wiesbaden: Harrassowitz.

Kropp, Manfred. 2008. "Rapport annuel de la Chaire européenne 'Études coraniques.'" *Annuaire du Collège de France 2007 – 2008. Résumé des cours et travaux.* 108:783–801.

Kropp, Manfred. 2014. " . . . und sagen: 'Er ist ein Ohr!' Sprich: 'Ein Ohr zum Guten für Euch!' (Q 9,61). Synthetische Körperauffassung im Koran? Über einige Körper(teil) bezeichnungen und ihre Bedeutungen. Ein Versuch unter teilweiser Einbeziehung der altarabischen Poesie. In *Synthetische Körperauffassung im Hebräischen und den Sprachen der Nachbarkulturen*, edited by Katrin Müller and Andreas Wagner, 185–222. Münster: Ugarit Verlag.

Paret, Rudi.1966. *Der Koran. Übersetzung*. Stuttgart: Kohlhammer.

Paret, Rudi. [1971] 2007. *Der Koran. Kommentar und Konkordanz*. Stuttgart: Kohlhammer.

Pohlmann, Karl-Friedrich. 2012. *Die Entstehung des Korans. Neue Erkenntnisse aus Sicht der historisch-kritischen Bibelwissenschaft*. Darmstadt: WBG.

Rubin, Uri. 2006. "Qurʾān and Poetry: More Data concerning the Qurʾān *jizya* verse (*ʿan yadin*)." *Jerusalem Studies in Arabic and Islam*. 31:139–46.

Seidensticker, T. *Altarabisch "Herz" und sein Wortfeld*. Wiesbaden: Harrassowitz, 1992.

Sima, Alexander. 2001. "Altsüdarabisch lb 'Herz,' yd 'Hand' and lsn 'Zunge.'" *Acta Orientalia* 62:65–80.

Sister, Moses. 1931. *Metaphern und Vergleiche im Koran*, Phil-Diss., Berlin.

Werning, Daniel. "Der 'Kopf des Beines,' der 'Mund der Arme' und die 'Zähne' des Schöpfers. Zu metonymischen und metaphorischen Verwendungen von Körperteil-Lexemen im Hieroglyphisch-Ägyptischen." In *Synthetische Körperauffassung im Hebräischen und den Sprachen der Nachbarkulturen*, edited by Katrin Müller and Andreas Wagner, 107–61. Münster: Ugarit Verlag, 2014.

Wolff, Hans Walter. 2010. *Anthropologie des Alten Testaments.Mit zwei Anhängen neu herausgegeben von Bernd Janowski*, 29–128. Gütersloh: Gütersloh Verlagshaus.

Jillian Stinchcomb

The Queen of Sheba in the Qur'ān and Late Antique Midrash

Surah al-Naml, the twenty-seventh surah of the Qur'ān, includes a suggestive account of the Queen of Sheba's visit to King Solomon. At first sight, the account seems to resemble the biblical story of her visit in 1 Kings 10:1–13, yet all the significant details differ. Where the biblical account describes the Queen coming to test Solomon with riddles, for instance, the Qur'ān presents Solomon testing the Queen with the help of his servant jinn. The Qur'ān emphasizes the Queen's conversion to proper religious practice, Solomon's magical powers and ability to speak the language of birds, and the oddities of the land of Sheba, all of which are absent from the biblical account. Already in 1833, however, Abraham Geiger noticed significant parallels with the *Targum Sheni Esther* (i.e., *Second Targum of Esther*).[1] Here too, for instance, one finds Solomon able to speak the language of birds, the Queen lifting her skirts in confusion at the floor of the site of their meeting, and improper religious devotion in Sheba.

Since the 19th century, this parallel has been adduced to support a model of dependence linking early Islam with late antique Jewish material in general.[2] Positing a date for this Targum in the sixth century, Geiger cited this parallel as part of his broader argument for Muḥammad's dependence on Rabbinic Jewish material in the creation of the Qur'ān. In his 1994 book *Demonizing the Queen of Sheba*, Jacob Lassner offers a less simplistic model of reception; nevertheless,

1 Geiger 2005, 147. Geiger dated Qur'anic material based on his understanding of Muḥammad's changing relationship to Jews. In his understanding, earlier material reflects a more accommodating and appreciative attitude towards Jewish interlocutors, while later material denounces or ridicules Jews.

2 For a discussion of the problematic aspects of such a model, as well as alternative approaches in recent research, see Pregill 2007 and Pregill 2020. For an example of a literary study of Qur'anic elaborations, see Waldman 1985. For an example of a historical-literary study of Qur'anic reception, see Neuwirth 2001. For an example of scholarship which discusses Jewish writers receiving Islamic material, see Wheeler 1998. All three of these modes of resistance to the Geiger model of dependence, however, implicitly assume a hierarchy of priority. They flip the direction of influence, or emphasize the unique literary and historical importance of the Qur'ān over its various sources, but they nevertheless assume the importance of "influence."

Jillian Stinchcomb, Brandeis University

https://doi.org/10.1515/9783110675498-005

in this case, he explains the Qur'anic episode through appeal to its dependencies on "Talmudic haggadic material" akin to this Targum.[3]

In what follows, I would like to re-consider the parallel material on the Queen of Sheba in the Qur'ān and *Targum Sheni Esther* as a test-case in exploring "New Perspectives and Contexts in the Study of Islamic Origins," not limited to dependence. In my view, the similarities between the Qur'anic and Targumic accounts of Solomon and the Queen of Sheba need not suggest direct lines of textual dependence in either direction. Rather, the shared material may point to a matrix of common discourses in the seventh-century Arabian peninsula between nebulously Islamic and Jewish groups that later came to be sharply defined against one another. In the following pages, I will introduce the Targumic and Qur'anic material, describing their literary context, similarities, and differences, before concluding with a reflection on potential comparanda which might further illuminate the literary dynamics of these early narratives about the Queen of Sheba.

Targum Sheni Esther

Before focusing on the narrative in question, some genre and historical information will be useful. *Targum Sheni Esther* has long presented a challenge to Jewish Studies scholars looking to classify this meandering, often long-winded text. Traditionally, a targum is a translation of a biblical book into Aramaic meant to enable Jews to understand weekly Tanakh (Hebrew Bible) readings in synagogue. The translator, known as a meturgeman, would translate alongside a cantor during synagogue services. Crucially, the meturgeman was to translate without any written text as a guide during services in order to delineate the difference between the biblical text and the translation to any onlookers.[4] This prohibition on written guides during services did not prevent the eventual textualization of targumim in Late Antiquity, where they were used in private devotional settings as well as in schools alongside the Hebrew Bible.[5] Targumim are often expansive translations, including exegetical traditions also found in Rabbinic midrashim, but without characteristically Rabbinic phrases, citation of specific Rabbis by name, or the

3 Lassner 1993. Earlier discussions include Pritchard 1974; see also Powers 2011;

4 For further reading, see Alexander 1985; Alexander 1988.

5 Today, Targum Studies is a rich field that often focuses on recovering early readings of biblical texts along with a focus on early reception in Jewish circles. For a useful overview, see Lasair 2012.

inclusion of multiple or contradictory accounts. These texts thus exhibit some overlaps with Rabbinic Judaism, while differing enough to raise the possibility of their formation in other or related Jewish settings.

Targum Sheni Esther is an incomplete translation but also the most expansive example of a targum. Here, the Aramaic translation of the text of Esther is often buried in excurses and tangents that move far afield from the biblical text itself.[6] The text contains some Eastern Aramaic vocabulary but primarily uses Western Galilean Aramaic grammar and vocabulary, consistent with a Palestinian provenance, and it has a preponderance of Greek loan words consistent with a Byzantine-era date. The earliest manuscript evidence of *Targum Sheni* is MS Sassoon 282.[7] This manuscript has a colophon that dates it to 1189. It is written in square German script and consists of sixty-eight pages, each of which has three columns of about 40 lines, which have Tiberian vocalization with interlined Hebrew. There are fourteen other manuscripts ranging in date from the twelfth- to the fifteenth-centuries and of Ashkenazic, Italian, and Yemenite provenance. The manuscript evidence attests its broad diffusion as well as textual fluidity and pluriformity. The reliance on Greek loan words and the use of Western Galilean Aramaic grammar, however, have led scholars to suggest a seventh-century Byzantine Palestinian context for its initial formation, prior to the Arabic rhetorical and literary dominance that later came to characterize the Jewish literature of the region.[8]

The Targum introduces the Queen of Sheba in a tangent presented in an excursus on Esther 1:2 ("In those days, the king Ahasuerus sat upon the throne of his kingdom, which was in Shushan the castle"). In a manner unusual for a targum, the text is theologically oriented and takes a meta-textual narrative voice

---

6 Its expansiveness led Alexander Sperber to question whether it is a targum at all; see Sperber 1968. More recent developments in the field of translation studies, as well as qualitative work by Targum Studies scholars, have now laid that question to rest, in part by establishing that some seventy percent of the text of Esther is embedded in the text of *Targum Sheni Esther* and that translation need not be limited to word-for-word dependence. See now Hayward 2011.

7 This manuscript is the basis for Bernard Grossfeld's critical edition (Grossfeld 1991). Grossfeld here discusses the Eastern Aramaic vocabulary that has led to some disputation of the origins of the text, but he ultimately concludes that the text was originally composed in Palestine.

8 Grossfeld 1991, 19–25. The text has an unusually wide range of dates attested to it: Allegra Iafrate has recently suggested that it may be from as late as the eleventh century (see Iafrate 2016, 147–51) while Stephen Kaufmann has suggested that it is a part of a group of texts which represent "Late Jewish Literary Aramaic" (Kaufmann 2013, 145). For the purposes of this paper, particularly because the dynamics of the text do not suggest Qur'anic influence, I accept Grossfeld's somewhat early date, although further study on the *Targum Sheni Esther* might shed more light on the literary dynamics of the text.

at various points, including in the hugely expansive first chapter. Here, the story of Esther is connected to the history of salvation of Israel, emphasizing the lamentation that sprung up in response to the Babylonian monarch Nebuchadnezzar's exile of Jewish leaders in 586 BCE.[9] It is while proclaiming the lost glory of David as the crown of Israel that the Targum discusses the theft of Solomon's throne by Alexander the Great, which occasions the tale of the Queen of Sheba.[10]

While Israel metonymically laments the fate of its people under Nebuchadnezzar, the narrator presents a story of the glory of Solomon who, cheerful from wine, calls all the local kings to his court. The text notes for a second time that Solomon was cheerful through wine with the kings when he presents all the beasts, birds, reptiles, demons, and spirits as a display of his greatness. However, a wild rooster was missing from his otherwise comprehensive presentation of every animal. When called to account, this wild rooster tells Solomon of the city of Qitor, located in the land of Sheba, ruled by a woman, with dust so precious "gold and silver sit like dung in the street."[11] Solomon sends a letter to the woman, promising great respect for willing submission, but threatening violence from his animals and demons should the land of Sheba refuse Solomon. Receiving the letter while she worshipped the sea, the Queen of Sheba consults with her advisors and decides to send a richly laden ship full of perfectly uniform youths and gold, and she comes herself some three years later to Jerusalem. The Queen is impressed by Solomon's court, descending from her carriage prematurely at the sight of an extremely beautiful youth. Solomon seats himself in a bathhouse when she arrives, and so she lifts her skirts when she approaches him, thinking he is in water. She reveals hairy legs, for which he chides her, saying her beauty is feminine but her hair is for men. The Queen of Sheba does not dignify this with a response. Instead, she challenges him with three riddles, all of which he answers correctly, resulting in her admiration and a mutually beneficial relationship in which she gives him gold and he gives her all that she desires, as in 1 Kings 10. All the local

9 For a fuller discussion, see Ego 1993.

10 The Targum discusses the theft of the throne by Alexander the Great after Nebuchadnezzar and its misadventures with various kings in Egypt at some length. This is particularly intriguing in light of the assertion in the seventh-century *Apocalypse of Pseudo-Methodius* that Alexander's mother was an Ethiopian princess and the suggestive argument, discussed below, that the *Kebra Negast* was originally composed in the sixth century. See further Pseudo-Methodius 2012, 23 and 97. Ra'anan Boustan discusses the significance of the throne in the imagination of Byzantine Jews and notes that the appearance of the throne in Targum Sheni Esther "may preserve the earliest extant form of the medieval throne tradition"; see Boustan 2013.

11 Grossfeld 1991, 116.

kings present their gifts tremblingly after this affair, the text reports, before shifting to speak of Jeremiah and Nebuchadnezzar.[12] The text is elaborate, including much more detail and several sub-tangents of its own, but clearly lays out its narrative logic, which differs somewhat from the Qur'anic account, to which we will now turn.

Q. 27:15–44

One in a series of narratives the Qur'ān exhorts one to "mention," the episode in Surah 27 about the Queen of Sheba is especially terse, even by Qur'anic standards.[13] The two opening verses to this episode (vv. 15–16) emphasize the prophetic status of Solomon and David by highlighting the knowledge of the language of birds granted by God to both men.[14] Notably, this power is also the premise of the Targumic story; there, too, birds, alongside jinn and men, act as Solomon's soldiers. The Qur'ān, however, uses this information to introduce the ants (*al-naml*) of the valley who are intimidated by this legion, who provide the name of the surah (al-Naml).

In verse 20, Solomon questions the absence of the hoopoe from his roster of birds. In the Targum, he is presenting his birds to fellow kings who have come to do him honor; no such context is given in the Qur'ān. The hoopoe, upon his return in verse 22, reports that he has news of Sheba, a land ruled by a woman where people worship the sun because of Satan's deceptions (Q 27:23–24). Solomon commands that the hoopoe bring a letter to the land of Sheba, and the scene shifts abruptly to the Queen as she consults with her advisors who, unlike the advisors in the Targum, refuse to give her political advice. She asks how she should respond to the letter, which requests that she submit with Solomon to God (Q 27:29–31). It is unclear if this submission should be read explicitly as a

12 This matrix of Jeremiah, Nebuchadnezzar, Solomon, and the Queen suggests a clear dependence by the ninth/tenth-century *Alphabet of Ben Sira* on the Targum. There is very little justification for this jumble of characters in the Targum, whereas the *Alphabet* presents these characters within a much more coherent frame narrative, giving a reasonably firm *terminus ad quem* for the date of composition of Targum Sheni Esther.

13 Further discussion can be found in Toy 1907; Pirenne 1979.

14 Jamal Elias suggests that the laconic character of this narrative means that it is most easily read against a backdrop of thematically similar stories about Solomon and the Queen from later Islamic literature (Elias 2009). Elias utilizes ibn Munabbih, al-Thaʿlabī, and al-Ṭabarī alongside later writers to present a wide, if partial, reading of the story as understood in classical Islamic writing. Here, my interest is in the comparison with *Targum Sheni Esther*.

desire for her to become a Muslim (which would be anachronistic at the time of the composition of the Qur'ān but an easily naturalized option in the wake of the development of Islam) or simply to worship properly. She decides to send a gift, but this idea backfires as it offends Solomon, who contemplates military action but decides to have a jinn bring her throne to his court and disguise it through the jinn's magic (Q 27:35–41). Solomon's reaction to her gift is entirely missing from the Targumic account, which also shows no interest in Solomon's throne as a factor in the interaction between the two monarchs. In the Qur'ān, the Queen of Sheba partially recognizes her throne in verse 42, suggesting that it is "as though it was" her own, but she is completely fooled by the glass floor of the palace, where she lifts her skirts as if to wade through a body of water, as in the Targumic account. Upon realizing her mistake, she submits with Solomon to God (v. 44).

Scholarship on this narrative episode provides a range of interpretations, from Jamal Elias' assertion that its focus is on Solomon and the negotiation of his role as prophet and ruler, to Lassner's argument that Solomon and the Queen of Sheba are foils to one another with respect to gender, political leadership, and religious worship.[15] The variety of possible readings underscores the fecundity of such a suggestive, sparse text. Despite its brevity, however, the Qur'ān includes elements that the Targumic account ignores completely, such as the movement and concealment of the throne and Solomon's offense at the gifts from the Queen. Simultaneously, it leaves out elements the Targum includes, such as the other kings to whom Solomon was showing his birds and the Queen's initial astonishment at Solomon's court. The two accounts are thus parallel in many ways, but it is not possible to read one simply as assuming the other.

These two stories also simply contradict one another in the details they present. In *Targum Sheni Esther*, the Queen's advisors urge her to reject Solomon, advice which she ignores; in the Qur'ān, they tell her they will defer to her decision. The Qur'ān incorporates the Queen's throne in its story, where in the Targum the throne of Solomon is a part of a frame story into which the narrative of Solomon and the Queen is woven. The type of bird missing from Solomon's roster differ from one another, a hoopoe in the Qur'ān and a wild rooster in the Targum. Furthermore, the Queen is riddled by Solomon in the Qur'ān rather than riddling him, as she does in *Targum Sheni* (which here follows the biblical accounts). Still, in both texts, Solomon has magical powers that give him control over both birds and demons, and he knows the language of birds. The Queen of Sheba improperly worships natural elements (i.e., the sea and the sun, respectively) – a detail entirely missing from the biblical account. In both, she reveals her legs as she mistakes the

15 Lassner, 1993; Elias, 2009.

ground for water. Both present a Solomonic concern with completeness of knowledge, emblematized by Solomon missing a single bird from his repertoire. But in his quest to display a complete form of knowledge, Solomon learns of an entirely new land of which he had no previous knowledge.

In the case of *Targum Sheni Esther*, this story replicates in microcosm an effect of its entire project: knowledge is never complete, but always ripe for addition, elaboration, and association. The impossibility of truly comprehensive knowledge is reflected in the form of the text, which resists neat knowledge enumeration just as Solomon's birds resist full submission to his desire to show them off. By contrast, the Qur'anic account negotiates the complex relationship of Solomon's prophethood with his position as a ruler by contrasting his divinely ordained rule with the land of Sheba.[16] Sheba is ruled by a woman, misled by Satan, and even where there are men in positions of power, like the Queen's advisors, they preemptively submit to the decisions of the Queen, who thus has an unusual degree of power, a distorted reflection to Solomon. Lassner suggests that the Queen is "demonized" variously, her gender presentation marking her as Other in contextually specific ways, especially through the recurring motif of her hairy legs.[17]

The Qur'ān makes no statement on the relative hairiness of her legs, but Elias has argued that the skeletal, elliptical nature of the text suggests that the tale is intended for an audience that already knew the story of the royal encounter.[18] The accounts thus differ in important ways, speaking to the divergent interests and aims of the respective texts in which they are found, but they also contain significant points of overlap that – as Geiger noticed long ago – invite speculation into their precise relationship.

Dating and Dependence

The final section of this paper will suggest further lines of research and more productive questions scholars might ask of the late antique iterations of narratives about the Queen of Sheba. Thus far, I have compared the presentation of the visit of the Queen of Sheba to Solomon's court and have argued that despite their similarities, the form, details, and structure of both do not suggest dependence in

---

16 For more see Elias 2009.

17 Lassner 1993, 12–15. Descriptions range from inappropriately many legs (i.e., related to her inappropriate rule) to goat legs which signify that the Queen is an actual demon (e.g., even conceptualized as the queen of demons in later Ashkenazic Jewish literature).

18 Elias 2009, 60.

either direction; this argument stands in contrast to earlier treatments of these narratives. As noted above, Geiger argued that Surah 27 was dependent on *Targum Sheni Esther* for its material on the Queen of Sheba,[19] while Lassner argued that the Qur'anic account is instead dependent on what he loosely calls "Talmudic haggadic material."[20] The potential objection to both of these suggestions, however, is the uncertain dates of the composition (let alone wide circulation) of the texts. As noted, the earliest manuscripts of this Targum date to the twelfth century, but linguistic evidence suggests a possible seventh-century date for its initial composition. The precise dates of the composition, textualization, and finalization of the Qur'ān, of course, remain debated. Such questions may recede in importance for explaining this particular parallel, however, when we reframe the quest for diachronic dependencies in terms of a discussion of common synchronic contexts. With some confidence, after all, one can situate both *Targum Sheni Esther* and the Qur'ān in a loosely seventh- or eighth-century milieu, at the end of Late Antiquity.[21] Can we instead ask about a matrix of common discourses and concerns that could result in these parallel versions of the royal interaction?

There is no clear line of dependence in either direction, and in fact, one could argue from the available evidence for both positions simultaneously. If the evidence we have can be utilized to argue both sides of the question, then perhaps we should ask different questions of our evidence. Since Geiger, after all, the question of the direction of dependence for this particular parallel has been asked primarily for the sake of considering the relationship of "Judaism" and "Islam" as "religions." But what might be missed if this material is read primarily through the rubric of religious difference? As most recently articulated by Brent Nongbri, religion is a modern second-order category, which has no direct analogue in the premodern period. It can be a useful heuristic lens but its use reflects modern scholarly discourse, not late antique concepts.[22] Islam is an emergent but not stable category at the time that the Qur'ān was written. Though it might be tempting to read the longer history of Jewish literature and communities in terms of an already stable conceptual category of "Judaism," Daniel Boyarin argues in his 2018 book that the term remains anachronistic into Late Antiquity and beyond.[23]

The problems with understanding these materials retrospectively in terms of the relationship between "religions" is perhaps especially sharp with the

19 Geiger 2005, 147–49.

20 Lassner 1993, 36.

21 Angela Neuwirth *et alii* 2011 offers a wide discussion of some of the considerations of dating and reading the Qur'ān.

22 Nongbri 2013.

23 Boyarin 2018.

Targumim. Geiger used the classical Rabbinic literature as the main basis for reconstructing the "Judaism" that, in his view, influenced Muḥammad and early Islam so strongly. Yet the production of the Targumim seems to have emerged in a non-Rabbinic or para-Rabbinic context, indicating that a conceptualization of these differences under the rubric of "religions" might be too anachronistic to be useful here. Furthermore, the relative position of the Rabbis in Late Antiquity and the early medieval period has come into question in recent scholarship.[24]

Lassner has argued that the presentation of the Queen not only in Islamic literature such as the Qur'ān, Munabbih (d. 732), and al-Thaʿlabī (d. 1035), but also Jewish literature such as *Targum Sheni Esther*, the *Alphabet of Ben Sira*, and later Ashkenazic Jewish sources offers an important window into the development and differentiation of Islamic identity in the context of a shared biblical past. In this, however, his approach remains historically unrooted, not least by virtue of his appeal to a broad range of sources and his framing of the question in terms of the relationship between "Judaism" and "Islam" more broadly. Especially suggestive for understanding this particular episode, in more specific and synchronic terms, is the argument put forth by Muriel Debié for a sixth-century dating for some material from the *Kebra Negast*, the Ethiopian Christian royal chronicle that represents the most extensive premodern treatment of the Queen of Sheba.[25] Over forty chapters of the text are devoted to the Queen of Sheba, who is named Makeda in the text, which "so radically departs from the Judaic and Islamic versions that it can no longer be compared."[26] Medieval and early modern manuscripts of the *Kebra Nagast* show a significant amount of variation, suggesting it represents an evolving tradition of earlier materials.[27]

24 For a discussion of period at which Rabbinic texts became normative, see Fishman 2011.

25 Debié 2010. *Kebra Negast* is the longest premodern narrative about the Queen of Sheba, and it serves as a major inflection point for any discussion of the character of the Queen. The text is well over one hundred chapters long, describing a national origin myth of Ethiopia (here used anachronistically and metonymically to refer to the area controlled by the Aksumites in the first millennium and the Abyssinians in the Middle Ages). For a discussion of the term "Ethiopia" as a complex, national (rather than ethnic) signifier, see Kaplan 2009.

26 Belcher 2009, 450.

27 Belcher, in her discussion of this aspect of the *Kebra Nagast*, calls it a "true palimpsest" (Belcher 2009, 445). The earliest manuscripts of the *Kebra Nagast* describe the translational history of the text, which has been summarized usefully by Wendy Belcher: "The scribe Yeshaq (a historical figure who was the leading ecclesiastical officer of the ancient city of Aksum in Abyssinia), working with five orthodox monks, states in the last paragraph of the Kebra Nagast that they are translating the work into Ge'ez from Arabic just before 1322. They also state that the work they are translating was itself a translation, from Coptic into Arabic in 1225." Belcher 2006, 202.

Debié points to the *ex-eventu* prophecy embedded in the *Kebra Negast* of the Christian persecution in Najran, a city in the southern part of the Arabian peninsula. This event, the last historical event recorded in the text of the *Kebra Nagast*, resulted in Ethiopian military intervention which brought about the fall of the Jewish Himyaritic kingdom of South Arabia and resulted in Ethiopian dominance of the region in the sixth century.[28]

We see, then, in the period of imperial instability that marks the end of Late Antiquity, Byzantine Jewish, Islamic, and possibly Ethiopian Christian traditions, which utilize disparate genres and textual forms, to exhibit a sharp interest in the cosmopolitan encounter between Solomon and the Queen of Sheba. In the first half of the first millennium, there is no example of any sustained narrative about the Queen of Sheba. Is there something about the Queen of Sheba that held particular resonance in this late antique Arabian context and its neighboring Palestinian and Ethiopian locales? What would happen were one to consider this constellation of texts in conjunction with other seventh-century texts, such as the *Apocalypse of Pseudo-Methodius*? Especially in light of the recent arguments for placing both 3 Enoch and *Sefer Zerubavel* in seventh-century Byzantine Palestine, by Klaus Hermann and Martha Himmelfarb respectively, might it be possible to situate this shared discourse further?[29] Whether or not any single historical event inspired the proliferation of stories about the Queen of Sheba, the parallel material offers a useful reminder of the diverse forms of a shared heritage in the time of Islamic origins.

Bibliography

Alexander, Phillip. 1985. "The Targumim and the Rabbinic Rules for the Delivery of the Targum." In *Congress Volume Salamanca 1983*, edited by J. A. Emerton, VT Supplement 36, 14–28. Leiden: Brill.

Alexander, Phillip. 1988. "Jewish Aramaic Translations." In *Mikra: Text, Translation, and Interpretation of the Hebrew Bible*, edited by M. J. Mulder and H. Sysling, 217–53. Philadelphia: Fortress Press.

Belcher, Wendy. 2009. "African Rewritings of the Jewish and Islamic Solomonic Tradition: The Triumph of the Queen of Sheba in the Ethiopian Fourteenth-Century Text *Kebrä Nägäst*."

28 For more information, see Shahid 1971. Belcher 2006, 202; Belcher is working on a forthcoming English translation of the *Kebra Nagast* with Michael Kleiner which will be a welcome alternative to Budge's translation, which is helpfully in the public domain but has many problems, as Belcher, and many others have noted.

29 Hermann 2013; Himmelfarb 2017.

In *Sacred Tropes: Tanakh, New Testament, and Qur'ān as Literary Works*, edited by Roberta Sabbath, 441–459. Boston/Leiden: Brill.

Belcher, Wendy. 2006. Review of Munro-Hay, *Quest for the Ark of the Covenant*, Research in African Literatures 37.2:199–204.

Boustan, Ra'anan. 2013. "Israelite Kingship, Christian Rome, and the Jewish Imperial Imagination: Midrashic Precursors to the Medieval 'Throne of Solomon.'" In *Jews, Christians, and the Roman Empire: The Poetics of Power in Late Antiquity*, edited by Natalie Dohrmann and Annette Yoshiko Reed, 167–182. Philadelphia: University of Pennsylvania Press.

Boyarin, Daniel. 2018. *Judaism: The Genealogy of a Modern Notion*. Key Words in Religious Studies. New Brunswick: Rutgers University Press.

Debié, Muriel. 2010. "Le Kebra Negast éthiopien: une réponse apocryphe aux événements de Najran?" In *Juifs et chrétiens en Arabie au Ve et VIe siécles: regards croisés sur les sources*, edited by J. Beaucamp, F. Briquel Chatonnet, and C.J. Robin. Centre de Recherche d'Histoire et Civilisation de Byzance, Monographies 32, 255–78. Paris: ACHCByz.

Ego, Beate. 1993. "The Concept of History in the Targum Sheni to Esther." In *Proceedings of the World Congress of Jewish Studies* 11:131–34 (Hebrew).

Elias, Jamal. 2009. "Prophecy, Power and Propriety: The Encounter of Solomon and the Queen of Sheba." *Journal of Qur'ānic Studies* 9.1:57–79.

Fishman, Talya. 2011. *Becoming the People of the Talmud: Oral Torah as Written Tradition in Medieval Jewish Cultures*. Philadelphia: University of Pennsylvania Press.

Geiger, Abraham. 2005 *Was hat Muhammad aus dem Judenthum aufgenommen?* Berlin: Parerga. Reprint (1833).

Grossfeld, Bernard. 1991. *The Two Targums of Esther*. Collegeville, Minnesota: The Liturgical Press.

Hayward, Robert. 2011. "Targum a Misnomer for Midrash? Towards a Typology for the Targum Sheni of Esther." *Aramaic Studies* 9.1:47–63.

Hermann, Klaus. 2013. "Jewish Mysticism in Byzantium: The Transformation of Merkavah Mysticism in 3 Enoch." In *Hekhalot Literature in Context: Between Byzanitum and Babylonia* ed. Ra'anan Boustan, Martha Himmelfarb and Peter Schäefer, 85–116. Tübingen: Mohr Siebeck.

Himmelfarb, Martha. 2017. *Jewish Messiahs in a Christian Empire*. Cambridge: Harvard University Press.

Iafrate, Allegra. 2016. *The Wandering Throne of Solomon: Objects and Tales of Kingship in the Medieval Mediterranean*. Mediterranean Art Histories 2. Leiden: Brill.

Kaplan, Steven. 2009. "Dominance and Diversity: Kingship, Ethnicity, and Christianity in Orthodox Ethiopia." *CHRC* 89.I–3:291–305.

Kaufmann, Stephen. 2013. "The Dialectology of Late Jewish Literary Aramaic." *Aramaic Studies* 11.2:145–48.

Lasair, Simon. 2012. "Current Trends in Targum Research." *Currents in Biblical Research* 10.3: 442–53.

Lassner, Jacob. 1993. *Demonizing the Queen of Sheba: Boundaries of Gender and Culture in Postbiblical Judaism and Medieval Islam*. Chicago: University of Chicago Press.

Neuwirth, Angela. 2001. "Qur'ān, Crisis, and Memory: The Qur'ānic Path towards Canonization as Reflected in the Anthropogonic Accounts." In *Crisis and Memory in Islamic Societies*, edited by A. Neuwirth and A. Pflitsch, 113–52. Beirut: Ergon Verlag.

Neuwirth, Angela, Nicolai Sinai, and Michael Marx, eds. 2011. *The Qur'ān in Context: Historical and Literary Investigations into the Qur'ānic Milieu*. Leiden: Brill.

Nongbri, Brent. 2013. *Before Religion: A History of a Modern Concept*. New Haven: Yale University Press.

Pirenne, Jacqueline. 1979. "La Reine de Saba dans le Coran et la Bible." *Dossiers de l'archeologie* 33:6–10.

Powers, David. 2011. "Demonizing Zenobia: The Legend of al-Zabba in Islamic Sources." In *Histories of the Middle East: Studies in Middle Eastern Society, Economy, and Law in Honor of A. L. Udovitch*, edited by Petra Silverb, Adam Sbra and Roxani Markoff, 127–82. Leiden: Brill.

Pritchard, James, ed. 1974. *Solomon and Sheba*. London: Phaidon Press.

Pregill, Michael. 2007. "The Hebrew Bible and the Qur'ān: The Problem of the Jewish 'Influence' on Islam." *Religion Compass* 1:643–59.

Pregill, Michael. 2020. *The Golden Calf Between Bible and Qur'an: Scripture, Polemic, and Exegesis from Late Antiquity*. Oxford Studies in Abrahamic Religions. Oxford: Oxford University Press.

Pseudo-Methodius. 2012. *Apocalypse. An Alexandrian World Chronicle*. Edited and translated by Benjamin Garstad. Cambridge: Harvard University Press.

Segovia, Carlos A. and Basil Lourié, eds. 2012. *The Coming of the Comforter: When, Where, and to Whom? Studies on the Rise of Islam and Various Other Topics in Memory of John Wansbrough*. Orientalia Judaica Christiana 3. Piscataway, NJ: Gorgias Press.

Shahid, Irfan. 1971. *The Martyrs of Najran: New Documents*. Wetteren: Imprimerie Cultura.

Sperber, Alexander, ed. 1968. *The Bible in Aramaic, based on old manuscripts and printed texts*. Leiden: Brill.

Toy, C.H. 1907. "The Queen of Sheba." *Journal of American Folklore* 20:207–12.

Waldman, Marilyn. 1985. "New Approaches to 'Biblical' Materials in the Qur'ān." *Muslim World* 75.1:1–16.

Wheeler, Brannon. 1998. "The Jewish Origins of Qur'ān 18:65-82? Reexamining Arent Jan Wensinck's Theory." *Journal of the American Oriental Society* 118.2:153–71.

Isaac W. Oliver

Standing under the Mountain: Jewish and Christian Threads to a Qur'anic Construction

At several points, the Qur'ān recalls the revelation given at Mount Sinai and the Israelite response to this awesome manifestation. The Qur'ān draws attention to this event already in Surah 2 (*al-baqara*) – which is replete with materials building on biblical and extrabiblical traditions – and recounts Israel's fortunes, from the exodus out of Egypt to the covenant cut with the Israelite deity in the wilderness. To the biblically initiated, many features in this extensive Qur'anic chapter are immediately discernible: Pharaoh's slaughter of the Israelite boys (2:49), the splitting of the sea (2:50), and the (golden) calf incident (2:51), to name a few. Some aspects, however, appear nowhere in the Jewish Scriptures or the New Testament. They are only known from extrabiblical sources.[1] Of special interest are two verses in Q 2 that convey the impression that God *raised* Mount Sinai above the Israelites (v. 63; 93).[2] The raised mountain features also in Q 4:154 and Q 7:171. Despite these extraordinary circumstances announcing

1 Two noteworthy examples that immediately stand out include the references to the twelve springs that gushed water at Moses' request (Q 2:60) and the death and resurrection of the Israelites during the Sinaitic theophany (vv. 55–56). Ezekiel the Tragedian 1:250 (Charlesworth ed.) mentions a rock whence flowed twelve springs; Tosefta Sukkah 3:11 (Lieberman ed.) refers to a well resembling a rock that brought forth water before the princes of Israel. Cf. Liber antiquitatum biblicarum (LAB) 20:8 (Jacobson ed.); Targum Pseudo-Jonathan 21:17–19. The closest parallel to the Qur'ān, however, seems to be on the wall paintings of the Dura Europos synagogue. It depicts Moses standing with a rod next to a well with twelve streams. See Gutmann 1983, 99–100. On the resurrection of Israel at Sinai, see below. All translations of primary sources are mine unless noted otherwise.

2 English translations of the Qur'ān are taken and slightly adapted from Droge 2013.

Notes: This article is based on a paper presented at the The Eighth Nangeroni Meeting held in Florence from June 11–16, 2017. Another article treating the same topic appeared after I submitted my piece for publication (Graves 2018). I have tried, when possible in this late hour, to interact with Graves' work. I trust nonetheless that our research overlaps in meaningful ways, not least because I consider additional evidence, especially targumic and early Christian literature. A special thanks goes to both Guillaume Dye and Mihai Vlad Niculescu who provided me with very helpful feedback on my work.

Isaac W. Oliver, Bradley University

https://doi.org/10.1515/9783110675498-006

the delivery of the Torah, the Qur'ān stresses that the Israelites transgressed and even defiantly refused to observe the Sinaitic covenant.

Several Islamic commentators interpret the Qur'anic references to the raised mountain *literally*, inferring that God actually lifted the mountain above the Israelites.[3] A number of modern interpreters have pointed to rabbinic texts that strengthen this supposition.[4] Indeed, a well-known rabbinic midrash claims that God raised Mount Sinai above the Israelites. While this rabbinic midrash offers the best "background" for illuminating the Qur'anic passages in question, the Qur'ān does not simply "borrow" this feature from rabbinic tradition. It retells the Sinai story in its own creative fashion. Moreover, the Qur'ān envelops its presentation of the raised mountain with polemical statements that find precedent in a long stream of Christian anti-Judaic discourse that predates the rise of Islam. The Qur'anic references to the raised mountain, therefore, should not be appreciated solely in light of rabbinic parallels.

To complicate the picture even further, many scholars now stress the diversity of early Judaism and Christianity in the centuries after 70 CE. Rabbinic Judaism did not become normative immediately after the Second Temple was destroyed. Rabbinic consolidation took centuries in the making. In the aftermath of 70, many Jews carried on with their lives unaware or even dismissive of rabbinic teaching.[5] Jewish synagogues, especially in the Hellenistic Diaspora, were not dominated or headed by "rabbis." Unfortunately, we know little about non-rabbinic forms of Judaism that persisted and developed after 70. Rabbinic writings remain our principal literary source for understanding Jewish life and thought throughout Late Antiquity. However, other sources do exist, including the targumim, the Jewish Aramaic translations of the Hebrew Scriptures. These preserve non-rabbinic Jewish traditions even if they were eventually "rabbinicized." Given the mounting scholarly interest in investigating the Qur'ān in light of Syriac (Christian Aramaic) sources, the Jewish targumic literature certainly warrants greater attention in Qur'anic studies.

Early Christianity, for its part, remained just as diverse as Judaism. Given this diversity, it is no longer possible to simply assume that early Christian-Jewish relations were marked exclusively by antagonism and clearly defined boundaries differentiating all Christians and Jews from one another. Many Christian and Jews interacted throughout Late Antiquity in meaningful ways, much

3 See Oberman 1941; Nasr 2015, 32–33, for references and a brief discussion.

4 Geiger (1833) 1970, 129; Obermann 1941, 34–35; Speyer 1961, 303–4; Witztum 2011, 22–23.

5 This is not to say that rabbinic Judaism exerted no influence at all. See Hezser 1997; Schwartz 2004, 103–28; Eliav 2010, 565–86. Lapin 2012, 151–67, situates the expansion of rabbinic norms from the fourth century to the early Abbasid era.

to the concern of church fathers and rabbinic sages alike, who wished for a clearer demarcation between Judaism and Christianity.[6] Yet Christians continued to negotiate their Israelite heritage in diverse ways, some stressing the novelty of their faith and therefore the rupture of Christianity with its Jewish past, others affirming continuity with Israel's Scripture and past. The scholarly debate over whether many of the so-called Old Testament Pseudepigrapha originated as "Jewish" or "Christian" compositions finely illustrates the complexity of this matter.[7] The same observation applies in various degrees to Ethiopic and Syriac expressions of Christianity. Before the discovery of the Dead Sea Scrolls, some supposed that the Book of Jubilees and 1 Enoch, which survive in their entirety only in Geez, the sacred language of the Ethiopian Orthodox Church, were Christian compositions. These documents, however, are unquestionably Jewish.[8] Similarly, the core of the Old Testament Peshitta is a Syriac translation of the Hebrew Scriptures from the second century CE that is informed by Jewish exegesis.[9] Although the translators of the Old Testament Peshitta were undoubtedly Jewish, this work soon made its way into Christian circles, illustrating how some Christians remained interested in how Jews understood the Scriptures that both communities shared in common.[10] All of this underscores the necessity to investigate the Qur'ān in light of Jewish (including non-rabbinic) *and* Christian sources – even those Qur'anic passages that find close correspondence with rabbinic texts – bearing in mind the complex mosaic of early Jewish-Christian relations.

---

6 The research on the "partings of the ways" between Jews and Christians is immense. See Boyarin 2004; Reed and Becker 2007; Baron, Hicks-Keeton, and Thiessen 2018.

7 See Davila 2005.

8 Singer 1898 singularly identified Jubilees as a Jewish-Christian polemic written against the apostle Paul. Rönsch (1874) 1970 believed that Jubilees was written in order to unite all Jewish parties against the rise of Christianity (c. 50–60 C.E.). Milik 1976, 96 considered the Book of Parables, one of the books now contained within 1 (Ethiopic) Enoch, to be a "Christian Greek composition" from the end of third century. His thesis had lasting effect on New Testament scholarship. The recent consensus among Second Temple specialists affirms its original Jewish provenance. See Boccaccini 2007.

9 Joosten 2013.

10 Brock 2006, 3–4 claims that some targumic books may even derive from the Peshitta. See, however, the contributions in Flesher 1998.

Rabbinic Midrash

Mekhilta de Rabbi Ishmael

According to Exodus 19:17, when the Israelites made a covenantal deal at Sinai, "Moses brought the people out from the camp to meet God, *and they took their stand at the foot of the mountain*" (emphasis mine). In the Masoretic Text, the italicized phrase reads, *wayyityatṣṣwû bətaḥtît hāhār*.[11] The Mekhilta de Rabbi Ishmael (MRI), the earliest rabbinic commentary on the book of Exodus,[12] comments on these words in the following way:

> "And they took their stand" (*wayyityatṣṣwû*): They were closely pressed together. This teaches that Israel feared because of the sparks, because of the earthquakes, because of the thunders, because of the lightnings that were coming.
>
> "At the foot of the mountain" (*bətaḥtît hāhār*): This teaches that the mountain was plucked (*nitlaš*) from its place, and they drew near and stood under the mountain (*taḥat hāhār*), as it says, "And you drew near and stood under the mountain (*taḥat hāhār*)" (Deut 4:11). Concerning them it is stated in the Written Tradition, "O my dove in the clefts of the rock, in the hidden place of the cliff, show me your appearance, let me hear your voice, for your voice is sweet and your appearance is delightful" (Song 2:14). "Show me your appearance": these are the twelve pillars for the twelve tribes of Israel. "Let me hear your voice": these are the Ten Utterances. "For your voice is sweet": after [receiving] the [Ten] Utterances. "And your appearance is delightful": "And the whole congregation drew near and stood before the LORD".[13] (Lev 9:5)

The MRI first expounds the verb *yityatṣṣwû* (root: *y-ṣ-w*), taking it to mean that the Israelites huddled or were pressed together during their exclusive rendezvous with God. At first, this interpretation may seem odd, seeing that the verb often connotes in biblical Hebrew the act of stationing or taking one's stand *firmly*.[14] The verb, however, can occasionally refer to the act of "presenting oneself" before a royal or divine figure for accountability or service.[15] Ultimately

11 For the transliteration of Hebrew, Aramaic, and Greek words, I have followed the academic style in the SBL Handbook (2nd ed.). For Arabic, I follow the rules of IJMES.

12 According to Stemberger 2011, 282, MRI was probably completed in the second half of the third century CE.

13 Mek. *Yitro – Baḥodeš* 3 (Horovitz-Rabin ed.).

14 See Koehler and Baumgarten 1994–2000 (BibleWorks 10v.).

15 See Exod 9:13; Deut 31:14; Josh 24:1; Judg 20:2; Prov 22:29; 1 Sam 10:19; Job 1:6; 2:1; Zech 6:5. Consider the remarks of Gilchrist 1981 (BibleWorks 10v.): "One who thus stands before kings implicitly makes himself available and ready for service . . . . One further idea may be considered. If they who stand before kings are servants and couriers ready to serve, how much more should those who present themselves to the great king, the Lord of lords, be submissive

though, it seems that the awesome sound-and-light presentation reported in Exod 19:16 determined the rabbinic exegesis of *yityatṣṣwû*. This verse refers expressly to thunder, lightning, blasts, smoke, and fire that enveloped the mountain – fearful sights that would have terrified any mortal soul (cf. Exod 19:18). No wonder, the Israelites packed together in fear.

Further aggrandizing the magnitude of the Sinaitic event, the MRI claims that the Israelites stood *under* the hovering mountain, interpreting the prepositional phrase *bətaḥtît hāhār* in a unique way. Several English translations of the Bible render this construction straightforwardly as "at the foot of the mountain."[16] The construction consists of the preposition *bə* followed by *taḥtît*, an adjective used here as a substantive, meaning "lower" or "base," in the construct form with *hāhār*, yielding an idiom that can be translated as "at the base/foot of the mountain" or "at the lowermost of the mountain." The adjective *taḥtît*, however, is related to *taḥat* ("below" or "under"), which appears in the parallel passage of Deut 4:11. Rather than understanding *taḥat hāhār* in Deut 4:11 in idiomatic fashion, the MRI takes this formulation quite literally, resulting in the claim that the Israelites stood under the mountain.[17] According to the Tannaitic midrash, this happened after the mountain was displaced: it was "plucked" or "detached" (*nitlaš*) from the ground. The Israelites then drew near so that they stood under the mountain. The MRI connects the opening of Song of Songs 2:14, "O my dove in the clefts of the rock," with the phrases *bətaḥtît hāhār* and *taḥat hāhār*. Israel, like a dove flying to seek refuge in the clefts of a rock, headed under the mountain.[18] What began as a rather frightful session turned out to be an intimate encounter celebrating Israel's induction into the covenant.[19]

---

to his will and command. This seems to be the thought in Exo 19:17 where 'Moses brought the people out of the camp to meet God, and they stood at the foot of the mountain.' The people gave a response of reverent obedience, 'All the words which the Lord has spoken we will do, and we will be obedient' (Exo 24:3, 7)."

16 See the New Revised Standard Version, the New Jewish Publication Society Translation, and the New American Standard Version.

17 Novick 2015, deems the rabbinic inference reasonable, since *taḥtît* mostly describes the underworld, a place of death, in the Hebrew Bible.

18 Cf. Graves 2018, 146: "the association of Exodus 19:17 with Song 2:14 depicts Israel standing beneath Mt. Sinai as a positive experience. God pulled up the mountain and Israel came willingly to stand beneath it. For Israel, the shelter of the mountain provided protection, security, and intimacy, where the people could respond sweetly to God by accepting His commandments." Cf. Urbach 1987, 328; and Blidstein 2004, 83.

19 A parallel midrash in the Mekhilta of R. Simeon b. Yoḥai also links Exod 19:17 with Song 2:14, much like the MRI (for the Hebrew text see Epstein and Melamed 1979, 143). I do not discuss this particular section of the MRS because it does not deal with the key phrase *bətaḥtît hāhār*.

Mekhilta de Rabbi Simeon b. Yoḥai

Another midrashic work, the Mekhilta de Rabbi Simeon b. Yoḥai (MRS), recounts this unique episode in a slightly different manner:

> And they took their stand at the foot of the mountain" (*wayyityatṣṣwû bətaḥtît hāhār*): this teaches us that the Holy One Blessed Be He turned (*kāpâ*) the mountain over them like a tank (*gîgît*) and said: "If you accept upon yourselves the Torah, that is good, but if not, here will be your burial." At the same moment they all lowed and poured out their heart like water in repentance and said: "everything that the LORD has spoken, we will do and we will hear.[20]
> (Exod 24:7)

Instead of saying that the mountain was "plucked" (MRI: *nitlaš*) from the ground, the MRS states that God "overturned" or "bent" (*kāpâ*) the mountain over (*ʿal*) the heads of the Israelites like a "tank" (*gîgît*). In rabbinic literature, the verb *kāpâ* can refer to such mundane acts as the overturning of vessels or beds (for mourning). Several rabbinic texts follow a similar syntactical construction as the one employed in the MRS: verb + preposition with a pronominal suffix followed by a direct object (*kāpâ ʿălêhem ʾēt hāhār*). Thus m. Tamid 5:5 recalls the time when the Jerusalem temple still stood and the priests would invert a large vessel over cinders on the Sabbath (*kôpîn* + *ʿălêhen* + *psktr*). The Babylonian Talmud even discusses the proper punishment for one who "inverts a vat over someone" (*kāpâ gîgît ʿālāyw*).[21] The mountain, then, could be envisioned as a tank that has been bent or flipped over, threatening to spill its content upon the people or to suffocate them.[22] Alternatively, the passage may assume that the mountain had

---

20 MRS 19:17. My translation is based on the critical edition of Epstein and Melamed 1979, 143. For a brief discussion of this passage, see Kaplan 2015, 73–74. This section of MRS is attested in Midrash ha-Gadol, a late medieval commentary (see Epstein and Melamed 1979, 143, who reproduce this passage in a small print; cf. Nelson 2006, 229). Yet the manuscript evidence, at least 140 manuscript fragments excluding Midrash ha-Gadol, accounts for approximately 75 percent of the critical text reconstructed by Epstein and Melamed. Indeed, the majority of MRS preserves traditions that developed during the Tannaitic period (c. 70–200 CE) even if it also contains Amoraic materials (c. 200–500 CE, so still prior to the composition of the Qur'ān). I include it here therefore for consideration, absence of additional manuscript evidence notwithstanding. Nevertheless, further research on the final date of MRS and a new critical edition of its text remain a desideratum. See Nelson 2006, xi–xxix; Stemberger 2011, 286–87.

21 B. Sanh. 77a according to the Soncino translation (Epstein 1978).

22 Alternatively, one could picture the mountain as an inverted vault, dome, or arched roofing. This is suggested by the possible associations between the Hebrew words *gîgît* and *gag* ("roof"), on the one hand, and *kāpâ* and *kîppâ* ("arch" or "dome"), on the other hand. According to Jastrow (1943) 2005, the term *gîgît* can mean "something arched, roofing, a huge vessel, tub, tank (for brewing beer); reservoir." Levy 1924, 1:298 has "Becken, Wanne, die gew. von

been unrooted from one side only with one edge in the ground, threatening to fall upon the people.[23]

However the rabbinic imagery is conceived in the MRS, it seems more frightening than its counterpart in the MRI. This is suggested by the verb *kāpâ*, which also means "to compel."[24] A double entendre may be at play here: by threatening to bury the Israelites alive with the suspended mountain, God *coerced* the Israelites to sign the contract. In the parallel midrash from the MRI, the threat to bury the Israelites as well as the verb *kāpâ* are entirely absent. According to the MRI, the Israelites may have been *impressed*, even conditioned, to accept God's "offer," but certainly not caught between a rock and a hard place, with no choice but to sign the contract or die. However, the MRS provides a reason for God's coercion: once the mountain loomed over the Israelites, they "lowed and poured out their heart like water *in repentance*." This suggests that there were trespasses that made repentance necessary. Israel immediately confesses and enters into a covenant with its God.[25]

Thon bereitet war, eig. gewölbtes Gefäss." The Soncino translation (Epstein 1978) has "overturned the mountain upon them like an [inverted] cask" (b. Šabb. 88a) or "suspended the mountain over Israel like a vault" (b. ʿAbod. Zar. 2b). The latter translation would agree with Nelson 2006, 229, who interprets *gîgît* as "roof." Novick 2015 supposes that the overturned mountain threatens to kill the Israelites through asphyxiation rather than crushing, like a tub blocking access to air. He surmises that the notion of killing by means of an overturned vessel would bring to mind in a Babylonian context magic bowls that were inverted on the ground. In a personal communication (April 30, 2020), Novick informs me that he is inclined to interpret *kāpâ* as "suspended." The idea, then, would not be that God inverted but suspended the mountain over the Israelites like an overturned tub. Interestingly, in a related statement in ʾAbot de Rabbi Nathan A 33 (Schechter ed.), R. Eliezer says that God "turned (*kāpāh*)" the deep over Israel from above when splitting the sea. In MIR *Bešalaḥ* – *Širah* 6 Exod 15:8, an anonymous Tannaitic interpretation claims that God made the deep like a "dome" (*kîppâ*). On the relation of these passages to the rabbinic midrash on the suspended mountain, see Novick 2015.

23 The mountain would be in a slant position (/), with Israel standing below: /. (the dot representing Israel). I thank my colleague Mihai Vlad Niculescu for this insight on how to possibly envision the rabbinic conception(s) of the uprooted/overturned mountain.

24 As noted by Novick 2015.

25 I thank Niculescu for underscoring this theme, which I had neglected. The expression "they poured out their heart like water" derives from Lam 2:19: "Pour out your heart like water before the face of the Lord." Rabbinic midrash understands this expression as an act of repentance. See Midrash Psalms 119 § 76 (Buber ed.).

The Babylonian Talmud: B. Šabbat 88a

The rather intimidating portrait recorded in the MRS is paralleled in the Babylonian Talmud:

> "And they took their stand under the mountain": R. Abdimi bar Ḥama bar Ḥasa[26] said: "this teaches that the Holy One, Blessed Be He, turned the mountain over them like a tank [or vault] and said to them, 'If you accept upon yourselves the Torah, good, and if not, there will be your burial'". (b. Šabbat 88a)

The language here is nearly identical to the parallel text in the MRS save that the Talmud credits the Amora R. Abdimi bar Ḥama bar Ḥamsa (Israel/Palestine, fourth century CE) for interpreting the overturned mountain in a menacing way. The Talmud, however, continues with a reflection on the legal implications stemming from R. Abdimi's conceptualization of God's terms of offer:

> R. Aḥa bar Jacob said: "From here there is a great protest (*môdāʿāʾ*) against the Torah." Raba said: "Even so, the generation received it [i.e., the Torah] in the days of Ahasuerus as it is written, 'The Jews confirmed and accepted. . ..' (Esther 9:27). They confirmed what they had already accepted."
>
> Hezekiah said: "What is [the meaning of] that which is written, 'From the heavens you caused judgment to be heard; the earth feared and was at peace' (Ps 76:9)? If it feared, why was it at peace? And if it was at peace, why did it fear? Rather, at the beginning it feared, and at the end it was at peace." And why was it afraid [in the first place]? As Resh Laqish [explains], for Resh Laqish said: "What is [the meaning of] that which is written, 'And there was evening and there was morning, the sixth day?' Why do I need the extra 'the' [the definite article before "sixth day"]? This teaches that the Holy One, Blessed Be He, stipulated with the acts of creation and said to them: 'If Israel accepts the Torah, you will remain; but if not, I will return you to being formless and void.'"[27]

In this fascinating discussion, R. Aḥa b. Jacob brings to the forefront a serious issue prompted by R. Abdimi's reflection on the uplifted mountain: if the Israelites had no alternative besides death to accept the Torah, then there are strong grounds for filing an objection against its observance. From a legal standpoint, the covenant would not be binding because it was unfairly forced upon Israel. R. Aḥa b. Jacob makes this point by employing the Aramaic word *môdāʿāʾ*, a legal term that refers to "a document of protest made in advance before witnesses in order to invalidate a transaction or a legal action to be made under duress."[28]

26 The spelling of this rabbinic sage varies by manuscript, sometimes abbreviated as Dimi, but also written as Abudimi. See Graves 2018, 147 fn. 8.
27 Translation mine based on the text of the Steinsaltz edition.
28 Sokoloff 2002, 645.

The Jewish people, then, would be exempt from observing the Torah, given the questionable circumstances in which it was originally delivered.[29] Raba responds to this objection by pointing out that the Jewish people willingly confirmed to observe the Torah at a later period in history, namely, during the time of Esther.[30] This position is still somewhat faulty though because it would not account for the period prior to Esther when Israel apparently kept the Torah out of coercion.[31] A second solution, therefore, is proposed: the very heavens and earth depended on Israel saying yes to God's demands. At creation, God imposed a special condition for the continual existence of the universe: the cosmos would remain if Israel later accepted the Sinaitic covenant. Israel's positive response to its divine calling was of such magnitude that God had no choice but to compel Israel to sign the "agreement."[32]

The Babylonian Talmud: b. ʿAbodah Zarah 2b

Another passage in the Talmud reflects on the theological ramifications of the uprooted mountain in a radically different way. According to b. ʿAbodah Zarah 2b, at the final judgment the nations will be condemned because they declined the Torah that God had offered them long ago:

> [I]t is written: "The Lord came from Sinai and rose from Seir unto them, He shined forth from Mount Paran" (Deut 33:2) And it is also written: "God comes from Teman" (Hab. 3:3). What did He seek in Seir, and what did He seek in Mount Paran? R. Johanan says: "This teaches us that the Holy One, Blessed Be He, offered the Torah to every nation and every tongue, but none accepted it, until He came to Israel who received it." [. . .]

---

29 As the Soncino translation to this passage tersely puts it: "It provides an excuse for non-observance, since it was forcibly imposed in the first place."

30 "Confirmed" for Raba refers to something preceding the time of Esther, namely, the covenant at Sinai. See Graves 2018, 149 n. 12.

31 Traditional rabbinic commentators of the Talmud have noted the (theological) problem involved here. For example, Rashba (1235–1310 CE) remarks that the Jewish people could not have been punished and exiled for violating the Torah if God had forced them to accept it. Rashba, accordingly, understands the imagery of the uprooted mountain in a positive way: the overturned mountain represents the abundance of the divine love bestowed upon Israel during the exodus. Rashba's understanding aligns better with the depiction of the uprooted mountain as expressed in the MRI but not so much with the interpretation of R. Abdimi in b. Shabbat 88a (or even with the anonymous tradition in the MRS). For a brief discussion of Rashba's viewpoint, see Steinsaltz 2012b, 31.

32 Graves 2018, 149: "For the sake of all creation God had to take extreme measures to ensure that Israel would receive the Torah."

> This, then, will be their contention [i.e., the nations in their defense will say before God on the day of judgment]: "Lord of the Universe, did you turn the mountain upside down over us like a vault as you did unto Israel and did we still decline to accept it?" As it is written, "And they stood together at the foot of the mountain" (Exod 19:17).
>
> R. Abdimi b. Ḥama said: "This teaches us that the Holy One, Blessed Be He, turned the mountain upside down over Israel like a vault, and said unto them: 'If you accept the Torah, that will be well, but if not, there will be your burial.'"[33]

R. Abdimi's interpretation of the dislocation of Mount Sinai is repeated here verbatim. A novel, positive spin, however, is ascribed to the overturning of the mountain.[34] On the day of judgment, the nations in their defense will argue that the Torah was not offered to them under the same terrifying circumstances that coerced Israel into submission. Otherwise, they would have presumably accepted the covenant like Israel. God's threat to bury Israel with the overturned mountain will in the end benefit the Jewish people. God, it turns out, was favoring Israel by bullying Israel!

This conclusion, however, raises questions about whether God plays favorites with Israel. The ensuing discussion in b. ʿAbod. Zar. (not quoted here) addresses this matter by asserting that the nations had received well before Sinai the seven Noahide commandments, a moral code that all humans (the children of Noah) are supposed to observe, according to rabbinic understanding.[35] Yet even these minimal requirements the nations failed to observe. Thus, b. ʿAbod. Zar. 2b considers the Mosaic covenant that took place under Sinai in conjunction with the universal covenant made with Noah after the flood.

Song of Songs Rabbah 8:5 § 1

The final rabbinic text of relevance for our purposes appears in Song of Songs Rabbah (Song. Rab.).[36] It comments on the wording from Song 8:5 in the following way:

---

33 English translation taken and adapted from the Soncino edition (Epstein 1978).

34 This new spin suggests that it was based on and produced *after* the parallel passage in b. Šabb. 88a. Cf. Graves 2018, 150 n. 15.

35 On the Noahide commandments, see Oliver 2013a.

36 This work originating from Israel/Palestine dates from the second half of the sixth century CE. See Stemberger 2011, 349.

> "Under the apple tree I roused you": Paltion, a man from Rome, expounded: "The mountain of Sinai was plucked (*nitlaš*) and was tied (*neʿĕnab*)[37] in the high heavens (*bišmê mārôm*), and Israel was placed under it, as it says, 'And you drew near and stood under the mountain.'" (Deut 4:11)
>
> Another interpretation of "under the apple tree I roused you": this is Sinai. And why is it likened to an apple tree? Just as an apple tree produces its fruit in the month of Sivan, so the Torah was given in Sivan.
>
> Another interpretation of "under the apple tree I roused you": Why not a nut tree or some other tree? The way of every tree is first to make its leaves come out and then its fruit. But an apple tree first makes its fruit come out and then makes its leaves come out. Thus Israel placed doing before hearing, as it says: "We will do and we will hear" (Exod 24:7). Said the Holy One, Blessed Be He: "If you accept upon yourselves my Torah, good, but if not, behold I will press (*kôbēsh*) this mountain upon you and kill you.'"[38]

This rabbinic commentary expounds Song 8:5 in light of the midrash attested already in the MRI. Like the MRI, Song Rab. employs the verb *nitlaš* to refer to the uprooting of Sinai, based on the literal understanding of the phrase "under the mountain" (Deut 4:11), which it also connects with the phrase "under the apple tree," from Song 8:5. However, Song Rab. describes the elevation of the mountain in a unique way, claiming that Sinai was "tied" to "the high heavens," once it was uprooted from its base. This language conveys the impression that mountain rose to the top of the sky. Heaven and earth met. They were "tied" together at Sinai. Perhaps, Song Rab. drew inspiration from Deut 4:11, which further states that "the mountain was burning with fire up to the very heavens." Indeed, one textual witness to Song Rab. includes this additional phrase from Deut 4:11.[39] Interestingly enough, Genesis Rabbah (Israel/Palestine, c. fifth century CE) declares that Mount Sinai reached the heavens when commenting on the ladder of Jacob's dream whose "top reached the sky" (Gen 28:12), quoting from Deut 4:11 as it equates the ladder with the mountain.[40] Sinai, like Jacob's ladder, stretched up to the celestial heights, linking heaven and earth.

---

37 The Vilna edition has *nitsav* (נצב: "stood"). However, Kadari's synoptic edition (https://schechter.ac.il/midrash/shir-hashirim-raba) includes variants such as נענב ("was tied" or "folded up") and נערב ("was mixed"). In a personal communication (April 16, 2020), Kadari suspects that נענב is the correct reading (attested in ms. Oxford – Bodleian 102, Neubauer – Cowley Catalogue 164.1) and that נצב is an attempt to correct an unclear text.

38 Translation of Song Rab. 8:5 § 1 mine. My translation is based on the Hebrew text of the Vilna edition. However, I have also consulted Kadari's synoptic edition, which contains all of the textual witnesses to Song. Rab.

39 Ms. Oxford – Bodleian 102: וההר בוער באש.

40 See Gen Rab. *Parašat Wayyēṣē* 68 on Gen 28:12 (Theodor-Albeck ed.).

Song Rab. also offers two original comparisons between Mount Sinai and the apple tree. First, apple trees yield their fruit during Sivan, the same month when the Torah was given at Sinai according to rabbinic tradition (the sixth of Sivan when Shavuot is celebrated). Second, apple trees, it is claimed, show their fruit before their leaves. This illustrates Israel's readiness to observe God's commandments. According to rabbinic understanding, when the Israelites said, "we will do and will hear" (Exod 24:7: *naʿăśeh wənišmāʿ*), they declared their willingness to keep the Sinaitic covenant even before they heard its stipulations, rabbinic exegesis noting that the biblical phrase mentions the "doing" before the "hearing." So far, the assessment of the uprooted mountain and Israel's response is positive. Yet surprisingly Song Rab. appends to this favorable evaluation God's threat to obliterate the Israelites. In fact, the language is formulated in even more violent terms than in the parallel passages from the MRS and the Babylonian Talmud: God threatens to *crush and kill* the Israelites if they do not accept the Torah. Perhaps, the midrash is inspired by the verb "rouse" in Song 8:5, which follows "under the apple tree." Yes, Israel eagerly declared its commitment to observe God's commandments when it stood under the mountain. But God "roused" them to do so. This agrees with the parallel text from the MRS, which claims that Israel promised to keep the Torah after God threatened to bury them. Thus Song Rab. mixes its apples and oranges, combining two opposing perspectives on the uprooted mountain, one rather favorable, the other quite dreadful.

Targumim

Worthy of equal attention for Qur'anic studies are the targumim, Jewish Aramaic translations of the Hebrew Scriptures. The translation of the Hebrew Scriptures into Aramaic began already during the Second Temple period, as attested by the Dead Sea Scrolls.[41] Tannaitic sources, moreover, presuppose their existence.[42] Undoubtedly, many of the materials found in Targum Onqelos (Tg. Onq.), Targum Neofiti (Tg. Neof.), and other targumic documents predate the rise of Islam

41 For a fragmentary targumic text of Job, see Sokoloff 1974. An Aramaic text of Leviticus also survives in fragmentary form (4Q156, 4Q157). The Genesis Apocryphon also merits mention here, although these Second Temple Aramaic texts differ from the targumim of the rabbinic period, especially by omitting and transposing the biblical materials from their Hebrew subtexts. See Shepherd 2020.

42 See Fraade 1992, 253–86 for references and a discussion. The Talmud attributes a targum of the Pentateuch to Onqelos and a targum of the Prophets to Jonathan ben Uzziel (see e.g., b. Megillah 3a).

in the seventh century CE.[43] The dating of Targum Pseudo-Jonathan (Tg. Ps.-J) is more problematic. According to Gavin McDowell, it was not completed before the twelfth century CE.[44] Indeed, at one point T. Ps.-J. refers explicitly to Muslim figures.[45] This, however, does not preclude the possibility that Tg. Ps.-J. contains older materials, as many scholars have indeed maintained.[46] Nevertheless, its late redaction calls for special caution. Passages in Tg. Ps.-J. should be evaluated on a case-by-case basis to determine their relevance for the historical-literary investigation of the Qur'ān. Overall though, the targumic writings contains a wealth of materials that predate the Qur'ān.[47] Interestingly, the targumim share exegetical traditions with the Old Testament Peshitta, the Syriac translation of the Hebrew Scriptures. Not only is the Peshitta's translation of the Hebrew Bible close to the Masoretic Text. As noted earlier, it is informed by Jewish exegesis. In fact, the Peshitta bears notable resemblances with interpretations attested in early rabbinic *and* targumic literature.[48] This suggests that the Aramaic and Syriac translations of Scripture share common Jewish sources.[49]

The extant targmumim of both Exod 19:17 and Deut 4:11 follow for the most part their Hebrew *Vorlage*.[50] This is especially true of Targum Onqelos, the more disciplined of the targums, which inserts paraphrastic materials to its translation of the Hebrew text far less than Tg. Ps.-J.: "And Moses took the people from the camp towards the Memra of the Lord, and they stood together at the lower part of the mountain (Exod 19:17)."[51] The only notable difference here

43 The precise dating of targumic materials is extremely challenging. In the context of New Testament studies, their relevance continues to be debated. See McNamara 2010, 387–427, for a discussion. For a critical overview of the Targums, see Flesher and Chilton 2011.

44 McDowell 2017; cf. Gottlieb 2014.

45 The names of Aisha and Fatima feature in Tg. Ps.-J. Gen 21:21.

46 Hayward 2010; Flesher and Chilton 2011; Mortensen 2006, 1:12–13. These scholars situate the final redaction of Tg. Ps.-J., save for any obvious interpolation, before the Middle Ages.

47 For a case on behalf of the early dating of Tg. Neof., see Boccaccini 1994, 260–69.

48 Maori 1998, 57–73, shows that many interpretations shared between the Old Testament Peshitta and rabbinic literature appear in the targumim as well.

49 See Flesher 1998, xi–xii.

50 This is true for the Samaritan text of Exod 19:17 and Deut 4:11 (von Gall ed.), which is similar to the Masoretic Text, and arguably the Septuagint: although both Exod 19:17 and Deut 4:11 LXX (Wevers ed.) have *hypo to oros*, the Greek phrase should probably not be taken literally. Cf. the English translation of Exod 19:17 and Deut 4:11 LXX by Pietersma and Wright 2007: "below the mountain." The Septuagint's choice to render the Hebrew *yityaṯṣṣwû* with *parestēsan* probably conveys the notion of standing before the presence of a divine authority at a specific location (see Judith 4:14; Luke 1:19; cf. fn. 16 above).

51 The Aramaic texts of the targums are taken from *The Comprehensive Aramaic Lexicon* (*CAL*) online database.

is Onqelos's substitution of "God" with "the Memra of the Lord," a distinctive feature of the targumic writings that has attracted significant scholarly debate.[52] Otherwise, Tg. Onq. renders *bətaḥtît hāhār* in a straightforward manner as *bšpwly ṭwr'*, that is, "at the lower part (or bottom) of the mountain." There is nothing that excites the imagination here, although, as we will see, the appearance of the Aramaic noun for mountain (*twr'*) is pertinent for the analysis of the Qur'ān. Tg. Neof. Exod 19:17 is essentially identical to Tg. Onk., save for its usage of the wordy construction "glory of the Shekinah of the Lord" instead of "Memra of the Lord." This targum also states that the Israelites were stationed "at the foot of the mountain" (*bšplwy dṭwr'*).[53]

As is often the case, Targum Pseudo-Jonathan's paraphrase of Exod 19:17 is far more expansive, drawing from the rich Jewish lore attested in rabbinic tradition and beyond:

> And Moses took the people out from the camp before the Shekinah of the Lord, and right away the Master of the Universe uprooted (*tlš*) the mountain and raised (*zqf*) it in the air, and it was clear (*zyyg*) as a window glass (*'spqlry'*), and they were stationed under the mountain (*tḥwty twwr'*).

This rendition of Exod 19:17 shows clear dependence on rabbinic tradition. It uses the verb *tlš*, attested in both MRI and Song. Rab. (*nitlaš*), albeit in the active voice to describe how the "Master of the Universe" (cf. the Hebrew rabbinic phrase, *ribbônô šel 'ôlām*) ripped the mountain from its place. Notably, Tg. Ps.-J. claims that God "raised" (*zqf*) the mountain "in the air" (*b'wyr'*). This wording finds no exact correspondence in the rabbinic midrashim we have assessed, the closest parallel being in Song. Rab., which declares that the mountain "was tied" or "stood" (if one accepts the reading from the Vilna edition) in the "high heavens." The word for "air" in Tg. Ps.-J. (a loanword from the Greek *aēr*) probably means here "sky," as it does in Tg. Ps.-J. Gen 1:26: "birds that are in the atmosphere of the sky" (*b'wyr' dbšmyy'*). The mountain seems to be floating in the air.

---

52 Traditionally, the Memra is understood as a means of avoiding anthropomorphic depictions of the divine. Boyarin 2004, 113–17, however, interprets the Memra as evidence for the widespread belief among (non-rabbinic) Jews in binitarianism, which, in turn, accounts for the origins of the Christian belief in the divinity of Jesus.

53 The Fragment Targums exhibit nothing noteworthy either: manuscripts P and V of the Fragment Targum as well as Cairo Geniza manuscript F all read "at the foot of the mountain," with minor variations in spelling. The translation of Exod 19:17 in the Old Testament Peshitta (Peshitta Institute Leiden ed.) is just as sober: "and Moses took the people from the camp to meet God, and they stood at the bottom of the mountain" (*bšpwlwhy dṭwr'*).

Tg. Ps.-J. Exod 19:17 contains the intriguing simile that the lifted mountain became as "clear" (*zyyg*) as a "window glass" or "mirror" (*'spqlr'*).[54] Interestingly, the word *'spqlr'* is used in a metaphorical sense in rabbinic literature to speak of prophetic or divine revelation.[55] For example, one passage from the Babylonian Talmud claims that the righteous are privileged to contemplate the divine in the hereafter through a "bright glass" (*'îspaqlaryâ hamē'îrâ*).[56] Similarly, a midrash in Leviticus Rabbah (fifth to sixth century CE) claims that the prophets of Israel saw the divine through "nine mirrors/lenses" (*tēša' 'îspaqlaryôt*) while Moses alone saw the divine through "one mirror/lense" (*'îspaqlaryâ 'aḥat*). This view is ascribed to R. Judah b. Ilai, who bases himself on Ezek 43:3 and Num 12:8. Ezek 43:3 refers to a "vision" (*mar'eh*) of the prophet Ezekiel. R. Judah b. Ilai, however, reads the noun *mar'eh* (מראה) as *mar'â* (מראה), namely, "mirror."[57] According to R. Judah b. Ilai's tally, the word *mar'ēh* and its related verb *rā'â* ("saw") appear no less than nine times within Ezek 43:3.[58] This amounts to "nine mirrors" (or lenses). Thus Ezekiel, and by extension all Hebrew prophets, saw God

54 Did the *mountain* or the *air* become as clear as a window glass? Both options are possible, since "mountain" and "air" are masculine in Aramaic. Picturing the air (i.e., the sky), rather than a mountain, as a clear glass might seem more straightforward. However, the latter option is not unthinkable. According to Midrash Psalms 8 § 4 (Buber ed.), at Sinai, God demanded from the Israelites their infants as a pledge that they would keep the Torah. The infants, it is said, some nursing from their mothers' breasts, others still in their mothers' bellies, assumed full responsibility for their parents' (future) wrongdoings. The midrash claims that the mothers' abdomens became like "glass" (*zəkûkît*) so that the infants could see God from their wombs. In the very next section of Midrash Psalms (§ 5), Rav claims that they became like a "bright glass" (*'îspaqlaryâ hamē'îrâ*). Cf. the parallel passage in b. Sotah 30b–31a, which is set at the Red Sea, and claims that the mothers' abdomens became like a "bright glass" (*'îspaqlaryâ hamē'îrâ*). This statement, however, appears in the Vilna edition of the Bavli but not in ms. Vatican, Biblioteca Apostlica ebr. 110 (for the text, see the *Ma'agarim* online database).

55 The word *'spqlr'* is a loanword (Latin *specularis*; Greek: *speklarion*). Translations, lexicons, and commentaries translate this word variously. For example, Jastrow (1943) 2005, 96 proposes "window glass" for Tg. Ps.-J. Exod 19:17. Strack and Billerbeck 1922–1926, 3:453, have "Glas" (German). *CAL* provides "shiny stone, mirror," based, it seems, on Jastrow as well as Levy 1924. Kittel (see below) prefers "mirror."

56 B. Sukkah 45b (Steinsaltz ed.). According to Gen. Rab. *Parašat Miqeṣ* 91 (Theodor-Albeck ed.), Jacob "sees through a glass" that Joseph is alive and well in Egypt. Cf. Paul in 1 Cor 13:12 and 2 Cor 3:18 (discussed below).

57 In his translation of Lev Rab., Neusner (1986) 2003, 160 translates *'îspaqlaryâ* as "lense"; Strack and Billerbeck 1926, 3:454 as "Glassscheibe" ("glass pane"). Kittel, (1964) 1983, 1:179, however, is adamant that it should be rendered as "mirror," based on the wordplay between *mar'eh* and *mar'â*. On mirrors in antiquity, see the next section of this article dealing with Paul.

58 The plural *mar'ôt*, which appears once in Ezek 43:3, counts as "two mirrors."

only through nine mirrors/lenses. By contrast, Num 12:8 mentions *mar'eh* only once: "Mouth to mouth I speak to him and [in] appearance (*mar'eh*) but not in riddles; he [i.e., Moses] beholds the form of the LORD." From this, R. Judah b. Ilai infers that Moses beheld the form of God more closely, through one mirror only.[59] Lev. Rab., however, also includes an alternative opinion ascribed to "the rabbis" who claim that the prophets saw the divine through a "stained mirror/lense" (*'îspaqlaryâ məlûkhlekhet*) rather than through nine mirrors/lenses, citing Hos 12:11 as their proof: "I spoke to the prophets, and I multiplied visions, and spoke parables through the prophets." Moses, on the other hand, the same rabbis claim, contemplated the divine through a "polished mirror/lense" (*'îspaqlaryâ məṣûḥṣeḥet*), as Num 12:8 states: "he beholds the form of the LORD." The rabbis take the reference in Hos 12:11 to the multiplication of visions and communication *via parables* to mean that the prophets experienced revelation less clearly than Moses. Finally, Lev. Rab. concludes with a parable attributed to R. Hoshaya about a king who "makes his appearance to his courtier in his informal garb [as an intimate]."[60] R. Hoshaya avers that the Shekinah is revealed only to a few privileged individuals in this world but to many in the world to come in accordance with Isaiah 40:5: "the glory of the LORD will be revealed, and all flesh will see it together."[61]

The reference in Tg. Ps.-J. Exod 19:17 to a transparent window pane/mirror highlights therefore the special character of the Sinaitic revelation. It was a lucid disclosure of the divine presence. Moreover, the *entire* nation of Israel was privileged to experience God's revelation in a way that rabbinic tradition would tend to reserve for Moses only.[62] Just as Moses saw God's glory through a polished mirror (Hebrew: *'îspaqlaryâ məṣûḥṣeḥet*), so too did the Israelites see the Shekinah of the Lord, once the mountain was raised and became clear as a mirror (Aramaic: *zyyg hy 'spqlr'*). In Tg. Ps.-J., the nation of Israel is elevated along

59 Cf. MIR *Yitro* – *'Amaleq* 2: commenting on Exod 18:21, "you [i.e., Moses] will see (*teḥezeh*) from all the people," R. Eleazar of Modiim states, "you will see for them through a glass, like the glass (*maḥazît*) that the kings see (*ḥôzîn*) through."

60 Following here the translation of Neusner (1986) 2003, 160, who depends on Lieberman and Margulies.

61 Lev. Rab. *Parašat Wayyiqra'* 1:XIV (Margulies ed.). Cf. the baraita in b. Yebamot 49b.

62 Recall, however, Midrash Psalms 8 § 4–5 (cited above), which claims that even unborn Israelite infants saw God at Sinai through their mothers' bellies, which became like "glass" (*zəkûkît*) or a "bright glass" (*'îspaqlaryâ hamē'îrâ*). Cf. MIR *Yitro* – *Baḥodeš* 3.

with Mount Sinai in a most positive way: God removed the mountain so that the people could enjoy a clear vision of the divine.[63]

Early Christian Interpretations

Before turning to the Qur'ān, we should not fail to appreciate some of the early Christian interpretations of the Sinaitic revelation. Even if they do not reveal any awareness of the rabbinic midrash on the raised mountain, they are pertinent because they frequently display pronouncements on the Torah and Israel that are paralleled in the Qur'ān.

Paul

Paul is the earliest "Christian" author who reflects on Israel's response to God's revelation when they pitched their tents in the wilderness. In 2 Corinthians, this reflection surfaces as Paul accounts for the Jewish resistance to the kerygma. Paul observes that when "the ministry of death engraved in letters on stone tablets" appeared "in glory" to the Israelites, they could not bear to contemplate the glory emanating from Moses' face, a glory in Paul's estimation that is now "passing away" (3:7).[64] Moses instead had to veil his face whenever he appeared before the

---

63 Mortensen 2006, 1:3–4, defines Tg. Ps.-J. as a "Handbook for Priests," and interprets the displacement of the mountain in Tg. Ps.-J. as a mechanism meant to instill reverence among Israel for sacred places: "The only reason a creator would bother to raise a mountain, is to impress his audience. The priest's job is to mediate between the holy place of the mountain and his people'" (1:177). However, in Tg. Ps.-J. Exod 19:17 *all of Israel*, not simply Levites and priests, witnesses the glorious spectacle. This contrasts with Tg. Ps.-J. Exod 24:10, where only *Nadav and Abihu* (priests) contemplate the divine glory along with the seventy elders, and with Exod 24:12–17, where Moses alone ascends to the top of the mountain. Perhaps, it is better to say that the priests experience a closer encounter with the divine than the laity: the former see the divine glory *on* the mountain, the latter *under* the mountain (see further Tg. Ps.-J. 24: 12–17). For Shinan 1992, 138, the reference to the uplifted mountain is part of a tendency in Tg. Ps.-J. to relate folk beliefs about the supernatural. The depiction of the flying mountain is thus intended to impress the imagination of the common folk. More is at play here though than just the relaying of popular beliefs, since the source of inspiration for Tg. Ps.-J. Exod 19:17 is rabbinic midrash.

64 Much debate in New Testament scholarship now centers on whether Paul only exempted *gentile* Christ-followers (the epithet "Christian" is an anachronism at this primitive stage of "church history") from observing the Mosaic Torah while advocating its observance *in toto* for

Israelites (v. 13). Paul then contrasts this former glory, which is associated with the tablets given to Moses at Sinai, with the glory of the "ministry of the spirit" or the "ministry of righteousness." The latter's glory is greater and permanent (vv. 8–11). Furthermore, Christ's followers behold this glory without a veil (vv. 13, 18) in contrast to the Jewish people whose spiritual perception remains impaired whenever they read "Moses" or the "old covenant" (vv. 14–15).[65]

Paul depends on Exodus 34:29–35, which reports that Moses would veil his face whenever he descended from the mountain. However, according to the book of Exodus, Moses began this habit only after a number of critical ascents and descents from Mount Sinai (Exod 19:3, 7–8, 14, 25). Additionally, the Israelites had received the Decalogue and other statutes (Exod 19:9–20:17; 20:22–23:19). After the ratification of the covenant (24:1–8), Moses ascended Sinai again in order to receive instructions about the Tabernacle and the consecration of the priests and their vestments (25:1–31:17). During this particular visit on the mountain top, Moses received two tablets of stone inscribed by the very finger of God (31:18). However, he angrily destroyed them when he returned to the Israelite camp and saw them worshipping a golden calf, in direct infringement of the covenant they had just signed (ch. 32–33:23). This meant that Moses had to undertake yet another ascent to the mountain, where he made a new set of tablets and received additional laws (34:1–28). Only *after* Moses returned from this latest visit does Exodus report the Israelites' fright at seeing his face glow (35:29–35).[66]

It is unclear whether Paul took this narrative progression into consideration in this instance. Did the Jewish apostle in 2 Cor 3 distinguish Israel's responses to God's revelation *before* and *after* the calf incident? Subsequent Christian thinkers, as we will shortly see, certainly zeroed in on the golden calf incident.[67] Paul, however, does not directly address the reaction of the Israelites the first time they stood at the foot of the mountain before they adored the

---

Jewish followers of Jesus. From a Jewish viewpoint, it is certainly startling that Paul compares the Torah to a "ministry of death" and a "ministry of condemnation" (2 Cor 3:7–9), while associating Mount Sinai with Hagar and slavery (Gal 4:24). See nevertheless the analysis of 2 Cor 3 by Duff 2015 and the insightful treatment of Galatians by Thiessen 2016. For a critical and charitable assessment of the "Radical New Perspective," see Oliver 2019.

65 Translations of the New Testament are based on Nestle-Aland's 28th edition of the Greek text (2012).

66 Many devout readers imagine the giving of the law at Sinai as a single, dramatic event. In reality, the Pentateuch presents the revelation of the Torah(s) as a lengthy process with multiple visits by Moses to the mountain and the Tabernacle. For a concise, accessible discussion of this matter from a source critical perspective, see Schwartz 1997.

67 Rabbinic texts also single out the sin of the golden calf. For a discussion of the golden calf as a polemic between Jews and Christians, see Bori 1990.

golden calf. Paul, rather, underscores the Israelites' inability to contemplate the divine splendor related to the "old covenant" (v. 14) in order to account for the (supposed) spiritual blindness of his Jewish contemporaries. Many Jews, like their Israelite ancestors, fail to perceive the divine glory now manifested through Christ. By contrast, Christ's followers according to Paul see "with unveiled faces the glory of the Lord as though reflected in a mirror" (v. 18). Interestingly, Paul, like Tg. Ps.-J. Exod 19:17, uses mirror imagery to describe the contemplation of the Lord's glory, the verb *katoptrizomenoi* ("seeing as though reflected in a mirror") deriving from the noun *katoptron* ("mirror").[68] This triumphant declaration stands somewhat in tension with the more sober assessment delivered in 1 Cor 13:12: "For now we see in a mirror (*dia esoptrou*), dimly (*en ainigmati*), but then we will see face to face."[69] This verse admits a more limited, indirect contemplation of the divine. For the time being, one can only see in a mirror *en ainigmati*, literally, "in a riddle." It is noteworthy that the Septuagint employs a similar phrase in Num 12:8 as it highlights the exceptional mode of divine communication afforded to Moses: "Mouth to mouth I will speak to him, in visible form and not through riddles (Greek: *dia ainigmatōn*). And he has seen the glory of the Lord."[70] We have already seen how rabbinic midrash capitalized precisely on this verse to exalt Moses above all other prophets. Quite possibly, Paul alludes to Num 12:8 in 1 Cor 13:12, given the close correspondence between *en ainigmati* and *dia ainigmatōn*. Perhaps, Paul even knew of a midrash like the one on Num 12:8 attested in (admittedly later) rabbinic sources, which interpreted the Hebrew *mar'eh* as *mar'â* ("mirror"), since both 1 Cor 13:12 and 2 Cor 3:18 speak variously of beholding the divine glory through a mirror.[71] If so, Paul would be ascribing to the followers of Christ a prophetic level of revelatory experience equal to that of Moses, for they, like Israel's greatest prophet, see through (one) mirror the very "glory of the Lord" (2 Cor 3:18 = Num 12:8: *tēn doxan kyriou*). Furthermore, Paul believed that they would see the divine "face to face" in the (imminent) eschatological future (1 Cor 13:12).[72] Thus Paul claims for the body of Christ's followers a revelatory experience that Tg. Ps.-J. and some rabbinic texts reserve only *for Moses*

68 On mirrors in antiquity, see Hurschmann, Prayon, and Pingel 2006.

69 Translation from the NRSV. Keener 2005, 110 harmonizes the two passages as follows: "Christians could see a reflection of God's glory now as in a mirror . . .. Compared to the final revelation and transformation into his image, however (1 Cor 15:48–49), Christians presently see a mere reflection, only a little beyond what Moses and the prophets saw."

70 Translation taken from Pietersma and Wright 2007.

71 As suggested already by Kittel (1964) 1983, 1:180. Alternatively, Paul and rabbinic midrash draw from a common pool of Jewish exegetical tradition.

72 Cf. Gen 32:31 LXX; Judg 6:22 LXX.

and the Israelite nation at Sinai. The conviction of the former stems from eschatological and messianic beliefs; the reservation of the latter implies that the messianic age has not yet dawned and that the righteous, therefore, can only see God more clearly in the hereafter. These conflicting claims may have been formulated in reaction to the "other." Paul ascribes the kind of revelation reserved for Moses to Christ-followers, having Jews who do not believe in Jesus' messiahship in mind. Similarly, the kind of praise for Israel and the Sinaitic revelation that one encounters in Tg. Ps.-J. and rabbinic literature may have taken Christian messianic and supersessionist declarations into account by pointing back to Sinai as a *past and unequaled event*. Some Christian writers, as we will see, may have been aware of these assertions and perceived them as threats to their Christian faith.

The Acts of the Apostles

No other New Testament passage deals specifically with the moment when Israel was first stationed at Sinai's base to receive the Torah. However, the Acts of the Apostles does refer to the revelation of the Law of Moses, which it claims was given through angels (Acts 7:53; perhaps echoing Gal 3:19). This report appears in Stephen's speech, which also exalts Moses as a prophet of Israel. The Stephen of Acts relates that God communicated with Moses at the burning bush (vv. 32–33) and on Mount Sinai, where he received "living words," a positive evaluation of the Torah (v. 38).[73] However, Stephen's speech especially underlines Israel's rejection of Moses and its transgression of the Torah. It glosses over the people's initial readiness to observe the Torah (Exod 24:7; cf. 19:8) as it retells Israel's history, rehearsing instead the golden calf incident. Additionally, it links Israel's rejection of Moses with the rejection of Jesus by his fellow Jews (vv. 37, 40–41). Stephen in Acts further indicts his Jewish interlocutors, whom he considers to be "stiff-necked and uncircumcised in their hearts and ears," for the slaughter of Israel prophets, including the murder of Jesus. All of this they committed despite the fact that they possess(ed) the Torah (vv. 51–53).

Although the writer of Acts hardly disparages the Torah, he condemns Jews who reject Jesus, portraying them as spiritually blind and misguided (cf. Acts 28:

73 More consistently and clearly than Paul, in my opinion, the author of Luke-Acts affirms a place for Torah practice for Jewish Christ-followers, on the one hand, who are to continue observing their ancestral Jewish customs, and gentile Christ-followers, on the other, who need only uphold the so-called Apostolic Decree. See Oliver 2013.

26–27) and charging them of the same violent crimes purportedly committed by their Israelite ancestors against God's messengers.[74]

The Synoptic Gospels

The Synoptic Gospels repeat some of the same tropes found in Acts, although they may have originally been targeted at specific subgroups withing Jewish society, for example, Pharisees who did not recognize Jesus's messianic status. Both Mark and Matthew submit that at least one commandment of the Torah, the license to divorce, was issued by Moses because of Israel's "hardness of heart" (Matt 19:8; Mark 10:5).[75] In both Mark and Matthew, this statement is directed at Jesus' Pharisaic audience. It is unquestionably polemical, especially in Matthew, which singles out the Pharisees for their supposed stubbornness.[76] However, seeing that Jesus' declaration points back to a particular stipulation in the Mosaic Torah, it may also concern Israel as a whole. After all, the Israelites who left Egypt, not the Pharisees, were the ones who were first granted license to divorce under the Mosaic legislation. Matthew and Mark, therefore, may imply that Moses had to concede in one legal area because of Israel's rebellious nature.[77] In any case, subsequent Christian writings will emphasize that Jews do not believe in Jesus because they supposedly have stubborn hearts.

74 The author of Acts nevertheless does not so much charge the Jews for the *crucifixion* of Jesus so much as for their *ongoing* disbelief in his messianic status. The crucifixion of Jesus, Acts underlines, was committed out of *ignorance* by those Jews who were in Jerusalem at that time. See Oliver 2021.

75 The Torah, nonetheless, maintains its authority, particularly for Matthew (5:17–21). Some have argued that Matthew views the Mosaic laws on oaths in a negative light. But see Oliver 2013b, 24–25.

76 Runesson 2008 views Matthew's polemics as part of an intra-Pharisaic controversy between Pharisees who believe in Jesus' messiahship and those who don't.

77 The concept would not prove to be altogether novel or antinomian in the context of Second Temple Judaism. In Gen 9:3, God grants humankind the right to eat flesh (without the blood). But this permission comes as a *concession*, as the original diet formulated in Genesis was vegetarian (1:29–30). On the unease of the Priestly writers of the Pentateuch with eating meat, see Milgrom 2009, 705–12. A person, therefore, who adopts a vegetarian diet does not *violate* any prohibition in the Torah, but, in fact, goes *beyond* its requirements. The same conclusion could be drawn from Matt and Mark concerning their rejection of divorce. Cf. Davies 2004, 80: "The OT *permits* but does not *command* divorce." Consider also the critique of the institution of slavery in 1 Enoch 98:4, which claims that "it was not ordained . . . but it happened because of oppression." Commenting on this passage, Nickelsburg, 2001, 477 states: "The argument is

The Epistle of Barnabas

Subsequent Christian writers rearranged and added to the blocks set by their New Testament predecessors to further condemn Israel. The Epistle of (Pseudo-) Barnabas repeatedly blames the Israelites for worshipping the golden calf, which invalidated their covenantal rights (4:7–8; 14:1–4).[78] Barnabas goes as far as accusing the Israelites for misunderstanding the true sense of the Mosaic Law. Commandments concerning such things as food were never intended to be taken literally. Yet the Israelites because of their "fleshly desire" (10:9) mistook the dietary laws prescribed in the Torah as concerning actual food. Likewise, an evil angel misled the Israelites into thinking that circumcision was a matter of the flesh rather than of the heart (9:4). This latter interpretation represents a radical departure from Paul, the (canonical) Gospels, and the Acts of the Apostles.[79] On the other hand, the depiction of the Israelites as a rebellious people is widely attested in the New Testament.

---

paralleled in Mark 10:2–9, where Jesus contrasts God's intention in creation with the concession made to human 'hardness of heart' in the Mosaic divorce law."

78 Barnabas is a post-70 text (see 16:5), perhaps written during the Bar Kokhba Revolt, although the ambiguity of 16:3–4 makes it hard to posit this dating with absolute certainty.

79 Some scholars esteem it inaccurate to characterize the Epistle of Barnabas as "anti-Jewish," since this document purportedly draws from Jewish sources. After all, the "radical allegorizers" whom Philo critiques for their exclusively non-literal interpretation of the Mosaic commandments were Jewish themselves. This argument is valid only to a certain degree. For one thing, Barnabas makes the radical claim that an *evil* angel misled the Israelites (see Paget 1991 and 2006, who thinks that Barnabas may be responding to a perceived threat of Judaism or Judaizers). A critical question concerns the social and theological standpoint of the author of Barnabas: does (s)he engage in such polemics by identifying with the Jewish people (as Paul does in Romans) or solely against and from outside of Judaism? For Mimouni 1998, 191, Barnabas is not anti-Jewish but reflects an internal conflict between two currents within "Jewish Christianity," one attached to the (literal) observance of the Torah, the other opposed. This social-historical approach though does not consider the implications of the author's theological outlook on Judaism. Taylor 1995, on the other hand, sees the anti-Judaic expressions in second and third century Christian literature as mainly due to internal theological reflections seeking to explain how and why Christianity differs from Judaism. This observation is important but risks reducing Christian reflections on Judaism to theological or rhetorical abstractions, as if Christians did not interact with Jews in antiquity and remained oblivious to the challenge presented by the persistent vitality of (non-Christian) Judaism.

Justin Martyr

For Justin Martyr (c. 100–165 CE), the sinful ways and stiff hearts of the Israelites explains why they received laws on the Sabbath, circumcision, and the like (*Dialogue with Trypho* chs. 18; 27; 45). These precepts were designed to guard Israel against its sinful proclivities. Thus, they were instituted only as temporary measures until Christ's formal entry into human history (see e.g., *Dial.* ch. 20). Justin admits that the Sinaitic revelation burst forth with incredible *éclat*, but the divine fireworks were so overwhelming that the Israelites could not even bear hearing God's word during the whole spectacle. By contrast, God instituted a new covenant with the Christians, one established without "fear and trembling and lightning flashes" in order to distinguish the divine precepts that are truly eternal and universal from those prescribed to the Israelites because of their heavy hearts (*Dial.* 67:9–10). In this way, Justin simultaneously downplays the magnitude of the Sinaitic revelation while coloring the people of Israel in negative light. The Israelites did not fully experience the divine revelation when they stood in fear at Sinai; many of the Mosaic commandments were of a transitory, even punitive, measure, necessary because of Israel's chronic addiction to idolatry (*Dial.* 19:5–6). To back his point, Justin emphasizes that the patriarchs who lived before the Mosaic covenant did not keep the Sabbath or circumcision yet were still counted as righteous (e.g., *Dial.* 67:7). In fact, Justin goes as far as to claim that the commandment of circumcision was given to set Israel apart for future chastisement, making it easy for the Romans to identify Jews and banish them from Jerusalem after the failure of the Bar Kokhba Revolt (*Dial.* ch. 16).[80] What Israel's Scriptures favorably casts as a sign of covenantal status Justin transforms into a definitive curse.[81] Had the Israelites known about the (invisible) fine print Justin identified in the Mosaic contract, perhaps they would have thought twice before signing below the dotted line!

---

80 Here, Justin conveniently overlooks what Barn. 9:6 foregrounds, even if only to dismiss Jewish circumcision, namely, that other ancient peoples (e.g., Syrians) purportedly practiced circumcision. On Justin Martyr's views on the Bar Kokhba Revolt and "the partings of the ways" between Judaism and Christianity, see Oliver 2014.

81 Nevertheless, despite his negative views on the ritual commandments of the Mosaic Torah, Justin tolerates their observance by Jewish Christ-followers, provided they do not force them upon gentile Christians. Justin contrasts his more accommodating position on this matter with Christians who will not fellowship with Torah observant Jewish Christ-followers (*Dial.* 47). On Justin's views on Jewish Christ-followers and gentile Judaizers, see White 2018.

Eusebius

The "father of church history," Eusebius of Caesarea (c. 260–339 CE), shares some points in common with his patristic predecessor Justin concerning Sinai and Israel. In a neglected work known as the *Eclogae propheticae*,[82] Eusebius, similar to Justin, emphasizes that God had to descend on Sinai with "great amazement and pomp" (*pollēs kataplēxeōs kai phantasias*), citing Exod 19:16–18.[83] This was so because the Israelites were still "childish and uninitiated in their souls," "habituated to Egyptian ways," and therefore in need of "great repentance." The terrifying theophany was supposed to make the Israelites keep the commandments. Eusebius further contends that the Israelites did not actually *see God*, who remained shrouded by fire and an angelic host. Eusebius contrasts the Sinaitic theophany with previous divine apparitions to the patriarchs Abraham, Isaac, and Jacob. These, unlike the Israelites, did see God, without the need for a glamorous show to impress their minds. Even Moses, so Eusebius stresses, did not see God in the wilderness but only *heard* God speak as he beheld an angel. If Eusebius' comments are not to be taken solely as theological reflections internal to Christianity, then perhaps he magnified pre-Mosaic theophanies in response to Jewish claims that exalted Moses above all other prophets and celebrated the Sinaitic theophany as a revelatory encounter experienced by all of Israel.[84]

Proclus

In one of his homilies, the archbishop of Constantinople, Proclus (died c. 446 CE), makes a similar point as Eusebius denying that the Israelites saw God during their stay at Sinai:

> There may per chance be a Jew in our midst, like the fox of Judah lurking in the vineyard of Christ. After the congregation is dismissed, he might stand outside and mock our words, saying such things as these: "Why do you Christians invent such novelties and boast of things which cannot be proved? When did God ever appear on earth? Never, except in the time of Moses." But even then, O Jew, he did not appear. Moses himself testifies to this when he says: "Take heed to thyself and place within thy heart all the words which thine eyes have seen. And thou shalt teach them to thy sons and thy sons' sons. Remember the day of the Lord thy God, the day of the assembly, when the Lord said to

82 A French translation of this work exists in the unpublished dissertation by Philippe 2003.
83 *Eclogae propheticae*, p. 30 lines 4–19. The Greek text is that of Gaisford 1842 (retrieved online through the *Thesaurus Linguae Graecae* database).
84 This point, however, awaits further investigation that goes beyond the scope of this article.

> me: 'Assemble all the people to me and let them hear my words and teach them to their sons.' And ye drew nigh and stood at the foot of Mount Sinai (*hypo to oros to Sina*). And the mountain burned with fire up to heaven, and ye heard the voice of the Lord your God out of the midst of the fire. Ye heard a voice of words, but ye saw no likeness.[85]

Proclus delivers these comments in response to Jews, whether real or imaginary, who question the veracity of the virgin birth.[86] Earlier on in the same homily, Proclus also roundly condemns the "children of the Jews" for questioning the perpetual virginity of Mary.[87] Proclus's pointed interest in the status of Mary stemmed from theological debates internal to Christianity. The status of Mary as Theotokos, that is, the mother of God, was intensely debated in his day. This issue had much to do with how Christians understood the relationship between the humanity and divinity of Christ. Nestorius, Proclus' contemporary, deemed the title Theotokos inappropriate. Mary, a human, could not be the mother of God but only "Christoforos" (bearer of Christ), Nestorius and his followers dividing the incarnate Christ into two separate Persons, the one divine and the other human. For holding this belief, Proclus spared Nestorius no rebukes in his homilies. To a certain degree, therefore, some of Proclus' condemnations of Jewish views may have also been aimed at *Christians* who did not share his Christology and Mariology.[88] Nevertheless, we may suppose that Proclus targeted Jews as well in his sermons.[89] A Jewish community, after all, did reside in Constantinople, and Proclus addresses what appear to be Jewish objections: his homiletical Jew questions the very incarnation of God in the person of Christ, pointing back to the sole moment and place in history when God was made manifest to (Israelite) humans – below Mount Sinai (*hypo to oros to Sina*).[90] Proclus argues accordingly that the Israelites did not see God when they converged at the foot of the mountain. They only heard

85 *Homilia de incarnatione* 2.9.104–118. Translation taken from Constas 2003, 171–73.
86 There was a Jewish community in Constantinople. See Barkhuizen 1999.
87 *Homilia de incarnatione* 2.6.64–65: "Let then the children of the Jews be ashamed, those who disparage the virgin birth saying: 'If a virgin gave birth she is no longer a virgin.'"
88 The work of Taylor 1995 proves more pertinent for this stage of church history when the label "Jewish" largely became a signifier of alterity, not least to condemn Christian heresy. On the usage of the word "Jew" as the constitutional "other," see Baker 2017.
89 Proclus also highlights the golden calf incident in his condemnation of Jewish feasts. See Barkhuizen 1999, 39.
90 Barkhuizen 1999, 40, argues that non-Christian Jews as well as "heretics" attended Proclus' services; otherwise, his references to Jews listening to his sermons would have a very weak rhetorical effect if they were not present at all.

utterances. Thus, Proclus, like Justin and Eusebius, also downplays Israel's revelatory experience of the Sinaitic theophany.[91]

Cyril of Alexandria

Cyril of Alexandria (c. 375–444 CE) comments on Exodus 19:17, including the phrase "at the foot of the mountain," in his commentary on the Gospel of John. This occurs as Cyril discusses Jesus's healing of a lame man on the Sabbath. According to John, Jesus not only healed but also commanded this man to carry his mattress on the Sabbath day (John 5:8). These acts are normally forbidden for Jews to perform on the Sabbath.[92] "The Jews" (this is the problematic way that John often names Jesus' adversaries) therefore confront Jesus for his apparent disregard of the Sabbath. Jesus makes the situation only worse in the eyes of his opponents when he appears to equate himself with God, wondering why he should refrain from healing on the Sabbath if God is always on active duty, even on the seventh day (5:17). In this confrontation, Jesus condemns "the Jews," going as far as to claim that they never heard God's voice nor saw God's form (5:37: *oute phōnēn autou pōpote akēkoate oute eidos autou heōrakate*). Cyril takes this declaration to mean that the Jewish people did not see or hear God at Sinai. In Cyril's imagination of this Johannine scene, Jesus' Jewish adversaries ("Pharisees" for Cyril)[93] wonder in their minds how Jesus could transgress the Sabbath since God had descended on Mount Sinai and clearly instructed the Israelites to keep this day holy: "And we heard none other than God saying these things, it says. The multitude of fathers heard the voice from God, and after them the word of God was in us. But who is this fellow?"[94] Cyril reprimands the Pharisees for their lack of understanding: "these events they do not understand, nor do they take them as images of spiritual realities, but they think that the divine nature can be seen with bodily

---

91 There is some exegetical basis to the reasoning of both Eusebius and Proclus. Modern biblical scholarship has noted the preference in Deuteronomy to cast the Mosaic revelation as an aural rather than ocular experience. See Brettler 2008, 24–25. For (rather late) rabbinic texts that understand Deut 4:12 as precluding seeing God or the divine voice, see Fraade 2008, 259 n. 32.

92 On the question of healing non-life-threatening ailments on the Sabbath in first-century Judaism, see Oliver 2013b, 47–53.

93 According to Azar 2016, 193, Cyril often identifies John's "Jews" with the Pharisees, whom he considers to be the rulers of the people. The Pharisees bear the brunt of Cyril's exegetical opposition in his commentary on John, although the Pharisees and the Jews are occasionally used interchangeably.

94 The English translation of *Comm. John.* is from Maxwell 2013.

eyes, and they believe that it uses a corporeal voice." For Cyril, these Pharisees may think that their ancestors beheld and heard the divine but in reality "they have never heard the voice of God the Father, nor has anyone seen with bodily eyes his form." Cyril adds: "I think that we *must even now charge the Jews* with sinking into absurdity concerning the glory of God because they both thought they saw his very form and heard a voice that was inherent in the divine nature" (*Comm. John.* 3.2; emphasis mine).[95]

It is difficult to determine to what extent Cyril has contemporary Jewish views in mind here. According to Michael Azar, Cyril's primarily employs the tension between Jesus and the Johannine Jews for inner-ecclesial debate. Within this framework, the Jesus of John becomes the orthodox theologian par excellence who combats Christian "heretics."[96] Yet Cyril was also not particularly fond of Jews.[97] His exegetical writings often polemicize against Judaism, singling out the Jewish people for their spiritual blindness.[98] Besides being well versed in the Old Testament, he was familiar with extra-biblical Jewish traditions, some found in the Talmud, which he occasionally deemed useful for interpreting Scripture.[99] He was also acquainted with Josephus' writings, and had personally interacted with Alexandrian Jews.[100] Thus, it cannot be completely ruled out that Cyril has actual Jews in mind when he condemns them for their spiritual ineptitude. To be sure, Cyril mainly expounds Scripture for pastoral purposes, seeking to strengthen and clarify the Christian faith for his parishioners.[101] Thus, in the same pericope of his commentary on John, Cyril considers what it means for a Christian believer to stand "at the foot of the mountain" (*hypo to oros*):

> Standing at the foot of the mountain . . . when God has already descended and is on it, suggests the readiness of mind and the eagerness of those who are called to serve him, not refusing in any way to apply themselves even to things that are above their power or

---

95 For the Greek text, see Pusey 1872, 1:379–81.

96 Azar 2016, 155. In a personal communication, Azar suggests that Cyril may have in mind here the Eunomian controversies of the preceding decades in which Eunomius had claimed (as his opponents understood it) to know the essence of God. Cyril, then, would be projecting something similar upon the Jews (or Pharisees), claiming that they, like Eunomius, thought that they could know God's nature.

97 He may have been instrumental in the expulsion of some Jews from Alexandria. For a critical treatment of this event as reported by Socrates, Cyril's (unfriendly) Christian contemporary, see Wilken (1971) 2004, 54–58; Azar 2016, 196–97.

98 Wilken (1971), 2004, 61.

99 Wilken (1971) 2004, 58–59.

100 Wilken (1971) 2004, 58.

101 Azar 2016, 162.

higher than their nature, since God is with them. The partakers of the Savior are certainly like this.[102]

Cyril pursues this theological reflection, specifying that God's descent on the *top* of the mountain implies that no one can ever truly apprehend God's essence. Sinai thus serves as a locus for theological and spiritual instruction.[103] This is evident from one of Cyril's earliest works, *De adoratione et cultu in spiritu et veritate*.[104] Here too Cyril draws lessons from the reference in Exod 19:17 to standing at the foot, rather than the top, of Mount Sinai. According to Cyril, God does not descend into the minds of humans who have earthly, debase thoughts but appears only to those who earnestly strive to reach spiritual heights. At the same time, however, Cyril contrasts the revelation of the "Old Law" given to the Israelites with the revelation of Christ granted to the Christians. At Sinai, God remained on the mountain far and above the people of Israel.[105] God, furthermore, had to descend on Sinai with fire to fill the Israelites with fear so that they would not neglect the commandments. This contrasts with the revelation made possible through the incarnation of Christ that Christian believers are privileged to experience.[106]

Ephrem

As noted in the introduction to this article, Syriac Christian writings are enjoying increased attention in Qur'anic studies. Ephrem's commentary on Exodus is remarkable for its inclusion of aggadic materials attested in early Jewish texts.[107] Unfortunately, Ephrem (fourth century) does not comment directly on Exod 19:17 (or Deut 4:11). He nevertheless has much to say about the status of the Law of Moses and the Jewish people. As he reflects on the Ten Commandments and the statutes of the Covenant Code (Exod 20:19–23:33), Ephrem like his Greek patristic

102 *Comm. John.* 3.2 (Pusey, 1872, 1:380 lines 2–8).

103 See also Gregory of Nyssa, *The Life of Moses*, Book II, for a similar theological reflection on standing and ascending the mount.

104 The Greek text I consulted is from Migne 1857–1866, vol. 68. According to Azar 2016, 157, *De Adoratione*, among other works, betrays Cyril's unease over the continuing intellectual and liturgical challenge of Judaism. However, in his later career, Cyril shifts greater attention to combatting Christian "heresies."

105 οὐκ ἔνθα περ ἦν ὁ λαὸς, ἀλλ' ὑψοῦ καὶ μακράν (Migne 1857–1866, vol. 68, p. 488, lines 39–40).

106 Migne 1857–1866, vol. 68, p. 488, lines 44–46.

107 See Matthews and Amar 1994.

counterparts, highlights the golden calf incident, remarking that the Israelites committed this sin after persistently rejecting the amazing signs God had performed on their behalf.[108] Ephrem also stresses that Moses did not actually see God, as "eyes that have been fashioned and created cannot look at that essence, which is neither fashioned nor created."[109] Otherwise, Ephrem has many positive things to say about the Mosaic Law although he discriminates between what considers to be permanent and temporary commandments in the Torah. For example, Ephrem believes that the Sabbath commandment was given to the Jews only for a limited time because of their immaturity.[110]

Aphrahat

The *Demonstrations* by Aphrahat is another Christian work written in Syriac that frequently overlaps with extra-biblical Jewish tradition.[111] In his comments on the Old Testament, the "Persian sage" (c. 280–345) repeatedly condemns Jewish practice and belief, accusing Jews for (supposedly) boasting about their ancestral practices (e.g., *Demonstrations* 15.9), their election (16.8), and confidence in their eschatological regathering (19.2).[112] Unfortunately, Aphrahat does not quote or comment on Exod 19:17 or Deut 4:11.[113] Yet like so many other early Christian writers, Aphrahat highlights the sin of the golden calf. Idolatry, according to Aphrahat, was the quintessential sin committed by the Israelites.[114] The people's idolatrous tendencies explains why God decreed for Israel commandments concerning sacrifices and diet. Given their attraction to idolatry, not to mention their "avarice" and "shamelessness," God forbade the Israelites from eating animals the Egyptians consumed (e.g., pigs) while ordering them to consume and sacrifice animals the Egyptians adored. These commandments, however, were merely designed to

108 Ephrem, *Homily on Our Lord* 17.3.
109 Ephrem, *Homily on Our Lord* 29.1. Translation taken from Matthews and Amar 1994.
110 *Commentary on Genesis*, Prologue 4: "He [Moses] wrote about the true commandments that had become forgotten, while adding those that were necessary for the infantile state of the [Jewish] people." Cf. *Hymn on the Nativity* II: "Praise be to Him Who made void the Sabbath by fulfilling it!" (227). For a discussion of the "Jewishness" of Ephrem, see Narinskaya 2010.
111 For a list of parallels, see Pierre 1988, 1:115–16 n. 12. Despite the interesting parallels with Jewish aggadic materials, Neusner 1971, 227, rules out contact between Aphrahat and the Babylonian sages of the Talmud.
112 Walters 2016 views Aphrahat's Jews entirely as a rhetorical device used to construct Christian identity.
113 For citations of Genesis and Exodus in Aphrahat's writing, see Owens 1983.
114 Pierre 1988, 39 n. 27.

prevent the Israelites from succumbing to the superstitions and sins they had committed in Egypt (*Demonstrations* 15.3–4). Otherwise, in Aphrahat's estimation, the Mosaic laws concerning food and offerings are useless, resulting from Israel's transgression (15.8). Jews, therefore, have no reason to boast about these commandments, which were ordained only after the golden calf incident.[115] On this matter, we should observe that Aphrahat is not too distant from another work that survives in Syriac, the *Didascalia Apostolorum*, which evinces awareness of rabbinic tradition yet relegates all of the laws enacted at Sinai *after* the golden calf, food laws included, to what it calls the "Second Legislation," a supposedly burdensome imposition from which Christ has liberated Christians.[116]

The Qur'ān

Textual Analysis

The Qur'ān refers to the raised mountain on four different occasions:

> Q 2:63: "(Remember) when We took a covenant with you, and raised above you the mountain (*rafaʿnā fauqakumu ṭ-ṭūra*): 'Hold fast what we have given you, and remember what is in it, so that you may guard (yourselves).'"

> Q 2:93: "And when We took a covenant with you, and raised the mountain above you (*rafaʿnā fauqakumu ṭ-ṭūra*): 'Hold fast what We have given you, and hear,' they said, 'We hear and disobey' (*samiʿnā wa-ʿaṣainā*). And they were made to drink the calf in their hearts because of their disbelief."

115 Aphrahat accordingly only deems the Ten Commandments to be of permanent value since it was given to Israel before the adoration of the golden calf (15.8). Aphrahat also draws other meaningful applications from the biblical narration about the Sinaitic revelation. For example, Aphrahat argues on behalf of the ideal of celibacy, this, in response to supposed Jewish criticisms of this practice. In defense of celibacy, Aphrahat singles out severable notable Israelites, not least Moses, who became a great prophet only *after* he forsook his marital duties to devote himself exclusively to God's calling. Aphrahat further infers the ascetic practice of celibacy from the fact that God appeared to the Israelites at the foot of the mountain (Exod 19:15) only after they themselves had refrained from sexual relations for three consecutive days. The people, however, could barely withstand the awesome manifestation of God in contrast to Moses who had permanently abandoned the cares of marriage and children (*Demonstrations* 18.4–6).

116 On the relationship between the "Second Legislation" in the *Didascalia* with the Mishnah, see Fonrobert 2001.

Q 4:154: "And We raised the mountain above them (*rafa'nā fauqahumu ṭ-ṭūra*), with their covenant, and We said to them, 'Enter the gate in prostration.' And We said to them, 'Do not transgress the Sabbath.' And We made a firm covenant with them."

Q 7:171: "(Remember) when We shook the mountain above them (*nataqna l-ǧabala fauqahum*), as if it were a canopy (*ẓullatun*), and they thought it was going to fall on them: 'Hold fast what We have given you, and remember what is in it, so that you may guard (yourselves).'"

Q 2:63, 93 and 4:154 all employ identical wording to describe the raising of the mountain: *rafa'nā fauqakumu/fauqahumu ṭ-ṭūra*. The verb *rafa'a* means to "raise," "lift," or "exalt."[117] Of all the rabbinic and targumic texts surveyed above, this verb resembles mostly the Aramaic *zqf* (Hebrew cognate, *zaqāf*), which is attested in Tg. Ps.-J. Exod 19:17. On the other hand, the combination *rafa'a* + the preposition *fauqa* ("over"/"above") + the pronominal suffix *kum/hum* + the direct object *ṭ-ṭūra* approximates the Hebrew construction *kāpâ* +*'ăl* + *hem* + *'ēt hāhār*. However, it would seem that *kāpâ* means primarily to "bend" or "turn over" in rabbinic Hebrew, while the simile of the mountain as a "tank" is entirely missing from the Qur'ān. Still, the combination of the verb *rafa'a* with the preposition *fauqa* means "to raise up over,"[118] and strengthens the supposition that the Qur'ān envisages a mountain that indeed *looms above and over* the Israelites. In this regard, the Qur'anic usage of *ṭūra* ("mountain") is particularly intriguing, given its Aramaic/Syriac origins. All of the targums surveyed above as well as the Peshitta use this Aramaic word to translate the Hebrew *har* in both Exod 19:17 and Deut 4:11. Indeed, *ṭūra* is used invariably in the Qur'ān in relation to Mount Sinai.[119] This word choice may suggest that Aramaic served somehow as a vehicle of transmission for the rabbinic midrash of the uprooted mountain.[120]

The language of Q 7:171 is distinctive in several ways. First, it employs *nataqna* (instead of *rafa'nā*), a hapax legomenon in the Qur'ān. This Arabic word shares cognates with Hebrew and Aramaic. In Hebrew and Aramaic, the root *n-t-q* denotes primarily the act of "detaching," "tearing away," or "luring away." This is its primary meaning in biblical Hebrew.[121] The meaning of "tearing out,"

117 Lane 1863.

118 Badawi and Haleem 2007, 374.

119 See Badawi and Haleem 2008, 575. The Jewish convert to Islam, Muhammad Asad (1980) 2008, 22 n. 51, even opts to translate *aṭ-ṭūra* as "Mount Sinai" throughout his translation of the Qur'ān.

120 Cf. Obermann 1941, 30.

121 See the Hebrew entry for *nātaq* in Brown, Driver, and Briggs 1907 (Bibleworks 10v.) as well as Baumgarten and Kohler 1994–2000.

or "withdrawing" persists in Babylonian Jewish Aramaic from the Talmudic period.[122] This meaning is not too distant from act of "plucking" connoted by the Hebrew root *t-l-š*, which is attested in rabbinic midrashim and Tg. Ps.-J. 19:17 (*tlš*). The *Study Quran* edited by Nasr essentially adopts this understanding albeit without acknowledging any rabbinic precedents: "*We lifted* translates *nataqnā*, a verb that means literally to pluck something out from its roots and suggests God's removing the mountain physically from its earthly base and causing it to hover above them . . .."[123]

However, we should also observe that *ntq* can apparently mean "to shake off" in Christian Palestinian Aramaic.[124] Some lexicons therefore render the Arabic *nataq* either as "detach" or as "shake."[125] Badawi and Haleem expand the range of options, proposing "to shake" but also "to raise," "to lift up," and even "to overturn, to pour out by overturning." The latter, we should note, corresponds to the Hebrew *kāpâ*.[126] The countless English translations of the Qur'ān reflect this variation. Some favor the act of shaking: "we shook"[127] or "we caused to quake."[128] Others prefer the notion of raising or lifting: "we raised,"[129] "we made (the mountain) loom high,"[130] or "we suspended."[131] The idea of shaking would align with Exod 19:18, which states that the mountain "trembled" (Hebrew: *wayyeḥĕrad*).[132] Whatever the exact correspondence (if there can be any) with biblical or early Jewish texts, it does seem that Q 7:171, like Q 2:63, 93 and 4:154, depicts a mountain lifted from its base looming over the Israelites. This is suggested by the preposition *fauqahum* ("above them") and the explicit statement that the Israelites thought that the mountain would fall upon them.

---

122 Sokoloff 2002, 781; Jastrow 1943 (2005), 945.

123 Nasr 2015, 466. On the ideological eschewal of historical criticism of *The Study Quran*, published by HarperCollins, in stark contrast to its biblical counterpart, *The HarperCollins Study Bible*, see Oliver (forthcoming).

124 Brown, Driver, and Briggs 1907; Baumgarten and Kohler 1994–2000; *CAL*.

125 Brown, Driver, and Briggs 1907 and Baumgarten and Kohler 1994–2000 provide both meanings for the Arabic root. Lane supplies no entry for the verb.

126 In the end though, Badawi and Haleem 2008, 918, offer "to raise, to hoist" for Q 7:171.

127 So Yusuf Ali Abdullah (1934) 2012; Droge 2013; McAuliffe 2017, following Arberry (1955) 1996.

128 Asad (1980) 2008.

129 Khan and Khanam 2014, without reference to cognate Semitic languages.

130 M. A. S. Abdel Haleem 2010.

131 Khan and Khanam, *The Quran*.

132 See Neuwirth 2019, 412, who connects Q 7:171 with Exod 19:18–19, and translates *nataqnā* accordingly as "we shook."

Most intriguing is the simile in Q 7:171, which states that the mountain was like a "canopy" or "shadow" (*ẓullatun*).[133] On the one hand, this imagery could be understood in a protective sense: God raised the mountain to provide the Israelites with shade or protection. This understanding would align with the positive assessment of the uprooted mountain attested in some of the rabbinic sources (e.g., MRI). Indeed, the Hebrew and Aramaic cognates *ṣēl* and *tll* ("shadow") often connote the notion of protection or refuge in biblical, targumic, and rabbinic literature, including finding shelter in God's shade.[134] On the other hand, the shadow may carry a more sinister connotation as suggested by Q 26:189: "the punishment of the Day of Shadow (*ʿaḏābu yaumi ẓ-ẓullati*) seized them."[135] Here, we cannot fail to reproduce two passages from Song Rab. that use the word "shadow" in reference to Israel and the granting of the Torah at Mount Sinai:

> "I am a rose (*ḥăbaṣṣelet*) of Sharon" (Song 2:1): I am the one, and beloved (*ḥabibâ*) am I. I am she that was hidden (*ḥăbûyyâ*) in the shadow (*ṣel*) of mount Sinai, and in a brief space I blossomed forth in good deeds before Him like a lily with hand and heart, and I said before Him, "All that the Lord has said we will do and we will obey" (Exod 24:7).

> "As an apple tree among the trees of the wood" (Song 2:3): R. Huna and R. Aḥa in the name of R. Yose b. Zimra [first-generation Amora from Palestine/Israel] said: "The apple tree is shunned by all people when the sun beats down, because it provides no shadow (*ṣel*). So all the nations refused to sit in the shadow (*ṣel*) of the Holy One, blessed be He, on the day of the giving of the Law. Think you that Israel was the same? No, for it says, 'For His shadow (*bĕṣillô*) I longed, and I sat there' (Song 2:3): I longed for Him and I sat; it is I that longed, not the nations. R. Aḥawa b. R. Zeʿira[136] made two comparisons. One is this. The apple tree brings out its blossom before its leaves. So Israel in Egypt declared their faith before they heard the message, as it says, "And the people believed; and they heard that the Lord had remembered" (Exod 4:31).[137]

The first passage cited above comments on Song of Songs 2:1, focusing on the word *ḥăbaṣṣelet* ("rose"), which it breaks down in two words, *ḥăbûyyâ* ("hidden")

---

133 Obermann 1941, 36, sees *ẓullatun* as the local Arab equivalent for the Hebrew *gîgît*, understood as *gag* ("roof") in the sense of "canopy."

134 For divine protection, see Isa 49:2; 51:16 (cf. Tg. Isa 51:16); Hos 14:7; Ps 17:8; 36:8; 57:2; 63:8; 91:1. Cf. Gen 19:8: "shadow (i.e., shelter) of my roof"; Isa 4:6; 25:4 (shade from the heat).

135 As pointed out by Speyer 1961, 304. But see Q 2:57: "And We overshadowed (*ẓallalnā*) you (with) the cloud." The reference here is to the pillar of cloud that accompanied Israel in the wilderness (Exod 13:21; 33:9–10; 40:38; Num 49:15; 14:14), surely positive. Cf. Q 2:210.

136 This name is spelled variously in the manuscripts, mostly as R. Aḥa b. R. Ze'ira. I have opted for this spelling, which is attested in manuscript Vatican Cod. Ebr. 249.9. R. Aḥawa b. R. Ze'ira is a fourth-generation Amora from Israel/Palestine. See Stemberger 2011, 110.

137 Song Rab. 2:1 § 1 & 2:3 § 1, respectively. Translation taken and modified from Freedman and Simon 1983.

and “shadow” (*ṣel*).[138] It does so under the premise that the assembly of Israel is God’s “beloved,” *ḥabibâ*, a word that shares Hebrew consonants with *ḥăbûyyâ*, and therefore provides an opportunity for a midrashic reflection on what it means for Israel to be God’s “loved one” while “hidden in the shadow.”[139] As we saw earlier, Song Rab. refers to the uprooted mountain (8:5 § 1). It is quite possible that this imagery is envisaged here as well: Israel stood in the shadow of Sinai once the mountain had been uprooted and raised to the high heavens.[140] The second passage quoted above from Song Rab. references Song 2:3, “For His Shadow I longed for,” which suggests intimacy, shade, and comfort. However, Song Rab. alleges that the nations of the world declined to sit in God’s shadow on the day the Torah was revealed, perhaps because they were scared of the mountain (or, alternatively, uninterested in God’s offer). If so, then in contrast to b. ʿAbod. Zar. 2b (see above), God *did* suspend Sinai over the nations (and not only over Israel). Yet they still declined to observe the Torah.[141] In any case, the two aforementioned pericopes from Song Rab. praise Israel for its response. When Israel stood in the shadow of the mountain, it abided by the Torah, declaring, “we will do and we will hear” (Exod 24:7). In fact, R. Aḥawa b. R. Zeʿira maintains that Israel expressed faithfulness to God even before exiting Egypt, quoting Exod 4:31.

Literary Analysis

All four Qur’ānic passages on the raised mountain appear in wider literary contexts that have to do with the Mosaic covenant and Israel.

138 *Torah Temimah* on Song Rab. 2:1 § 1 by Epstein (1902) 2005; Wünsche 1880, 52.

139 Song Rab. 2:1 § 1 in fact offers several more examples of when Israel was hidden in the shadow (e.g., in the shadow of Egypt, the shadow of the Sea, etc.).

140 Epstein, *Torah Temimah* (1902) 2005 understands the shadow in this way, referencing b. Šabb. 88a.

141 See Epstein (1902) 2005 on Song Rab. 2:3 § 1, who references b. ʿAbod. Zar. 2b. We may observe, however, that in this section of Song Rab. the shadow does not have so much to do with the *mountain* as it does with *God*: the text expressly refers to the shadow of the *Holy One, Blessed Be He*. The nations in other words reject the relationship with God made possible through the Torah.

Surah 2 (al-baqarah)

Surah 2, the largest chapter of the Qur'ān, is immense, and we cannot do justice here to its literary intricacies.[142] In brief, this chapter opens testifying about the veracity of "the Scripture" as "guidance" (v. 2), and then contrasts the "believers" or "God-fearers" with the "disbelievers" (vv. 2–29). First it defines the believers (vv. 2–5): they believe in the "unseen," observe prayer, assist the needy, believe in present and past revelations ("what has been sent down"), and are certain about the hereafter. By contrast, the disbelievers (vv. 6–20) are faithless and hopeless. Indeed, God has "set a seal on their hearts and on their hearing"; their sight is covered (v. 7). Some of them claim to believe in God and the Final Judgment but are disbelievers nonetheless, even deceivers (vv. 8–9). Their hearts are sick (v. 10). They bring corruption (vv. 11–12), are foolish (v. 13), hypocrites (vv. 14–15), and more.[143] The interest in defining the profiles of the believers versus the disbelievers resurfaces throughout Q 2, especially when it is matter of Israel.

Q 2 deals with Israel after recounting the story of Adam and his wife (vv. 30–39). First, the Qur'ān reminds "the children of Israel" of the divine "blessing" or "favor" (*niʿmah*) bestowed on them, admonishing Israel to fulfill the covenant (v. 40). God's preferential favor shown to Israel is underscored in vv. 47 and 122 as well.[144] At one level then, the Qur'ān affirms Israel's covenantal election, but often with added qualifications, especially the warning not to disbelieve in what God has in more recent times "sent down, confirming what is with you" (v. 41). This reference to disbelief points back to the opening of Surah 2, which distinguishes between people based on their confession of past and present revelations. Here, Israel is confronted in a similar way, the past revelation at Sinai is summoned in order to exhort Israel to accept the more recent revelation contained in the Qur'ān.[145]

In v. 49, the Qur'ān begins recounting Israel's biblical history, starting with Israel's redemption from Egypt. Verse 51 refers to Moses' forty-night stay on Mount

---

142 See Sinai 2017, 97–104 for a literary and thematic analysis of Q 2 in light of its redactional macrostructure.

143 For a social-historical analysis of the category of "believers" in the Qur'ān, see the contribution of Lindstedt in this volume.

144 Pohlmann 2015, 163–164, notes the literary correspondence between v. 40 and v. 47 as well as one key difference: the declaration in v. 47 affirming God's preference for Israel over other nations is conspicuously missing in v. 40. For Pohlmann, this absence is intentional. Q 2: 40–46 was redacted after Q 2:47f. with a sharper criticism of Israel in mind.

145 Pohlmann 2015, 164 interprets this exhortation, made directly in the second person, as addressing contemporary Jews from the time and milieu in which vv. 40–46 were redacted.

Sinai and especially the sin of the golden calf that immediately ensued. The Qur'ān stresses that God forgave the Israelites for their wrongdoing (vv. 52, 54) yet immediately follows with an episode unattested in the Hebrew Bible: the Israelites purportedly told Moses, "We shall not believe you until we see God openly." Their request was answered, though not in the way that they expected: "and the thunderbolt took you while you were looking on" (v. 55). God, fortunately, had mercy on the mortal Israelites, and restored them to life "so that you [i.e., the Israelites] might be thankful" (v. 56).[146] While this scene and others underline God's mercy upon Israel, it also portrays the same people in negative light.[147] They need signs to believe – a polemical motif that is also attested in the New Testament with respect to Jewish adversaries of Jesus (Pharisees and Sadducees in the Synoptics, "the Jews" in John).[148] Furthermore, the demands of the Israelite people for signs are excessive, even defiant. In any case, Israel proves unfaithful despite the evidence as the subsequent scenes in Q 2 illustrate: in the wilderness, God showered blessings upon the Israelites but they repeatedly did wrong (vv. 58–59, 60, and 61). In fact, they even "disbelieved in the signs of God and killed the prophets without any right." Here, the Qur'ān's narration points well beyond the exodus from Egypt and Israel's stay in the wilderness, castigating the Israelite people for murdering the prophets who came after Moses. Indeed, within almost the same stroke, Q 2 transitions to addressing "those who believe, and those who are Jews, and the Christians, and the Sabians" (v. 62). Israel's past is harnessed and refurbished to provide a message for the present, which concerns Jews, Christians, and Sabians alike.

This brings us to v. 63 in which the first reference in Q 2 to the raised mountain appears. The mountain was lifted when God struck a covenant with the Israelites, ordering them to follow its stipulations. The nation of Israel, however, immediately went astray. God, nevertheless, had mercy on Israel (v. 64), but the people continued to err nonetheless. For example, some of them broke the

146 This Qur'anic scene is probably a reworking of a rabbinic midrash concerning the resurrection of the Israelites. According to b. Šabb. 88b (Steinsaltz ed.), the souls of the Israelites departed when they heard the divine utterances. God, however, rained upon them the "dew through which the dead will be revived." Cf. Exodus Rabbah *Parašat Yitrô* 29 (Vilna ed.); Tg. Ps.-J. Exod 20:18: "all the people saw . . . the sound of the shofar how it was reviving the dead." Tanḥuma *Parašat Šemot* 25 (Warsaw ed.) claims that the nations heard the Sinaitic revelation in their own languages but passed away. Israel was the only nation to hear the divine voice and escape unharmed.

147 Cf. Q 4:153. In Q 7:155, only *the seventy elders along with Moses* risk dying from an *earthquake* but are spared once Moses intercedes on their behalf.

148 Matt 12:38–39; 16:1–4; Mark 8:11–12; Luke 11:16, 29–30; John 2:18; 3:2. Cf. Paul in 1 Cor 1:22: "Jews demand signs and Greeks desire wisdom."

Sabbath and transformed into apes (vv. 65–66)![149] Surah 2 goes on retelling Israel's biblical story, intermingling its narration with expressed criticism of Israel, notably its stubborn heartedness (v. 74) and repeated rejection, even slaughtering, of God-sent prophets, not least, "Jesus, the son of Mary" (v. 87). Curiously, the Qur'ān presents the people of Israel defending themselves for committing these crimes by declaring, "Our hearts are covered." However, in the Qur'ān, this self-declaration of ignorance hardly exempts the Jewish people who are cursed for their supposed rejection of God's messengers (v. 88). Along the way, Q 2 also accuses some Jews for distorting God's word (v. 75), others for writing Scripture (or what they claim to be Scripture) for personal gain (v. 79).[150]

It is in this polemical vein underlining Israel's unbelief that the raised mountain appears once again in Surah 2. Prior to its reintroduction, the Qur'ān notes that the Jewish people only believe in prior revelations, "what has been sent down on us," but "disbelieve in anything after that." The Qur'ān further questions whether the Jewish people ever heeded their own prophets: "Why did you kill the prophets of God before, if you were believers?" (v. 91) The Qur'ān then repeats the calf incident, which transpired after Moses had shown the people "clear signs" (v. 92). Thus, Israel is portrayed as serial-prophet killers and chronic idolaters just as the raised mountain resurfaces in Q 2, this time with a striking new feature further illustrating Israelite unbelief: as God lifted the mountain over the Israelites and commanded them to follow the Torah, the people defiantly replied, "we hear and disobey" (v. 93). The Israelites were accordingly "made to drink the calf *in their hearts*," the seat of their spiritual stubbornness and unbelief.[151] The focus on Israel then recedes in Q 2, though not completely (see, e.g., vv. 122–123), until v. 246, where the history of Israel resumes with the appointment of Saul as the first Israelite king.

From the overview just provided, it is evident that Israel is often solicited as part of a much larger and sustained endeavor that reifies the distinctions between the believers and the disbelievers of the Qur'ān. This no more obvious than at the conclusion of Surah 2, which parallels the introduction of Q 2 by rehearsing the defining qualities of the believers, who, along with the Qur'anic Messenger, profess

---

149 Cf. Q 7:163–167. On this troubling episode, see Firestone 2015.

150 On the concept of *taḥrif* ("scriptural falsification," broadly understood) in the Qur'ān and Islamic tradition, see Reynolds 2010.

151 This episode is reported in Exod 32:20 (cf. Deut 9:21) but without mention of the potion reaching the people's *hearts*. Thus, the Qur'anic retelling of this biblical episode stresses the unbelief of the Israelites as manifested in their hearts. B. ʿAbod. Zar. 44a interprets this episode in light of the bitter water mixed with dust that the suspected adulteress had to drink in order to prove her innocence (Num 15:12–31).

their belief "in what has been sent down . . . in God, and His angels, and His Books, and His messengers." Additionally, the believers should make "no distinction between any of His messengers" (v. 285). The true believer, unlike unbelieving Israel, accepts the revelations granted to the Israelite Prophets *and* the Qur'anic Messenger. Quite tellingly, the believers declare: "We hear and obey" (v. 285: *sami'nā wa-'aṭ'nā*).[152] This declaration of faith(fulness) by the Qur'anic believers is extremely striking, given its close resemblance to Exod 24:7, "we will do and we will hear" (*na'ăśeh wənišmā'*) and especially Deut 5:27, "we will hear and obey" (*šāma'nû wə'āśînû*).[153] In Surah 2 (and elsewhere), the Qur'ān denies Israel the opportunity to make this biblical confession, transferring its utterance to those who embrace the revelation of the Qur'anic Messenger. In fact, according to Q 2, the Israelites affirmed the very opposite when they stood under Mount Sinai, saying, "we hear and disobey." Q 2 fittingly ends with the following petition: "Help us against the people who are disbelievers" (v. 286).

Surah 4 (an-nisā')

Surah 4 contains much of the same as Q 2 as far as the Jewish people are concerned. Verse 47, which draws attention to those "who have a portion of the Book," begins a diatribe that ends in v. 57.[154] The attacks are familiar in light of what has already been noted in Q 2. The "Jews" (*hādū*)[155] "alter words from their positions" (cf. Q 2:75). They say, "We hear and disobey" (v. 46 = Q 2:93). As in Q 2, the Jews are called upon to "believe in what We have sent down, confirming what is with you" (Q 4:47). Otherwise, Q 4 also reiterates the dichotomy in Q 2 that discriminates between the believers and the disbelievers (vv. 51–57).

A second diatribe against the "people of the Book" appears in Q 4:153–162. The terrain and tone are similar to Q 2 here as well. The Jews make unreasonable demands that exemplify their disbelief. They ask the Qur'anic Messenger

---

152 See Q 5:7 and 24:51.

153 See Firestone 1997 for a discussion. The Arabic *sami'nā wa-'aṭ'nā* in Q 2:285 is closer to the Hebrew *šāma'nû wə'āśînû* in Deut 5:27 although the phrase, *na'ăśeh wənišmā'* from Exod 24:7 became widely known among Jews. Notice too that the Old Testament Peshitta has the order "we will hear and we will do" (rather than "doing" preceding "hearing") for Exod 24:7. The same is true for the Samaritan Pentateuch.

154 The reference to a "portion of the Book" may mean that the Jews only have a part of the divine revelation sent from above. See Droge 2013, 51.

155 Droge 2013, 51: "lit. 'those who have judaized,' or follow Jewish law, punning on the name Yahūd." Cf. the German translation in *Corpus Coranicum* (corpuscoranicum.de): "die dem Judentum angehören."

"to bring down on them a Book from the sky." In other words, they make unfair demands as their ancestors did in the wilderness: "They had already asked Moses for (something) greater than that, for they said, 'Show us God openly!' So the thunderbolt took them for their evildoing. Then they took the calf, after the clear signs had come to them (v. 153)." As noted earlier, this episode also appears in Q 2:55–57. Here, it is phrased in even more polemical terms: God's merciful resurrection of the Israelites is left out and substituted by the people's idolatrous adoration of the calf. This polemical edge is further sharpened after the raised mountain is mentioned in Q 4:154, which contains nothing that is controversial *en soi* ("And We raised the mountain above them, with their covenant, and We said to them, 'Enter the gate in prostration.' And We said to them, 'Do not transgress the Sabbath.' And We made a firm covenant with them."). The following verse, however, suggests that God's extraordinary feat of raising the mountain and earnest exhortations hardly sufficed to impress Israel away from sin. The people, rather, went on to "kill the prophets without any right" (Q 4:155 = Q 2:61). In their defense for such alleged crimes, the people repeat the same excuse provided in Q 2:88: "Our hearts are covered" (v. 155). In reality, however, "God set a seal on them for their disbelief so they do not believe, except for a few" (v. 156). Q 4 adds to the list of Israel's self-damning confessions the claim that "surely we killed the Messiah, Jesus, son of Mary, the messenger of God" (v. 157). The Jews, however, according to the Qur'ān, did not kill Jesus, despite their boasting, but will be held accountable by Jesus himself on the day of the resurrection (v. 159). Finally, we should notice the following observation concerning the food laws and other Torah regulations given to the Jewish people: "So for the evildoing of those who are Jews, We have made (certain) good things forbidden to them which were permitted to them (before)" (v. 160). This verse affirms that some Torah regulations were given because of Israel's transgressions. The motif of the raised mountain, therefore, is bracketed in Q 4 by verses that underscore Israel's incredulity and infidelity towards God's message and messengers.

Surah 7 (al-ʾarʿāf)

In Q 7, Israel appears after a series of stories, the "punishment legends" or "punishment narratives," which recount the chastisement of various past peoples for their rejection of God's messengers and signs (vv. 59–102).[156] Before introducing

---

156 For a discussion of punishment legends, see Neuwirth 2019, 131–35.

Israel proper, Q 7 relates Moses' confrontation with Pharaoh (vv. 103–137). Here, Pharaoh appears as particularly opposed to God's messenger. By contrast, his magicians confess in prostration their belief in "the Lord of the worlds, the Lord of Moses and Aaron" (v. 121–122), which leads Pharaoh to threaten to crucify them (v. 124; cf. Q 20:71). Eventually, the Egyptian people join Pharaoh in resisting divine will (v. 136) before the Israelites succumb to the same kind of behavior as well.[157] Q 7 highlights Israel's love for idols. As soon as the Israelites cross the sea, they bid Moses to make them a false god for which they are sternly rebuked (v. 138). The people get their idol anyways, during Moses' absence, when they make a golden calf out of their own ornaments (vv. 148–153; cf. Q 20:83–98). Some of the other episodes that follow are attested in both Q 2 and Q 4 (e.g., the desecration of the Sabbath).[158] There is one additional feature, however, that is noteworthy in this context. After his anger abates (due to the calf incident), Moses, along with the seventy men, go out to meet the Lord (v. 154–155).[159] During this meeting, God declares that "the messenger, the prophet of the common people,[160] whom they find written in their Torah and Gospel," will "command them what is right and forbid them what is wrong, and he will permit them good things and forbid them bad things, and he will deliver them of their burden and the chains that were on them" (v. 157). The messenger in question is the Qur'anic prophet, purportedly predicted in the "Torah and Gospel" (v. 157).[161] Here, he is cast as a liberator from burdensome restrictions imposed on the people, which, undoubtedly, includes the Jewish food laws (cf. Q 6:146–147; 4:160; 2:168–173).

Next, follows what seems to be a theological reflection on Jewish exile (vv. 167–70). Apparently, God has appointed nations throughout history as instruments of punishment against Israel (v. 167). Nevertheless, the Qur'ān grants that there are some righteous Jews in the diaspora (v. 168). On the other hand, v. 169 refers to a successive generation that inherited "the Book" yet sinned by reasoning presumptuously that God would always forgive its transgressions. They accordingly lost "the covenant of the Book." V. 170, on the other hand, affirms that "those [Jews?] who hold fast the Book [Torah?] and observe the prayer" will

157 The immediate focus of the narration, therefore, is not on the exodus, that is, the *redemption* of Israel from Egypt but on the proper response to God's messenger, as exemplified by the confrontation between Pharaoh and Moses. Cf. Neuwirth 2019, 408–9.

158 For Pohlmann 2015, 170, Q 7:141–166 is older than Q 2:47ff. The latter was composed based on the former.

159 Cf. Exod 24:1, 9–11; Num 11:16–23.

160 It is possible to interpret *al-nabī al-ummī* as "the gentile prophet." See the contribution of Lindstedt in this volume; Droge 2013, 102.

161 Passages such as Deut 18:15, 18 and John 14:16; 15:26; 16:7 have been interpreted in Islam as foretelling the coming of the prophet Muḥammad.

surely be rewarded (v. 170). It is here that the raised-mountain motif appears in Q 7 (v. 171). Given its inclusion at this juncture of the surah, it seems reasonable to consider its content in connection with the topics on the revelation of the Torah and Israel's election and exile that are treated in the preceding verses.[162] Israel was firmly admonished with a looming mountain to observe the Torah yet neglected God's instructions. Thus, Israel remains dispersed, bereft of the covenantal blessings.[163] They experienced a lot not altogether different than that of the "foregone peoples" mentioned earlier in Q 7:59–101. Finally, right after considering Israel's covenantal status in relation to its exile, Q 7 discusses the obligation of all human beings, "the children of Adam," to follow the one true God. Since at some point (in primordial history?) all of Adam's descendants were notified about God's sovereignty, they will not be able to declare "on the Day of Resurrection, 'Surely we were oblivious of this,' or say, 'Our fathers were idolaters before (us), and we are descendants after them . . ..'" (v. 172).[164]

Source, Historical, and Rhetorical Analysis

The textual and literary analysis performed above reveals (at least to this author) a remarkable acquaintance on the part of the Qur'ān with rabbinic interpretations of the exodus story, especially Israel's reception of the Torah at Sinai. Expert hands, furthermore, have ably integrated this information into the Qur'ānic text for rhetorical effect and theological purposes.

Of all the Jewish literature surveyed in this article, the Qur'ān bears the greatest affinities with Tg. Ps.-J. Exod 19:17, b. ʿAbod. Zar. 2b, and Song Rab. (2:1 § 1; 2:3 § 1; 8:5 § 1). The affinity with Tg. Ps.-J. is terminological: both the Qur'ān and the Targum employ the same (Aramaic) word for mountain (*ṭūra*/*twr*ʾ) and refer to its "raising" (*rafaʿa* = *zqf*). These similarities, notwithstanding, there are insufficient grounds for positing any direct dependence of the Qur'ān upon Tg. Ps.-J. After all, all the targumim contain the Aramaic *twr*ʾ. In fact, it is fair to wonder in

162 On divine election in the Qur'ān, see Firestone 2011.

163 Q 7:169 can be related to the question raised earlier in Q 7:129. In the latter, Moses tells the Israelites that perhaps God "might make them successors on earth" (*wa-yashtaḫlifakum fī l-ʾarḍi*). This, provided that they remain faithful to God (7:128). In Q 7:169, a new generation (of Israelites) *succeeds* its biblical ancestors (*fa-ḫalafa min baʿdihim ḫalfun*) and loses the covenant of the Book because of its transgression.

164 Perhaps, this universal reflection arises from a consideration of Israel's particular covenantal status, as is the case, for example, in b. ʿAbod. Zar. 2b. See Neuwirth 2019, 414–15 and especially Hartwig 2008. The latter shows how Q 7:171–174 should be treated as a unit that can be effectively elucidated by rabbinic midrash.

this instance whether Tg. Ps.-J. could be reacting to the Qur'ān, given its late date (12th cent. CE). Several considerations, however, make this unlikely. First, Tg. Ps.-J. exhibits little influence from Islam.[165] Indeed, Tg. Ps.-J. Exod 19:17 uses a Greek/Latin loanword (*'spqlr'*), and incorporates pre-Islamic rabbinic materials. If Tg. Ps.-J. Exod 19:17 responds in any way to views external to Judaism, these are probably *Christian*. Paul had posited long before Tg. Ps.-J. that a veil covers Jewish minds as at Sinai, whereas Christ's followers gaze at the glory of the Lord as if through a mirror (2 Cor 3:18). Tg. Ps.-J., to the contrary, affirms that Israel had a splendid view of the divine glory as it stood under Sinai, which was as clear as a glass mirror (or pane).

Conceptually, the Qur'ānic perspective(s) of the raised mountain aligns more with b. ʿAbod. Zar. 2b and Song Rab. (8:5 § 1) in so far as these rabbinic texts view the looming mountain as a threat and reflect on Israel's covenantal relationship in relation to other groups (the nations or humankind in general). The Qur'ānic and rabbinic interpretations, however, depart from one another in how they evaluate Israel's *response* to this extraordinary phenomenon. None of the rabbinic or targumic texts assessed above claim that Israel *refused* to keep the Torah when they arrived at Sinai – especially when the mountain hovered over their heads. Not even R. Abdimi bar Ḥama in b. Šabb. 88a portrays Israel as recalcitrant in this instance even though his views raise questions about the binding status of the Sinaitic covenant. Instead, some rabbinic texts *commend* Israel for its response, underscoring the people's readiness to embrace the Torah. This is true of the earliest rabbinic midrash on Exodus, the MIR, which claims that Israel ventured to go under the mountain once it was uprooted. Otherwise, rabbinic tradition discerns in the collective declaration, *naʿăśeh wənišmāʿ*, "we will do and we will hear" (Exod 24:7), the people's eagerness to follow the Sinaitic covenant.[166] Far from defying God, the Israelites unconditionally accepted to observe the Torah,

165 As noted already by Hayward 1989. According to McDowell (personal communication on May 6, 2020), the reference to Aisha and Fatima in Tg. Ps.-J. 21:21 derives from the rabbinic work Pirqe de Rabbi Eliezer. Otherwise, McDowell suspects that Tg. Ps.-J. is a European composition, which would explain the absence of Arabic loanwords and its mixed Aramaic dialect.

166 To be sure, some rabbinic texts voice criticism against Israel for its response at Sinai. Speyer 1961, 301–2, references Numbers Rabbah 7:3 and Pesiqta de Rab Kahana 14, which both view Israel's declaration, *naʿăśeh wənišmāʿ*, in negative light. Concerning Pes. Rab. Kah., it is doubtful that "Mohammed konnte auch folgende Sache gehört haben" (Speyer 1961, 301). As for Num Rab., its composite nature and very late redaction complicate its historical use for Qur'anic studies. See Stemberger 2011, 343–44. Obermann 1941, 43–44 points to other rabbinic texts, notably Exod Rab. 42:8, which is quite critical of Israel's attitude at Sinai. The same problems of dating though apply here as well. More recently, Hartwig singles out Pes. Rab. Kah. 14:4 as a possible background. Indeed, even biblical texts (e.g., Ps 78:36–37), as Hartwig

whatever its requirements, prioritizing the doing before the hearing.[167] Their responsiveness to God's call contrasts with the reaction of the nations, who either rejected or declined to keep the Torah. According to b. ʿAbod. Zar. 2b, the nations will have no legitimate excuse to offer on the day of judgment, despite their complaint that they were not compelled as Israel was with an intimidating, looming mountain, because they neglected even to keep the Noahide commandments. Song Rab., for its part, uses shadow imagery to contrast the dispositions of Israel and the nations: only Israel desired to dwell in God's shadow, that is, accept the Torah at Sinai, even if it did not offer immediate respite.

The Qur'ān, by contrast, underlines Israel's *disbelief and disobedience*. Beyond all hutzpah, the Israelites replied to God, *samiʿnā wa-ʿaṣainā*, "we hear and disobey," despite the threatening shadow of the mountain looming over their heads. Although the Arabic formulation *samiʿnā wa-ʿaṣainā* is closest in its wording to Deut 5:27, Qur'anic knowledge of the declaration, *naʿăśeh wənišmāʿ* (Exod 24:7) made popular by rabbinic tradition, should not be ruled out, given the Qur'ān's rather extensive interaction with extra-biblical materials. The writer(s) of the Qur'ān has overturned rabbinic tradition on its head not only to condemn Israel but also to construct its own portrait of the ideal believer who accepts the revelation of the Qur'anic Prophet. In this process, Israel becomes a foil for the Qur'anic believers who truly say "we hear and obey" (*samiʿnā wa-ʾaṭʿnā*).[168]

This Qur'anic construct though is not performed in an unprecedented and isolated manner. It joins rather the Christian *Adverus Judaeos* tradition that preceded (and followed) the Qur'ān. Although no early Christian text (to my knowledge) alludes to the rabbinic midrash on the uprooted mountain, many early Christians, as we saw, interpreted the Sinai event in various ways, including to account for and even condemn Israel for its rejection of Jesus as the messiah. With Paul begins a trajectory that will cast the Jewish people as spiritually blind, because of their unbelief in Jesus. To be sure, the Jewish Scriptures themselves underline the moral and spiritual deficiencies of Israel (e.g., Isa 6:9–11). Christianity, however, amplified and aimed such materials at the Jewish people to convict them for rejecting Jesus. The Qur'ān joins the Christian chorus,

---

observes, underscore the insincerity of the Israelites. The Qur'ān, however, uniquely claims that Israel said, "we will do and *disobey*." See further fn. 169.

167 Philo, *On the Confusion of Tongues* 58–60, already commends the Jewish people for their response when commenting on Exod 24:7/Deut 5:27.

168 Rather than assuming an oral *Sitz im Leben* in which Muḥammad initially misunderstood Hebrew speech, I find it more compelling to see the Qur'anic declaration, "we will do and disobey" (and other similar critical statements in the Qur'ān) as a *deliberate parody penned* by someone rather familiar with Jewish retellings of the biblical story of the exodus.

reiterating the sins of Israel, its idolatrous adoration of the calf but also its alleged assassinations of the prophets, from Moses to Jesus. While the Hebrew Bible occasionally relates that the Israelites slew some of their own prophets, many early Christian texts set these reports as a cornerstone of Jewish history and identity. Interestingly, the Qur'ān repeats these allegations *sans plus* as if it its audience shares these Christian assumptions.[169] This is especially evident in Q 2 and Q 4. The following statement certainly resonates with a particular Christian outlook from the time, both in its confessional and polemical tone: "Surely we [i.e., the Jewish people] killed the Messiah, Jesus, son of Mary, the messenger of God" (Q 4:157). This declaration, which appears only three verses after the raised mountain, affirms at once that Jesus is the messiah, the son of Mary, and that the Jews are (wannabe) "Christ-killers."[170] What is more, this self-damning confession is preceded by the assertion that God sealed Jewish hearts for their disbelief (v. 155–156) after they transgressed the Torah, which they had just received at Sinai (v. 154). Remarkably, all of these elements – the revelation of the Torah, the hardening of the hearts, the massacre of the prophets, including Jesus, the Christian messiah – converge already in Stephen's speech in the Acts of the Apostles.[171]

The Qur'ān further mingles other elements from the Christian *Adversus Judaeos* tradition, including the claim that numerous ritual commandments were imposed on the Jewish people as a punishment for their sins (e.g., Q 4:160). Noteworthy, is the presentation of the Qur'anic messenger as a liberator from these supposedly burdensome commandments (Q 7:157). This perspective on Torah praxis is hardly Jewish, certainly not rabbinic, but finds its precedent in early Christian discourses. The Didascalia Apostolorum is especially illustrative in this regard. According to this text, Jesus has freed the Christian believers from the

169 Reynolds 2012a.

170 Is the Qur'ān aware of Jewish claims such as those found in b. Sanhedrin 43a, which asserts that the Jewish Sanhedrin *did* kill Jesus, not to mention the anti-Gospel materials that eventually morphed into the *Toledot Yeshu* (some of which are attested by the pagan writer Celsus)? This is possible given the allusion in Q 4:156 (i.e., Jews slander Mary). In any case, these polemical Jewish sources are hardly reliable for research on the historical Jesus. Their date and provenance, not to mention their anachronisms, rule this out. On Jesus in the Talmud, see Schäfer 2007. On the *Toledot Yeshu*, see Alexander 2018. The Qur'ān does not necessarily deny that Jesus *died* on the cross, only that the *Jews killed him*. The Qur'ān, however, does not rule this act out of concern to exempt Jews from christocide. On the contrary, it portrays them as boastful (and delusional) Christ-killers, depriving them from having accomplished this feat. On the crucifixion of Jesus in the Qur'ān, see the contribution by Dye in this volume.

171 See the contribution of Dye in this volume for other possible intersections between Acts and the Qur'ān.

"bonds" and "burdens" of the Second Legislation, which include the Jewish food laws (chs. 2; 4; 24).[172] As we saw, several early Christian authors share this sentiment, deeming the "ceremonial" laws of the Mosaic Law to be of temporary and punitive value resulting from Israel's sinful and idolatrous inclinations.

Thus, while the Qur'anic references to the raising of Mount Sinai ultimately originate from rabbinic midrash, their inclusion within the Qur'ān cannot be ignored from their literary surroundings. The Qur'ān reproduces the rabbinic midrash on the lifted mountain attached with anti-Judaic ribbons of a Christian fabric. This repackaging serves specific functions and needs, among other things, the establishment of a new identity, that of the Qur'anic community, which is distinguished from other social-religious groups and constructed categories. From a source critical viewpoint, this means that the midrashic teaching about the raised mountain may not have made its way directly from rabbinic circles into a Qur'anic milieu. At least two other possibilities present themselves: 1) the transmission occurred via Jewish Aramaic-speaking synagogues or 2) Syriac/Aramaic Christian circles. The Aramaic provenance of the raised mountain is suggested by the Qur'anic usage of the word *ṭūra*. At this time, however, the only Jewish Aramaic translation (or paraphrase) known to us that includes the raised mountain is Tg. Ps-J., but has been ruled out as a candidate for transmission because of its late date and unique character. Consequently, some scholars have suggested an *oral* setting and transmission of the midrash on the raised mountain (and other Jewish aggadah), which was translated from Aramaic (or Hebrew) and heard in Arabic.[173] At any rate, the Tg. Ps.-J and the Qur'ān probably testify to the consolidation of rabbinic Judaism toward the end of Late Antiquity. By this time, rabbinic teaching had extended beyond the specialized houses of rabbinic learning, reaching non-rabbinic synagogues and occasionally even non-Jewish circles.

As for the possible transmission of rabbinic midrash into the Qur'ān via Christian channels, we must understand that Christianity was a real force to be reckoned with in Late Antiquity. Northwest of the Arabian Peninsula, there was of course the Christian Byzantine Empire, often in conflict with the Sasanian Empire in the east, which itself contained sizeable Christian communities. Already by the fourth century CE, the kingdom of Aksum (Ethiopia) had become a Christian polity and ally of the Byzantines, extending its political and economic influence throughout the Red Sea region.[174] Eastern Arabia for its part became

172 On the Didascalia and the Qur'ān, see Zellentin 2013.
173 Obermann 1941, 30.
174 Bowersock 2013.

home to a thriving Christian culture by 400 CE.[175] Southern Arabia also boasted a Christian presence although Judaism too had rooted itself in this region.[176] The pre-Islamic Arabian peninsula, therefore, was no "pagan wasteland." The evidence internal and external to the Qur'ān suggests that it was produced in a milieu where Christian influence was widespread. This becomes even more likely when the Qur'ān is viewed as a *composed* and *composite* text, whose final form may have acquired shape beyond the Hijaz.[177] In such a milieu, it would not be surprising to encounter Christians exhibiting the type of acquaintance with rabbinic teaching that one finds for example in Ephrem or the Didascalia. Yet perhaps the genesis of the "Qur'anic midrash" on the raised mountain arose in an encounter with(in) a Jewish setting that at first envisaged the election of the Jewish people apart from any Christian supersessionist understandings. This motif was subsequently redacted in light of Christian anti-Judaic teachings.[178]

Conclusion

The shared features between the Qur'ānic and rabbinic descriptions of the raised mountain of Sinai show that the Qur'ān is informed in one way or another by a rabbinic midrash on Exod 19:17 and Deut 4:11 that goes back to Tannaitic times. Prior to the composition of the Qur'ān, rabbinic midrash imagined that God had

175 For a concise, accessible presentation of the evidence see Reynolds 2012b. See also the contribution of Grasso in this volume.

176 On Judaism in pre-Islamic Arabia, see Robin 2015.

177 See Dye (forthcoming), who nevertheless acknowledges that Muḥammad's community and certain layers of the Qur'ān are anchored in the Hijaz. Cf. Sinai 2017, who, to a large extent, follows the Weil-Nöldeke chronological partitioning of the Qur'ān into Meccan and Medinan layers.

178 A thorough redactional-critical analysis of the relevant verses (including Q 20:80, "the right side of the mountain"; cf. Q 28:44) and pericopes might shed further light on this question. For the time being, it is tempting to see Q 7:171 as the earliest rendition of the raised mountain motif, followed perhaps by Q 2:63 or Q 4:154 and then Q 2:93. According to this working hypothesis, the unique wording of Q 7:171 was modified in Q 2:63, 93 and Q 4:154 (e.g., the unique *ğabala* replaced by the standardized *ṭūra*). Interestingly, Q 7 happens to have a shorter "mean verse length" than Q 2 and Q 4, which could further suggest an earlier dating for Q 7:171, pending further demonstration on redactional grounds (e.g., the "standard deviation" of Q 7:171 and surrounding verses). On "mean verse length" as a method for dating Qur'anic verses, see Sinai 2017, 111–37. Q 2:93 seems later than Q 2:63: the parallelism between the two and the pronounced polemical materials in Q 2:93 suggest that it came later. See Pohlmann 2015, 164–68.

uprooted Sinai above the Israelites when offering them the Torah. Initially, this imagery was viewed favorably, symbolizing God's protection (so MRI), but eventually it was also interpreted in a threatening sense that even menaced to invalidate the Mosaic covenant (so R. Abdimi b. Ḥamsa in b. Šabb. 88a). Some rabbinic sources incorporated both views (e.g., MRS and Song Rab. 8:5 § 1). Others, provided novel, creative spins to what standing under the mountain or in its shadow signified (b. ʿAbod. Zar. 2b; Song Rab. 2:1 § 1; 2:3 § 1).

The Christian authors surveyed in this article were apparently unfamiliar with this rabbinic midrash. Similarly, the targumim did not include it, save for Targum Pseudo-Jonathan, whose final composition postdates the Qurʾān. Targum Pseudo-Jonathan celebrates the raised mountain as a unique opportunity afforded to Israel to peer at God as it were through a clear glass pane. This positive portrait, which elevates both Israel and the Torah, contrasts with many early Christian interpretations of Israel's experience at Sinai, from Paul to Proclus. Though a Jew himself, Paul wrestled with the nonbelief in Jesus of his fellow Jews. In his estimation, this was due to a veil covering the minds of the Jewish people, a veil like the one Moses used to cover his face whenever he descended from Mount Sinai (2 Corinthians 3). Paul did not belittle the Torah, which he considered to be part of a glorious, albeit passing, revelation now being surpassed (but perhaps not yet supplanted) by the manifestation of God made possible through Christ. Whatever his true intentions, Paul initiated a (regretful) legacy that stigmatized the Jewish people as spiritually blind and seemingly relativized the enduring relevance of the Mosaic Torah. At least subsequent Christian writers understood Paul in this way, magnifying Israel's spiritual incompetence while minimizing its cherished encounter with God at Sinai and discarding much from the Mosaic Law. Although the author of Acts carved a space for Torah practice among Jewish Christ-followers and remained hopeful that Jews would confess Jesus as their messiah, he highlighted their opposition to divine will. Stephen's speech in Acts singles out Israel's adoration of the golden calf and its repeated rejection, even murder, of the prophets, including and especially Jesus (Acts 7). The writer of Acts concurred with Paul that this stemmed from Israel's spiritual condition. For the time being at least, their hearts remained dull, their eyes blind, and their ears deaf to the gospel, as the Jewish Scriptures themselves had allegedly predicted (Acts 28:26–27 quoting Isa 6:9–11). This trope is repeated in the Synoptic Gospels, although it originally targeted internal Jewish audiences (e.g., Pharisees who did not confess Jesus as the messiah). The Epistle of Barnabas and Justin Martyr, on the other hand, raised the polemics against Judaism to new levels. Some of the Torah's stipulations were delivered to Israel through deception (Barnabas) or as punishment (Justin but also the Didascalia, Aphrahat, etc.). In any case, Israel's encounter with God at Sinai was not so great as the Jewish people might have imagined. Israel didn't see God (so Justin, Eusebius, and Proclus) but remained at the bottom (rather than the top) of the mountain (Cyril). Moreover, the Sinaitic party was ruined soon after by Israel's idolatrous sin of the golden calf, which virtually all of the aforementioned Christian authors did not fail to emphasize.

This survey of early Christian and Jewish materials sheds light on the Qur'ān. First, it shows that the author(s) of the Qur'ān did not simply "copy and paste" rabbinic aggadah. The rabbinic midrash on the raised mountain was effectively repurposed in the Qur'ān to serve the needs of a burgeoning community in search of establishing its own identity. It was furthermore integrated into a literary texture that shares much in common with Christian views about Judaism. Jewish and Christian threads have been interwoven into the Qur'anic text as the lifted mountain enables the construction of a new entity, the community of the believers who confess the revelation given to the Messenger of the Qur'ān. These are contrasted with non-believing Jews and ultimately all non-believers, including Christians who do not recognize the Qur'anic Prophet. In a certain sense, then, the Qur'ān is both "Jewish" and "Christian": Jewish, given the many contents in its text that stem from Jewish Scripture and rabbinic tradition; Christian, because of its confession of Jesus as the messiah, the son of the virgin Mary, and participation in the *Adversus Judaeos* discourse. These observations are not meant to deny the Qur'ān its own distinctive identity and originality, but are valid for *any* religious text, which, from a historical point of view, emerges from an interaction with the cultures and actors already present on the ground. This is true of the Hebrew Bible, whose writings show that the ancient Israelites were part and parcel of their ancient Near Eastern surroundings, and the New Testament documents, now widely viewed by biblical scholarship *as part* of its Second Temple Jewish matrix. All canonical texts, the Qur'ān included, reflect the genius of the religious traditions they represent, creative expressions but local productions nonetheless.

Perhaps, then, the time is coming to view the Qur'ān as a "Jewish" *and* "Christian" text just as many documents of the New Testament are now appreciated as Jewish writings (or, at the very least, as important sources for the understanding of Judaism in antiquity).[179] In this vein, the Qur'ān can also complement our understanding of Christianity and Judaism during the late antique period. For one thing,

179 My designation of the Qur'ān as "Jewish" and "Christian" is meant to be taken in an *inclusive* sense, with the hope that there will be further integration between Jewish, Christian, and Islamic studies as well as biblical and Qur'anic studies. Additionally, this designation puts into question one of the general assumptions associated with the problematic term "Judeo-Christian," which in Western usage normally *excludes* Islam. Jews, Christians, and Muslims alike can be challenged to rethink the interrelationship between their Scriptural traditions.

it seems to attest to the rising influence of rabbinic teachings. In the milieu where the Qur'an originated, Jews and maybe even non-Jews took note of rabbinic interpretations of Scripture. In addition, the Qur'ān points to a milieu fermenting with religious disputes centering on the proper understanding of Scripture and revelation. For Jews during the late antique period, Sinai as a revelatory event had become paramount for self-understanding: the Sinaitic theophany was unprecedented, witnessed by an entire nation, and of lasting *durée*, the Mosaic Torah and covenantal election of Israel remaining in full force. These Jewish assertions countered in part Christian supersessionist claims to the contrary that heralded the replacement of the Torah and Israel by the Gospel and the Church. However, the more Judaism aggrandized the significance of the Sinaitic revelation, the more this could be perceived to undermine Christian belief, since it implied that the advent of Christ had not surpassed the advent of the Torah, that the divine glory had not yet returned as in former times. Christianity, of course, could provide its counter arguments (e.g., that the incarnation of God the Son exceeded all prior theophanies), but the controversy had started ever since Jesus' first Jewish followers, in their apocalyptic enthusiasm, proclaimed Jesus as Israel's messiah and the incoming inauguration of a new age – without succeeding in convincing the majority of the Jewish people that this was so. The Qur'ān tries to clear a third path that in some ways transcends the divide between Jews and Christians (see e.g., Q 2:113; 5:18) yet repeats some of the common Christian anti-Judaic tropes that cast the Jewish people as idolatrous, spiritually blind, and murders of the prophets and Jesus (the latter in a delusional way). To contemporary Jews, Christians, and Muslims, these religious disputes may prove disheartening, but today there is no need for such competition. Members from all three communities can share with one another what they see as they stand *together* at the foot of the mountain.

Bibliography

Primary Sources and Reference Tools

Aland, Barbara, Kurt Aland, Johannes Karavidopoulos, Carlo M. Martini, and Bruce M., Metzger, eds. *Novum Testamentum Graece* (Nestle-Aland). 28th Revised Edition. Stuttgart: Deutsche Bibelgesellschaft, 2012.

Ali, Abdullah Yusuf. (1934) 2012. *The Qur'an: Text, Translation, and Commentary*. New York: Tahrik Tarsile Quran.

Arberry, Arthur John. (1955) 1996. *The Koran Interpreted*. New York: Touchstone.

Asad, Muhammad. (1980) 2008. *The Message of the Qur'ān*. Bristol: The Book Foundation.

Badawi, Elsaid M., and Muhammad Abdel Haleem. 2008. *Arabic-English Dictionary of Qur'anic Usage*. Brill: Leiden.
Brown, Francis, S. R. Driver, and Charles A. Briggs. *The Brown-Driver-Briggs Hebrew and English Lexicon*. Oxford: Clarendon Press, 1907.
Buber, Solomon. 1892. *Midrash on Psalms*. Vilna: Romm.
Bushell, Michael S., Michael D. Tan, and Glenn L. Weaver. 1992–2015. *BibleWorks 10*. BibleWorks, LLC.
Charlesworth, James H., ed. 1983–1985. *The Old Testament Pseudepigrapha*. 2 vols. New York: Doubleday.
Constas, Nicholas. 2003. *Proclus of Constantinople and the Cult of the Virgin in Late Antiquity*. Supplements to Vigiliae Christianae 66. Leiden: Brill.
Droge, A. J. 2013. *The Qur'ān: A New Annotated Translation*. Sheffield: Equinox.
Epstein, I., ed. 1978. *The Babylonian Talmud Translated into English with Notes, Glossary, and Indices*. London: Soncino Press.
Epstein, J. N., and Ezra Zion Melamed, eds. 1979. *Mekhilta de Rabbi Shimon bar Yochai*. Jerusalem: Sumptibus Hillel Press.
Exodus Rabbah. 1878. Vilna: n.p. Online Responsa Project. https://www.responsa.co.il.
Freedman, H., and Maurice Simon. 1983. *Midrash Rabbah: Song of Songs*. London: Soncino Press.
Gaisford, Thomas. 1842. *Eusebii Pamphili. Episcopi Caesariensis. Eclogae propheticae*. Oxford: Oxford University Press.
Gall, August Freiherrn von, ed. *Der Hebräishe Pentateuch der Samaritaner*. 5 vols. Giessen: Alfred Töpelmann, 1914–1918.
Gilchrist, P. R. 1981. "יצב." In *Theological Wordbook of the Old Testament*, edited by R. Laird Harris, Gleason L. Archer Jr., and Bruce K. Waltke. 2 vols. Chicago: Moody Press. BibleWorks 10v.
Gurtner, Daniel M., and Loren Stuckenbruck, eds. 2020. *T&T Clark Encyclopedia of Second Temple Judaism*. 2 vols. London: T&T Clark.
Horovitz, Haim S., and Israel A. Rabin. 1970. *Mekilta de Rabbi Ishmael: Cum variis lectionibus et adnotationibus*. 2nd ed. Jerusalem: Wahrmann.
Jacobson, Howard. 1996. *A Commentary on Pseudo-Philo's Liber Antiquitatum Biblicarum: With Latin Text and English Translation*. 2 vols. AGJU 31. Leiden: Brill.
Jastrow, Marcus. (1943) 2005. *Dictionary of the Targumim, the Talmud Babli and Yerushalmi, and the Midrashic Literature*. Peabody: Hendrickson Publishers.
Kadari, Tamar. *Midrash Shir HaShirim Rabbah: Synoptic Edition*. https://schechter.ac.il/midrash/shir-hashirim-raba.
Kaufman, Stephen A., et al. *The Comprehensive Aramaic Lexicon*. http://cal.huc.edu.
Khan, Maulana Wahiduddin, and Farida Khanam. 2014. *The Quran*. New Delhi: Goodword Books.
Kittel, Gerhard. (1964) 1983. "αἴνιγμα." In *Theological Dictionary of the New Testament*, edited by Gerhard Kittel and Gerhard Friedrich, translated by Geoffrey W. Bromiley. 10 vols. Grand Rapids: Eerdmans.
Koehler, Ludwig, Walter Baumgartner, and Johann Jakob Stamm. 1994–2000. *The Hebrew and Aramaic Lexicon of the Old Testament*. Leiden: Brill. BibleWorks 10v.
Lane, Edward William. 1863. *Arabic-English Lexicon*: Williams & Norgate.
Levy, Jacob. 1924. *Wörterbuch über die Talmudim und Midraschim*. 4 vols. Berlin/Vienna: Benjamin Harz.

Lieberman, Saul. 1955–1988. *The Tosefta*. 5 vols. New York: Jewish Theological Seminary.
Margulies, Mordecai. 1953–1960. *Midrash Vayyikra Rabbah: A Critical Edition Based on Manuscripts and Genizah Fragments with Variants and Notes*. 5 vols. Jerusalem: Ministry of Education and Culture of Israel.
Matthews Jr. Edward G., and Joseph P. Amar. 1994. *St. Ephrem the Syrian: Selected Prose Works. Commentary on Genesis. Commentary on Exodus. Homily on Our Lord. Letter to Publius*. The Fathers of the Church 91. Washington D.C.: The Catholic University of America Press.
Maxwell, David R. 2013. *Commentary on John, Volume 1. Cyril of Alexandria*. Ancient Christian Texts. Downers Grove: IVP Academic.
McAuliffe, Jane. 2017. *The Qur'ān*. Norton Critical Editions. New York: W. W. Norton & Company.
Migne, J.-P. 1857–1866. *Patrologiae cursus completus*. Series Graeca 68. Paris: Migne.
Nasr, Seyyed Hossein, ed. 2015. *The Study Quran: A New Translation and Commentary*. New York: HarperCollins.
Nelson, David. 2006. *Mekhilta de-Rabbi Shimon bar Yohai*. Philadelphia: Jewish Publication Society.
Neusner, Jacob. (1986) 2003. *Judaism and Scripture: The Evidence of Leviticus Rabbah*. Eugene: Wipf and Stock.
Owens Jr., Robert J. 1983. *The Genesis and Exodus Citations of Aphrahat the Persian Sage*. Monographs of the Peshitta Institute Leiden 3. Leiden: Brill.
Philippe, Monique Jaubert. 2003. "Les extraits prophétiques: Au sujet du Christ d'Eusèbe de Césarée. Introduction, traduction, annotation." PhD diss., Université de Provence Aix-Marseille I.
Pietersma, Albert, and Benjamin G. Wright, eds. 2007. *A New Translation of the Septuagint*. Oxford: Oxford University Press.
Pierre, Marie-Joseph. 1988. *Aphraate le sage person*. 2 vols. Sources Chrétiennes 349. Paris: Cerf, 1988.
Pusey, P. E. *Sancti patris nostri Cyrilli archiepiscopi Alexandrini in D. Joannis evangelium*. 3 vols. Oxford: Clarendon Press, 1872.
Schechter, Salomon. 1979. *ʾAbot de Rabbi Nathan: Edited from Manuscripts with an Introduction, Notes and Appendices*. Hildesheim: n.p.
Sokoloff, Michael. 1974. *The Targum to Job from Qumran Cave XI*. Bar Ilan Studies in Near Eastern Languages and Culture. Ramat Gan: Bar Ilan.
Sokoloff, Michael. 2002. *A Dictionary of Jewish Babylonian Aramaic of the Talmudic and Geonic Periods*. Ramat-Gan: Bar Ilan University Press.
Steinsaltz, Adina. 2012a. *Koren Talmud Bavli: The Noé Edition*. Jerusalem: Koren Publishers.
Steinsaltz, Adina. 2012b. *Koren Talmud Bavli: Shabbat – Part Two*. Jerusalem: Koren Publishers.
Stemberger, Günter. 2011. *Einleitung in Talmud und Midrasch*. 9th ed. Munich: C. H. Beck.
Talmud Bavli. 1961. Vilna Edition, Punctuation Using Machon Tevel Edition. Bnei Brak: n.p. Online Responsa Project. https://www.responsa.co.il.
Tanhuma. 1875. Warsaw: n.p. Online Responsa Project. https://www.responsa.co.il.
Theodor Juda, and Chanoch Albeck. 1965. *Midrash Bereshit Rabbah*. Jerusalem: Wahrmann.
Wevers, John Williams, ed. 1991. *Septuaginta Vetus Testamentum Graecum: Exodus*. Göttingen: Vandenhoeck & Ruprecht.

Wevers, John Williams, ed. (1977) 2006. *Septuaginta Vetus Testamentum Graecum: Deuteronomium*. Göttingen: Vandenhoeck & Ruprecht.
Wünsche, August. 1880. *Bibliotheca Rabbinica: Eine Sammlung alter Midraschim. Der Midrasch Schir Ha-Schirim*. Leipzig: Otto Schulze.

Secondary Sources

Alexander, Philip S. 2018. "Narrative and Counternarrative: The Jewish Antigospel (The *Toledot Yeshu*) and the Christian Gospels." In *The Ways That Often Parted: Essays in Honor of Joel Marcus*, edited by Lori Baron, Jill Hicks-Keeton, and Matthew Thiessen, 377–401. Atlanta: SBL Press.
Azar, Michael. 2016. *Exegeting the Jews: The Early Reception of the Johannine "Jews."* The Bible in Ancient Christianity 10. Leiden: Brill.
Baker, Cynthia M. 2017. *Jew*. New Jersey: Rutgers University Press, 2017.
Barkhuizen, J. H. 1999. "Jews, Heretics and Pagans in the Homilies of Proclus of Constantinople." *Acta Patristica et Byzantina* 10.1:33–48.
Baron, Lori, Jill Hicks-Keeton, and Matthew Thiessen, eds. 2018. *The Ways That Often Parted: Essays in Honor of Joel Marcus*. Atlanta: SBL Press.
Blidstein, Gerald J. 2004. "כפה עליהם הר כגיגית – מקורות חדשים." In *Studies in Halakhic and Aggadic Thought*, *idem*, 83–85. Beersheba: Ben-Gurion University of the Negev. [Hebrew]
Boccaccini, Gabriele. 1994. "Targum Neofiti as a Proto-Rabbinic Document: A Systemic Analysis." In *The Aramaic Bible: Targums in Their Historical Context*, edited by Derek Robert George Beattie and Martin McNamara, 260–69. Sheffield: Sheffield Academic Press.
Boccaccini, Gabriele, ed. 2007. *Enoch and the Messiah Son of Man: Revisiting the Book of Parables*. Grand Rapids: Eerdmans.
Bori, Piere Cesare. 1990. *The Golden Calf and the Origins of the Anti-Jewish Controversy*. Atlanta: Scholars Press.
Bowersock, Glen W. 2013. *The Throne of Adulis: Red Sea Wars on the Eve of Islam*. Oxford: Oxford University Press.
Boyarin, Daniel. 2004. *Borderlines: The Partition of Judaeo-Christianity*. Philadelphia: University of Pennsylvania.
Brettler, Marc Zvi. 2008. "'Fire, Cloud, and Deep Darkness (Deuteronomy 5:22): Deuteronomy's Recasting of Revelation.'" In *The Significance of Sinai: Traditions about Sinai and Divine Revelation in Judaism and Christianity*, edited by George J. Brooke, Hindy Najman, and Loren T. Stuckenbruck, 15–27. Leiden: Brill.
Brock, Sebastian. 2006. *An Introduction to Syriac Studies*. Revised edition. Piscataway: Gorgias Press.
Davies, W. D., ed. 2004. *Matthew: A Shorter Commentary*. London: T&T Clark.
Davila, James. 2005. *The Provenance of the Pseudepigripha: Jewish, Christian, or Other?* Supplements to the Journal for the Study of Judaism 105. Leiden: Brill.
Dye, Guillaume. "The Qur'ān and Its Hypertextuality in Light of Redaction Criticism." In *Early Islam: The Sectarian Milieu of Late Antiquity?* Edited by Guillaume Dye. Late Antique and Medieval Islamic Near East. Chicago: The Oriental Institute of the University of Chicago.
Duff, Paul. 2015. *Moses in Corinth: The Apologetic Context of 2 Corinthians 3*. Leiden: Brill.

El-Badawi, Emran Iqbal. 2014. *The Qur'an and the Aramaic Gospels*. New York: Routledge.
Eliav, Yaron Z. 2010. "Jews and Judaism 70–429 CE." In *A Companion to the Roman Empire*, edited by David S. Potter, 565–86. Oxford: Blackwell Publishing.
Epstein, Baruch. (1902) 2005. *Torah Temimah*. Jerusalem: Chad V'Chalak. https://www.responsa.co.il.
Firestone, Reuven. 1997. "The Failure of a Jewish Program of Public Satire in the Squares of Medina." *Judaism* (Fall):439–52.
Firestone, Reuven. 2011. "Is There a Notion of 'Divine Election' in the Qur'ān?" In *New Perspectives on the Qur'ān: The Qur'ān in Its Historical Contexts 2*, edited by Gabriel Said Reynolds, 393–410. Routledge: New York.
Firestone, Reuven. 2015. "Apes and the Sabbath Problem." In *The Festschrift Darkhei Noam: The Jews of Arab Lands*, edited by Carsten Schapkow, Shmuel Shepkaru, and Alan T. Levenson, 26–48. Leiden: Brill.
Flesher, Paul Virgil McCracken, ed. 1998. "Looking for Links in All the Wrong Places: Targum and Peshitta Relationships." In *Targum Studies: Targum and Peshitta*, vol. 2., edited by Paul Virgil McCracken Flesher, xi–xii. Atlanta: Scholars Press.
Flesher, Paul Virgil McCracken, ed. 1998. *Targum Studies: Targum and Peshitta*. Vol. 2. Atlanta: Scholars Press.
Flesher, Paul Virgil McCracken, and Bruce H. Chilton. 2011. *The Targums: A Critical Edition*. Waco: Baylor University Press.
Fonrobert, Charlotte Elisheva. 2001. "The Didascalia Apostolorum: A Mishnah for the Disciples of Jesus." *Journal of Early Christian Studies* 9:483–509.
Fraade, Steven D. 1992. "Rabbinic Views on the Practice of Targum and Multilingualism in the Jewish Galilee of Third–Sixth Centuries." In *The Galilee in Late Antiquity*, edited by Lee I. Levine, 253–86. New York/Jerusalem: The Jewish Theological Seminary.
Fraade, Steven D. 2008. "Hearing and Seeing at Sinai: Interpretive Trajectories." In *The Significance of Sinai: Traditions about Sinai and Divine Revelation in Judaism and Christianity*, edited by George J. Brooke, Hindy Najman, and Loren T. Stuckenbruck, 247–268. Leiden: Brill.
Geiger, Abraham. (1833) 1970. *Judaism and Islam*. Prolegomenon by Moshe Pearlman. Translated by F. M. Young. New York: Ktav Publishing House.
Gottlieb, Leeor. 2014. "Composition of Targums after the Decline of Aramaic as a Spoken Language." *Aramaic Studies* 12:1–8.
Graves, Michael Wesley. 2018. "The Upraised Mountain and Israel's Election in the Qur'ān and Talmud." *Comparative Islamic Studies* 11:141–77.
Gutmann, Joseph. 1983. "The Illustrated Midrash in the Dura Synagogue Paintings: A New Dimension for the Study of Judaism." *Proceedings of the American Academy of Research* 50:91–104.
Hachlili, Rachel. 1998. *Ancient Jewish Art and Archaeology in the Diaspora*. Handbook of Oriental Studies, Section 1, The Near and Middle East 35. Leiden: Brill.
Hartwig, Dirk. 2008. "Der 'Urvertrag' (Q 7:172): Ein rabbinischer Diskurs im Koran." In *Die Wissenschaft des Judentums und die Anfänge der kritischen Koranforschung*, edited by Dirk Hartwig, Walter Homolka, Michael J. Marx, and Angelika Neuwirth, 191–202. Würzbug: Ergon, 2008.
Hayward, Robert. 1989. "Targum Pseudo-Jonathan and Anti-Islamic Polemic." *Journal of Semitic Studies* 34:77–93.

Hayward, Robert. 2010. *Targums and the Transmission of Scripture into Judaism and Christianity*. Studies in the Aramaic Interpretation of Scripture 10. Leiden: Brill.
Hezser, Catherine. 1997. *The Social Structure of the Rabbinic Movement in Roman Palestine*. Texte und Studien zum Antiken Judentum 66. Tübingen: Mohr Siebeck.
Hurschmann, Rolf, Friedhelm Prayon, and Volker Pingel. 2006. “Mirror.” In *Brill’s New Pauly*, edited by Christine F. Salazar. Brill: Leiden. Consulted Online on 23 June 2020.
Joosten, Jan. 2013. *Language and Textual History of the Syriac Bible: Collected Studies*. Texts and Studies 9. Piscataway: Gorgias.
Kaplan, Jonathan. 2015. *My Perfect One: Typology and Early Rabbinic Interpretation of the Song of Songs*. Oxford: Oxford University Press.
Keener, Craig S. 2005. *1-2 Corinthians*. The New Cambridge Bible Commentary. Cambridge: Cambridge University Press.
Lapin, Hayim. 2012. *Rabbis as Romans: The Rabbinic Movement in Palestine, 100–400 CE*. Oxford: Oxford University.
Maori, Yeshayahu. 1998. “The Relationship between the Peshitta Pentateuch and the Pentateuchal Targums.” In *Targum Studies: Targum and Peshitta*, vol. 2., edited by Paul Virgil McCracken Flesher, 57–73. Atlanta: Scholars Press.
McDowell, Gavin. 2017. “The Sacred History in Late Antiquity: *Pirqe de-Rabbi Eliezer* and Its Relationship to the *Book of Jubilees* and the *Cave of Treasures*.” PhD diss., École Pratique des Hautes Études.
McNamara, Martin. 2010. “Targum and the New Testament: A Revisit.” In *The New Testament and Rabbinic Literature*, edited by Reimund Beiringer, Florentino García Martínez, Didier Pollefeyt, and Peter J. Tomson, 387–427. Leiden: Brill.
Milgrom, Jacob. 2009. *Leviticus 1–16: A New Translation with Introduction and Commentary*. New Haven: Yale University Press.
Milik, J. T. 1976. *The Books of Enoch: Aramaic Fragments of Qumrân Cave 4*. Oxford: Clarendon Press.
Mimouni, Simon Claude. 1998. *Le judéo-christianisme ancien: essais historiques*. Paris: Editions Cerf.
Mortensen, Beverly P. 2006. *The Priesthood in Targum Pseudo-Jonathan: Renewing the Profession*. 2 vols. Studies in the Aramaic Interpretation of Scripture 4. Leiden: Brill.
Narinskaya, Elena. 2010. *Ephrem, a “Jewish” Sage: A Comparison of the Exegetical Writings of St. Ephrem the Syrian and Jewish Traditions*. Turnhout: Brepols.
Neusner, Jacob. 1971. *Aphrahat and Judaism: The Christian-Jewish Argument in Fourth-Century Iran*. Leiden: Brill.
Neuwirth, Angelika. 2019. The Qur’an and Late Antiquity: A Shared Heritage, translated by Samuel Wilder. Oxford: Oxford University Press.
Nickelsburg, George W. E. 2001. *1 Enoch 1*. Hermeneia. Minneapolis: Fortress.
Noth, Martin. (1943) 2002. *The Deuteronomistic History*. Sheffield: Sheffield Academic Press.
Novick, Tsvi. 2015. “Standing Under Sinai: On the Origins of a Coerced Covenant.” TheTorah.com. https://thetorah.com/article/standing-under-sinai-on-the-origins-of-a-coerced-covenant (accessed on May 20, 2021).
Obermann, Julian. 1941. “Koran and Agada: The Events at Mount Sinai.” *The American Journal of Semitic Languages and Literatures* 58:23–48.
Oliver, Isaac W. 2013a. “Forming Jewish Identity by Formulating Legislation for Gentiles.” *Journal of Ancient Judaism* 4.1:105–32.

Oliver, Isaac W. 2013b. *Torah Praxis after 70 CE: Reading Matthew and Luke-Acts as Jewish Texts*. Wissenschaftliche Untersuchungen zum Neuen Testament II/355. Tübingen: Mohr Siebeck.

Oliver, Isaac W. 2014. "Jewish Followers of Jesus and the Bar Kokhba Revolt: Re-examining the Christian Sources." In *The Psychological Dynamics of Revolution: Religious Revolts*. Vol. 1 of *Winning Revolutions: The Psychology of Successful Revolts for Freedom, Fairness, and Rights*, vol. 1., edited by J. Harold Ellens, 109–27. Santa Barbara: Praeger, 2014.

Oliver, Isaac W. 2019. "Does Paul Have to Be a Covenantal Jew in Order to Be a Jew?" In *The Message of Paul the Apostle within Second Temple Judaism*, edited by František Abel, 75–87. Lanham: Lexington Books/Fortress Press.

Oliver, Isaac W. 2021. *Luke's Jewish Eschatology: The National Restoration of Israel in Luke-Acts*. Oxford: Oxford University Press.

Oliver, Isaac. W. Forthcoming. "The Historical-Critical Study of Jewish, Christian, and Islamic Scriptures." In *Early Islam: The Sectarian Milieu of Late Antiquity?* Edited by Guillaume Dye. Late Antique and Medieval Islamic Near East. Chicago: The Oriental Institute of the University of Chicago.

Oliver, Isaac W., and Gabriele Boccaccini, eds. 2018. *The Early Reception of Paul the Second Temple Jew: Text, Narrative and Reception History*. London: T&T Clark.

Paget, James Carleton. 1991. "Barnabas 9:4: A Peculiar Verse on Circumcision." *Vigiliae Christianae* 45:242–54.

Paget, James Carleton. 2006. "The Epistle of Barnabas." *The Expository Times* 117.11:441–46.

Pohlmann, Karl-Friedrich. 2015. *Die Entstehung des Korans: Neue Erkenntnisse aus Sicht der historisch-kritisch Bibelwissenschaft*. 3rd ed. Darmstadt: WBG.

Reed, Annette Yoshiko, and Adam H. Becker, eds. 2007. *The Ways That Never Parted*. Minneapolis: Fortress.

Reynolds, Gabriel Said. 2010. "On the Qur'anic Accusation of Scriptural Falsification (*taḥrif*) and Christian Anti-Jewish Polemic." *Journal of the American Oriental Society* 130.2: 189–202.

Reynolds, Gabriel Said. 2012a. "On the Qur'ān and the Theme of Jews as 'Killers of the Prophets.'" *Al-Bayān Journal* 10.2:9–32.

Reynolds, Gabriel Said. 2012b. *The Emergence of Islam: Classical Traditions in Contemporary Perspective*. Minneapolis: Fortress Press.

Robin, Christian Julien, ed. 2015. *Le judaïsme de l'Arabie antique. Actes du Colloque de Jérusalem (février 2006)*. Turnhout: Brepols.

Rönsch, Hermann. (1874) 1970. *Das Buch der Jubiläen oder Die kleine Genesis*. Leipzig: Fues. Reprint Amsterdam: Rodopi.

Runesson, Anders. 2008. "Rethinking Early Jewish-Christian Relations: Matthean Community History as Pharisaic Intragroup Conflict." *Journal of Biblical Literature* 127.1:95–132.

Schäfer, Peter. 2007. *Jesus in the Talmud*. Princeton: Princeton University Press.

Schwartz, Baruch J. 1997. "What Really Happened at Mount Sinai? Four Answers to One Question." *Biblical Archaeology Society* 13:20–30, 46.

Schwartz, Seth. 2004. *Imperialism and Jewish Society: 200 BCE to 640 CE*. Princeton: Princeton University Press.

Shepherd, David. 2020. "Targumim." In *T&T Clark Encyclopedia of Second Temple Judaism*, vol. 1, edited by Daniel M. Gurtner and Loren T. Stuckenbruck, 523–26. London: T&T Clark.

Shinan, Avigdor. 1992. *The Embroidered Targum: The Aggadah in Targum Pseudo-Jonathan of the Pentateuch*. Jerusalem: Magnes Press. [Hebrew]

Sinai, Nicolai. 2017. *The Qur'an: A Historical-Critical Introduction*. Edinburgh: Edinburgh University Press.

Singer, Wilhelm. 1898. *Das Buch der Jubiläen oder die Leptogenesis 1: Tendenz und Ursprung zugleich ein Beitrag zur Religionsgeschichte*. Stuhlweissenburg: Singer.

Speyer, Heinrich. 1961. *Die biblischen Erzählungen im Qoran*. Darmstadt: Wissenschaftliche Buchgesellschaft.

Thiessen, Matthew. 2016. *Paul and the Gentile Problem*. Oxford: Oxford University Press.

Urbach, Ephraim E. 1987. *The Sages: Their Concepts and Beliefs*. Translated by Israel Abrahams. Cambridge: Harvard University Press.

Walters, James Edward. 2016. "Aphrahat and the Construction of Christian Identity in Fourth-Century Persia." PhD diss., Princeton Theological Seminary.

White, Ben. 2018. "Gentile Judaizing in the *Dialogue with Trypho*: A Test Case for Justin's Reception of Paul." In *The Early Reception of Paul the Second Temple Jew: Text, Narrative and Reception History*, edited by Isaac W. Oliver and Gabriele Boccaccini, 252–64. London: T&T Clark.

Wilken, Robert L. (1971) 2004. *Judaism and the Early Christian Mind: A Study of Cyril of Alexandria's Exegesis and Theology*. Eugen: Wipf & Stock.

Witztum, Joseph Benzion. 2011. "The Syriac Milieu of the Quran: The Recasting of Biblical Narratives." PhD diss., Princeton University.

Zellentin, Holger. 2013. The Qur'ān's Legal Culture: The Didascalia Apostolorum as a Point of Departure. Tübingen: Mohr Siebeck, 2013.

Guillaume Dye

Mapping the Sources of the Qur'anic Jesus

Reading the Qur'ān as a Late Antique text has become a motto of recent research—a motto, however, which should not remain an empty slogan.[1] Indeed, we cannot just say that the Qur'ān shares ideas, stories, tropes, and the like, which are present in religious and literary traditions of Late Antiquity, and refer to "oral dissemination" as a sufficient explanation, since it does not tell us anything about the precise circumstances in which these materials were transmitted and appropriated by the communities involved in such a process. For sure, our documentation remains very patchy, but there are several questions and lines of inquiry (e.g., the profile of the producers of the Qur'anic text, the search for plausible specific textual parallels between the Qur'ān and other Late Antique traditions, or the idea that the Qur'ān is a text with several layers) that should be explored further and could shed light on the context(s) and genesis of the Qur'ān.

In this regard, the Qur'ān, significantly so, often displays a Christian context.[2] Yet it is supposed to have originated in a context—7th century Western Arabia—where, according to our evidence, the Christian presence seems marginal.[3] In other

1 This paper is a work in progress and a sequel to previous articles, where more detailed arguments for some of the claims presented here can be found (Dye 2012, Dye 2018, Dye 2019, Dye forthcoming). It is also in dialogue with the works of several colleagues, like Pohlmann 2015, 175–95, Pohlmann forthcoming, Shoemaker 2018, Segovia 2019, Oliver forthcoming, and Wood forthcoming.

2 By "Christian context," I refer to several things (Dye 2019, 764–70): 1) several important Qur'anic characters are typically Christian figures: Jesus, Mary, John, Zachariah, the Sleepers of the Cave, and so on; 2) quite often, when Qur'anic narratives refer to figures shared by Jews and Christians (Adam, Joseph, Moses, etc.), they seem to mirror more closely Christian narratives than Jewish ones (see e.g., Witztum 2011): in short, the subtexts of many (para-)biblical stories in the Qur'ān tend to be closer to Christian texts than Jewish ones, as far as we can tell; 3) some Qur'anic rhetorical arguments or *topoi* are directly borrowed from Christian sources: the anti-Jewish polemics, the use of the character of Abraham, and also Qur'anic demonology; furthermore, 4) many formulas and metaphors in the Qur'ān suggest a Christian background; 5) some texts are clearly addressed to Christians and attest to deep interactions between "Believers" (*mu'minūn*) and Christians; finally, 6) some of the Qur'anic texts have been composed by *literati* who display a very deep and precise knowledge of Christian texts and traditions (a knowledge which cannot be gained by simple hearsay).

3 Christianity encircled Western Arabia, but that does not imply it was similarly widespread in Western Arabia: no evidence speaks for that (either materially or in the literary sources), and scanty knowledge of Western Arabia does not allow us to imagine whatever we want.

Guillaume Dye, Université libre de Bruxelles

https://doi.org/10.1515/9783110675498-007

words, we face the following aporia, with four propositions which do not appear easily reconcilable:[4]

1) Substantial layers of the Qur'ān have a Christian background.
2) The Qur'ān is only a record of Muḥammad's preaching.
3) Muḥammad's career took place in Western Arabia.
4) The Christian presence in Western Arabia was at best marginal.

Of course, some layers of the Qur'ān, which display ideas, attitudes, and practices pointing to a Christian background, might be explained as the outcome of a phenomenon of oral dissemination that would have reached Western Arabia in one way or the other. However, other aspects of the Qur'ān (especially categories 5 and 6, see footnote 2) suppose a context with highly competent scribes of a Christian background and deep interactions between the "Believers" and Christian groups: it does not fit what we know, or what we can reasonably suppose, about Western Arabia at the time, given the nature of our evidence.

In other words, a consistent approach implies introducing some Christianity in Mecca and Medina, and/or placing some of the Qur'ān outside of the Ḥijāz, the whole question being how exactly this should be done. The present paper, which seeks to sketch out how the figure of Jesus was appropriated by the Qur'anic corpus, can be seen as a preliminary attempt to shed some more light on this issue.

Four Paradoxes

The Qur'anic Jesus is a very ambivalent figure—even a paradoxical figure in at least four respects.

First, there are many passages in the Qur'ān where Jesus is wholly absent. For example, surahs 7, 20, 26, 37, and 41 narrate various biblical and parabiblical stories; they refer to numerous prophets—but they say nothing about Jesus. Does this silence imply that the communities using these texts did not count Jesus as one of God's prophets? Or was Jesus simply not the focus of homiletic attention in these passages (as in Christian homilies about episodes of the Hebrew Bible, which might be silent about Jesus)? I will leave this issue open here. Note also that the brief surahs of the end of the corpus (from surah 69 on-

4 See Dye 2019, 764–85, for a full discussion.

wards) display a remarkable Christian background,[5] without mentioning the name of Jesus.

However, in other passages the Qur'ān makes Jesus into one character among others—and even, it seems, a rather secondary character:

> Surely We have inspired you as We inspired Noah and the prophets after him, and as We inspired Abraham, and Ishmael, and Isaac, and Jacob, and the tribes, and Jesus, and Job, and Jonah, and Aaron, and Solomon, and We gave David (the) Psalms, and messengers We have already recounted to you before, and messengers We have not recounted to you—but God spoke to Moses directly—(and) messengers bringing good news and warning, so that people might have no argument against God after (the coming of) the messengers. God is mighty, wise.[6] (Q 4:163–165)

> And We granted him Isaac and Jacob—each one We guided, and Noah We guided before (them)—and of his descendants (were) David, and Solomon, and Job, and Joseph, and Moses, and Aaron—in this way We repay the doers of good—and Zachariah, and John, and Jesus, and Elijah—each one was of the righteous—and Ishmael, and Elisha, and Jonah, and Lot—each one We favored over (all) the people[7]—and some of their fathers, and their descendants, and their brothers. We chose them and guided them to a straight path. (Q 6:83–87)

This should be puzzling for anyone inclined to see the Qur'ān as *simply* mirroring a Jewish, a Christian, or a Jewish Christian environment: the mention of Jesus dismisses a purely Jewish background, but the rather marginal role devoted to Jesus apparently excludes Christian and Jewish Christian backgrounds as well, since Jesus' role does not look central enough.

Elsewhere, Jesus is placed among the privileged prophets: he is clearly raised, with a few figures (Adam, Noah, Abraham, Moses in Q 3:33–34, or the Qur'anic messenger, Noah, Abraham, Moses in Q 33:7 and 42:13), above the other prophets (Q 2:136 and 3:84 could be placed mid-way between the former category and this one):

> Surely God has chosen Adam and Noah, and the house of Abraham and the house of 'Imrān over (all) the people (*'alā l-'ālamīn*), some of them descendants of others. (Q 3:33–34)

> Those are the messengers—We have favored some of them over others. (There were) some of them to whom God spoke, and some of them He raised in rank. And We gave Jesus, son of Mary, the clear signs, and supported him with the holy spirit. (Q 2:253)

---

5 See e.g. Andrae 1955, Sinai 2017, and the relevant commentaries in Amir-Moezzi & Dye 2019.
6 Translations of the Qur'ān are taken from Droge 2013, with occasional minor modifications.
7 *'alā l-'ālamīn*, usually (but questionably) translated "over the worlds."

Here, Jesus belongs to the most important figures in the Qur'ān. Furthermore, in other passages, he is even the most eminent character, since he alone enjoys a very high status: he is the only one called the word and spirit of God (Q 4:171); he is born miraculously of the virgin Mary (the only woman named in the Qur'ān); he is the only prophet to receive a revelation from the cradle (Q 19:30–33); his return to earth is the sign of the end of time (Q 43:61); moreover, the holy spirit (*rūḥ al-qudus*) is mentioned only four times in the Qur'ān, and in three cases, precisely about Jesus (Q 2:87, 253; 5:110). Here is the *first paradox* of the Qur'anic Jesus: it seems that there are different layers in the Qur'anic corpus, where the role of the figure of Jesus is very variable— sometimes Jesus is absent, sometimes he seems to be a minor figure, sometimes he belongs to the few most important figures, sometimes he appears as the most eminent character.

Second, the figure of Jesus is both a figure of convergence and cleavage (this alone, of course, is not paradoxical). Jesus is a figure of convergence, in certain passages, with the Christians/*naṣārā:*[8] various verses testify to a tendency to find a kind of compromise, or convergence, with Christians (see e.g., Q 3:33–63; 19:1–33; 61:14).[9] But Jesus is also a cleaving figure: sometimes in relation to the Christians, and systematically in relation to the Jews. The Jews, indeed, did not recognize Jesus as a messenger of God, in spite of all the proofs he brought (Q 2:87, 253; 3:52; 43:63–65; 61:6); they were incredulous and even called him a magician (Q 5:110; 61:6), an accusation that implies he has trading with the demons. The Jews even accuse themselves of having killed and crucified Jesus (Q 4:155–159). The Christians, for their part, have a false understanding of Jesus' real nature: they divinize Jesus, they make him the son of God (what the Qur'ān denies vigorously: "God did not take a son," see Q 2:116; 17:111; 18:4; 19:35, 88–92; 21:26; 23:91; 25:2; 39:4; 72:3; "They have disbelieved, those who say that God is the Messiah, son of Mary" (Q 5:17)); and they are wrong about the Trinity (Q 4:171–172; 5:72–77).

Here is the *second paradox*: the Qur'ān shows contradictory attitudes towards Christians (and this is in part related to Christological controversies), who are sometimes presented in a very positive light (Q 5:82), and sometimes

---

8 Sg. *naṣrānī*. There has been some debate about the meaning and translation of this term (see De Blois 2002; Gallez 2008; Griffith 2011, 2015; about the Syriac word *nāṣrāyē*, see Jullien & Jullien 2002). I am inclined to take it as a general term referring to the main denominational Christian communities of the Late Antique Near East, and not a reference to a marginal (for example Jewish Christian) group.

9 See van der Velden 2007; Dye forthcoming.

are the target of violent polemics (Q 5:51; 19:34–40). The concomitance of such hardly reconcilable verses in surah 5, for example, is striking:[10]

> You who believe! Do not take the Jews and the Christians as allies. They are allies of each other. Whoever of you takes them as allies is already one of them. Surely God does not guide the people who are evildoers. (Q 5:51)

> Surely those who believe, and those who are Jews, and the Sabians, and the Christians— whoever believes in God and the Last Day, and does righteousness— there will be no fear on them, nor will they sorrow. (Q 5:69; see also Q 2:62)

> Certainly you will find that the most violent of people in enmity to the believers are the Jews and those who associate (*mushrikūn*). Certainly you will find that the closest of them in affection to the believers are those who say, 'We are Christians.' That is because (there are) priests and monks among them, and because they are not arrogant. When they hear what has been sent down to the messenger, you see their eyes overflowing with tears because of what they recognize of the truth. (Q 5:82–83)

The *third paradox* can be stated briefly: the Qur'ān mentions Jesus' eschatological role only in passing (Q 43:57–67; see also Q 4:159), whereas the eschatological Jesus is often mentioned in early Islamic traditions.[11] Why such a contrast, since eschatological and apocalyptic issues are almost everywhere in the Qur'ān? Is there a deliberate tendency in the Qur'ān to downplay this aspect of the early Islamic Jesus, and if so, why?

Fourth, the reader who is used to the Jesus of the canonical Gospels, or to the Jesus of the mainstream Christian traditions, might think (wrongly) that the Qur'anic Jesus does not have much to do with the character he or she knows. So, here is a *last paradox*: who is this Jesus who *seemingly* does not look at all like the Jesus of the Christians, but who might be, in many respects (as we shall see), very close to it? And this does not pertain only to the contents of the Qur'anic verses about Jesus: it also pertains to what the Qur'ān chooses to tell, and to what it chooses *not* to tell, about Jesus. Indeed, the Qur'ān insists on certain aspects of the figure of Jesus (his conception and birth, his death, real or apparent, and a few other things, which we shall return to), but it is strikingly silent on others (e.g., there are very few references to the contents of Jesus' preaching, like his parables).

---

10 There is also a paradox in relation to the Jews. On the tensions in the Qur'anic treatment of the Jews, see e.g. Pohlmann (2019, 312–313).
11 See e.g. Reynolds 2001; Amir-Moezzi 2018.

The Heresiological Model

How should we explain this somewhat strange Jesus? For a long time, the model favored by scholars has been what might be called a *heresiological model*: the Qur'anic message, which displays Christian stuff, and the Qur'anic description of Christians should come from marginal, heretical Christian groups. A single example is better than a long discourse:

> When God will say,[12] 'Jesus, son of Mary! Did you say to the people: 'Take me and my mother instead of God (alone)?' (Q 5:116)

The text *seems* to imply that the Christians took Mary as the third person of the Trinity. Scholars have therefore supposed that the Qur'ān (and Muḥammad, as its author) had a mistaken view of the Trinity, or attributed to Christianity as a whole the tenets of a marginal Christian sect. The issue, then, has been to determine where this mistaken idea came from. Various explanations have been proposed,[13] such as: a) this verse refers to a specific Christian sect, the Collyridians who, according to Epiphanus, liked to bake cakes for the Virgin Mary; b) Muḥammad could have mistaken Mary for the Holy Spirit out of ignorance or because the word for "spirit" (*rūḥ*) is feminine in Arabic; c) a particular group of Jewish Christians, the Nazoreans, could be targeted here. De Blois has argued for the last hypothesis,[14] referring, for example, to Origen and Jerome:

> But in the gospel written according to the Hebrews which the Nazoreans read, the Lord [Jesus] says: "Just now, my mother, the holy spirit, lifted me up." (Jerome, *in Esaiam* 40:9)

> Just now my mother, the holy spirit, lifted me up by one of my hairs and brought me to the great mountain Thabor. (Origen, *in Johannem* 2:12)

This is basically how the heresiological model works, where almost nothing in the Qur'ān is supposed to come from Chalcedonian Christianity. Sometimes scholars argue for an influence of Miaphysitism or Diophysitism—a sensible approach, for sure, since these were widespread Christian affiliations at the time. However, generally speaking, they rather look for more marginal movements. A

---

12 *'idh qāla llāhu*. Translators (Droge included) often translate: "(Remember) when God said," but I take *qāla* here as an extra-temporal perfect, understanding the event referred to as taking place at the moment of the Last Judgment (the same is true of Q 5:110; the verbs in Q 5:111–115, on the other hand, should be translated as perfects).

13 See Reynolds 2014, 52–53.

14 De Blois 2002, 14–15.

survey of the secondary literature yields the following list of possible candidates behind this or that aspect of the Qur'anic Jesus (in alphabetical order):

> Adoptianists / Arians / Bardaysanists / Collyridians / Docetists / Gnostics / Jewish Christians: Ebionites, Elkesaites, Nazoreans – Pseudo-Clementine literature / Julianists (Aphtartodocetists) / Manichaeans[15] / Mandaeans / Monarchianists / Montanists / Paulicians / Samosatenists (Paul of Samosate) / Tritheists.

This list is not exhaustive, and it might be hard to find a sect that has not been related to the Qur'ān (not to mention possible influences from Jewish sects, the Sadducees, Qumran, or from Iranian movements like Zurvanism or Mazdakism).

My main goal here is not to criticize in detail the "heresiological" model. So I will be quite brief.[16] The main weaknesses of this model should nevertheless be highlighted.

First, some of the "heresies" already mentioned exist only in the minds of the heresiographers or are based on confusing and questionable categories (e.g., Docetists, Gnostics, Jewish Christians).

Second, most of these heresies are not attested at the time and/or in Western Arabia. Concretely, the heresiological model is therefore unverifiable and unfalsifiable, since it presupposes oral dissemination between the Qur'anic community and marginal groups that have left no traces.[17] Strictly speaking, this does not entail that this model is wrong—only that it is irredeemably speculative, at best.

Third, any global explanation of the Qur'anic Jesus needs to appeal to several "heresies" to get a comprehensive picture of the Qur'anic Jesus. This is not impossible, but it implies a quite baroque picture of the Qur'anic Jesus (Ebionite Christology with a Julianist understanding of crucifixion, for example), and also a baroque picture of ancient Arabia, which is implicitly considered as a kind of Jurassic Park for ancient "heresies."[18]

Fourth, this model presupposes a wholly passive attitude from the author(s) of the Qur'ān, as if some of the Qur'anic teachings in relation to Christianity could not be explained by irony, hyperbole, *reductio ad absurdum*, and so forth.[19]

---

15 Contrary to the other denominations, a widespread movement at the time. See Tardieu 2019.

16 See van der Velden 2007, 198–203; Tannous 2018, 225–69; Reynolds 2014; Wood forthcoming, and about Jewish Christianity, Dye 2018.

17 Dye 2018, 16–18; about the merits and limits of an appeal to oral dissemination, see Dye 2019, 777–783.

18 I borrow this nice formula from Tannous 2018, 247.

19 See Reynolds 2014.

Fifth, very often, the explanatory power of the heresiological model is rather weak. Let us go back to Q 5:116.[20] Is it really plausible that, because *rūḥ* is feminine, the author of this passage (be it Muḥammad or someone else) took the holy spirit for Mary? About the Collyridians: we have no evidence that they ever considered Mary as a person of the Trinity, and no evidence whatsoever of their presence in Western Arabia (or elsewhere) in the 7th century. Finally, the Nazorean explanation is hardly convincing, and not only because our evidence about Nazoreans is at best ambiguous (in general and in relation to Muḥammad's movement in particular). In fact, the content of the verse itself goes against such a reading.

Indeed, the text says "Jesus, son of Mary!"; and then it *immediately* refers to Jesus' mother. "Jesus son of Mary" might be a stereotyped formula, but the obvious reading is to identify "my mother" (Jesus' mother) with Mary. Moreover, the text clearly does not aim at simply describing Christian beliefs and practices; it is rather a polemical text, which draws the Theotokos formula and the idea of Jesus' divine sonship to absurd consequences: if you make Jesus God and the son of God, and if you say that Mary is not only the mother of Jesus but also the mother of God (Theotokos), then the only logical conclusion (to be rejected, of course) is that Mary should be divine too.

Sixth, this model does not answer the decisive question raised by the fourth paradox above, namely why the Qur'ān is talkative on some topics but so silent on others.

Seventh, when we manage to find promising subtexts or sources of Qur'anic pericopes, they belong to the Chalcedonian, Miaphysite, or Diophysite Christianities. No need therefore to look for exotic movements.[21]

Eighth, there are other—and more economical—ways to explain the contents of the Qur'ān.

Let us travel forward in time and consider a remarkable example: Socinianism. The Socinians, in the 16th century, did not believe in Jesus' divine nature, the Trinity, or in original sin—yet it would be absurd to suppose behind the

20 See Dye 2018, 22–23. Note that Gallez, who often favors the heresiological model, provides here another explanation: designating the Holy Spirit as a "mother" is simply here a manner of speaking, influenced by Aramaic usage (Gallez 2005, 74–83).

21 For example: the Syriac homiletic literature, especially Narsai and Jacob of Serugh; the liturgical traditions of the Palestinian (and Chalcedonian) Kathisma Church, the (pro-Byzantine) *Alexander Legend*, the monastic literature as attested in the *Leimon* of John Moschos, various passages from the Bible, the Gospels, or pseudepigraphical and apocryphal works largely disseminated, and so on. See, more generally, the commentaries in Amir-Moezzi & Dye 2019, vols. 2a and 2b.

birth of Socinianism the existence of a kind of marginal pre-Nicean sect, which survived miraculously, hidden from our sources, from the 2nd or 3rd century to the Tuscany (Poland, the Polish Brethen) and Transylvania (the Unitarian Church of Transylvania) of the 16th century.[22] The following explanation is much more straightforward: Socinianism was born in an environment of debates about and around Scripture, of challenges and defiance concerning the magisterium of the Church and the authoritativeness of its method of interpreting Scripture. At the same time, Socinianism was based on a close reading of Scripture. For sure, cultural transfers from anti-Christian Islamic polemics are possible, and Socinian and Unitarian authors, as well as their "orthodox" opponents, could stress the affinities between Socianism and Islam.[23] However, this does not imply that, without the existence of anti-Christian Islamic polemics, Socinianism would have been impossible.

This brings us to the core of the issue: how to generate "heresy" or "wrong belief."[24] What is needed is not a relation with a "heretic" movement or teacher— we should not posit unnecessary entities. What is needed is to read Scripture (which admits many possible readings, and which contains multifarious, not to say contradictory, elements) in a way that is not consonant with the "orthodox" reading. Any reading of Scripture supposes taking some passages as fundamental and others as secondary, ignoring others, reading some passages literally and others metaphorically, and so on. The various so-called "heretics" and the so-called "orthodox" believers all do this; they only differ in their choices about the passages they rely on (and those they neglect) and the ways they read them.[25] If, moreover, there is no agreement on what should count as Scripture (the hierarchy between canonical and non-canonical books was not really implemented at this time, and the sources of religious authority have always been more diverse than what the "orthodox" authorities and the "guardians of the temple" want people to believe), the range of available interpretations expands even more.

In other words, Scripture (taken in a large sense, and not only as the Jewish or Christian canon) is a literary, thematic, symbolic, and formulaic repertoire, the tank where so-called "heretics" and "orthodox" take their stuff, in different

---

22 This is one of the most serious oddities of the heresiological model: for the needs of its cause, it can even invent ghost entities, which have no evidence (even ambiguous or confused) in our sources, but whose existence needs to be assured, precisely to explain later "heresies."

23 Mulsow 2010.

24 Tannous 2018, 247–50; Dye 2018, 28–29. I use the (value-laden, and inappropriate) terms "heresy" and "wrong belief" here only for the sake of convenience (ideally, we should say "how to generate different beliefs, based on the same scriptural canon").

25 For a recent example of this phenomenon, see Irons, Dixon, and Smith 2015.

and even sometimes opposed ways, through acts of reinterpretation, appropriation, and subversion of competing readings and tenets. I suggest that this is precisely the kind of phenomenon that we should refer to when we seek to explain the Qur'anic Jesus.

Before moving further, three remarks are in order: first, the rejection of the heresiological model does not mean denying that Early Islam was born in a sectarian milieu, that is, in a context of deep confessional competition—between the various "religions" and also inside each religious tradition, "Islam" included. Second, it is not because we do not want to posit hypothetical marginal groups that we should deny the existence of a wide range of possible views *within* the mainstream Christian groups, both among the laymen and the clergy. Third, the Qur'ān is not simply a passive receptor of various sources, but we should not stop our investigations at this point: the Qur'anic Jesus does not come from nowhere, and we should try to determine its sources and subtexts so that we understand how the Qur'ān uses them.

Overview of the Qur'anic Jesus

Here is a list of the Qur'anic passages where Jesus is explicitly mentioned.

2:87 / 2:136 / 2:253 / 3:33–63 / 3:84 / 4:155–159 / 4:163 / 4:171–172 / 5:17 / 5:46 / 5:72–75 / 5:78 / 5:110–118 / 6:84–87 / 9:30–31 / 19:16–36 / 21:91 / 23:50 / 33:7–8 / 42:13 / 43:57–64 / 61:6 / 61:14 / 66:12

It is possible to determine several networks for these texts (some passages, in part or as a whole, can belong to several networks)—something that I cannot do exhaustively in the context of this short paper. For example, there is a rather small network of similar texts providing long lists of messengers ("the tribes" are mentioned in three of them), where Jesus appears as one character among several others (Q 2:136; 3:84; 4:163–165; 6:84–87), another network of texts against the Trinity (Q 4:171–172; 5:72–75), and so on.

One of the most important networks consists in texts related to the conception and birth of Jesus. They can be arranged in the following (rough) chronological order:

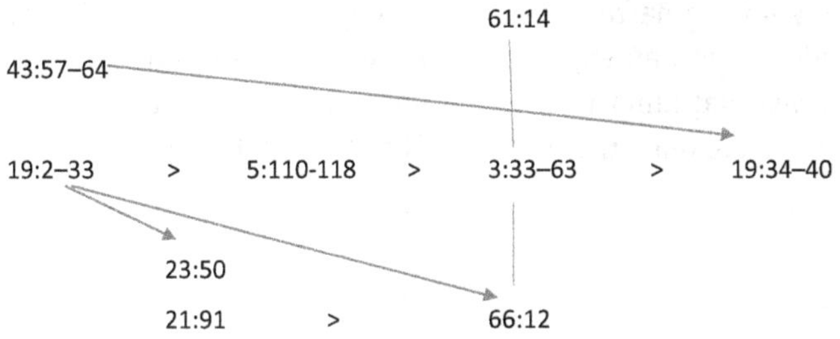

We can take Q 19:2–33 as a starting point. Q 5:110–118 is probably later than Q 19:2–33. There are good reasons to think that the author of Q 3:33–63 uses both Q 19:2–33 and Q 5:110–118, and that Q 19:34–40 is a patchwork of Q 3:47 and Q 43:64–65.[26] Q 23:50 refers allusively to the palm tree miracle in Q 19 and probably also to the site of the Kathisma church, whereas the relative chronology between (the almost identical verses) Q 21:91 and 66:12 mirrors some aspects of Q 5 and Q 3 (see below). Q 3:52 and Q 61:14 are roughly identical, and Q 66:12 and Q 3:33 echo each other (it is hard to design a relative chronology for these four verses). Q 66:12 is certainly later than Q 19:2–33; however, establishing a relative chronology between Q 19:2–33 and Q 21:91 seems tricky. I have added Q 43: 57–64, which does not mention the Nativity but has been used by the author of Q 19:34–40.

Qur'anic pericopes about Jesus rely on extra-Qur'anic sources and also on intra-Qur'anic sources, when they are the reworking of a previous (proto-Qur'anic) *Textgut*. For example, Q 19:2–33 is deeply indebted to Palestinian traditions (no need to look for heretics), especially the popular, liturgical, and homiletic traditions of the Kathisma church, and more generally the Jerusalem Marian liturgy.[27] Moreover, this passage is based on widely-disseminated Christian traditions (the *Protoevangelium of James*, Luke, the Dormition narratives, and the Infancy Gospels). Even the presentation of Jesus (Q 19:30–32) is scripturally warranted. In Q 3: 33–63, on the other hand, we have an author who uses Q 19 (and also Q 5) but also other passages from some of the Christian sources already used in Q 19 (above all, the *Protoevangelium of James*).[28]

26 See respectively Pohlmann 2015, 186–88 and Dye forthcoming.
27 Shoemaker 2003; Dye 2012, forthcoming.
28 Dye forthcoming.

This accounts only for the narrative on the conception and birth of Jesus, but it does not provide us with an explanation of the *skeleton* of the Qur'anic Jesus. However, it seems that almost all of the bones of this skeleton can be found, quite unexpectedly, in one brief passage of the New Testament.

Acts 2:22–24

Let us look at Acts 2:22–24,[29] an excerpt from the speech of Peter (Acts 2:14–36), supposedly delivered on the day of Pentecost in Jerusalem:

> Men of Israel, hear these words: Jesus the Nazorean, a man attested to you by God with mighty works and wonders and signs that God did through him in your midst, as you yourselves know—this Jesus, delivered up according to the definite plan and foreknowledge of God, you crucified and killed by the hands of lawless men. God raised him up, loosing the pangs of death, because it was not possible for him to be held by it.

This text is remarkable for several reasons. First, as we will see, it has striking similarities with the Qur'anic Jesus. Even if some of its main ideas have parallels elsewhere,[30] there is apparently no single text that displays with such a density of elements that are central in the Qur'ān. Second, as far as I know, it does not seem to have enjoyed a wide popularity in the Christian homiletic literature of Late Antiquity (and Acts is seldom used in the lectionaries—except in the lectionaries of the Church of Jerusalem).

Let us sketch the main points of this text:

a. Men of Israel, hear these words:
b. Jesus the Nazorean,
c. a man
d. attested to you by God with mighty works and wonders and signs that God did through him in your midst,
e. as you yourselves know,
f. this Jesus, delivered up according to the definite plan and foreknowledge of God, you crucified and killed by the hands of lawless men. God raised him

---

29 I am indebted here to Räisänen 1980, 127–129, who noticed the parallels between the Qur'ān and a) Lk 9:20 ; Acts 3:18 (Jesus described as God's messiah) ; b) Acts 2:22 (Jesus portrayed as a man dependent on God) ; c) Acts 3:13, 18; 4:27 (Jesus as God's servant) ; d) Lk 9:35; Acts 3:20 (Jesus is the chosen one); Acts 2:23 (Jesus was killed according to God's plan and raised from the dead).

30 The whole speech of Peter (Acts 2:14–39) has several parallels in the Acts:3:12–26; 4:9–12; 5:29–32; 10:34–43; 13:16–41 (in this last case, the speech is by Paul).

up, loosing the pangs of death, because it was not possible for him to be held by it.

Roughly speaking, each point has striking correspondences with the Qur'ān. Some of them do not necessarily prove much; others are very significant.

a) *Men of Israel, hear these words*

The Greek is Ἄνδρες Ἰσραηλῖται, and the Syriac *gabrē banī Isra'el*, "men from the Sons of Israel,"—a formulation that evokes the Qur'anic *Banū Isrā'īl*. The speech of Peter is addressed to the Jews, and its point is that some of the "Men of Israel" followed Jesus (the disciples, or apostles), and some of them did not. The same idea is central in the Qur'ān: some of the *Banū Isrā'īl* followed Jesus (his disciples), many of them did not:[31]

> You who believe! Be the helpers of God, as Jesus, son of Mary, said to the disciples: 'Who will be my helpers to God?' The disciples said, 'We will be the helpers of God.' One contingent of the Sons of Israel believed, and (another) contingent disbelieved. So We supported those who believed against their enemy, and they were the ones who prevailed.
> (Q 61:14; see also Q 2:253; 3:49–57; 4:155; 5:72, 110–112; 43:63–65; 61:6)

b) *Jesus the Nazorean*

I do not want to speculate here about the origins of the word *naṣrānī/naṣārā* in the Qur'ān (see above, footnote 8). There are not many passages, however, in the New Testament where this word is used (Mt 2:23; 26:71; Lk 18:37; Acts 24:5).

c) *A man*

This is of course a decisive element. *Nothing* in Acts 2:22–24 suggests that Jesus could share a parcel of divinity—everything tells he is an exceptional man, chosen by God, through whom God schemes His plan. This is in fact the Qur'anic conception of Jesus. The Qur'anic Jesus might be an outstanding character, but he is not described as a pre-existing being. Jesus eats food (Q 5:75), that is, he is neither divine nor an angel, he is a prophet (Q 19:30: *nabī*), a messenger (*rasūl*) of God (Q 4:171), a messenger to the Sons of Israel (Q 3:48), a servant of God (Q 4:172; 5:72, 117; 19:30–31)—a formula used for other figures in the Qur'ān, which recalls how the Hebrew Bible speaks of the prophets. Jesus is also defined by a series of negations: he is not a divinity beside God (Q 5:116); God is not Jesus (Q 5:17, 72); Jesus is not the third person of a trinity (Q 4:171; 5:73,

31 This theme of the "divided house of Israel" is arguably central not only to the speech of Peter, but also the entirety of Acts; see Jervell 1972. I thank Isaac Oliver for the remark and the reference.

116); he is not the son of God (Q 4,71; 9:30; 19:35). Indeed, like Adam, Jesus was born without a father, but it is not for this reason that, according to the Qur'ān (which implicitly takes sides here against Lk 1:35; 3:38) he should be called "son of God" (Q 3:59).

d) *Attested to you by God with mighty works and wonders and signs that God did through him in your midst*

This is another very striking point. Once again, the text highlights the fact that Jesus is *specifically* sent to the Sons of Israel ("attested *to you*"), that it is the work of God which is visible through Jesus ("*attested . . . by God . . . that God did through him*"), and that this attestation takes the form of miracles, signs, wonders. This corresponds precisely, once again, to the Qur'anic Jesus. The Qur'anic Jesus is a prophet sent to the *Banū Isrā'īl*, not to the gentiles or the whole humanity (see however Q 21:91); God made him an example for the Sons of Israel (Q 43:59). His prophetic office is attested by the miracles and wonders God does through him, in the midst of the Children of Israel, who do not believe. Yet Jesus came with the "clear proofs" (*al-bayyināt*):

> Certainly We gave Moses the Book, and followed up after him with the messengers, and We gave Jesus, son of Mary, the clear proofs, and supported him with the holy spirit. Whenever a messenger brought you what you yourselves did not desire, did you become arrogant, and some of you called liars and some of you killed? And they say: "Our hearts are uncircumcised." No! God has cursed them for their disbelief, and so little will they believe.[32] (Q 2:87, see also Q 2:253; 5:110; 43:63; 61:6)

Jesus is also sent to the Sons of Israel with a sign (*āya*):[33]

> And (God will make Jesus) a messenger to the Sons of Israel. "Surely I (Jesus) have brought you a sign from your Lord. I shall create for you the form of a bird from clay (. . .). And (I come) confirming what was before me of the Torah, and to make permitted to you some things which were forbidden to you (before). I have brought you a sign from your Lord, so guard (yourselves) against God, and obey me. Surely God is my Lord and your Lord, so serve Him! This is a straight path.[34]" (Q 3:49–51)

32 Q 2:87–88 directly echoes in almost all its details Acts 7:51–53.

33 A very significant use of *'āya*, since generally the *'āyāt* are the signs of God, and come "directly" from God (they can be observed, understood, without the need of a messenger, for example, the signs of divine providence and power), whereas the *bayyināt* pertain rather to the divine investiture of the messenger. See Haddad 1977, 520, n. 4.

34 "God is my Lord and your Lord": for the origins of this formula (see also Q 19:36; 43:64), see John 20:17.

The "proofs" and the "sign" are clearly related to Jesus' miracles, not unlike the "mighty works, wonders and signs (σημείοις)" in Acts. The Qur'ān alludes several times to Jesus' miracles. It might be useful to compare here two Qur'anic passages (identical words are in italics).

Q 3:49	**Q 5:110 (middle of the verse)**
49 wa-rasūlan 'ilā banī 'isrā'īla 'annī qad ji 'tukum bi-'āyatin min rabbikum	
And (He will be) a messenger to the Sons of Israel. 'Surely I have brought you a sign from your Lord.	
49 'annī '*akhluqu* lakum *mina l-ṭīni ka-hay'ati l-ṭayri fa-'anfukhu fīhi fa-*yakūnu *ṭayran bi-'idhni* llāhi	110 wa-'idh ta*khluqu mina l-ṭīni ka-hay'ati l-ṭayri* bi-'idhnī *fa-*tan*fukhu fī*hā *fa-*ta*kūnu ṭayran bi-'idhn*ī
I shall create for you the form of a bird from clay. Then I will breathe into it [masc. referring to the bird], and it [masc.] will become a bird by the permission of God.	And when you created the form of a bird by My permission, then you breathed into it [fem., referring to the form], and it [fem.] became a bird by My permission.

The subtext is a tradition related to the *Infancy Gospel of Thomas* 2:2–4. But it is not the subtext of these Qur'anic passages which is my focus here. I would rather highlight two different points.

The first one pertains to the formula *bi-'idhni (A)llāh* (*bi-'idhnī* in Q 5:110). This expression is usually translated by "with the permission of God." Yet this translation is awkward at best. Strictly speaking, "the permission of God" would mean that Jesus has himself the power to accomplish such wonders but needs the authorization of God. I doubt this is what is intended here: rather, the idea is that the real agent of the miracle is God, who does miracles *through* Jesus. In other words, a translation by "by the will of God, by the order of God," or even "by the grace of God," would certainly be better. Consider, for example, the following verses:

> Those (people)—they call (you) to the Fire, but God calls (you) to the Garden and forgiveness *bi-'idhnihī*. He makes clear His signs (*yubayyinu 'āyātihī*), so that they make take heed. (Q 2:221)

> By means of it God guides those who follow after His approval (in the ways) of peace, and He brings them out of the darkness to the light, *bi-'idhnihī*, and guides them to a straight path. (Q 5:116)

In these passages (see also, e.g., Q 2:97, 213, 249, 251; 3:49; 4:64; 5:110; 7:58; 8:66; 10:100; 14:1, 11, 23, 25), a translation by "by His permission" does not make much sense. The idea, on the contrary, is that it is God's will and power which are implied here, and which become *manifest and visible*. This idea fits perfectly with what is expressed in Acts 2:22.

The second point is related to a significant difference between Q 3:49 and Q 5:110 concerning the miracle where a bird is created by Jesus on the model of God's creation of Adam.

In Q 5:110, Jesus makes from clay "like the form of a bird" (*hay'ati l-ṭayri*), then breathes into the form (the Qur'ān uses the feminine pronoun), and the form (implicit feminine pronoun in Arabic) becomes a (real) bird. In Q 3:49, Jesus does the same, but the Qur'ān uses the masculine pronoun, so Jesus is supposed to breath not into the form but, apparently, into the bird (which does not exist yet as a bird): *fa-'anfukhu fīhi fa-yakūnu ṭayran bi-'idhni llāhi*, "he breathes into it (the bird?) and it (the bird?) becomes a bird by God's will." The context shows that the real referent of the masculine pronoun should be *ṭīn*, "clay," which is also masculine in Arabic.

There is an interesting and striking parallel in the Qur'ān.

Q 66:12	**Q 21:91**
wa-maryama bnata imrāna *llatī aḥṣanat farjahā fa-nafakhnā fī*hi *min rūḥinā.*	*wa-llatī aḥṣanat farjahā fa-nafakhnā fī*hā *min rūḥinā.*
And Mary, daughter of ʿImrān, who guarded her private part: We breathed into it/him from/some of Our spirit.	And she guarded her private part: We breathed into her from/some of Our spirit.

If Q 21:91 is considered as the earliest version, then one can ask why the quite natural formula (God breathes his Spirit inside Mary) is changed with a clumsy and ambiguous formula which either means that God breathes his Spirit in Mary's private part (*farj*), or that He breathes His Spirit inside Jesus. Pohlmann suggest the following explanation:

> On the one hand the important Christian assertion of faith "Jesus, son of the Virgin Mary" is obviously essential and indispensable in a later phase of the genesis of the Qur'ān; on the other hand the relevant text passages try increasingly to avoid a misunderstanding of the mention of God's spirit and the Holy spirit in the context of Jesus' birth.
>
> (. . .) That's why the author [of sura 3] consistently avoids mention of the Spirit of God in his passage. His aim is to rule out the possibility of misunderstandings and misinterpretations, namely that mentioning any participation or assistance of some kind by God's spirit in the context of Jesus' birth—in whatever manner—could evoke the idea of Jesus being the son of God—an idea not acceptable to the Qur'anic community. This is clearly demonstrated

> by the fact that the author finally ensures in Q 3:47, that Jesus' birth is just the effect of the Word of God.[35]

That such an embarrassment was at stake seems confirmed by the following point: the mention of God's breathing His spirit is present only in the two earliest versions of the creation of Adam (Q 38: 72; 15:29); in the later reworkings of the story (surahs 7, 20 and 2), this element disappears—and the parallel between Adam's creation and Jesus' birth are highlighted by the Qur'ān itself (Q 3:59).

There were indeed, inside the community(ies) behind the genesis of the Qur'ān, debates on various contentious issues related to Jesus. This is reflected in the way the Qur'anic pericopes are rewritten and reworked, clearly in a context of deep interactions with Christians.

e) *As you yourselves know*
Another possible translation is "as you have seen yourselves" (καθὼς αὐτοὶ οἴδατε). This is a very important rhetorical and polemical device: the unbelievers really know what they deny, and have no excuse for their disbelief, since all the proofs have been given to them. Such a device is often used in the Qur'ān, particularly when anti-Jewish polemics are at stake (Q 2:87–89; 4:46, 155–157; 5:70; 19:27–33).

f) *This Jesus, delivered up according to the definite plan and foreknowledge of God, you crucified and killed by the hands of lawless men. God raised him up, loosing the pangs of death, because it was not possible for him to be held by it."*
Of course, in the Qur'ān, the "lawless men"—the Romans—are absent. But the accusation is the same: Acts 2:23 claims that the Jews (some Jews, rather) are responsible for the death of Jesus; in the Qur'ān, the Jews accuse themselves— or rather pride themselves— of having killed Jesus in a famous but unclear and controversial passage:

> So for their breaking of the covenant, and their disbeliefs in the signs of God, and their killing the prophets without any right, and their saying, "Our hearts are uncircumcised" – No! God set a seal on them for their disbelief, so they do not believe, except for a few – and for their disbelief, and their saying against Mary a great slander, and for their saying, "Surely we killed the Messiah, Jesus, son of Mary, the messenger of God" – yet they did not kill him, nor did they crucify him, but it (only) seemed like (that) to them (*wa-lākin shubbiha lahum*)." (Q 4:155–157)

35 Pohlmann forthcoming.

Much has been written about these verses, from the *topos* of Jews as killers of the prophets,[36] to the understanding of the formula *wa-lākin shubbiha lahum*. For most scholars (and the mainstream Islamic tradition), the text means that Jesus did not really die on the cross, and that a substitute was crucified instead of him (or that the whole event was a sort of collective hallucination). However, various Qur'anic passages refer to Jesus' death (Q 3:55; 5:17, 75, 116–118; 19:33) and resurrection (Q 3:55; 19:33). It seems, therefore, that there are three possibilities: a) consider that the Qur'ān displays a docetist understanding of crucifixion and therefore interpret metaphorically the passages that refer to Jesus' death (the majority view, to my mind highly questionable); b) consider that the Qur'ān admits Jesus' real death on the cross throughout all its layers and therefore interpret Q 4: 155–157 in a resolutely non-docetist way, namely: Jesus was really crucified, but the Jews thought they had the real power to make him die, whereas this was only God's decision to make Jesus die that was really determinative here;[37] c) consider that some layers affirm Jesus' real death and some do not, since the Qur'ān is a corpus that might display different conceptions of Jesus.

I will not decide here between the last two options. I only want to point out that in some passages the Qur'ān displays an understanding of Jesus' death that is consonant with Acts 2:23–24:

> No positive effect is ascribed to the death of Jesus; this is characteristic of Acts as a whole (. . .). He was wickedly killed by a conspiracy of Jews and Gentiles, but God (who, as the OT shows, had foreseen both the conspiracy and his response to it) did not allow this to be the last word and appointed the apostles as witnesses of the fact that he had raised Jesus from the dead.[38]

No positive (soteriological) effect is ascribed in the Qur'ān to Jesus' death either, as can be seen in the following passage, where it is hard *not* to see the sameness with Acts:

> They (the Jews) schemed, but God schemed (too), and God is the best of the schemers. (Remember) when God said, 'Jesus! Surely I am going to make you die (*'innī mutawaffika*) and raise you to Myself (*wa-rāfi'uka 'ilayya*), and purify you from those who disbelieve. And I am going to place those who follow you above those who disbelieve until the Day of Resurrection. (Q 3:54–55)

36 See Reynolds 2012.
37 See Reynolds 2009; Mourad 2011.
38 Barrett 1994, 131.

Some Reflections

What should we make of all this? Roughly, we can find the skeleton of the Qur'anic Jesus in just one brief New Testament passage, which accounts for most of what the Qur'ān tells about Jesus. Otherwise, some Qur'anic pericopes focus on Jesus' conception and birth—certainly a very sensitive topic inside the "proto-Qur'anic" communities. Moreover, several Qur'anic verses (mainly, but not only, from Luke and Acts) complete the picture of the Qur'anic Jesus by adding various details and elements to this skeleton. Most of these elements are *scripturally warranted*:

Jesus heals the blind and the leper (Q 3:49; 5:110): see, for example Luke. 18:35–43; Mark 8:22–26, 10:46–52; John 9:1–15; Matt 9:27–31 (the blind); Mt 8: 1–4; Mark 1:40–45; Luke 5:12–16, 17:11–19 (the leper).

Jesus gives life to the dead (Q 3:49; 5:110): a common topic in Christian literature (see Luke 7:11–17, 8:40–56). I take Q 5:110, with its peculiar formulation (*wa-'idh tukhriju l-mawtā*, "when you make the dead go out"), to refer specifically to the resuscitation of Lazarus (John 11:17–44).

Jesus confirms the Torah (Q 3:50; 5:46; 61:6): what is meant exactly here is not clear. Strictly speaking, it can mean that the prophecies of the Torah are accomplished through Jesus, or it can mean that Jesus does not abolish the Law (see, e.g., Matt 5:17–18). Indeed, according to the Qur'ān, Jesus permits his followers things that were not permitted before (i.e., to the Sons of Israel; Q 3:50; cf. 4:160), or informs his followers what to eat (Q 3:49). Here, we have striking parallels with the *Didascalia*[39]—something which, to my mind, does not prove the presence of a Jewish Christian community behind the Qur'ān, but rather hints to debates within or around "proto-Qur'anic" communities, between people of different backgrounds and competing attitudes to dietary laws, these debates finding their solutions in ways akin to those found earlier in similar contexts such as the *Didascalia*.

Jesus informs his followers what to store in their houses (Q 3:49), a possible allusion to Lk 12:13–34.

Jesus is also the main character in the *mā'ida* miracle (Q 5:112:15), a transposition of elements from Ps 78:19 (see Exod 16–17) to a context recalling John 6:22–71.

Jesus is a servant of God (Q 4:172; 5:72, 117; 19:30; 43:59): see Acts 3:13; 4:27.

39 See Zellentin 2013, 127–154.

Jesus is a prophet (Q 19:30): see Matt 13:57, 21:11; Mark 6:4; Luke 4:24, 7:16, 13:33, 24:19; John 4:19, 44; 6:14; 7:40; 9:17.

If we wish to gain a clearer picture of the process involved in the making of the Qur'anic Jesus, I think we should consider the following points.

First, we should acknowledge how much the Qur'anic Jesus is a strange and exceptional figure compared to other biblical figures. There are various layers in the Qur'ān, and the figure of Jesus, as well as the variations in the attitudes towards Christians, are extremely relevant criteria for determining different strata of the Qur'anic corpus as well as providing clues about the building of the confessional identity of the movement of the *mu'minūn* and its relations with Jews and Christians.

Second, the Qur'anic Jesus is often used as a polemical figure (which is not completely surprising, since the Qur'ān itself is a very polemical text): systematically in relation to the Jews, sometimes in relation to the Christians. In other words, it seems that some producers of the Qur'anic corpus were more interested in the use of Jesus as a polemical weapon than, for example, in the teachings of Jesus.

Third, there is much evidence of several reworkings inside the Qur'ān of texts, narratives, and tenets related to Jesus. This is a sign of debates inside the proto-Qur'anic community, and also a sign of deep interactions with (mainstream) Christians (interactions that might very possibly have taken place after Muḥammad's death and the conquests[40]).

Fourth, it is very probable that early in the history of the proto-Qur'anic community there was a kind of unitarian (or better, non-trinitarian) sensitivity.[41] At one side of the spectrum, several Qur'anic passages (e.g. Q 19:1–33 and Q 3:33–63) try to achieve a kind of convergence between this non-trinitarian sensitivity and higher conceptions of Jesus[42] (strikingly, through anti-Jewish polemics). Such pericopes were written by people having a good knowledge of Christianity and Christian Scriptures—in a word, *literati* with a Christian background. At the other side of the spectrum, there are polemical passages that do not necessarily display a good command of Christian doctrines (see e.g., "God did not take a son" in Q 2:116; 17:111; 18:4; 19:35, 88–92; 21:26; 23:91; 25:2; 39:4; 72:3), and simply amount to a rejection of a basic Christian dogma. However, in between these two extremities are

---

40 See Pohlmann 2012, Pohlmann forthcoming, Dye 2012, Dye forthcoming.

41 See also the remarks in Wood forthcoming, about non-trinitarian tendencies in 7th century Iraq. The non-trinitarian sensitivity in the Qur'ān might be a possible reaction to the preaching of Christian missionaries. For some reflections on this explanatory model (reinterpretation/misinterpretation of the teaching of missionaries), see Dye 2019, 781–83.

42 See Dye forthcoming.

many passages, neither explicitly converging with nor explicitly polemical against Christians, which articulate a picture of Jesus that is consonant with the non-trinitarian sensitivity mentioned above yet grounded in Scriptural formulas. In other words, the authors of such texts knew how to use (Christian) Scripture as a thematic, symbolic, and formulaic repertoire, which they could use to subvert competing views of Jesus and support their own. Possibly, they felt the need to justify their own view of Jesus against the discourse, arguments, and objections of Christians. Only a small part of these debates is known to us, but we have good reasons to think that Acts 2:22–24 played a crucial role in this process.

References

Amir-Moezzi, Mohammad Ali. 2018. "Muḥammad the Paraclete and ʿAlī the Messiah: New Remarks on the Origins of Islam and of Shiʿite Imamology." *Der Islam* 95.1:30–64.

Amir-Moezzi, Mohammad Ali, and Guillaume Dye, eds. 2019. *Le Coran des historiens. Vol. 1: Études sur le contexte et la genèse du Coran. Vols. 2a et 2b: Commentaire et analyse du texte coranique.* Paris: Éditions du Cerf.

Andrae, Tor. 1955. *Les origines de l'Islam et le christianisme*, trans. Jules Roche. Paris: Adrien-Maisonneuve.

Barrett, Charles Kingsley. 1994. *A Critical and Exegetical Commentary on The Acts of Apostles. Volume 1: Preliminary Introduction and Commentary on Acts I-XIV.* Edinburgh: T&T Clark.

de Blois, François. 2002. "*Naṣrānī* (*Ναζωραῖος*) and *ḥanīf* (*ἐθνικός*): Studies in the Religious Vocabulary of Christianity and Islam." *Bulletin of the School of Oriental and African Studies* 65.1:1–30.

Droge, A. J. 2013. *The Qur'ān: A New Annotated Translation.* Sheffield: Equinox Publishing.

Dye, Guillaume. 2012. "Lieux saints communs, partagés ou confisqués : aux sources de quelques péricopes coraniques (Q 19 :16–33)." In *Partage du sacré : transferts, dévotions mixtes, rivalités interconfessionnelles*, edited by Isabelle Depret and Guillaume Dye, 55–121. Bruxelles-Fernelmont: EME.

Dye, Guillaume. 2018. "Jewish Christianity, the Qur'ān, and Early Islam: Some Methodological Caveats." In *"Jewish Christianity" and Early Islam. Papers presented at the Eighth Annual ASMEA Conference*, edited by Francisco del Rio Sanchez, 11–28. Turnhout: Brepols.

Dye, Guillaume. 2019. "Le corpus coranique: contexte et composition." In *Le Coran des historiens*, edited by Mohammad Ali Amir-Moezzi & Guillaume Dye, vol. 1, 733–846. Paris: Éditions du Cerf.

Dye, Guillaume. Forthcoming. "The Qur'ānic Mary and the Chronology of the Qur'ān." In *Early Islam: The Sectarian Milieu of Late Antiquity?*, edited by Guillaume Dye.

Gallez, Édouard-Marie. 2005. *Le messie et son prophète. Aux origines de l'islam*, vol. 2, Versailles : Éditions de Paris.

Gallez, Édouard-Marie. 2008. "'*Gens du Livre*' et *Nazaréens* dans le Coran: qui sont les premiers et à quel titre les seconds en font-ils partie?" *Oriens christianus* 92:174–186.

Griffith, Sidney H. 2011. "*Al-Naṣārā* in the Qur'ān: A Hermeneutical Reflection." In *New Perspectives on the Qur'ān. The Qur'ān in its Historical Context 2*, edited by Gabriel Said Reynolds, 301–322. London: Routledge.

Griffith, Sidney H. 2015. "The Qur'ān's 'Nazarenes' and Other Late Antique Christians: Arabic-Speaking 'Gospel People' in Qur'ānic Perspective." In *Christsein in der islamischen Welt. Festschrift für Martin Tamcke zum 60. Geburstag*, edited by Sidney H. Griffith and Sven Grebenstein, 81–106. Wiesbaden: Harrassowitz Verlag.

Haddad, Yvonne Yazbeck. 1977. "An Exegesis of Sura Ninety-Eight." *Journal of the American Oriental Society* 97.4:519–530.

Irons, Charles Lee, Danny André Dixon, and Dustin R Smith. 2015. *The Son of God. Three Views of the Identity of Jesus*, foreword by James F. McGrath. Eugene: Wipf & Stock.

Jervell, Jacob. 1972. "The Divided People of God: The Restoration of Israel and Salvation for the Gentiles." In *Luke and the People of God: A New Look at Luke-Acts*, 41–74. Minneapolis: Augsburg Publishing House.

Jullien, Christelle, and Florence Jullien. 2002. "Aux frontières de l'iranité: "*nāṣrāyē*" et "*krīstyonē*" des inscriptions du *mobad* Kirdīr: enquête littéraire et historique." *Numen* 49:282–335.

Mourad, Suleiman A. 2011. "Does the Qur'ān Deny or Assert Jesus' Crucifixion and Death?" In *New Perspectives on the Qur'ān. The Qur'ān in its Historical Context 2*, edited by Gabriel Said Reynolds, 349–57. London: Routledge.

Mulsow, Martin. 2010. "Socinianism, Islam and the Radical Uses of Arabic Scholarship." *Al-Qanṭara* 31.2:549–86.

Oliver, Isaac. Forthcoming. "The Historical-Critical Study of Jewish, Christian, and Islamic Scriptures." In *Early Islam: The Sectarian Milieu of Late Antiquity?*, edited by Guillaume Dye.

Pohlmann, Karl-Friedrich. 2015. *Die Entstehung des Korans. Neue Erkenntnisse aus Sicht der historisch-kritischen Bibelwissenschaft*, 3rd ed. (2012). Darmstadt: WBG.

Pohlman, Karl-Friedrich. 2019. "Commentaire de la sourate 7." In *Le Coran des historiens*, edited by Mohammad Ali Amir-Moezzi and Guillaume Dye, vol. 2a, 271–334. Paris: Éditions du Cerf.

Pohlmann, Karl-Friedrich. Forthcoming. "Conversion from Jewish and Christian Milieus to Islam and Its Influence on the Formation of the Qur'ān." In *Early Islam: The Sectarian Milieu of Late Antiquity?*, edited by Guillaume Dye.

Räisänen, Heikki. 1980. "The Portrait of Jesus in the Qur'ān: Reflections of a Biblical Scholar." The Muslim World 70:122–133.

Reynolds, Gabriel Said. 2001. "Jesus, the Qā'im and the End of the World." *Rivista degli studi orientali* 75:55–86.

Reynolds, Gabriel Said. 2009. "The Muslim Jesus: Dead or Alive?" *Bulletin of the School of Oriental and African Studies* 72.2:237–258.

Reynolds, Gabriel Said. 2012. "On the Qur'ān and the Theme of Jews as 'Killers of the Prophets'." *Al-Bayān – Journal of Qur'ān and Ḥadīth Studies* 10:8–32.

Reynolds, Gabriel Said. 2014. "On the Presentation of Christianity in the Qur'ān and the Many Aspects of Qur'anic Rhetoric." *Al-Bayān – Journal of Qur'ān and Ḥadīth Studies* 12:42–54.

Segovia, Carlos A. 2019. *The Qur'anic Jesus. A New Interpretation*. Berlin: de Gruyter.

Shoemaker, Stephen J. 2003. "Christmas in the Qur'ān: The Qur'ānic Account of Jesus' Nativity and Palestinian Local Tradition." *Jerusalem Studies in Arabic and Islam* 28:11–39.

Shoemaker, Stephen J. 2018. "Jewish Christianity, Non-Trinitarianism and the Beginnings of Islam." In *"Jewish Christianity" and Early Islam. Papers Presented at the Eighth Annual ASMEA Conference*, edited by Francisco del Rio Sanchez, 105–16. Turnhout: Brepols.

Sinai, Nicolai. 2017. "The Eschatological Kerygma of the Early Qur'an." In *Apocalypticism and Eschatology in the Abrahamic Religions, 6th–8th Centuries*, edited by Hagit Amirav, Emmanouela Grypeou, and Guy Stroumsa, 219–66. Leuven: Peeters.

Tannous, Jack. 2018. *The Making of the Medieval Middle East: Religion, Society, and Simple Believers*. Princeton: Princeton University Press.

Tardieu, Michel. 2019. "Le manichéisme: recherches actuelles." In *Le Coran des historiens*, edited by Mohammad Ali Amir-Moezzi and Guillaume Dye, vol. 1, 467–95. Paris: Éditions du Cerf.

Van der Velden, Frank. 2007. "Konvergenztexte syrischer und arabischer Christologie: Stufen der Textentwicklung von Sure 3, 33–64. *Oriens Christianus* 91:164–203.

Witztum, Joseph. 2011. *The Syriac Milieu of the Qur'ān: The Recasting of Biblical Narratives*. PhD diss., Princeton University.

Wood, Philip. Forthcoming. "Christianity in the Arabian Peninsula." In *Early Islam: The Sectarian Milieu of Late Antiquity?*, edited by Guillaume Dye.

Zellentin, Holger. 2013. *The Qur'ān's Legal Culture: The Didascalia Apostolorum as a Point of Departure*. Tübingen: Mohr Siebeck.

Julien Decharneux

The Natural Theology of the Qur'ān and Its Late Antique Christian Background: A Preliminary Outline

Introduction

As William Graham rightly stated, "in the Qur'anic message, nature is the most manifest token of the majesty and sovereignty as well as the bounty and mercy of God."[1] Indeed, one of the most recurring themes in the Qur'ān is certainly the idea that Creation overflows with "signs" hinting at the existence of the divine Creator. This Qur'anic particularity, which can be named the Qur'anic natural theology, encourages the aspiring believer to contemplate[2] the universe and its natural phenomena so as to grasp the existence of the Creator hidden behind, or rather beyond, the material world.

In this paper, I would like to provide some background to this Qur'anic natural theological framework in focusing on the Christian tradition of natural contemplation. Although one can certainly find its premises in Scripture already (e.g., Rom 1: 18–23), natural theology as such slowly started flourishing in the 2nd century among Christian writers and steadily developed between the 4th and the 7th centuries, especially in Syriac Christian writings, which are of great interests for us here.

I will argue that the Qur'anic development of a natural epistemology of the divine should be read in light of these late antique Christian traditions in which natural contemplation played a key role. Despite attempts to highlight subtexts of various cosmological pericopes (cf. *infra*), I do not find in modern scholarship any real attempt to resituate the very natural theology of the Qur'ān within the broader spectrum of late antique Christian natural theological systems. Departing from the seemingly tacit agreement among Qur'anic scholars that the Christian and Jewish

1 Graham 2010, 111.

2 Although the word "contemplation" can conjure up the idea of transcending the object in question so as to grasp the metaphysical reality hiding behind it, I use it here in the broader sense of "meditation". Part of the debates surrounding the contemplative activity in late antique Christianity precisely touched upon the issue of whether the contemplator needed to observe and meditate upon natural or scriptural objects or more strenuously inquire and aim at the higher reality behind them (cf. *infra*).

Julien Decharneux

https://doi.org/10.1515/9783110675498-008

influences in the Qur'ān can only be suggested by means of *textual* parallels, the major goal of this preliminary survey is to suggest that the Qur'anic natural theological model *structurally* hinges upon the natural theological tradition that slowly developed from the $2^{nd}/3^{rd}$ century onwards in the Christian world. Although my objective is foremost to highlight the theological framework within which the Qur'ān looks at nature and show its homology with the late antique natural theological tradition, I will also look into some specificities of the natural theology of the Qur'ān which might help pin down the source through which the Qur'anic authors came to be acquainted with this particular Christian worldview.

I do not claim to offer here a comprehensive study of the late antique background to the Qur'anic natural theology. My main goal is rather to signal new trails in the study of the origin of the Qur'ān and to flag aspects of the text that might benefit from this approach, pending deeper investigations. In the first part of my article, I offer a broad outline of the Qur'anic natural theology. The second section is dedicated to a quick summary of the Christian natural contemplation from Clement and Origen of Alexandria until the 7th century. After highlighting similar patterns in both traditions, I turn towards more precise Qur'anic motifs that I see particularly connected to specific authors and texts admonishing natural contemplation in the immediate centuries preceding the emergence of the Qur'ān. Section 3 focuses on the central notion of signs in the Qur'ān, while section 4 looks at the use of scribal and scholastic metaphors to describe Creation.

Qur'ānic Natural Theology

To begin with, it should be stressed that the Qur'anic cosmology is eminently *theological*. Although the Qur'ān repeatedly alludes to the cosmos and its natural phenomena, it very seldom describes them. On the contrary, a close scrutiny of the text indicates that the Qur'anic interest in the universe is mostly – though not solely – motivated by the assumption that the universe reflects God's bounty, sovereignty, and more broadly God's role as supreme Creator. Within this theological framework, the universe is regarded as providentially ordered to the benefit of human beings, whose main purpose in life is to acknowledge the immanent presence of God in the natural order. Accordingly, the universe is nothing but a sum of natural wonders through which the single, merciful, and almighty Creator reveals himself to those willing to open their eyes to the truth. The Qur'ān thus constantly invites its audience to contemplate nature so as to gain knowledge of the divine.

This natural theological thought is mainly expressed by means of the so-called "sign-passages", pericopes typically presenting themselves as lists of cosmological phenomena. Though not systematically, these phenomena are often described as "signs" (*āyāt*)[3] hinting both at the sovereignty of God over Creation and the divine grace bestowed upon humankind through the supplying of everything needed for its sustenance. These passages are quite numerous, vary in length (see for instance Q 16:3–16 for one of the longest examples of the genre), and typically enumerate any kind of natural objects, from the most glorious and elevated cosmical items to the most insignificant ones: the sky, the earth, the sun, the moon, stars, the night and the day, rains, seas and water in general, mountains, the trees, livestock, camels, fruits, date-palms, grains, herbs, husk, fishes, and so on.

On the one hand, these *āyāt* attest to God's sovereignty (*mulk*) over the universe (e.g., Q 3:189–91; 10:5–6; 13:2–4; 34:9; 45:1–6). The signs show God's rule over the cosmos since God did not only create the cosmic phenomena mentioned but also sustains them,[4] and will destroy them in due time before their final re-creation. On the other hand, the divine *āyāt* in the universe also prove God's grace and mercy (*niʿma, faḍl, raḥma*) towards humans, for God created nature in such a perfect fashion that it constantly provides humankind with its necessary sustenance: rain makes crops, fruits, and grains grow, darkness allows humans to rest, shade provides natural shelters from the sun rays, and so forth.[5]

It is important, as Graham notes, to understand that in the Qur'ān "nature not only reflects the handiwork of God", but "*exists* to do so; its *raison d'être* from the Qur'anic viewpoint is to remind humankind of God's sovereignty, bounty, and mercy, and to serve as constant admonition to humans to recognize the power of God that will bring ultimately the world to its end."[6] It is indeed God who shows signs to humans "on the horizons and in themselves" (Q 41:53; cf. 51:20–1). The human ability to grasp the divine in Creation is therefore not merely a logical consequence of the divinely created universe. More specifically, the universe was conceived in order that humankind finds the divine in it. Creation serves the purpose of putting humankind to the test and see who among them is grateful and worships God after having witnessed God's *āyāt* (Q 11:7; 18:7–8; 67:2).

---

3 A natural phenomenon acting as a sign is mostly called an *āya* (pl. *āyāt*), but can also be named *bayyina* or *ʿibra* ("lesson"; Q 3:13; 12:111; 16:66; 23:21; 24:44; 79:26; see Abrahamov 2006, 2–11).

4 E.g., Q 3:189–91; 6:95–99; 10:6; 16:77–83; 30:46–53; 31:31; 36:33–47; 42:29–35; 45:1–6; 47:37–39; 57:2–6.

5 Graham 2010, 114–15.

6 Graham 2010, 124.

The recognition (or lack thereof) of God's signs clearly has soteriological implications. Those who accept the underlying presence of God in the natural phenomena described, will enjoy eternal rewards in the afterlife, whereas those who deny them are simply considered *kāfirūn* ("unbelievers") and regularly scolded and promised hellfire (e.g. Q 3:70; 17:89; 21:1–10; 30–33, or the integral Q 45). As said above, God's manifest role of Creator points towards the divine ability to recreate and thus to God's dominion not only over the present world but also over the next one: protology points towards eschatology (e.g., Q 22: 5–7; 23:12–22; 23:78–90; 67:14–26; 71:15–20). Hence, behind God's *āyāt* in the present world one can find comfort of the promised resurrection and salvation.[7]

The key role played by this concept of *āyāt* in the Qur'anic spiritual system can only be fully understood in encompassing its entire semantic range. Aside from obviously designating cosmic phenomena, the term *āyāt* also specifically characterizes other types of objects. On the one hand, the Qur'ān often designates the stories of the prophets as *āyāt*; on the other hand, it also very often characterizes the miracles performed by these prophets. We therefore see that the *āyāt* of God also encompass sacred history. Finally, *āyāt* is in a series of cases explicitly connected to the notion of Scripture. The word *āyāt* is indeed used in the Qur'anic text in the sense of "verses" or "pieces of his revelation" that supposedly hail from or form the heavenly *kitāb* ("Writing", "Scripture"), which contains God's universal knowledge and plan in Creation.

It appears to me, however, that when the text alludes explicitly to those "scriptural *āyāt*", it does not refer to specific objects, distinct from "cosmic phenomena" or "stories of the prophets." I take here for granted Daniel Madigan's study on the word *kitāb* in the Qur'ān, which in my eyes convincingly shows that *kitāb* does not refer to an actual physical book in the Qur'ān but is most likely used in a symbolical sense to designate God's knowledge, parts of which (the *āyāt*) are revealed and made accessible through Nature and sacred history to humankind. Thus, when the Qur'ān affirms that someone has been granted the *kitāb*, or part of the *kitāb* (cf. *min al-kitāb*), it does not refer to someone being granted a sacred heavenly book but it means rather that one is being "given some access to that divine realm where everything is 'written,' that is known and determined."[8] In other words, for the Qur'anic authors, gaining access to the *kitāb* means to have a glimpse through God's *āyāt* at God's salvific plan in Creation, that is the Divine Economy to use a Christian vocabulary. In this context, the *āyāt* of Nature (cosmic phenomena) and the *āyāt* of sacred history

7 Graham, 2010, 114–15.
8 Madigan 2001, 75–77.

(stories of the prophets, miracles, etc.) presumably constituted two means through which one gains access to this "divine knowledge," God's *kitāb*.

I will suggest below a possible source for the origin of this imagery of the heavenly *kitāb* as well as the notion of *āyāt*. For the time being, one should bear in mind that the Qur'ān regards God's *āyāt* as epistemological tools leading to a knowledge of God's plan in Creation. These divine signs are divided in two distinct realms (Nature and sacred history) pointing towards the same metaphysical reality. In the next section, I will show how in this regard the Qur'anic epistemology and its understanding of the access to the divine is in line with the natural and scriptural contemplative life among Christian writers as promoted from the 2nd/3rd century.

Natural and Scriptural *theôria* in Late Antique Christianity

To the modern reader, the listing of natural phenomena hinting at God's grace in the universe might look like a rather banal trope in ancient texts. Contemporary scholarship has drawn attention to the fact that such passages echo at times biblical and parabiblical writings. Tor Andrae, for instance, stressed that the "sign-passages" in the Qur'anic text, Q 16:3–18 in particular, reflected to a certain extent Ps 104, which invites the audience to the contemplation of divine good deeds in Creation.[9] It is likely that this type of psalmic "sign-passages" stands as the archetype of several other texts of the same trend in Christian and Jewish literature. Other examples of this genre would include, for instance, 1 Clement 19–26 or Acts 14:15–17, although none of these texts seem really closer than another to Qur'anic excerpts as Andrae himself already acknowledged.[10] What interests me here, however, is not the content of these "sign-passages" or even their peculiar genre but rather their function: urging people to contemplate the cosmos and acknowledge God's dominion over and grace in it.

Contemplation, of course, as a tool to acquire knowledge is deeply rooted in the Greek philosophical tradition. It is therefore not a surprise that as early as the late 2nd/beginning of the 3rd century philosophically-educated Christians such as Clement and Origen of Alexandria instrumentalized natural contemplation (*theôria physikê*) for their own theological purpose. Whereas *theôria* was limited in the

9 Andrae 1955, 172–80

10 Andrae 1955, 172–80; Pregill 2017, 193; cf. Decharneux 2019.

Greek philosophical tradition to physical (and metaphysical) objects, Christians considered early on that a second type of contemplation was indissociable from the first one. This second contemplation was the contemplation of Scriptures (*theôria graphikê*), in which God was revealed all the same.[11] In many different forms, Christian authors coming in the wake of Clement and Origen, even those formally opposed to the Alexandrian school of exegesis, always understood both Nature and Scripture as unavoidable and indivisible means to reach a knowledge of the triune Creator.

To be sure, the degree to which natural and scriptural contemplations related varied a great deal depending on the periods and authors in question. Clement of Alexandria, for instance, even though he considered the contemplation of the cosmos a helpful tool to grasp the divine, thought that a proper knowledge of Scripture was a prerequisite for rightly reading God's presence in the universe. Moreover, the status granted to natural and scriptural contemplation also differed depending on the authors. Origen and Clement thought that the interpretation of both Scripture and Nature in quest of knowledge (*epistemê*) was only a preliminary stage on the "heuristic journey," a prerequisite towards a different kind of "spiritual insight," *gnôsis*.[12] If this view was particularly emphasized later on, especially among ascetical and monastic writers, other thinkers, as we will see, had a less optimistic view of the accessibility to God's knowledge.

Apart from these differences, divine *theôria* through Creation (Nature) and sacred history (Scripture) abundantly developed from the 4th century onwards. Thinkers such as Ambrose of Milan and all three Cappadocian Fathers started considering the cosmos as an object of contemplation in its own right, parallel to the revealed Scripture, and constituting an "alternative witness to the history of salvation."[13] For example, in his *Homilies on the Hexaemeron*, Basil of Caesarea famously described the cosmos as an "amphitheater" (*theatron*) in which his congregants should not only be spectators but also side by him "as fellow combatants" so as to know themselves and know God (6:1).[14] Elsewhere he characterizes the cosmos as a training ground, a school, in which reasonable souls should exercise themselves to know God (1:6). Indeed, Basil and some of his contemporaries

11 Blowers 2012, 315–18.

12 Blowers 2008b, 149.

13 Blowers 2008a, 918.

14 Greek text in Giet 1968. For the English translation, see Way 2003. Basil's *Homilies on the Hexaemeron* was translated into Syriac soon after his death and was widely read in the Syriac world. Cf. Thomson 1995 for the Syriac text and its translation. On the Cappadocian Fathers in the Syriac tradition, see for instance Taylor 2007.

regarded not only the universe but also human nature itself as the place where one could contemplate God's creative and redemptive activity.[15] For these authors the universe is not merely an object of simple wonderment (*thauma*) but has become an object of ascetic practice towards the reaching of the knowledge of God and thus the grasping of the divine plan for Creation.

Natural and Scriptural contemplations were not only encouraged in the liturgical and homiletical contexts in which the Cappadocians Fathers were writing. On the contrary, contemplating nature made even more sense in the context of monastic desert retreat that gained in popularity in the 4th and 5th century.[16] In fact, the idea of natural contemplation was particularly developed by two fourth-century "monastic," or "proto-monastic," writers who had a tremendous influence in the later period of Christian Late Antiquity up to the time of the emergence of the Qur'ān.

The first of these writers is of course Evagrius of Pontus, student of the Cappadocian Fathers and true Origenist, who developed a particularly complex system of natural contemplation that he regarded as a prerequisite for the contemplation of Scripture, especially Psalms, Proverbs, and Ecclesiastes.[17] It is not the place to describe in detail here Evagrius' intricate natural contemplative model, but it is worth noting that for him the purpose of natural contemplation was to grasp the underlying "spiritual principles" (*logoi*) present in Nature and in Scripture. He regarded these *logoi* as the imprints of the immanent Logos in the universe. In reaching them, through divine grace and strong ascetic practice, the gnostic was therefore able to gain knowledge of the Logos himself. Evagrius, however, thought that the contemplation of corporeal and incorporeal objects was only a first step in the spiritual life before reaching a stage where the contemplator could enjoy a more direct kind of contemplation of the divine, and eventually reach a stage of union with the Godhead (*theôsis*).[18]

In the Syriac world, a no less important writer independently developed a whole theology of nature. Perhaps writing a bit earlier than Evagrius, Ephrem of Nisibis too understood the universe as well as Scripture as media through which one could grasp the presence and a knowledge of the divine. Although Ephrem also integrated into his system of thought the possibility of a form of divinization of humanity through the process of divine contemplation, he neverthe-

15 Blowers 2008a, 918.
16 Blowers 2008a, 920.
17 Blowers 2008a, 920.,
18 Blowers 2008b, 154–66.

less emphasized the idea that God would remain a fundamentally hidden being, occasionally accessible through "points of revelation" or "revealed things" (*galyātā*) extant in Nature and in Scripture.[19]

I will develop aspects of these two authors' respective thoughts in subsequent sections. What seems important to emphasize here is that the impact of both Ephrem and Evagrius on the later Syriac Christianity was unprecedented. The effects of their influence were perhaps best felt in the East-Syrian Church, where both authors were abundantly read, studied, and, in the case of Evagrius, translated. To give a single example, the influence of these two writers was particularly tangible in the School of Nisibis, where the reception of Evagrius, Ephrem, and Neoplatonism gave rise to an original model of divine contemplation with which the Qur'ān shares several motifs.

In this section, my goal was to show that the Qur'anic call to observe God's signs in both cosmos and revelation seems, at least in broad outline, rooted in the late antique tradition of divine *theôria* that developed both in liturgical/homiletical and (proto-)monastic spheres. For authors such as Basil of Caesarea, Gregory Nazianzen, Ephrem, Evagrius of Pontus, and others coming in their wake (Narsai, Maximus the Confessor, etc.), Nature and Scripture were considered the two feet on which Christian *theology* stood. Through a path that is yet to be determined, it seems that the authors of the Qur'ān inherited this specific worldview to the extent that it transpires in the text as a fully integrated model.

The Signs of God

I highlighted above that the Qur'ān's urging call to find the divine in Nature and sacred history structurally corresponds to the Christian tradition of divine *theôria* that developed throughout Late Antiquity and that regarded both Nature and Scripture as the two inseparable means through which one could get to know the divine. In this Qur'anic divine epistemological model, the key notion is that of "signs", *āyāt*. The term *āya* is certainly not the only word that designates something like a divine sign in the Qur'ān (cf., for instance, *bayyina*) but the overflowing presence of this word in the Qur'ān (87 times in the singular and 291 times in the plural) and its occurrence within quite stereotypical formulas suggests that it was endowed in the Qur'anic authors' minds with a technical sense. I already mentioned above that it referred in the Qur'ān to stories of the

19 Brock 1992, 27–29.

prophets and cosmic phenomena. Besides, the Qur'ān often uses the notion of *āyāt* in the seemingly sense of "verse" or "piece of revelation," which has led scholars to think that the word *āya* in the Qur'ān has a twofold meaning: "sign" (cosmic or stories of the prophets) and "verse/piece of revelation". It should be emphasized, however, that these two meanings are not etymological but contextual. It is only because the word *āya* is frequently used in correlation with *kitab* and *qur'ān*, and in contact with verbs such as *talā* ("to recite")[20] that one infers a scriptural/textual/revelatory meaning for this term. From there, modern scholars posit the meaning of "verses" or "pieces of revelation" (somewhat teleologically, since this is the meaning that the word will eventually acquire later).

In fact, scholars agree that etymologically the term *āya* probably derives from the Syriac *ātā* and entered Arabic at an unknown stage. As Jeffery indicates, the semantic range of the word *āya* in the Qur'ān reflects quite closely the use of the word *ātā* in the Peshitta, where it translates both in the Septuagint and in the New Testament the Greek *sêmeion* ("sign"). For example, in Gen 1:14 and 9:12–17, the word *ātā* (pl. *ātūtā*) designates cosmic phenomena. In other passages the term also denotes miraculous signs hinting at God's presence (Exod 8:19; Deut 4:34; Ps 48:43), as well as tokens of prophetic activities (Exod 3:12; 1 Sam 10:7–9).[21] A key Syriac text using the term *ātā* is the Gospel of John and more precisely the section following the prologue, commonly known as the "Book of Signs" (John 1:19–12:50). This part of the book relates the signs that "are written [in the book] so that you may believe that Jesus is the Christ, the Son of God, and that believing you may have life in his name" (John 20:31).

Thus, the word *āya* in the Qur'ān maps fairly well the use of the word *ātā* in the Bible except for one particular meaning, which is the scriptural one. Indeed, to my knowledge, *ātā* is not used at all in the Peshitta to designate a "piece of the scripture," whereas it is explicitly so in the Qur'anic context. Why is it then that the Qur'ān seems so prompt to use the term *āyāt* in connection with the semantic field of scripture? One should of course not discard the possibility of a Qur'anic innovation here but it is noteworthy that a somewhat similar development can be observe in the Christian tradition under scrutiny.

The notion of "sign" is of course present in many late antique Christian writings across linguistic boundaries.[22] Among the Cappadocians, for instance, it is worth mentioning Gregory of Nyssa, who says in one of his speeches that

---

20 The expression "to recite the *āyāt* of God" occurs 31 times in the Qur'ān in various forms (Madigan 2001, 96).
21 Jeffery 1938, 72–73.
22 In the Latin world, the notion of *signa* is particularly developed by Augustine, for example Blowers 2012, 324–25.

during creation God left behind "signs" or "traces" (*gnôrismata*) in the cosmos and that these traces point towards the divine Creator.[23] But this notion is not developed as a key concept within Gregory's contemplative system. In fact, I have so far only come across two authors developing concepts endowed with a comparable technicity and used at a same frequency as the Qur'ān's use of the word *āyāt*: Evagrius of Pontus and Ephrem of Nisibis.

Under Origen's influence, Evagrius indeed developed in his ascetic writings the notion of *logoi*. This key concept, taken over later by Maximus the Confessor, is at the heart of Evagrius' contemplative model. The *logoi* as he understood it are the "principles" embedded in Nature and Scripture through which God, and more precisely the Logos, is made accessible. As a matter of fact, the *logoi* are the imprints left by Christ the Logos in Nature and Scripture, through which he is therefore immanent.[24] Evagrius distinguishes between two different kinds of *logoi*: those of rational beings and those of providence and judgement, both of which are sought through *theôria physikê*. Just as the universe is filled with these *logoi*, so does Scripture – and especially Psalms, Proverbs, and Ecclesiastes – contain *logoi* that reveal God's purpose in Creation and redemption.[25]

Though not equivalent, the Evagrian concept of *logoi* shares characteristics with the notion of *āyāt*. First of all, just as the word *āya* is used in the Qur'ān to refer to two different sorts of objects ("signs" and "pieces of revelation"), the Evagrian *logoi* enjoys in Greek a twofold meaning. On the one hand, it refers to the "constitutive principles" of things, which ascetics seek through contemplation, and, on the other hand, it simply means "words." Evagrius is aware of this ambiguity and, as we shall see in the next section, he willingly plays on it so as to create the sense that the "principles" of Creation are to be read as the "words" of a book.[26]

The second shared characteristic is that the *logoi* are understood to be extant not only in Nature and Scripture (*logoi* of providence and judgment) but also in humans (*logoi* of reasonable beings). This echoes passages of the Qur'anic text emphasizing the presence of *āyāt* in humans themselves. Signs are indeed said to be in the "chests of those who have been given knowledge" (*fī ṣudūr al-ladhīn ūtū al-ʿilm*), namely, among those who believe in the *āyāt* present

23 Blowers 2012, 315–18; 2016, 12.

24 Blowers 2012, 320–21.

25 Blowers 2008b, 163–64.

26 The word was often translated by *mellē* ("words") in Syriac. Nevertheless, the translation was not always so mechanical. The revised translation of Evagrius' *Gnostikos* for instance often has *sūkālē* ("intelligence", "reason"), but other words can be used as well. Cf. Guillaumont 1989, 29; 164–65.

in the "book" (*kitāb*) sent down by God (Q 28:45–52). Elsewhere, the Qur'ān also declares that God will show humans the "*āyāt* at the horizons and in themselves" (*fī al-afāq wa-fī anfusihim*; Q 41:53; 51:20–21), although this could also simply be an allusion to the creation of human beings and their reproduction.[27]

Nevertheless, both notions ultimately differ from one another. First of all, the Evagrian *logoi* constitute the signified of the contemplated objects whereas the Qur'ānic *āyāt* are merely signifiers. Secondly, for Evagrius the divine *logoi* are only accessible through a long "process of discernment engaging mind (*nous*), reason (*logos*), and even the lower affective faculties of desire (*epithymia*) and aversion (*thymos*)."[28] In the Qur'ān however, the access to the *āyāt* and the higher reality to which they are pointing is much more "democratic": anyone "who thinks, reflects, or ponders" can reach them. Perhaps this has to do with the fact that Evagrius writes for ascetics engaged in solitary life while the Qur'ān is more likely directed to a communal audience, thus promoting an easier access to divine knowledge.

Ephrem, as for him, also develops a precise terminology to designate objects worthy of contemplation in Nature and Scripture. He indeed often resorts to the notion of *galyātā*, literally "revealed things," to which he systematically opposes the notion of *kasyātā* ("hidden things"). Through these *galyātā*, the fundamentally and ultimately hidden God manifests himself and these points of divine self-manifestation therefore constitute what one should inquire in order to reach a knowledge of the Creator. The term *galyātā* is used several times in Ephrem's *Hymns on Faith* (2:9; 8:9; 9:4^2; 9:7; 23:8; 31:3; 35:10; 43:3; 47:4; 47:6; 47:12^2; 48:4^2; 76:11) and elsewhere in reference to both natural and scriptural objects.

Although, neither the Ephremian concept of *galyātā* nor the Evagrian concept of *logoi* fully maps the Qur'anic notion of *āyāt*, the fact that Qur'ān possesses a technical notion to designate the media through which the contemplator reaches divine knowledge already constitutes a distinctive feature that the Qur'ān shares with these two authors. Moreover, all three of these corpora conceive of Nature and Scripture as networks of signs through which God is made known to humans. The Qur'ān indeed repeatedly implies that these *āyāt* are sent, recited, and explained by God, who otherwise would not allow them to be visible (*idhn*; Q 13:38; 40:78).

Given the fact that both Ephrem and Evagrius were extremely influential throughout from the 5th to 7th centuries, one wonders how much their respective concepts of *galyātā* and *logoi* were taken over in subsequent ascetic writings. I do not find in the Syriac world any authors who seem to take over in particular

---

27 Droge 2013, 355 n. 13.
28 Blowers 2008b, 162.

Evagrius or Ephrem's vocabulary of *logoi* and *galyātā*. This, however, does not mean that they had fallen into disuse since, as we mentioned already, many read and commented on the works of these two authors during this period. Moreover, the depiction of Nature and Scripture as interfaces full of "signs" between the Creator and its creatures was still in vogue at the time of the Qur'ān's composition.

I noted above that scholars agree on the fact that the Qur'anic term *āya* is originally a loanword from the Syriac word *ātā*. It is quite striking therefore to note that in the *Cause of the Foundation of the Schools*, a central text of the late 6th century at the School of Nisibis, the very term *ātā* is employed in a technical sense that echoes quite closely the notion of *āyāt* and its twofold meaning in the Qur'ān. The *Cause of the Foundation of the Schools* is "a late sixth-century address to the incoming class at Nisibis that purports to give a history of education, beginning with God's instruction to the angels at the time of Creation and concluding with the tenure of Ḥenana of Adiabene, the head of the school at the time of the speech's composition."[29] It is difficult to determine precisely how impactful was the text of the *Cause*, but it appears that students and teachers in Nisibis were acquainted with its contents, which reflect the specific worldview taught and promoted there at the end of the 6th century.

The *Cause* lies in many ways at the intersection of several different traditions and systems of thought: Neoplatonism, Aristotelian logic, but also Evagrius of Pontus, Ephrem of Nisibis, and Theodore of Mopsuestia. The influence of the latter on the East-Syrian Church can hardly be overstated. As it is widely accepted, the fourth-century Antiochene thinker Theodore of Mopsuestia was indeed probably the most important theologian and exegete for the Church of the East. As many scholars have pointed out, the *Cause of the Foundation of the School* relies very much on Theodore of Mopsuestia's model of divine *paideia*, according to which the present world was seen as a providentially guided educational ground directed to and preparing for the world to come. Creation itself is regarded in this model as highly didactic insofar as it serves the purpose of testing the virtues of each person according to providentially granted rational faculties, bodies, and laws.[30] This understanding of Creation is also assumed by the Qur'ān, which describes the universe as a means to put humankind on trial and see who among them is grateful and worships God after having witnessed the *āyāt* (Q 11:7; 18:7–8; 67:2).[31]

---

29 Becker 2004, 174.

30 Becker 2006, 114.

31 Additionally, Theodore develops the idea that a human's ability to reason entails the capacity to choose between good and evil, and thus to prove his or her virtue in choosing good in

Developing the Theodorian metaphor of a divine classroom of Creation in which God taught the angels, the text compares the learning process of understanding the cosmos to the teaching of the reading of the alphabet to children:

> In a similar manner we have a practice, after we have a child read the simple letters (*ātwātā pšīṭātā*) and repeat them, we join them one to another and from them we put together names that he may read syllable by syllable and be trained. Thus also that eternal teacher did, after he had them [angels] repeat the alphabet, then he arranged it [the alphabet] with the great name of the construction of the firmament and he read it in front of them that they might understand that he is the creator of all of them, and as he orders them, they complete his will, and because they are quick-witted, they receive teaching quickly. (*Cause* 349; Syr. Scher 1981, 349; Eng. Becker 2008, 118–19)

We see here the strategy of the text which consists in metaphorically speaking of the cosmos as a divine arrangement of letters. This metaphor runs through the entire passage so as to create the impression that God's creative process is one of "performative writing." The universe is God's written text. I will return in the next section to this very imagery but what seems particularly important to emphasize here is the expression *ātwātā pšīṭātā* used to designate the "simple letters."

It is likely, as Adam Becker argues, that the expression *ātwātā pšīṭātā* is originally a calque of the Greek *ta hapla stoicheia* used in Greek physics. What interests us, however, is the pun in the Syriac text itself. The term *ātwātā* used in this passage of the *Cause* has in fact a twofold meaning since it is the plural of two distinct words. On the one hand, *ātwātā* is the plural of the word *ātūtā*, which designates "a sign, a character, or a letter of the alphabet." On the other hand, it is also the plural of *ātā*, which means "sign" or "mark," the scriptural use of which has already been discussed earlier.[32]

The twofold meaning of the term *ātwātā* comes out at two different levels. On the basic level, God writes letters in the universe and teaches them. The universe itself is a revelation, a divine Scripture. On the second level, however, these "simple letters" shown to angels are also the "signs" of God, that is, the divine immanence in the cosmos through natural phenomena. In using the

---

the present world. This Theodorian idea evidently found its way into the text of the *Cause of the Foundation of the School*, as Becker showed (2006, 118–20), and I would see an extension of this reasoning in the multiple Qur'anic formulaic expressions alluding to the fact that the natural phenomena are clear divine signs for a "people who ponder" (*li-qawmin ya'qilūn*; Q 2:164; 13:4; 16:12; 16:67; 29:35; 30:24; 30:28; 45:5) or "for a people who reflect" (*li-qawmin yatafakkarūn*; Q 10:24; 13:3; 16:11; 30:21; 39:42; 45:13). In this way, the text implies that humans out of freewill choose evil in denying the divine character of the signs.

32 Becker 2006, 131–32.

ambiguous word *ātwātā*, the literary purpose of the writer of the *Cause* is in fact to make the distinction between Nature and Scripture implode so as to create a sense that Nature does not disclose God's knowledge differently than Revelation but rather that Nature and Scripture are one and the same.

This seems like quite an unbelievable coincidence that the term *āyāt* in the Qur'ān is used in a similar twofold meaning as the word *ātwātā* in the text of the *Cause*. Not only is there a structural homology between the referents of both terms, but both words are etymologically linked since the word *āyāt* is originally a loanword from the singular form of the Syriac *ātwātā*. To be sure, the term *ātwātā* is not as profusely used in the *Cause of the Foundation of the Schools* as *āyāt* is in the Qur'ān. Nonetheless, given that this text was seemingly a "classic" in the School of Nisibis, one wonders how much this metaphor could have impacted members of the institution.[33]

In any case, we see that the technical notion of *āyāt* is not devoid of antecedent in previous natural theological systems. Sharing functional characteristics with the Evagrian *logoi* and the Ephremian *galyātā*, the term *āyāt* also shares operative and striking linguistical aspects with the Syriac word *ātwātā* used in a central text at the School of Nisibis. The *Cause of the Foundation of the Schools* indeed plays on the polysemy of the word *ātwātā* so as to create the impression that the universe is in fact an arrangement of divine letters forming a book of Creation. This distinctive Nisibene feature results from the development of a broader motif rooted in the early Christian tradition already and with which the Qur'ān is apparently also acquainted.

---

33 One wonders whether this new insight on the potential origins and meanings of the word *āyāt* does not open up new vistas with regards to the famous "mysterious letters" put at the beginning of certain surahs in the Qur'ān. As a matter of fact, seven of the twenty-nine occurrences of these mysterious letters are followed by a clause of the type *tilka āyāt al-kitāb* ("these are the *āyāt* of the Scripture"; Q 10:1; 12:1; 13:1; 15:1; 26:2; 27:1; 28:2; 31:2; cf. also 41:2–3; 45: 2–3), while others do not mention the *āyāt* but do make reference to the *kitāb* (Q 2:2; 7:2, 32:2; 40:2; 43:2; 44:2; 46:2), more rarely to the *qur'ān* only (Q 20:2; 36:2; 38:1; 50:1), or simply to the notion of writing (Q 68). We therefore see that these mysterious letters are tightly connected to the semantic field of the act of writing or reciting. In light of what we have said of the word *āyāt* and *ātwātā* above, perhaps should we understand the word *āyāt* in expressions of the type *tilka āyāt al-kitāb* that often follow these isolated letters in the very sense of "letters" (Ar.: *āyāt* > Syr.: *ātwātā* > *atūtā* (sg.): "a sign", "a character", or "a letter of the alphabet"). Though this deserves much more investigation, the hypothesis is certainly worth pursuing, considering that these isolated letters remain an unsolved issue in modern scholarship.

The Classroom of Creation: When Nature is Revelation

Attention has been raised to the fact that the twofold meaning of the *āyāt* in the Qur'ān ("natural signs" and "verses, pieces of revelation") suggests a literary strategy aiming at identifying the cosmos to an open-air book one reads to learn about the Creator.[34] Although to my knowledge, the Qur'ān never makes explicit the comparison of the universe to a book, I find this idea quite compelling. Of course, many passages in which the word *āyāt* is used do not allow to determine whether it refers to scriptural or natural signs. Nevertheless, the Qur'ān seems very much aware of the two different uses it makes of this word, and in some cases we are left wondering whether it does not purposefully entertain its ambivalent meaning so as to create a sense that Nature and Scripture reflect one another. The Qur'ān indeed never makes explicit the ontological difference between scriptural signs and natural ones, but rather treats them as equals and even suggest their pointing towards the same metaphysical reality: the *āyāt* of heavens and earth (Nature) and the *āyāt* of the Revelation (sacred history) point towards God in a similar fashion. The beginning of Q 45 for instance is a good example where the word *āyāt* is used no less than nine times in both senses in the lapse of a few verses. It is worth quoting here verses 2 to 6, which present a particularly ambiguous use of the word *āyāt*:

> The sending down of the Book is from God, the Mighty, the Wise. Surely in the heavens and the earth (there are) *āyāt* indeed for the believers. And in your creation, and what He scatters of the creatures, (there are) *āyāt* for a people who are certain. And (in the) alternation of the night and the day, and what God sends down from the sky of (His) provision, and by means of it gives the earth life after its death, and (in the) changing of the winds, (there are) *āyāt* for a people who understand. Those are the *āyāt* of God. We recite them (*natlūhā*) to you in truth. In what (kind of) proclamation – after God and His *āyāt* – will they believe?[35]

Herein, the heaven and the earth, together with other cosmic natural objects and phenomena, are designated as *āyāt* (vv. 3–5). Yet, right after, the text affirms that these same signs are recited (*talā*) by God to the Qur'anic prophet. We are here left in some kind of *flou artistique* in which God's signs in nature are not seen or witnessed, shown or displayed, but recited and listened, as if the universe was itself revealed, or one should say, as if the universe was itself the Revelation. The example of Q 45, however, is quite unique in this regard.

---

34 Peterson 2001, 62–63; Graham 2010, 116.

35 Droge's translation slightly modified for the purpose of demonstration (2013, 337).

If the merging of Scripture and Nature is indeed what the Qur'ān seeks to achieve in designating as *āyāt* both items pertaining to sacred history and the cosmos, then it echoes a motif developed in the writings of several Christian writers treating divine *theôria*. The understanding of Creation and Revelation as two equal and indissociable means to reach a knowledge of God eventually led some late antique authors to identify the former to the latter. While Origen and the Cappadocians often compared Nature and Scripture to show their interrelation, the first explicit comparison of nature to a book in the Christian tradition seems to appear in Athanasius of Alexandria who affirms that Creation "as it were in writing, indicates and proclaims its master and maker."[36] Roughly at the same time, the two most influential champions of natural contemplation, Evagrius of Pontus and Ephrem of Nisibis, do not merely use the comparison of nature to a book but, so to say, genuinely "bookify" Creation. In his *Practicus*, Evagrius declares: "My book, O Philosopher, is the nature of [created] beings, and it is there when I want to read the words (*logoi*) of God".[37] Elsewhere, Evagrius compares Creation to written letters that once read allow for the grasping of the one who wrote them (*Epistula ad Melaniam* 2).[38] A similar imagery is used by Ephrem. In his *Hymns on Paradise*, for example, the Syrian metaphorically speaks of the "book of creation":

> The keys of doctrine, which unlock all Scripture's books, have opened up before my eyes the book of creation (*sefrā d-brītā*), the treasure house of the Ark, the crown of the Law. This is a book which, above its companions, has in its narrative made the Creator perceptible and transmitted His actions; it has envisioned all His craftsmanship, made manifest His works of art.[39] (6:1)

The comparison is repeated in his *Hymns on Faith*, where he also declares that "Nature is like the Scripture,"[40] (35:1) and both are said in many passages to reflect one another (e.g. *Hymns on Faith* 35:7; *Hymns on Paradise* 5:2–3; *Hymns against Heresies* 28:11; 38:4).

Evagrius and Ephrem's respective conceptions enjoyed further developments in later centuries among various authors. Around the time of the Qur'anic composition in the Greek-speaking world, Maximus the Confessor will take over Evagrius's imagery and build on it quite substantially.[41] In the Syriac-speaking world,

36 Blowers 2012, 318–19.
37 Sinkewicz 2003, 112 as quoted in Blowers 2012, 319. Mary Hansbury affirms that this passage is thought to be "the earliest mention of the 'book' of Creation" (1993, 209 n. 64).
38 Blowers 2012, 319.
39 Translation by Brock 1990, 108–9. For the Syriac text, see Beck 1957, 19.
40 Translation from Wickes 2015, 203 slightly modified. Syriac text in Beck 1955, 114.
41 Blowers 2012, 320–22.

Narsai, the famous founder and director of the School of Nisibis at the end of the 5th century, resorts to this motif in his *Homilies on Creation*. Having in mind Theodore of Mopsuestia's image of the God being a pedagogue for angels, he affirms:

> Through the six days, He taught them [the rational beings] the ordering of His power, and He made them skillful scribes by the work of His hands.
>
> They studied a learned book (*sefrā mhīrā*), in the Creation in front of them, and they started arranging with their intelligence the beings without discernment.[42] (5:137–140)

The motif of a "book of creation" flourishes several times in Narsai's *Homilies on Creation*. Whereas at one point he designates Creation as a "new book" (*sefrā ḥadtā*; 2:250–254), he also depicts Creation as a book "written in God's palm," which he calls the "book of His eternity" (*sefrā d-amīnūteh*; 5:451).[43]

This sort of imagery probably finds its roots in Ephrem already and will particularly develop in the School of Nisibis as attested by the *Cause of the Foundation of the Schools*.[44] We already saw that the author of the *Cause* subtly plays on the double meaning of the word *ātwātā* ("letters" and "signs") so as to convey the meaning that in writing letters God also creates "signs" in the universe. This literary strategy is made explicit when, in the same passage, the text mentions the creation of the firmament. God arranged letters of the alphabet to create "the great name of the construction of the firmament" and then read it in front of the angels (*Cause* 312).[45] Everything unfolds as if divine Creation was first the writing of the name of the created object and that its pronunciation by God in front of the angels made it come into being. God's role as pedagogue for humans is also emphasized in the text. The *Cause* indeed has God whisper in Adam to allow him to read "in this first tablet the names for all the domestic animals and for all the wild animals of the field and all the birds of the heavens" (*Cause* 353).[46]

---

42 My translation. Syriac text and French translation in Gignoux 1968, 646–47.

43 Gignoux 1968, 568–69; 664–65.

44 Brock 2017, 243–44.

45 Syriac text in Scher 1981, 349; English translation in Becker 2008, 119. The origin of this metaphor, as Becker argues, is doubtless Evagrius of Pontus who regularly uses the lexical field of "reading" and "writing" in relation to natural contemplation. In his *Letter to Melania*, for instance, Evagrius compares Creation to a letter (*ktībātā*) sent to communicate with someone from afar (Becker 2006, 131–33).

46 Syriac text in Scher 1981, 352; English translation in Becker 2008, 123. Note that, just as in the Qur'ān, it is not Adam who names the animals but God. Indeed, in the *Cause*, Adam is only responsible for reading the tablet on which God wrote the names beforehand. Similarly, this text shares with the Qur'ān and other parabiblical writings the idea that Satan was in fact an angel who rebelled against God.

Such a complex Creation imagery does not explicitly appear in the Qur'ān but it seems that the Arabic text was also keen on seeing God in the role of a pedagogue. It is, for instance, quite remarkable that one of the verbs most commonly associated with the term *āyāt* is *talā*, "to recite" (31 times). Connecting the notion of recitation with that of revelation or "verses" obviously makes sense but in the passage of Q 45 (cited above) *talā* is used to refer to cosmic signs as if both natural and scriptural signs could be recited all the same. Although Q 45 remains to my knowledge an isolated example; in many respects the Qur'ān still portrays a God with the characteristics of a pedagogue. Besides the fact that God is repeatedly described as "reciting" (*talā*) the signs, "bringing down" (*ātā*) the signs, and "explaining" (*faṣṣala*) them, God is also ascribed the role of "teaching" (*'allama*) in many passages (Q 2:31; 2:32; 2:39; 2:251; 2:282; 3:48; 4:113; 5:4; 5:110; 12:6; 12:21; 12:37; 12:68; 12:101; 18:65; 21:80; 36:69; 53:5; 55:2; 55:4; 96:4; 96:5).

In some cases, we come very close to the "classroom imagery" so specific to Narsai's writings and conveyed in the *Cause*.[47] In Q 96, for instance, God is said to "teach [humans] by the pen" (vv. 4–5) and Q 68 starts by an oath, with scholastic overtones, "By the pen and what they [angels] write" (v. 1). Considering the following passage in Narsai, one wonders if these Qur'anic verses do not owe something to the Nisibene tradition:

> As if with a finger he was showing them the power of his essence, "See, Angels, that I am the power over every power." As if with a pen (*ak d-b-qanyā*) he was writing them a book (*sefrā*) in the mind, and he was making them read syllable by syllable (or: meditate upon) the writings (*ktībātā*) of the creator of all.[48] (2:352-355)

To these metaphors, we can also add the fact that the Qur'anic God is very often described as a writing deity. Not only does the text tell us that God had written down from all eternity a plan for Creation, but God's writing activity is mentioned as an ongoing process in several passages.[49] Finally, it should be added that the notion of a divine *kitāb* concealing God's universal and absolute knowledge in the universe is central in the Qur'ān as we saw above.[50] This knowledge is often epitomized by the use of the word *ghayb* (literally "absence", "hidden"):

---

47 As Becker explains, although the *Cause* borrows from Theodore of Mopsuestia the whole idea of Creation as divine pedagogy, the rich imagery developed in Narsai and then the *Cause* of Creation as a classroom is not derived from Theodore but proper to them. Moreover, whereas Narsai only use this imagery as a comparison (i.e., Creation is *like* a classroom), the text of the *Cause* steps up and completely projects the school imagery on the Creation (Becker 2006, 124–25).

48 As translated by Becker (2006, 124). Syriac text in Gignoux 1968, 576–79.

49 See Madigan 2001, 107–17 for the precise references.

50 On the notion of *kitāb*, see Madigan 2001.

> With Him are the keys of the *ghayb*. No one knows them but Him. He knows whatever is on the shore and the sea. Not a leaf falls but He knows it. (There is) not a grain in the darkness of the earth, and nothing ripe or withered but (it is recorder) in clear Scripture (*kitāb mubīn*). (Q 6:59)

A similar idea occurs in Q 34:3:

> (He is the) Knower of the *ghayb*. Not (even) the weight of a speck in the heavens and the earth escapes from Him, nor (is there anything) smaller than that or greater, except (that it is) recorded in a clear Scripture. (*kitāb mubīn*)

Besides the depiction of God as a divine pedagogue, one could add that the Qur'ān at times, though not often, relies on metaphors relating to the semantic field of "writing" in the depiction of certain aspects of the cosmos. The speech of God, for instance, is compared to a sea of ink (Q 18:109; 31:27). In addition, trees are paralleled with pens (Q 31:27) and some passages compare the shape of the sky in the *eschaton* to "the rolling up of a scroll for the writings" (Q 21:104; 39:67; cf. also Is 34:4; Rev 6:14).[51]

I am tempted to draw a more specific parallel between the *Cause* and the Qur'ān. In the Syriac text, the world is said to be akin to an alphabet written on a tablet:

> As if upon a tablet (*lūḥā*), He wrote and composed all the visible bodies that it [mind] might read them and from them know that one who was the cause of this learning [. . .].[52] (*Cause* 345)

The image of the "tablet" used here and in several other passages of the same text,[53] is likely, as Becker suggested, to ultimately derive from Aristotle who had compared the human mind to a tablet.[54] Besides this, however, I find the idea of a Creation divinely engraved tablet quite intriguing. The Syriac word for "tablet" here is *lūḥā* and this calls to my mind the well-known *lawḥ maḥfūẓ* in which is said to be inscribed "a glorious recitation" (Q 85:22: *qur'ānan majīd*). Given the fact that the Qur'ān has a tendency to equate Creation and Revelation,

---

51 Note that scribal metaphors are used in various Syriac authors and texts of the 5th and 6th centuries: John of Apamea's *Dialogue on the Soul*, the *Teaching of Addai*, Philoxenus of Mabbug. Most importantly perhaps, Jacob of Sarugh also resorts to this imagery in his *Homilies against the Jews* and in a letter to Stephen bar Sudaili, coming very close from the *Cause*'s turns of phrases. There seem to be little doubt that the development of this scribal imagery originated in Edessa. See Becker 2006, 28–30 for the references to the various texts mentioned. For Jacob of Sarugh, see Frothingham 1886, 12; Albert 1976, 44–45; 120–23; 206–7.

52 Scher 1981, 345; Becker 2008, 113–14.

53 Becker 2008, 123^2–124^2; 128.

54 Becker 2006, 148.

could it be that the "Guarded tablet" of which the Qur'ān speaks has something to do with the tablet metaphors found in the *Cause*? This would certainly be a lead worth following.

In this section, I tried to show that the late antique Christian understanding of Nature and Scripture as two inseparable objects of contemplation through which one can gain knowledge of God made certain Christian thinkers see Nature as a mirror of Scripture and eventually led some of them to speak of nature as a book. Under the influence of previous literature, this conception seems to have reached another degree of importance in the School of Nisibis and gave rise to the depiction of Creation as a written piece composed and taught by God to created beings. Although this motif is not explicitly developed in the Qur'ān, in many respects a comparable imagery of God as pedagogue and of the cosmos as a classroom is definitely involved therein.

One wonders to what extent the presence of this imagery in the Qur'ān informs us of the socio-historical context in which the text saw the light of day. Concerning the Syriac texts and authors mentioned above, the cause of their resort to scribal terminology to describe Creation is easy to understand. As Becker puts it, "transformations above often conform to developments below."[55] The very institutional and scholastic setting in which these authors were writing and their texts were produced explains by itself the appetite for such scribal metaphors in their description of the universe. However, the *Sitz im Leben* of these Qur'anic metaphors is much less obvious: How did it end up in the Qur'ān? What does it tell us of its authors and/or their informants? And how were these images meaningful to the addressees of the text?

Conclusion

In this article, I tried to show that the Qur'ān shared with a whole current of the Christian late antique *theôria* the idea that both Nature (Creation) and Scripture/ Revelation (Sacred history) were regarded as the two means through which believers could train themselves to find God and acquire knowledge of the divine plan in Creation. Two goals, a major one and a minor one, were pursued in this regard. The main objective was to show at the macro-level the existence of a clear structural homology between the Qur'anic "contemplative model" and a certain Christian model of divine *theôria* that developed from Clement and Origen of Alexandria. This tradition flourished in the 4th century in the writings of various

55 2006, 125.

authors such as Ephrem and Evagrius, and carried on between the 5th and 7th centuries in various places, not least the School of Nisibis.

On the micro-level, I suggested a likely route by which this whole natural theological tradition might have reached the Qur'ān. Although this might perhaps have been a bit speculative, some specificities of the Qur'anic *theôria* find particular echoes with writings read in or related to the School of Nisibis, mostly Ephrem, Evagrius, Narsai, and the *Cause of the Foundation of the Schools*. The concept of *āyāt* and the representation of the universe as a readable book and a divine classroom echo similar tropes developed in the Nisibene rendition of natural theological tradition.

Far from being comprehensive, our survey aimed at opening up new perspectives with regards to the origin of the Qur'ān's theological cosmology. Several other motifs identified in the text would certainly reveal more connections with the Christian tradition of divine *theôria*, including the Qur'anic doctrine of God's incomprehensibility, the central and seemingly complex role of the messenger (*rasūl*), and other distinctive aspects of the Qur'anic contemplative system. Not unlike some of the authors mentioned in the previous pages, our article shows how a thorough contemplation of the Qur'ān in light of the *long* late antique Christian tradition will help future investigations lay hands on the origins and structure of the Qur'anic theological system.

Bibliography

Abrahamov, Binyamin. 2006. "Signs." In *Encyclopaedia of the Qur'ān*, edited by Jane Damen McAuliffe, 2–11. Leiden: Brill.

Albert, Micheline. 1976. *Jacques de Saroug: Homélies contre les Juifs*. Patrologia Orientalis 38/1. Turnhout: Brepols.

Andrae, Tor. 1955. *Les Origines de l'Islam et le Christianisme*. Paris: Adrien-Maisonneuve.

Beck, Edmund. 1955. *Des Heiligen Ephraem des Syres: Hymnen de Fide*. Corpus Scriptorum Christianorum Orientalium 154. Leuven: Imprimerie orientaliste L. Durbecq.

Beck, Edmund. 1957. *Des Heiligen Ephraem des Syrers: Hymnen de Paradiso und Contra Julianum*. Corpus Scriptorum Christianorum Orientalium 174. Leuven: E. Peeters.

Becker, Adam H. "Bringing the Heavenly Academy Down to Earth: Approaches to the Imagery of Divine Pedagogy in the East Syrian Tradition." In *Heavenly Realms and Earthly Realities in Late Antique Religions*, edited by Ra'anan S. Boustan and Annette Yoshiko Reed, 174–90. Cambridge: Cambridge University Press, 2004.

Becker, Adam H. 2006. *Fear of God and the Beginning of Wisdom: The School of Nisibis and Christian Scholastic Culture in Late Antique Mesopotamia*. Philadelphia: University of Pennsylvania Press.

Becker, Adam H. 2008. *Sources for the History of the School of Nisibis*. Liverpool: Liverpool University Press.

Blowers, Paul M. 2008a. "Doctrine of Creation." In *The Oxford Handbook of Early Christian Studies*, edited by Susan Ashbrook Harvey and David Hunter, 906–31. Oxford: Oxford University Press.

Blowers, Paul M. 2008b. "Entering 'this Sublime and Blessed Amphitheatre': Contemplation of Nature and Interpretation of the Bible in the Patristic Period." In *Interpreting Nature and Scripture: History of a Dialogue in the Abrahamic Religions*, edited by Jitse van der Meer and Scott Mandelbrote, vol. 1, 148–76. Leiden: Brill.

Blowers, Paul M. 2012. *Drama of the Divine Economy: Creator and Creation in Early Christian Theology and Piety*. Oxford: Oxford University Press.

Blowers, Paul M. 2016. "Beauty, Tragedy and New Creation: Theology and Contemplation in Cappadocian Cosmology." *International Journal of Systematic Theology* 18:7–29.

Brock, Sebastian. 1990. *Saint Ephrem: Hymns on Paradise*. Crestwood: St Vladimir's Seminary Press.

Brock, Sebastian. [1985] 1992. *The Luminous Eye: The Spiritual World Vision of Saint Ephrem*. Kalamazoo: Cistercian Publications.

Brock, Sebastian. 2017. "God as the Educator of Humanity: Some Voices form the Syriac Tradition." In *Jewish Education from Antiquity to the Middle Ages: Studies in Honour of Philip S. Alexander*, edited by George J. Brooke and Renate Smithuis, 236–51. Leiden/ Boston: Brill.

Decharneux, Julien. 2019. "La navigation dans le Coran: entre *Psaumes* et *topoï* tardo-antiques." *Acta Orientalia Belgica* 32:127–42.

Droge, Arthur J. 2013. *The Qur'ān: A New Annotated Translation*. Sheffield/Bristol: Equinox.

Frothingham, Arthur L. 1886. *Stephen bar Sudaili: The Syrian Mystic and the Book of Hierotheos*. Leiden: Brill.

Giet, Stanislas. 1968. *Basile de Césarée, Homélies sur l'Hexaéméron: texte grec, introduction et traduction*. Éditions du Cerf: Paris.

Gignoux, Philippe. 1968. *Homélies de Narsaï sur la Création: édition critique du texte syriaque, introduction et traduction*. Patrologia Orientalis 34. Turnhout: Brepols.

Graham, William A. 2010. "'The Winds to Herald His Mercy': Nature as Token of God's Sovereignty and Grace in the Qur'ān." In *Islamic and Comparative Religious Studies: Selected Writings*, 111–25. Farnham: Ashgate.

Guillaumont, Antoine. 1989. *Evagre le Pontique, Le Gnostique ou A celui qui est devenu digne de la science*. Paris: Éditions du Cerf.

Hansbury, Mary Teresa. 1993. "Nature as Soteric: Syriac and Buddhist Traditions." *ARAM* 5: 197–217.

Jeffery, Arthur. 1938. *The Foreign Vocabulary of the Qur'ān*. Baroda: Oriental Institute.

Madigan, Daniel. 2001. *The Qur'ân's Self-image: Writing and Authority in Islam's Scripture*. Princeton and Oxford: Princeton University Press.

Peterson, Daniel C. 2001. "The Language of God: Understanding the Qur'an." *BYU Studies Quarterly* 40/4:51–68.

Pregill, Michael. 2017. "Commentary on QS 16." In *The Qur'an Seminar Commentary: A Collaborative Study of 50 Qur'anic Passages*, edited by Mehdi Azaiez, Gabriel Said Reynolds, Tommaso Tesei, Hamza M. Zafer, 193. Berlin/Boston: De Gruyter.

Scher, Addai. 1981. *Mar Barḥadbšabba ʿArbaya, évêque de Halwan (Vie siècle): Cause de la Fondation des écoles*. Patrologia Orientalis 4/4. Turnhout: Brepols.

Sinkewicz, Robert E. 2003. *Evagrius of Pontus: The Greek Ascetic Corpus*. Oxford: Oxford University Press.

Taylor, David G. K. 2007. "Les Pères cappadociens dans la tradition syriaque." In *Les Pères grecs dans la tradition syriaque* (Études syriaques 4), edited by Andrea Schmidt and Dominique Gonnet, 9–26. Paris: Librairie Orientaliste Paul Geuthner.
Thomson, Robert W. 1995. *The Syriac Version of the Hexaemeron by Basil of Caesarea*. Corpus Scriptorum Christianorum Orientalium 550–551. Leuven: Peeters.
Way, Agnes Clare. 2003. *Saint Basil: Exegetic Homilies*. Washington: The Catholic University of America Press.
Wickes, Jeffrey T. 2015. *St. Ephrem the Syrian: The Hymns on Faith*. Washington: The University of America Press.

III Early Islam and the Qur’ān: Social, Political, and Religious Contexts

Gilles Courtieu and Carlos A. Segovia

Q 2:102, 43:31, and Ctesiphon-Seleucia

New Insights into the Mesopotamian Setting of the Earliest Qur'anic Milieu

1 Introduction: Q 2:102, Babylon, and Ctesiphon

By Late Antiquity, the onetime center of the earth, Babylon had all but vanished. It was just a small village surrounded by mud, ruins, and dust.[1] Its memory, though, had been both persistent and recurrent in the Judaeo-Christian imagery, where in fact Babylon is never innocent – nor are the references to it fortuitous: there is always something wicked, something bad, something vile about it. There is surely little need to recall here, for instance, the famous verses of the Book of Revelation where Babylon is attacked as the source of every evil – the designation is no longer a metaphor but rather an archetype.[2]

Is this also the case – i.e., metaphorically – that we must also understand the reference to Bābil (i.e., Babel = Babylon) in Q 2:102? If so, how then are we to explain the simultaneous allusion, in the same verse, to a brace of Zoroastrian deities, Hārūt and Mārūt, whose presence is somewhat odd in what seemingly should be viewed as a para-biblical passage?[3] And why, moreover, the reference to Babylon in a verse that mentions, at its very outset, the biblical figure of Solomon, with whom Babylon simply has nothing to do?

We would like therefore to open our article with a different hypothesis: might Q 2:102 be said to contain rather, an encrypted reference to the powerful but ill-famed city-complex of Ctesiphon (as we will call it for now, even if this is an oversimplification), later-forgotten due to the fame of Bagdad,[4] which was still closely associated, in the 7th century, with Zoroastrianism, the contemporary Sassanian religion, as well as with the Sassanian Empire, since it was the latter's administrative capital? Did the authors of Q 2:102, following the ancient

1 Boiy 2004, 51: "When the Muslim armies conquered Mesopotamia, Babylon was no more than a small village."
2 Rev 17:1–18.
3 See further Courtieu forthcoming b.
4 For an overview on the town and its destiny after the Arab conquest, see Bowen Savant 2013:169–186.

Gilles Courtieu, Université Jean Moulin Lyon III
Carlos A. Segovia, independent scholar

https://doi.org/10.1515/9783110675498-009

and rather frequent assimilation of Ctesiphon with Babylon given the latter's prestigious fame,[5] which thereby became the almost-natural name for any big town in Southern Mesopotamia – as was the case with the Manichaeans?[6]

Indeed Ctesiphon had been the major town of the Near East for a long period of time: it had been a political capital, a monumental center, and a religious center for Jews,[7] Christians,[8] Mazdaeans,[9] and Manichaeans[10] alike,[11] as well as a crowded and rich metropolis to the north of the Arabia Peninsula. In fact, its influence, fame, and oppressive power marked the adjacent peninsula for centuries, both directly and through Hira,[12] in particular regarding the lifestyle of Arab elites, who were impressed by the court of the Persian *Reichshauptstadt*.[13]

2 Q 43:2-45, The Qur'anic Prophet, and His community

Yet Q 2:102 with its allusion to Babylon may not be the *only* reference to the capital of Sassanian Iran contained in the Qur'anic corpus. A careful analysis of Q 43:31, 33–5 proves revealing in this respect. But before examining these verses we must turn to the pericope where they belong, namely, vv. 2–45 in surah 43.

5 Since Apollonius of Tyana (Dilley 2014, 30). Cf. McDowell 1972, 149 on the prestige of the name and the confusion between Babylon as both a town and a region; examples of this can be found in Chaumont 1988:93.

6 For instance, the Coptic homilies from Egypt call Mani "Lord of the Great Babylon," and the Turfan texts from China "a physician from Babylon." Cf. Baker-Brian 2011:104, 134; Henning 1942, 944.

7 As demonstrated by the Babylonian Talmud.

8 Cf. Chaumont 1988, 52, 42, 71–72 for the first rank assigned to the see of Ctesiphon in the Persian Church; Wood 2013, 189–207 for Ctesiphon as the place of ordination (and burial site) of the Catholicos; Wood 2013, 22–23 for the literary focus on the town in the East-Christian literature of Late Antiquity.

9 Because of the presence of the royal court and its religious officials, as noticed during the Mani's mission.

10 See *infra* for Mani and his followers.

11 For a presentation of the mixture of religions in Ctesiphon, see Neusner 1976, 139.

12 The distance between both cities was c. 100 km. Besides, Hira acted as a southern *emporion* for the capital; see Toral-Niehoff 2013a, 117.

13 Toral-Niehoff 2013b, 106: "Die nahe Reichshauptstadt Ktesiphon war ein unmittelbarer kultureller und politischer Bezugspunkt für die städtische Elite von al-Ḥīra, die sich in ihrem Lebensstil am persischen Hof orientierte."

Q 43:2–45 may be divided into 7 thematic segments whose distribution follows a zigzagging *binary* model: (A_1) vv. 2–8 // (B_1) vv. 9–22 // (A_2) vv. 23–25 // (B_2) vv. 26–28 // (A_3) vv. 29–31 // (B_3) vv. 32–39 // (A_4) vv. 40–45, with all A-segments aiming at *supporting* the Qur'anic prophet in his mission, and all B-segments variously elaborating on the attitude of the *disbelievers* – be they real or imaginary – vis-à-vis prophecy and their punishment in both the present and the next life:

(A_1) 2By the clear book! 3Surely we have made it an Arabic recitation, so that you[14] may understand! 4And indeed it is [contained] in the "mother" of the book [that is] with us, [which is] sublime and wise! 5Shall we take the reminder away from you because you are a wanton people? 6How many prophets have we sent to former people? 7Yet not one prophet came to them whom they did not mock! 8So we destroyed [those who were] stronger than them[15] in power – thus the example of the [men] of old has gone [before them].

(B_1) 9If you ask them, "Who created the heavens and the earth?," they will say, "The [all-] mighty, the [all-]knower created them." 10[He is] the one who has made the earth as a cradle for you; and roads in it for you, so that you may be guided; 11and the one who sends down from the sky water in due measure – then we revive with it a barren land, and in this way [too] you shall be brought forth [from your graves]; 12and the one who created the pairs, all of them, and made for you, from the ship[s] and the cattle, what you ride on, 13so that you may mount their backs, [and] then remember the blessing of your Lord when you are mounted on them, and say, "Glory to the one who has subjected this to us, as we [ourselves] were not fit for it. 14Indeed we will surely return to our Lord." 15Yet they attribute to him a number of his own servants. Surely men are clearly ungrateful indeed. 16Or is it that he has taken daughters [for himself] from what he has created, and chosen for you sons [instead]? 17[But behold,] when one of them is given good tidings of [the birth of] what he has [thus] assimilated to the Merciful, his face turns dark and he is filled with grief. 18Then [there is] he who is brought up in luxury but lacks clarity in the [time of] dispute. 19Yet they have made [of] the angels – who are themselves servants of the Merciful – females. Did they witness their creation? Their testimony will be written down and they will be questioned [thereof]. 20They say, "If the Merciful had so pleased, we would not have worshipped them." They have no knowledge about this, [hence] they are lying! 21Or have we given them a book before it, to which they are holding fast? 22No! They say, "Surely we found our fathers [set] on a community, and it is on their footsteps that we are guided."

(A_2) 23Thus we have not sent any warner before you to a town, except that its affluent ones said, "Surely we found our fathers [set] on a community, and it is on their footsteps

14 *You*: pl.
15 It should be *you* here (cf. v. 3), yet the prophet's opponents are here (and in the following verse) alluded to as "them," which further strengthens the view that *they* are his opponents and that the prophet's mission is to be supported against *them* – a contention that only makes full sense if it is addressed to the prophet's own community (see our remarks on v. 24 below).

that we are guided."[16] [24]He said,[17] "Even if I bring you better guidance than what you found your fathers [set] on?" They said, "Surely we do not believe in what you are sent with." [25]So we took vengeance on them. See how the end was for the deniers!

(B_2) [26][Remember] when Abraham said to his father and his people, "Surely I am free of what you worship, [27]except for the one who created me. Surely he shall guide me." [28]And he made it a lasting word among his descendants, so that they may return [to God].

(A_3) [29]No! I gave these [people] and their fathers enjoyment [of life] until the truth and a clear messenger came to them. [30]But when the truth came to them, they said, "This is magic. Certainly we do not believe in it." [31]They said, "If only this recitation[18] had been sent down upon a great man from the two towns!"

(B_3) [32]Do they distribute the mercy of your Lord? We have distributed their livelihood among them in this life, and raised some of them above others in rank, so that some of them may take others to serve them. But the mercy of your Lord is better than what they accumulate. [33]If it were not[19] that humankind would have [thereby] become a single community [of disbelievers], we would have made for those who disbelieve in the Merciful silver roofs for their houses and stairways on which to ascend, [34]and doors for their houses, and couches on which to recline, [35]and [all kind of] ornaments. Yet all this is but

16 Cf. the preceding verse. Originally, this repetition may have served there purpose of connecting the two sections formed by vv. 9–22 and 23–24, respectively. Also, it is interesting to note that those who oppose God's prophets are the wealthy. Should the opponents of the Qur'anic prophet in vv. 2, 5, 8-14-17, 19–22, 29–32, 41–42 be represented, too, as an economic elite – and, more precisely, as we shall see below, as an economic elite somehow connected to Ctesiphon, the capital of Sassanian Iran?
17 *He said*: one of the former prophets, that is. Other readings have *Say*, in the imperative. Droge (2013:329 n. 30) dismisses this alternative reading as meaningless in this context, yet the somewhat blurring boundary between the Qur'anic prophet and his alleged predecessors is made patent in the corpus, especially *AD* 11:35, 49, on which see Segovia 2015:85–6.
18 Like most Muslim exegetes, modern scholars tend in their majority to read the latter noun as an equivalent to the Qur'an itself, which they therefore portray as displaying, here and elsewhere, some kind of more or less straightforward self-referentiality (see e.g. Wild 2007; Boisliveau 2014). Yet such identification proves problematic, as there is no reason to believe that the Qur'an formed a single unitary text (i.e., something like a "book") prior to its collection and subsequent canonization. See further Wansbrough 2004, 20–52; de Prémare 2004, 29–46. It should be noted, anyway, that the term "recitation" (*Qur'an*) in v. 31 goes back to v. 3, where we find it too – as also in v. 21. Actually, in vv. 2–4 we find three different textual (or metatextual) things: a "book" (in v. 2, but which is mentioned again in vv. 21 and 31), its "recitation" (in v. 3), and the so-called "mother the the book" (in v. 4) whose reference is largely obscure (cf. Q 3:7; 13:39).
19 The beginning of this verse mirrors that of v. 31, since they both include the conditional particle *lawlā*. Were they to be read consecutively, v. 32 could therefore represent an interpolation.

the enjoyment of this life, while the hereafter with your Lord is for the righteous.[20] [36]Whoever turns away from the remembrance of the Merciful – we allot him a satan as his companion [37](indeed they [the satans] surely turn them from the [straight] path, though they think they are [rightly] guided)[21] – [38]until, when he comes to us, he says [to him],[22] "Would that [there were] between me and you the distance of the two easts!"[23] "How wretched is the companion! [39]This will not profit you, since you have wronged – and so you will be partners in the punishment."[24]

(A_4) [40]"Can you make the deaf to hear, or guide the blind or one who is clearly astray? [41]Whether we take you away [in death] – surely we will take vengeance on them! – [42]or show you what we have promised them – surely we are powerful over them! [43]So hold fast to what has been inspired to you. Surely you are on a straight path! [45]Surely it is indeed a reminder for you and your people, and soon you will [all] be questioned! [45]Ask those whom we sent before you as our messengers, 'Did we appoint any other gods than the Merciful to be worshiped?'" (Our translation.)

Prophetic rejection and vindication are the two sides of a single literary *topos* distinctive of Qur'anic prophetology. They figure prominently, for instance, within the corpus's para-biblical narratives, whose heroes often provide a *model* – or to some extent, eventually, an *alter-ego* – for the Qur'anic prophet himself.[25] More generally, they constitute a key component of Qur'anic counter-discourse.[26] Interestingly enough, however, this passage presents an elsewhere *unmatched* feature.

As it becomes apparent in vv. 29–31, the main purpose of the whole pericope is to vindicate the Qur'anic prophet (i.e. the sing. "you" in vv. 9, 23, 40–45, who is also described as a "clear messenger" in v. 29) *and* implicitly his community (cf. the pl. "you" in v. 24 in allusion to the community behind the Qur'anic prophet's imaginary/archetypal prophetic model, and the Qur'anic prophet's own community alluded to in v. 44) against their *opponents*, who are alternately referred to as (pl.) "you" (in vv. 2, 5, 10–13, 16), "them" (in v. 8–9, 17, 21, 30, 32, 41–42), "we" (in v. 14, 30), "they" (in v. 15, 19–20, 22, 30–32), and "these" (in v. 29). The conflict between the Qur'anic prophet, his followers, and their opponents, is moreover presented as *echoing*, on the one hand, that between a previous

20 Or the "fearful" (*al-muttaqūn*).
21 The grammatical shift from the third-person singular in v. 36 to the third-person plural in v. 37, and then its reversion back again to the third-person singular in v. 38 allows to read v. 37 as an interpolation.
22 I.e., to his appointed satan; alternatively, though, one might take the addressee of the speech to be God, as the speech's meaning is difficult to grasp (see the following note).
23 *the distance of the two easts*: the reference of this expression is obscure.
24 This exclamation, in turn, is normally attributed to God.
25 See further Segovia 2015.
26 On which see Azaiez 2015.

archetypal prophet (called "he" in v. 24), his community, and their opponents (who are alternately referred to as "they" and "we" in vv. 23–24, "you" in v. 24, and "them" in v. 25, and different from the archetypal disbelievers "them," "they," and "you" in vv. 37–8), and, on the other hand, that between *Abraham* and his opponents (vv. 26–28).[27]

In short, it looks as though vv. 2–8 + 23–25 + 29–31 represent the thematic *core* of this Qur'anic pericope, with vv. 9–22 and 33–39 functioning, say, as two *supplementary* homilies, while vv. 40–45 connect *back* to the core. Perhaps these three additional parts – which may be further divided into smaller units – date from the time when the core itself was composed, or perhaps they do not and are later instead. Be that as it may, the defense of the Qur'anic prophet's community that results from comparing vv. 24 and 44 is elsewhere unparalleled and hence *unique* to this very pericope.

3 Ctesiphon and the "Two Towns" in Q 43:31

We would now like to focus on Q 43:31, which has perplexed commentators for centuries. In fact exegetes and translators have frequently found it necessary to employ various tricks to make it meaningful, adding to it unprovable data to make it fit within the so-called "Circumstances of Revelation."

This verse presents a provocative (and rhetorical) one-way question, uttered by some anonymous opponents who seem to be offended because some kind "Qur'ān" – if social hierarchy was to be respected – should have been sent to an important man, rather than to the prophetic candidate the verse purports. And it provides a small detail at the end, perhaps just sufficient to specify that important man's identity: he should be from "two towns," as the unambiguous use of dual indicates. Such an addition can be said to be rhetorically useless[28] – it would have been enough to express his social prominence – but it creates the problem and provides contemporaneously the solution, *li-ulī al-albāb* ("for those of understanding").

As we have seen the Qur'anic prophet is confronted with the claim allegedly made by his opponents that God's revelation should have been sent instead to *a man from the two towns*:

27 The specificity of each prophet seems here to be respected, but their missions clearly overlap.
28 Unless there is also some sort of anti-urban discourse at stake here.

وَقَالُوا لَوْلَا نُزِّلَ هَٰذَا الْقُرْآنُ عَلَىٰ رَجُلٍ مِنَ الْقَرْيَتَيْنِ عَظِيمٍ
wa-qālū lawlā nuzzila hāḏā l-Qur'ān 'alà rağul min al-qaryatayn 'aẓīm

> They said, "If only this recitation had been sent down upon a great man from the two towns!"[29]

The (dual) noun القريتين *al-qaryatayn* in this verse – lit. "the two towns" – is a *hapax*. The *denotandum* is obscure (Droge 2013, 330 n. 36) though the expression is normally taken to refer to the towns of Mecca (Makka) and Ṭā'if in the Ḥiğāz (on which see section 4 below). The syntax of the sentence, however, *defies* this common interpretation: the distance between Mecca and Ṭā'if amounting to c. 40 miles (64 km), it is difficult to fancy that anyone could be said to *simultaneously* come from both towns – put differently: a man could be said to come *either* from Mecca *or* Ṭā'if, but not from Mecca and Ṭā'if. Consequently, translations of the kind of "And they said, 'Why was this Qur'ān not sent down upon a great man from [one of] the two towns?'" abound too.[30] Yet this is *not* what the text says. For the sake of coherence, one must assume that, in all likelihood, *al-qaryatayn* does not mean *two* different towns, but a place called "the two towns" or "the twin towns."

Now, we do know of a place, namely Ctesiphon (Syr. ܟܛܝܣܦܘܢ *kṭysfwn*), the administrative capital of the Sassanian empire, which could very well *match* such denomination. Ctesiphon had ben founded in 129 BCE by the Parthians as a royal suburb adjacent to the Hellenistic town of Seleucia about 21 miles (35 km) southeast of the modern Baghdad, and resettled by the Sassanians, together with Seleucia, which they in turn renamed Beh-Ardashir [Syr. *bh-'rdšyr* ܒܗܐܪܕܫܝܪ] in honor of Ardashir I,[31] towards the end of the first quarter of the 3rd century CE – for Ctesiphon had been destroyed and Seleucia depopulated during the Roman sack of the dual city complex in 165 CE. "[D]uring the Sassanian period," writes Jens Kröger, "Ctesiphon developed into a metropolis, consisting of a series of towns and suburbs along both banks of the Tigris.[32] It thus became known as 'the towns,'"[33] Syr. ܡܚܘܙܐ *mḥwz'*, post-Qur'anic Arab. المدائن *al-madā'in*.[34] Yet this urban development was gradual, and it must be stressed that, in spite of it,

29 Droge (2013:330) translates this verse as follows: "They said, 'If only this Qur'an had been sent down on some great man of the two towns.'"

30 E.g. Sahih International trans.: https://quran.com/43/31.

31 See Morony 1989.

32 For the river's role in the topography of the city complex, see Fiey:1967.

33 Kröger 1993, 2011.

34 See however our comments on Tabari in n. 36 below.

Ctesiphon and Seleucia/Beh-Ardashir remained the two *main* towns or districts,[35] with all others, in contrast, being established *ad hoc.*[36] This moreover explains the fact that Ctesiphon-Seleucia was also called in Syriac ܬܪܬܝܗܝܢ ܡܕܝܢܬܐ *mdynt' trtyhyn*, i.e. "the two towns."[37] Interestingly enough, in addition to being the winter home of the Persian king, Ctesiphon was also the residence of the Jewish Exiliarch, the seat of the Catholicos of the Church of the East, and that of the Manichaean Archegos.[38]

Hence, despite its frequent designation as "the towns," in the *plural*, in a number of post-Qur'anic Arabic sources, it is well within the evidence to affirm that Ctesiphon was known too in the late-antique world as "the *two* (or the *twin*) *towns*."[39] And it is likewise possible to surmise that, even if in post-Qur'anic

---

35 Thus in the Synod of the Church of the East of 544 the clergy from Beh-Ardašīr and the clergy from Ctesiphon signed the acts separately; see Chabot 1902; see also Fiey 1967, 415.

36 Thus, for instance, one of them was founded in 540 CE, when Khusraw I had part of the population of Antioch deported to Iraq.

37 Lieu 1992, 5.

38 The archaeological surveys (see the maps in Neusner 1966, 16–17) and literary testimonies agree as to the overall picture of the area which we have provided in the preceding lines. The river separated in meanders a complex conurbation (Lieu 1994, 5) dividing the whole area into two parts connected by floating bridges (Fiey 1967a, 11). It had perhaps more than seven centers (el-Ali 1968–1969, 422–423), some growing, some in decay, plus fortresses, palaces, suburbs, places of worship and for the performance of public executions which are known to us from martyrological reports (Fiey 1967, 8). The river divided or disrupted the urban space with its changing bed, provoking floods and destructions, not to mention the results of foreign invasions and, as a reaction, the powerful efforts initiated by Parthian and Sassanian dynasties to rebuild here and there, and to maintain the balance on both banks; for if mud brick architecture proves very fragile with time, and the lack of maintenance quickly leads to ruins, it also gives the opportunity to build even more quickly. The result was that of two equally-populated sides and a plan, since the Parthians, to separate their functions (Chaumont 1988:48): in the west a mixed, economically active, populous bank; in the east a more administrative, monumental bank (where there is still the Arch of the famous Tāq Kasrā). About one century before the rise of Islam, the western "town" was composed mostly by Beh Ardashir (i.e. "Good [city of) Ardashir," also named Dardeshir [Neusner 1966, 129] and Bahurasir [Fiey 1967, 14), called *Kōḵē* (a mysterious name, cf. Fiey 1967, 402: "The Huts"?) by the Christians and *Māḥozā* (the "Town") by the Jews. But these two names could otherwise indicate specific suburbs, the areas where both populations were concentrated, the Christian population around the Catholicos' See, with its churches and schools (Fiey 1967:398, 404, 406, 418; Wood 2013, 23); the Jewish population around the famous school that produced the Bavli and the residence of the Exilarch (Neusner 1966, 247, 232; Neusner 1969, 200–202, etc.; Bowen Savant 2013, 171). And further south one would find Vologesias as a place for trade (Maricq 1959, 264–76).

39 The exceptionally-complex geographical configuration of Ctesiphon is reflected in its toponymy from the outset until ultimate abandonment, during the formative period of the Qur'an, and even afterwards. Relating some Byzantine campaign reaching the area in the same

Arabic the city complex was frequently called *al-madāʾin* in the plural (with a noun, therefore, from the root *m.d.n.*), Ctesiphon could just as well have been designed in the *dual* in Arabic in former times, that is, when the Qur'anic *grundschriften* were composed. And if so, it need not have been necessarily named in the dual with a noun from the root *m.d.n.*, as there is another root *equally* used in the Qur'ān – even more often than *m.d.n.* – to refer to towns and settlements, namely: the root *q.r.y.* So the question is: is it possible that the Qur'anic authors used the *dual* noun *al-qaryatayn* (from the root *q.r.y.*) to refer to Ctesiphon?

In our opinion this question has an *affirmative* response. The nouns مدينة *madīna* (sing.) and مدائن *madāʾin* (pl.) are used in the corpus, with only four exceptions,[40] to denote legendary towns, often in the context of narratives retelling the biblical story of the Israelites in Egypt.[41] Conversely, the nouns قرية *qarya* (sing.) and قرى *qurà* (pl.) are used to denote various real if unspecified towns and villages and, more broadly, the notion of township itself.[42] Besides, *unlike* in post-Qur'anic Arabic the term *qarya* does not seem to have been used at first to denote a small village, but a village or a town – indistinctly, that is.[43] From all this one may infer that the root *q.r.y.* might have proved suitable for the Qur'anic authors in order to name a dual city-complex like Ctesiphon; based on the previous remarks apropos de referent of the nouns *madīna/ madāʾin* and

period, Procopius of Caesarea (*History of Wars* 2.28.4–6) described the cities thus: "at the place where there are two towns, Seleucia and Ctesiphon, built by the Macedonians . . . These two towns are separated by the Tigris river only, for they have nothing else between them." Cf. the references in Fiey 1967, 15; Chaumont 1988, 161–62. In turn the Talmud takes into account the separate presence of Jews in both cities and mentions the frequent crossing of the river from one town to the other (Fiey 1967). Yaʿqūbī, on his part, writes that "*al-Madāʾin* consisted of several cities on the banks of the Tigris," and that "between the two cities [sic] there is a distance of a mile" (*Kitāb al-Buldān* 107, quoted by Bowen Savant 2013, 172). And Ṭabarī informs us that "on the banks of the Tigris, opposite the city of Ctesiphon (which is the city that forms the eastern part if *al-Madāʾin*), he [= Ardashir I] built a city on the western site, which he called Bih Ardashir" (Ṭabarī *Tārīḫ* 13.819), and he calls both towns the "two royal cities" (859). In sum, topography changed a lot over the centuries, and the toponymy presented as many difficulties for travellers, rulers, and/or settlers, as it presents to us today, given that every community had its own word(s) to name it. But during all those changes, for centuries, there always were two prominent centres always acknowledged as such on each bank of the river, so that for centuries it was normal to call the place the "Two Cities."

40 Q 9:101, 120; 33:60; 63:8.

41 Cf. Q 7:111, 123; 12:30; 15:67; 18:19, 82; 26:36, 53; 27:48; 28:15, 18, 20; 36:20

42 Cf. Q 2:85, 259; 4:75; 6:92, 123, 131; 7:4, 82, 88, 94, 96–8, 101, 161, 163; 10:98; 11:100, 102, 117; 12:82, 109; 15:4; 16:112; 17:16, 58; 18:59, 77; 21:6, 11, 74, 95; 22:45, 48; 25:40, 51; 26:208; 27:34, 56; 28:58–9; 29:31, 34; 34:18, 34; 36:13; 42:7; 43:23; 46:27; 47:13; 59:7, 14; 65:8.

43 See Shahid 1995:245 n.134; Fioriani Piacentini 1994.

qarya/qurà, respectively, one may even venture that such *might* have been, perhaps, their preferred option – and hence that, quite possibly, *al-qaryatayn* in Q 43:31 alludes to Ctesiphon. Attempts to Arabization like the one arguably *reflected* in 43:3 could be explained, furthermore, against a non-Arabic background of this sort.

To sum up: Q 43:31, is, to the best of our knowledge, the only occurrence in the Qur'ān where the Qur'anic prophet is alluded to in the context of polemic and counter-discourse *together with* his community; and they are, moreover, mentioned therein in connection to the *capital* of the Sassanian empire – for what sense would it have to claim that God's revelation should have been sent to someone from the "Two Towns" if it were not that such place (and hence Ctesiphon, upon our reconstruction) was fully meaningful to them? If we are on the right track, then, it seems we are before something not only important but indeed crucial, as the Qur'ān is usually silent about its *Sitz im Leben* – and we presumably have here a very early fragment that provides us with one.

Our reasons for considering Q 43:31 and, more broadly, Q 43:2-45 – or, at the very least, its textual core, that is, Q 43:2–8, 23–25, 29-31 – as an early Qur'anic text are basically *two*. First, in his *Geschichte des Qorâns* Nöldeke lists Q 43 among those he proposes to label "*Mittelmekkanische Suren*," that is, Middle-Meccan surahs (Arab. *suwar*). However problematic talking of "Meccan" and "Medinan" surahs as may be – for in our view the Qur'ān is an heterogeneous textual corpus that cannot be just said to go back to the unitary figure of a prophet living in the Arabian Peninsula between 570 and 632, and the corpus's chapters often prove intricate multilayered textual surfaces[44] – assuming that the Qur'anic texts grouped by Nöldeke's under the rubrics "Meccan-I" (*Frühmekkanische*), "Meccan-II" (*Mittelmekkanische*), and "Meccan-III" (*Spätmekkanische*), do represent the oldest texts of the corpus is, we think, still valid in general terms given their similar concerns, style, and vocabulary.[45] Secondly, the claim in Q 43:36 that "[w]hoever turns away from the remembrance of the Merciful . . . [is] allot[ed] . . . a satan as his companion" is clearly reminiscent of Q 17:79; 73:1–8; 74:43; 76:26 and, above all, the Syriac *Vorlage* of Q 108:1-3[46] – a series of texts with a more-than-probable Messalian background[47] which also pertain, as per

44 See further Dye 2015.
45 On Nöldeke's periodization, see Stefanidis 2008. See also Angelika Neuwirth's, Nicolai Sinai, and Nora Schmid's reassessment of Nöldeke's chronology at http://corpuscoranicum.de/kommentar/uebersicht.
46 On which see Luxenberg 2007:295–300. See now too Guillaume Dye's and Manfred Kropp's comments in Azaiez *et alii* 2016, 444, 445–7.
47 See Segovia 2020.

Nöldeke (as well as Neuwirth, Sinai, and Schmid), to the *Frühmekkanische* (thus Q 73, 74, 108) and *Mittelmekkanische* (so Q 17, 76) textual layers of the Qur'ān.

Yet there is an additional if oblique *clue* for considering Q 43:20–45 (or, again, its textual core) not just an early Qur'anic fragment, but also one of the Qur'ān's earliest *pro-prophetic* fragments. Explaining it will somehow demand a longer detour. But this, in turn, will help us to *locate* with more of accuracy – on the map of Sassanian Iraq – the setting of the early Qur'anic community.

4 A Manichaean/Messalian milieu?

In a nutshell: if (1) Q 43:36, with its tacit reference to the remembrance of God as an efficacious mean to expel the demons from the soul (which parallels the explicit reference to praying as constituting such mean in Q 108 and the repeated allusions to the virtues of extended praying in Q 17:79; 73:1–8; 74:43 and to the need of remembering God in Q 73:1–8; 76:26), does then also have a Messalian background; and if (2) Q 43:31 provides to Q 43:36 a possible and indeed plausible context: Ctesiphon or, better perhaps, its region – where we know the Messalian question was intensely dealt with and debated from 596 to 628[48] (notice how these dates overlap with those commonly assigned to Mu ammad's lifetime); then (3) it is fair to deduce that the polemics hinted at in Q 43:2–8, 23–25, 29–31 (and later in Q 43:2–45) had, in all probability, a *Messalian* setting, and that Messalian *too* must have been the setting of the earliest Qur'anic community – which in Q 43:2–45 we encounter supporting its still anonymous leader[49] against their opponents from Ctesiphon's region.[50] A supplementary clue to this is offered in Q 74:43,

---

48 On the Messalians, in general and in the context of the monastic crisis registered in the Church of the East at the beginnings of the 7th-century, see further Tamcke 1988; Fitschen 1993; Escolan 1999; Camplani 2007; Bettiolo 2007; Fiori 2010:463–4; Reinink 2009; Wood 2013: 147–48. For a discussion of Columba Stewart's and Brouria Bitton-Ashkelony's nominalistic approaches to the Messalian problem, see once more Segovia 2020.

49 An interpretation of Q 17:79–80 as representing a first incomplete shift beyond such anonymity, see Segovia 2020.

50 Is the "great man" of Q 43:31 a real figure, or is he merely a rhetorical device? Sadly, we cannot tell – see the next section, though. What is beyond doubt is that those whom the followers of the Qur'anic prophet are willing to confront in Q 43:2–8, 23–5, 29–31 claimed, or were in their eyes susceptible of claiming, that the divine "recitation" of which the Qur'anic prophet presented himself, or was presented by his followers, as the recipient, should have been sent to a great man from Ctesiphon instead. But how exactly must we understand the opponents' claim? Supposing they ever made it, did the problem consist for them in that the recitation had not been sent down (*a*) upon *a man*, i.e. upon *someone* from Ctesiphon

with its implicit assimilation of the righteous with the مصلّون *muṣallūn*, which is the Arabic equivalent of the Syriac ܡܨܠܝܢܐ *mṣallyānē*, "Messalians."

We are, of course, aware of the discussion on the meaning of the term "Messalianism" raised by C. Stewart in his seminal book of 1991, which has influenced the recent work of B. Bitton-Ashkelony and her definition of "Messalianism" as a *rhetorical* category contradictorily applied to different targets.[51] Yet in my view Ph. Escolan's approach, which takes Messalianism as a *diffuse* underground phenomenon within the Church of the East, cannot be ruled out as easily Bitton-Ashkelony does.[52] To be sure, heresiologists reified what lacked a cut-clear definition, and polemicists used whatever terms to describe their opponents, but in order to escape their artificial categorization's one should not lose sight of a reality that cannot be reduced to a simple label.[53] Thus the synods of the Church of the East of 576 and 585 point to the existence of ascetics and monks who exceedingly devoted themselves to prayer,[54] were reluctant to confer soteriological validity to the sacraments,[55] and separated from the Sunday ecclesiastical gatherings and festivals;[56] moreover, their canons established penitences for such people and commanded the bishops to have them submitted to their authority.[57] As Daniel Carner observes, "[w]e are dealing [here] with a post-Constantinian ecclesiastical process of defining, consolidating, homogenizing, or rejecting forms of Christian life and expression that . . . came under the direction of a . . . [specific]

additionally qualified as "great"; or (*b*) upon *a great man* from Ctesiphon? There probably is no satisfactory answer to this question; but see our comments on Q 43:32–5 below. Finally, it should be added the epithet عظيم *'aẓīm* ("great") is somewhat odd in this context, as it is normally applied elsewhere in the corpus to God's punishments and rewards or to God himself, but never to a human being. We are grateful to Paul Neuenkirchen for kindly drawing our attention to this latter issue.

51 Bitton-Ashkelony 2013, 226

52 Escolan 1999.

53 Thus Fiori (2010, 463–464) persuasively argues, *pace* Stewart, that views traditionally labelled as "Messalian," including the dismissal of baptism, are positively documented in Stephen Bar Sudhaile's *Book of Hierotheos* (late 5th century). Cf. Fitschen (1993, 352), who speaks in turn of an "amorphous movement."

54 Due to their peculiar interpretation of Luke 18:1 and 1 Thess 5:7.

55 Basically, the eucharist and the baptism.

56 Thus constituting an anarchic and hence potentially rebel community in the very margins of the Church.

57 See "Synod of Mar Ezekiel (576 CE)," canon no. 1; "Synod of Mar Isho'yahb I (585 CE)," canons nos. 8–9, after J.-B. Chabot's ed. of ms. Alqosh Syr. 169/Vat.Borg.Sir. 81–82 (Chabot 1902, 115–116, 144–146, 374–375, 406–407).

hierarchy with its own institutional perspective and concerns"[58] – a process that Philip Wood has carefully examined against the background of the ecclesiastical *reform* implemented in the Church of the East in the late 6th century,[59] which aimed, he writes, at shaping an "'anti-Messalian' [type of] Christianity."[60] Put differently: a *post-nominalist* (or nuanced) realist use of the term "Messalian," different from its *pre-nominalist* (or naive) realist rendition, is by all means necessary if instead of just paying attention to the rhetorically inflated writings of the Christian *heresologists*, one goes on to examine the concrete, daily issues reflected in the *synodical* canons.

Yet we do not mean to say that either the Qur'anic prophet or his community were in fact Messalians. Our *prise de position* is more nuanced indeed. Messalians – like Manichaeans for that matter – divided into two complementary and interdependent human groups: the "perfect" and their supporters, the "upright." Obviously, the boundaries of the latter group are unclear to us. The more we can say is that belonging to the "upright" allowed, quite probably, various degrees of engagement. And yet, as it is always the case with all religious groups,[61] it is also likely that there existed here and there, in addition to these more-or-less then defined groups (the "perfect" and the "upright"), *sympathizers* of the Messalian movement – which was chiefly a monastic movement, albeit one significantly lacking any center and pervasive throughout the social structure of east-Syrian Christianity. Accordingly, one would expect to find them almost everywhere in Iraq, northern Syria, and western Iran. So, of course, the question is: were there *Arab* groups among the sympathizers of the Messalians? Unfortunately, we do not know – that is to say, we do not have direct evidence of it. Still no one would surely dispute that Q 17:79; 43:36; 73:1–8; 74:43; 76:26; 108, which do look like Messalian or pro-Messalian texts, have all an *Arab* background. And we have information that several *Arab* groups linked to the Arabian Peninsula camped regularly in the surroundings of al-Ḥīra, the former capital of the Persian-allied Nasrid kingdom in the outskirts of present-day Najaf (former Kūfa) and the capital of Persian Arabia. Let us also add that al-Ḥīra was only c. 125 miles (200 kms.) southwest from Ctesiphon and a Christian city dependent on the patriarchal see of Seleucia; its relevance in the ecclesiastical map of Sassanian

58 Carner 2002, 84. See now also Berzon (2016, 73–97). On the tensions between Basilian, Homoiousian, and a more anarchic type of asceticism represented *inter alios* by the Messalians, see Elm (1994, 194–226).

59 Wood 2013, 147–148.

60 Ibid., 174.

61 W. James (1985, 267) was one of the first psychologists to mention it in his Gifford Lectures in Edinburgh, which were published in 1902 as *The Varieties of Religious Experience*.

Iraq is moreover attested by Sabrisho I's intervention in the political and religious affairs of the city at the beginnings of the 7th century (Fisher and Wood 2016).

Now, the 8th-to-9th-century Kufan historian Hishām b. al-Kalbī reports that the Arabs living in al-Ḥīra and its surroundings formed three distinct groups: (α) the إباد *ʿibād* or inhabitants of the city, who had submitted to the Sassanian authority and were legally, therefore, Sassanian subjects; (β) the تنوخ *tanūkh*, i.e. the tent-dwellers camping east of the Euphrates, who had also submitted to Sassanian rule; and (γ) the "confederates" or أحلاف *aḥlāf*, who had an agreement with the people of al-Ḥīra but had not themselves become Sassanian subjects.[62] In religious terms, the *ʿibād* were, as it happens, Christians who spoke Arabic but used Syriac as their church language. As for the *tanūkh* and the *aḥlāf*, we ignore what was their religious affiliation and linguistic habits; yet it is not absurd to imagine that they might have known some Syriac and that they were exposed to, perhaps even influenced by, the religious views prevalent in the region – Messalianism (which had disseminated through all Iraq) and Manichaeism (which had spread from Ctesiphon to al-Ḥīra) included.[63]

In short, then, it is possible that the Qur'anic prophet and his community originally belonged to the *tanūkh* or, more likely, the *aḥlāf*. This would actually make all the pieces of the puzzle match. Their opponents, in turn, might have pledge a *stronger* alliance to the religious communities and/or leaders of Ctesiphon, or else *protested*, judging them spurious, against the claims made at some point by the Qur'anic prophet and/or his community. Be that as it may, the name given to the cave near Mecca where, as the legend has it, Mu ammad received his first revelations, is most eloquent in this respect – its name is Ḥirāʾ, with a slight orthography shift, therefore. Its obliquity notwithstanding, this curious fact can be seen as an intriguing additional clue pointing to the original *scenario* in which the Qur'anic prophet faced opposition and got support from his followers – who, paraphrasing the words in Q 17:79–80, subsequently raised him to a praised, that is, authoritative position.

Furthermore, eventual *exchanges* between Manichaeans and Messalians cannot be ruled out, as there are a number of interesting clues that hint at it, for example, their parallel twofold division, their common emphasis on extensive prayer, their pneumatological soteriology, and the accusations raised against the Messalians for their angelomorphic Christology, which some sources describe as being similar to that of the Manichaeans.[64]

---

62 Toral-Niehoff 2010; 2013a; Fisher and Wood 2016

63 On the Manichaean background of al-Ḥīra, see Tardieu 1992; Tardieu 1994.

64 For an assessment of the crucial role played by the act of praying in Manichaean ascetics, see BeDhun 2000. On the depiction of Messalian Christology as being crypto-Manichaean, see

In turn, the influence of Manichaeism upon formative Islam has often been underlined.[65] The mediation of an angel in the transmission of revelation, the view that the latter must be preserved in a book, the notion that its new qualified human recipient of God's is the seal of all previous prophets (who are like the epiphanies of an eternal Prophet), and the simultaneous identification of the last prophet with the Johannine Paraclete[66] – all these motifs are usually evoked to prove formative Islam's debt to the Manichaean worldview, which, despite its *liminal* nature at the crossroads of the religious traditions of the late antique Near East[67] constituted not so much a separate religion as a *variant* understanding of the Christian faith, "heterodox" in the eyes of the Christian heresiologists, more "authentic" in those of the Manichaeans themselves.[68] For, as Timothy Pettipiece writes, Manichaeism was ultimately "an indigenous form of Persian Christianity."[69] In fact, the boundaries between Manichaeism and east-Syriac Christianity remained *fluid* until the late 620s – when, it should be added, the Messalians, too, were asked to submit to the hierarchy of the Persian Church under the threat of being otherwise excommunicated as heretics.[70] In short, even if Manichaeism was *permeable* to influences from other various religions – which, as Nicholas Baker-Brian[71] perspicaciously observes, does not justify its definition as a "syncretic" religious tradition[72] – and did not envisage the

---

Van Reeth 2012a, 32, 35. Overall, however, these at first sight eloquent analogies are still in need of thorough study.

65 E.g. Simon 1997; de Blois 2004a; 2004b; Van Reeth 2011; 2012b.

66 As described in John 14:16, 26; 15:26; 16:7; conversely, 1 John 2:1 equates him with Jesus – an assimilation which is absent from the Qur'an.

67 Pettipiece 2015:299.

68 Lim 2008:154.

69 Pettipiece 2015, 302.

70 Segovia 2020.

71 Baker-Brian 2011, 7–8.

72 "Cultural interaction in Manichaeism," he writes, "has not only tended to be discussed in terms of syncretism, but Mani and his followers have in addition been portrayed as conscious syncretists, in the sense that they are believed to have intentionally appropriated terminological and cortical features from other traditions, and displayed a tendency to activate particular 'borrowed elements' as the need arose . . . from within the context of missionary activity: a process viewed as being undertaken in order to increase the share of converts during those periods when the religion was engaged in proselytising activities. Assessments of Manichaeism in this vein are now slowly being re-evaluated by many commentators, not least because of the problems surrounding the notion of syncretism in relation to the historical application of the term. As Charles Stewanrt and Rosalind Shaw have highlighted, syncretism tends towards being 'an "othering" term applied to historical distant as well as geographically distant societies,' and as [Karen] King has demonstrated in her study on Gnosticism, it replaces that more ancient 'othering' term, heresy, by reduplicating its prejudicial assumptions about competitor

historical Jesus – unlike mainstream Christianity – as the *key* soteriological figure upon whom everything else depended in both theory and practice, the dividing line between the Manichaean and the east-Syrian Churches was *not* altogether obvious. The case of the *bēma* may contribute to briefly illustrate this fact. In Syrian Christianity, the *bēma* or "throne" was a raised platform in the nave of the church before the sanctuary from where the Scripture was read (similar to the Seat of Moses in the synagogue, therefore); yet in the east-Syrian Church, in addition to this and to serving as the episcopal seat, it symbolized the throne on which, upon his return in the end of times, Christ will seat to judge humankind. In Manichaeism the *bēma*, which was also called the "Throne of Light" and of the "Paraclete" – and was, moreover, the name of the major festival of the liturgical year – was the key cultic structure employed to celebrate Many's martyrdom and invested too with an eschatological role, as it was likewise symbolically connected to Christ's second coming as the Judge of humankind.[73]

Now, just like Messalianism, which was a monastic movement not restricted to cenobitic boundaries – like in general east-Syriac monasticism – was widespread throughout Sassanian Iraq, Manichaeism had its official center in Ctesiphon, whence it had spread to al-Ḥīra and south-westwards from it. We would like to draw the reader's attention, in this sense, to the somewhat understated fact that the Islamic tradition portrays Mu ammad's opponents in Mecca and Medina as *Manichaeans* who had exported their religious views *from* al-Ḥīra.[74] One is tempted to interpret this as a circuitous declaration concerning the provenance of the early opponents of the Qur'anic prophet and his community as described in the textual core of Q 43:2–45. Accordingly, it is possible to depict the Qur'anic-prophet group, we think, as initially inhabiting the *periphery* of the Manichaean and Messalian communities of present-day Iraq. The aforementioned relevancy of Messalian themes in the earliest Qur'anic layers militates in favor of what one might thus call – paraphrasing the title of William

traditions, most notably in its conveying of the sense of contamination and distance from 'authentic' faiths (as illustrated by the juxtaposition between *syncretism* [= contaminated tradition] vs. *anti-syncretism* [= pure tradition])." We should like to add that all religious traditions – including those commonly viewed as "uncontaminated" – are in fact the result of complex superimpositions. Christianity, with its original (in the two senses of the term) merging of Jewish and Hellenistic beliefs, is a good example of this; see further (to only mention a few relevant titles) Engberg-Pedersen 2001; van Henten and Verheyden 2012; Lieu 2016.

73 Cf. Ries 1976; Cassis 2002; Loosley 2003; Sundermann n. d.

74 See however de Prémare 2002:252–3, who conveniently highlights the notice thereof provided by the Kufan polymath Ibn Qutayba (9th century).

Friedkin's 1971 famous crime thriller – the "Messalian connection" of the early Qur'ān. But which are the Manichaean elements present in it?

We essentially follow here Daniel Beck's thought-provoking re-assessment of the Manichaean background of the so-called "early-Meccan" *sūra*-s.[75] Among their encrypted Manichaean *features*, one finds (*a*) repeated *oaths* that echo the turmoil descent of the lights bringing redemption to the world, and that speak too of the sun and the moon as their cosmic vehicles;[76] (*b*) a *polymorph* monotheism susceptible of being reconstructed through a symptomatic analysis of several pronominal shifts,[77] but which was later replaced by a human prophetology and a more strictly monotheistic theology that entailed its foreclosure; and (*c*) an equally important motif, as is that of the *szygos* or heavenly alter-ego of every men.[78] Similarly, the *correlation* between "prayer" and "almsgiving" in passages where there is no trace of the five Islamic pillars[79] might be said to reflect a Manichaean background; and the same applies – even more clearly – to identification of the Qur'anic Prophet (like that of Mani) with the Paraclete.[80] Finally, we wonder if the criticism raised against the portrayal of God's angels in *feminine* terms in Q 43:16[81] is not to be understood as a denunciation of the Zoroastrian representation of every person's heavenly counterpart as a maiden of light – which, once more, would only make sense in, instead of outside, the Sassanian world.

5 Who is the "Important Man" in Q 43:31?

Let us now return to the Qur'anic-prophet's arch-rival mentioned in Q 43:31.

Muslim commentaries have tried to satisfy natural curiosity about this by all accounts fictive opponent, and therefore to assign him a name and a story. Ṭabarī in his *Tafsīr*[82] found a simple and complete, though hardly convincing solution, naming not one but two persons (in fact more) from both cities, the most prominent of which are Mu ammad's adversary al-Walīd b. al-Mughīra

75 Beck 2018, Beck 2020. We are also very grateful to D. Beck for sharing with us an early draft of paper he is offering to this conference, in dialogue with which we have partly written ours.
76 Notice the imagery in Q 52, 75, 77, 79, 85, 86, 89, 90–3, 95, 100, 103.
77 Especially in Q 75–86, 89–92, 95–6, 99–104, 107, on which see also Segovia 2020.
78 In Q 86:4.
79 E.g. in Q 73:20; cf. 58:12.
80 In Q 61:6.
81 Cf. Q 16:57; 17:40.
82 Ṭabarī, *Tafsir* 43.31.

al-Makhzūmī, belonging to the recalcitrant tribe of Makhzūm, a powerful man, a warlord from Mecca; and coming from Ṭāʾif an opponent called Abū Masʿūd ʿUrwa b. Masʿūd al-Thaqifī. These choices were favored by most subsequent commentators, who tended to avoid taking risks, and so other Qurʾanic commentaries, from all persuasions, followed Ṭabarī's view, despite the fact that it is not supported by the syntax. There is definitely one man here only, and two distinct cities, as the singular linked to the dual proves. It means, as the text says, someone born, living, active, known in two different places. In Antiquity – let us repeat it again – everyone was from somewhere, a specific place on Earth, from cradle to grave (if possible at the same location), and Mu ammad had a special fate, switching from Mecca to Yathrib, but never settling in either city and viewed as hailing from both cities.

In turn, the *Sira* adopts a similar, even more subtle and in a way astute, strategy. The thesis is presented, this time, within a statement purportedly made by al-Walīd b. al-Mugīra himself: "al-Walīd said: 'Does God send down revelation to Mu ammad and ignore me, the greatest chief of the Quraysh, to say nothing of Abū Masʿūd ʿUrwa b. Masʿūd al-Thaqifī, the chief of the Thaqif, we being the greatest ones of Ṭāʾif and Makka? So God sent down concerning him, so I am told, they said, if this Qurʾān had been revealed to a great man of the two towns.'"[83] So the enigma is diluted on two levels of narration, a trick proof again of the trouble stemming from the interpretation of this verse. The first important man speaks of the second as an eventuality . . . The aporia remains, for demanding minds; those who do not look away and recite.

Finally, in modern times, some orientalists, when translating the Qurʾān, have substituted Medina for Ṭāʾif (so Blachère), while others (including Paret) have chosen an even more desperate solution, again inapplicable to the text as we have it; in short they insert/dissolve the dual within a distributive formula of the type: "(one of) the two cities." Yet most translators have either accepted there is no clear solution to the problem or, often in resignation, follow Muslim traditions (e.g., Buhl and, more recently, Droge), or else guess some other and even more extravagant option, as in the case of Bell: "The reference is uncertain, and variously explained; it may perhaps be the Jewish colonies outside Medina, in which case this will be a Jewish objection."[84]

Might it be possible to propose a more-suitable name? If we pursue our Mesopotamian thesis, we must ask who could be illustrious enough to be alluded in such way, given that the adjective *ʿaẓīm* (which occurs 120 times in the Qurʾanic

---

83 *Sira*, ed. Guillaume, 164.
84 Bell 1991, 493.

corpus) is, with the sole exception of v. 31, always used in the Qur'ān to qualify the supernatural.[85] Could it be the King of Kings, that is, the Persian Shah himself, as Ctesiphon was overtly associated with royal power? But then how could a hypothetical descent of a Qur'ān focus on him? There is, we think, a better option: that of a reputed Mesopotamian prophet. Mani, whose homeland was very, very close to Ctesiphon. A short name, merely four letters, but an essential figure in the history of Middle East, the cradle of capital innovations, still influential during the formative centuries of the Qur'ān, always at the crossroad of religions, and very frequently involved in polemical statements. In fact, as we have already underlined, emergent Islam did not escape the influence of the religious system he created. Could Mani, then, be the *or* an important man in Q 43:31?

To gather evidence of Mani's link with Ctesiphon is not a difficult task. The only trouble is that it forces us to collect information from biographical, in fact hagiographical, sources as opposed to polemical ones, and the meeting of both has resulted in a methodological brainteaser for historians of religion. It will be sufficient to underline here the main elements, not necessarily the facts in their entirety, merely well-known accounts which circulated in the area throughout the Late Antique period. Ibn al-Nadīm writes in his *Fihrist* that Mani's father was originally from Hamadan and had moved to Babylon, settling in al-Madāʾin, in the place called Tisfun.[86] Mani himself was said to have been born in a small village just outside of Ctesiphon (Mardinu?), in the southern suburbs, near a canal connecting the two major rivers.[87] The big city, the metropolis always attracted him, throughout his career, even if he was said to have been a great traveler, above all, because of the position he wanted to assume in the royal court, the closest he could be with the kings and the ruling elite.[88] After years abroad, he returned to Ctesiphon to begin his public mission amidstthe population,[89] and even if he frequently moved, compelled by necessities, he always came back, viewing the city as his home.[90] This, however, is anything but a mystery, since,

85 Our thanks to P. Neuenkirchen for this remark.
86 Quoted by Baker-Brian 2011, 44.
87 See Widengren 1965, 24, and Baker-Brain 2011, 43 on the various reports we have in this respect; other sources prefer a location to the east of the towns, in Gaukhay; it has also been suggested that his birthplace and his homeland could be different, cf. Sundermann 2009.
88 See Widengren 1965, 30, as a key of his behavior; Baker-Brian 2011:62; on (the) Mani (chaeans)' fascination for the royal court, see Dilley 2014, 37; Gardner 2014, 240–45.
89 Sundermann 2009; the fact is recorded in Manichaean documents, cf. Gardner 2015a, 75–97 comment on K76: "Here Mani is explicitly placed in Ktesiphon where Shapur keeps asking for him and the apostle must go back and forth between the demands of the king at court and his own community in the city."
90 Henning 1942, 941, 943–44; Sundermann 1986:278–98.

looking at the map, the city was just in the middle of his world to which all roads, real and proverbial, led. More important, all the missions he sent forth, led by his disciples,[91] departed from Ctesiphon.[92] The Manichaean documents themselves (e.g., M 216) recount that he kept Beh Ardashir as his permanent base during his lifetime.[93] And a populous city gives more opportunities to hide, for a new faith and a delicate prophet to flourish, so he remained there during difficult periods.[94] Indeed he met his fate in another capital, and just after his execution, the remains of his corpse were possibly taken back to Ctesiphon (and if so, it probably was the starting point of a *martyrion*, as some texts suggest).[95] For his disciples the situation did not change much: as the new religion expanded, Mani's disciples still travelled to Beh-Ardashir,[96] Ctesiphon remained Manichaeism's ecclesiastical center,[97] the official head, the *archegos*, had his see there[98] until it was moved to Baghdad[99] and a number Manichaean communities persisted nearby, despite numerous persecutions.[100]

In a word the connection between Mani and his homeland cannot be challenged, and in fact it remained tight long after Mani's death, in Mesopotamia and probably beyond. And so too he is our candidate for the anonymous figure mentioned in Q 43:31, whose allusion to Mani we therefore understand to be rhetorical, as though it meant to say: they have insulted our prophet saying: "if you were just like Mani!" or: "who do you think you are, another (a new) Mani?" And hence neither fully real (Mani was well dead by the time Q 43:31 was composed) nor fully irreal (for Mani had existed and his person could still be evoked to make a difference).

91 Sundermann 2009.

92 Baker-Brian 2001, 71.

93 I.e., between 244 and 261 CE; cf. Widengren 1965:34; Lieu 1994, 26.

94 Gardner 2015b:160, 184.

95 Widengren 1965, 42, quoting the *Manichaean Homelies* and the *Psalm Book*; Sundermann 2009.

96 Asmussen 1975, 21.

97 Toral-Niehoff 2013b, 55.

98 Sundermann 2009c.

99 Lieu 1994, 15.

100 Glassé 2009, 129–44.

6 An Architecture of Pride and Shame

The following verses (Q 43:32–33) lend unexpectedly support to the proposed Mesopotamian trope, and it is a pity that so far they have not been exploited as they deserve; however, material culture broached in the Qur'ān is scarcely studied despite its relevance. The rhetorical attacks continue against the same people countered on the preceding verses with a well-known theme. The disbelievers got some obvious mundane benefits in terms of both material and social life (*ma'īshat, darajat*). They obtained welfare (periphrastic *mimmā yajma'ūna*, what they accumulated), and surely they are proud of it, nor they do not hide it, a behavior which is moreover typical of nobility or the high classes. Clearly, this usual discourse is a desperate one indeed, without any hope of converting them.

The following verse (v. 34) is more complex, and rhetorically ambitious, not to say risky: it wants to express absolute divine power to the extreme, even to the absurd, against its own purpose. If we follow the text, it claims that God could have found even more favor in them if he had wanted, and by doing so, he would have gathered one community (*umma*), for unbelievers, of course.[101]

This confirms that material welfare was a fundamental issue, a central debate at that time for both (those who have it, and those without). Nothing new under the sun, but the poor hold the *kalām*, this time. If the redactors dared to reach these logical extremities, it is because their audience was very sensitive to these topics, and it even goes further: after this highly sophisticated argument, the images used as examples became monumental, to say the least. Surely, the way they express themselves was obscure for some and it demands stunning examples for (or against) people scandalously favored by life fate. So, their imaginations produced some original extravagance about the unbelievers' houses, as the most apparent element of their prosperity. Their domestic architecture had already reached an outstanding level of comfort and splendor, and the next step could only be, for God, to furnish them some "terraces of silver." The first word, *suquf*, is something translated as roof but this is misleading, or imprecise: it is an elevated place and the following section explains that people can go there, by some stairs (*ma'ārij*, an item leading upstairs) and the element is related to a verb *ẓahara*. Most of translations proposed a pleonastic sense: to climb, to go upstairs. But most of its 35 other occurrences are verbal connoting to appear, and in this precise situation it should hence be understood as: by staircase, they appear on the roof and to the people who are already there. So it is a place to rest and enjoy

101 This sense is possible because the Qur'anic use of *umma* is very generic and not yet associated with the Muslim community; it implies gathering people, for example, against something.

fresh air at night, during the suffocating summers, in the lowlands.[102] That some houses are moreover provided with doors appears not to be a great privilege in and of itself. Seemingly, it implies impressive, colossal gates as it can be seen in palaces, not normal houses, perhaps with columns or arcs.[103] The last element involved is set there deliberately, because it marks a climax, and a link to another theme: the beds, or more precisely the benches (*surur*), for the verb next to it describes a physical gesture (*yattaki'u*), to lean, not to lie, and that is enough to evoke banqueting activities here and now, and furthermore hereafter, in Paradise.[104]

As an afterthought, the text uses a word whose function is surely to reiterate the whole idea, and its importance might have later provided the choice of the *sūra*'s title: *al-zukhruf*, a difficult word, not exactly understood, whose derivation is still discussed.[105] The general picture is clear: something rich, beautiful, luxurious (no use to add "gold" as in most of the translations . . .). A look at other occurrences in the Qur'ān confirms this sense.[106]

Now, if the authors used these striking images here, taken and derived from a domestic architecture, it means they were impressed themselves by these models, surely in some advanced urban area, where people and wealth enabled the erection of ostentatious buildings. Certainly not in the midst of *Arabia Deserta*, in the middle of nowhere. All of this evidence is much better fitted to an imperial capital,[107] or a frontier society like that found in contemporary Hira, again.[108] Besides, the flamboyant use of silver (*fiḍḍat*) as flat roofing, instead of

102 A more fitting example of large-scale domestic architecture is Dura Europos, and of course, some areas excavated in Seleuceia. This type of building has a very conservative shape, because the climate and hence the basic materials never change (before the rise of concrete).

103 Besides their natural suspicion against town and urban people, it is easy to imagine how nomads would be suitably impressed by arcs and vaults as architectural marvels.

104 Note that the Qur'anic redactors placed the next Paradise verse at some distance from the present verse. For the gesture, see Courtieu forthcoming a.

105 Jeffery 1938, 150; cf. Carter 2006, 147: "something highly embellished."

106 E.g. Q 6:112, 10:25.

107 Lieu 1994, 37 calls it "a major center for the distribution of luxury goods."

108 Toral-Niehoff 2013a, 123–24: "The evidence of the pre-Islamic Arab poetry, archeological material and Persian loanwords in Arabic, all suggest that this contact resulted in a voluntary cultural orientation of the Hiran elites towards the court culture of Ctesiphon, by assimilating Persian luxury items, aristocratic values and power semiotics. However, this transculturation process requires a much deeper and actualized analysis in light of current research methodologies in Cultural studies, especially those which relate to frontier societies."

earth, straw and reeds,[109] leads directly to Iran, considered the "land of Silver" (more than gold), where accordingly the (silver) *dirham* was minted in bulk for centuries,[110] and the semi-luxurious silverware was so widespread it can be found even in the Qur'anic descriptions of Paradise.[111]

Singularly the *Tafsīr* and the *Sunna* provide us with useful information, which again points nigh exclusively to Iran. Thus for instance Ibn Kathīr elaborates on Q 43:31 by quoting a *ḥadīth* thereby showing where the archetype lies:

> When 'Umar bin Al-Khattab, may Allah be pleased with him, visited the Messenger of Allah in seclusion, when he was keeping away from his wives, and he saw him resting on a rough mat which had left marks on his side, his eyes filled with tears and he said, "O Messenger of Allah, look at this Chosroes and this Caesar with all that they have, and you are the best of Allah's creation." The Messenger of Allah was reclining, but he sat up and said:
>
> "Are you in doubt, O son of Al-Khattab."
>
> Then he said:
>
> "Those are people for whom the enjoyments are hastened in this world."
>
> According to another report [he said]:
>
> "Does it not please you that this world is for them and the Hereafter is for us?"
>
> In the two *sahihs* and elsewhere, it is reported that the Messenger of Allah said:
>
> "Do not drink from vessels of gold and silver, and do not eat from plates of the same, for these things are for them in this world and for us in the Hereafter. Allah has granted these things to them in this world because it is insignificant . . . "[112]

As for the *Sunna* it develops the same rejection of luxury as materialized in (Sassanian) silverware:

> While Hudhaita was at Mada'in, he asked for water. The chief of the village brought him a silver vessel. Hudhaifa threw it away and said,
>
> "I have thrown it away because I told him not to use it, but he has not stopped using it.
>
> The Prophet forbade us to wear clothes of silk or Dibaj, and to drink in gold or silver utensils, and said:
>
> 'These things are for them in this world and for you in the Hereafter.'"[113]

109 This fantasy of building in precious metals is widespread (cf. Nero's *domus aurea* in Rome). But a fact can explain the exaggeration in mind: in Mesopotamia, even the most impressive buildings, for the most powerful rulers or gods, are in fact made of very rude materials: crude earth, straw, reeds, palm-trees and plaster, rocks, metals, and precious stones tend to be unwonted – hence desired – imports.

110 As Ṭabarī himself records (*Tārīḫ* 14.1056–1057).

111 In the next paradisiac verse, as a surprise, the dishes are not made out of silver, but, as an exception (see Courtieu forthcoming a) gold; perhaps a means to disconnect from the aforementioned metallic roofs . . .

112 Ibn Kaṯīr, *Tafsīr* AD 43:31.

113 Buḫārī, *Ṣaḥīḥ* 5632.

Note how the sudden appearance of this precious metal, though not in Paradise, but the real life, is the most striking image, with obvious exaggeration, designed to impact suitably the audience.

In conclusion, the study of the Qur'ān's material culture's additionally supports the idea of a Mesopotamian background for Q 43:2–45, and thereby too the hypothesis that the setting of the earliest Qur'anic milieu must be searched for in the environments of Ctesiphon-Seleucia, the administrative capital of the Sassanian empire.

7 Addendum

Is it possible that Q 43:2–45, while being about Ctesiphon, was, however, written elsewhere, somewhere in the Arabian Peninsula, maybe even Mecca? It is not impossible, of course. But why keep a non-Mesopotamian setting at whatever price – the passage's vivid fascination with Ctesiphon's richness, the close comparison of the Qur'anic prophet with a man from Ctesiphon? Must one not be sensitive to the warm blood running through the aforementioned examined verses. Besides, what could require such caution – a sense of conformity, despite all, to the grand narrative of Islam's origins, a sense of scholarly custom or habit? It would be easy to evoke, say, Mu ammad's informants – like in the early days of the study of the Qur'ān. We have opted to follow a different path. From the infinite combinatory options one could venture apropos the interpretation of the passage in question, we have set forth a possible combination: the one we feel to be more methodologically sound and historically plausible; the one that proves more fascinating.

References

el-Ali, Saleh Ahmad. 1968–9. "Al-Madā'in and its Surrounding Area in Arabic Literary Sources." *Mesopotamia* 3–4:417–39.

Asmussen, Jes Peter 1975. *Manichaean Literature.* Delmar, NY: Scholars Facsimiles and Reprints.

Azaiez, Mehdi. 2015. *Le contre-discours coranique.* Berlin: De Gruyter.

Azaiez, Mehdi, Gabriel Said Reynolds, Tommaso Tesei, and H. M. Zafer, eds.. 2016. *The Qur'ān Seminar Commentary / Le Qur'ān Seminar: A Collaborative Study of 59 Qur'ān Passages / Commentaires collaborative de 50 passages coraniques.* Berlin: De Gruyter.

Baker-Brian, Nicholas J. 2011. *Manichaeism: An Ancient Faith Rediscovered.* London and New York: Continuum.

Beck, Daniel A. 2018. *Evolution of the Early Qur'ān: From Anonymous Apocalypse to Charismatic Prophet*. New York: Peter Lang.

Beck, Daniel A. 2020. "The Astral Messenger, The Lunar Redemption, The Solar Salvation: Manichaean Cosmic Soteriology in the Qur'ān's Archaic Surahs (Q 84, Q 75, Q 54)." In *Remapping Emergent Islam: Texts, Social Contexts, and Ideological Trajectories*, edited by C. A. Segovia, Amsterdam: Amsterdam University Press.

BeDhun, Jason D. 2000. *The Manichaean Body: In Discipline and Ritual*. Baltimore and London: Johns Hopkins University Press.

Bitton-Ashkelony, Brouria 2013. "'Neither Beginning nor End': The Messalian Imaginaire and Syriac Asceticism." *Adamantius* 19:222–39.

de Blois, François. 2004a. "Elchasai – Manes – Muhammad: Manichäismus und Islam in religionshistorischen Vergleich." *Der Islam* 81/1:31–48.

de Blois, François. 2004b. "Sabians." In *Encyclopaedia of the Qur'ān*, vol. 4, edited BY Jane Dammen McAuliffe, 511–13. Leiden and Boston: Brill.

Boiy, Tom. 2004. *Late Achaemenid and Hellenistic Babylon*. Leuven: Peeters.

Bowen Savant, Sarah. 2013. "Forgetting Ctesiphon: Iran's Pre-Islamic Past, c. 800–1100." In *History and identity in the late antique Near East*, edited by Ph. Wood, 169–86. Oxford and New York: Oxford University Press.

Berzon, Todd S. 2016. *Classifying Christians: Ethnography, Heresiology, and there Limits of Knowledge in Late Antiquity*. Berkley, Los Angeles, and London: University of California Press.

Bettiolo, Paolo. 2007. "Contrasting Styles of Ecclesiastical Authority and Monastic Life in the Church of the East at the Beginning of the Seventh Century." In *Foundations of Power and Conflicts of Authority in Late-Antique Monasticism*, edited by A. Camplani and G. Filoramo, 297–331. Leuven: Peeters.

Boisliveau, Anne-Sylvie 2014. *Le Coran par lui-même. Vocabulaire et argumentation du discours coranique autoréférentiel*. Leiden and Boston: Brill.

Camplani, Alberto. 2007. "The Revival of Persian Monasticism (Sixth to Seventh Centuries): Church Structures, Theological Academy, and Reformed Monks." In *Foundations of Power and Conflicts of Authority in Late-Antique Monasticism*, edited by A. Camplani and G. Filoramo, 277–95. Leuven: Peeters.

Carner, Daniel F. 2002. *Wandering, Begging Monks: Spiritual Authority and the Promotion of Monasticism in Late Antiquity*. Berkley, Los Angeles, and London: University of California Press.

Carter, Michael. 2006. "Foreign Vocabulary." In *The Blackwell Companion to the Qur'ān*, edited by A. Rippin, 120–39. Oxford and Malden, MA: Blackwell.

Cassis, Marica. 2002. "The Bema in the East Syriac Church In Light of New Archaeological Evidence." In *Hugoye: Journal of Syriac Studies* 5/2. URL: https://hugoye.bethmardutho.org/article/hv5n2cassis (accessed May 21, 2021).

Chabot, Jean-Baptiste. 1902. *Synodicon Orientale, ou recueil de synodes nestoriens*. Paris: Imprimerie Nationale.

Chaumont, Marie-Louise. 1988. *La christianisation de l'empire iranien*. Louvain: Peeters.

Courtieu, Gilles. Forthcoming a. "Cushions, Bottles and Roast Chickens." Proceedings of the 1st Nangeroni Meeting of the Early Islamic Studies Seminar (EISS), Milan, 2015.

Courtieu, Gilles. Forthcoming b. "Why Hārūt, why Mārūt, why Hārūt and Mārūt? Some Simple Questions on a Long-Standing Problem – and the Search for a Not-So-Very-Sectarian *Milieu*." Proceedings of the 2nd Nangeroni Meeting of the Early Islamic Studies Seminar (EISS), Florence, 2017.

Dilley, Paul. 2014. "Mani's Wisdom at the Court of the Persian Kings: The Genre and Context of the Chester Beatty *Kephalaia*." In *Mani at the Court of the Persian Kings, Studies on the Chester Beatty Kephalaia Codex*, edited by I. Gardner, J. BeDuhn, and P. Dilley, 15–51. Leiden and Boston: Brill.

Droge, Arthur D. 2013. *The Qur'ān: A New Annotated Translation*. Sheffield and Bristol, CT: Equinox.

Dye, Guillaume. 2015. "Pourquoi et comment se fait un texte canonique? Quelques réflexions sur l'histoire du Coran." In *Hérésies. Une construction d'identités religieuses*, edited by G. Dye, A. Van Rompaey, and Ch. Brouwer, 55–104. Brussels: Université Libre de Bruxelles.

Elm, Susanna. 1994. *"Virgins of God": The Making of Asceticism in Late Antiquity*. Oxford: Clarendon Press.

Engberg-Pedersen, Troels (ed.). 2001. *Paul beyond the Judaism/Hellenism Divide*. Louisville, KY: Westminster John Knox Press.

Escolan, Philippe. 1999. *Monachisme et Église. Le monachisme Syrien du VIe au VIIe siècle: un monachisme charismatique*. Paris: Beauchesne.

Fiey, Jean-Maurice. 1967. "Topographie chrétienne de Mahozé." *L'Orient syrien* 12:265–302.

Fiori, Emiliano B. 2010. "Dionigi l'Areopagita e l'origenismo siriaco. Edizione critica e studio storico-dottrinale del trattato sui Nomi divini nella versione di Sergio di Reš'aynā." PhD dissertation, University of Bologna.

Fioriani Piacentini, Valeria. 1994. "Madīna/shahr, qarya/deh, nā iya/rustāq – The City as Political-Administrative Institution: The Continuity of a Sassanian Model." *Jerusalem Studies in Arabic and Islam* 17:85–107.

Fisher, Greg, and Philip Wood. 2016. "Writing the History of the 'Persian Arabs': The Pre-Islamic Perspective on the 'Naṣrids' of al-Ḥīrah." *IS* 49/2:247–90.

Fitschen, Kiel K. 1993. "Did 'Messalianism' Exist in Asia Minor after A.D. 431?" *Studia Patristica* 25:352–55.

Gardner, Iain. 2015a. "The Final Ten Chapters." In Mani at the Court of the Persian Kings: Studies on the Chester Beatty Kephalaia Codex, ed. Iain Gardner, Jason BeDhun, and Paul Dilley, 75–98. Leiden and Boston Brill.

Gardner, Iain. 2015b. "Mani's Last Days." In Mani at the Court of the Persian Kings: Studies on the Chester Beatty Kephalaia Codex, ed. Iain Gardner, Jason BeDhun, and Paul Dilley, 159–208. Leiden and Boston Brill.

Glassé, Cyril. 2009. "How We Know the Exact Year the Archegos Left Baghdad." In *New Light on Manichaeism*, edited by J. D. BeDuhn, 129–44. Leiden and Boston: Brill.

Henning, Walter B. 1942. "Mani's Last Journey." *BSOAS* 10:941–53.

Henten, Jan W. van, and Joseph Verheyden (eds.). 2012. *Early Christian Ethics in Interaction with Jewish and Greco-Roman Contexts*. Leiden and Boston: Brill.

James, William. 1985. *The Varieties of Religious Experience: A Study in Human Nature*. Cambridge, MA: Harvard University Press.

Jeffery, Arthur. 1938. *The foreign vocabulary of the Quran*. Baroda: Oriental Institute.

Kröger, Jan. "Ctesiphon". 1993, 2011. In *Encyclopaedia Iranica*, edited by E. Yarshater. New York. URL: http://www.iranicaonline.org/articles/ctesiphon (accessed May 21, 2021).

Lieu, Judith. 2016. *Neither Jew Nor Greek? Constructing Early Christianity*. 2nd ed. London and New York: Continuum.

Lieu, Samuel N. C. 1992. *Manichaeism in the Later Roman Empire and Medieval China*. 2nd ed. Tübingen: Mohr Siebeck.

Lieu, Samuel N. 1994. *Manichaeism in Mesopotamia and the Roman East*. Leiden and Boston: Brill.

Lim, Richard. 2008. "The Nomen Manichaeorum and Its Uses in Antiquity." In *Heresy and Identity in Late Antiquity*, edited by Eduard Iricinschi and Holger M. Zellentin, 143–67. Tübingen: Mohr Siebeck.

Loosley, Emma. 2003. *The Architecture and Liturgy of the* Bema *in Fourth- to Sixth-Century Syrian Churches*. Kaslik, Liban: Parole de l'Orient.

Luxenberg, Christoph. 2007. *The Syro-Aramaic Reading of the Koran: A Contribution to the Decoding of the Language of the Koran*. Berlin: Schiler.

Maricq, André. 1959. "Vologésias, l'emporium de Ctésiphon." *Syria* 36/3–4:254–76.

Morony, Michael. 1989. "Beh-Ardašīr." In *Encyclopaedia Iranica*, ed. E. Yarshater. New York. URL: http://www.iranicaonline.org/articles/beh-ardasir-mid (accessed May 21, 2021).

Morony, Michael. 2009. "Madā'en.", In *Encyclopaedia Iranica*, ed. E. Yarshater. New York. URL: http://www.iranicaonline.org/articles/madaen-sasanian-metropolitan-area (accessed May 21, 2021).

Neusner, Jacob. 1966. *A History of the Jews in Babylonia*, vol. 2. Leiden and Boston: Brill.

Neusner, Jacob. 1969. *A History of the Jews in Babylonia*, vol. 4. Leiden and Boston: Brill.

Neusner, Jacob. 1976. *Talmudic Judaism in Sassanian Babylonia. Essays and Studies*. Leiden and Boston: Brill.

Neuwirth, Angelika, Nicolai Sinai, and Nora K. Schmid. N.d. "Mekkanischen Suren." URL: http://corpuscoranicum.de/kommentar/uebersicht (accessed May 21, 2021).

Nöldeke, Theodor. 1860. *Geschichte des Qorāns*. Göttingen: Dieterich.

Pettipiece, Timothy. 2015. "Manichaeism at the Crossroads of Jewish, Christian and Muslim Traditions." In *Patristic Studies in the Twenty-First Century: Proceedings of an International Conference to Mark the 50th Anniversary of the International Association of Patristic Studies*, edited by, 299–313 B. Bitton-Ashkelony, Th. de Bruyn, and C. Harrison. Turnhout: Brepols.

de Prémare, Alfred-Louis. 2002. *Les fondations de l'islam. Entre écriture et histoire*. Paris: Seuil.

de Prémare, Alfred-Louis. 2004 *Aux origines du Coran: questions d'hier, approaches d'aujourd'hui*. Paris: Téraèdre.

Van Reeth, Jan M. F. 2011. "La typologie du prophète selon le Coran: le cas de Jésus." In *Figures bibliques en Islam*, edited BY G. Dye and F. Nobilio, 81–105. Brussels: EME.

Van Reeth, Jan M. F. 2012a. "Melchisédech le Prophète éternel selon Jean d'Apamée et le monarchianisme musulman." *Oriens Christianum* 96:8–46.

Van Reeth, Jan M. F. 2012b. "Who Is the 'Other' Paraclete?" In *The Coming of the Comforter: When, Where, and to Whom? – Studies on the Rise of Islam and Various Other Topics in Memory of John Wansbrough*, edited by C. A. Segovia and B. Lourié, 423–52. OCJ 3. Piscataway: Gorgias Press.

Reinink, Gerrit J. 2009. "Tradition and the Formation of the 'Nestorian' Identity in Sixth- to Seven-Century Iraq." *Church History and Religious Culture* 89/1–3:217–50.

Ries, Julien. 1976. "La fête de Bêma dans l'Église de Mani." *Revue d'Études Augustiniennes* 22: 218–33.

Segovia, Carlos A. 2015. *The Qur'anic Noah and the Making of the Islamic Prophet: A Study of Intertextuality and Religious Identity Formation in Late Antiquity*. Berlin and Boston: De Gruyter.

Segovia, Carlos A. 2020. "Messalianism, Binitarianism, and the East-Syrian Background of the Qur'ān." In *Remapping Emergent Islam: Texts, Social Contexts, and Ideological Trajectories*, edited by C. A. Segovia, 111–127. Amsterdam: Amsterdam University Press.

Shahid, Irfan. 1995. *Byzantium and the Arabs in the Sixth Century*. Washington, DC: Dumbarton Oaks.

Simon, Robert. 1997. "Mani and Muihammad." *Jerusalem Studies in Arabic and Islam* 21: 118–40.

Guillaume, Alfred. 1955. *The Life of Muhammad: A Translation of Isḥāq's* Sīrat Rasūl Allāh *with Introduction and Notes*. Oxford & New York: Oxford University Press.

Segovia, Carlos A. "Messalianism, Binitarianism, and the East-Syrian Background of the Qur'ān." In *Remapping Emergent Islam: Texts, Social Settings, and Ideological Trajectories*. Edited by Carlos A. Segovia, 111–127. Amsterdam: Amsterdam University Press, 2020.

Stefanidis, Emmanuelle. 2008. "The Qur'ān Made Linear: A Study of the *Geschichte des Qorâns* Chronological Reordering." *Journal of Qur'ānic Studies* 10/2:1–22.

Stewart, Columba. 1991. *"Working the Earth of the Heart": The Messalian Controversy in History, Texts, and Language to AD 431*. Oxford: Clarendon Press.

Sundermann, Werner. 1981. *Mitteliranische manichäische Texte kirchengeschichtlichen Inhalts*. Berlin: Akademie-Verlag.

Sundermann, Werner. 1986. "Studien zur kirchengeschichtlichen Literatur der iranischen Manichäer II." *Altorientalische Forschungen* 13:40–92, 241–319.

Sundermann, Werner. 2009. "Manicheism. General survey." In *Encyclopædia Iranica*, edited by E. Yarshater. New York URL: http://www.iranicaonline.org/articles/manicheism-1-general-survey (accessed May 21, 2021).

Sundermann, Werner (n. d.). "BĒMA." In *Encyclopaedia Iranica*, ed. E. Yarshater. http://www.iranicaonline.org/articles/bema-festival-manicheans (accessed May 21, 2021).

Tamcke, Martin. 1988. *Der Katholikos-Patriarch Sabrīšō' I. (596–604) und das Mönchtum*. Frankfurt: Peter Lang.

Tardieu, Michel. 1992. "L'Arrivée des Manichéens à al-Ḥīra." In *La Syrie de Byzance à l'Islam, VIIe–VIIIe siècles*, edited by Pierre Canivet and Jean-Paul Rey-Coquais, 15–24. Damascus: Institut Français de Damas.

Tardieu, Michel. 1994. "L'Arabie du nord d'après les documents manichéens." *Studia Iranica* 23/1:59–75.

Toral-Niehoff, Isabel. 2010. "The 'Ibād of al-Ḥīra: An Arab Christian Community in Late Antique Iraq." In *The Qur'ān in Context: Historical and Literary Investigations into the Qur'ānic Milieu*, edited by Angelika Neuwirth, Nicolai Sinai, and Michael Marx, 323–48. Leiden and Boston: Brill.

Toral-Niehoff, I. 2013a. "Late Antique Iran and the Arabs: The Case of al-Hira." *Journal of Persianate Studies* 6:115–26.

Toral-Niehoff, I. 2013b. *Al-Ḥīra, Eine arabische Kulturmetropole im spätantiken Kontext*. Leiden and Boston: Brill.

Wansbrough, John. 2004. *Qur'anic Studies: Sources and Methods of Scriptural Interpretation*. Amherst, NY: Prometheus.

Wild, Stefan. (ed.). 2007. *Self-referentiality in the Qur'ān*. Wiesbaden: Harassowitz.

Widengren, Geo. 1965. *Mani and Manichaeism*. London: Weidenfeld & Nicolson, and New York: Holt, Rinehart and Winston.

Wood, Philip. 2013. *The Chronicle of Seert: Christian Historical Imagination in Late Antique Iraq*. Oxford and New York: Oxford University Press.

Peter von Sivers

Prophecies Fulfilled: The Qur'anic Arabs in the Early 600s

Few reliable reports exist about the history of the Qur'anic Arabs during the first half of the 600s. There are the near contemporary accounts in Christian sources of the foundation of the Arab kingdom (622 CE), the beginning expansion of this kingdom into Sasanid Mesopotamia (628 CE), the failure of the first Arab campaign against Roman Syria (629 CE), and the first civil war among the Arabs (660–661 CE). All other events are known only from the Islamic Tradition, which date to about 150 years later. These other events could very well be factually true, but so far, no method has been developed that reliably separates fact from fiction for any time prior to ca. 720 CE. If the historical method is to be upheld, documentation from the Islamic Tradition has to be set aside before any conclusions beyond the well-attested events cited above are drawn.[1]

This essay is intended to contribute to the writing of early Islamic history by searching for additional clues in the available sources, including the Qur'ān, of which we know now that it was largely complete toward the end of the seventh century CE.[2] In this search I will first (1) identify the Qur'anic pericopes that advance an anti-Sasanid prophecy of doom at the beginning of the 600s and therefore constitute a critical beginning of its composition. Second (2) I will look at the dispersal of the prophecy into the Syrian steppe after 602 and its presence in Arabia Petraea.[3] Third (3), the focus will move to the circumstances surrounding the emergence of the kingdom of the Arabs in 622. And fourth (4), the essay will conclude with a discussion of the generally accepted anti-Sasanid curse in 7/628, when the East Roman emperor Heraclius (610–641) defeated the

1 On two occasions in this essay (concerning the word *quraysh* and the chronology of early Arab campaigns in Mesopotamia) I am referring to information from the Islamic Tradition.

2 Nicolai Sinai argues for the date of ca. 650 of the closure of the *rasm*, an argument identical with the Islamic Tradition which asserts that the third ruler of the Arab kingdom, 'Uthmān, ordered the redaction of an official Qur'ān. See Sinai 2014. The earliest (incomplete) copies date to the second half of the seventh century. A list and description of the earliest extant Qur'āns dating to the second half of the first century AH/seventh century CE can be found in https://www.islamic-awareness.org/quran/text/mss/, "First Century Hijra.' Accessed 11–22-2019.

3 The official name of the East Roman province during the sixth century was "Tertia Palaestina." In this essay I will use the more common name "Arabia Petraea" or "Petraea." On the late history of Petraea see Fiema 2002:192.

Peter von Sivers, Emeritus, Department of History, University of Utah

https://doi.org/10.1515/9783110675498-010

Sasanid shah Khosrow II (590–628) and when the prophecy broadened into the vision of a post-Roman apocalyptic end of the world.

1 The Qurʾānic Curse of Khosrow II

The first person to doubt the veracity of the Islamic Tradition of Abraha's failed siege of Mecca in 570 CE,[4] allegedly told in Q 105, was Alfred-Louis de Prémare. In an article dating to 1998 he proposed to replace the traditional exegesis of this sura as a past story of punishment (*Straflegende*) of Abraha and his elephant-equipped army besieging Mecca with the prophecy of a Sasanid defeat at Qādisiyya by the Arabs.[5] In a follow-up article of 2000 he suggested that in addition to Qādisiyya also the Sasanid defeat by an eastern Arab tribal coalition at Dhū Qār, assumed to have occurred sometime between 604 and 611, should be considered as belonging to the Qur'anic "eschatological intention" (*visée*) in the sura.[6] As ingenious as these proposals are to move us away from Abraha's siege of Mecca, they unfortunately replace the original Islamic tradition with two further Islamic traditions (Qādisiyya and Dhū Qār) and thus do not bring us any closer to any of the "occasions of revelation" (*asbāb an-nuzūl*) in the Qur'ān that can stand up to modern requirements of documentation. Nevertheless, the shift in focus from southern Arabia to Mesopotamia was trailblazing.

A scholar who blazed Prémare's trail further, Daniel Beck, argues that Q 105 is a prophecy by God, revealed to a warner (*nadhīr*), of a disaster which will befall the ungodly Sasanid empire and its tyrant, Shahinshah (*shāhān shāh*) Khosrow II.[7] Sura 105, of course, consists of just four verses, which are a reminder about how God dealt with the army of elephants, how he made the stratagems of this army go awry, and how flocks of birds destroyed the army by pelting it with stones of clay so that nothing but chewed-up straw remained. The sura, according to Beck, reminds of the fate of the Seleucid and Ptolemaian armies with their Indian elephants from whose grip God saved the Jews according to Maccabees 2 and 3, as well as the sinful people of Sodom whom God pelted to death with stones of clay after he had sent two angels to lead Lot and the faithful remnant to safety (Q 15:72 and 51:32).

4 On this tradition see, for example, Horovitz 1926:10–11.
5 de Prémare 1998.
6 de Prémare 2000:346–359.
7 Beck 2018:1–78.

Listeners, so Beck, would have no problem applying the prophecy to Khosrow and understanding it as God's prophecy of the shahinshah's eventual punishment. It is this reapplication of the existing *Straflegenden* concerning the Sodomites, Ptolemies, and Seleucids to the Sasanids at the beginning of the 600s scholars of early Islam have supposedly overlooked. Beck insists that this concrete prophecy must be distinguished from the general, geographically and historically indistinct "eschatological orientation" of the Qur'ān, assumed in existing scholarship.

On the basis of sura 105, Beck extends his exegesis to an entire group of suras – Q 111, 96, 74, 68, 85, and 80 – which in his opinion flesh out the anti-Sasanid prophecy.[8] In my judgment, this extended exegesis is less convincing: Either the underlying scriptural background remains unidentified or the application of the pericopes to events contemporary with the composition of the Qur'ān does not quite fit. Two examples may suffice.

First, in the case of the *Straflegende* of Q 111:1–5 and its application as a prophecy predicting the doom of Khosrow, Beck argues that the shahinshah of the fire temple-worshiping Zoroastrians is the addressee when he is called "Abū Lahab" (Father of the Flame). He adduces a suggestive testimony of the seventh-century Armenian chronicler Sebeos, to frame how contemporaries viewed Khosrow: The Sasanids "consumed with fire the whole inner [land]" during Khosrow's conquests and brought "destruction on the whole earth."[9] However, on reflection, the suggested application does not really work well: Verses 4–5 speak of Abū Lahab's wife as an accomplice, even though there is nothing in the historical record which would implicate either of Khosrow's two wives. Their role remains unaddressed in Beck's exegesis.

One can only agree, of course, with Beck's critique of the Islamic Tradition which makes a certain Abū Lahab, assumed uncle of Muhammad and fierce enemy of Muhammad's during his early preaching career, the intended target of sura 111. Since there is nothing outside the *Sīira* that would corroborate the existence of Abū Lahab, he seems to be doubtful as a true candidate among the *asbāb an-nuzūl* for the pericope. Unfortunately, however, Beck does not investigate the underlying scriptural source in order to clarify whether the verses could have functioned as a prophecy of Khosrow's doom. Surprisingly, a satisfactory explanation of who is meant with the sobriquet "Abū Lahab" is still lacking in scholarship in general even though it is actually in plain view in the scripture.

8 Beck 2018: chs. 2–6.

9 Beck 2018:13. For Sebeos, see n. 12 below.

I am suggesting that the explanation lies in Q 28:76–81 (cf. also 29:39–40 and 40:23–24). Here, Abū Lahab turns up under his real name Qārūn, the immensely wealthy and arrogant rebel against Moses whom God destroyed by having the earth swallow him. Qārūn, as is generally recognized in Qur'anic scholarship, is the Korah of Numbers 16:1–40, which narrates at length his rebellion against Moses, together with some 250 followers, after the latter's descent from the mountain.[10] God ended this rebellion and saved Moses by not only having the earth swallow Korah but also by sending down a fire consuming all the followers.

Neither Numbers nor the Qur'ān (outside Q 111) mentions the wife of Korah/Qārūn, but the Midrashim feature her prominently. There she appears as a clever and wily person who actually instigates Korah into his rebellion.[11] Her description in Q 111 as a firewood carrier with a rope of palm fiber around her neck seems to be inspired by Numbers 16:6–7, 17–18, and 39, which speak of the burning of incense with charcoal (made by firewood) in 250 censers to garner God's favor for the rebellion. Midrash Mishlei, furthermore, mentions rope and gallows for the rebel Hāmān, whom the Qur'ān associates with Qārūn (Q 29:39).[12] The incorporation of these details from the Jewish scriptural tradition into the Qur'ān make sura 111 actually a sort of Qur'anic Midrash. In this role, the pericope has to be seen as a *Straflegende*, warning about God's inescapable earthly punishment of a rebel (together with his wife) who is sinful and acts against his command.[13] It would be difficult to apply to a king, such as Khosrow.

The second case of debatable application is Q 85:1–9 where the "people of the ditch" (*aṣḥāb al-ukhdūd*) are condemned to burn in hellfire because they "persecute the faithful men and women and do not repent." Beck applies it to the Sasanids after their conquest of Jerusalem in 614.[14] On first reading, one wonders, however, if the application really fits well since one would have to imagine the Persians as

---

10 Reynolds 2018:610.

11 Kadari 2009.

12 See: Le champ du Midrash, "A propos des fibres," https://www.lechampdumidrash.net/index.php?option=com_content&view=article&id=87:a-propos-de-fibres&catid=81&Itemid=483, accessed 7-13-2019. For further details on the wife of Korah see also *Babylonian Talmud*, Tractate Sanhedrin, folio 109a-110a, in http://come-and-hear.com/sanhedrin/sanhedrin_109.html, accessed 7-13-2019. On Hāmān see Reynolds, 2010, 97–106.

13 The identification of Abū Lahab with Korah/Qārūn (as well as with the Abū Lahab of the Islamic Tradition) was proposed in 1885 by an English Presbyterian missionary in India who composed a lengthy commentary on the Qur'ān. It was apparently never picked up in Islamic scholarship. See 1882–1896: III, 265–266: "The Quraishite facsimile of Qārūn against whom this revelation [Q 111- PVS] is directed, is most likely Abū Lahab, the rich and influential and defiant opposer of Muhammad."

14 Beck 2018:45; Beck 2019:16–18.

bearing the otherwise unknown sobriquet "people of the ditch." As he continues his argument, Beck mentions the Islamic tradition of the Jewish king Dhū Nuwās (517–527 CE) of Ḥimyar in Yemen as the antecedent that inspired Q 85:1–9. This tradition points to the king as the persecutor of the Christians of Najran – martyrs figuratively thrown into a ditch. Beck confronts the tradition with an essay by Manfred Kropp, who sees the sura as "an enraged outburst of a frustrated missionary directed to his followers" and proposes a new translation of verse 4: "To hell with (you), the 'people of the glazing flame' . . . You exactly know what you are doing to us, the believers."[15] If one accepts Kropp's translation, the sura could indeed dispel the first reading and be applicable to Jerusalem in 614, provided one associates the Sasanids with their fire temples, as Beck does.

Q 85:1–9, of course, trails a long history of research in which authors, dissatisfied with the alleged Dhū Nuwās antecedent of Islamic Tradition, have looked for alternative answers. This history began with Adam Geiger's brief suggestion in 1833 of the Book of Daniel 3 as the root of the pericope.[16] Daniel 3 contains the long story of three Christian youths thrown by Nebuchadnezzar into the flames of a furnace because of their refusal to pray to the Babylonian king's golden statue. God saves them unscathed in a miracle and puts Nebuchadnezzar to shame. Numerous investigations followed Geiger's suggestion, in search of an explanation of how in the *Straflegende* a furnace became a trench and how martyrs in the trench were replaced by perpetrators.[17] Marc Philenko gave the search a new twist in 1967 by suggesting that the scriptural antecedent is provided by the Qumran scrolls which refer repeatedly to the ditch of hell (*aneshey ha-Shaḥat* or *beney ha-Shaḥat*) as the fate for sinners.[18] Accordingly, one would have to read Q 85:1–9 not as a *Straflegende* but as an announcement of the ultimate fate of people who disobey God's commandments. This latter reading has found general favor with Islamic scholars, as Adam Silverstein points out, replacing Geiger's *Straflegenden* suggestion.[19] It is, of course, not impossible for the scriptural Qumran antecedent to have been applied in Q 85:1–9 to the Sasanids, but in my judgment this application remains speculative – certainly more so than in the case of Q 105. Nevertheless, in overall terms Beck's return to the neglected prophetic content of the Qur'ān deserves serious consideration and is definitely meritorious.

---

15 In Kropp's translation, the Arabic word for "trench" (*ukhdūd*) is emendated with the Aramaic loanword "(glazing) flame (*ujdūd*)." The translation can be found in Azaiez *et alii* 2016: 408–409. An earlier, but more detailed, analysis can be found in Kropp 2009:483–491.

16 Geiger 1833:192–193.

17 See Silverstein 2019.

18 Philonenko 1967:553–556.

19 Silverstein 2019:314–315.

In view of the overwhelming attention in the Qur'ān to past cases of God carrying out punishments on earth rather than postponing them to the eschatological future, it would indeed be surprising not to expect God to continue such punishments in the present. Consequently, to take *Straflegenden* of the past and apply them to concrete examples in the present would be a staple in the preaching of an often-frustrated missionary before obstreperous listeners, to use Kropp's image. That evidence in the Qur'ān of such pronouncements of divine punishment in the present is rare, however, is to be expected since prophesies need to be fulfilled in order to be remembered and recorded as true. Prophecies have to be *vaticinia ex eventu*, as the saying goes.

In my judgment, there are perhaps two fulfilled prophecies concerning events in the first half of the seventh century CE in the Qur'ān, that is, the *Straflegende* of Sasanid doom and possibly the prediction of the Roman victory just prior to the arrival of the Apocalypse (Q 30:2–7), both obviously connected. All others – if they indeed existed – did not survive the redaction process of the Qur'ān. Instead we have a proliferation of unspecific warnings of the impending Eschaton, often accompanied by announcements of divine actions of salvation or punishment in God's Final Judgment. Prophecy, Apocalypse, and Eschaton will figure prominently in the following sections of this essay.

2 The Arabs "Gained Power" in the Syrian Steppe

If at least one sura of the Qur'ān (that is, Q 105) has Khosrow II and the Sasanids as its contemporary prophetic target, what then was the historical "occasion of revelation" for this sura to be composed? As argued in Section 1, Dhū Qār of the Islamic Tradition is not a good candidate, on account of belonging to the Islamic Tradition dating to 150 years after the composition of the Qur'ān. Interestingly, however, Ṭabarī, one of the stalwarts of the Islamic Tradition, makes clear, that Dhū Qār itself had an"occasion," arguing that "the fate of Nuʿmān was the cause for Dhū Qār."[20] He is referring to Khosrow II's abolition of the Arab vassal kingdom under the Nasrid (Lakhmid) king Nuʿmān III (582–602 CE), centered on the town of Ḥīra at the western edge of Mesopotamia, and the subsequent suppression of the Arab revolt – a revolt dating to 602 that is well-documented outside the Islamic Tradition.

20 Ṭabarī 1879: III, 1029; Ṭabarī 1999:V, 358.

In this context, Ṭabarī also mentions Muhammad twice, first to establish the date of the beginning of his prophethood as coinciding with the aftermath of Nuʿmān's death[21] and second, to have him exclaim that Dhū Qār was the first contest (*yawm*) for the Arabs to "demand justice" (*intaṣafa*) from the Persians.[22] This exclamation sounds like an echo, even if faint, of the thunderous curse in sura 105 hurled against the Sasanids surviving in the Islamic Tradition.

The historical documentation for the abolition of Nuʿmān's kingdom and the subsequent revolt of the Arabs is quite detailed and allows us to establish a solid "occasion of revelation."[23] Much of it deals with a court intrigue that led to Nuʿmān's arrest and death by poison.[24] The specifics of this intrigue are not of importance here except that one can gather from the documents that this last ruler of the Nasrid kingdom was perhaps no longer at the height of his power. He had originally been crowned by Khosrow's father Hormizd IV in ca. 580. When Hormizd was confronted in 590 with a coup by his relative Bahrām Chōbīn and was planning his flight from the capital Ctesiphon to Ḥīra, Nuʿmān was evidently still influential. But when the plan was forestalled by Hormizd's two brothers-in-law dynastic politics in the capital changed drastically. The two brothers-in-law deposed, blinded, and finally murdered Hormizd in a palace coup before placing his son Khosrow II on the throne. Instead, Bahrām Chōbīn, posing as Hormizd's avenger, took the throne himself and defeated Khosrow, forcing the latter to flee to Maurice. The East Roman and Persian Empires were at that time still technically at war, but in a shrewd move, Maurice extracted territorial concessions from Khosrow to make peace and equipped him with an army to regain his throne.[25]

During these events, Nuʿmān had kept his distance and did not accompany Khosrow into exile, perhaps assuming that the rule of the then still young Khosrow was finished. He may also have suspected Khosrow as an accomplice in the palace coup. Q 80:1–10 can perhaps be read as an allusion to Khosrow's assumed

---

21 Ṭabarī 1879: III:1038; Ṭabarī 1999:V, 372.

22 Ṭabarī 1879: III:1016; Ṭabarī 1999:V, 338.

23 The two major sources are *Khuzistan Chronicle* and *Chronical of Seert*. A new edition and translation of the *Khuzistan Chronicle*, replacing the older but still valuable works by Guidi and Nöldeke, was published by al-Kaʿbī in 2016 (*Khuzistan Chronicle* 2016). The *Chronicle of Seert* is available as *Histoire nestorienne* in *Chronicle of Séert* 1983. Both sources were composed by East Syriac/Nestorian Christians; the first author was an eyewitness to events up to 658 and the second, while writing in the middle of the fourth/tenth century, made extensive use of now lost pre-Islamic sources. For evaluations of these sources see Robinson 2004 and 2013:2–8.

24 al-Kaʿbī 2016:25–27 (ed.), 24–26 (trans.).

25 On these events see Pourshariati 2008:397–404 and Shahbazi 2016:514–522.

complicity, if one follows Beck.[26] The *Chronicle of Seert* seemingly agrees with the charge of complicity, by asserting point blank that Khosrow blinded his father.[27] But a few pages later, with much greater detail, the *Chronicle* rolls the assertion back by stating that Bahrām minted coins in the name of Khosrow as he was marching on the capital Ctesiphon, thereby arousing Hormizd's suspicion of a plot by his son. To save his life, so the source states, Khosrow fled the palace and returned only after his two uncles had blinded Hormizd and offered the throne to Khosrow.[28] Three other sources agree with the more detailed account of the Chronicle of Seert[29] and it seems that Khosrow's complicity was more a suspicion than a proven fact.[30] This nuanced evaluation in the sources of Khosrow's inauspicious beginnings as shah, of course, would not have merited any consideration in the eyes of the Eastern Christian Arabs who were outraged by the murder of Nuʿmān III and the suppression of their kingdom.[31] For them, Khosrow was a bloody tyrant from his youthful start onwards.

Nuʿmān presumably redeemed himself after Khosrow's return to power when he sent one of his sons to save the shah in a new plot against him a few years

26 Beck 2019:18–20.

27 *Chronicle of Seert* 1983:439.

28 Ibid.:443–444.

29 The anti-Sasanid East Syriac *Khuzistan Chronicle* reports on the accession of Khosrow only briefly and does not charge Khosrow with complicity. See *Khuzistan Chronicle* 2016:5–7 (ed.), 4–6 (trans.). The anti-Khosrow Sebeos writes in a similar vein, taking Khosrow's youth at that time into account. See Sebeos 1999:17–18. The chronicle, with an ending date of ca. 660, is based on now lost sources and is generally considered reliable up to the rise of the Qur'anic Arabs. The anti-Khosrow Roman chronicler Theophylact Simocatta, in a much longer story, agrees with the longer version of the *Chronicle of Seert* and with the *Khuzistan Chronicle*, charging no complicity, but has the doomed Hormizd nevertheless implore his two brothers-in-law in a lengthy speech to elevate another of his sons on the throne, in place of the in his mind unworthy Khosrow. See Theophylact Simocatta, *History*, IV.3.4–IV:7.6.

30 In their entries in the *Encyclopaedia Iranica*, Abdallah S. Shahbazi ("Hormozd IV," "Bestam o Bendoy," and "Vahram Chubin") and James Howard-Johnson ("Kosrow") go farther than the above sources, without however presenting contemporary documentation. Shahbazi charges Khosrow with having been "in league" with his two uncles and assenting to their actions with "full complaisance (despite the claim to the contrary in the official history)," while Howard-Johnson describes Khosrow as a puppet in the hands of his uncles who gave "at least his tacit consent" to the overthrow of his father.

31 There is evidence of emotions being at a fever pitch during 590–602. Bahrām had his followers proclaim a Zoroastrian apocalyptic prophecy according to which he was the savior (*saoshyant*) at the end of the third millennium when the "deaf and blind" last tyrant would be overthrown, the world would end, and the original creation of Ahura Mazda would be restored. See Payne 2013:25–26, Skjaervö 2011:343, and Pourshariati 2008:403–414.

later.[32] But the king's influence at court must have been diminished: The *Chronicle of Seert* is explicit about Nu'mān's solicitousness to receive permission for his conversion from paganism to Eastern Christianity in 594.[33] All things told, Khosrow and Nu'mān did not have a close and trusting relationship and since the latter's power was waning, Khosrow expedited the demise of his vassal with his murder.

From a modern, geostrategic perspective one can conclude that the king had become expendable by the late 500s. In 582, the East Roman emperors had downgraded the Arab vassal kingdom of the Jafnids (or Ghassanids) in Syria and Arabia Petraea on the border of the steppe, which was the counterpart to that of the Nasrids. Prior to this time, both the Romans and the Sasanids had subsidized the buildup of mobile Arab auxiliary forces on the fluid Syrian steppe border between them, to act as proxies in their own prolonged wars against each other. But eventually, for reasons of economy as well as religion, Emperor Maurice exploited a failed campaign with Mundhir against the Persians to depose the Arab king and appoint instead a set of 15 lower-ranked tribal shaykhs (some of whom Jafnid) for the defense of the border.[34] The Jafnids had embraced the Jacobite Monophysite Christian confession of their subjects in the province of Arabia during the mid-500s but remained loyal to the Chalcedonian emperors, continuing to receive rich subsidies in kind or money during their reign. But when schisms divided the Jacobites in the second half of the 500s, which the Jafnids were unable to mend, Maurice decided to reassert Chalcedonian church authority and reduce their power.[35] With the Jafnids weakened after 582, Khosrow evidently decided to follow Maurice's example and assert Sasanid power over his Arabs as well.

Like Maurice, Khosrow appointed a lower level leader, Qiyās b. Qabīṣa, to the position of *qā'id* over the Arabs. Because of the Arabs' "strength of power" (*li-shidda l-shawka*), however, Ibn Qabīṣa was unable to maintain himself in Ḥīra. In his place, a more resolute frontier commander (*marzubān*), Rūzbī b. Marzūq, took up residence in a fortified place near Ḥīra, "to guard the frontier and battle the Arabs in the desert (*bi-l-barriyya*)."[36] Eventually, Rūzbī was able to defeat the Arabs, as well as "escape the trap" (*ḥīla*) that Khosrow intended for him to fall

32 *Chronicle* of *Seert* 1983:469.

33 Discussed in von Sivers 2021. An English version will appear in early 2022 on the Academia.edu website.

34 See: Shahid 1995a:418–420, 455–461, and 545.

35 Ibid.:467–468; Shahid 1995b:805–806, 922–935. The schisms are discussed in von Sivers 2020.

36 *Chronicle* of *Seert* 1983:546.

into."[37] The sources do not elaborate on this trap. Perhaps it was Rūzbī's Eastern Christian leanings – he was an admirer of a cenobitic monk and healer near Ḥīra – that made him suspect to the shah whose relations with his Eastern Christian subjects in the early 600s had turned indifferent or even outright hostile.

The Nasrid dynasty had owned large agricultural properties in Mesopotamia, from which its rulers drew subsidies for the tribal alliance system that characterized their kingdom. Ḥīra's inhabitants, the bodyguard of Nuʿmān, as well as the nearby and farther away tribal leaders were all recipients of subsidies doled out by the king. Hence, once the subsidies disappeared and the initial revolt was crushed, the *Chronicle of Seert* does not hold back in its overall assessment:

> When Khosrow, through a ruse, had poisoned and killed al-Nuʿmān b. al-Mundhir, king of the Arabs, and his son, the Arabs rose in the Persian as well as the Byzantine empires, dispersed [into the Syrian steppe] according to their own whims, caused quarrels (*munāziʿāt*) with Heraclius and Khusrow, and gained power (*takammanū*). They continued with their unrest until the appearance (*ẓuhūr*) of the creator of Islamic Law. [Muḥammad – PVS][38]

In the absence of documentation, we can only guess who all dispersed into the Syrian steppe. Possible candidates are Eastern Christian priests, monks, scribes, and learned men of Ḥīra, called the "Pious" (sing. *ʿibād*). In addition, we can think of the remnants of the Eastern Christian Nasrid dynastic family, allied Eastern Christian and Monophysite local tribes, and branches of (Eastern Christian as well as pagan?) desert tribes.[39] What they likely carried with them, apart from older Eastern Christian, Manichaean, and Chaldaean texts, was God's curse of Khosrow II, perhaps in written form, to be preached among the dispersed people. The prophecy and texts might have traveled from Ḥīra more deeply into the Syrian steppe than any human groups and as such might have become common lore among the Arabs in the years after 602, even without anyone from Ḥīra directly involved. Agnosticism as to how this literature spread among the Arabs of the Syrian steppe is probably the most prudent approach here.

Before we follow the Arabs or their prophecy more deeply into the Syrian steppe a brief return to Khosrow's battle against Bahrām Chōbīn in 591 might illuminate sura 111 from an unexpected perspective. In the *History* attributed to Bishop Sebeos is the text of a message sent by an Armenian military commander, Musegh II Mamikonean, to Bahrām Chōbīn, the usurper of the Sasanid throne in 591

---

37 Ibid.:549.
38 Ibid.:539–540.
39 Kister 1968:143–169; Donner:1980, 5–38.

discussed above. Emperor Maurice had given Khosrow II troops with which to fight his way back to the Persian throne. These troops included an Armenian contingent under Mussegh who answered a taunt of Bahrām's with the following prophecy:

> And now I say to you that if God so wills it, tomorrow you will be embroiled in a battle with braves who will explode upon you and your multitude of elephants like the most violent clouds in the sky. An enormous explosion will be heard from on High, and a flash of lightning, and armed men on white horses with unerring spears will attack you and pass through your hosts the way lightning does through an evergreen forest, burning the branches as the bolts rain down from Heaven to earth, burning the brush of the fields. For, should God will it, a whirlwind will carry off your might like dust . . .[40]

Are we dealing here with some standard battle messaging that chroniclers like Sebeos and the composer of sura 105 were using at the turn of the 600s, threatening the opponent with catastrophic consequences? Or is the imagery merely coincidental, conveniently at hand during military confrontations? However these questions are to be answered, at a minimum the example of Mussegh's oration illustrates the kind of holy fury a few years later a contingent of East Christian Arabs was capable of when facing their elephant-equipped pagan foe.

3 Christianity in Arabia Petraea

The spread of the Qur'anic prophecy into the Syrian steppe coincided with Khosrow's great war of annihilation against East Rome (602–628), shortly after the murder of Nuʿmān. It must have received, therefore, powerful reinforcement especially during the Sasanid conquest of northern Syria in 612 and southern Syria in 614 when Chalcedonians and Monophysites fled from the enemy. That there was such a flight of, among others, monks (presumably both Chalcedonoians from Jerusalem and Palestine and Jacobites from Syria), into the Syrian steppe we can take from Bernard Flusin, who examined the available sources for the Persian massacres and deportations of Christians from Jerusalem.[41] One logical place to flee to was to the southwestern end of Arabia Petraea, the former kingdom of Nabataea. The area around Petra, the capital of the province, and along the Wadi Musa had been developed by the Romans into an important urban and agricultural

---

40 Sebeos 1999:22.

41 Flusin 1992:164–170. While the Sasanid conquest had a definite human impact, material destruction remained limited; see for a summary see Stoyanov 2011:13–22.

province, a development that continued throughout the sixth century.[42] Christianity had arrived in the province in the middle of the 300s[43] and by the late 500s Arabia Petraea possessed a bishop, a basilica, monasteries, and churches.[44] How deep the inroads of the Jacobites into the province were during the later 500s is impossible to determine: Parts of the province belonged to the Jacobite Arab kingdom of the Jafnids, but the nearby Negev remained Chalcedonian. Presumably there was a degree of sectarian diversity among the Christians in the province.

Sura 106 allows us perhaps to catch a glimpse of the situation of the Qur'anic believers in the province of Petraea. The sura is grammatically connected to Sura 105 discussed above and might have been conjoined with it at some point in the Qur'anic redaction process:[45]

> He did this [God prophesying the destruction of the Sasanids in sura 105? – PVS)] to make the *quraysh* feel secure, secure in their winter and summer journeys. So, let them worship the Lord of this House (*rabb hadhā l-bayt*) who provides them with food to ward of hunger, safety to ward of fear.[46]

The word *quraysh* in the sura has caused much ink to be spilled. Islamic Traditionists found it difficult to explain why the word was apparently not a tribal name. Ṭabarī for example, cites first the genealogist Ibn al-Kalbī, for stating that "Quraysh is a collective name and cannot be traced back to a father and a mother or to a male or female guardian." After citing a number of further traditions, however, Ṭabarī mentions a report that invokes descent: " . . . they [the descendants of an-Naḍr b. Kināna, ancestor of Muhammad – PVS] were then called "Quraysh" because they had been gathered together, which is the meaning of the verb *taqarrasha*." Another report, also cited by Ṭabarī, is silent about descent but similarly focuses on the verb *taqarrasha*. According to this report, the Umayyad caliph ʿAbd al-Malik (r. 66–86/685-705 CE) inquired about the origin of the Quraysh and learned that their existence began "[when] they were

42 See Nasarat *et alii* 2012. See also Caldwell 2001. Caldwell uses new evidence from the decipherment of burned papyri dating to as late as 593 that reveal a still strong class of East Roman landowners administering their affairs in the province. In an article of 2005 Patricia Crone expresses her puzzlement about the "quranic pagans" being described as farmers even though Mecca is infertile. She mentions farming in Arabia Petraea but fails to disconnect these quranic pagans from Mecca (Crone 2005:387–399). In another article, of 2007, she mentions Petra but wonders why it is not mentioned in the Qur'ān (Crone 2007:83).

43 Politis 2007:190–194.

44 Michel 2001:3–7.

45 See Cuypers in Azaiez *et alii* 2016:438–439; Cuypers 2018:254.

46 Trans. Abdel Haleem in *The Qur'ān* 2004, 437–438.. The translator also believes that suras 105 and 106 were originally linked.

gathered into the sacred precincts (Ḥarām) from their dispersion. This gathering together is *taqarrush*."[47] Thus, if we can give any credence to these accounts from the Islamic Tradition it appears that the Quraysh did not have an eponymous ancestor and were some sort of an assembly of persons coming together only recently.

Would it be too speculative to conclude from Q 106 that there was a preacher in Arabia Petraea who either belonged to or was close to a people named "Quraysh" some of which journeyed with their wares during winter and summer journeys and had to always be vigilant against competitors who disputed the transit routes with them? In my judgment, this speculation is certainly less audacious than that of traditional Islam scholars who assume that the journeys of the Quraysh were pilgrimages-cum-trade journeys from Mecca to Jerusalem, once to celebrate Easter in Spring and to commemorate the discovery of the Cross in September.[48] If my version were acceptable, one would have to think that the Quraysh of Q 106 were people who considered Arabia Petraea their center and the "Lord of this House" as their central place of prayer, regardless of where the seasonal journeys took them.

The reading "Lord of this House" in sura 106 is close to the phrase "lord of the house (*mrʿ byt'*)," which, appears in Nabataean temple inscriptions in Petra, Ayn Shellaleh, Iram, Higra, and Madeba.[49] The temples were dedicated to the supreme god Dushāra, sometimes also with female associates, such as ʿUzzā, Manāt, or Allāt. If the term in sura 106 is indeed harking back to a Nabataean pagan origin, the question arises how it survived Christianization in the fourth and fifth centuries. Was it adopted into Christianity, in the sense that "the Lord" of a place of worship became "God"? Prémare and Dye assert such a Nabataean-Christian genealogy, but do not give further details.[50] John F. Healy, who investigated Nabataean religion in detail, suggests that one can understand the words *mrʿ byt'* in a generic sense, similar to how they appear in Arabic in the Qur'ān, as in sura 106:3.[51] Thus, the conclusion would have to be that Dushāra – a name derived from an escarpment near Petra[52] – was the lord of a place of worship who did not have to be named and that such places became churches when the Nabataeans were converted to Christianity.

---

47 Ṭabarī 1879:I, 1103–1104. Ṭabarī 1999:VI, 29–31. For a further discussion see Morris 2014.

48 Peters 1985:139–140, and 203. The September pilgrimage, called the "Encaenia," commemorated the discovery of the Holy Cross, as well as the inauguration of the Martyrium Basilica.

49 Healy 2001:75, 92, and 192.

50 Dye, in Azaiez *et alii* 2016:439; de Prémare 1998:263.

51 Healy 2001:92.

52 Healy 2001:85–86; see also Alpass 2013:48–50; Patrich 1990:99–104; Peterson 2006:23–31.

If we furthermore accept Q 6:92 as relevant in this context, it is perhaps indeed possible to localize the faith in God's prophecy about the Sasanid doom in the first and second decades of the 600s in a small community of scriptural believers in the region of Petra, which itself was likely inhabited by a mixture of Chalcedonian and Jacobite Arabs, as mentioned above:

> Blessed is this Book that we have sent down, confirming what was [revealed] before it, so that you may warn the Mother of Cities (*umm al-qurā*) and those around it. Those who believe in the Hereafter believe in it, and they are watchful of their prayers.[53]

Emperor Trajan (r. 98–117 CE) gave Petra the status of a "metropolis" (mother city, from *meter*, Gr. for "mother") in 114 CE, a few years after the Roman conquest of the kingdom of Nabataea (106 CE).[54] Consequently, we can understand this verse as God saying that he has sent a book down to a warner who is preaching to the people of Petra and surroundings about the Hereafter.[55]

If we look at the preceding verses 83–91 of sura 6, we learn that God has sent written texts of divine guidance previously to a whole series of (biblical) figures in this area of Petraea who all believed in God's oneness, rejected the possibility that God has partners, and to whom he gave "the Book, judgment, and prophethood." But evidently, according to verse 91, there are critics who object that the book sent down is not delivered in the proper way (by an angel, cf. verse 50 in the same sura).[56] Verse 92 cited above is thus the assertion, with the help of a scriptural typology of figures selected by God in support, that the warner is indeed being sent with a genuine revelation to Petra, angels or no angels aiding in this mission.

---

53 Trans. Ali Quli Qarai, in Reynolds 2018:235.

54 Tracy 1999:51–58. The idea of *umm al-qurā* being a calque of "metropolis" was perhaps first formulated by Dan Gibson, although he mistakenly assumes that it was Emperor Elag Abūlus (r. 218–222 CE) who gave Petra the status of a metropolis. See "Sneaker's Corner #2," https://www.youtube.com/watch?v=-x-wIbKU2mY, accessed 5-28-2019. Dan Gibson, of course, is a controversial author whose standards of scholarship I do not consider as measuring up to those of a professional historian. However, I also do not think that the intemperate reply to Gibson by the Islamic Traditionalist historian of astronomy David King in 2017 is what one thinks should be an appropriate form of academic exchange. See his "From Petra back to Makka – From 'Pibla' back to Qibla," http://www.muslimheritage.com/article/from-petra-back-to-makka, accessed 5-28-2019. Neither of the two takes a critical stance vis-à-vis the Islamic Tradition which assumes that the Arabs in western Arabia were pagans rather than Chalcedonian and Jacobite Christians, a stance which in my judgment is a precondition for any serious discussion of early Islam or, for that matter, Islamic civilization.

55 Jan Retsö 2003:48–50.

56 I am following here Reynolds 2018:234–235.

There is a parallel verse, Q 42:7, where God makes the announcement to the warner that he has revealed an Arabic Qur'ān to him so that he may alert the people of the "mother of towns" and environs of the Day of Gathering when people will be sent to Paradise and Hell. The sura, in which this verse is embedded, consists of a description of the many powers of the one God who has no partners, the blessings he bestows on the believers, and the punishments he meets out against the evildoers. Verse 13 announces that it is "hard on the associators (*mushrikūn*)" to what "you summon them" to. The following verse 14 tells the believers that they are to support the religion (*din*) enjoined upon Noah, Abraham, Moses, and Jesus and not be divided in it. The people, so we learn, did not divide until knowledge (*'ilm*) reached them and they became jealous of each other. At the end of the sura God assures the warner that he has imbued him with the Spirit of his Command (*al-rūḥan min amrinā*). Qur'ānic scholars understand this expression as meaning that God, through the Spirit, bestows his Command or Word on warners and others.[57] Looking at the sura as a whole, it is evidently an assertion of God's unchanging revelation from Noah to Jesus that also happened in Petra.

The name of the city of Petra seems to appear in yet another sura – 18:9 – although this time not in the shape of a calque, as above, but in the form of the Arabic expression *ar-raqīm*, which happens to be a *hapax legomenon*: "Do you suppose that the Companions of the Cave and *ar-raqīm* were among Our wonderful signs?" There are strong reasons to assume that the *rasm r-q-m* is of a Semitic origin and indicates a toponym, that is, the name of Petra,[58] and does not have the meaning of "inscription," as assumed by most commentators, most recently Sydney Griffith.[59] The meaning of "inscription" is rare in Arabic and plays no role in the sura, whereas a "tablet" inscribed with the names of the companions figures prominently in the Syriac version of the story. In both the Monophysitic and Eastern Christian traditions, in which the story of the Companions of the Cave was transmitted, the cave is associated with Ephesus in northern Mesopotamia.[60] By contrast, the Qur'anic version can be understood as both seeking to take pride

57 Ibid.:732, citing Jeffery 1938:6, for the possibility to view the Arabic *amr* as being related to Aramaic *memra*, with the meaning of word (*logos*), invoking the Johanine *logos* theology.

58 This translation has been championed recently by Mehdy Shaddel in Shaddel 2017. Not cited in Shaddel is Ernst A. Knauf who advanced the same translation several years earlier. See Knauf 2003.

59 Griffith derives the meaning of "inscription" from the East Syriac Christian Jacob of Serough's (451–521) version of the Companions story, which features a leaden tablet with the names of the youths in the cave inscribed and is repeatedly referred to in the story. See Griffith 2008. Reynolds (2018:450–451) continues to embrace Griffith's interpretation.

60 Theodosius:1882:27. Theodosius (530–566 CE) was a coenobitic monk and pilgrim.

of place for Petra and emphasizing divine Unitarianism (mentioned twice in the sura, as opposed to Trinity in the Syriac version). There is furthermore, of course, plenty of linguistic evidence for Arabia Petraea as the homeland of the Qur'ān.[61] Overall, it seems fair to state that this growing list of names pointing to the northwest of the Arabian Peninsula as the place of Islamic origins can no longer be dismissed easily.

From the above investigations of suras it is possible to deduce without undue speculation that the Qur'anic warner was a Christian preacher of the oneness of God, addressing himself to fellow Christians in Arabia Petraea who were divided among themselves as to what the true faith was. Apparently, these Christians were "associators," that is, Christians who added partners to the one God. Worse, once "knowledge," that is, theology, was introduced into the true faith, jealousy among the theologians deepened the divisions. We have here, in my judgment, a perfect description of the religious situation that prevailed in Syria, Mesopotamia, and the Syrian steppe since the second half of the 500s. The Syrian Jacobite Monophysites were split into the three branches of Severism, Tritheism, and Julianism; Chalcedonians were split into appeasers and hardliners vis-à-vis the Monophysites, and the Eastern Christians were split into the two branches of Henanism and Nestorianism.[62] In another essay,[63] I point to evidence according to which the theological splits caused considerable spiritual unrest among the monks of monasteries further north on the steppe rim of Syria. In my judgment, the Qur'ān is proof of both this unrest stirring also in Arabia Petraea and the unitarian faith intended for the warner to overcome it.

4 The Emergence of the Arab Kingdom

The curse of Khosrow entered a new phase with the emergence of the Arab "kingdom" in 622, as documented in seventh-century sources. One of these sources comes from the Arabs themselves in a Greek inscription affixed on a plaque to the thermal baths of Gader (today in northern Israel). The Umayyad *amīr al-mu'minīn* Muʿāwiya (r. 661–680 CE) had ordered its renovation which was dated according to

61 Durie 2018; Al-Jallad 2017:99–186; Fisher 2011:135–144; and Kerr 2014.

62 In this essay I am avoiding the term "Nestorianism" for the period prior to 612 and use instead the names "East Syriac Christians" or "Eastern Christians." Given Nestorius' condemnation in 431, the term "Nestorianism" was used by the Chalcedonians and Monophysites in a derogatory sense until the 800s when it became so common that East Syriac Christians began to use it for themselves. Reinink 2009:1–3 and 217–250.

63 von Sivers 2021.

the two chronologies of the Romans and the Arabs, in the latter case to 42 AH (662/663 CE).[64] The other documentation is by the seventh-century Eastern Christian chronicler John Bar Penkaye (d. ca. 685 CE) who dated a plague in Mesopotamia and Syria to the "sixty-seventh year of the kingdom (*malkutā*) of the Arabs."[65] No further information exists on who the rulers were, where the capital was located, and how the Arab kingdom looked like. But given that the new chronology was primarily used by East Syriac Christians it is perhaps not too speculative to assume that we are talking here about the project of a restored Arab kingdom of Nuʿmān III, that is, a kingdom under a single ruler with a military force.

The date of Summer 622 is also the time of Emperor Heraclius' (r. 610–641 CE) first tentative foray against Khosrow in Cilicia. Fortunately, it was successful but the emperor was not strong enough yet to follow up with more systematic campaigning until 624.[66] Since the foray was prepared with, and accompanied by, an intensive Chalcedonian Christian propaganda, chroniclers remembered it as more significant than it actually was in terms of results.[67] It is possible to assume, as does Tommaso Tesei, that news of Heraclius' propaganda reached Arabia Petraea, especially since western Arab military contingents participated in the Roman operations in Ciclicia.[68]

Tesei, who has reservations about the traditional chronology of the Qur'ān but nevertheless continues to hold on to it, leaves the nature of events in the Hijaz open since he is interested in the prophecy of the Romans' victory of 628, seemingly proclaimed 622 in Q 30:2–7 out of sympathy for Rome and a hatred for Persia.[69] He opposes dating the proclamation to 622 and declares it to be a *vaticinium ex eventu* after the final victory of the Romans over the Sasanids in 628. One might quibble here about the *ex eventu* part of the prophecy since the defeat of the Sasanids was assured from 626 onwards when Heraclius turned the tide against them in Armenia. But Tesei's point is nevertheless well taken: Even if one does not

64 For the inscription of Gader see https://www.islamicawareness.org/history/islam/inscriptions/hammat.html, accessed 3-31-2019. See also Kerr 2014.

65 Bar Penkaye 1907; Trans. Mingana and Roger Pearse in http://www.tertullian.org/fathers/john_bar_penkaye_history_15_trans.htm, accessed 7-20-2019. For later examples of East Syriac dating according to the Arab kingdom see Brock 2005.

66 Ekkebus 2009; Howard-Johnston 1999. The article is also available in Howard-Johnston 2006: VIII.

67 Howard-Johnston 1999:14–15.

68 Tommaso Tesei argues that "there is no reason to doubt" this participation, citing the *Chronicon Paschale* and the sources in Greatrex and Lieu 2002:199. See Tesei 2018:20–21. Shahid cites the three sources of Theophanes, *Chronicon Paschale*, and Pisides that suggest Arab participation in the campaign of 622:Shahid 1995a: I, 641–646.

69 Tesei 2018:18 and 26.

necessarily go by the Islamic Tradition one can nevertheless conclude that beginning in 622 Heraclius' propaganda reached the Arabs, causing them to begin hoping for an eventually final Roman victory. Then, in 628, when the anti-Sasanid prophecy was fulfilled, the year 622 was declared to have been the year of Prophet Muhammad's Hijra from Mecca to Yathrib (Medina), and the formal establishment of his community.

If one disregards the alleged Hijra event and replaces it with that of the emergence of an Arab kingdom in 622 it would follow that this state was at that time still more the projection of a revived kingdom of Ḥīra than a reality. This projection, fitting closely with the then still unfulfilled prophecy of doom for Khosrow, became eventually more real in 628 with the first Arab raids into Mesopotamia following the death of Khosrow, as we know now through Parvaneh Pourshariati's reconstructed timeline of the Arab expansion into Mespoopotamia.[70] The patient waiting for God to fulfill the prophecy gave thus finally way in 628 first to military action and then, after 636, to the outright conquest of the Sasanid empire.

The Roman victory over the Sasanids was, of course, the fulfillment of the prophecy of Khosrow's doom. In the Qur'ān, this victory is presented, however, as something even more significant. The pericope Q 30:2–7 mentioned above contains the enigmatic verses 4–5 which appear to endorse Rome as the Danielic final empire before the imminent Eschaton. The fulfillment of the prophecy of doom for Khosrow thus seems to give way to the arrival of the Apocalypse, that is, a brief revival of the Roman empire before the end of the world.

For a proper understanding of apocalyptic thought in the Qur'ān, these verses have to be read together with the Qur'anic rendering of the so-called *Alexander Legend.* According to Kevin van Bladel, the inclusion of a synopsis of this legend in the Qur'ān (Q 18:83–102) has to be dated to shortly after the Roman victory in 628, probably to around 630.[71] The date is dependent on the completion of the Syriac text of the *Alexander Legend*, the so-called *Glory (neṣḥānā) of Alexander*, which Gerrit Reinink dates to 628 or 629 and which then served as a model for the Qur'ān.

In a series of articles, Reinink has demonstrated convincingly that immediately after his victory over Khosrow Emperor Heraclius sought to demonstrate to the Jacobites, who were passionate opponents of Chalcedonian Christology, that he was the new Alexander and that Rome was as solid as before, returning to its role as the final empire of history to be handed over by its Christian king

70 Pourshariati 2008:164–173 and 281–285.
71 van Bladel 2008:184–185.

(*basileus*) to Jesus when he would come for the second time.[72] By reestablishing the salvation history of Chalcedonian Rome Heraclius' Syriac version of the *Alexander Legend* returned to the traditional imperial ideology. This ideology was formulated originally by Eusebius of Caesarea (ca. 239–340) when he merged the histories of church and empire and thereby unified the idea of a world already changed with Jesus's first coming and Vergil's *Roma aeterna*.[73] Needless to say, the Jacobites composed their own version of the Alexander Legend which ends with the prediction of no Roman revival and the imminent Eschaton.[74]

The Qur'anic *Alexander Legend* in 18:83–102 is considerably shorter than the Syriac one and ends, like that of the Jacobites, with the prediction of the immediate end of Rome. It sketches the Apocalypse with its disasters leading up to the Eschaton, albeit in a highly compressed version.[75] As the End arrives, so we read, God will level the iron gates in the north which until now (thanks to God's mercy) have kept the barbarian nations Gog and Magog from Central Asia at bay. "That day We will let them [the nations] surge over one another and the Trumpet will be blown" (Q 18:99). At the same time the faithless will be sent to Hell. Thus the Qur'ān leaves open what will happen to Rome and merely sketches a general apocalyptic horizon for the future (assuming that the trumpet that will be blown in Q 18:99 is the same as the trumpet in 78:18 that will sound soon).

The image of the nations surging over one another, as van Bladel points out, is an allusion to Luke 21:25 where Jesus speaks of the "distress of nations confused by the roaring of the sea and the waves," in his own apocalyptic vision of the destruction of Jerusalem and the following collapse of the Roman empire – an apocalypse fully laid out in Matthew 24.[76] The rejoicing of the Qur'ānic believers is thus but a prelude to the imminent general apocalypse and end of the world. As brief as this prediction of the apocalypse is it makes it clear that the Qur'ān is definitively not a work that delays the completion

72 Reinink 2003:163–168; Reinink 1999:152–154; and Reinink 1985:279–280.
73 Mitchell 2011:53–55; Fowden 1993:89–90.
74 Reinink 2003:165–168.
75 Remarkably, this is also the sense of the Sasanid-Zoroastrian apocalypse, which Theophylact Simocatta, the historian of emperors Maurice and Heraclius, puts into the mouth of Khosrow II during his sojourn in the Roman empire 590/591. According to this prophecy, Khosrow II predicted that the Persians would be victorious for three hebdomads (3x7 years), then the Romans would "enslave" the Persians for one hebdomad, and finally the fifth hebdomad would be when "the day without evening will dwell among men." See Theophylact Simocatta, *History*, ed. in Theophylact Simocatta 1888 V:15, 3–7; trans in Theophylact Simocatta 1986:153; and Reinink 2000:86–90, who is "tempted to assume" that Heraclius used the Khosrow prophesy to develop "a completely reversed scenario."
76 van Bladel 2008:193–194.

of salvation history into the indefinite future. Quite on the contrary, as the believers are assured throughout the Qur'ān, even though only God knows the Hour, it will come soon and suddenly. No human action is required for God to bring about the end. We thus arrive at the paradox that after the fulfillment of the prophecy of Sasanid doom any further human enterprise will be overtaken in the blink of an eye by the collapse of the Roman empire and the sound of the Trumpet, regardless of whether the Roman Empire still exists or which situation the Qur'ānic community finds itself in.

There is, however, the possibility of an alternate understanding of Qur'ān 30: 2–7. In 629, the Qurānic Arabs mounted a punitive campaign against the Jafnids in Syria, after the latter had killed an emissary seeking to invite the "Christian Arab nations" to the Arabs' Unitary interpretation of Christianity. This campaign failed after a "Qurayshite" betrayed the Arabs and a Jafnid/Roman army was able to defeat them at Mu'ta, southeast of the Dead Sea.[77] If one were to read Q 30:2–7 with a different vocalization one would learn that the Romans were victorious in a nearby land (in 629) but would be defeated "in a few years (*fī biḍʿi sinīn*)" to the joy of the Qur'ānic believers. With this vocalization, vv. 2–7 appear as a *vaticinium ex eventu* pronounced in 636 at the earliest when the Romans suffered their first heavy defeat at Yarmuk. One could apply Ockham's razor and come to the conclusion that this alternate understanding is the better one, because it explains the Arab "rejoicing" (Q 30:4) in more logical terms.[78]

5 Conclusion

In this essay I have laid out a case for the chronological and geographical locations of the Qur'ān in Mesopotamia and Arabia Petraea between the Sasanid and Roman empires during 602–630. The Qur'ān, so I conclude, has roots reaching back to the Christological crisis of the second half of the sixth century CE, which

77 Theophanes 1883:335; 1997:466.

78 The Mu'ta interpretation is offered by Manfred Kropp in Azaiez *et alii* 2016:290, Stephen Shoemaker 2012:154, and Edouard Gallez 2005. Tommaso Tesei seeks to refute this interpretation by arguing that the Islamic Tradition embraced the version of the Roman victory over the Sasanids for a reason and adduces for proof examples of non-Islamic apocalyptic prophecies of the 600s that are in his view worded similarly. There are two problems, however, with this refutation. First, Q 30-1-7 does not mention the Persians whereas the apocalypses do and second, there is no documentation outside the Islamic Tradition for a pro-Roman stance of the Arabs dating back to 622 and shifting inexplicably in 628 with their Mu'ta campaign against the Romans/Jafnids.

is reflected in the Eastern Christian and Jacobite elements identifiable in the Qur'ān, notably the anti-theopaschite polemic against the Jacobite and Chalcedonian "associators" (*mushrikūn*), which I have dealt with in another essay and which is presupposed here.[79] The chronological and geographical locations discussed in this essay are circumscribed by the violent end of the Arab kingdom of the Nasrids in 602 at the hands of Khosrow II and the Sasanids, the formulation of a prophecy predicting the end of Khosrow, the emergence of a congregation of Unitarian Christian anti-Jacobite and anti-Chalcedonian believers in the Roman province of Arabia Petraea, the (re)foundation of an Arab kingdom, the fulfillment of the anti-Sasanid prophecy, and the expectation of an apocalyptic end of history in 630 or a few years later.

This outline of the time frame and geographical location of the Qur'ān presupposes an analysis that dispenses with the inner Qur'ānic chronology proposed originally in the so-called Nöldeke-Schwally history of the Qur'ān[80] and modernized by Angelika Neuwirth, Nicolai Sinai, and other members of the *Corpus Coranicum* project.[81] This chronology is built around the framework of Muhammad's biography imposed by the Islamic Tradition on the Qur'ān 150 years after its redaction. At the end of this essay I do not want to enter into a detailed discussion of the questionable methodology of arranging the content of the Qur'ān according to the Islamic Tradition.[82] Suffice it to state here that a far more cautious and methodologically defensible procedure consists in considering the Qur'ān as a heterogenous corpus with a nearly indeterminable internal chronology and plenty of redactions up to the second half of the first/seventh century.[83] When reading the Qur'ān, one is advised to think that in the background of every sura there is the full range of expressions of prophecy, scriptural heritages, theological polemics, and apocalyptic expectations of the remaining suras.

This does not mean, however, that the Islamic Tradition is worthless: Quite on the contrary, while occasionally valuable for shedding light on the 600s, it is invaluable for the understanding of Islam in the Abbasid empire. The present

79 von Sivers 2021.

80 Originally published by Theodor Nöldeke in 1860. The second edition, with the additional authors, dates to 1909. English translation of the second edition: Nöldeke *et alii* 2013.

81 Neuwirth 2014 and Nicolai Sinai https://corpuscoranicum.de/, accessed 4-14-2019.

82 Gabriel Reynolds lays out the full array of arguments against a Muhammadan chronology in Reynolds 2011. Sean Anthony describes the notion that this external chronology cannot be modernized along the lines of the Neuwirth-Sinai method of an internal Qur'ānic chronology as a "common canard." But the five contemporary "historical events" which he argues are contained in the Qur'ān are clearly not historical but rely on the Islamic Tradition. See Anthony 2020, 16, n. 59, and 13, n. 45.

83 This is also the approach most recently of Friedrich-Karl Pohlmann (Pohlmann 2015).

essay with its corner dates of 602 and 630 and its locales of Mesopotamia and Arabia Petraea is offered as an effort to use the historian's tools to provide the Qur'ān with a seventh-century context. Reading the Qur'ān while suspending one's knowledge of the Islamic Tradition of the eighth and ninth centuries is not easy but is perhaps not without at least a few results.

Bibliography

Al-Jallad, Ahmad. 2017. "Graeco-Arabica I: The Southern Levant." In *Arabic in Context*. Edited by Ahmad Al-Jallad, 99–186. Leiden and Boston: Brill.

Alpass, Peter. 2013. *The Religious Life of Nabataea*. Leiden and Boston: Brill.

Anthony, Sean W., 2020. *Muhammad and the Empires of Faith: The Making of the Prophet of Islam*. Berkeley and Los Angeles: University of California Press.

Azaiez, Mehdi, Gabriel S. Reynolds, Tommaso Tesei, and Hamza M. Zafer. 2016. *The Qur'ān Seminar Commentary, Le Qur'ān Seminar: A Collaborative Study of 50 Qur'anic Passages, Commentaire collaboratif de 50 passages coraniques*. Berlin: Walter de Gruyter.

Beck, Daniel. 2018. *Evolution of the Early Quran: From Anonymous Apocalypse to Charismatic Prophet*. Apocalypticism, Cross-Disciplinary Perspectives 3. New York, Berlin, Bern: Peter Lang.

Beck, Daniel. 2019. "Anti-Sasanian Apocalypse and the Early Qur'ān: Why Muhammad Began His Career as a Prophet Who Genuinely Prophesied. Essay on Academia.edu: https://www.academia.edu/38029465/Anti-Sasanian_Apocalypse_And_The_Early_Qur%C4%81n_Why_Mu%E1%B8%A5ammad_Began_His_Career_As_A_Prophet_Who_Genuinely_Prophesied (accessed March 15, 2019).

Brock, Sebastian. 2005. "The Use of Hijra Dating in Syriac Manuscripts. A Preliminary Investigation." In *Redefining Christian Identity: Cultural Interaction in the Middle East since the Rise of Islam*. Edited by Jan J. van Ginkel, Hendrika, L. Murre van den Berg, and Theo M. van Lint, 275–291. Orientalia Lovaniensa Analecta 134. Leuven, Paris, and Dudley, Mass.: Peeters and Departement Oosterse Studies.

Caldwell, Christopher. 2001. *Between State and Steppe: New Evidence for Society in Sixth-Century Southern Transjordan*. PhD Dissertation, Ann Arbor: University of Michigan.

Chronicle of Seert. 1983. *Histoire nestorienne (Chronique de Séert)*. In Patrologia Orientalis 13, Part 2, Fasc. 2. Ed. and trans. Addaï Scheer and Robert Griveau. Turnhout: Brepols. Reprint 1919. Paris: Firmin-Didot.

Crone, Patricia. 2005. "How Did the Quranic Pagans Make a Living?" *Bulletin of the School of Oriental and African Studies* 68: 387–399.

Crone, Patricia. 2007. "Quraysh and the Roman Army: Making Sense of the Meccan Leather Trade," *Bulletin of the School of Oriental and African Studies* 70: 63–88.

Cuypers, Michel. 2018. *A Qur'anic Apocalypse: A Reading of the Thirty-Three Last Suras of the Qur'ān*. International Qur'anic Studies Association Studies in the Qur'ān 1. Atlanta: Lockwood Press.

Donner, Fred. 1980. "Wā'il Tribes and Politics in Northeastern Arabia on the Eve of Islam." *Studia Islamica* 51: 5–38.

Durie, Mark. 2018. "On the Origin of Qurʾanic Arabic," draft article on Academia.edu: https://www.academia.edu/37743814/On_the_Origin_of_Qur%CA%BE%C4%81nic_Arabic (accessed April 10, 2019).

Ekkebus, Bob: 2009. "Heraclius and the Evolution of Byzantine Strategy." *Constructing the Past* 10: 73–96.

Fiema, Zbginiew T. 2002. "Petra and Its Hinterland during the Byzantine Period: New Research and Interpretations." In *The Roman and Byzantine Near East*, vol. 3: *Some New Discoveries*. Edited by John H. Humphrey, 191–252. Supplementary Series, 49. Portsmouth, R.I.: Journal of Roman Archaeology.

Fisher, Greg. 2011. *Between Empires: Arabs, Romans, and Sasanians in Late Antiquity*. Oxford: Oxford University Press.

Flusin, Bernard. 1992. *Saint Anastase le Perse et l'histoire de la Palestine au début du VIIe siècle*. 2 vols. Paris: Editions du Centre de la Recherche Scientifique.

Fowden, Garth. 1993. *Empire to Commonwealth: Consequences of Monotheism in Late Antiquity*. Princeton, N.J.: Princeton University Press.

Gader Inscription. https://www.islamicawareness.org/history/islam/inscriptions/hammat.html (accessed March 31, 2019).

Gallez, Edouard-Marie. 2005. "Défaite de Muhammad en Terre Sainte et sourate 30 'les Byzantins' (ar-Rûm)." http://www.lemessieetsonprophete.com/annexes/mou_ta.htm (accessed June 9, 2020).

Geiger, Theodor. 1833. *Was hat Mohammed aus dem Judenthume aufgenommen? Eine von der Königl. Preussischen Universität gekrönte Preisschrift*. Bonn: F. Baaden.

Gibson, Dan. Cited on Emperor ElagAbūlus in Sneaker's Corner #2. https://www.youtube.com/watch?v=-x-wlbKU2mY (accessed May 28, 2019).

Greatrex, Geoffrey, and Samuel N.C. Lieu, eds.. 2002. *The Roman Eastern Frontier and the Persian Wars. Part 2. AD 363–630: A Narrative Sourcebook*. London and New York, Routledge.

Griffith, Sydney. 2008. "Christian Lore and the Arabic Qur'ān: The 'Companions of the Cave' in *Surat al-Kahf* in in Syriac Christian Tradition." In *The Qur'ān in Its Historical Context*. Edited by Gabriel Said Reynolds, 109–137, London and New York: Routledge.

Healy, John F. 2001. *The Religion of the Nabataeans: A Conspectus*. Leiden, Boston, and Cologne: Brill.

Horovitz, Josef. 1926. *Koranische Untersuchungen*, Studien zur Geschichte und Kultur des islamischen Orients 4. Berlin and Leipzig: Walter de Gruyter.

Howard-Johnson, James. 1999. "Heraclius' Persian Campaigns and the Revival of the East Roman Empire, 622–630." *War in History* 1: 1–44. Repr. in Howard-Johnston, James, ed. 2006. *East Rome, Sasanian Persia, and the End of Antiquity: Historiographical and Historical Studies*. Variorum Reprints, Aldershot and Burlington, Vt.: Ashagate Variorum.

Howard-Johnson, James. "Kosrow II." In *Encyclopaedia Iranica*. http://www.iranicaonline.org/articles/khosrow-ii (accessed June 5, 2020).

Jeffery, Arthur. 1938. *The Foreign Vocabulary of the Qur'ān*. Baroda: Oriental Institute.

Kadari, Tamar. 2009. "Wife of Korah: Midrash and Aggadah." *Jewish Women: A Comprehensive Historical Encyclopedia*. https://jwa.org/encyclopedia/article/wife-of-korah-midrash-and-aggadah (accessed July 13, 2019).

Kerr, Robert. 2014. "Ist der Qur'ān in Mekka oder Medina entstanden?" In *Die Entstehung einer Weltreligion III. Die heilige Stadt Mekka – eine literarische Fiktion*. Edited by Markus Groß and Karl-Heinz Ohlig., 39–45. Inârah, Schriften zur frühen Islamgeschichte und zum Koran 7, Berlin and Tübingen: Hans Schiler.

Kerr, Robert. 2014. 2014. "Der Islam, die Araber und die Hiğra." In *Die Entstehung einer Weltreligion III. Die heilige Stadt Mekka – eine literarische Fiktion*. Edited by Markus Groß and Karl-Heinz Ohlig, 46–51. Inârah, Schriften zur frühen Islamgeschichte und zum Koran 7. Berlin and Tübingen: Hans Schiler.

Khuzistan Chronicle. 2016. *Khuzistan Chronicle: A Short Chronicle of the End of the Sasanian Empire and Early Islam*. Ed. and trans. Nāṣir al-Kaʿbī. Gorgias Chronicles of Late Antiquity 1. Piscataway, N.J.: Gorgias Press.

King, David. 2017. "From Petra back to Makka – From 'Pibla' back to Qibla." http://www.muslimheritage.com/article/from-petra-back-to-makka (accessed May 28, 2019).

Kister, Meir J. 1968. "Al-Ḥīra: Some Notes on Its Relations with Arabia." *Arabica* 15: 143–169.

Knauf, Ernst A. 2003. "Review of J. Frösén & al., The Petra Papyri, Vol. 1, American Center of Oriental Research, Publications 4. Amman: American Center of Oriental Research." *Scripta Classica Israelica* 22, 350–355.

Koran: *Der Koran. Handkommentar*. Vol. 1: *Frühmekkanische Suren, poetische Prophetie*. 2011. Trans. Angelika Neuwirth. Berlin: Verlag der Weltreligionen.

Kropp, Manfred. 2009. "Koranische Texte als Sprechakte am Beispiel der Sure 85." In *Vom Koran zum Islam*. Edited by Markus Groß and Karl-Heinz Ohlig, 483–491. Inârah, Schriften zur frühen Islamgeschichte und zum Koran 4. Berlin: Hans Schiler.

Michel, Anne. 2001. *Les églises d'époques byzantine et umayyade de Jordanie. Étude de typologie et inventaire*. Turnhout: Brepols.

Midrash: *Le champ du Midrash*. "A propos des fibres." https://www.lechampdumidrash.net/index.php?option=com_content&view=article&id=87:a-propos-de-fibres&catid=81&Itemid=483 (accessed July 13, 2019).

Mitchell, Roger Haydon. 2011. *Church, Gospel, and Empire: How the Politics of Sovereignty Impregnated the West*. Eugene, OR: Wipf and Stock.

Morris, Ian D. 2014. "Quraysh and Confederacy." http://www.iandavidmorris.com/quraysh-and-confederacy/#comments (accessed November 24, 2019).

Nasarat, Mohammed, Fawzi Abudanh, and Slameh Naimat. 2012. "Agriculture in Sixth-Century Petra and Its Hinterland: The Evidence from the Petra Papyri." *Arabian Archaeology and Epigraphy* 23: 105–115.

Neuwirth, Angelika, 2014. *Scripture, Poetry, and the Making of a Community: Reading the Qurʾan as a Literary Text*. Oxford: Oxford University Press.

Nöldeke, Theodor, Friedrich Schwally, Gotthelf Bergsträßer, and Anton Pretzl. 2013. *The History of the Qur'ān*. Trans. Wolfgang S. Behn. Texts and Studies of the Qur'ān 8. Leiden and Boston: Brill.

Patrich, Joseph. 1990. *The Formation of Nabataean Art: Prohibition of a Graven Image Among the Nabataeans*. Jerusalem and Leiden: Magnes Press and Brill.

Payne, Richard. 2013. "Cosmology and the Expansion of the Iranian Empire." *Past and Present* 220: 3–33.

Penkaye, Yohanan Bar. 1907. *Sources syriaques*, I, 1: *Mshiha-zkha (texte et traduction) et Bar-Penkayé (texte)*. Ed. and trans. Alphonse Mingana. Mosul: Imprimerie des Pères Dominicains.

Penkaye, Yohanan Bar. "Summary of World History (Rish melle) (2010), book 15." Trans. Alphonse Mingana and Roger Pearse. http://www.tertullian.org/fathers/john_bar_penkaye_history_15_trans.htm (accessed July 20, 2019).

Peters, Frank E. 1985. *Jerusalem: The Holy City in the Eyes of Chroniclers, Visitors, Pilgrims, and Prophets from the Days of Abraham to the Beginnings of Modern Times*. Princeton, N.J.: Princeton University Press.
Peterson, Stephanie B. 2006. *The Cult of Dushara and the Roman Annexation of Nabataea*. MA Thesis, Hamilton, Ontario: McMaster University.
Philonenko, Marc. 1967. "Une expression qumranienne dans le Coran." In *Atti di Terzo congresso di studi Arabi e islamici*, Ravello, 1–6 settembre 1966, 553–556. Naples: Istituto Universitario Orientale.
Pohlmann, Karl-Friedrich. 2015. *Die Entstehung des Korans. Neue Erkenntnisse aus Sicht der historisch-kritischen Bibelwissenschaft*, 3rd Ed. Darmstadt: Wissenschaftliche Buchgesellschaft.
Politis, Konstantinos D. 2007. "Nabataean Cultural Continuity into the Byzantine Period," In *The World of the Nabataeans*. Edited by Konstantinos D. Politis, 190–194. The World of the Herods and the Nabataeans: International Conference Held at the British Museum, 17–19 April 2001. Oriens et Occidens 15. Stuttgart: Franz Steiner.
Pourshariati, Parvaneh. 2008. *Decline and Fall of the Sassanian Empire: The Sassanian-Parthian Confederacy and the Arab Conquest of Iran*. London: I.B. Tauris.
Prémare, Alfred Louis de. 1998. "Les éléphants de Qādisiyya." *Arabica* 45: 261–269.
Prémare, Alfred Louis de. 2000. "'Il volut détruire le Temple.' L'attaque de la Kaʿba par les rois yéménites avant l'islam. Akhbār et Histoire." *Journal Asiatique* 288: 261–367.
Qur'ān: *The Qur'ān: A New Translation*. 2004. Trans. A.M.S. Abdel Haleem. Oxford: Oxford University Press.
Qur'ān: "First Century Hijra Manuscripts." https://www.islamic-awareness.org/quran/text/mss (accessed November 22, 2019).
Reinink, Gerrit J. 1985. "Die Entstehung der syrischen Alexanderlegende als politisch-religiöse Propagandaschrift für Herakleios' Kirchenpolitik." In *After Chalcedon: Studies in Theology and Church History Offered to Professor Albert van Roey for His Seventieth Birthday*. Edited by Carl Laga, Joseph A. Munitz, and Lucas van Rompay, 263–281. *Orientalia Lovaniensia Analecta* 18. Leuven: Departement Oriëntalistiek and Peeters.
Reinink, Gerrit J. 1999. "Alexandre et le dernier empereur du monde. Les développements du concept de la royauté chrétienne dans les sources syriaques du septième siècle." In *Alexandre le Grand dans les littératures occidentales et proche-orientales*. Edited by Laurence Harf-Lancner, Claire Kappler, and Françoise Suard, 149–159. Actes du Colloque de Paris, 27–29 novembre 1997. Paris: Nanterre: Centre des Sciences de la Littérature de l'Université Paris X.
Reinink, Gerrit J. 2000 "Heraclius, the New Alexander: Apocalyptic Prophecies during the Reign of Hercalius." In *The Reign of Heraclius (610-641): Crisis and Confrontation*. Edited by Gerrit J. Reinink and Bernard Stolte, 81–94. Groningen Studies in Cultural Change 2. Leuven, Paris, and Dudley, Mass.: Peeters.
Reinink, Gerrit J. 2003. "Alexander the Great in Seventh-Century Syriac 'Apocalyptic' Texts." *Byzantinorossica* 2: 150–178.
Reinink, Gerrit J. 2005. *Syriac Christianity under Late Sasanian and Early Islamic Rule*. Aldershot and Burlington, Vt.: Ashgate Variorum.
Reinink, Gerrit J. 2009. "Tradition and the Formation of the 'Nestorian' Identity in Sixth- to Seventh-Century Iraq." *Church History and Religious Culture* 89: 1–3 and 217–250. Reprint in Bas ter Haar Romeny, ed. 2010. *Religious Origins of Nations? The Christian Communities of the Middle East*. Leiden and Boston: Brill.

Retsö, Jan. 2003. *The Arabs in Antiquity: Their History from the Assyrians to the Umayyads*. London and New York: RoutledgeCurzon.
Reynolds, Gabriel S. 2010. *The Qur'ān and Its Biblical Subtext*. London and New York: Routledge.
Reynolds, Gabriel S. 2011. "Le problème de la chronologie du Coran." *Arabica* 58:477–502.
Reynolds, Gabriel S. 2018. *The Qur'ān and the Bible: Text and Commentary*. New Haven, Ct.: Yale University Press.
Robinson, Chase F. 2004. "The Conquest of Khuzistan: A Historiographical Assessment." *Bulletin of the School of Oriental and African Studies* 67:14–39.
Sebeos. 1999. *The Armenian History Attributed to Sebeos*. Trans. Robert W. Thomson, historical commentary James Howard-Johnston, assistance from Tim Greenwood. Translated Texts for Historians 31, 2 vols. Liverpool: Liverpool University Press.
Shaddel, Mehdy. 2017. "Studia Onomastica Coranica: *Al-Raqim*, Caput Nebataeae." *Journal of Semitic Studies* 62:303–318.
Shahbazi, Abdollah S. 2016. "Bahrām VI Čōbīn." In *Encyclopaedia Iranica* III:5, 514–522.
Shahbazi, Abdollah S. 2012. "Hormozd IV." In *Encyclopaedia Iranica* XII:466–467.
Shahbazi, Abdollah S. 1989. "Bestam o Bendoy. *Encyclopaedia Iranica* IV:180–182.
Shahid, Irfan. 1995a. *Byzantium and the Arabs in the Sixth* Century. Vol. I, Part 1: *Political and Military History*. Washington, D.C.: Dumbarton Oaks Research Library and Collection.
Shahid, Irfan. 1995b. *Byzantium and the Arabs in the Sixth* Century, Vol. I, Part 2: *Ecclesiastical History*. Washington, D.C.: Dumbarton Oaks Research Library and Collection.
Shoemaker, Stephen J. 2012. *The Death of a Prophet: The End of Muhammad's Life and the Beginning of Islam*. Philadelphia: Pennsylvania University Press.
Silverstein, Adam. 2019. "Who Are the *Aṣḥāb al-Ukhdūd*?: Q 85:4–10 in Near Eastern Context." *Der Islam* 96:281–323.
Sinai, Nicolai. 2014. "When did the Consonantal Skeleton of the Quran Reach Closure?" *Bulletin of the School of Oriental and African Studies* 77:273–292 and 1–13.
Sinai, Nicolai. "Das Projekt eines ausführlichen Korankommentars." https://corpuscoranicum.de/kommentar/einleitung (accessed April 14, 2019).
Sinai, Nicolai, with Nora K. Schmid, "Sure 111, Kursorischer Kommentar." In *Corpus Coranicum*, https://corpuscoranicum.de/kommentar/index/sure/111/vers/1 (accessed June 16, 2019).
Skjaervö, Prods Oktor. 2011. "Zarathustra: A Revolutionary Monotheist?" In *Reconsidering the Concept of Revolutionary Monotheism*. Edited by Beate Pongratz-Leisten, 317–350. Winnona Lake, IN.: Eisenbrauns.
Stoyanov, Yuri. 2011. *Defenders and Enemies of the True Cross: The Sasanian Conquest of Jerusalem in 614 and Byzantine Ideology of Anti-Persian Warfare*. Veröffentlichungen zur Iranistik 61. Vienna: Verlag der Österreichischen Akademie der Wissenschaften.
al-Ṭabarī, Abū Jaʿfar Mu ammad b. Jarīr. 1879, *Ta'rīkh rusūl wa-l-muluk*. Edited by Michael Jan de Goeje. Leiden: Brill.
al-Ṭabarī, Abū Jaʿfar Mu ammad b. Jarīr. 1999. *The History of aṭ -Ṭabarī*. Vol. 5: *The Sasanids, the Byzantines, the Lakhmids, and Yemen*. Trans. Clifford E. Bosworth. Albany, NY: State University of New York Press.
Talmud: *Babylonian Talmud*, Tractate Sanhedrin. 1961. Folio 109a-110a. http://come-and-hear.com/sanhedrin/sanhedrin_109.html (Accessed June 13, 2019).
Tesei, Tommaso. 2018. "'The Romans Will Win!' Q 30:2–7 in Light of 7th-C. Political Eschatology." *Der Islam* 95:1–29.

Theophanes. 1883. *Chronographia*. Edited by Carl G. de Boor. Leipzig: Teubner.

Theophanes. 1997. *The Chronicle of Theophanes Confessor: Byzantine and Near Eastern History AD 284-813*. Trans. Cyril Mango and Roger Scott. Oxford: Clarendon Press.

Theophylact Simocatta. 1888. *Theophylacyti Simocattae Historiae*. Edited by Carl G. de Boor. Leipzig: Teubner.

Theophylact Simocatta. 1986. *The* History *of Theophylact Simocatta*. Trans. Michael and Mary Whitby. Oxford: Clarendon.

Theodosius. 1882. *De situ Terrae Sanctae im ächten Text und der Brevarius Hierosolyma vervollständigt*. Edited by Johann Gildemeister. Bonn: Adolph Marcus.

Tracy, Stephen. 1999. "The Dedicatory Inscription to Trajan at the 'Metropolis' of Petra." In *The Roman and Byzantine Near East*. Vol. 2: *Some Recent Archaeological Research*. Edited by John H. Humphrey, 51–58. Supplementary Series 31. Portsmouth, R.I.: Journal of Roman Archaeology.

Van Bladel, Kevin. 2008. "The Alexander Legend in the Qur'ān 18:83–102." In *The Qur'ān in Its Historical Context*. Edited by Gabriel S. Reynolds, 175–203. London and New York: Routledge.

Von Sivers, Peter. 2021. "Koranische Hintergründe: Tritheismus, Theopaschitismus und Doppelqnōmā." In *Die Entstehung einer Weltreligion VI: Vom umayyadischen Christentum zum abbasidischen Islam*. Edited by Markus Groß and Robert M. Kerr, 734–762. Inârah, Schriften zur frühen Islamgeschichte und zum Koran 10. Berlin and Tübingen: Hans Schiler and Tim Mücke. 734-763.

Wherry, Elwood M. 1882–1896. *A Comprehensive Commentary on the Quran: Comprising Sale's Translation and Preliminary Discourse*, 4 vols. London: Kegan Paul, Trench, and Trübner.

Whitby, Mary. 2003. "George of Pisida and the Personal Word: Words, Words, Words . . ." In *Rhetoric in Byzantium*. Edited by Elizabeth Jeffreys, 173–186. Society for the Promotion of Byzantine Studies 11. Aldershot and Burlington, Vt.: Ashgate Variorum.

Wood, Philip. 2013. The Chronicle of Seert: Christian Historical; Imagination in Late Antique Iraq. Oxford: Oxford University Press.

Boaz Shoshan

The Sasanian Conquest of Ḥimyar Reconsidered: In Search of a Local Hero

I Introduction

It is widely agreed that the South Arabian kingdom of Ḥimyar was subdued by the Ethiopian kingdom of Aksum sometime in the 520s[1] in response to the massacre in 523 of the Christian inhabitants of Nagrān (Arabic Najrān) by Yūsuf As'ar Yath'ar (Masrūq, in Syriac), the Ḥimyarite king, also known as Dhū Nuwās. Yūsuf had converted to Judaism about a year earlier and sent his agent of the Dhū Yaz'an clan to perform the atrocity.[2] Some of the Christian victims were Nestorians, others had contacts with Christians of the Persian Empire and still others were converted through missionary efforts initiated in northern Syria by anti-Chalcedonian circles. To a meeting called by Yūsuf at Ramla, in Southern Iraq, shortly after the massacre, the Byzantine emperor sent a delegate. A Greek source provides an account which includes information on Emperor Justin I asking Timothy, the archbishop of Alexandria, to intercede with the Ethiopian ruler to take action against Yūsuf.[3] Even if one considers the emperor's call in 525 to "attack, by land or by sea, the abominable and criminal Hebrew" as apocryphal, the tragedy of the Christians must have reached many ears.[4] Following the Ethiopian invasion, Abraha, a former slave in the service of Aksum, succeeded in taking control of South Arabia. Arabic tradition and Qur'ān exegesis identified him as the man implicated in surah 105 in the attempt to capture Mecca and punished through divine intervention. Abraha was succeeded by his two sons, then a Persian invasion in ca. 570 terminated the approximately 50 years of Ethiopian nominal control of Ḥimyar. The region remained a Persian province till the rise of Islam.[5]

What do we know of the Persian conquest of Ḥimyar? No sources originating in the Sasanian Empire have survived and there is only little that is provided by Christian-Byzantine writers. According to Theophanes of Byzantium, a late

1 Dates in this article are in terms of the Christian era.
2 Robin 2012, 282; Robin 2015, 147–148; Fisher 2015, 447–49.
3 Bowersock 2013, 88–90, 96–97; Greatrex 2014, 255–56.
4 Robin 2012, 282–83; Robin 2015, 148.
5 Robin 2012, 297.

Boaz Shoshan, Ben-Gurion University of the Negev

https://doi.org/10.1515/9783110675498-011

sixth-century Roman author, in other words, a contemporary of the events, King Khosrau marched against the Ethiopians and "with the aid of Miranos, the Persian general, he captured Sanatources, king of the Ḥimyarites, sacked their city and enslaved the inhabitants."[6] Although we lack details about the reasons for this operation it stands to reason that Khosrau decided that he had to curtail the aggressive policy of the Romans and their Ethiopian ally in that region. They, in their part, had their own interests in countering Sasanian influence along the eastern part of the Arab peninsula, as well as improving naval routes to the East.[7] An expedition led by the Ḥimyarite king Ma'di Karib Ya'fur in 521 against al-Ḥīra, the foremost outpost of the Sasanian regime in Southern Iraq, probably had Roman imperial backing.[8] According to Procopius, in 530 or 531, Justinian "had the idea of allying himself with the Ethiopians and the Ḥimiarites in order to work against the Persians," and he dispatched two embassies to South Arabia and to Aksum to invest in the trade of Chinese silk, to test new economic and political possibilities in the war against the Sasanians and to divert the trade with India.[9] Procopius adds that around the mid sixth century Abraha (Abramus) promised Justinian "many times" to invade the land of Persia, but only once did he begin a journey and then turned back straightaway.[10] In 547, according to an inscription attributed to Abraha, Roman and Persian delegates came to the town of Ma'rib for a diplomatic conference, possibly to discuss the division of the spheres of influence between the two main powers.[11]

The Persian king's success in ca. 560 to subdue the Hephthalites, his longtime enemies, could have encouraged him now in taking action in the far south.[12] There could be other reasons as well. Al-Ṭabarī, a leading Muslim historian, would report hundreds of years later of a truce – he probably refers to that in 545 – that Khosrau signed with the Byzantines, after which he turned his attention to Aden, blocked "with large ships, rocks, iron columns and chains" part of the sea adjacent to the land of Ethiopia and "killed the great men of state of that land." Later, after receiving a deputation (not specified precisely wherefrom) that sought help against the Ethiopians, the Persian ruler "sent back with them one of his commanders

6 Hoyland 2014, 273–275. Miranos is presumably the Greek adaptation of the Persian name Mihran and Sanatources (Parthian Sanatruk) was probably a royal title. See also Rubin 2007, 190.

7 Dijkstra and Fisher 2014, 18.

8 Greatrex 2014, 255–256.

9 Robin 2012, 284; Robin 2015, 149; Bowersock 2013, 107, 108–110. For Nonnosus' account of the embassies, see Bowersock 2013, 135–42. For Procopius' report, see Robin 2014, 35–36; Fisher 2015, 237.

10 Robin 2014, 66; Bowersock 2013, 115–116.

11 Robin 2012, 285; Robin 2015, 150, 164–67; Bowersock 2013, 114.

12 Wiesehofer 2010, 110–111.

heading an army of the men of Daylam . . . they killed the Abyssinian Masrūq in Yemen and remained there."[13] As we shall see below, al-Ṭabarī's synoptic account, quite surprisingly, stands in almost total oblivion to other accounts he provides on this matter elsewhere.

II The Arabic Sources

How did the Arabic writers treat the Persian conquest? As it turns out, not only did they see it differently from the non-Arabic sources but there are major and secondary differences between a number of Arabic versions. At the risk of repeating a fairly well-known episode, it is worthwhile to reconsider the available Arabic material and point out some conclusions.

Let us begin with some six major Arabic versions. The first version, which is ascribed to Ibn Isḥāq as featured in Ibn Hishām's recension of his biography of the Prophet, focuses on Sayf, of the Dhū Yazan (Yaz'an, in the South Arabian dialect). This clan, of Western Ḥaḍramawt, is mentioned in an inscription presumed to have been carved in the year 360 to commemorate the clan's campaigns and construction work.[14] According to Ibn Hishām, Sayf goes to the Byzantine emperor and asks him to drive the Ethiopians ("Abyssinians," *ḥabasha*) out and take control of Ḥimyar. As the emperor pays no attention to the request, Sayf turns to the ruler of al-Ḥīra in Southern Iraq (here wrongly identified as al-Nʿumān b. al-Mundhir).[15] The Ḥīran suggests to Sayf to join him in his upcoming audience with Khosrau. Here Ibn Hishām adds that upon entering the royal hall Sayf bends his head and that the king regards him as a fool. What follows is a detailed description of the audience that leads the reader (or the listener) to glimpse behind the scene, so to speak. Accordingly, the king's crown, which was inlaid with rubies, gold and silver, was definitely heavy. This is why, so it is implied, it was hooked onto a chain in the ceiling, for this way his majesty's head did not have to carry the crown's weight. Now, before giving audience, the king used to be sheltered by a screen in order that none of the visitors see the preparations for the reception, apparently so as not to detract from his royal image. As soon as he appeared in sight, all those in audience prostrated. One could envisage such a folkloric scene to be of the utmost interest to South

13 Bosworth, 1999, 159–160.
14 Fisher 2011, 6; Hoyland 2014, 271–272; Robin 2015, 139–42.
15 Al-Nuʿmān was the last of the local Naṣrīd dynasty, who came to power in ca. 580, that is, about ten years after the event discussed here. See Shahid 1995.

Arabian listeners, curious about how things looked like at a royal court so far removed from their land geographically, materially, as well as culturally.

Given permission to address the king, Sayf complains about "ravens" who took possession of his country. As if unaware of the political situation in Yemen, Khosrau asks whether by ravens is meant "Abyssinians or Sindians" (of Sind in India). Sayf answers that he meant the former, yet the king declines anyhow the offer to receive control there because, so he claims, the region has little attraction to him and he cannot endanger a Persian army in marching to Arabia. Instead, he gives Sayf 10,000 dirahms (which should be *drahms*, the Persian silver currency) and a fine robe. Then he is informed about Sayf scattering the money and after interrogating him he learns that Ḥimyar is full of gold and silver. The transmitter (or is it rather Ibn Hishām?) notes at this point that Sayf did what he did to increase the king's desire to conquer the region. Here one may add Robert Hoyland's intervention, who considers Sayf's petulant reply understandable since a silver mine, located northeast of Ṣanʿā (and recovered not long ago) and later reported by a geographer of the region, possibly surpassed any ancient Persian mine.[16] However, this piece of information is not crucial for our purpose, and one may consider Sayf's reply as part of a concocted narrative that has a point to make about the man's shrewdness.

Be that as it may, Khosrau accepts the advice given to him to send 800 prisoners as a military expedition under the command of the old-aged, yet noble Wahriz.[17] This force sails on eight boats, two of which are lost on the way. Sayf meets Wahriz and promises him his unconditional loyalty. In the engagement with the forces of Masrūq, Abraha's son, Wahriz loses his own son. Enraged, he shoots an arrow at Masrūq – there are a few piquant details interwoven into this scene – and kills him. The Ethiopian army is defeated, Wahriz enters Ṣanʿā and orders to dismantle its gate and that his standard "should never be lowered."

At this point Ibn Isḥāq's version gives voice to three poems. The first is allegedly Sayf's, in which the Ḥimyarite accredits both Wahriz and himself ("we") with Masrūq's death adding that Wahriz swore that he would drink no wine until he captured prisoners and spoil. The second poem, by Abū 'l-Ṣalt, the father of the Jāhilī poet Umayya, is in praise of Ibn Dhī Yazan – the specific name is not mentioned – who had been forced to stay at the Byzantine court no less than ten years before moving on to the Persian ruler. Interestingly enough, the poem omits Wahriz altogether yet depicts the Persian fighters as "lions." It is rather Sayf who is being urged to drink his fill and walk proudly in his robes. A

16 Hoyland 2001, 111–12.
17 The Arabic Wahriz could have derived from the Persian Vehrez.

third poem is ascribed to the poet ʿAdī b. Zayd of al-Ḥīra, who served al-Nuʿmān b. al-Mundhir (sic) and whose ancestors had settled in al-Ḥīra long before.[18] The poem speaks of the glorious past of Ṣanʿā and of fate causing the Persian army and the Persian generals to settle there. Sayf, however, is not mentioned.[19]

Ibn Isḥāq's second version was reproduced by al-Ṭabarī and has some minor differences when compared to that in Ibn Hishām. Most significant is an addition of the circumstances bringing about the death of Wahriz's son, who had been sent on a reconnaissance mission. Another addition is about Wahriz returning to the Sasanian court after the victory over the Ethiopians and Sayf assuming the post of the ruler. It is after interrupting Ibn Isḥāq's version in order to introduce Ibn al-Kalbī's version (for which see below) that al-Ṭabarī returns to what, it turns out, is missing in Ibn Hishām. It sheds some unexpected light on Sayf's politics. Accordingly, after Wahriz's departure, Sayf starts killing the Ethiopians and is extremely cruel to the point of "ripping open the pregnant womenfolk to tear out the fetuses." Only a few are spared and made into his slaves, which proves to be a grave mistake, since they take revenge and murder him. Subsequently, one of them assumes power and begins killing the Yemenites. Anxious about this development, the Persian king sends Wahriz once again, this time with no less than 4,000 troops. He orders him to exterminate all the blacks and their offspring. Wahriz accomplishes the mission, stays as a viceroy and establishes a dynasty till the removal of his descendant and the appointment of one named Bādhān.[20] Ibn Ishaq's two versions differ then in presenting Sayf. In the first, we learn only about his positive acts. In the second, the end of Sayf's career overshadows the initial acts and forces the Persian ruler to intervene. Sayf appears as a victim of haughtiness.

We turn now to the version ascribed to Ibn al-Dāya (d. ca. 340/951), which is claimed to come from Ibn al-Muqaffaʿ (d. 142/756) who, befittingly, as his origins would require, purportedly received it "from the Persians." Had it been the

18 Involved in political intrigues, despite his marriage to Hind, al-Nuʿmān's daughter, ʿAdī was imprisoned and murdered by his father-in-law. Later, however, his son Zayd was picked up by al-Nuʿmān to succeed him as a scribe in charge of messages dispatched to "the land of the Arabs." His lost dīwān is claimed to have been reconstructed some decades ago but doubt had been cast on its authenticity already in the ninth-century. See on him Seidensticker 2009. For a convenient summary of his "biography," see Hainthaler 2005. For a detailed retelling of the plot, which brought about ʿAdī's murder, see Sizgorich 2007, 1012–13; Powers 2011, 134–38. For samples of the poems ascribed to him, see Bosworth 1999, 37 n. 116; 81n. 219. For his poetry, see Toral-Niehoff 2008; Dmitriev 2010; Talib 2013, 129–32.

19 Ibn Isḥāq 1955, 30–33. See also, for example, al-Iṣfahānī 1970, vol. XVII, 303; Thaʿālibī 1900, 618, in the context of the report on Sayf's murder.

20 Bosworth 1999, 235–42, 251–52.

case this version would have to be considered one of the earliest versions. Now, it has its focus elsewhere, on the deceit masterminded by the "king of the Abyssinians" who bribed the Sasanian king's interpreter in order to subvert Sayf's request for help. Only after the deceit is revealed (and the interpreter executed) is Sayf's request for the aid of a force of prisoners explicated. However, there is certainly a dissonance between the alleged Persian source of this version and its actual content, as there is no mention of Wahriz; implied is that Sayf is solely responsible for the victory.[21] This reflects sympathy for Arab historical heroes, which is, after all, conventional with Arabic sources, and could raise doubt about the claim that the report originated in Persian circles.

A version ascribed to the Kūfan Hishām b. Muḥammad Ibn al-Kalbī (d. 204/820) is another one reproduced by al-Ṭabarī. It differs substantially from Ibn Isḥāq's version and provides the reader with a thicker description, so to speak. Its Ḥimyarite hero is Abū Murra al-Fayyāḍ Dhū Yazan, whose wife Rayḥāna, the mother of his son Maʿdī Karib, was forcibly taken by Abraha, thus adding a personal grudge to the collective resentment to the foreign oppression of Ḥimyar. Abū Murra goes to ʿAmr b. Hind – not al-Mundhir, as erroneously stated in Ibn Isḥāq's version[22] – and thus, unlike the sequence elsewhere, the Ḥimyarite notable addresses *kisrā* before going to the Byzantine emperor. The dialogue between the two is not significantly different in this account, except that the detailed description of the preparation before giving audience is missing. Here as well the Persian king does not know who the "ravens" are but at least he is more polite. He finds it difficult to decide about Abū Murra's request and, as if to buy time, offers him lodging. Eventually, Abū Murra stays at the Persian court to his death. This may be seen as a counterpart to his seven-year (and even longer) stay at the Byzantine court as reported in other versions.

Ibn al-Kalbī's narrative now shifts to Abraha's court, where Maʿdī Karib, Abū Murra's son, has been raised. Believing the Ethiopian ruler to be his father, he regards Masrūq, the man destined to play a crucial role in Ibn Ishāq's version as the ruler to be defeated in the invasion, as his brother. However, by sheer chance Maʿdī Karib learns that this is not the case, and after Abraha's death he sets out to the Byzantine court, "avoiding *kisrā* because he had delayed so long in helping his father." But the request is rejected because the Byzantines and the Ethiopians share (Christian) religion. Maʿdī Karib is forced to turn to *kisrā*, where his father had seen no luck, and the encounter between the two, unlike in Ibn Isḥāq's version, is not at the king's audience but rather accidental. Feeling

21 Ibn al-Dāya 1987, 99–101.

22 Bosworth 1999, 237 n. 587; 242 n. 596.

guilt for neglecting Maʿdī Karib's father, *kisrā* turns to his advisors and one of them suggests sending prisoners to invade Yemen. The numerical superiority of Masrūq's troops is belabored, as well as the circumstances leading to the death of Wahriz's son. Another striking feature of this version is the detailed description of Wahriz's determination, despite his advanced age, to fight the Ethiopian army ("I shall fall upon this sword of mine until it comes out of my back"). He also delivers a flamboyant speech to his troops in order to lift up their spirits. The description of the battle is largely similar to Ibn Isḥāq's. After Masrūq's defeat each of the Persian soldiers receives a few dozen prisoners as booty. Whariz orders his men to let Masrūq's defeated troops massacre the black soldiers.[23]

What can we make of the comparison between Ibn Isḥāq's and Ibn al-Kalbī's versions? Clearly, both agree that by going to the Persian king the Ḥimyarite nobleman of the Dhū Yazan family – they differ on his precise identity – was instrumental to the Persian conquest. A modern commentator has concluded, presumably on that basis, that Ibn Kalbī's is a pro-Yemenite version,[24] but so appears also Ibn Isḥāq's first part. However, in the second part Wahriz becomes the main protagonist, since thanks to his experience and military skills the expeditionary force prevails. This is especially detailed in Ibn al-Kalbī's version, where Wahriz disowns his son ("he was not my son, but only the son of a whore") for betraying him and breaking the truce with Masrūq. He also pushes his troops against the wall by destroying their ships and commanding them to finish up all their food. Sayf, however, has no role in the battle.

Next we have al-Dīnawarī's brief version, which downplays Sayf's role. The Yemenite is described as a Dhū Nuwās's descendant, the implication being that he stemmed from Judaized origins. He goes to the Byzantine ruler in Antioch and, unlike in other versions, the emperor appears to know who are the "ravens" yet declines the request because the blacks (Ethiopians) are Christians, while "you [Sayf and his folks] are pagans [!]" When Sayf goes to meet the ruler of al-Ḥīra, the latter emphasizes the blood ties between his dynasty and the Yemenites: "Our grandfather Rabīʿa b. Naṣr the Yemenite and our settling here had been especially for this," namely, assisting their relatives, the Ḥimyarites.[25] It is as if an auspicious hour for a Yemenite brotherhood arrived. The Persian

23 Bosworth 1999, 242–250.

24 Daghfous 1995, vol. I, 143–53.

25 The claim was that Rabīʿa headed the Lakhm clan who consulted a soothsayer about a terrifying dream he had and was told that the Ethiopians would invade. Thereafter, he sent his son with the whole clan to the Persian king who settled them in al-Ḥīra. For sources see Bray 1998, 114 n. 15 (she errs in identifying the Lakhm as Ghassānids).

king's instant decision is to send troops to Yemen. The military encounter with Masrūq receives only one line and then this version echoes Ibn Isḥāq (in al-Ṭabarī's reproduction) by turning to Sayf's murder and the need to send Wahriz once again.[26] This version ends with Wahriz's death, his burial and Bādhān's (it is not specified who he was) accession.[27] In the end, this version appears as less favorable to Sayf.

Coming to Ibn Qutayba, there are two different versions, both allegedly drawn from Persian (ʿ*ajam*) sources. The version in ʿ*Uyūn al-akhbār* is perhaps the least Arab, so to speak, for Sayf is not even mentioned and it is the Sasanian king's initiative to send Wahriz to fight which propels the event. The major part of this version deals with the criteria by which Wahriz chooses the arrow to be shot at the Ethiopian ruler.[28] Possibly, what we have here is a piece of folklore current among Persian circles in the post-conquest time. Ibn Qutayba's second version, although, once again, claimed to be taken from Persian romances (*siyar*), has the main ingredients of the familiar Arab version. Its original contribution is in the number of Wahriz's troops (7500!) and in comparing the split of the regime in Ḥimyar, after Sayf's murder, to a pattern of *mulūk al-ṭawāʾif*.[29]

III What to make of the Arabic Sources

Thus far, we have examined the main versions in the Arabic sources. Other versions contain variants on secondary matters. According to some Sayf stays with the Byzantine emperor no less than seven years before hearing from him the reason for the negative decision: "You are Jews and the Abyssinians are Christians."[30] Learning from Sayf that the mountains in his homeland are made of gold and silver, and that there is no need for the king's gift, the Persian ruler

26 Bonner glosses over the differences between al-Dīnawarī's and al-Ṭabarī's accounts. However, he notes the former's pride in Iranian culture and his scoffing at ideas of Arab supremacy, emphasizing Iran at the expense of distinctly Arabian themes, see Bonner 2014, 58, 61, 65, 106. For al-Dīnawarī's possible connection with the cultural movement of the *shuʿūbiyya*, see Bonner 2014, 63–64.

27 Al-Dīnawarī 2002, 62–63.

28 Ibn Qutayba 1925–30, vol. I, 149.

29 Ibn Qutayba 1969, 638–639; Ibn Hishām 2008, 354. This is a reference to the situation in ancient Iran following the death of Alexander.

30 Al-Masʿūdī 2005, Vol. II,88; al-Iṣfahānī 1970, vol. XVII, 308.

reacts: "This poor man (*miskīn*) thinks he knows his land more than I do." It is an intriguing reaction and could be variously interpreted. For one, it could be seen as subverting the king's alleged lack of interest in Arabia. Further, according to an unidentified book on the conquests (*futūḥ*), Khosrau feels sorry for Sayf after he approaches him. Contemplating his request, his answer is the flip side of the afore-mentioned answer given by his Christian rival, that is, his religion bans him from sending sea-borne troops to assist someone who is not his co-religionist. However, not being banned from sending prisoners, the number he sends is 809 (sic).[31] Sayf appeals to the Persian king by also using a racial argument: "I am closer to you than they [the Abyssinians] are because I am of a fair color (*abyaḍ*), as you are, while they are black (*sūdān*)."[32] In the version provided by the rather late Nashwān al-Ḥimyarī (d. 573/1178) Sayf adds: "I am your cousin."[33]

Turning to the scene of the fighting, also here there are some variants. Thus the Persian prisoners sail on the Tigris down to Baṣra (at that time non-existent) and in Arabia they face no less than 100,000 Ethiopian troops, of which 30,000 are killed. In the last stage of the battle Masrūq is forced to ride a camel.[34] After Wahriz's son is killed, the Ethiopians "raise the cross," by which they signal their Christian creed. In his message to the king, Wahriz adds that "this is Arab land of old (*al-qadīma*) where their kings had ruled."[35] The Persian king allows his troops to initiate marriage with Yemenite women but, so it appears, bans a similar Yemenite initiative.[36] Two poems are said in praise of the Persians by "one of the Persians" and by al-Buḥturī.[37]

---

31 Al-Iṣfahānī 1961, 52–53. For a reference to his source, see al-Iṣfahānī 1961, 114–15. For a recent treatment of some of his sources for Iranian history, see Rubin 2008. According to al-Jāḥiẓ 1965–79, vol. II, 346, the number of prisoners was 300.

32 Al-Masʿūdī 2005, vol. II, 88; al-Iṣfahānī 1970, vol. I, 308.

33 Nashwān al-Ḥimyarī 1958, 150. See "Nashwān b. Saʿīd,"*Encyclopaedia of Islam*, Second Edition; Al-Qāḍī Ismāʿīl 1987.

34 Al-Masʿūdī 2005, vol. II, 88–89. One may note that he is aware of the anachronism involving Baṣra.

35 Al-Iṣfahānī 1970, Vol. XVII, 309, 310.

36 Al-Masʿūdī, Vol. II, 89.

37 Ibid, 90–91.

IV The Aims of the Sources

Variants apart, the Arabic versions address two major questions: Was Sayf a Jew? Even more importantly, was he instrumental to the conquest and subsequent events? About the first question, al-Dīnawarī's version is intriguing. On the one hand, in a statement made by the Byzantine emperor, Sayf is characterized as an idolater. On the other hand, this is contradicted by the note that Sayf was a descendant (*min walad*) of Dhū Nuwās, the implication being that he could have professed the Jewish faith. Now, it is assumed that from ca. 380–400 until ca. 525–530 Judaism was the only religion attested to in Ḥimyarite inscriptions. The association of the Dhū Yazan, Sayf's clan, with Judaism is therefore of relevance. Archaeological evidence in the form of a massive inscription dated to July 523 and carved on a rock at the wells of Ḥima, 90 km north-east of Nagrān, was initiated by Sharaḥ'īl Yaqbul Dhū-Yaz'an, who was appointed by Yūsuf to crush the Christians there and attests to a complicated situation. It contains a vague allusion to Sharaḥ'il's religious belief: "Lord of the Jews, with the Praised One (*Mḥmd*)." Other inscriptions invoke terms such as "people of Israel," and "Israel and their god."[38] Yet things appear to have changed. The tributary ruler of Southern Arabia during the Ethiopian phase was probably Christian, and it seems that we have no indication of Yazanī association with Judaism afterwards. Churches were founded in great numbers, an ecclesiastical hierarchy was established and Jews were systematically massacred. Abraha's inscription dedicated to the consecration of a church at Ma'rib, for example, mentions the Messiah and the Holy Ghost.[39] Interestingly enough, al-Ṭabarī records that Byzantine artisans, stone masons, and mosaic artists helped to construct a church in San'a out of materials sent from Constantinople.[40]

This notwithstanding, the aim of Arabic tradition was to distance Sayf from the Jewish creed and represent him as a proto-Muslim. In analogy to other reports of a similar nature – consider, for example, Baḥīrā and his warning to Abū Ṭālib to protect Muḥammad the boy from his potential enemies, be they Jews or Chrisians – Sayf, ironically, is made to warn ʿAbd al-Muṭṭalib, the Prophet's grandfather, about the danger associated with the Jews. The occasion is a visit paid to him by Arab delegates after his victory. Wearing fancy attire and his guests next to him on his left and right, Sayf is presented as having blood ties with the Prophet's

---

38 Robin 2012, 265, 269, 270–272, 282–283; Robin 2015, 158–159. Robin (2012, 297) characterizes Sayf, a kinsman of Sharaḥ'īl, as a "Yemenite Jewish prince." For his characterization as a Jew, see also Bowersock 2013, 117.

39 Robin 2012, 284, 294–295; Robin 2015, 150–154.

40 Bosworth, 1999, 221.

grandfather. He addresses him as "our sister's son," a reference to the claim that Āmina originated in Yemen. To be tailored to the task, Sayf had to be purged and Islamized. This explains not only why there is no mention of his Jewish confession but also why he is made to vow not to drink wine or touch a woman before he takes revenge on the Ethiopians.[41] Perhaps this also accounts for not detailing the circumstances of his death, more precisely, his murder, which surely was not to his credit.[42] One scholar seems to have been carried away as seeing in Sayf the earliest Arab hero.[43] A propos of this claim, one should note Hoyland's point that Sayf belonged to an ancient Ḥaḍramite family whose members would not have considered themselves as Arabs, the concept of Arab identity retrospectively applied to all the inhabitants of pre-Islamic Arabia notwithstanding and emerging relatively late.[44]

To turn to the second major issue, to what extent was Sayf, or his son, for that matter, instrumental to the Sasanian conquest? Here one can see a clear divide between writers with Persian sentiments and writers who saw here an opportunity to play up Arab importance. Thus, on the one hand, we find Ibn Qutayba, who claims to have relied on Persian sources, and al-Dīnawarī, who was of Persian stock and his history book displays his interest in Persian history. To these two one may add al-Iṣfahānī, of Persian stock as well, who notes that after a fighting of five hours Wahriz carried a banner on which the name of Allāh and the name of the [Persian] king was inscribed.[45]

On the other hand, versions generated by opposite interests leave no doubt as to Sayf's crucial role and that the Persian conquest was a result of Sayf's initiative. Some versions even go so far as simply erasing any trace of Wahriz.[46] Here, perhaps, was an opportunity to repeat the pattern known from references to politics in Central Arabia, which is rewriting the past by focusing on the Arab

41 Ibn ʿAbd Rabbihi 1983, vol. I, 293; al-Iṣfahānī 1970, vol. XVII, 311, 315; Bray 1998, 26–33; Rubin 2007, 199. However, the version in the Aghānī, despite what has been noted earlier and Sayf's image there as a proto-Muslim, is ambivalent and self-contradictory in "allowing" Sayf to drink wine. See Bray 2005, 33.

42 See also Thaʿālibī 1900, 618; al-Masʿūdī 2005, vol. II, 91–92 (Maʿdī Karib, Sayf's son, is the one who receives ʿAbd al-Muṭṭalib and is murdered after four years into his reign).

43 Manqūsh 2004, 35–66.

44 Hoyland 2001, 229. For a detailed exposition of the argument about the retrospectively forged identity of Arabs in pre-Islamic and early Islamic periods in Arabic historiography, see Webb 2016.

45 Al-Iṣfahānī 1961, 52–53.

46 Ibn ʿAbd Rabbihi 1983, vol. I, 289; al-Azraqī 1858, 98–99. Al-Azraqī (d. ca. 222/837?), together with his grandfather, collected mainly materials allegedly going back to Ibn ʿAbbās. See "al-Azraḳī,"*Encyclopaedia of Islam*, Second Edition.

princes of Kinda, to whom the Ḥimyarites granted the dignity of kings over the Maʿadd confederation. Like the emphasis on the descendants of Ḥujr b. ʿAmr of Kinda and their role in Arabian politics in the late fifth and sixth centuries, so was, most likely, Ibn al-Kalbī's emphasis on Sayf.[47] Add to this the degree of drama that could be imparted to the Arabic point of view.[48] First we see Sayf's turning to the Roman emperor for help, only to be rejected. Then, if not for Sayf's shrewdness, the appeal to Khosrau would also have gone unnoticed. In between, we have a secondary plot of the abduction of Sayf's wife, and then the detailed descriptions of the battle in Yemen and the political intrigues that followed the Persian conquest. Is this history or a local legend? To reach a possible answer to this question one must contrast the lionization of Sayf in the Arabic version with his total omission from the Roman tradition.[49]

V Conclusion

In an article published more than ten years ago Ze'ev Rubin assessed the considerably later Arabic narratives as much more detailed than the four-line account in Theophanes Byzantinus' Historika on the Persian conquest. However, they suffered from their own problem being too rich in apparently fanciful details. Rubin also detected differences between the versions, especially regarding the identity of the Ethiopian local ruler at the time of the conquest. However, for Rubin these were minor differences that could not challenge the existence of a factual kernel. The Sasanian conquest was close enough chronologically to the advent of Islam to have left some residue of genuine reminiscences in the Arabic sources about the central role of a member of the Dhū Yazan – either Sayf or his son.[50] Working under the premise that we have before us a true story, for Rubin the question was: How could the Yazanī dignitary hope to find sympathy with the Christian emperor against the Ethiopian, Christian as well, ruler of Ḥimyar? Here Rubin ruled out the possibility that doctrinal differences between the Byzantine and Ethiopian courts might have been harped upon. Such fine tuning would

47 Robin 2012, 272; Robin 2015, 138; Fisher 2015, 443–47.

48 The drama is also pointed out by Hoyland (2014, 275), who examines Ibn Hishām's version.

49 See also Hoyland 2014, 275. However, for a recent analysis that implies support of the Arabic tradition on Sayf, see Bowersock 2017, 28–29. See also Bowersock 2013, 117–18.

50 Despite his interest in the popular romance on Sayf, that is, in literature more than in history, Tharyā Manqūsh has also deemed the traditional reports of the Arab writers to be a basically factual account.

not be expected of the Ḥimyarites. Hence, Rubin speculated on the opportunism or miscalculation that motivated the Yazanī in the affair under consideration.[51]

It is my contention that Rubin spent his energy on a speculative solution to a historically false conundrum and that a more critical approach to early Arabic historiography on the event in question is required. The present article has put forward the argument that the factual kernel in the Arabic materials was much smaller than Rubin deemed it to be. What we see in the Arabic versions is the buildup of a legend of a local hero, possibly of historical existence, yet entangled in a political drama on which, in all likelihood, he exerted limited, if any, influence.

Bibliography

Al-Azraqī. 1858. *Kitāb akhbār Makka*. Leipzig: Brockhaus.

Bonner, Michael Richard Jackson. 2014. "An Historiographical Study of Abū Ḥanīfa al-Dīnawarī."Oxford D. Phil.

Bosworth C. E., trans. 1999. *The History of al-Ṭabarī, Vol. V, The Sāsānids, the Byzantines, the Lakhmids, and Yemen*. Albany: State University of New York Press.

Bowersock, G. W. 2013. *The Throne of Adulis: Red Sea Wars on the Eve of Islam*. New York: Oxford University Press.

Bowersock, G. W. 2017. *The Crucible of Islam*. Cambridge, MA: Harvard University Press.

Bray, Julia Ashtiany. 1998. "The Damnation of Gebala, a Habar in Context," in *Law, Christianity and Modernism in Islamic Society*, edited by U. Vermeulen and J. M. F. van Reeth, 111–24. Leuven: Peeters.

Bray, Julia Ashtiany. 2005. "'Abbasid Myth and the Human Act: Ibn 'Abd Rabbihi and Others," in *On Fiction and Adab in Medieval Arabic Literature*, edited by Philip F. Kennedy, 1–54. Wiesbaden: Harrassowitz.

Daghfous, Radhi. 1995. *Le Yaman islāmique des origines jusqu'à l'avènement des dynasties autonomies 1er-IIIemes/VIIeme-IXemes*. Tunis: Université de Tunis.

Dijkstra, Jiste H. F. and Greg Fisher. 2014. "General Introduction," in *Inside and Out: Interactions between Rome and the Peoples on the Arabian and Egyptian Frontiers in Late Antiquity*, edited by Jitse H. F. Dijkstra and Greg Fisher, 1–31. Leuven: Peeters.

Al-Dīnawarī. 2002. *Al-Akhbār al-ṭiwāl*. Beirut: Dar al-kutub al-ilmiyya.

Dmitriev, Kirill. 2010. "An Early Christian Arabic Account of the Creation of the World," in *The Qur'ān in Context: Historical and Literary Investigations into the Qur'ānic Milieu*, edited by Angelika Neuwirth, Nicolai Sinai, and Michael Marx,349–87. Leiden: Brill.

Fisher, Greg. 2011. *Between Empires: Arabs, Romans, and Sasanians in Late Antiquity*. Oxford: Oxford University Press.

Fisher, Greg, ed. 2015. *Arabs and Empires before Islam*. Oxford: Oxford University Press.

51 Rubin 2007, 194–99.

Greatrex, Geoffrey. 2014. "Procopius and Roman Imperial Policy in the Arabian and Egyptian Frontier Zones." In *Inside and Out: Interactions between Rome and the Peoples on the Arabian and Egyptian Frontiers in Late Antiquity*, edited by Jitse H. F. Dijkstra and Greg Fisher, 249–64. Leuven: Peeters.

Hainthaler, Theresa. 2005. '"Adī ibn Zayd al-'Ibādī, the Pre-Islamic Christian Poet of al-Ḥīra and his Poem nr. 3 Written in Jail." *Parole de l'Orient* 20:157–72.

Hoyland, Robert G. 2001. *Arabia and the Arabs from the Bronze Age to the Coming of Islam*. London: Routledge.

Hoyland, Robert G. 2014. "Insider and Outsider Sources: Historiographical Reflections on Late Antique Arabia," in *Inside and Out: Interactions between Rome and the Peoples on the Arabian and Egyptian Frontiers in Late Antiquity*, edited by Jitse H. F. Dijkstra and Greg Fisher,267–80. Leuven: Peeters.

Ibn 'Abd Rabbihi. 1983. *Al-'Iqd al-Farīḍ*. Beirut:Dār al-kutub al-'ilmīya.

Ibn al-Dāya. 1987. *Kitāb al-mukāfa'a wa ḥusn al-'uqbā*. Beirut:Dār al-kutub al-'ilmīya.

Ibn Hishām. 1995. *Al-Sīra al-nabawiyya I*. Cairo: maktabat al-turāth al-'arabī.

Ibn Hishām (ascribed). 2008. *Kitāb al-tijān fī mulūk Ḥimyar*. Ṣan'ā: Markaz al-dirāsāt wal-buḥūth al-yamanī.

Ibn Isḥāq. 1955. *The Life of Muhammad: a Translation of Ibn Isḥāq's Sīrat Rasūl Allāh*, translated by A. Guillaume. Oxford:Oxford University Press.

Ibn Qutayba. 1925–1930. *'Uyūn al-akhbār*. Cairo:Dār al-kutub al-miṣriyya.

Ibn Qutayba. 1969. *Al-Ma'ārif*. Cairo:Dār al-ma'arif.

Al-Iṣfahānī. 1961. *Ta'rīkh sinī mulūk al-'arḍ wal-anbiyā'*. Beirut: Dār maktabat al-ḥayā.

Al-Iṣfahānī. 1970. *Kitāb al-aghānī*. Cairo: Al-Hay'a al-miṣriyyat al-'amma lil-kitāb.

Al-Jāḥiẓ. 1965–79. *Rasā'il*. Cairo: Maktabat al-khalījī.

Manqūsh, Tharyā. (1980) 2004. *Sayf b. Dhī Yazan bayna al-ḥaqīqa wal-usṭūra*. Baghdad, rep. Ṣan'ā.

Al-Mas'ūdī. 2005. *Murūj al-dhahab wa-ma'ādin al-jawhar*. Beirut: Al-Maktaba al-'asriyya.

Nashwān al-Ḥimyarī. 1958. *Qaṣīdat mulūk Ḥimyar*. Beirut: Dār al-'awda, rep. 1978.

Powers, David S. 2011. "Demonizing Zenobia: The Legend of al-Zabbā' in Islamic Sources." In *Histories of the Middle East: Studies in Middle Eastern Society, Economy and Law in Honor of A. L. Udovitch*, edited by Roxani Eleni Margariti, Adam Sabra and Petra M. Sijpesteijn, 127–82. Leiden: Brill.

Al-Qāḍī Ismā'īl bin 'Alī al-'Akwa. 1987. "Nashwān Ibn Sa'īd al-Ḥimyarī and the Spiritual, Religious and Political Conflicts of His Era." In *Yemen: 300 Years of Art and Civilisation in Arabia Felix*, edited by Werner Daum, 212–31.Innsbruck: Umschau-Verlag.

Robin, Christian Julien. 2012. "Arabia and Ethiopia."In *The Oxford Handbook of Late Antiquity*, edited by Scott Fitzgerald Johnson, 247–332. Oxford: Oxford University Press.

Robin, Christian Julien. 2014. "The Peoples beyond the Arabian Frontier in Late Antiquity: Recent Epigraphic Discoveries and Latest Advances." In *Inside and Out: Interactions between Rome and the Peoples on the Arabian and Egyptian Frontiers in Late Antiquity*, edited by Jitse H. F. Dijkstra and Greg Fisher, 33–79. Leuven: Peeters.

Robin, Christian Julien. 2015. "Ḥimyar, Aksūm, and Arabia Deserta in Late Antiquity: The Epigraphic Evidence." In *Arabs and Empires before Islam*, edited by Greg Fisher, 127–71. Oxford: Oxford University Press.

Rubin, Ze'ev. 2007. "Islamic Traditions on the Sāsānian Conquest of the Ḥimyarite Realm." *Der Islam* 84:185–99.

Rubin, Zeev. 2008. "Ḥamza al-Iṣfahānī's Sources for Sāsānian History." *Jerusalem Studies in Arabic and Islam (JSAI)* 35:27–58.
Shahid, Irfan. 1995. "Al-Nuʿmān (III) b. al-Mundhir."In *The Encyclopaedia of Islam*, Two, vol. VIII, edited by C. E. Bosworth et al. Leiden: Brill.
Seidensticker, Tilman. 2009."ʿAdī b. Zayd." In *The Encyclopaedia of Islam*, Three, edited by Kate Fleet et al. Leiden: Brill.
Sizgorich, Thomas. 2007. "'Do Prophets Come with a Sword?' Conquest, Empire, and Historical Narrative in the Early Islamic World." *American Historical Review* 112:993–1015.
Talib, Adam. 2013. "Topoi and Topography in the Histories of al-Ḥīra," in *History and Identity in the Late Antique Near East*, edited by Philip Wood, 123–47. New York: Oxford University Press.
Thaʿālibī. 1900. *Ghurar akhbār mulūk al-furs wa-siyaruhum*. Paris: Imprimerie nationale.
Toral-Niehoff, Isabel. 2008. "Eine arabische poetische Gestaltung des Sündenfalls: Das vorislamische Schöpfungsgedicht von ʿAdī b. Zayd." In *"Im vollen Licht der Geschichte": Die Wissenschaft des Judentums und die Anfange der kritischen Koranforschung*, edited by Dirk Hartwig et al.235–56.Würzburg: Ergon.
Webb, Peter.2016. *Imagining the Arabs: Arab Identity and the Rise of Islam*. Edinburgh: Edinburgh University Press.
Wiesehofer, Josef. 2010. "The Late Sasanian Near East." In *The New Cambridge History of Islam, Vol. I: The Formation of the Islamic World Sixth to Eleventh Centuries*, edited by Chase F. Robinson, 98–152. Cambridge: Cambridge University Press.

Marcus Milwright

Contextual Readings of Religious Statements in Early Islamic Inscriptions

In 2014 a metal detectorist discovered a unique silver coin, minted for the Anglo-Saxon king, Aethelberht II of East Anglia. The obverse carries a circular inscription in Latin script, pairing the name of the king with the title, *rex* (king).[1] It has been speculated that the placing of the regal title on the same face of the coin that bore his name was a means to assert his independent kingship. This message to his more powerful neighbor, Offa of Mercia (r. 757–96) provoked a swift and violent reaction; according to the late ninth-century *Anglo-Saxon Chronicle*, Aethelberht was beheaded by order of the Mercian ruler in 794.[2] Only a handful of other coins of Aethelberht II survive. One of these also bears the title, *rex*, but this time on the reverse of the coin. The remainder of the reverse shows Romulus and Remus suckled by a wolf (Figure 1a).[3] This striking design had not previously been employed on Anglo-Saxon coinage, and may have been an attempt by Aethelberht to connect himself with the illustrious Wuffing dynasty, who claimed a mythological ancestry back to both Julius Caesar and Wōden (Odin).[4] If the motivations of Aethelberht and his moneyer, Lul, remain unclear, the visual source for this

1 The story is outlined in "Cambridge Expert identifies rare Anglo Saxon Coin." ITV News, 14 May 2014: https://www.itv.com/news/anglia/update/2014-05-19/cambridge-expert-identifies-rare-anglo-saxon-coin/ (accessed: 22 November 2019).

2 Swanton 1997, 54–55.

3 The coin is in the British Museum (BMC 2). See: North 1994, 29, 102, pl. 6.12; Naismith 2016, 93.

4 This claim is recorded in the *Textus Roffensis* (Rochester Cathedral Library Ms. A.3.5), an early twelfth century legal compilation. The genealogy of Aelfwald appears on fol. 103v. Available

Note: A different, but related paper was presented at the *Eighth Nangeroni Meeting: New Perspectives and Contexts in the Studies of Islamic Origins*, held in Pratolino in June 2017. I am grateful to Guillaume Dye, Tommaso Tesei and the other the participants for their constructive critiques of my interpretations. My thanks also to Denis Genequand, Marie Legendre, Glaire Anderson, Andrew Rippin, Adam Walker, and Scott Lucas for their help and advice.

Many of the inscriptions discussed in this article can be found on the website, Islamic Awareness. The site provides the original publications for each inscription. I have made slight adjustments to some of the translations given below for the purposes of consistency. For example, the Arabic *rasūl* is translated exclusively as "messenger," even though it is given also as "prophet" and "apostle."

Marcus Milwright, Professor of Islamic Art and Archaeology, Department of Art History and Visual Studies, University of Victoria, Canada

https://doi.org/10.1515/9783110675498-012

design is easier to establish: numerous Roman coins, including copper issues of emperor Constantine I (r. 306–37), carry the motif of the suckling of Romulus and Remus (Figure 1b). Some coins like this must have still been in circulation in late eighth-century England, either as currency or heirlooms.

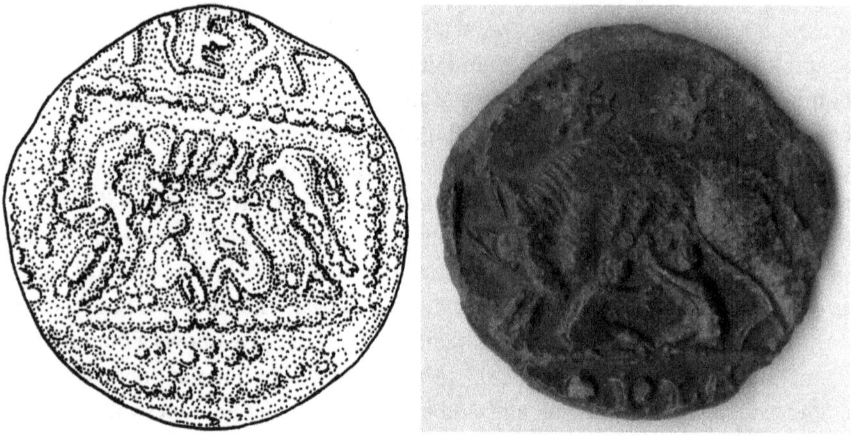

Figure 1: A) Reverse of copper coin issued by Aethelberht II of East Anglia, before 794 (drawing: Marcus Milwright); b) Commemorative coin of Constantine I, minted in Constantinople, early fourth century. Collection of the author.

The creative reuse of the Roman past can also be found in early Medieval monumental epigraphy across Europe. Dating from a few decades after Aethelberht's coin, a fragmentary inscription from the monastery of San Vincenzo al Volturno exhibits a revival, or continuation of the ancient practice of embedded cast bronze lettering into ashlar masonry. The metal letters (probably gilded) of this inscription would each have been about 30cm in height, and adorned the façade of the nave of the monastery church.[5] The tradition of applying metal lettering into stone continued in Constantinople, as is seen in the example of the narrow inscription band running around the exterior of the monastery complex of Constantine Lips, dated 907.[6] In both cases, one can imagine the potential symbolic value for the original patrons of asserting a continuity with the practices of imperial Rome.

---

online at: https://luna.manchester.ac.uk/luna/servlet/detail/Man4MedievalVC~4~4~990378~142729 (accessed: 28 November 2019).

5 Mitchell 1990, 205–216. Only one other Western European building of this period employed metal lettering: the west façade of the Abbey of Corvey, dating between 873 and 885.

6 Millingen 1974 [1912], 131, Figure 42. On the reading of this and later text bands, see James 2007, 191–193, Figures 44–47.

The Syrian site of Qaṣr al-Ḥayr al-Gharbī includes a ruined building, known in publications as the *khān*, that was originally accessed by an impressive doorway, comprising finely carved jambs and a lintel taken from an earlier building. The Arabic foundation inscription is carved across the lintel, and reads: "In the name of God. There is no god but God alone without partner. The execution of this work has been ordered by the slave of God, Hishām, Commander of the Faithful (*amīr al-mu'minīn*) . . . in Rajab 109 (November 727 CE)."[7] If the text itself is largely unremarkable for its structure and content, the same cannot be said for the way it was designed. The presence of regular drill holes among the intaglio Arabic characters indicates that they provided the support for cast copper alloy lettering (Figures 2 and 3). The architectural historian, K. A. C. Creswell (d. 1974), had no doubt about the significance of this find, writing: "It is an extraordinary example, unique of its kind, of the survival of antique methods in early Islam."[8] It is also worth remarking on the technical challenges of casting the Arabic inscription with the variant forms of selected letters in their initial medial and terminal forms and the requirement for ligatures. This can be contrasted with the stable forms of upper case letters in Latin or Greek. Thus, it seems likely that in many cases the artisans responsible for the inscription had to fashion unique casts for complete words, rather than assembling words from individual graphemes (which would allow for the repeated use of the same mould[9]).

The inscription must have been costly to produce, particularly if the exterior surface of the bronze elements was covered with gold leaf. Set into the limestone of the lintel, the letters would have had a powerful visual impact, especially when picked out in sunlight. The ambition of this commission can be appreciated through a comparison to the crude intaglio inscription that appears on the lintel of the entrance to another structure associated with the Umayyads, Qaṣr al-Burquʿ, dating to 81/700.[10] Caliph Hishām's (r. 724–43) interest in the aesthetic dimensions of inscriptions can be shown also in the gold on blue mosaic foundation plaque recovered from the excavation of his market in Baysān (Bet Shean).[11] Inscriptions of this type in glass mosaic were, of course, a signature feature of Umayyad patronage, but have their origins in imperial architecture of

7 For a transcription and translation, see Combé, Sauvaget and Wiet (eds.) 1931), 23 (no. 27). Also: Schlumberger with Écochard and Saliby 1986), 5–6, pl. 49.d; Creswell 1989, 136–137; Genequand 2006, 64.

8 Creswell 1989, 137.

9 On sand moulds for repeated casting of small objects, see Wulff 1966, 18–19.

10 Gaube 1974, 93–100. On the inscription, see also: Islamic Awareness: https://www.islamic-awareness.org/history/islam/inscriptions/burku.html (accessed: 28 November 2019).

11 On these excavated panels, see Khamis 2001, 159–176.

Figure 2: Inscription from the lintel of the entrance of the *khān* at Qasr al-Hayr al-Gharbi, 109/727. Now in the garden of the Syrian National Museum, Damascus. Photograph: Denis Genequand.

Figure 3: Detail of the inscription from the *khān* at Qasr al-Hayr al-Gharbi. Photograph: Denis Genequand.

Late Antiquity. Like Aethelberht's adoption of Romulus and Remus on his coins, Hishām's decision to order this elaborate foundation text must have derived from having seen or, at least, heard of surviving examples of gilded bronze inscriptions.[12] Furthermore, to have such an inscription executed would also have required an Arabic scribe to collaborate with stonemasons and metalworkers who possessed the requisite skills. These types of interaction can also be seen in the mosaic inscriptions in the Dome of the Rock in the 690s.[13]

Alain George has gathered persuasive evidence for the imposition of proportional systems in the Arabic epigraphy of the Umayyad period, spanning everything from coins and Qurʾanic manuscripts through to monumental inscriptions.[14] The scribe(s), metalworkers, and stonemasons working on the *khān* inscription needed to share the same understanding of the proportional characteristics of each grapheme. This system was already being codified in the 690s in the Dome of the Rock, though there is evidence in these mosaic inscriptions for experimentation.[15] The *khān* inscription shares with the Dome of the Rock the use of the invocation (*basmala*) followed by the profession of faith that emphasizes the oneness of God (*waḥdahu lā sharīka lahu*). Closer links can be made with more compressed script employed on the two painted and gilded copper plaques that were originally located in the north and east entrances to the building.[16]

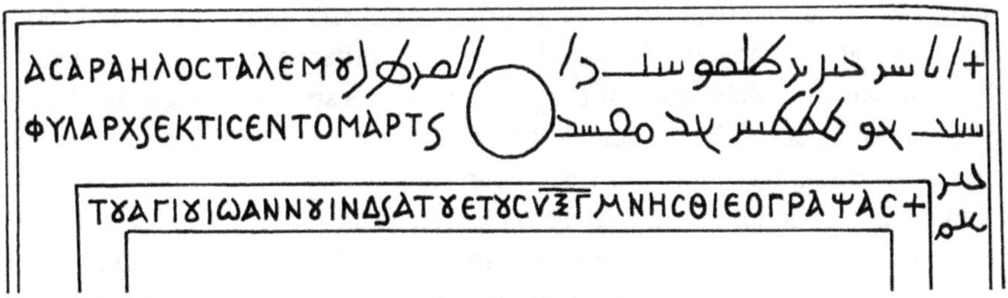

Figure 4: Lintel with Greek and Arabic inscriptions from the martyrium of St John, Ḥarrān, Syria, 568 CE. After Schroeder, 1885. Drawing: Marcus Milwright.

Other points of visual comparison can be made with lintel inscriptions from Late Antique Syria. The scale, compression, and angular character of the *khān* inscription are all present in Greek inscriptions. Notable too is the tendency to

12 Bloom 1993, 21–28.
13 Milwright 2016, 135–138.
14 George 2010.
15 Milwright 2016, 109–122.
16 Transcriptions and translations of these panels appear in: Berchem 1927. Reprinted Geneva: Slatkine 2001, 248–250. See also Milwright 2016, 75–77, Figures 2.8, 2.9.

leave minimal spacing between individual words.[17] The inscribed lintels discovered at Zebed (512 CE) and Ḥarrān (568 CE) are significant in this context because they show the contrast between the orderly Greek epigraphy and the more experimental Arabic.[18] In the Ḥarrān example (Figure 4), the Arabic inscription was probably added first, with the scribe running over the central roundel on the first line of text. Individual graphemes also vary in height and width, with somewhat indiscriminate spacing between unjoined letters and between separate words. By contrast, the mason carving the Greek lettering was able to employ an established set of guidelines to work around this spatial infringement without any noticeable adjustment in the fundamental proportionality of the script.

The remainder of this essay offers interpretations of selected early statements of religious belief in the monumental Arabic epigraphy of the seventh and first half of the eighth centuries. The reason for dwelling at some length on the inscription from the *khān* of Qaṣr al-Ḥayr al-Gharbī is to demonstrate the importance of establishing context as part of reading of a given inscription. In other words, an appreciation of the explicit content of the text is enriched through consideration of a variety of other factors, including, but not limited to: the structural characteristics of the text itself and the presence of recurrent phrases and sentiments; script morphology and its relationship to other examples of the period; the materials and techniques of the inscription; the strategies employed in the physical laying out of inscriptions in other linguistic traditions; and the relationship of the inscription to its wider environment. The potential audience for an inscription is also conditioned by geographical features; for example, a text placed on an urban mosque communicated with more varied social groups than the ones at Qaṣr al-Ḥayr al-Gharbī, which would have been seen by such people as the entourage of the caliph, Arab tribes of the Syrian desert, and merchants travelling the ancient *Strata Diocletiana*.[19]

None of the factors listed above are peculiar to the early Islamic period, and it will be argued that the creation of monumental Arabic inscriptions in the seventh and early eighth centuries was meaningfully informed by past practices. Partly, this can be explained by the resilience of craft traditions in the Middle

17 On the spacing of words in Greek inscriptions, see Papalexandrou 2001, 59–83. Also Milwright 2016, 83–106.

18 On these inscriptions, see Gründler 1993, 13–14. Also Islamic Awareness: https://www.islamic-awareness.org/history/islam/inscriptions/zebed.html (Zebed); https://www.islamic-awareness.org/history/islam/inscriptions/harran.html (Ḥarrān) (accessed: 28 November 2019).

19 On the relationship between the Umayyad *quṣūr* and trade routes, see King 1987, 91–105; Genequand 2004, 3–44.

East, and also by the need to project messages in a visual language that was comprehensible to its target audiences. This reliance upon the past was not slavish in nature, and one of the fascinations of Umayyad and early Abbasid art and architecture is its creative refashioning of earlier styles and motifs in order to generate novel meanings. The process also required the artists, patrons, and scholars of early Islam to formulate viewpoints – positive and negative – about the cultures of the pre-Islamic past. The next section looks at the appearance of different forms of professions of faith and requests for intercession in Arabic inscriptions and early Islamic written sources. The second section suggests ways in which a survey of the wider context can augment the interpretation of these formulae.

Professions of Faith and Pleas for Intercession

The *khān* inscription begins with the invocation and a profession of faith. The former component appears in the earliest surviving Islamic graffiti, while the latter is first seen on the gravestone of ʿAbāssa bint Jurayj (71/691) (Figure 5), and is then repeated in slightly variant forms in the mosaic inscription of the Dome of the Rock (dated 72/691–92, and probably completed in the mid 70s/690s).[20] While the profession of faith carried a doctrinal potency in interactions with Christian communities during the 690s and 700s, it probably possessed a more formulaic character by 109/727. Disputes over matters of religion were evidently occurring between Muslims and Christians during the reign of ʿAbd al-Malik (r. 685–705),[21] and later sources implicate the profession of faith in these discourses. For example, the *History of the Patriarchs of the Coptic Church of Alexandria* records an event during the patriarchate of Isaac (686–89) in which the governor of Egypt, ʿAbd al-ʿAzīz ordered the destruction of crosses. The account continues that the governor instructed that the doors of churches should be inscribed with the words, "Muḥammad is the great Messenger (*rasūl*) of [He who is] God, and Jesus is also the Messenger of God. But verily God is not begotten and does not beget (cf. Q 112:3)."[22] The simple profession (the so-called "short *shahāda*") involving only the statement of Muḥammad as God's Messenger first appears on Zubayrid "Arab-Sasanian" drachms in 65/685.[23]

---

20 Bacharach and Anwar 2012, 60–69. Also Islamic Awareness: https://www.islamic-awareness.org/history/islam/inscriptions/abasa.html (accessed: 28 November 2019).

21 Summarized in Milwright 2016, 223–226.

22 See *History of the Patriarchs of the Coptic Church of Alexandria* 1910, 24–25 (slightly adapted).

23 Johns 2003, 426–427.

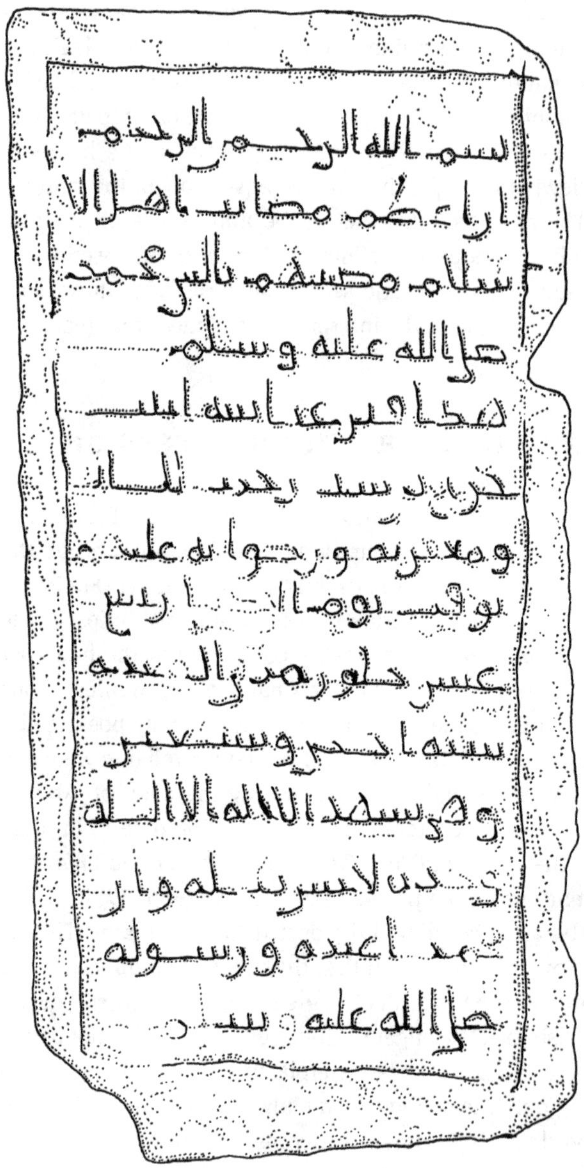

Figure 5: Funerary plaque of ʿAbāssa bint Jurayj (71/691). Museum of Islamic Art, Cairo. After el-Hawary, 1932. Drawing: Marcus Milwright.

The profession of faith (or *shahāda*) takes on a relatively stable form following its appearance in the Dome of the Rock, but there is evidence in surviving inscriptions to support the implication in the *History of the Patriarchs* that variant forms existed.[24] For example, an undated graffito on the walls of the Byzantine fortress of Rujm Sfar (Rogem Safir) in Israel reads, "I, Yūsuf bin Zubayd al-Aylī, do not associate with anything but God."[25] Another early graffito appears as part of a group located on Mount Salʿ, near Medina. Some parts are no longer legible, with Muhammad Hamidullah offering the following: "I testify that there is no God [but God] and I testify that Muḥammad is His servant (*ʿabd*) [and] His messenger. With Thy Mercy O God. There is no God but [Him. I] God is my Trust and He is my Lord."[26] Each one places emphasis on the fact that these professions have to be testified (using the verb, *shahida*) by the one making the inscription. The grave marker 71/691 asserts that ʿAbāssa bint Jurayj died testifying to the oneness of God and the prophethood of Muḥammad. This strategy is also employed in an even more urgent fashion in a graffito dated 78/697–98 from near Taʾif. The first part reads: "Al-Rayyān b. ʿAbdullāh testifies that there is no god but God and he testifies that Muḥammad is the Messenger of God then reiterates to those who come to testify to that, God have mercy on al-Rayyān."[27] Presumably, this verbal addition brought the profession of faith closer to the person being recorded, perhaps encouraging the viewer to make an oral declaration of faith.[28]

This idea of an active testament statement of faith appears in early Islamic literature. For example, in his *Kitāb al-Aṣnām* (Book of Idols), Ibn al-Kalbī (d. 819) quotes the poet and companion of the Prophet, Hassan ibn Thabit's (d. 674) verses offering a rejection of a statue of the pagan goddess, al-ʿUzzā, in Mecca:

> Through the grace of God I testified that Muḥammad / Is the Messenger of Him who reigneth above the Heavens; / And the Zacharias and his son John have worshipped Him with acceptable and meritorious works; / And that which standeth (i.e. the statue of al-ʿUzzā) by the dam in the valley of Nakhlah / And those who worship her are removed from truth, hopelessly lost.[29]

---

24 For a detailed analysis of statements of faith on pre-Islamic and early Islamic inscriptions, see Imbert 2011, 57–78. Also Hoyland 1997, 77–101.

25 Islamic Awareness: https://www.islamic-awareness.org/history/islam/inscriptions/sfar.html (accessed: 28 November 2019).

26 Hamidullah 1939, 438 (inscription E).

27 Islamic Awareness: https://www.islamic-awareness.org/history/islam/inscriptions/haram1.html (accessed: 28 November 2019).

28 Lindstedt 2017. https://iqsaweb.wordpress.com/tag/arabic-inscriptions/ (accessed: 20 November 2019).

29 Ibn al-Kalbī 1950, 39 (slightly adapted).

This formula could also be used to testify against the revival of pagan practices, as is seen in al-Ṭabarī's report of a poem of Aʿsha Hamdān, written in Kufa in 66–67/685–87: "I testify against you that you are Subaʾiyya (Sabaean)."[30] The eighth part of the *Kitāb al-Iklīl* by al-Hamdānī (d. 945) draws on Ibn al-Kalbī in the presentation of the antiquities of pre-Islamic Arabia. Al-Hamdānī provides numerous instances of the supposed discovery of ancient tombs, some of which carry inscriptions bearing parallels to Muslim formulae; for example, an inscribed tablet on a gold-lined coffin, reads: "This is the tomb of Tubbaʿ, who died a Ḥanīf (*ʿalā al-ḥanīfiyya*). He testified that there is no god but Allah."[31] The author gives several variant reports about the recovery of the bier of the daughters of the Yemenite king, Tubbaʿ, one of which reads: "I am Ruḍwā and beside me is her sister. We are the two daughters of Tubbaʿ. We believed in God and associate Him with no other [god]."[32] Another statement of faith located on a tomb states:

> I am Qidār ibn Ismāʿīl ibn Ibrāhīm, the friend of the Compassionate God. From among a people whose king is unbelieving I fled carrying the torch of the true faith. I testify that there is no god but Allah; I associate none with Him and turn to no other than Him for help.[33]

There is no reason, of course, to accept these as objective records of the excavation of pre-Islamic burials. For example, one of the accounts of the inscription of the daughters of Tubbaʿ finishes with the anachronistic formula: "We testify that there is no god but Allah and that Muḥammad is His Messenger."[34] The readers of the *Kitāb al-Iklīl* were provided with pre-Islamic inscriptions of people who had failed to heed the call of God, either directly or through the guidance of the prophets Hūd and Shuʿayb.[35] Another text is attributed to Hūd and expresses regret about the unbelief of the people of ʿĀd, concluding, "Verily nothing can forestall what God has ordained."[36]

Al-Hamdānī populates his accounts with implausible and entertaining details about ancient monuments, such as one would expect to find in a work of *adab*. While these features support Gerald Hawting's contention that such early

30 Hawting 1999, 71.

31 Al-Hamdānī 1931, 173, 201. Translated by Nabih Amin Faris as *The Antiquities of South Arabia. Being a Translation from the Arabic with linguistic, geographic and historic Notes of the eighth Book of al-Hamdani's al-Iklīl* (Faris 1939, 92–93, 107–108).

32 Al-Hamdānī 1931, 169; Faris 1939, 90.

33 Al-Hamdānī 1931, 199; Faris 1939, 107.

34 Al-Hamdānī 1931, 170; Faris 1939, 91 (slightly adapted).

35 Al-Hamdānī 1931, 160–164; Faris 1939, 84–87.

36 Al-Hamdānī 1931, 154; Faris 1939, 79–80.

Islamic texts cannot be used as objective evidence to reconstruct the true nature of "pagan" religious practice in Arabia,[37] it is still possible that al-Hamdānī's references to pre-Islamic professions of faith reflect a conviction among Muslims of his time that the *shahāda* had forerunners in other religious traditions of Late Antiquity (see below). Furthermore, the supposed texts recorded in the *Kitāb al-Ilkīl* tend to adopt forms found in early inscriptions. Compare, for example, the rejection of unbelief/paganism of Qidār ibn Ismāʿīl ibn Ibrāhīm with a graffito from al-ʿAqra, dated 83/702–703 by ʿĀfir bin al-Madārib, which starts, "I believed in what was rejected by the people of al-Ḥijr (*aṣḥāb al-ḥijr*; cf. Q 15:80)."[38]

The mosaic text bands running around the octagonal arcade in the Dome of the Rock are perhaps most significant for the fact that they are the first dated inscriptions to carry complete verses from the Qur'an. While short Qur'anic phrases appear in earlier graffiti, no earlier Islamic inscription can compete with the scale and complexity of the engagement with Muslim scripture in ʿAbd al-Malik's monument on the Temple Mount. There is, however, other religious content that may not come from a Qur'anic source. Scott Lucas has argued that the wording on the outer face (northeast side) and inner face (south side), which has commonly been interpreted as a "conflation" of Q 64:1 and 57:2 ("To Him belongs dominion and to Him belongs praise. He gives life and makes die; He is powerful over all things") is better understood as an early *ḥadīth*. The instance in the Dome of the Rock does, however, add a feature not seen in *ḥadīth* collections: the phrase, "He gives life and makes die (*yuḥyī wa-yumītu*)."[39]

Some circumstantial support for Lucas' interpretation is provided by the immediate reference to the Prophet after the point where this passage first appears on the outer face of the octagonal arcade. The remainder of the northeast side of the outer face carries the non-Qur'anic statement, "Muḥammad is God's Messenger, may God bless him and accept his intercession on the day of resurrection (*yawm al-qiyāma*) for his community." The Prophet's role in intercession (*shafāʿa*) is also mentioned in the plaque from the eastern entrance. Writing in 2003, Jeremy Johns remarks that the reference to the intercession of the Prophet is not found again in Islamic monumental inscriptions for about another 150 years.[40] Recent studies of early graffiti demonstrate that the Prophet was evoked in this manner and through the use of other terminology during the seventh and early eighth

37 Hawting 1999.
38 Islamic Awareness: https://www.islamic-awareness.org/history/islam/inscriptions/kilabi4.html (accessed: 28 November 2019).
39 Lucas 2017, 215–230 (see especially, 225–230).
40 Johns 2003, 429.

centuries. For example, the first extant epigraphic reference to Muḥammad appears in a plaque from Jerusalem, probably dated 32/652–53. This inscription speaks of "the protection of God and the guarantee (*ḍamān*) of His messenger."[41] Most important in this context, however, is a graffito from the Hisma plateau in northern Arabia, reading:

> O Lord, bless Muḥammad, the Prophet (*al-nabī*), and accept his intercession on behalf of his community, and show us mercy through him in the Hereafter (*al-ākhira*) just as You have shown us mercy through him in this world. Written by Bakr ibn Abī Bakrah al-Aslāmī in the year 80.[42] (699–700 CE)

Figure 6: Graffito near Mecca containing Q 4:87, written by ʿUthmān b. Wahran in 80/699–700. Photograph: Saad Abdulaziz Al Rashid.

The word, *al-ākhira*, is frequently used in the Qurʾan, and stands in for *yawm al-qiyāma* in the Dome of the Rock inscriptions. Two graffiti inscribed by ʿUthmān ibn Wahran in 80/699–700 use Qurʾanic verses (38:26 and 4:87 respectively) to reflect on the impending Day of Reckoning (*yawn al-ḥisāb*) and Day of Resurrection (Figure 6). The third by this scribe employs a longer quotation (56:28–40) dealing

41 Sharon 2018, 100–111; Islamic Awareness: https://www.islamic-awareness.org/history/islam/inscriptions/jerus32.html (accessed: 28 November 2019).
42 Islamic Awareness: https://www.islamic-awareness.org/history/islam/inscriptions/hisma7.html (accessed: 28 November 2019).

with paradise.[43] This desire for paradise is a common refrain, appearing in the same year in another inscription from Mecca. The last part reads, "And he seeks from God dwelling (*nazl*) in paradise and message-carrying (?) angels." Another graffito made in Dhū al-Ḥijja 85/January 704 and found in the central Negev desert names Ḥākim b. ʿAmr, expressing the desire that the subject be admitted "into the paradise (*al-janna*)." A rock inscription of 100/718–19, located on the Syrian hajj route concludes with a similar plea: "We ask God for paradise as our abode."[44]

The concept of intercession is dealt with by early Islamic authors in discussions of practices in pre-Islamic Arabia. For example, Ibn al-Kalbī reports that the Quraysh of Mecca venerated the "daughters of Allah" (i.e. Allāt, al-ʿUzzā, and Manāh). After circumambulating the Kaʿba, they would say, "Verily they are the most exalted females. Whose intercession is to be sought." A later passage in the book deals with the reasons why the people of Arabia first came to practice idolatry (*shirk*), remarking:

> Another century followed during which people venerated and respected those statues (i.e. ones carved by the children of Cain) more than they did in the first century. Then a third century followed, and the people said, "Our forefathers venerated these statues for no other reason than the desire to enjoy their intercession before God."[45]

Many Christians prayed to saints for intercession, often through the mediation of icons. While this was evidently a popular practice, the involvement of painted or sculpted representations could promote charges of idolatry, as occurred periodically through Late Antiquity, and most famously during the Iconoclastic controversy (c. 726–843).[46] This general context may provide reasons why early Muslims were relatively slow in committing to monumental inscriptions claims that Muḥammad could act as an intercessor for fear that this could lead to the improper veneration of the person of the Prophet. That this represented a genuine concern is shown by the steps taken to discourage circumambulation of the burial place of the Prophet within the mosque in Medina.[47]

---

43 Discussed in Milwright (2016), 153–154, 241, Figures 5.14, 15. Also Islamic Awareness: https://www.islamic-awareness.org/history/islam/inscriptions/makkah2.html; https://www.islamic-awareness.org/history/islam/inscriptions/makkah5.html; https://www.islamic-awareness.org/history/islam/inscriptions/makkah6.html (accessed: 28 November 2019).

44 Islamic Awareness: https://www.islamic-awareness.org/history/islam/inscriptions/negev1.html; https://www.islamic-awareness.org/history/islam/inscriptions/kilabi6.html (accessed: 28 November 2019).

45 Ibn al-Kalbī 1950, 17.

46 On Christian attitudes to representational art prior to the eighth century, see: Kitzinger 1950, 85–150; Haldon 1977, 161–184.

47 Crone and Hinds 1986, 28–29; Robinson 2005, 90–91.

Establishing Spatial and Cultural Context

One aspect of the context can be broadly defined as the relationship developed between the monumental text and its natural and built surroundings. Hamidullah provides some intriguing insights into this issue in his analysis of the graffiti located on Mount Salʿ, near Medina. The site itself is connected to the life of the Prophet, having been visited by him for prayer during the Battle of al-Khandaq in 5/627. *Salʿ* refers to the act of slicing, and reflects the fact that the natural rock formations are cut through in several places to create ravines. Hence, the connection with the life of the Prophet made it a suitable site for inscriptions, while the geology provided numerous vertical flat surfaces that could be easily seen by visitors. Hamidullah notes that near the summit is an L-shaped rock, continuing that "the lower part of the base presents a big couch on which a dozen people can easily sit and take rest." Perpendicular to this sitting area is one of the early graffiti, reading, "Night and day ʿUmar and Abū Bakr take shelter (?) with God from everything unpleasant." The left side of the same rock carries two further inscriptions.[48]

It is tempting to find a connection between the existence of a natural resting place and the placement of these graffiti, as well as the choice of content. The confluence of natural rock formations and religious practice is described by early Islamic sources dealing with *al-jāhiliyya*. For example, Ibn al-Kalbī writes about an idol called al-Fals that was venerated by the Tayyiʿ. This was a "red [rock], in the form of a man, projecting from the centre of their mountain, Aja, which was black." In this case, it appears that the unusual color contrast stimulated the acts of veneration as much as the supposedly anthropomorphic form of the rock. Another idol named Sād comprised simply of a "long rock," presumably meaning that its form was not the result of subsequent sculpting.[49] Al-Hamdānī records a slab bearing the images of the sun and the crescent moon located outside a palace in Yemen that the ruler would genuflect toward (*kaffara lihā*) each time he passed.[50] Islamic writers exhibit some interest in the aesthetic qualities of stone, a preoccupation that is also apparent in the ekphrastic literature of Late Antiquity.[51]

Scholars have noted the role of natural features such as springs and rock formations in the siting of ancient shrines across the Middle East, and it is plausible that similar processes could be at work in the locations of some early

48 Hamidullah 1939, 434.

49 Ibn al-Kalbi 1950, 31, 50.

50 Al-Hamdani 1931, 83; Faris 1939, 46–47.

51 On this issue, see Milwright 2005, 211–221. Also Barry 2007, 627–654.

Islamic graffiti. Other factors relating to placement can be identified on the basis of available evidence. Many inscriptions are located near to major trade routes through the Arabian Peninsula, Greater Syria, and Iraq. The proximity of Qasr al-Hayr al-Gharbi to the *Strata Diocletiana* has already been mentioned, and this stop was made more desirable through the plentiful supply of water via a canal running from the nearby Ḥarbaqa dam. Qaṣr al-Burquʿ, the site with the lintel inscription naming Walīd ibn ʿAbd al-Malik is located in the eastern desert, and owes its existence to a lake.[52] Pilgrimage (*ḥajj*) is specifically referenced in some early inscriptions, including two on the southern part of Syrian route dated 91/710 and 100/719 respectively. Ḥāʾil, a stop on the Darb Zubayda, has another inscription dated 82/701–702 also asking for the acceptance of the pilgrimage performed by two named individuals. This example is interesting for the presence of overlapping Arabic graffiti on the same panel, including one dated 74/693, suggesting that this flat patch of rock was deemed especially attractive for its visibility to the pilgrims, merchants and other travellers who would pass it.

The choice of rock surface appears to have been an important consideration for the earliest Arabic graffiti, with scribes looking for relatively flat surfaces that were not obscured by other geological features. The tendency toward more lengthy inscriptions carried with it challenges, from the identification of suitable patches of stone to measuring out of the lines for the text itself. The three texts composed by ʿUthmān b. Wahran in about 80/699–700 illustrate well the sophistication of the best graffiti produced after the completion of the Dome of the Rock. These are far from being spontaneous expressions of piety, and required careful consideration of how to measure out the chosen text and accommodate it to the rock surface. ʿUthmān b. Wahran focuses on Qurʾanic citations, using an impressive control of the lettering to convey to the reader the seriousness of the message. This same concern for proportionality and visual impact is seen in later graffiti with scriptural passages, including examples dated 84/703–704, 98/716–17, and an undated inscription from Ṭāʾif carrying Q 33:56 (this verse also employed in the Dome of the Rock) (Figure 7).[53]

---

52 Gaube 1974.

53 For the Taʾif inscription, see: Miles 1948, 241–242; Milwright 2016, 153, Figure 5.16. Also Islamic Awareness: https://www.islamic-awareness.org/history/islam/inscriptions/makkah1.html; https://www.islamic-awareness.org/history/islam/inscriptions/makkah3.html; https://www.islamic-awareness.org/history/islam/inscriptions/muwinsc2.html (accessed: 28 November 2019).

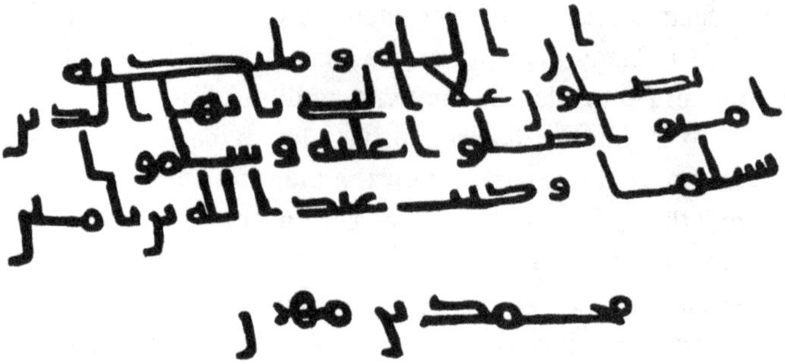

Figure 7: Undated graffito with Q 33:56. Found near Ta'if, late seventh or early eighth centuries. After Miles, 1948. Drawing: Marcus Milwright.

A general tendency toward proportionality can be discerned, which can be matched with parallel developments in portable objects, Qur'an manuscripts, and inscriptions applied to buildings. There is no doubting the sincerity of the sentiments expressed on, for example, the earliest known grave marker of 31/652,[54] but the uncontrolled nature of the lettering and uneven delineation provide a radically different visual experience to the three texts produced by ʿUthmān b. Wahran five decades later.[55] This correlation of aesthetic qualities and the nature of message conveyed likely reflects the changing expectations of those who commissioned inscriptions as well as the people who saw them. Even illiterate observers would have appreciated the contrast between rapidly executed work and a considered inscription by a trained scribe. No familiarity with Arabic is required to appreciate that the addition of bronze lettering to the doorway of the *khān* at Qaṣr al-Ḥayr al-Gharbī lent the inscription a sense of majesty not possessed by the equivalent one at Qaṣr al-Burquʿ. Similarly, contemporary viewers of the bilingual lintel inscription at Ḥarrān would presumably have contrasted the ease with which the Greek text fitted itself to the available space and the expansive nature of the Arabic lettering.

I have argued elsewhere that the emergence of Qur'anic citation should be understood in the context of Late Antique practices, and particularly the employment of selected passages from the Psalms in Christian monumental inscriptions.[56] Geoffrey Khan has noted that early Islamic inscriptions borrow formulae, such as the demonstrative pronoun in the opening of the text, that

54 Islamic Awareness: https://www.islamic-awareness.org/history/islam/inscriptions/hajri.html (accessed: 28 November 2019).

55 On the evolution of Arabic writing in the first decades, see Ghabban 2010, 89–102.

56 Milwright (forthcoming).

can be traced back to South Arabian documents. He locates this structure in significant examples such as the grave marker of 31/652, the graffito recording the completion of caliph al-Muʿāwiya's dam at Ṭāʾif from 58/677–78, and the foundation inscription at Qaṣr al-Burquʿ.[57] While oral testimony was given primacy in legal matters to in the Hijaz before the birth of Islam, there was a practice of hanging texts in the Kaʿba. As Khan notes, this "gave the documents the status of public monuments."[58] A comparison can be made between this treatment of agreements between individuals or groups and early Islamic inscriptions, such as the one from Jerusalem dated 32/652, that lists the men who witnessed it.[59] Later legal texts record other documents of this early phase that also list witnesses to an agreement, using the verb, *shahida*. The context of orality is maintained in some early Islamic inscriptions; for example, one undated example from the Negev desert states, "O God, forgive Salāmah, son of Malik, all the sins he has ever committed and [forgive] the one who reads [aloud this writing] and the one who hears [it] and then says amen."[60]

Returning to the early manifestations of the profession of faith, it is also possible to provide further cultural context through a consideration of comparable statements developed among the other confessional communities of the Middle East. Scholars have drawn attention to the wording of the Samaritan creed ("There is no god but the One"), and that this formulation may have developed in reaction to the Christian concept of the Trinity.[61] Jere Bacharach and Sherif Anwar note that the presence of *waḥdahu lā sharīka lahu* as part of the profession of faith on the grave marker of ʿAbāssa bint Jurayj (72/691) may also be a reaction to the beliefs of local Christians, some of whom may have been family members.[62] Hawting points to the Samaritan hymn that includes the words, "O Being of Unity, who hast no fellow, no second, nor colleague (*shateph*)." This last term corresponds to the Arabic, *sharīk*. The Babylonian Talmud contains a passage explaining that Adam was created on the Sabbath so that sectarians would not claim that "God had a partner in the work of creation."[63] The Jewish prayer, *Shema Yisrael*, comprises the words, "Hear, O Israel: the Lord our God, the Lord is one (Deuteronomy 6:4)." Christians circulated credal statements through inscriptions, including "One God alone and Christ" and "There is

57 Khan 2019, 27–28.
58 Khan 2019, 29.
59 Sharon 2018.
60 Lindstedt 2017.
61 Montgomery 2006 [1907], 207–208; Macuch 1978, 20–38; Hawting 1999, 72.
62 Bacharach and Anwar 2012, 64–65, 68–69.
63 Hawting 1999, 72. The reference in the Babylonian Talmud is Sanhedrin 38a.

only one God, who protects him that has engraved [the inscription] and him who reads it."[64] In addition, epigraphic surveys have demonstrated the ubiquity of the trinitarian statement, "In the name of the Father, the Son, and the Holy Spirit," on Christian buildings from the sixth century onward.[65] Intercession is also a very common theme in pre-Islamic inscriptions across the Middle East. The same ideas, coupled with pleas for salvation and forgiveness, are expressed on portable objects, such as the liturgical silver produced for churches in Greater Syria and Egypt.[66]

Conclusion

Figure 8: Palestinian Aramaic inscription from the monastery church at Hayyan al-Mushrif, Jordan. Sixth century. Drawing: Genevieve Neelin.

This chapter has argued that the ways in which early Arabic inscriptions were understood by their audiences went beyond the textual content to encompass the material and aesthetic dimensions, the location, and the broader context of Late Antique epigraphic and oral culture. Muslim writers such as Ibn al-Kalbī and al-Hamdānī propagated the idea that the profession of faith itself existed in Arabia prior to the time of the Prophet; while this may be a literary fiction, it is clear that statements about the oneness of God were in use among the Abrahamic faiths of Late Antiquity. The evidence suggests that the engagement with the past was creative and varied. For example, a graffito from the Hisma region encloses the text with a type of frame commonly known as a *tabula ansata* ("tablet-with-handles"). This device has its origins in the classical world, and is

64 Milwright 2016, 222–223. The oneness of God is also stated in 1 Corinthians 8:4, Romans 3:30, and 1 Timothy 2:5.
65 Leatherbury 2016, 133–156.
66 See examples in Mango 1986. Also Milwright 2016, 189–197.

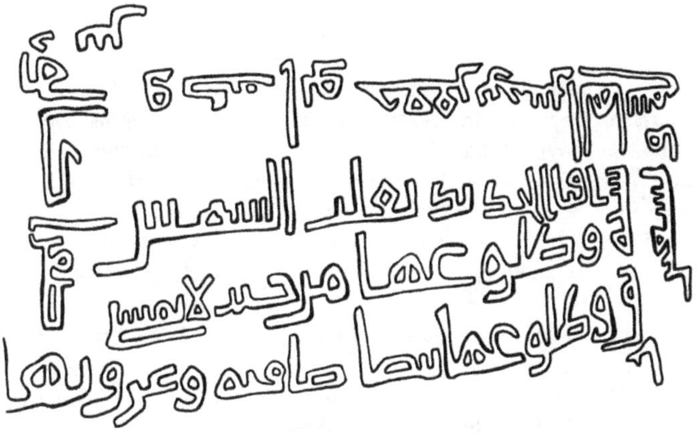

Figure 9: Graffito from Mecca region with poetry by Tubbaʿ, dated 98/716–17. After Muhammad al-Thenayin, 2015. Drawing: Marcus Milwright.

a common feature of floor mosaics of Late Antique churches (Figure 8).[67] Another demonstration of this point is a graffito, dated 98/716–17, that contains lines of poetry attributed by Ibn Qutayba (d. 889) to the pre-Islamic Yemenite king, Tubbaʿ. Most remarkable in the present context is the arrangement of the inscription with the first two lines written in conventional manner and the remainder of the words enclosing them on four sides with two lines arranged vertically and one upside-down (Figure 9).[68] This type of visual play is more familiar from later centuries, but illustrates the ways in which early texts can anticipate future developments in Islamic epigraphy,[69] while also remaining rooted in the cultures of Late Antiquity.

67 The graffiti on this site were discovered by Maysaʾ al-Ghabban. For a discussion and a photograph, see Al-Jallad: https://www.academia.edu/36680785/_May_God_be_mindful_of_Yazīd_the_King_Reflections_on_the_Yazīd_Inscription_early_Christian_Arabic_and_the_development_of_the_Arabic_scripts?email_work_card=title (accessed: 22 November 2019). On *tabula ansata* inscriptions, see Leatherbury 2019, 380–404.

68 Islamic Awareness: https://www.islamic-awareness.org/history/islam/inscriptions/makkah8.html (accessed: 28 November 2019).

69 I discuss the evolution of encircling inscriptions of this type in a forthcoming study. See also Milwright 2016, 172–213. For a general survey of visual dimensions and content of inscriptions, see Blair 1998.

Bibliography

Al-Jallad, Ahmad. "'May God be mindful of Yazīd the King': Reflections on the Yazīd Inscription, early Christian Arabic, and the Development of Arabic Scripts." https://www.academia.edu/36680785/_May_God_be_mindful_of_Yazīd_the_King_Reflections_on_the_Yazīd_Inscription_early_Christian_Arabic_and_the_development_of_the_Arabic_scripts?email_work_card=title (accessed: 22 November 2019).

Bacharach, Jere and Sherif Anwar. 2012. "Early Versions of the *Shahāda*: A Tombstone from Aswan of 71 A.H., the Dome of the Rock, and contemporary Coinage," *Der Islam* 89: 60–69.

Barry, Fabio. 2007. "Walking on Water: Cosmic Floors in Antiquity and the Middle Ages," *Art Bulletin* 89.4: 627–654.

Berchem, Max van. 2001 [1927]. *Matériaux pour un corpus inscriptionum Arabicum, Deuxième partie: Syrie du sud*. Cairo 1927. Reprinted Geneva: Slatkine, 2001.

Blair, Sheila. 1998. *Islamic Inscriptions*. New York: New York University Press.

Bloom, Jonathan. 1993. "On the Transmission of Designs in Early Islamic Architecture," *Muqarnas* 10: 21–28.

Combé, Etienne, Jean Sauvaget and Gaston Wiet, (eds.). 1931. *Répertoire chronologique d'épigraphie arabe* I. Cairo: Institut Français d'Archéologie Orientale (no. 27).

Creswell, K. A. C. 1989. *A short Account of early Muslim Architecture*, revised and expanded by James Allan. Aldershot: Scolar Press.

Crone, Patricia and Martin Hinds. 1986. *God's Caliph: Religious Authority in the first Centuries of Islam*. Cambridge: Cambridge University Press.

Faris, Nabih Amin, (trans.) 1939. *The Antiquities of South Arabia. Being a Translation from the Arabic with linguistic, geographic and historical Notes of the eighth Book of Hamdani's al-Iklil*, Princeton Oriental Texts 3. Princeton NJ and Oxford: Princeton University Press.

Gaube, Heinz. 1974. "An Examination of the Ruins of Qasr Burquʿ," *Annual of the Department of the Antiquities of Jordan* 19: 93–100.

Genequand, Denis. 2004. "Châteaux omeyyades de Palmyrène," *Annales Islamologiques* 38: 3–44.

Genequand, Denis. 2006. "Some Thoughts on Qasr al-Hayr al-Gharbi, its Dam, its Monastery, and the Ghassanids," *Levant* 38: 64.

George, Alain. 2010. *The Rise of Arabic Calligraphy*. London and Berkeley CA: Saqi.

Ghabban, ʿAli. 2010. "The Evolution of Arabic Script in the Period of the Prophet Muhammad and Orthodox Caliphs in the Light of new Inscriptions discovered in the Kingdom of Saudi Arabia," in *The Development of Arabic as a Written Language*, ed. Michael Macdonald, Supplement to the Proceedings of the Seminar for Arabian Studies 40. Oxford: Seminar for Arabian Studies and Archaeopress.

Gründler, Beatrice. 1993. *The Development of the Arabic Scripts: From the Nabataean Era to the first Islamic Century*, Harvard Semitic Studies 43. Atlanta: Scholars Press.

Haldon, John. 1977. 'Some Remarks on the Background to the Iconoclastic Controversy," *Byzantine Studies* 38: 161–184.

Al-Hamdānī, Ḥasan Ibn Aḥmad. 1931. *Kitāb al-iklīl*, ed. A. M. al-Karmali. Baghdad: Dar al-Salam.

Hamidullah, Muhammad. 1939. "Some Arabic Inscriptions of Medinah of the early Years of the Hijrah," *Islamic Culture* 13: 427–438.

Hawting, Gerald. 1999. *The Idea of Idolatry and the Emergence of Islam: From Polemic to History*. Cambridge: Cambridge University Press.

History of the Patriarchs of the Coptic Church of Alexandria (III: Agathon to Michael [766]). 1910. Trans. and ed. Basil Evetts, *Patrologia Orientalis* 5: 1–215.

Hoyland, Robert. 1997. "The Content and Context of early Arabic Inscriptions," *Jerusalem Studies in Arabic and Islam* 21: 77–101.

Ibn al-Kalbī, Hishām. 1950. *The Book of Idols. Being a Translation from the Arabic of the Kitāb al-Aṣnām*, trans. Nabih Faris, Princeton Oriental Studies 14. Princeton NJ: Princeton University Press.

Imbert, Frédéric. 2011. "L'Islam des pierres: L'expression de la foi dans la graffiti arabes des premiers siècles," *Revue des Mondes musulmans et de la Méditerranée* 129: 57–78.

James, Liz. 2007. '"And shall these mute Stones speak?" Text as Art', in *Art and Text in Byzantine Culture*, ed. Liz James. Cambridge: Cambridge University Press.

Johns, Jeremy. 2003. "Archaeology and the History of early Islam: The first Seventy Years," *Journal of the Economic and Social History of the Orient* 46.4: 411–436.

Khamis, Elias. 2001. "Two Wall Mosaic Inscriptions from the Umayyad Market Place in Bet Shean/Baysan," *Bulletin of the School of Oriental and African Studies* 64: 159–176.

Khan, Geoffrey. 2019. "The Opening Formula and Witness Clauses in Arabic legal Documents from the early Islamic Period," *Journal of the American Oriental Society* 139.1: 23–40.

King, Geoffrey. 1987. "The Distribution of Sites and Routes in the Jordanian and Syrian Deserts," *Proceedings of the Seminar for Arabian Studies* 20: 91–105.

Kitzinger, Ernst. 1950. "The Cult of Icons in the Period before Iconoclasm," *Dumbarton Oaks Papers* 8: 85–150.

Leatherbury, Sean. 2016. "Reading and Seeing Faith in Byzantium: The Sinai Inscriptions as Verbal and Visual 'Text'," *Gesta* 55.2: 133–156.

Leatherbury, Sean. 2019. "Framing Late Antique Texts as Monuments: The Tabula Ansata between Sculpture and Mosaic," in *The Materiality of Test – Placement, Perception, and Presence of inscribed Texts in Classical Antiquity*, eds. Andrej Petrovic, Ivana Petrovic, and Edmund Thomas. Leiden and Boston: Brill.

Lindstedt, Ilkka. 2017. "Writing, Reading and Hearing in early Muslim Era Arabic Graffiti," *International Qur'anic Studies Association* website, 2 January 2017. https://iqsaweb.wordpress.com/tag/arabic-inscriptions/ (accessed: 20 November 2019).

Lucas, Scott. 2017. "An efficacious Invocation inscribed on the Dome of the Rock: Literary and epigraphic Evidence for a first-Century *Ḥadīth*," *Journal of Near Eastern Studies* 76.2: 215–230.

Macuch, Rudolf. 1978. "Zur Vorgeschichte der Bekenntnisformel *lā ilāha illā llāhu*," *Zeitschrift der deutschen Morgenländischen Gesellschaft* 128: 20–38.

Mango, Marlia. 1986. *Silver from early Byzantium: The Kaper Koraon and related Treasures*. Baltimore MD: Trustees of the Walter's Art Gallery.

Miles, George. 1948. "Early Islamic Inscriptions near Ṭā'if in the Ḥijāz," *Journal of Near Eastern Studies* 7.4: 236–242.

Millingen, Alexander Van. 1974 [1912]. *Byzantine Churches in Constantinople*. London: McMillan and Co., 1912. Reprinted London: Variorum Reprints, 1974.

Milwright, Marcus. 2005. "'Waves of the Sea': Responses to Marble in written Sources (9th-15th Century)," in *The Iconography of Islamic Art. Studies in Honour of Professor Robert Hillenbrand*, ed. Bernard O'Kane. Edinburgh: Edinburgh University Press.

Milwright, Marcus. 2016. *The Dome of the Rock and its Umayyad Mosaic Inscriptions*, Edinburgh Studies in Islamic Art. Edinburgh: Edinburgh University Press.

Milwright, Marcus (forthcoming). "The Shock of the New? Qur'anic Content in the Inscriptions of the first Islamic Century,' in *From Oriens Christianus to the Islamic Near East: Theological, Historical, and Cultural Cross-Pollination in Late Antiquity*, eds. Manolis Ulbricht and Adam Walker.

Mitchell, John. 1990. "Literacy displayed: The Uses of Inscriptions at the Monastery of San Vincenzo al-Volturno in the early ninth Century," in *The Use of Literacy in early Medieval Europe*, ed. Rosamond McKitterick. Cambridge and New York: Cambridge University Press.

Montgomery, James. 2006 [1907]. *The Samaritans, the earliest Jewish Sect: Their History, Theology, and Literature*. Philadelphia: John C. Winston, 1907. Reprinted Eugene OR: Wipf and Stock, 2006.

Naismith, Rory. 2016. "Kings, Moneyers, and Royal Imagery," in *Anglo-Saxon England and the Visual Imagination 2016*, eds. John Niles, Stacy Klein, and Jonathan Wilcox. Tempe AR: Arizona Center for Medieval and Renaissance Studies.

North, J. J. 1994. *English Hammered Coinage. Volume I: Early Anglo-Saxon to Henry II, c. 600–1272*. London: Spink and Son

Papalexandrou, Amy. 2001. "Text in Context: Eloquent Monuments and the Byzantine Beholder," *Word and Image* 17.3: 59–83.

Robinson, Chase. 2005. *ʿAbd al-Malik*, Makers of the Muslim World. Oxford: One World.

Schlumberger, Daniel with Michel Écochard and Nessib Saliby. 1986. *Qasr el-Heir el-Gharbi, texte et planches*, Institut Français d'Archéologie du Proche-Orient. Bibliothèque Archéologique et Historique 120. Paris: Librairie Orientaliste Paul Geuthner.

Sharon, Moshe. 2018. "Witnessed by three Disciples of the Prophet: The Jerusalem 32 Inscription from 32 AH/652 CE," *Israel Exploration Journal* 68.1: 100–111.

Swanton, Michael (trans. and ed.). 1997. *The Anglo-Saxon Chronicle*. London and New York: Routledge.

Wulff, Hans. 1966. *The traditional Crafts of Persia: Their Development, Technology, and Influence on Eastern and Western Civilization*. Cambridge MA and London: The MIT Press.

Valentina A. Grasso

The Gods of the Qur'ān: The Rise of Ḥijāzī Henotheism during Late Antiquity

Reflections on the Sources

In a recently published paper on the pre-Islamic *talbiyāt*, invocations of Allāh made during the *ḥajj* (pilgrimage) to Mecca, Tilman Seidensticker has claimed that "our knowledge of the religious history of [pre-Islamic Arabia] is considerably poorer than it appeared to be as recently as a generation ago."[1] In the same article, he has argued that the most relevant testimonies for a study of the period are the Islamic sources. This is true only if we isolate the Ḥijāz from its surroundings. Although "it is impossible to transfer information from other regions and centuries"[2] to the area where Muḥammad lived, it is equally impossible to imagine this area as completely isolated from the remaining parts of Arabia, such as the better documented northern fringes of the Arabian desert and the southern part of the Arabian Peninsula. With this section, I aim to offer some reflections on the sources for the religious history of Arabia between the fourth and the sixth centuries CE, comparing and contrasting all available sources and contextualizing the history of this region with its surroundings. In doing so, I will demonstrate that evidence for pre-Islamic Arabia has never been so abundant, while illustrating how they can expand our knowledge of its religious history.

There is virtually no independent historical information for the Ḥijāz during Late Antiquity. The Qur'ān imparts little information regarding its immediate religious context. In addition to biblical figures (e.g., Abraham and Jesus), the only names that appear are those of three Arab prophets (Hūd, Ṣāliḥ and Shuʿayb), Muḥammad and a certain Abu Lahab. Four religious communities (Jews, Christians, Magians and the Sabians) and only two peoples (the Romans and the Arab Quraysh) appear. Overall, we should hardly consider Scriptures as historical sources; we should treat the Qur'ān, with its self-presentation as the speech of God, in similar fashion. Even the remaining Muslim sources, which date to at least two hundred years after the events they describe, are similarly unreliable.

1 Seidensticker 2010, 293.
2 Seidensticker 2010, 293.

Valentina A. Grasso,

https://doi.org/10.1515/9783110675498-013

By the end of the nineteenth century, Gustav Weil[3] and Ignác Goldziher[4] had already asserted that the *aḥādīth* were later fabrications. The works of these scholars also led to a widespread skepticism towards the historical use of the first Islamic *tawārīkh* ("histories"), the *tafāsīr* and the *Sīrat Rasūl Allāh* ("Biography of the Messenger of God," also known as *al*-Sīrat al-Nabawīya, "Prophetic Biography"). The historical prejudice towards the Muslim sources grew even further with the works of Crone, who labeled the whole Islamic tradition "tendentious" because it was composed in a later, and hence changed, cultural environment.[5] In her works, Crone chose to give prominence instead to non-Muslim literary accounts composed in Semitic languages (Arabic, Hebrew, Syriac, Aramaic) as well as in Greek, Latin, Armenian and Coptic.[6]

This approach, however, was not universally accepted. Wansbrough, for example, defined the types of sources Crone used as "a discrete collection of literary stereotypes composed by alien and mostly hostile observers."[7] Others, such as Robert Hoyland, nevertheless utilized an approach similar to Crone's though in a more measured way,[8] though recognizing that the use of external sources is mostly valid after the Muslim conquests.[9] The scholarly consensus up to that point was therefore that the traditional Muslim sources were not contemporary to the events they portray but were rather the result of a literary process carried out by the early Islamic community. As such, they were likely inspired by exegetical impulses and/or composed under the influence of later debates. Moreover, this creative re-elaboration of existing literature may have attempted to emphasize the supremacy of Muḥammad's revelation at a time when the *querelle* among the scriptural communities was surely vivid. Nevertheless, some literary sources, such as the traditions on the life of the Prophet, have been demonstrated to be consistent and "have an authentic kernel."[10]

Traces of early discussions about the trustworthiness of these testimonies can still be found. Some recently published works have attempted to verify the historicity of the Muslim sources. This has been done through an analysis of the accounts which portray Muḥammad in a negative way, and also through the examination of their *asānīd* (lists of authorities who transmitted a report). These

3 Weil 1846–62.

4 Goldziher 1889-90.

5 Crone 1987, 230.

6 E.g., the accounts of the Armenian bishop Sebeos, those in Greek of the Patriarch of Jerusalem Sophronius, and the Syriac accounts by Jacob of Edessa.

7 Wansbrough 1978a, 156.

8 Hoyland 1997.

9 Hoyland 2007, 591.

10 Görke 2011, 141.

publications have successfully shed some light on the redactional process of this material. Indeed, like the non-Muslim literary accounts, which, despite their evident apologetic intents, have the merit of being contemporary to the events narrated, the Muslim literary sources constitute a useful instrument of inquiry. Even if not considered historical documents, these works reflect some of the tendencies of the early Islamic community. Currently, although there are still some attempts to contextualize the Qur'ān using only biblical literature while denying the trustworthiness of Muslim literary sources, other scholars at least esteem the latter's usefulness as "evidence for the [Islamic] history of ideas."[11] Collaborative works uniting contributions by specialists in both Muslim and non-Muslim materials aim to produce a more balanced perspective, but this approach is still in its infancy.[12]

The use of pre-Islamic poetry for reconstructing the history of Arabia is also very controversial. In 2001 Hoyland labelled this corpus an "insider" source, since it was composed by the inhabitants of Arabia at the time of the events therein depicted.[13] Nevertheless, many scholars believed that a large portion of the so-called pre-Islamic poems is not pre-Islamic at all, but instead represents a group of later elaborations. According to this theory, this material was produced to support the idea that the Qur'ān was born in a savage polytheistic milieu. Two of the most provocative texts published in this regard were written by David Margoliouth[14] and Ṭāhā Ḥusayn[15] in the 1920s, largely inspired by the preceding works of Nöldeke[16] and Wilhelm Ahlwardt.[17]

Later, in the wake of Milman Parry's work on the Homeric poems,[18] James Monroe convincingly demonstrated that pre-Islamic poetry originated orally and was written down only some centuries after its composition.[19] The use of writing was then no more than auxiliary, and it was only during the Umayyad period (661–750) that the corpus was systematically written down. This view was rejected by Gregor Schoeler, who instead claimed that "poets and *ruwāt* (transmitters) possessed written notes and even substantial collections."[20]

If we accept that pre-Islamic poetry was written down after a long period of oral transmission, many problems regarding the authenticity of this corpus

11 Robinson 2003, 12.
12 E.g. Neuwirth, Sinai, and Marx 2010. For pre-Islamic Arabia, see Fisher 2015.
13 Hoyland 2001, 8–10.
14 Margoliouth 1925.
15 Ḥusayn 1926.
16 Nöldeke 1864.
17 Ahlwardt 1872.
18 Parry 1928.
19 Monroe 1972.
20 Schoeler 2006, 67.

become negligible.[21] If the order of the verses was vulnerable to the fallible memory of the *ruwāt*, many of the inconsistencies of these texts are attenuated. It is plausible to imagine that some rewriting of the content took place during early Islamic times. A later reshaping of the texts can easily explain the style of the poems, written down in a form of standardized Arabic *koinè* which does not substantially diverge from the language of the Qur'ān. However, it does not alter the striking contrast between the libertine context of pre-Islamic poetry and the inspired preaching of the Qur'ān, a text that also teems with literary motifs and strands of narratives, but of a very different nature.

Today, we are often lucky enough to be able to integrate the study of the literary materials with a range of archaeological finds. New archaeological finds in the Arabian Peninsula are rapidly expanding our understanding of the pre-Islamic milieu and the political structures of the Middle East. Although the archaeology of the Roman Near East has received consideration from early times, studies on the religion of late antique Arabia are, however, still in their infancy.[22] Projects on epigraphic corpora such as those based at the CNR and the University of Oxford are uncovering the material culture of ancient civilizations. These digital archives are useful instruments which enable researchers to study the history of pre-Islamic Arabia by allowing them easy access to epigraphic materials. These epigraphic corpora can help offer a corrective reading to the literary accounts. A comparison between the sources is desirable; writing the history of Arabia exclusively through a study of its epigraphic documents is as dangerous as attempting to do so only using the literary sources. The works of the archaeologists Nevo and Koren, who interpreted the rise of Islam through a study of the archaeological evidence of the Negev desert, are a good example of this misguided practice.[23]

Material culture has to be integrated *aliorsum* with the literary sources; archaeology is one of the tools we possess to confirm or disprove the historical accuracy of the Qur'ān, itself a monument, and to illuminate its complex genesis. In the following section, I will offer some reflections on the idols mentioned in two parts of the Qur'ān: the *Sūrat al-Najm* and the *Sūrat Nūḥ*. Following the findings of this section, I will draw some conclusions on the existence of polytheism in Arabia at the rise of Islam.

21 An early confutation of Margoliouth's and Ḥusayn's works is in Arberry 1957, 228–54.
22 The journal *Arabian Archaeology and Epigraphy* was founded barely thirty years ago.
23 Nevo and Koren 2003.

The Goddess of Sūra al-Najm

Muslim accounts such as those written by al-Ṭabarī, Ibn al-Kalbī and Ibn Isḥāq have been favorite sources for uncovering the polytheistic cults of Arabia during the last century,[24] and still are for some.[25] This material broadly describes most of the Arabians contemporary to Muḥammad as idolatrous. The inhabitants of Arabia are said to have once been *ḥunafā'* (lit. "those inclined"), "[a] loan-word from Aramaic through Nabatean."[26] This term denotes those Arabians who professed the *dīn* or millat *Ibrahīm*, "creed of Abraham,"[27] who "was no idolater" (*mushrik*),[28] but a follower of the "straight path" (*al-ṣirāṭ al-mustaqīm*) and "right religion" (*dīn qiyām*).[29] Little is known of this peculiar Arabian monotheistic creed and what little information we can deduce is often controversial.

The Muslim sources describe how the monotheistic belief of the *ḥunafā'* was corrupted by a man called ʿAmr b. Luḥayy. He is reported to have gone to Syria, gathered some idols there, and then erected them around the Kaʿba in Mecca. Afterwards, people started worshipping stones and irremediably forgot the true religion of Abraham. This story is reported by the biographer of the prophet, Ibn Isḥāq (d. 767), whose work is known through the edition of Ibn Hishām (d. 833),[30] and by Ibn al-Kalbī (d. 821).[31] Another version by Ibn al-Kalbī, who is the main source for pre-Islamic idolatry, claims that the corruption of monotheism in Arabia was established once the inhabitants of Mecca left the city due to its overpopulation; no one then left Mecca without a stone from the *ḥarām* (holy shrine), and after a while these were mistaken for idols.[32]

The Qur'ān often engages in polemic with a group called *al-mushrikūn* ("those who associate [with Allāh]"[33] and "make [equal] with Allāh another deity").[34] The term is often translated as "polytheists" in modern English translations. The presence of this group, altogether with the mentions of idols names and betyls in the Muslim Holy Book, has led early Muslim historians to conceive the Ḥijāzi milieu at

24 Wellhausen 1897.
25 Lecker 1993.
26 Hitti 1970, 108.
27 Q 6:161.
28 Q 6:161.
29 Q 6:161.
30 Ibn Isḥāq, *Sīrat*, 51–56.
31 Ibn al-Kalbī, *al-Aṣnām*, 5–6.
32 Ibn al-Kalbī, *al-Aṣnām*, 4.
33 Q 3:64; 12:108
34 Q 15:96.

the rise of Islam as extensively polytheist. This view is further reflected in later Muslim and Western scholarship and is still in vogue today.

In his groundbreaking *The Idea of Idolatry and the Emergence of Islam*, G. R. Hawting has argued that the Qur'ānic *mushrikūn* were Jews or Christians.[35] Hence the Qur'ānic polemic against the *mushrikūn* reflects a debate among monotheists, not necessarily taking place in Arabia.[36] However, if the redaction of the Qur'ān in Arabic would not be enough to make it an Arabian product, the presence of deities widely attested in the Arabian Peninsula links the Qur'ān to its Arabian background. I agree with Hawting's suggestion that the Qur'anic *mushrikūn* are not polytheists. However, in the next section I will argue that these were not Jews or Christians.

Different communities were present in the religious milieu at the rise of Islam, as suggested by a verse in the *Sūrat al-Ḥajj*,[37] where the *mushrikūn* are considered a separate category. I will argue that these were sympathizing monotheists who venerated Allāh. This was a pagan god who had assumed biblical character due to the intense contact between the monotheistic communities in Arabia. I argue therefore that the idols mentioned in the Qur'ān are the reminiscent memory of an old past, and their presence in the *Sūrat al-Najm* is a direct consequence of the assembly of orally transmitted *logia* during the written composition of the Qur'ān. The absence of Qur'anic textual variants further reflects this long period of oral transmission.

There are only eight pagan deities named in the Qur'ān. Three Arabian goddesses, al-Lāt, al-'Uzzā and Manāt, are mentioned in the *Sūrat al-Najm* (Q 53, "The Star").

> Have you considered al-Lāt and al-'Uzzā?
> and Manāt, the third, the other?
> What, have you males, and He females?[38]

The Muslim tradition reports in this regard a story known as *Qiṣṣat al-Gharānīq* ("Story of the Cranes"). Found in the exegetical literature on the authority of Ibn 'Abbās as well as in the *Suwar Maghāzī* ("Stories of Military Expeditions"), this *qiṣṣah* narrates that after *Sūrat al-Najm* was revealed to Muḥammad, he recited it in front of the pagan tribe of the Quraysh. However, when he got to the names of the "Daughters of Allāh," which were venerated by this powerful tribe, he supposedly added the phrase: "Indeed they are the high cranes, and indeed their intercession is to

---

35 Hawting 1999, 137.
36 Hawting 1999, 16.
37 Q 22:17
38 Q 53:19–21.

be desired,"[39] because he was misled during a moment of inattention. That this was a possibility is explicitly acknowledged in the Qur'ān.[40] Versions of the story are also found in the monumental *History* by al-Ṭabarī (d. 923)[41] and in the *Book of Idols* by Ibn al-Kalbī.[42]

Al-Lāt, al-'Uzzā and Manāt are also named in the pre-Islamic poetic corpus. For example, they appear in the encyclopedic collection *Book of Songs* by the historian al-Iṣfahānī (d. 967), who explicitly mentions the custodian of al-'Uzzā.[43] Moreover, these deities are often mentioned as the "Daughters of Allāh" (*banāt Allāh*) in the Muslim sources.[44] Other Semitic deities were also considered as the daughters of a higher god in other contexts.[45]

Non-Muslim authors repeatedly mention al-Lāt, al-'Uzzā and Manāt in literary accounts produced between the fifth century BCE and the Middle Ages. The Arab cult of Aphrodite is connected with al-Lāt on the basis of a passage by the Greek historian Herodotus (d. 425 BCE) ("the 'heavenly' Aphrodite [. . .] is called by the Assyrians Mylitta, by the Arabians Alilat").[46] One millennium later, the Syrian bishop of Cyrrhus Theodoret (d. c. 466) argued that the Ishmaelites (a term often used to refer to the inhabitants of the Arabian Peninsula) converted to Christianity renouncing the "ceremonies for Aphrodite."[47] Theodoret of Cyrrhus further states in the same section of his *Church History* that the Arabians smashed their idols and converted thanks to the preaching of Symeon Stylite.

Theodoret's contemporary Procopius of Caesarea (d. c. 554) also records the Arabians' veneration of Aphrodite. While narrating the conflict between the Naṣrid leader al-Mundhir and the Jafnid leader al-Ḥārith during the sixth century, Procopius states that the first captured the son of the second, and then "sacrificed him to Aphrodite."[48] There are also attestations of the veneration of Aphrodite among the Arabians in the later work of the Syrian priest John of Damascus (d. in the 740s) ("they used to be idolaters and worshiped the morning star and Aphrodite, whom in their own language they called *Khabâr*, which means great").[49] A vague mention of this cult appears in the anonymous Arabic

39 E.g., the classical Sunni *Tafsīr al-Jalālayn.*
40 Q 22:52.
41 Al-Ṭabarī, *Ta'rīkh,* 1192–1196.
42 Ibn al-Kalbī, *al-Aṣnām*, 12.
43 Al-Iṣfahānī, *al-Aghānī,* 21.57–8.
44 Ibn al-Kalbī, *al-Aṣnām*, 12.
45 Robin 2000.
46 Herodotus, *Histories,* 1.131.3.
47 Theodoret, *Life of Symeon*, 13.
48 Procopius, *Wars*, 2.28.20.
49 John of Damascus, *On Heresies*, 218.

Chronicle of Seert. In a passage on the Naṣrid leader al-Nuʿmān's conversion to Christianity in the sixth century, it is said that al-Nuʿmān "used to venerate the star named Venus (*al-Zohra*)."[50]

Like many Semitic idols, the "Daughters of Allāh" possessed astral characteristics.[51] Al-'Uzzā was probably seen as a personification of Venus, no differently from the Greek Aphrodite. Since Herodotus associated Alilat (i.e., al-Lāt) with the Greek goddess, scholars postulated that al-Lāt and al-'Uzzā were in an initial phase attributes of the same female goddess.[52]

Three works attest the worship of al-'Uzzā during the fifth and sixth century CE. This is the case of the fifth-century Syriac work of Isaac of Antioch and the sixth-century work of Pseudo-Zachariah Rhetor, bishop of Mytilene. The first states that 'the Arabians (*'rby'*) sacrifice to "Uzzāi when they worship."[53] Zachariah Rhetor mentions the veneration of al-'Uzzā in connection with the violent raids of the Naṣrid leader al-Mundhir, also found in Procopius.[54]

Another mention of the veneration of al-'Uzzā/Aphrodite appears in the West Syrian recension of the legend of the Christian monk Sergius/Baḥīrā, said to have recognized Muḥammad in Syria as the prophet-to-be. The Christian version of this story is found in two Syriac (one eastern "Nestorian" and one western Syrian "Jacobite") and two Arabic versions, dated between the eighth and the twelfth century CE. They consist of various parts that must have circulated independently.[55] Muslim versions of this material are scattered all over Islamic literature: the story is, for example, contained in Ibn Isḥāq's aforementioned *Sīra*. Whereas two of the three "Daughters of Allāh" are clearly mentioned in the Muslim account ("Baḥīrā got up and said to him: 'Boy, I ask you by al-Lāt and al-'Uzzā to answer my question'"),[56] only one of them (al-'Uzzā) is found in the (Christian) West Syrian recension. In this account, a correspondence between the two deities is clearly established ("the star al-'Uzzā, who is Aphrodite Venus").[57]

According to the archaeological sources, the cult of at least two of the three goddesses mentioned in *Sūrat al-Najm* seems to have been widespread in the northern and central part of the Arabian Peninsula. Already in the first millennium BCE, inscriptions attesting to the veneration of al-Lāt are widely distributed.

50 *Chronicle of Seert*, 60.
51 Nielsen 1904.
52 Starcky 1981, 120.
53 Isaac of Antioch, *Homilies*, 11.101.
54 Ps.-Zachariah, *Chronicle*, 8.5.78.
55 Szylágy 2008, 201.
56 Ibn Isḥāq, *Sīrat*, 116.
57 *West-Syrian Recension*, 49a.31.

This is because this name literally means "the goddess," as al-Lāh means "the god" (in Arabic, words ending in *t* are usually feminine). The main archaeological sites where the cults of this deity and "her sisters" are attested likely belonged to the Nabateans. Nevertheless, the Nabatean epigraphic corpus is dated too early to offer useful information on the religious milieu of Arabia just prior to the rise of Islam. Moreover, barring the onomastic of the later "Nabateo-Arabic" or "transitional"" inscriptions (e.g., JSNab 17, dated to 267 and mentioning a certain 'Abd-Manātw), there is no epigraphic attestation of the "Daughters of Allāh" in this later corpus. In any case, using names as indicators is risky.[58]

On the other hand, in the Safaitic corpus, part of the broader Ancient North Arabian corpus, dated between the first century BCE and the fourth century CE,[59] a deity named *'Lt* or *Lt* is mentioned more than one thousand times. *Mny*, literally meaning "fate" and possibly treated as its personification,[60] recalls the name Manāt Furthermore, there are ca. one hundred mentions of *Lt* in the Hismaic corpus (formerly called Thamudic E), dated to the same time of the Safaitic. Al-'Uzzā is, instead, attested in Sabaic inscriptions, part of the wider Ancient South Arabian corpus.[61] She is also attested in the Qatabanic corpus.[62]

These South Arabian inscriptions are all dated before the end of the fourth century CE. The epigraphic evidence coming from the North also points to the fact that these three deities, after having long been venerated in the Arabian Peninsula, ceased to be mentioned in inscriptions after the fourth century. This consideration mainly relies on the fact that the fourth century is the *terminus ad quem* of the inscriptions composed in the North Arabian scripts. However, this *terminus ad quem* "is entirely conventional since it is based on an *argumentum ex silentio*."[63] Although this chronology is unsatisfactory, it is significant that not even one of the "Nabateo-Arabic" or "transitional" inscriptions bear religious *formulae*. For example, among the 32 transitional texts dated to the period 200–500 CE and recently analyzed by Laïla Nehmé,[64] only one mentions a deity, a very generic "Lord of Eternity" (*mry 'lm'*).[65] Neither have polytheistic *formulae* been found in

58 A similar comment appears in Macdonald 1999.
59 Al-Jallad 2015, 17.
60 Al-Jallad 2015, 328.
61 E.g. A-50-506; A-50-858; CIAS 35.21/o 6.
62 E.g. CIAS F 24/s 4/95.11; CIAS 95.11/o 2; H 2c.
63 Al-Jallad 2015, 18.
64 Nehmé 2010.
65 JSNab 17.

the nine inscriptions which Michael Macdonald defines as "Epigraphic Old Arabic."[66]

We do not possess many inscriptions dated between the fourth and sixth centuries CE. The inhabitants of the northern part of the Arabian Peninsula decreased their habit of writing on rocks, asking for the protection of pagan deities. Yet there are consistent epigraphic mentions for this period of Allāh in association with those Christian communities which inhabited the Arabian Peninsula during Late Antiquity.[67]

As for material culture, portraits of al-Lāt, sometimes represented with the same iconography as the Greek Athena,[68] are scattered all over Arabia, but they are not dated after the third century. We also lack testimonies of pagan temples dated after the fourth century. Nabatean temples and later temples with architectural Nabatean influences, with cult-niches and steles,[69] have been found in the north. However, only one of these, the one found at Umm al-Jimāl, can be dated to the fourth century.[70] There is hence no archaeological evidence for the veneration of polytheistic deities after the fourth century CE.

The Gods of Sūrat Nūḥ

In addition to the "Daughters of Allāh," the Qur'ān mentions five deities in the *Sūrat Nūḥ* ('Noah').[71] In Qur'ān 71:23, Noah complains to God that his people venerate Wadd, Suwāʿ, Yaghūth, Yaʿūq and Nasr.

> And [the people of Noah] said, "Never leave your gods and never leave Wadd or Suwāʿ or Yaghūth and Yaʿūq and Nasr."[72]

66 OCIANA.

67 E.g., some fifth century inscriptions found near Najrān bear a cross next to certain names. Two of them also bear the mention ʾl-ʾlh. See Robin, al-Ghabbān, and al-Saʿīd 2014. An important Christian epigraphic attestation of Allāh in the sixth century comes from Zabad, see Kugener 1908.

68 Hoyland 2001, 187; al-Azmeh 2017, 170.

69 Patrich 1990 50–113.

70 Healey 2001, 65. For the Nabateans see also Alpass 2013.

71 Suwāʿ was also venerated by the Banu Hudhayl in al-Ḥijāz.

72 Q 71:23.

Three of these deities are clearly connected to South Arabia by Ibn Isḥāq[73] and Ibn al-Kalbī.[74] The latter claims that the Quraysh, the Thaqīf, the Aws, the Khazraj and all the northern and central Arabian tribes preferred al-Lāt, al-'Uzzā and Manāt to all other deities. These tribes did not hold the five idols of *Sūrat Nūḥ*[75] in the same regard. The latter were conceived as less important than the "Daughters of Allāh" because venerated far away from the Ḥijāzi milieu ("for their distance from them").[76]

Wadd was surely the national god of the Mineans,[77] and was possibly also venerated in Dūmat al-Jundal, the capital of Kinda.[78] In addition to representing the moon, he was also a fertility god.[79] This god also appears in the *Dīwān* (collection of poems by one author) of the pre-Islamic poet al-Nābigha (c. 535–604),[80] as reported by Ibn al-Kalbī. He is also mentioned in an inscription found in al-ʿUlā (in north-western Saudi Arabia), recording the offering of a young slave boy by a priest of *Wd* and his two sons to the chief god of the kingdom of Liḥyān.[81] The veneration of *Wd* is further attested in the south of the Arabian Peninsula by more than one hundred inscriptions composed in Ḥaḍramitic, Sabaic, Qatabanic and Minaic and dated up to the late third century CE. Suwāʿ's name was heard by Ibn al-Kalbī in a "poem by a man from Yemen."[82] On the other hand, he states that the names of Yaʿūq and Nasr were never heard by him.[83]

Before ca. 275, South Arabia was divided into several small kingdoms. These kingdoms also possessed distinct religious pantheons. The main god of Ḥaḍramawt was then Sayīn, of Qatabān ʿAmm, of Maʿīn ʿAthtar and of Sabaʾ ʾAlmaqah.[84] Temples and sacrifices were dedicated to the main gods in each kingdom. The multiplicity of religious features in these kingdoms thus mirrors the political and cultural fragmentation of the region. Around 300, the infant kingdom of Ḥimyar achieved what no other kingdom had, unifying the southern part of the Arabian Peninsula. Around 380, king Malkīkarib Yuha'min (r. 375–400) and the ruling

73 Ibn Isḥāq, *Sīrat*, 52.
74 Ibn al-Kalbī, *al-Aṣnām*, 6–7
75 Ibn al-Kalbī, *al-Aṣnām*, 16.
76 Ibn al-Kalbī, *al-Aṣnām*, 17.
77 Ryckmans 1989, 163.
78 Ibn al-Kalbī, *al-Aṣnām*, 9.
79 Ryckmans 1989, 164.
80 Nallino 1921.
81 JSLih 049.
82 Ibn al-Kalbī, *al-Aṣnām*, 6.
83 Ibn al-Kalbī, *al-Aṣnām*, 7.
84 Robin 2015a, 97.

class of Ḥimyar adopted a monotheism influenced by Judaism.[85] No monumental inscription attests the survival of polytheism after the fourth century. Differently from the segmentary and chaotic picture we possess of North Arabia society, we can almost safely say that there were no polytheistic cults in South Arabia at the time of Muḥammad's prophetic career.

The break from polytheism by the Ḥimyarite kings has often been defined as radical and abrupt.[86] However, Malkīkarib Yuha'min's monotheism was vague and syncretistic, so as to homogenize the kingdom's populations in a less abrupt way. The god venerated by kings and princes is an omniscient god, often called "Lord of Heaven" (*Mrʾ s¹my*).[87] In the brand-new reign of Ḥimyar, the cult of a single, institutionalized, and trans-local deity provided a strong criterion for establishing identities.[88] These were reshaped in a wider syncretistic social framework through a socio-political exploitation of cults, as characteristic of the broader late antique world.[89] In some aspects, this god resembles the "High God" venerated in the Graeco-Roman world and in buffer state regions. Buildings for "the one whose name is blessed forever," "the Lord of the World," and "the Merciful One" are commonly found in Palmyra.[90] Greek inscriptions dedicated to a *Theos Hypsistos* are also found in the Syrian city. As the god of South Arabia, *Theos Hypsistos* was a single, remote, and abstract deity.[91] Moreover, as the Ḥimyarite god, it was anonymous and never represented in human form.[92]

The monotheism of Ḥimyar shares features with that of the Hypsistarians as well as with the early phase of Ethiopian Christianity.[93] Moreover, the Ḥimyarite kingdom's official conversion to monotheism shares some features with that of the first Christian Roman emperors.[94] Overall, the beliefs of the early late antique inhabitants of South Arabia were the social response to the changes of the period. They arose from the evolution of indigenous cults emerging during the fourth century but were also inspired by the Jews of the Diaspora who are attested living in South Arabia at the time.

No archaeological source attests the cult of the gods of *Sūrat Nūḥ* as the "Daughters of Allāh" after the fourth century. Muslim historians claim that the

85 Grasso 2020.
86 Robin 2015b, 129.
87 E.g. Gar Bayt al-Ashwal 2.
88 Grasso 2020.
89 Grasso 2020.
90 Teixidor 1977, 122–43.
91 Mitchell 1999, 92.
92 Mitchell and Van Nuffelen 2010, 12.
93 Grasso 2020.
94 Grasso 2020.

inhabitants of pre-Islamic Arabia were mostly idolatrous on the eve of Islam. The Qur'ān itself mentions the belief in eight pagan deities. For their part, the non-Muslim authors argue that some leaders of the Arabians began converting to Christianity from the fifth century onwards. The names of the pagan deities which these authors mention correspond to those named by the Muslim scholars and the Qur'ān itself, in addition to being attested by the archaeological sources.

Overall, if the literary extracts convey the idea of the existence of widespread polytheistic beliefs in pre-Islamic north Arabia, the archaeological material points to the abandonment of pagan cults during Late Antiquity. Of course, this lack of material evidence is not to be used as an *argumentum ex silentio*, as absence of evidence is not evidence of absence. Late-dated polytheistic inscriptions may simply not have been found yet. Therefore, at the moment, we can only acknowledge the abrupt epigraphic disappearance of pagan deities and the dismissal of pagan temples after the fourth century.

Ḥijāzī Henotheism during Late Antiquity

As previously mentioned, the Qur'ān directly testifies that most of the people living in Arabia during the sixth/seventh century were *mushrikūn* ("associators"[95]). These are defined as "those who set up with Allāh [the God] another god"[96] thus implying that these were not "polytheists" *tout court* because of their belief in Allāh.

The term "pagan monotheism" has often been used to indicate a monotheism, mostly independently of Judaism and Christianity, which was widespread by the time of Late Antiquity in the Near East.[97] Angelos Chaniotis has claimed that the term not only seems to be a paradox, but reduces the matter to a question of quantity.[98] Instead, he argues it represents a different interpretation of the divine, and hence a question of quality.[99] He has proposed to use the neologism "megatheism."[100] Other scholars have adopted the term "henotheism," but there is not a universally accepted definition of this term.[101]

95 E.g. Q 15:94.
96 Q 15:96.
97 First employed in 1999 by Athanassiadi and Frede.
98 Chaniotis 2010, 112.
99 Chaniotis 2010, 112.
100 Chaniotis 2010, 112.
101 Van Nuffelen 2010, 18.

Julius Wellhausen has proposed seeing Allāh as "der eigentliche Inhaber der Göttlichkeit" ("the true bearer of the divine"), and hence the supreme god of pre-Islamic Arabia.[102] Wellhausen claimed that the inhabitants of Arabia believed Allāh had created the world, and postulated that Allāh was a syncretistic abstraction of other local deities and that his cult was therefore inter-tribal. Carl Brockelmann later proposed to read the genesis of Allāh as a primitive *Urmonotheismus*; this was thus not an abstraction of other deities, but a primitive Arabian god resembling a *Deus Otiosus*.[103] This discussion was re-instigated in the 1970s by the works of Javier Teixidor and William Montgomery Watt. The former postulated the existence in the Hellenistic and Roman Near East of a main god which controlled lesser divine beings,[104] while Watt proposed seeing Allāh as a *Deus Otiosus*.[105] The genesis of Allāh can be hence seen as a historical process whereby a specific deity came to emerge as singular.[106] If we closely analyze the relevant sources on the creeds of the ***Jāhilīyah*** and attentively search for mention of Allāh as a High God, we obtain unexpected results.

From Qur'ānic passages, we can infer that the "pagans of ***Jāhilīyah***" were accustomed to associating lesser beings with a higher god only when not in need of protection. These passages do offer in fact substantial evidence of the existence of a pagan belief in Allāh.

> They [the evildoers, *aẓ-ẓalimūn*] appoint to God, of the tillage and cattle
> that He multiplied, a portion, saying,
> "This is for God" – so they assert – "and
> this is for our associates" (*shurakā'*). So what is
> for their associates reaches not God; and
> what is for God reaches their associates.
> Evil is their judgement![107]

> When they embark in the ships, they call on
> God (Allāh); making the religion sincerely His;
> but when He has delivered them to the land,

102 Wellhausen 1897, 217.
103 Brockelmann 1922.
104 Teixidor 1977.
105 Watt 1981. For an earlier exposition, see Watt 1971.
106 Al-Azmeh 2017, 47.
107 Q 6:136.

> they associate others (*yushrikūn*)
> with Him.[108]
>
> When some affliction visits mankind, they
> call unto their Lord, turning to Him; then,
> when He lets them taste mercy from Him,
> lo, a party of them assign associates (*yushrikūn*)
> to their Lord.[109]

Qur'ānic passages such as the aforementioned ones postulate the concurrent believe in a High God named Allāh and in other supernatural beings associated with it. An enlightening passage by Ibn al-Kalbī also points to belief in an Arabian *Urmonotheismus*. He mentions that the North Arabian tribe Nizār commonly said:

> Here I am Allāh! Here I am! (*Labbayka Allāhumma! Labbayka!*)
> Here I am! You have no partner (*sharīk*) save one who is yours!
> You have dominion over him and over what he possesses"
> They were used to declare his unity through the talbiyāt while associating their gods with him, placing their affairs in his hand.[110]

These passages attest simultaneous belief in Allāh and the intermission of lesser beings. The intercessors were sometimes perceived as "angels with the names of females."[111] Elsewhere they were conceived as demons. Ibn al-Kalbī regards the aforementioned al-'Uzzā as such: "al-'Uzzā was a demon (*shayṭān*) which used to frequent three trees in the valley of Nakhla."[112] The passage continues with the description of the mission of the companion of Muḥammad, Khālid Ibn al-Walīd, who was ordered to cut down the trees of al-'Uzzā. Around one of these trees, al-Walīd saw an Abyssinian woman (*ḥabashya*) gnashing her teeth.[113] Once Khālid had severed her head in two, she crumbled into ashes.[114]

Among the partners of Allāh, that is, the intercessors, we also find the *jinn*.[115] An entire *Sūra*, number 72, is called *al-Jinn*. This is a term borrowed from Aramaic[116] that designated "creatures of smoke, intermediate between the fiery

---

108 Q 29:65.
109 Q 30:33.
110 Ibn al-Kalbī, *al-Aṣnām*, 4.
111 Q 53:27; Q 17:40; Q 37:149–150.
112 Ibn al-Kalbī, *al-Aṣnām*, 15.
113 Ibn al-Kalbī, *al-Aṣnām*, 16.
114 Ibn al-Kalbī, *al-Aṣnām*.
115 Q 6:100. Ibn al-Kalbī also claims that an Arab tribe worshipped the "demons" known as jinn. *See al-Aṣnām*, 22.
116 Albright 1940, 292.

devils of hell and the angels of light."[117] This lexeme shows notable similarities with Zoroastrianism and Judeo-Christian angelology,[118] and at the same time recalls ancestral Bedouin cults, because it was from these *jinn* that poets and soothsayers derived inspiration and the ancient art of divination.[119] This *topos* of a liminal demonic creature also has many intriguing parallels and equivalences in Antiquity, such as the Roman *genii*[120] and the Greek *patrōoi theoi.*[121] Distinguished in later Islamic traditions from both humans and angels, and labelled as *shaytān*, *mārid* or *'ifrīt*, the *jinn* are re-elaborations of pagan Arab conceptions which grew to represent interfaces between the sacred and secular spheres, while occupying an ambiguous position neither wholly good nor evil.

Al-Azmeh has argued that supernatural beings such as the *jinn* did not have a cultic infrastructure in pre-Islamic times and were later "Islamised and made to be subservient to and created by the supreme being."[122] I instead propend to see the *jinn* and the other supernatural being found in the Qur'ān (and in the later Muslim literature) as already subjected to a High God in pre-Islamic times. The Islamization of the *jinn* and their molding to serve Muḥammad's strict monotheist propaganda is exemplified by their substitution with the *Shayṭān*, the Devil of the Christian tradition, in later *suwar*. The *jinn* are in fact almost completely absent in the Medinan *suwar*, with only one exception in the *Sūrat al-Raḥmān*. This may suggest an increase influence and appreciation of the preachings of the scriptural communities present in the Ḥijāz, as well as a re-adaptation of old indigenous beliefs to serve the new Islamic propaganda.

It is improbable that these associates were perceived as independent gods, as depicted by the later Muslim authors ("When a traveler stops to sleep, he would take four stones, pick the finest one and adopt it as his lord").[123] The supposed polytheism of the pre-Islamic Arabians was thus limited to the request of vague forms of intercession to a High God, to whom all creatures, whether humans, angels, demons or *jinn*, were subordinated ("Those on whom you call apart from God, are servants the likes of you; call them and let them answer you, if you speak truly").[124] The lack of a Ḥijāzī well-organized pantheon and the inconsistent, scattered mentions of guardians and temples found in literature

117 Albright 1940, 293.
118 Crone 2010, 192–200.
119 Al-Azmeh 2017, 206.
120 Kunckel 1974.
121 Ilberg 1884-1937.
122 Al-Azmeh 2017, 327.
123 Ibn al-Kalbī, *al-Aṣnām*, 21.
124 Q 7:194.

corroborate this thesis. Arabian animism and the veneration of a supreme god in pre-Islamic Arabia, suggested also by the reiterated supremacy of al-Ka'ba,[125] are documented in the Qur'ān and other Muslim sources (e.g., "By Allāt and al-"Uzzā and those who believe in them, and by Allāh, indeed he is greater than both").

Ibn al-Kalbī claims that the inhabitants of Arabia were "fond of worshipping idols".[126] However, they were not inclined to privilege one above the others. Different terms are used in the Qur'ān to refer to idols worshipped concurrently with Allāh. In addition to *andād* (equals) and *shurakā'* (partners), they are named as *ṭāghūt, jibt, anṣāb, awthān* or *aṣnām*. Ibn al-Kalbī explains that if statues were made of wood, gold, or silver and resembling human forms, they are then called *aṣnām*.[127] Instead, if they are made of stones, they are called *awthān*.[128] All the passages of the Qur'ān mentioning the *aṣnām* ("idols") relate of an old past, being part of accounts on Abraham,[129] or the Children of Israel. More ambiguous are the two occurrences of idols as *awthān*. Although the first, found in Q 29:17 and 25, may be also placed in the context of Abraham's narrative,[130] the situation is more complicated for the mention in the *Sūrat al-Ḥajj*. We read: "Whoever honors the sacred rites of Allāh – it is best for him in the sight of his Lord. And permitted to you are the grazing livestock, except what is recited to you. So avoid the abominations of idols and avoid false statements."[131] The surah also mentions Sabians, Christians, Magians and 'those who associate'.[132] However, clear the historical context of the surah is unclear, and the encouragement to "avoid false statements" can be interpreted in various ways.[133]

Finally, pre-Islamic formulae of ritual invocation, *talbiyāt*, further attest that pre-Islamic Arabians repeatedly invoke and pray to Allāh. It has been almost one century since the publication of S. M. Husain's article which collects twenty five pre-Islamic *talbiyāt*, utterance during the Meccan pilgrimage.[134] A later article by M. J. Kister, moving from Husain's pioneering work, claimed that the pre-Islamic talbiyāt of the tribe association of the Ḥums, including the Quraysh, expounded "clearly their belief in the authority of Allāh over the

125 Ibn al-Kalbī, *al-Aṣnām*, 21. Also in Ibn Isḥāq, *Sīrat*, 55.
126 Ibn al-Kalbī, *al-Aṣnām*, 21.
127 Ibn al-Kalbī, *al-Aṣnām*, 33. See also 21.
128 Ibn al-Kalbī, *al-Aṣnām*, 33.
129 Q 6:74; 14:35; 21:57; 26:71.
130 Q 29:17 and 25.
131 Q 22:30.
132 Q 22:17.
133 E.g. Al-Ṭabarī, *Tafsīr*, 17.113.
134 Husain 1937.

principal Arab deities".[135] This further claimed that the *talbiyāt* reflect the ideas of the existence of Allāh as a supreme God in pre-Islamic times. In more recent times, Al-Azmeh has suggested that these acclamations are "generic, intensified and superlative affirmation of devotion, used for a variety of deities and for any deity."[136] In the same work, he has claimed that Allāh was an undefined god, invoked in particular ritual moments, and far from being conceived as a cosmocratic deity.

To summarize, the Qur'ānic *mushrikūn* were imperfect monotheists who believed in the intercession of supernatural beings but venerated the same god of the Muslims. I have so far argued that polytheistic cults are only conspicuously attested until the fourth century CE, the *terminus ad quem* of the North Arabian Inscriptions, and the moment in which the kings of South Arabia adhered to monotheism. The inscriptions of the Arabian Peninsula dated after the fourth century attest the mention of more than one recurrent name to indicate god. This imperfect terminology is reflected in the Qur'ān. I will now briefly move to analyze the nature of this Ḥijāzi High God.

In the Qur'ān, both the words *Raḥmān* and *Allāh* appear in Medinan and Meccan *suwar* to indicate the god of Islam with no particular proportions. *Rabb* also often appears to indicate the god of Muḥammad. False gods are often mentioned as *ilah*. *Raḥmān* usually appears in the Qur'ān as an epithet. According to Al-Azmeh, a god named *Raḥmān* was assimilated to Allāh from the second Meccan period.[137] Al-Azmeh further claims that "Allāh had the distinct advantage of not having been anyone's cultic deity."[138] Although epigraphy has shown that Allāh was the god of the Christians, Azmeh is right in suggesting that the genesis of Allāh can be seen as a historical process whereby a specific deity came to emerge as singular.[139] Some passages of the Qur'ān give the impression that *Raḥmān* was not only an epithet of Allāh. In surah 25, for example, *al-Furqān*, *Raḥmān* is perceived with aversion by Muḥammad's community: "And when it is said to them, 'Prostrate to al-Raḥmān,' they say, 'And what is the al-Raḥmān? Should we prostrate to that which you order us?' And it increases them in aversion."[140]

As previously mentioned, a deity named *Lh*, "god," is sometimes found on his own in the Ancient North Arabian corpora. It is, however, uncertain whether

135 Kister 1980, 36
136 Al-Azmeh 2017, 231.
137 Al-Azmeh 2017, 313.
138 Al-Azmeh 2017, 314.
139 Al-Azmeh 2017, 47.
140 Q 25:60.

this deity corresponded to Allāh since his name was not attached to the North Arabian determinative article *h-*.[141] An Old Arabic inscription found at al-Jawf (Dūmat al-Jandal) dated to the sixth century clearly mentions Allāh[142] and a similar epigraphic evidence comes from north-eastern Jordan (*dkr ʾl-ʾlh yzydw ʾl-mlk*).[143] Allāh also features in the Christian inscriptions from Najran,[144] as well as in the Christian trilingual inscription from Zabad (Syria)[145] and in an Arabic epigraphic evidence dated to around 560 and found in the monastery of Hind the Elder at al-Ḥira (preserved in two transcriptions of al-Bakrī (d. 1094)[146] and Yāqūt (d. 1229)).[147] Al-Raḥmān, the other name of Allāh in the Qur'ān, appears in inscriptions found both the North and the South of the Arabian Peninsula. The name is used in both Christian and Jewish inscriptions from South Arabia.[148]

Overall, though the attestation of *Lah* appears widespread, the veneration of *Raḥmān* is more confined to the south among the Jewish-sympathizing and later Christian kingdom of Himyar in South Arabia.[149] It appears likely that this god was imported to the Ḥijāz from the south, where significant attestations are found for the fourth and fifth centuries. It is plausible to imagine that the belief in Raḥmān "migrated" from Ḥimyar after the collapse of the kingdom at the end of the sixth century. A close inspection of the Qurʾān confirms the identification of *Raḥmān* as a proper theonym, and not as a mere epithet of Allāh. The Qurʾān tries to syncretistically merge these two gods ("Say: Invoke Allāh or invoke the al-Raḥmān. Whichever you invoke, to Him belong the best names. And do not be too loud in your prayer or quiet but seek between that an [intermediate] way"),[150] but some echoes of the tension between the two are still to be found.[151]

Raḥmān is mostly present in Meccan *suwar*. It is significant that Allāh is not mentioned at all in the *Sūrat al-Raḥmān*. Allāh is also missing in Meccan *Sūrat al-Naba'* where *al-Raḥmān* is found twice.[152] Any explanation for *Raḥmān*'s prominence in early and middle Meccan *suwar* would be tentative. It is possible

141 Al-Jallad translates "Lh" with "Allāh" while analyzing some theophoric names, see al-Jallad 2015, 58.
142 Nehmè 2017.
143 Al-Shdaifat et al. 2017.
144 Ḥimà-Sud PalAr 8 and 10 in Robin et al. 2014, 1099–1102.
145 Robin 2006, 337.
146 Al-Bakrī, *Muʿjam* 2, p. 607.
147 Yāqūt, *Buldān* 2.542.
148 Grasso 2020.
149 Grasso 2020.
150 Q 17:110.
151 See already mentioned Q 25:60
152 Q 78:37–38.

that there was a stronger presence from the south in the region. Or, more plausibly, the mention of *Raḥmān* reflects the nomenclature employed at an embryonal phase of the formation of Islam. In Medina, a change of Muḥammad's perception of god is signalized by the adoption of the more generic Allāh over *Raḥmān*. This procedure does not reflect the abandonment of an Allāh as a "dreadful and inflexible Justiciary," or Muḥammad's renouncement to be an apocalyptic prophet for being a legislator.[153] Instead, it indicates Muḥammad's recognition that a generic name would have better fit Islam universalistic message. Muḥammad was possibly familiar with the nomenclature struggle dividing the Christian churches at the time. He may have thus opted to employ a simple, but firm, name and interpretation of God, over a more subjective and complex one.

The merging of the two high gods, bearer of similar attributes, took place therefore in Ḥijāz, at the center of the Arabian Peninsula, a location familiar with the merging of cultures and the exchange of goods and ideas due to the caravan trades. A Ḥijāzi High God, simply called al-Lāh ('the God'), had been always primitively venerated, but became prominent from the fifth century onwards, when it got merged with the southern, better defined, High God by the name of *Raḥmān*. It then started assuming the attributes of a biblical god, under clear influence of local Jewish-Christian communities.

Conclusion

At the end of the twentieth century, Hawting argued that the Qur'anic polemic against the *mushrikūn* "reflects disputes among monotheists rather than pagans and that Muslim tradition does not display much substantial knowledge of Arab pagan religion."[154] In order to sustain his thesis, Hawting cautiously embraced Wansbrough's theory which proposed an extra-Arabian redaction of the Qur'ān.[155] This idea fits well with the proposal of an empty Ḥijāz between the fifth and sixth century.[156] Nevertheless, if the Qur'ān had been composed outside the Arabian Peninsula, one would expect to find references to a non-Arabian milieu (not to mention a language different from Arabic). As we have just seen, the references to Arabian deities are abundant.

153 Robin 2019, 104–5.
154 Hawting 1999, 16.
155 Wansbrough 1978b.
156 Nevo and Koren 1990.

In a similar fashion, Crone has argued that "it is hard to avoid the impression that both Jews and Judaizing pagans are involved [with the *mushrikūn*]."[157] Nonetheless, interpreting the *mushrikūn* as Judeo-Christians is risky. One verse in the Qur'ān even mentions *mushrikūn* and People of the Book as distinct communities.[158] It is instead more appropriate to connect the religious attitudes of the Qur'anic *mushrikūn* with the "trend toward monotheism, namely toward the exclusion of other gods' existence," spread across the Near East during Hellenistic and Roman times.[159] After years of declining paganism, this trend was reaching maturation in Arabia on the eve of Islam.

Overall, the *mushrikūn* were not "monotheists" or "polytheists." They believed in a supreme god (Allāh) but also in lesser divine beings and in blurred Arabian concepts. These concepts gradually lost ground to external monotheistic influences. Put more simply, Muḥammad and the Qur'ānic *mushrikūn* concurrently believed and worshipped one common High God, whose attributes were slowly assimilated with the biblical god of the Jewish-Christian communities present in the Ḥijāz. The disputes between the Islamic prophet and his opponents may have been caused by a different perception of the unity of God, one being anchored to old pagan remembrance but sympathizing with the flourishing monotheistic streams, and the other more deeply influenced by the scriptural traditions.

The cult of deities such as al-Lāt, al-'Uzzā and Manāt declined after the end of the fourth century. Polytheistic cults were surely strong at the time of the Safaitic inscriptions but were already diminishing under the influence of the surrounding scriptural communities. This is suggested by several facts, i.e., the lack of polytheistic archaeological material, the ambiguous Qur'anic definition of *mushrikūn* and the testimonies of the non-Muslim scholars, which attest the conversion to Christianity of the Arab leaders. Under the influences of the scriptural communities, the veneration of an already existing high god became prominent, while local deities with their tribal identity were assuming a pan-Arab significance, becoming "intercessors" to Allāh.

However, remembrances of the ancient cult of pagan deities remained anchored to the collective imaginary of the tribes of north and central Arabia. As argued at the beginning of this work, poetry had long been transmitted orally, aiming to boost a tribe and bond individuals together. It then "became like archival documents, representing a tableau of a distant past."[160] In a similar fashion, the assembly of the biblical and typical Arabian *topoi* found in the Qur'ān

157 Crone 2016, 101; reiterated 111, 321.
158 Q 2:105.
159 Teixidor 1977, 17.
160 Drory 1996, 48.

and their creative production was a long process and the passages attesting pagan cults may have originated in remote times. The Qur'ān is thus both a response of the Jewish-Christian diatribes of the first millennium, as well as an echo of a more prominent Arabian religious past, resurfacing, in better resolution, in later collections such as Ibn al-Kalbī's *Book of Idols*.

Hawting claimed that works such as *The Book of Idols* "should not be understood [. . .] as collections of authentically Arabian ideas and traditions."[161] Epigraphy has proved the contrary. Stories on the "Daughters of Allāh" probably constituted the tradition of the pre-Islamic inhabitants of the northern and central part of the Arabian Peninsula. Their names and their stories were therefore inherited by the later Muslim scholars (and to a lesser degree by the Qur'ān itself) who made a clever use of declining cults to underline the supremacy of Muḥammad's revelation. This process was not different from that carried out by non-Muslim authors. These in fact exploited the old portrayal of Arab idolatry to emphasize the early Arab conversions to Christianity. Nonetheless, the Muslim sources were composed later than the non-Muslim ones; it is difficult to tell whether some of the stories on Arab idolatry were consciously fabricated or were the consequence of misinterpretations.

Arabian idolatrous cults had already ceased being prominent a few centuries before the preaching of Muḥammad, and the sociological milieu of Arabia was changing under external influences. In the fifth and sixth centuries, extensive monotheistic movements were flourishing. The neighboring monotheistic empires increased their influence on the tribal communities of Arabia. The echoes of different cultures and beliefs possibly also penetrated the Peninsula along with trade. Arabia was at that time experiencing both an ecological[162] and a political crisis. The great empire of South Arabia and the vassal states of the north had in fact disappeared, while a prophetic monotheistic movement was attempting to respond to a rampant age of fragmentation. It is not fortuitous that six prophets are said to have been preaching in Arabia c. 575–634.[163]

The sixth and seventh centuries were in fact a period of disorder and great uncertainty for the inhabitants of the Arabian Peninsula. The prophetic movement, which supposedly spread in this region during these centuries, was the natural outcome of this widespread and oppressive malaise. Among these prophets, there was Musaylima b. Ḥabīb, the great rival of Muḥammad, belonging to, perhaps not by chance, a clan called Banū Ḥanīfa. These changes explain the

161 Hawting 1999, 110.

162 Sigl et al. 2015. Extreme weather events in this period are recorded by historians such as Procopius, *Wars*, 4.14.4.

163 Robin 2012.

lack of archaeological polytheistic material and the appearance of churches all over the Arabian Peninsula and its northern extension. On the eve of Islam, the declining cults of lesser beings slowly lost ground to the monotheistic preachings of the Judeo-Christian communities.

Hence, it is plausible that later Muslim apologists exaggerated the residual polytheism in Arabia to emphasize Muḥammad's impact and establish a comparison between his prophetic career and those of the biblical prophets. We can also say that the information found in the Muslim material is often to be ascribed to later dogmatic needs, as evident in regard to the Christian Jafnid al-Ḥārith, said by Ibn Isḥāq to venerate Manāt,[164] and by Ibn al-Kalbī to venerate both Manāt[165] and al-Fals.[166] This dogmatic need is also found in the accounts of non-Muslim writers, who were willing to emphasize the Arab conversions to Christianity. We could also partially ascribe the misinformation of some non-Muslim writers to their "external background." It is, for example, significant that Jacob of Serug (d. 521) claims that Ethiopia (*Kwš*) "venerates the sun (*shmsh*) as a god (*'lh'*),"[167] when Aksūm had officially converted to Christianity at the beginning of the fourth century. Nonetheless, the literary sources are generally concordant.

Overall, Arabia before the fourth century was conspicuously polytheist, but it is highly likely that this was not the case of pre-Islamic Arabia at the time of Muḥammad's prophetic career. The surrounding late antique empires and the Arabian scriptural communities played an important role in the genesis of Islam. However, by the time of Muḥammad, henotheistic and monotheistic expressions had likely already fermented in the composite and distinctive milieu of late antique Arabia. In fact, at this time those deities appearing in the Qur'ān had been degraded to the status of "intercessors," the Qur'anic *mushrikūn* had become merely "associators," and Allāh was slowly assuming the attributes of the biblical god.

The Ḥijāzi "contingency of cults" reflects a tribal society which lacks an authoritative political system. It is only with the creation of a Ḥijāzi scriptural monotheism, greatly inspired by the monotheisms attested in the Arabian Peninsula at the time but plausibly for the first time in the region regulated by an organic *Kitāb* ("Scripture"), that Muḥammad unforeseeably flattened the divergences between the fragmented tribal societies of Arabia, supplying a brand-new civilized cultural identity to the next world conquerors of the first millennium.

---

164 Ibn Isḥāq, *Sīrat*, 55.
165 Ibn al- Kalbī, *al-Aṣnām*, 9.
166 Ibn al- Kalbī, *al-Aṣnām*, 38.
167 Jacob of Serug, *Homelies*, 101.65.

Bibliography

Literary Primary Sources

Ali, M. M. 1920. *The Holy Qur'ān Containing the Arabic text with English Translation and Commentary*. Lahore.
Al-Bakrī al-Andalusī. *Mu'jam mā ista'jama min 'asmā' al-bilād wa-al-mawāḍi'*, edited by M. al-Shaqqā. 1945-1949. Cairo.
Al-Iṣfahānī. *Kitāb al-Aghānī*, edited by R. E. Brünnow. 1888. Leiden.
Al-Ṭabarī. *Ta'rīkh al-rusul wa-l-mulūk*, edited by M. J. de Goeje. 1879-1901. Leiden: Brill.
Al-Ṭabarī. *Tafsīr = Jāmi' al-Bayān 'an Ta'wīl 'Ay al-Qur'ān*, edited by I. Fāris. 1905–1912.
Arberry, A. J. 1955. *The Koran*. London: Macmillan.
Herodotus, *Herodoti Historiae*, edited by C. Hude. 1926-1927. Oxford: Oxford University Press.
Ibn al-Kalbī, *Kitāb al-Aṣnām*, edited by R. Klinke-Rosenberger. 1941. Leipzig: Harrassowitz.
Ibn Isḥāq [Ibn Hishām], *Sīrat Rasūl Allāh*, edited by M. al-Saqqā, I. al-'Abyārī, and 'A. Shalba. 1937. Cairo.
Isaac of Antioch, *Homiliae S. Isaacs Siri Antiocheni*, edited by P. Bedjan. 1903. Paris.
Jacob of Serug, *Homiliae Selectae Mar-Jacobi Sarugensis*, edited by P. Bedjan. 1905-1910. Leipzig. (edited by S. Brock. 2006. Piscataway: Gorgias Press).
John of Damascus, *On Heresies* in *John of Damascus and Islam. Christian Heresiology and the Intellectual Background to Earliest Christian-Muslim Relations*, edited by P. Schadler, 218–32. 2017. Leiden: Brill.
Procopius, *History of the Wars = Procopii Caesariensis Opera Omnia*, edited by J. Haury. 1962–1964. Leipzig: Teubner.
Roggema, Barbara. 2009. "Christian Recension of the "Legends of Sergius Baḥīrā." In *The Legend of Sergius Bahira: Eastern Christian Apologetics and Apocalyptic in Response to Islam*. Leiden: Brill.
Scher A., and R. Griveau, ed. 1908–19. *Chronicle of Seert = Histoire Nestorienne Inédite*. Paris: Firmin-Didot.
Tafsīr al-Jalālayn, edited by J. Maḥallī. 2004. Cairo.
Theodoret, *Life of Syméon (Le Stylite) = Histoire des Moines de Syrie*, edited by P. Canivet and A. Leroy-Molinghen, 158–216. 1979. Paris: CERF.
Yāqūt. *Kitāb mu'jam al-buldān*. 1955–1957. Beirut.
Zacharia Rhetor, *Historia Ecclesiastica Zachariae Rhetori Vulgo Adscripta*, edited by E. W. Brook. 1919–24. Paris: E Typographeo Reipublicae; *The Chronicle of Pseudo-Zachariah Rhetor: Church and War in Late Antiquity*, edited by G. Greatrex, translated by R. R. Phenix. and C. B. Horn. 2011. Liverpool: Liverpool University Press.

Mentioned Safaitic inscriptions (accessible on OCIANA, http://krc.orient.ox.ac.uk/ociana/index.php/database*)*
AbaNS 352
C 3315
C 4351
JSLih 049

Mentioned South Arabian Inscription (accessible on DASI, http://dasi.humnet.unipi.it/*)*

A-50-506
A-50-858
CIAS 35.21/o 6.
CIAS F 24/s 4/95.11
CIAS 95.11/o 2
Gar Bayt al-Ashwal 2
H 2c

Secondary Sources

Ahlwardt, Wilhelm. 1872. *Bemerkungen über die Echtheit der Alten Arabischen Gedichte.* Greifswald: L. Bamberg.

Al-Azmeh, Azīz. 2017. *The Emergence of Islam in Late Antiquity: Allāh and His People.* Cambridge: Cambridge University Press

Albright, William F. 1940. "Islam and the Religions of the Ancient Orient." *Journal of the American Oriental Society* 60:283–301.

Al-Jallad, Ahmad. 2015. *An Outline of the Grammar of the Safaitic Inscriptions.* Leiden: Brill.

Alpass, Peter. 2013. *The Religious Life of Nabataea.* Leiden: Brill.

Al-Shdaifat, Younis, Ahmad Al-Jallad, Zeyad al-Salameen, and Rafe Harahsheh. 2017. "An early Christian Arabic graffito mentioning 'Yazīd the king.'" *Arabian Archaeology and Epigraphy* 28: 315–324.

Arberry, Arthur. 1957. *The Seven Odes: The First Chapter in Arabic Literature.* London: G. Allen & Unwin.

Athanassiadi, Polymnia and Michael Frede, eds. 1999. *Pagan Monotheism in Late Antiquity.* Oxford: Oxford University Press.

Brockelmann, Carl. 1922 "Allah und die Götzen, der Ursprung des islamischen Monotheismus." *Archiv für Religionswissenschaft* 21:99–121.

Chaniotis, Angelos. 2010. "Megatheism: The Search for the Almighty God and the Competition of Cults." In *One God: Pagan Monotheism in the Roman Empire*, edited by S. Mitchell and P. Van Nuffelen, 112–140. Cambridge: Cambridge University Press.

Crone, Patricia. 1987. *Meccan Trade and the Rise of Islam.* Oxford: Oxford University Press.

Crone, Patricia. 2010. "The Religion of the Qur'ānic Pagans: God and the Lesser Deities." *Arabica* 57:151–200.

Crone, Patricia. 2016. *The Qur'ānic Pagans and Related Matters.* Leiden: Brill.

Drory, Rina. 1996. "The Abbasid Construction of the Jahiliyya: Cultural Authority in the Making." *Studia Islamica* 83:33–49.

Fisher, Greg, ed. 2015. *Arabs and Empires before Islam.* Oxford: Oxford University Press.

Goldziher, Ignác. 1889-1890. *Muhammedanische Studien.* Halle: Max Niemeyer.

Görke. Andreas. 2011. "Prospects and Limits in the Study of the Historical Muḥammad." In *Transmission and Dynamics of the Textual Sources of Islam*, edited by N. Boekho-van der Voort, K. Versteegh and J. Wagemakers, 137–151. Leiden: Brill.

Grasso, Valentina. 2020. "A Late Antique Kingdom's Conversion: Jews and Sympathisers in South Arabia. " *Journal of Late Antiquity* 12: 352–82.

Hawting, Gerald R. 1999. *The Idea of Idolatry and the Emergence of Islam*. Cambridge: Cambridge University Press.
Healey, John F. 2001. *The Religion of the Nabateans: A Conspectus*. Leiden: Brill.
Hitti, Philip. 1970. *History of the Arabs: From the Earliest Times to the Present*. London: Macmillan.
Hoyland, Robert G. 1997. *Seeing Islam as Others Saw It: a Survey and Evaluation of Christian, Jewish and Zoroastrian Writings on Early Islam*. Princeton: Princeton University Press.
Hoyland, Robert G. 2001. *Arabia and the Arabs from the Bronze Age to the Coming of Islam*. London: Routledge.
Hoyland, Robert G. 2007. "Writing the Biography of the Prophet Muḥammad: Problems and Solutions." *History Compass* 5:581–602.
Ḥusayn, Ṭāhā. 1926. *Fi al-Shiʾr al-Jāhilī*. Cairo.
Husayn, Sayyid M. 1937. "Talbiyat al-Jahiliyya." *Proceedings of the 9th All-India Oriental Conference*: 361-69.
Ilberg, Johannes. 1884-1937. "Patrooi theoi." In *Ausführliches Lexikon d. griechischen u. römischen Mythologie*, edited by W. H. Roscher. Leipzig: Teubner.
Kister, Meir J. 1980. "Labbayka, Allāhumma, Labbayka: On a Monotheistic Aspect of a Jāhiliyya Practice." *Jerusalem Studies in Arabic and Islam* 2:33–57.
Kugener, Marc-Antoine. 1908. "Nouvelle note sur l'inscription trilingue de Zébed." *Rivista degli Studi Orientali* 1:577–586.
Kunckel, Hille. 1974. *Der Romische Genius*. Heidelburg: Kerle.
Lecker, Michael. 1993. "Idol Worship in pre-islamic Medina (Yathrib)." *Le Muséon* 106: 331–346.
Macdonald, Michael. C. A. 1999. "Personal Names in the Nabatean Realm: a Review Article." *Journal of Semitic Studies* 44:251–289.
Margoliouth, David S. 1925. "The Origins of Arabic Poetry." *Journal of the Royal Asiatic Society* 57:417–449.
Mitchell, Stephen and Peter Van Nuffelen. 2010. "Introduction: the debate about pagan monotheism." In *One God: Pagan Monotheism in the Roman Empire*, edited by S. Mitchell and P. Van Nuffelen, 1–15. Cambridge: Cambridge University Press.
Mitchell, Stephen. 1999. "The Cult of Theos Hypsistos between Pagans, Jews, and Christians." In *Pagan Monotheism in Late Antiquity*, edited by Polymnia Athanassiadi and Michael Frede, 81–148. Oxford: Oxford University Press.
Monroe, James T. 1972. "Oral Composition in pre-Islamic Poetry." *Journal of Arabic Literature* 3:1–53.
Nallino, Carlo A. 1921. "Il Verso d'Annabigah sul Dio Wadd." *Rendiconti Accademia Nazionale dei Lincei* 29:283–290.
Nehmé, Laila. 2010. "A Glimpse of the Development of the Nabatean Script into Arabic Based on Old and New Epigraphic Material." In *The Development of Arabic as a Written Language*, edited by M. C. A. Macdonald, 47–88. Oxford: Oxford University Press.
Nehmé, Laila. 2017. "New Dated Inscriptions (Nabataean and pre-Islamic Arabic) from a Site near al-Jawf, Ancient Dūmah, Saudi Arabia." *Arabian Epigraphic Notes* 3:121–164.
Neuwirth, Angelika, Nicolai Sinai, and Michael Marx, eds. 2010. *The Qurʾān in Context: Historical and Literary Investigations into the Qurʾānic Milieu*. Leiden: Brill.
Nevo, Yehuda D. and Judith Koren. 1990. "The Origins of the Muslim Descriptions of the Jahili Meccan Sanctuary." *Journal of Near Eastern Studies* 49:23–44.
Nevo, Yehuda D., and Judith Koren. 2003 *Crossroads to Islam*. New York: Prometheus.

Nielsen, Ditlef. 1904. *Die altarabische Mondreligion und die mosaische Ueberlieferung.* Strasbourg: Trübner.
Nöldeke, Theodor. 1864. *Beiträge zur Kenntnis der Poesie der Alten Araber.* Hannover: Rümpler.
Parry, Milman. 1928. *L'Epithèt traditionnelle dans Homère.* Paris: Les Belles Lettres.
Patrich, Joseph. 1990. *The Formation of Nabatean Art. Prohibition of Graven Images Among the Nabateans.* Jerusalem: Magnes Press.
Robin, Christian J. 2000. "Les 'Filles de Dieu' de Saba' à la Mecque: Réflexions sur l'agencement des panthéons dans l'Arabie ancienne." *Semitica* 50:113–92.
Robin, Christian J. 2006. "La réforme de l'écriture Arabe à l'époque du califat médinois." *Mélanges de l'Université Saint-Joseph* 59:319–364.
Robin, Christian J. 2012. "Les signes de la prophétie en Arabie à l'époque de Muhammad (fin VIe siècle et début VIIe siècle de l'ère chrétienne)." In *La raison des signes: Présages, rites, destin dans les sociétés de la Méditerranée ancienne*, edited by S. Georgoudi, R. K. Piettre, and F. Schmidt, 433–76. Leiden: Brill.
Robin, Christian. J., A. I. al-Ghabbān, and Sa'īd Fāyiz al-Sa'īd. 2014. "Inscriptions antiques de la région de Najrān (Arabie Séoudite Méridionale): Nouveaux jalons pour l'histoire de l'écriture, de la langue et du calendrier Arabe." *Comptes rendus des séances de l'Académie des Inscriptions & Belles-Lettres*: 1033–1128.
Robin, Christian. J. 2015a. "Before Ḥimyar: Epigraphic Evidence for the Kingdoms of South Arabia." In *Arabs and Empires before Islam*, edited by G. Fisher, 90–127. Oxford: Oxford University Press.
Robin, Christian J. 2015b. "Ḥimyar, Aksūm, and *Arabia Deserta* in Late Antiquity." In *Arabs and Empires before Islam*, edited by G. Fisher, 127–171. Oxford: Oxford University Press.
Robin, Christian J. 2019. "L'Arabie préislamique." In *Le Coran des Historiens*, edited by M. Ali Amir-Moezzi and G. Dye, 51–155. Paris: Le Cerf.
Robinson, Chase F. 2003. *Islamic Historiography.* Cambridge: Cambridge University Press.
Ryckmans, Jacques. 1989. "Le Panthéon de l'Arabie du Sud Préislamique: état des Problèmes et Brève Synthèse." *Revue de l'Histoire des Religions* 206 (1989): 151–169.
Schoeler, Gregor. 2006. *The Oral and the Written in Early Islam.* London: Routledge.
Seidensticker, Tilman. 2010. "Sources for the History of Pre-Islamic Religion." In *The Qur'ān in Context*, edited by A. Neuwirth, N. Sinai, and M. Marx, 293–321. Leiden: Brill.
Sigl, M., et al. 2015. "Timing and Climate Forcing of Volcanic Eruptions for the Past 2,500 years." *Nature* 523:543–549.
Starcky, Jean. 1981. "Allath, Athèna et la Déesse Syrienne." In *Mythologie Gréco-Romaine, mythologies périphériques. Études d'iconographie*, edited by L. Kahil and C. Augé, 119–39. Paris: Editions du Centre National de la Recherche Scientifique.
Szylágyi, Krisztina. 2008. "Muḥammad and the Monk: The Making of the Christian Baḥīrā Legend." *Jerusalem Studies in Arabic and Islam* 34:169–214.
Teixidor, Javier. 1977. *The Pagan God. Popular Religion in the Greco-Roman Near East.* Princeton: Princeton University Press.
Van Nuffelen, Peter. 2010. "Pagan Monotheism as a Religious Phenomenon in One God." In *One God: Pagan Monotheism in the Roman Empire*, edited by S. Mitchell and P. Van Nuffelen, 16–33. Cambridge: Cambridge University Press.
Wansbrough, John. 1978a. "Reviewed Work: Hagarism: The Making of the Islamic World by Patricia Crone, Michael Cook." *Bulletin of the School of Oriental and African Studies* 41: 155–56.

Wansbrough, John. 1978b. *The Sectarian Milieu*. Oxford: Oxford University Press.
Watt, William Montgomery. 1971. "Belief in a "High God" in pre-Islamic Mecca." *Journal of Semitic Studies* 16:35–40.
Watt, William Montgomery. 1981. "The Qurʾān and Belief in a 'High God.'" In *Proceedings of the Ninth Congress of the Union Européenne des Arabisants et Islamisants*, edited by R. Peters. Leiden: Brill.
Weil, Gustav. 1846–62. *Geschichte der Chalifen*. Mannheim: F. Bassermann.
Wellhausen, Julius. 1897. *Reste arabischen Heidentums*. Berlin: Reimer.

Ilkka Lindstedt

"One Community to the Exclusion of Other People": A Superordinate Identity in the Medinan Community

Introduction

Earlier Research on Early Islamic Identity

How did the early (seventh–eighth century CE) Muslims categorize and view themselves? What did their conceptions of themselves and the others entail? A number of studies concerning or touching on early Islamic identity have been published in recent years.[1] Most significant for my arguments are the studies written by Fred Donner.[2] According to Donner, the early movement lacked a specifically Islamic identity (until the late seventh century); rather, the Believers (the endonym of the group) began as a pious and strictly monotheistic reform movement that included Jews, Christians, and others.

However, the studies referenced above mostly lack a theoretical framework that would make cross-disciplinary comparison possible. Furthermore, terminology (such as "identity") is often used loosely in the literature on early Islam. A delightful exception to this is the recent book by Peter Webb, which utilizes theories of ethnicity and ethnogenesis from the field of anthropology.[3] My own studies on early Islam use theories having to do with identity from the field of social psychology.[4] These studies deal with the Qur'ān and Arabic epigraphy. Here, I will engage with the so-called Constitution of Medina, which has been

1 Bashear 1997; Hoyland 1997; Nevo and Koren 2003; Retsö 2003; Lecker 2004; Griffith 2008; Levy-Rubin 2011; Shoemaker 2011; Johnson 2012; Bowersock 2013; Al-Azmeh 2014; Penn 2015; Crone 2015–2016; Crone 2016; Pohl et al. 2016; Shaddel 2016; Bowersock 2017; Mortensen 2018.
2 Donner 1998, 2002–2003, 2010, 2018.
3 Webb 2016.
4 Lindstedt 2019, forthcoming a, b.

Note: I thank Sean Anthony, Juan Cole, Fred Donner, Guillaume Dye, Jaakko Hämeen-Anttila, Kaj Öhrnberg, and Mehdy Shaddel as well as the participants of the Early Islamic Studies Seminar for comments on an earlier draft of this article.

Ilkka Lindstedt, University of Helsinki, e-mail: ilkka.lindstedt@helsinki.fi

https://doi.org/10.1515/9783110675498-014

accepted by most scholars as an early, authentic text going back to the Prophet's time. I utilize the concept of recategorization (explained below) as a framework of analysis. In addition to the "Constitution," I will consider the text of the Qur'ān from this point of view.

Theoretical Premise

I put forward that *the social identity approach* (SIA) offers a significant framework for engaging with early Islamic identity-building processes and intergroup behavior. The SIA comprises theorization based on empirical experiments and observations in social psychology. The SIA, as a field of study, began in the 1970s with the works of Henri Tajfel (1978, 1981) and John Turner (1975, 1982). Of late, it has been advanced by, for example, S. Alexander Haslam.[5] The SIA helps understand and analyze group behavior as well as social competition and prejudice. The SIA consists of the social identity theory,[6] which explains intergroup behavior, and the self-categorization theory, which explains how people identify themselves as belonging to a set of groups ("I" becomes "we") and how this shapes individual behavior.

According to the SIA, group identification and conduct are a big part of the human experience, which cannot be reduced to the individual only. This groupness is characterized by 1) the urge of the group members to construe and strive for positive distinctiveness for themselves and their group, and 2) the eagerness to make a contrast between the "ingroup" that they identify with and, by contrast, what is construed as the "outgroup(s)." Groupness affects how the members act and view the world since "individuals who self-categorize themselves similarly also manifest similarities in their behavior and beliefs."[7] What is more, negative stereotypes are often projected to the outgroup, although, according to studies, ingroup favoritism is a more common form of bias than outgroup rejection.[8] What is more, preference for the ingroup and bias against the outgroup are

5 Haslam 2004; Haslam, Reicher, and Platow 2011.

6 This should not be confused with *identity theory*, discussed by Burke & Stets 2009. Identity theory concentrates on the self, the individual identity and roles, as well as interindividual behavior, whereas social identity theory concentrates on groups and social categorizations. Differently put, social identity theory focuses on group identities, while identity theory analyzes role identities. For a discussion of the similarities and dissimilarities of the two, see Stets & Burke 2000.

7 Ehala 2018, 36.

8 Gaertner and Dovidio 2000, 19, 40.

not always linked, and some groups even show outgroup favoritism.[9] Social psychological studies have noted that prejudice or discrimination can form against an outgroup but not against all outgroups. In an article by Verkuyten, for instance, a salient Muslim identity among people of Turkish descent living in the Netherlands went hand in hand with negative views about atheists but not about non-Muslim religious groups.[10] Clearly, ingroup favoritism and outgroup discrimination are phenomena that are not completely automatic results of social categorization. In some instances, social categorization only names and delineates groups, while in other contexts it results in intolerance between groups.[11]

A cognitive process related to stereotyping is the habit of viewing the outgroup as a homogeneous whole, an unchanging monolith. On the other hand, more heterogeneousness is allowed for the ingroup.[12] Although group identities are often perceived as stable, even primordial, they are, from a scholarly perspective, open to change if social factors so require. Changes can occur at the level of the group or the individuals: for instance, new people can join the group, changing its goals, or the old group members can themselves effect change.

The homogenizing and stereotyping tendency which is part of much categorization explains why authoritative texts such as the Bible, the Qur'ān, or other, sometimes present the world through stable categories. However, they also indicate, almost as if by accident, that the reality on the ground and lived experiences were much more complex: social identifications were often in flux, dynamic, and negotiated. There is much more overlap between the categories and groupings than would be evident at first glance. The SIA also explains why the interpreters of these texts (whether pre-modern or modern readers or scholars, Muslims or non-Muslims) have often read them as representing stable, distinct identities and groups. We look for unchanging, clearly defined and bounded groups, and because of this expectation, we find them in a text.

The social identity approach has been a fruitful one for engaging with pre-modern texts, including those considered sacred by religious communities. Philip Esler has been instrumental in introducing the SIA to biblical studies. For example, in a study of Paul's letter to the Romans, he suggests that Paul intended to recategorize the Judean and non-Judean recipients of the letter to be included in the new superordinate identity of Christ-believers.[13] Through this, Paul aimed to reduce tension and foster cooperation between the two groups,

---

9 Gaertner and Dovidio 2000, 132–133.
10 Verkuyten, 2007.
11 Lebedeva and Tatarko 2008.
12 Jones, Wood, and Quattrone 1981.
13 Esler 2003.

now understood as sub-groups. The concept of *recategorization* (or common ingroup identity model) is also of importance for the analysis of the text of the "Constitution of Medina" and the Qur'ān, as will be seen below. Esler's important studies have spurred other biblical scholars to apply the approach to the Bible, Judaism, and Christianity.[14]

Baker has followed Esler's lead in utilizing the concept of recategorization in the reading of another New Testament text, the book of Acts.[15] Paul's letters are a rather different type of text than the more narrative parts of the Bible. Hence, Baker finds it useful to engage with narrative theory in addition to the social identity approach. Baker finds the following common ingroup identity articulated and put forward in Acts:

> the core of the superordinate identity . . . developed in the narrative is belief that Jesus of Nazareth is the resurrected Messiah. Those who believe this message are invited to join the Christ group by undergoing the boundary crossing rituals of baptism in the name of Jesus Christ and being filled with the Holy Spirit. This core identity marker and its associated boundary crossing rituals form the essential marks of the superordinate Christ group identity and thus serve a crucial role in the recategorization process in which two subgroups within the authorial audience, one in favor of non-Judean inclusion and one opposed, are bought together in a superordinate group whose identity is centered on belief in Jesus as the resurrected Messiah.[16]

The SIA has featured prominently in biblical studies carried out at the Faculty of Theology at the University of Helsinki as well. For example, Jutta Jokiranta has applied SIA to the Qumran texts and community,[17] Nina Nikki to Paul's letters,[18] and Raimo Hakola to the Gospel of John.[19] These studies have yielded valuable insights into religious identity and group formation during the Second Temple period.

The importance of the SIA in offering theoretically refined interpretations in the study of religion and history is, I would argue, well demonstrated. Furthermore, in the past ten years or so, there has been interest in the social identity approach in studies of modern Islam, especially Islamic radicalism and related phenomena.[20] However, the SIA has not previously been applied to early Islam and its identity articulation.

---

14 Marohl 2008; Barentsen 2011; Lau 2011; Stargel 2018.
15 Baker 2011.
16 Baker 2011, 88.
17 Jokiranta 2012.
18 Nikki 2018.
19 Hakola 2005, 2015.
20 Jacobson 2006; Marranci 2009; Al Raffie 2013; Herriot 2014; Pely 2016.

Recategorization and Decategorization

Above, I referred to some works in biblical studies that utilize the concept of *recategorization* in their analysis. This concept, alongside *decategorization*, will be explained in this section in more detail. In the previous section, I also referred to the social psychological *social identity approach*. Since categorization itself often generates bias in favor of the ingroup and against the outgroup, the suggestion that has arisen in scholarship is that group recategorization (drawing the boundary lines differently) could help ameliorate intergroup tension and hostility.

An early example of scholarship looking at recategorization processes is the classic Robbers Cave study carried out by Muzafer Sherif and his team, although it did not yet use the terminology of the later social psychologists, such as those promulgated by Henri Tajfel.[21] To summarize this experiment briefly, the scholars conducted a three-week study with 12-year old boys from Oklahoma who took part in a summer camp at Robbers Cave State Park. The boys were divided into two groups. They spent the first week in isolation from the other group, letting the groups form. The two groups spent the next week in competitive sports. Intergroup bias and hostility, even fistfights, broke out between the two groups because of the competitive spirit and clear intergroup demarcation. To improve the intergroup relationship, Sherif and his team intervened and endeavored to direct the energy of the boys towards shared goals. Although this took some time, cooperation between the two groups reduced the hostility and, eventually, made it disappear completely. In fact, the salience and borders of the identities of the two groups became less important, and the boys began to view – recategorize – themselves as one group.[22]

Although the concepts of re- and decategorization have been present in social psychology more generally, Gaertner and Dovidio's monograph (2000) proffers an accessible and lucid overview on the topic. The book draws on decades of social psychological experimentation in both laboratory and natural settings as well as on a wide array of research literature. I will rely on this work in what follows.

The social identity approach, as mentioned above, suggests that ingroup favoritism and negative stereotypes against the outgroup are grounded on very deep-seated and natural cognitive processes. Gaertner and Dovidio base their work on the social identity approach and suggest that "attempts to ameliorate bias should be directed not at eliminating the [normal psychological categorizing] process but rather at redirecting the forces to produce more harmonious

21 Sherif et al. 1954 and 1961.

22 See Gaertner and Dovidio 2000, 6–8 and 172–177 for an overview of the study.

intergroup relations."[23] This redirecting they call *recategorization* or *the common ingroup identity model.* Simply put, recategorization means "changing the basis of categorization . . . [which] can alter who is a 'we' and who is a 'they'" (Gaertner and Dovidio 2000, 15). This is done not only by changing the group borders but also often by increasing "the level of category inclusiveness."[24] To give a concrete example of the common ingroup identity model, one survey study of white Americans found that, if their superordinate identity as "American" was more salient than their identity as "white," they were more likely to support affirmative action policies that do not aid them but benefit rather non-white Americans. However, if their identity as "white" was stronger, their support for such policies was rarer.[25]

Hence, for instance, a national identity such as "American" can function as a common identity, presenting a big-tent group consisting of different subordinate ethnic, religious, and other identities. A salient superordinate identity that connects people from different groups together makes it possible for individuals to accept and embrace policies and trajectories, for example, by helping and advancing people belonging to another subgroup.[26] However, the question of majorities and minorities and the power dynamics between them often come to the fore in such superordinate identities and challenge them. Minorities can often especially feel that their subordinate identities are rejected and the majority wants them to assimilate rather than accepts a pluralistic vision of the big-tent group where subordinate identities are not erased. A recent example is offered by Moss, who notes that the superordinate North Sudanese national identity construction has been a top-down effort to emphasize Arab and Muslim identity as well as Arabic as a shared language while rejecting other categorizations.[27] Those who do not identify as Arab or Muslim see this as discriminatory. In this instance, the creation of a superordinate identity is hierarchical, forced, and problematic for intergroup relations. Moss also emphasizes the importance of looking at who is carrying out the recategorization process, that is to say, the context and the agency of the group members and leaders: "Recategorization is not a passive process, and those who often invoke superordinate identities are an important part of the puzzle. Relatedly, focusing on leadership identity narratives also emphasizes how such processes may produce resistance."[28]

23 Gaertner and Dovidio 2000, 5.
24 Gaertner and Dovidio 2000, 43.
25 Gaertner and Dovidio 2000, 67.
26 Gaertner and Dovidio 2000, 67.
27 Moss 2017.
28 Moss 2017, 938.

Gaertner and Dovidio remark that, for the recategorization effort to work harmoniously, the common ingroup identity must be accommodating to subordinate identities: "demands to forsake these [former/subordinate] group identities . . . would likely arouse strong resistance."[29] There is ample evidence that identities can accommodate other identities and that accepting hybrid identities is often advantageous for social harmony. Dual identities or subgroup affiliations are not a threat to the superordinate ingroup identity.[30]

What are the benefits of the common ingroup identity model? Gaertner and Dovidio note that people are more eager to help members affiliated with the same group; hence, extending the boundaries of the group can be beneficial.[31] This is significant, given how much the "Constitution of Medina" emphasizes that the participants in the document help each other (articulated with words from the Arabic root *n-ṣ-r*, for example). The ingroup members cooperate to accomplish goals; furthermore, they share a sense of common fate and shared labor.[32] In fact, intergroup cooperation itself can lead to recategorization; on the other hand, discursive and cognitive recategorization can precede cooperation. For instance, in the Robbers Cave experiment cited above, recategorization ensued from collaboration between the two groups. On the other hand, Desmond Tutu and Nelson Mandela's "rainbow nation"[33] recategorization paved the way for increasing possibilities for cooperation between the blacks and whites in South Africa.

Although recategorization is one possible means of combating intergroup bias, de-emphasizing group membership or *decategorization* is another.[34] This more personal approach in interactions between two or more people coming from different groups diminishes ingroup preference and lessens the possibility that stereotypical outgroup representations will be projected to the other person. However, while recategorization can generalize positive descriptions to the (former) outgroup, this is not borne out in the case of decategorization to the same extent. In this study, I suggest that while recategorization is an apt term to describe the "Constitution of Medina," decategorization might be a more important concept for the analysis of the Qur'ān, especially its Medinan layer.

---

29 Gaertner and Dovidio 2000, 49.

30 Gaertner and Dovidio 2000, 86–87, 97, 146–148, 163–168.

31 Gaertner and Dovidio 2000, 7.

32 Gaertner and Dovidio 2000, 72–78.

33 In his inaugural speech, Nelson Mandela said, among other things: "We enter into a covenant that we shall build the society in which all South Africans, both black and white, will be able to walk tall, without any fear in their hearts, assured of their inalienable right to human dignity – a rainbow nation at peace with itself and the world." (https://www.africa.upenn.edu/Articles_Gen/Inaugural_Speech_17984.html). This is a prime example of recategorization.

34 Gaertner and Dovidio 2000, xi, 8, 33, 42–43.

I briefly note that social identity approach researchers have more recently begun to direct greater attention to intragroup processes, such as the relationship between the leader and the followers in a group. For example, Haslam, Reicher, and Platow note the importance of the leader in a successful recategorization process (and the other way around, since this process can bring the leader to holding power to begin with): "transformational leadership . . . can be seen to arise from the forging of a *shared* social identity around a new definition of the group that the leader comes to embody. In short, it is by becoming emblematic of a new sense of 'us' that leaders acquire their transformational power."[35] This remark is of utmost importance when considering the "Constitution of Medina" and the role of the Prophet.

The "Constitution of Medina"

The Question of the Date and Authenticity of the Text

The so-called Constitution of Medina can be characterized as a treaty[36] document that includes some legislation. Its purpose was, I submit, to recategorize groups (both tribal and religious) to belong to the same superordinate category as "one community" (*umma wāḥida*). The document has generated quite a bit of scholarship.[37] The most important and extensive study is the monograph by Michael Lecker (2004). Lecker's book contains the two versions of the Arabic text, their translations, and commentary. It is a crucial piece of scholarship for understanding the "Constitution." However, on key parts my interpretation of the text is rather different from Lecker's, who generally understands the text in the context of legislation on murder, retaliation, and blood money, which I see as too restrictive a reading. Moreover, he sees the social categorizations of the document in a different light than I do.

In what follows, I have often used Lecker's translation of the clauses of the document as the basis of my own translation; however, I usually diverge from

35 Haslam, Reicher, and Platow 2011, 89.

36 However, the text does not describe itself as a treaty (*ʿahd* or *mīthāq*), and some readers might oppose this characterization based on the claim that the text seems as it would have been simply ordered by the Prophet rather than negotiated between different parties. While it is true that the text refers to the Prophet as its authority and source, it appears rather unlikely that the tribal groups mentioned and partaking in the document would not have had any say in its formulation.

37 Wellhausen 1889, 65–83; Watt 1956, 221–226; Serjeant 1964; Gil 1974; Denny 1977; Serjeant 1978; Rubin 1985; Humphreys 1991, 91–99; Arjomand 2009; Munt 2014, 54–64.

his wordings. In his commentary, Lecker also quotes earlier translations and notes on the document.[38] In addition to the original texts, I refer below to Lecker's division of the document into 64 clauses (marked with §).[39] This differs from some earlier divisions, such as those of Wensinck and Watt, which have 47 clauses.[40]

The document survives in two versions: one in Ibn Isḥāq's *Maghāzī* in the recension of Ibn Hishām (*Sīra*, ed. Wüstenfeld, I, 341–344; ed. al-Saqqā, II, 110–112; the reference is to the former if not otherwise indicated),[41] the other in the *Kitāb al-Amwāl* of Abū ʿUbayd (II, 466–470, with an interpretative commentary by Abū ʿUbayd in II, 471–473). The former text is longer, although Abū ʿUbayd's version seems to me to include better readings of some parts of the document.[42] Lecker presents a detailed philological analysis on the texts of the two versions and their readings.[43] Later classical Arabic literary works sometimes quote the document in whole or in bits and pieces; these citations proffer some variant readings. The document calls itself *kitāb* (Ibn Hishām, *Sīra*, I, 341) and *ṣaḥīfa* (Ibn Hishām, *Sīra*, I, 343). Both words can be translated simply as "document." "Constitution of Medina" is a name given by modern scholars to describe it. Since the word "Constitution" is anachronistic and rather misleading, I will only use it in quotation marks as a conventional name for the text.

Almost all scholars of early Islam have accepted this document as authentic,[44] although they might otherwise doubt the authenticity of the material related to or stemming from the Prophet's era (which I think is very reasonable). For instance, according to the otherwise skeptical Patricia Crone, the "Constitution of Medina is preserved in Ibn Isḥāq's *Sīra*, in which it sticks out like a piece of solid rock in an accumulation of rubble."[45] By "rubble," she means

---

38 Lecker 2004, 88–190.

39 Lecker 2004, 32–39.

40 Wensinck 1928, 74–81; Watt 1956, 221–225.

41 The beginning of the document is quoted in another recension (by Yūnus ibn Bukayr) of Ibn Isḥāq's *Maghāzī* in al-Bayhaqī, *al-Sunan al-Kabīr*, XVI, 401–402 (not used by Lecker but brought to my attention by Sean Anthony, to whom I am grateful). This shows that the document was indeed part of Ibn Isḥāq's work.

42 As also noted by Lecker 2004, 191.

43 Lecker 2004, 7–26.

44 See, e.g., Watt 1956, 225: "No later falsifier writing under the Umayyads or ʿAbbāsids would have included non-Muslims in the *ummah*, would have retained the articles against Quraysh, and would have given Muhammad so insignificant a place. Moreover the style is archaic, and certain points, such as the use of 'believers' instead of 'Muslims' in most articles, belong to the earlier Medinan period."

45 Elide Patricia Crone 1980, 7.

the Arabic historiographical material that is dogmatic and late and that one cannot, in her opinion, work with when it comes to the Prophet's life.

My stance is that the "Constitution of Medina" is an authentic, early document going back to the 620s CE.[46] To borrow concepts from biblical studies, the criteria of *embarrassment* and *dissimilarity* can be cited to support the authenticity of the "Constitution": the document articulates, as I argue below, a view on the Medinan society that is at odds with the (other) reports contained in the historiographical literature. It does not contain any evidence of distinct Islamic identity. Moreover, Jews are not disparaged in the "Constitution" even with a single word. Rather, they are included as members of the community and their subordinate identity as Jews is accepted. What is more, the text does not contain a single Qur'anic quotation, which to me is further proof of its authenticity and early date: if it had been authored later, a Qur'anic flavor might have been included here and there in the text. One is also struck by how little (if any) overlap in the vocabulary, concepts, and formulae there is between the text of the "Constitution" and the *ḥadīth* material. According to my comparison of the clauses to Wensinck's *Concordance et indices de la tradition musulmane*, almost no similarities can be found.[47]

In my opinion, it is mistaken to divide the document into many different texts that would have been promulgated over a series of years.[48] The text shows a compositional and logical unity that does not allow this. Michael Lecker has put forward detailed criticism of the supposed composite nature of the document.[49] However, I add that I believe that the surviving textual witnesses of the document do not contain the original wording of the text with complete accuracy. In all likelihood it underwent some reworking in the two centuries or so during which it was transmitted.[50] My reading below contains some text-critical remarks on the two versions (Ibn Hishām and Abū ʿUbayd), although I do not endeavor to reconstruct the original wording of the document as a whole. For a discussion of all the surviving variants of the text of the document, I refer the reader to Lecker's study.[51]

---

46 Abū ʿUbayd (*Kitāb al-Amwāl*, II, 466 and 472–473) remarks that the document was drafted immediately when the Prophet Muḥammad came to Medina. We do not have to accept this statement but I think it is reasonable to suggest that the treaty dates to soon after the *hijra*. See also Lecker 2004, 182 for the date of the document.

47 Wensinck 1939–1969.

48 As suggested by Watt 1956, 226; Serjant 1964 and 1978.

49 Lecker 2004, 183–190.

50 For the transmission of the text, see Lecker 2004, 191–203.

51 Lecker 2004, 7–26.

If the document is authentic, then who was its author? I suppose that that the Prophet was likely behind many of its clauses, although it must have been to an extent a negotiated treaty, whose wording the partakers shaped.

A word on methodology: My approach is historical, meaning that only contemporary material is accepted as evidence. As for the topic of this discussion, I view the Qur'ān as the only surviving text that is more or less contemporary with the "Constitution." This has not been the methodological starting point of most people engaging with the text. Often, scholars have accepted the biography of the Prophet literature as having a historical basis to varying degrees,[52] but I treat it, for the most part, as part of the social (and mythic) memory of the burgeoning Muslim community.[53] Almost all commentators, with the exception of Fred Donner, appear to agree that the Jews and the Believers/Muslims mentioned in the document formed two clear-cut religious communities.[54] However, a good methodological starting point for historical research is to shed the preconceived notions one might have and work with contemporary evidence. Moreover, most scholars have discussed the "Constitution" with a naïve set of conceptions of ethnicity and identity.[55] My reading is somewhat, or in some cases totally,[56] different from the earlier scholarship. It comes close to Donner's treatment,[57] although I read the "Constitution" in the light of modern concepts of social psychology.

As stated in the previous paragraph, all too often scholars have read the "Constitution" in the light of the biography of the Prophet and other Arabic historiographical literature. This I find unwarranted. All sorts of anachronistic aspects have been projected to the document because of this. For example, it is common to say that the "Constitution" was a treaty between the *muhājirūn* and the *anṣār*,[58] because Arabic historiography claims that this is its function. Nonetheless, the *anṣār* are never mentioned in the text and the *muhājirūn* feature only in passing.[59]

How does the "Constitution" categorize the Medinans participating in the treaty? To anticipate the arguments of this study, the document refers to a

52 Lecker 2004, for example, treats the text in the context of other Arabic historical literature, which he by and large approaches uncritically.
53 Assmann 1992.
54 Donner 2002–2003, 29–34.
55 See, e.g., Rubin 1985, 6, who argues that the Jews mentioned in the text refer to "genuine Jewish groups" – whatever that might mean.
56 Contrast my reading with Gil 1974.
57 Donner 2002–2003, 29–34.
58 E.g. Lecker 2004, 142.
59 For the word *muhājirūn*, see also Lindstedt 2015.

superordinate group appellation *umma wāḥida min dūn al-nās*, "one community to the exclusion of other people." Although the word *umma* is used in different meanings in the document, as will be seen, here the sense of a bigger "community" is pertinent. The *umma wāḥida* encompasses subordinate identities, consisting of what could be considered both religious and tribal. The religious subordinate groups are in my reading the following: *mu'minūn*, "Believers," *muslimūn* "Submitters," and *yahūd*, "Jews."[60] The tribal groups are called Banū X, of which a number are listed in the text; in addition to these, *muhājirūn*, "Emigrants,"[61] can also be understood as a quasi-tribal group in the document. The group label *mu'minūn*, "Believers," seems to function on two levels: as a subordinate group (probably referring to Believers of Gentile background, see below) under the big tent *umma wāḥida*, but also as a superordinate category and synonym for the *umma wāḥida*. I hope to make this clearer below.

The Interpretation of the Document

I divide the document into four parts, which correspond to the following clauses in Lecker's division:

1. Lecker 2004, §1–12, the tribes participating in the treaty.
2. Lecker 2004, §13–26, legislation.
3. Lecker 2004, §27–48, the categorization of the Jews and Believers.
4. Lecker 2004, §49–64, legislation and ending.

This division is made simply to facilitate the discussion and interpretation of the document.

---

60 Cf. Lecker 2004, 90, according to whom only the Believers and Submitters are part of the *umma wāḥida*.

61 For the term *muhājirūn* in the Quran, see now Mortensen 2018, who argues (p. 210): "Emigration in the Qur'ān is the action of the devoted and the god-fearing, and the Qur'ān's use of the term *muhājirūn* and its derivatives embodies an ideal of creating and maintaining separation from the surrounding, unbelieving world. In this concept of an 'uprooting' into a new mobility also lies an idea of mobilization. The *muhājirūn* are spiritual secessionists, but they are also fighters. What seems clear from the Qur'ān's use of the root *h-j-r* is that the idea of emigration is closely linked to the idea of warfare in the path of God, and furthermore, that these activities are pivotal in the Qur'ān's definition of a true believer."

The First Part

Significantly, the document opens by saying that it is a *kitāb*, a document, from Muḥammad, called *al-nabī*, "the Prophet," in Ibn Hishām's version (*Sīra*, I, 341), and *al-nabī rasūl allāh*, "the Prophet, the Messenger of God," in Abū ʿUbayd's (*Kitāb al-Amwāl*, II, 466). The text hence starts by referring to Muḥammad's prototypical status as the leader of the group and the ultimate source and author(ity) of the text.

The clause after the mention of the Prophet states that this is a document "between the Believers and Submitters of Quraysh and Yathrib [i.e., Medina] and those who follow them,[62] join them, and struggle[63] alongside them (*jāhada maʿahum*): they are one community to the exclusion of other people (*umma wāḥida min dūn al-nās*)" (Ibn Hishām, *Sīra*, I, 341). Abū ʿUbayd (*Kitāb al-Amwāl* , II, 466) has *ahl yathrib*, "the people of Yathrib," as opposed to simply *yathrib*; his version also adds "(those who) reside with them" (*fa-ḥalla maʿahum*) after "(those who) join them."

The phrase "the Believers (*al-muʾminūn*) and Submitters (*al-muslimūn*) of Quraysh and Yathrib" has created some discussion in the scholarly literature.[64] The premise of much of this scholarly discourse has been that the words *mu'minūn* and *muslimūn* should be synonyms,[65] as is understood in later Islamic parlance. But this is a development belonging to the eighth century CE, as I argue elsewhere.[66] As can be seen in the Qur'ān, the word *muʾminūn* is the primary term signifying group affiliation, whereas *muslimūn* appears very infrequently and cannot be translated as "Muslims" at this stage of Islamic history. Indeed,

62 Arabic: *man tabiʿahum*, which Lecker (2004, 32, 45–46) translates as "those who join them as clients." I do not believe such a precise interpretation of the verb is necessarily required or warranted here.

63 The word *jāhada* denotes both physical fighting and other types of striving and struggling. Its usage in the Quran is often ambivalent, see Lindstedt, forthcoming b. In the "Constitution," the meaning seems to be related to fighting and warfare since this is a common theme in the text (see below), often indicated with unambiguous words such as *ḥāraba*, "to make war." But naturally, other types of striving might be meant here.

64 See, for example, Denny 1977, 43–44. Lecker's own view (2004, 40–45) on the matter is unclear, but he emphasizes that the two are distinct categories in the "Constitution." Nevertheless, he often replaces *muʾminūn* in his commentary simply with "Muslims," which cannot be defended.

65 Naturally, one way out of this problem would be to suppose that the pair *al-muʾminūn* and *al-muslimūn* is used as a hendiadys. In this interpretation, the words would indeed be synonyms. But as argued here, I do not see this as the preferable solution.

66 Lindstedt 2019, 193.

even the Quran remarks that these words are not really synonyms. The verse (49:14) in question should be quoted *in toto*:

> The nomads say: 'We believe' (*āmannā*). Say: You do not believe [yet]. Say instead: 'We submit' (*aslamnā*). Belief (*al-īmān*) has not entered your hearts. If you obey God and His messenger, He will not deprive you [of the reward] of any of your deeds. God is Forgiving, Merciful.[67]

In this passage, submission (*al-islām*) is clearly inferior to faith (*al-īmān*). The latter, not *al-islām*, is the term denoting communal belonging.[68] If we take Quran 49:14 at its word (as I think we should in this case), submission could be understood as the first stage of the process whereby the person wants to join the Prophet's group. Note also the connection to "nomads" (*al-aʿrāb*) in the passage. As the "Constitution" appears to include some references to the nomads (see below), it could be the case that the *muslimūn* at the beginning of it are a reference to people of nomadic background who are not yet considered to be full members of the in-group. Surah 49 is Medinan according to the traditional Islamic and to Nöldeke's dating (1909–1919, I, 206). If that dating is accepted, the surah is roughly contemporary with the "Constitution." To recapitulate, I suggest that the term *muʾminūn* at the beginning of the document refers to the full members of the Prophet's group whereas, *muslimūn* interpreted in light of Qur'ān 49:14 denotes those who wish to join the group but have not yet shown full commitment, possibly nomads. However, there is another, hypothetical, possibility: the word *muslimūn* is a later interpolation added by a scribe that was puzzled by the notion that the document only talked about "Believers," not mentioning "Muslims." However, there is no manuscript evidence that this was the case. So this suggestion remains in the realm of speculation.

Where are the Jews in the opening clause? As will become clear below, I believe that the Jews who belonged to the tribes mentioned in the document are part of the *umma wāḥida*. At the beginning of the document, the Jews should be understood to be part of either the Believers or, perhaps more likely, "those who follow them, join them, and fight/struggle alongside them." Indeed, later the text refers to "those Jews who follow us" (Ibn Hishām, *Sīra*, I, 342). I will return to the question of religious identities later.

Next, the document moves on to discuss tribal organization (Ibn Hishām, *Sīra*, I, 341–342). It lists a number of Medinan tribes, starting, however, with

67 Quranic quotations are based on the translation of Abdel Haleem, although I often modify the wording.

68 However, see below for Quranic passages 28:52–55 and 29:46–47 that categorize both the gentile Believers and the People of the Book as "Submitters" (*muslimūn*).

"the Emigrants from Quraysh," which would refer to people coming (supposedly) from Mecca to settle in Medina and who would be outside the tribal structure in Medina. The first part of the text mentions the following groups (Ibn Hishām, *Sīra*, I, 341; Abū ʿUbayd, *Kitāb al-Amwāl*, II, 466–467):

- *al-muhājirūn min quraysh*
- *banū ʿawf*
- *banū al-ḥārith* (Abū ʿUbayd's text reads *banū al-khazraj* instead)
- *banū sāʿida*
- *banū jusham*
- *banū al-najjār*
- *banū ʿamr ibn ʿawf*
- *banū al-nabīt*
- *banū al-aws*

As will be seen below, most of the groups mentioned here had members who identified as Jewish.[69] This is not necessarily obvious to the modern reader who is only glancing at the beginning of the text, but this was naturally clear to the contemporary participants in and observers of the treaty.[70] Jews, although not explicitly mentioned here yet, are important partakers in the "Constitution." Significantly and curiously, no Christians are mentioned in the treaty.[71]

What is said of these tribes, their rights and duties? Three things are repeated throughout: 1) that the tribe keeps their previous tribal organization (*banū X ʿalā ribʿatihim*),[72] 2) that the tribe pays their previous bloodwites (*yataʿāqalūna maʿāqilahum al-ūlā*),[73] and 3) that each subgroup of them ransoms

69 *Pace* Rubin 1985, 9, who argues that the "Jews of Banū X," mentioned later in the text, were Jews who were not real members of said tribes but had "almost affiliated into the Arab tribes whose *ḥalīf*s they became." Lecker (2004, 184) also sees "two distinct parts, the treaty of the Muʾminūn and the treaty of the Jews" in the text. But the beginning does not mention the Believers among the Banū X, but simply the Banū X. The latter category would include both gentile and Jewish Believers in the tribe. There are a number of problems in Rubin's and Lecker's views: 1) the idea of a clear Arab ethnicity being present, 2) the demarcation of "Arabs" and "Jews", and 3) the notion that ethnicity and religion are something primordial rather than identities that are socially negotiated and potentially changing.

70 Cf. Rubin 1985, 5, who refers to these tribes as consisting of simply "Muslims."

71 For charts on the genealogies of these tribes, based on later Arabic literature, see Lecker 1995, 5 and 7.

72 Abū ʿUbayd, *Kitāb al-Amwāl*, II, 467, has *ribʿātihim*, which does not change the meaning. Lecker (2004, 99–101) notes that *ribʿatihim* and *maʿāqilahum* could be understood as synonyms.

73 For the Emigrants from Quraysh, Ibn Hishām (*Sīra*, I, 341) has a different phrase: *yataʿāqalūna maʿāqilahum baynahum*. The word *baynahum* is not mentioned in connection with other

their captives according to what is acceptable and just among the Believers (*kull ṭā'ifa tafdī 'āniyahā bi-l-ma'rūf wa-l-qisṭ bayn al-mu'minīn*).

The first of these notions indicates the continuation of tribal identities under the big-tent group *umma wāḥida*. This is in accordance with what modern social psychologists have observed: recategorization to a superordinate identity (or the common ingroup model) works best if the previous identities are not rejected but rather understood as legitimate sub-identities.[74] The tribal identities are not abolished in the "Constitution" but accepted. As will be seen, the same is true for religious identities. What is more, the subgroups are in charge of their own financial obligations even though they are part of the common ingroup now. Like the rejection of earlier identities, a suggestion that also would have made the financial obligations of one tribe everyone's responsibility would have probably generated much opposition to joining the treaty.

The document specifies that each group is in charge of paying their previous bloodwites and ransoming their captives. What does this mean? Let us start with the verb *yata'āqalūna*. It might indicate reciprocity or locate the paying of bloodwites inside the tribe: "to pay among themselves." However, it could also mean "to pay conjointly".[75] I suggest that the latter is probable: the aim of the stipulation is that each tribe that takes part in the "Constitution" makes arrangements to pay the bloodwites that they owe currently (*ma'āqilahum al-ūlā*), perhaps primarily to the other tribes that take part in the document.[76] The idea is, I submit, that the tribes belonging to the *umma wāḥida min dūn al-nās* reset their relationships and start with a clean slate. Later in the document new legislation or norms concerning murder and bloodwite are put forward, which is part of the same phenomenon of starting over with a different set of categories; I will discuss this below. In these new norms, there is no suggestion that the Believers owe bloodwite for the non-Believers that they kill. It thus makes sense to suppose that the words *yata'āqalūna ma'āqilahum al-ūlā* refer to arrangements inside the Medinan *umma wāḥida* rather than bloodwite paid outside Medina, to tribal groups that are not party to the document.

---

groups. Abū 'Ubayd, *Kitāb al-Amwāl*, II, 467, adds here the word *al-ūlā* which is not present in Ibn Hishām's version. I believe that Abū 'Ubayd's reading here is better.

74 Gaertner and Dovidio 2000, 86–87, 97, 146–148, 163–168.

75 Lane 1863–1893, 2114. As al-Zabīdī, *Tāj al-'Arūs*, XXX, 25, says, *wa-ta'āqalū dam fulān: 'aqalūhu baynahum.*

76 Lecker (2004, §4) translates *yata'āqalūna ma'āqilahum al-ūlā* as "continuing to co-operate with each other in accordance with their former mutual aid agreements regarding blood money," which is rather cumbersome but not necessarily wrong.

Lastly, number three states that each group ransoms their captives according to what is acceptable and just among the Believers (*kull ṭāʾifa tafdī ʿāniyahā bi-l-maʿrūf wa-l-qisṭ bayn al-muʾminīn*). This too, can be interpreted in different ways. My interpretation is the following: the "Constitution," first and foremost, instructs that each tribal group must ransom the tribesmen and -women that have been captured by other tribal groups that are mentioned in and accept the document and perhaps outside Medina as well. We can speculate that, when the Prophet came to Medina, the tribal groups owed each other bloodwites and were holding captives, one from the other. This is hardly an ideal situation to start a new community. What the "Constitution" does, however, is to reset the situation and suggest an evenhanded solution to the previous bloodwites and hostage situations. The ransom should be paid "according to what is acceptable and just" (*bi-l-maʿrūf wa-l-qisṭ*), which suggests that the party that has taken the captive should not set her or his price too high. The phrase *bi-l-maʿrūf wa-l-qisṭ bayn al-muʾminīn* could be understood in two different ways: 1) *bayn al-muʾminīn* continues and modifies *bi-l-maʿrūf wa-l-qisṭ*, or 2) *bayn al-muʾminīn* continues *kull ṭāʾifa tafdī ʿāniyahā*. In my opinion, the second option is more probable, although this does not seem to have been preferred by earlier commentators.[77] I add that here it makes sense to understand *al-muʾminīn*, the Believers, as synonymous with *umma wāḥida*, a superordinate rather than subordinate category, although the latter seems to be the intended meaning at the beginning of the document. The section ends by noting that the Believers help other members pay ransoms and bloodwites if someone is in debt.[78]

To summarize my reading of this part of the document (Ibn Hishām, *Sīra*, I, 341–342; Lecker 2004, §1–12), the text has recategorized the religious groups of Believers, Submitters, and others, designating them as *umma wāḥida min dūn al-nās*, "one community to the exclusion of other people." There is already some indication here that the label "Believers" functions as a super-category, more or less synonymous with the "one community." These people possessing religious identities also had tribal affiliations. They are not challenged but, rather, their previous tribal structures are kept intact (*banū X ʿalā ribʿatihim*). What is commanded, though, is that the tribes belonging to the "one community" hit a reset button: settle their bloodwites and ransom their captives. Furthermore, the point appears to be that the financial matters of the tribes, now understood as sub-groups, are not meshed together.

77 See Lecker 2004, 105–106.
78 Lecker 2004, §12.

The Second Part

The next part moves on to discuss legal matters (Ibn Hishām, *Sīra*, I, 342; Lecker 2004, §13–26). This is also where we encounter the first mention of the Jews, though it is the next part of the text (Ibn Hishām, *Sīra*, I, 342–343; Lecker 2004, §27–48) that really deals with them and their categorization.

The second part contains stipulations on law and norms; the fourth part returns to this theme. It continues the common ingroup identity building effort begun in the first part, which recategorized different religious and tribal groups as "one community" and "Believers" that should be united and start anew. In the second part, the ingroup concord is buttressed by putting forward rules and regulations that the ingroup will agree upon, as well as the mention, for the first time, of the outgroup, "disbelievers" (sing. *kāfir*), "associators" (sing. *mushrik*),[79] and "sinners" (sing. *muḥdith*; this could be interpreted as a black sheep group inside the ingroup, though). The aim is that the participants in the treaty do not categorize the other participating groups as outgroups, as they might have done before the "Constitution," but draw the borders differently.

The section opens (Ibn Hishām, *Sīra*, I, 342; Lecker 2004, §13) with a somewhat ambivalent phrase that stipulates that "a Believer shall not make an alliance with[80] a *mawlā* of [another] Believer without his [the latter's] will (*dūnahu*)." How is the word *mawlā* to be translated here? It might refer to a client (often = freedwoman or freedman) of a Believer or, on the other hand, to an ally of a Believer. The meaning "ally" seems to be present at least a few lines down (Lecker 2004, §17), where it is stated that "the Believers are allies (*mawālī*) to each other to the exclusion of other people." However, the meaning "client" could be intended here.[81]

---

79 According to Lecker 2004, 44, 114, the word *kāfir* included (all?) Jews, Christians, and polytheists, while *mushrik* refers to polytheists. On the basis of my reading of the "Constitution," however, it cannot be claimed that the Jews belong to the category of disbelievers at all. What is more, the Quran does not categorize the Jews and Christians clearly as disbelievers but as borderline groups that included both Believers and disbelievers. See below and Cole 2020; Lindstedt, forthcoming a.

80 Arabic *yuḥālifu*, as in the *Sīra* of Ibn Hishām (see Lecker 2004, 12) and the *Kitāb al-Amwāl* of Abū ʿUbayd (II, 468). The edition of Wüstenfeld (I, 342) reads *yukhālifu*, "shall not oppose." It might be remarked in this connection that according to the corpus of Prophetical dicta, *ḥilf* agreements are forbidden in Islam (Crone and Hinds 1986, 78, n. 127), which is an example of the difference between the "Constitution" and the rest of the material traced to the Prophet.

81 Cf. Lecker 2004, 110, who argues, without citing any evidence, that the word *mawlā* always means "an ally" in the document. But there is no reason why the word could not be used in

Be that as it may, the document then spells out that the God-fearing Believers (*al-muʾminīn al-muttaqīn*)[82] are completely and totally against sinners and criminals among them (*ʿalā man baghā minhum aw ibtaghā dasīʿat ẓulm aw ithm aw ʿudwān aw fasād*).[83] It does not even matter if the sinner is someone's child (*wa-law kāna walad aḥadihim*). I suggest that this is an intragroup discourse: disreputable and deviant members are not tolerated in the Believers' community. However, neither this passage nor anything else in the document explains what should be done with such sinners.

After this, the outgroup "disbelievers" (sing. *kāfir*) is mentioned. This I take mainly as a reference to people outside Medina and outside the treaty, although it might be the case that these clauses continue the discussion of the sinners, who would, in this interpretation, be former ingroup members relegated to the outgroup, outside the "one community," though living in Medina. The passage in question states that "a Believer shall not kill [another] Believer in retaliation for a disbeliever, nor help[84] a disbeliever against a Believer." Above I suggested that the order to pay the "previous bloodwites" concerned in particular those owed to other participants of the treaty who are part of the Believer ingroup. This passage, though it does not mention bloodwite, notes that a Believer cannot be killed in retaliation for having killed a disbeliever. The disbelievers are a community apart, and they should not receive help from the Believers even, or especially, in the ancient custom of blood revenge. Rather the Believers succor each other, as the document goes on to say: "the protection of God is unvarying (*dhimmat allāh wāḥida*); *adnāhum* offers aid to them [scil., the Believers]." The

---

two different, though connected, meanings. As I argue, the word *umma*, for instance, is used in various ways in the text.

82 Abū ʿUbayd, *Kitāb al-Amwāl*, II, 468, has *al-muʾminīn wa-l-muttaqīn*. Might the word "God-fearers" (*muttaqūn*), here as in the Quran, be used, at least in some instances, as a technical tern meaning people of Gentile background who had adopted monotheism and some Jewish customs as well as visited synagogues but did not officially convert to Judaism? This is an interesting hypothesis. It might be remarked that Patricia Crone (2016, 315–339) suggested that the Prophet and many of his followers were originally God-fearers in this sense. However, Crone (2016, 330–331) denies that the Quranic *muttaqūn* is itself a translation of "*theosebeis* or *phoboumenoi/sebo[u]menoi* (*ton theon*)." Be that as it may, note that Crone's (2016, 338–339) insistence on the salience of the Arab ethnicity of the Prophet and his community seems unwarranted in the light of Peter Webb's work (2016). It is rather the Gentile identity that is put forward by the Quran.

83 Lecker (2004, §14) reads this clause, like the text in general, in the context of blood money, which I do not find very convincing. He translates: " . . . against whosoever of them demands an excessive sum of blood money . . . "

84 Lecker (2004, 119) interprets "help" as signifying help to secure blood money in the case of murder. I deem this too narrow.

word *adnāhum* is unfortunately rather ambivalent as to its exact meaning here since it could point to opposing things: "the richest of them," "the poorest of them," or "the closest of them." Whatever the signification intended by the drafter of the document, the basic idea seems to be that all Believers should help each other since what immediately follows reads "the Believers are allies (*mawālī*) to each other to the exclusion of other people."[85]

The Jews appear for the first time in the document before the text returns to the question of blood revenge and warfare. The text reads: "Those Jews who follow us shall have succor (*al-naṣr*)[86] and help (*al-iswa*); they shall not be wronged nor [shall their enemies be] helped against [them]" (Ibn Hishām, *Sīra*, I, 342; Lecker 2004, §18). Lecker translates the word *al-iswa* (or *al-uswa*) as "equal rights," noting that it means "parity" in some texts.[87] I think these are rather too modern concepts. The basic meaning of the word is "help," so I believe the word is simply used here synonymously with *al-naṣr*. The importance in the document of helping the other members of the recategorized common ingroup identity should be noted here. To quote Gaertner and Dovidio: "People are more helpful toward ingroup members,"[88] and hence a common ingroup identity model is useful for expanding the sphere of helping. In the "Constitution," recategorization entails succor, and succor, in turn, increases affinity and affiliation with the new superordinate group.

Who are (or is) the "us" in the clause, "Those Jews who follow us"? We have two possibilities. Either it is a plural of majesty referring to the Prophet, or "us" refers to the (gentile) Believers. According to Lecker, the first person plural in the document refers to the "main contracting parties."[89] It seems that at this stage of the document Jews and Believers are kept apart as distinct subgroups as part of the big-tent "one community." The label "Believers" has been used synonymously with the "one community" in some passages, but for the most part, I suggest, it denotes those followers of the Prophet who were of gentile background. The gentile identity is not borne out in the text of the "Constitution"

85 Compare this to Qur'ān 3:28: "The Believers should not take the disbelievers as allies (*awliyā'*) to the exclusion of the Believers," which has a rather similar wording and meaning.

86 Abū 'Ubayd, *Kitāb al-Amwāl*, II, 468, has *al-ma'rūf*, which could be translated as "amicability" or "fairness," instead of *al-naṣr*.

87 Lecker 2004, 118–120.

88 Gaertner and Dovidio 2000, 7.

89 Lecker 2004, 41. The main contracting parties did not, according to Lecker, include the Jews, but I think this is mistaken.

itself, but the contemporary Quranic evidence shows that the identity of the Prophet and many of his followers was gentile (*ummī/-yūn*, Q 3:20, 7:158, 62:2),[90] which I understand to mean non-Jewish and non-Christian.

The exclusiveness of the category of the Believers as including only people of gentile background will change in the third part of the "Constitution" where the text in Abū ʿUbayd's version (if this is the original wording of the document) categorizes the Jews as belonging to the Believers. Thus, in the text of the document, the category "Believers" functions both as a subordinate group ("Believers of gentile background") that is on the same conceptual level with the Jews *and* as a superordinate identity that is synonymous with the "one community" and that is further divided into different subordinate identities, be they gentiles or Jews.

The wording in the clause "those Jews who follow us," and so on, harks back to the passage at the beginning of the text where it is stated that the treaty is "between the Believers and Submitters of Quraysh and Yathrib [i.e., Medina] and those who follow them, join them, and fight/struggle alongside them: they are one community to the exclusion of other people."

What could be called the legislative part continues by stipulating some rules of warfare: "the peace (*silm*)[91] of the Believers is unvarying: a Believer shall not make peace in warfare in the path of God to the exclusion of another Believer except in equity and justice between them" (Ibn Hishām, *Sīra*, I, 342; Abū ʿUbayd, *Kitāb al-Amwāl*, II, 468; Lecker 2004, §19). In what preceded, the concept of "the protection of God" was cited. Here, it is "the peace of the Believers" that is "unvarying" (*wāḥida*). The idea is that the ingroup is supposed to be united in their approach to warfare. Above, it was mentioned that one of the benefits of recategorization is that people affiliated with the same ingroup often have a sense of common fate and shared labor (Gaertner and Dovidio 2000, 72–78). The groups partaking in the "Constitution" shared the sense of their fate as one community protected by God and, ultimately, judged by God. Their shared labor involved helping each other in waging war against the enemy.

The document then states that every fighting unit (*kull ghāziya*) among the community shall follow each other (*yaʿqubu baʿḍuhā baʿḍan*) in battle. In the ideal situation, the Believers make peace as one community and fight as one community. It should be remembered that in some passages the Quran is

90 See Shaddel 2016.

91 The word occurs only once in the Qur'ān (2:208): "You who believe, enter wholeheartedly into peace (*udkhulū fī al-silm kāffatan*) and do not follow in Satan's footsteps, for he is your clear enemy."

preoccupied with free-riding ingroup members that claim to be part of the community but stay behind and do not take part in fighting.[92]

Above, I argued that the Believers do not owe blood money to the outgroup members. However, this is not reciprocal. Indeed, the "Constitution" next states that the Believers shall avenge the community members whose blood was shed in the path of God (*inna al-muʾminīn yubīʾu baʿḍuhum ʿan baʿḍ bi-mā nāla dimāʾahum fī sabīl allāh*; Ibn Hishām, *Sīra*, I, 342; Lecker 2004, §21). This clause is missing in Abū ʿUbayd, *Kitāb al-Amwāl*. As suggested above, Ibn Hishām's version of the treaty offers a fuller text and should be the preferred basic version, although Abū ʿUbayd's edition contains some readings that fit the context better, as will be seen below.

Moving on (and skipping a formula insisting that the God-fearing Believers fulfill the treaty), we encounter a passage that differs in Ibn Hishām and Abū ʿUbayd and can be variously understood. In Ibn Hishām (*Sīra*, I, 342) it reads *innahu lā yujīru mushrikun mālan li-quraysh wa-lā nafsan lā yaḥūlu dūnahu ʿalā muʾmin*, "an associator shall not offer protection to any property or person belonging to Quraysh, nor intervene[93] for him/it against a Believer," and in Abū ʿUbayd (*Kitāb al-Amwāl*, II, 468) *innahu lā yujīru mushrikun mālan li-quraysh wa-lā yuʿīnuhā ʿalā muʾmin*, "an associator shall not offer protection to any property belonging to Quraysh nor aid it [scil., Quraysh] against a Believer." The interpretation of the feminine suffix in *yuʿīnuhā* in Abū ʿUbayd is more straightforward (scil., Quraysh) than Ibn Hishām's masculine in *dūnahu*, the referent of which can be either the word *māl*, "property," or *nafs*, "person."[94] Whatever the exact original wording of this clause and its interpretation, the point appears to be that no associator shall help the tribe of Quraysh against any Believer. Who is denoted by the word *mushrik*, "associator"? I would suggest that it refers here to the gentile non-Believers who were living in Medina but were not really participants in the "Constitution." Their existence is not questioned nor is their blood declared licit, but it is simply stated that they shall not help the Meccan Quraysh against the Medinan "one community." The beginning of the document refers to *al-muhājirūn min quraysh*, "the Emigrants from Quraysh" as one of the groups participating in the treaty but, here, Quraysh is portrayed as the outgroup.

---

92 Lindstedt, forthcoming b.

93 For the phrase *yaḥūlu dūna*, see Lecker 2004, 179, who argues convincingly that it means "intervening between something or someone and one who wants to take or harm it or him"

94 Although the word *nafs* is generally feminine in Arabic, it can be treated as masculine when the meaning is "a person, self." See also Lecker 2004, 125.

What follows are further clauses on the inviolability of the blood of the Believers (Lecker 2004, §24–26). To begin with, "who knowingly kills a Believer – there being evidence of this – will be killed in retaliation for him, if the relative of the killed is not content with bloodwite."[95] This continues the theme discussed earlier: the blood of the Believers is sacrosanct and shall be avenged.[96] Above, it was stated that the Believers shall avenge the blood of the community shed in the path of God: the context of that clause was about warfare and intergroup relations. The current clause, on the other hand, applies not only to intragroup contexts but also to cases where someone outside Medina might shed the blood of a Believer. The "Constitution" goes on to say that the Believers shall be against the murderer *in toto* (*kāffatan*). Moreover, a Believer shall not help or shelter a "criminal," *muḥdith*, which might be a reference to the murderer[97] discussed in the previous clause or be a broader category. Be that as it may, here we encounter a characterization of a Believer: one who "believes in God and the last day" (*āmana bi-llāh wa-al-yawm al-ākhir*), a common Quranic refrain and definition of the minimal requirements for being a Believer (e.g., 2:126 and 2:232). The second part ends by noting that "whatever you disagree about, refer it to God and Muḥammad." God is in particular the source of this treaty and more generally of jurisdiction. The Prophet, as the prototypical Believer, is the human arbiter of all legal matters.

The Third Part

The third part (Ibn Hishām, *Sīra*, I, 342–343; Abū ʿUbayd, *Kitāb al-Amwāl*, II, 469; Lecker 2004, §27–48) is crucial for the categorization of Jews and for the question of the contours of the Believers' community. As stated above, the first and second part of the document affiliate the Jews with the "one community to the exclusion of other people" and state that they shall receive help. But are they also Believers in the broader sense of the word that incorporates monotheists

---

95 The last word, *bi-l-ʿaql*, is only present in Abū ʿUbayd's version (*Kitāb al-Amwāl*, II, 468), but the context clearly requires it so I suggest that it was part of the original wording of the document.

96 Lecker (2004, 128) notes concerning this passage: "The clause attempts to prevent the settlement of accounts left open from the Jāhilī period." This is a good interpretation of the document in general: it aims to start the relationship between the tribes participating in the document with a clean slate.

97 Lecker (2004, 132) understands the word *muḥdith* as referring to a murderer rather than a criminal in general.

of whatever subgroup? This is a complex question that depends to some extent on the version of the text.

The part which I deem the third begins by stating that the Jews shall "spend" (*yunfiqūna*) with the Believers as long as they wage war. "Spending" refers rather clearly to expenses related to warfare, and the implication of the clause is that the Jews and Believers are fighting a common enemy. It might be remarked that "spending in the path of God" is a common Quranic requirement (e.g., 2:195, 8:60) for ingroup affiliation.

The document then moves on to mention Jews of different tribes, the names of which correspond to a large extent to those mentioned in part one. The Jews of the first tribe (and other tribes mentioned) are characterized in the following way: *inna yahūd banī ʿawf umma*[98] *maʿa/min al-muʾminīn*. The crux of the matter is the preposition. Ibn Hishām (*Sīra*, I, 342) has *maʿa*, while Abū ʿUbayd has *min* (*Kitāb al-Amwāl*, II, 469). We can translate the two different versions accordingly:

- Ibn Hishām: "The Jews of the Banū ʿAwf are a group (*umma*)[99] alongside/along with the Believers."
- Abū ʿUbayd: "The Jews of the Banū ʿAwf are a group from among the Believers."

Thus, the text preserved in Ibn Hishām's work is rather ambivalent about whether or not the Jews of the tribes mentioned are among the Believers. Abū ʿUbayd's text, however, explicitly categorizes the Jews here as belonging to the Believer ingroup. Which one is the original wording? A case can be made that Abū ʿUbayd's *min* is

98 Lecker (2004, 139–147) claims that we should replace the word *umma* with *amana* and translate: "The Jews of the Banū ʿAwf are secure from (*amana min*) the Muʾminūn." But this is based on extremely poor textual evidence and, frankly, special pleading. Lecker's contention in his study is that the Jews and Believers were distinct groups and, moreover, that the Jews were not really part of the "one community." Lecker (2004, 191) notes that Abū ʿUbayd's text has some superior readings, and indeed prefers the preposition *min* here, in opposition to Ibn Hishām's *maʿa*. However, his emendation of *umma* to *amana* should be rejected.

99 In contrast to earlier commentators (see Lecker 2004, 137–139), I do not interpret the word *umma* here as a synonym or reference to the *umma wāḥida* mentioned in the early part of the text. Rather, here we simply have to translate the word *umma* as "a group." (In the Qur'ān too, the word *umma* is used in divergent contexts and with different significations; Denny 1975.) If *umma* here were a reference to the *umma wāḥida*, I would expect a rather different wording, perhaps, for example, *inna yahūd banī ʿawf min* al-*umma maʿa al-muʾminīn*. But this is not the case in any surviving quotation of the "Constitution." Rather, here the word *al-mu'minīn* functions as a synonym for *umma wāḥida* and as a superordinate category incorporating the various participants in the treaty.

plausibly the original preposition in this clause: the criterion of dissimilarity supports it.[100] That is to say, there are reasons to suppose that the original *min* would have been changed to *maʿa*, which does not clearly incorporate the Jews among the community of the Believers, whereas there are fewer reasons why a copyist or an editor working with the text would have changed *maʿa* into *min*. Later Islamic dogma grew wary of the suggestion that Jews might have been among the Prophet's community (although it is of course a problematic issue to try to pinpoint when this aversion started). Indeed, the persecution of the Prophet by the Jews is one of the most important themes of the literature on the Prophet's biography.

My reading, then, is that Abū ʿUbayd's version – stating that the Jews participating in the treaty were a subset of the Believers – is the more authentic one here. This formulation of the treaty could be compared to Qur'ān 3:113–114 (this passage is discussed below in more detail): "There is among the People of the Book an upright group (*umma qāʾima*), who recite God's revelations during the night, who bow down in worship, who believe in God and the Last Day, who order what is right and forbid what is wrong, who are quick to do good deeds. These people are among the righteous." Both texts categorize a group (*umma*) among the Jews/People of the Book as Believers.

That Ibn Hishām's text was reworked (*min* → *maʿa*) in this passage is in my opinion also visible in what immediately follows. Abū ʿUbayd's text (*Kitāb al-Amwāl*: II, 469) continues: *li-l-yahūd d-y-n-hum wa-li-l-muʾminīn d-y-n-hum wa-mawālīhim wa-anfusuhum*.[101] Ibn Hishām, on the other hand, has *muslimīn* instead of *muʾminīn*. However, as has been argued above, the Qur'anic evidence does not suggest that the word *muslim* was used as an ingroup appellation. This is a later development, and the text in Ibn Hishām's work was probably reworked to agree with that.[102] Thus Abū ʿUbayd's *muʾminīn* is preferable in my estimation. In what immediately precedes, the "Constitution" has (re)categorized the Jews as belonging to the Believers. However, it goes on to elaborate that, despite the recategorization, the Jews and the gentile Believers keep some of their previous characteristics or possessions. The first thing mentioned is "their *d-y-n*." This word can be read in two different ways, both of them plausible. To begin with, we can read it as *dayn*, meaning "loan" or "money obligation" (owed not by but to them,

100 Thus also Rubin 1985, 19–20, in contrast to Crone 1980, 7, who sees Ibn Hishām's reading as preferable.
101 However, Lecker (2004, 24) notes different word orders in this clause in different editions.
102 Or, if Ibn Hishām's wording is preferable, it cannot refer to the (Gentile) Believers in general, since the Submitters and the Believers are different groups in the document.

since the preposition is *li-*).[103] The other possibility is *dīn*, meaning "religion," "judgment," or "law." While the latter reading (*dīnuhum*) might be preferable at first glance since the treaty discusses religious groups at this point,[104] what follows suggests that the reading *dayn* is also possible. The following words are *mawālīhim wa-anfusuhum*,[105] "their allies/clients and themselves." The document, then, seems to be discussing property: the Jews and those who are already Believers shall keep their existing finances, allies/clients, and themselves. The word *anfusuhum*, "themselves," probably means that neither subgroup can reduce members of the other subgroup to a servile or client status.[106] To borrow a term from modern legal terminology, the members of the subgroups keep their right to self-determination. Let me note that although the reading *li-l-yahūd daynuhum wa-li -l-muʾminīn daynuhum* is possible, *dīnuhum* too is completely sensible here (most commentators prefer this reading).[107] If *dīnuhum* is the correct reading, we must probably understand the word as referring to "law." The clause could then be paraphrased as: 1) the Jews and the gentile Believers can continue living according their separate laws and rites; 2) they keep their allies/clients to themselves according to the former categories; and 3) they preserve their right to self-determination.

The word *anfusuhum* is modified by what follows: *illā man ẓalama aw athima fa-innahu lā yūtighu illā nafsahu wa-ahla baytihi*. That is, the Jews who are now recategorized as belonging to the Believers keep their *anfusuhum*, their self-determination, except those who do wrong or commit sin (*ẓalama aw athima*). However, even these wrongdoers and sinners, although they might be subject to punishment because of their deeds, do not jeopardize the whole

---

103 Cf. Lecker (2004, 147–148) according to whom the reading *dayn* is unwarranted. He says (following Rubin 1985, 16, n. 44) that, to be a possible interpretation, *dayn* would require the preposition *ʿalā* and not *li-* as we have in the text. But this is not a very compelling argument since *lahu dayn* simply means "money is owed to him." See Lane 1863–1893, 944, who translates *lahu dayn* "*To him is due a debt*," i.e., "*he has a debt owed to him.*"

104 Quran 109 is often cited by commentators who prefer the reading *dīnuhum*: "Say, 'Disbelievers: I do not worship what you worship, you do not worship what I worship, I will never worship what you worship, you will never worship what I worship: you have your religion and I have mine (*lakum dīnuhum wa-lī dīnī*).'"

105 Ibn Hishām (*Sīra*, I, 342) has *mawālīhim wa-anfusuhum*, while Abū ʿUbayd has *wa-mawālīhim wa-anfusuhum* with *wa-* before the word *mawālīhim* (*Kitāb al-Amwāl*, II, 469).

106 My interpretation differs from that of earlier commentators (see Lecker 2004, 136–137). Lecker (2004, §28) translates: "The Jews have their religion and the Muslimūn have theirs. [This applies to] their allies and their persons."

107 See, for example, Donner 2002–2003, 31.

subgroup of Jewish Believers: they only bring calamity to themselves and their family (*fa-innahu lā yūtighu illā nafsahu wa-ahla baytihi*).

Jews belonging to the following tribes are mentioned in this context as having the same rights as *yahūd banī ʿawf* who were discussed above: *yahūd banī al-najjār, yahūd banī al-ḥārith, yahūd banī sāʿida, yahūd banī jusham, yahūd banī al-aws, yahūd banī thaʿlaba,*[108] *jafna baṭn*[109] *min thaʿlaba, banī al-shuṭayba,*[110] *mawālī thaʿlaba*, and *biṭānat yahūd* (Ibn Hishām, *Sīra*, I, 342–343; Abū ʿUbayd, *Kitāb al-Amwāl*, II, 469 contains the same groups up to *yahūd banī al-aws* but not what comes after that). All groups contain a tribal name except the *biṭānat yahūd*. Most tribal groups were mentioned at the beginning of the document without the word *yahūd* before them. It appears that many members of the tribes that took part in the treaty were Jewish.

Who are the *biṭānat yahūd*? Although the word *biṭāna* might simply signify "associates," as is its basic meaning, Lecker, referencing Arabic texts, suggests that it might denote in particular the nomadic or semi-nomadic allies of the Jews living outside Medina.[111] Perhaps then, we can translate *biṭānat yahūd* as "nomadic Jewish groups." If so, what follows (*innahu lā yakhruju minhum aḥad illā bi-idhn muḥammad*, "no one of them shall go out except with the permission of Muḥammad") might refer to the *biṭānat yahūd*, not Jews in general.[112] But this is unclear, as is the exact meaning of the clause, since the verb *yakhruju* might mean various things in this context ("go out [of Medina]," "quit [the treaty]," or even "rebel").[113] Perhaps the meaning is indeed that the *biṭānat yahūd*, nomadic Jews, should settle in Medina and not leave it and continue their nomadic way of life. It is also possible that *innahu lā yakhruju minhum aḥad illā bi-idhn muḥammad* might concern all Jews participating in the treaty or everyone, Jews and non-Jews. What follows immediately after is probably a qualification to this: "[but] no one is prevented from avenging an injury – for the one who

108 There is a rich discussion (on the basis of Arabic literary evidence) on the Banū Thaʿlaba in Lecker 2004, 75–79.

109 On the word *baṭn*, see the commentary in Lecker 2004, 150–151.

110 This clause (Lecker 2004, §36) reads: *inna li-banī al-shuṭayba mithl mā li-yahūd banī ʿawf*. Since the passage does not mention *yahūd banī al-shuṭayba* but simply *banī al-shuṭayba*, I would suggest that it should be understood that the tribe al-Shuṭayba was completely or predominantly Jewish. The Jewishness of al-Shuṭayba was taken for granted and did not need to be mentioned.

111 Lecker 2004, 154–155.

112 This is the understanding of Lecker 2004, 155.

113 The clause is further complicated by the fact that the text later says (Lecker 2004, §62 and see below): "Who leaves (*man kharaja*) is safe, and who remains (*man qaʿada*) is safe in Medina, except whoever does wrong and sins."

kills is responsible, in addition to his family (*ahl baytihi*), for it – except a wrongdoer (*illā man ẓalama*)"[114] (this is only in Ibn Hishām, *Sīra*, I, 343). That is, no one is allowed to leave Medina (since the community is busy fighting a war together) unless that person is avenging an injury (murder?).[115]

Next, the document returns to the question of expenses, probably related to warfare: *ʿalā al-yahūd nafaqatuhum wa-ʿalā al-muslimīn nafaqatuhum*, "the Jews have [at their responsibility] their expenses, and the *muslimūn* have [at their responsibility] their expenses" (Ibn Hishām, *Sīra*, I, 343, Abū ʿUbayd, *Kitāb al-Amwāl*, II, 469).[116] The sentence is puzzling in the light of what has been said above, namely that the word *muslimūn* was not used during the life of the Prophet to refer to the Believers in general, although it was suggested, in the light of a Qur'anic verse (49:14, cf. 3:64), that the word might have been used to denote people – perhaps in particular of nomadic background – who show willingness to join the ingroup but are not yet considered to be full members: "The nomads (*al-aʿrāb*) say: 'We believe' (*āmannā*). Say: You do not believe [yet]. Say instead: 'We submit' (*aslamnā*)." The word *al-muslimīn* is found in both Ibn Hishām and Abū ʿUbayd's versions of the text, so there is no evidence for claiming textual reworking here (although it is not impossible of course). It must be remembered that the document mentioned the *biṭānat yahūd* in the preceding section, which is according to Lecker a reference to the nomadic allies of the Jews.[117] If this is the correct interpretation of the *biṭāna*, the word *al-muslimīn* might be continuing the same discourse on the nomads who want to become Believers but of whom there was considerable suspicion according to the Qur'anic evidence. I might add that this suspicion is specifically connected with nomads around Medina in Qur'ān 9:101 (see also 9:120): "Some of the nomads around you are hypocrites, as are some of the people of Medina – they are obstinate in their hypocrisy. You [sing.] do not know them, but We know them well: We shall punish them twice and then they will be returned to a painful punishment."

---

114 The ending (*illā man ẓalama*) is somewhat obscure. Perhaps we could read the verb in the passive (*ẓulima*), and translate: "no one is prevented from avenging an injury; for the one who kills is responsible, in addition to his family (*ahl baytihi*), for it, except one who has been coerced." Or perhaps the *man ẓalama* refers to the victim killed (see the following note).

115 Lecker (2004, 155–159) does not connect these three clauses but presents them as separate (§40–42 in his numbering). He translates them as follows (square brackets in the original): "No-one of them [viz. of the Jews' nomadic allies] may go out [of Medina] without Muḥammad's permission" (§40). "There is no refraining from retaliation for a wound" (§41). "He who kills [someone entitled to security] kills himself and his agnates, unless he [viz. his victim] acted unjustly" (§42).

116 Lecker (2004, 184) simply considers this clause a duplication "due to a scribal error."

117 2004, 154–155.

Whatever the intended referent of *al-muslimīn*, the text continues (Lecker 2004, §45–47) by saying that between them (*al-muslimīn* and the Jews?), "there shall be help against those who make war against the people of this document (*ahl hādhihi al-ṣaḥīfa*); and there shall be good and sincere advice between them; and devotion without misdeed (*al-birr dūn al-ithm*)."[118] The phrase *ahl hādhihi al-ṣaḥīfa* is an interesting expression that functions similarly to the "one community to the exclusion of other people," as a big-tent superordinate category encompassing all participants in the treaty.

After a clause (Lecker 2004, §48) that can be skipped here, Ibn Hishām (*Sīra*, I, 343) repeats what has already been said, that the Jews shall spend money with the Believers as long as they wage war. This is not found in Abū ʿUbayd. Since the phrase is an exact repetition of what was at the beginning of part three, it is possible that it does not belong to the original text of the treaty but is a sign of corrupt text in Ibn Hishām at this point.[119] Another possibility is that it serves as a sort of refrain to close the section. Be that as it may, for my division this is the end of part three.

The Fourth Part

The two versions of the text have some differences in part four (Ibn Hishām, *Sīra*, I, 343–344; Abū ʿUbayd, *Kitāb al-Amwāl*, II, 469–470; Lecker 2004, §49–64). Ibn Hishām's version is once again fuller but is incomprehensible in some parts. Abū ʿUbayd's text reads better but some of the variants could be considered *lectio facilior* and hence discarded.

Both versions start by noting that the interior (*jawf*)[120] of Medina (Ibn Hishām: *Yathrib*; Abū ʿUbayd: *al-Madīna*) is an inviolable area (*ḥaram*/*ḥarām*) for the participants of the treaty (*li-ahl hādhihi al-ṣaḥīfa*). Uri Rubin has suggested that this clause decrees a shared religious center for the new community.[121] While this is possible, I would suggest that the word *ḥaram*/*ḥarām* is here primarily linked with the idea of an area where blood should not be shed. It has

118 Lecker (2004, §47) understands *al-birr dūn al-ithm* as forming a clause of its own, unrelated to what precedes. He reads *al-barr dūn al-āthim* and translates it: "The righteous man will restrain the sinner." I do not find this interpretation plausible.
119 Lecker 2004, 16 also omits it.
120 For the *jawf* of Medina and its possible location, see Lecker 2004, 167–169 and Munt 2014, 57–64.
121 Rubin 1985, 10.

been mentioned a number of times in the text that a Believer shall not be killed. The clause currently discussed is further connected with this notion.

The text (only in Ibn Hishām, *Sīra*, I, 343) continues by discussing *jiwār* arrangements, that is, covenants of protection between members of the community. It proclaims that the protected person is like the protector (*inna al-jār ka-l-nafs*): she or he shall not be injured or wronged. Next (Lecker 2004, §51), the text in Ibn Hishām reads *wa-innahu lā tujāru ḥurma illā bi-idhn ahlihā*. This has been variously interpreted by previous commentators. Watt translates: "No woman is given 'neighbourly protection' without the consent of her people."[122] Lecker, on the other hand, believes that the word ḥ*urma* refers to a state of protection.[123] He translates: "No protection will be granted without the permission of the parties to this treaty." However, there are reasons why Watt's interpretation is better. First of all, all instances of the verb *ajāra* in the document are connected with concrete social relations and not abstract nouns as Lecker takes *ḥurma* to be. Moreover, to translate *ahlihā* as "the parties to this treaty" is a stretch: it is unlikely that the possessive suffix would refer to the *ṣaḥīfa*, which is not mentioned in this clause. The word *ḥurma* is a much more likely candidate, and if that word means "woman/wife," the word *ahl* finds its natural referent as her family (or perhaps more precisely, her husband). I believe that Lecker's interpretation here is unfounded and should be discarded. The text will come back to interindividual or intergroup *jiwār* arrangements after a clause repeating the authority of the Prophet Muḥammad.

The next clause (Lecker 2004, §52) is both in Ibn Hishām and Abū ʿUbayd (with small variations). It once again emphasizes that God and Muḥammad are the ones to administer the law if an incident should arise. To quote Watt's translation (1956, 224) of Ibn Hishām's version: "Whenever among the people of this document there occurs any incident (disturbance) or quarrel from which disaster for it (the people) is to be feared, it is to be referred to God and to Muḥammad, the Messenger of God." Muḥammad is the prototypical member and leader of the group and the one who wields justice on earth as God's representative.[124]

Ibn Hishām's version now returns to the question of *jiwār* (this passage is missing in Abū ʿUbayd). It is possible that this clause is misplaced and should follow after the one mentioning ḥ*urmas* (wives or women). Earlier in the document it was stated, *lā yujīru mushrikun mālan li-quraysh wa-lā nafsan*, proclaiming it illicit for

122 Watt 1956, 224.

123 Lecker 2004, 171–172.

124 See also, e.g., Quran 4:59: "You who believe, obey God and the Messenger, and those in authority among you. If you are in dispute over any matter, refer it to God and the Messenger, if you truly believe in God and the Last Day: that is better and fairer in the end."

associators to make *jiwār* arrangements with Quraysh. Here (Lecker 2004, §54), the text expands the prohibition of *jiwār* towards Quraysh: *wa-innahu lā tujāru quraysh wa-lā man naṣarahā*, "a covenant of protection shall not be made with Quraysh nor with anyone who helps them." The prohibition is here categorical.

Indeed, the community shall help each other against anyone who should attack Medina (*man dahama yathrib*), as the text continues (Lecker 2004, §55). The word *dahama* often signifies a sudden attack, but Lecker suggests that it may also mean an attack with a large army.[125] Be that as it may, next comes a very messy part, continuing the topic of warfare and expanding it to peace treaties. Ibn Hishām's text (*Sīra*: I, 343) is especially difficult to comprehend.

Watt translates this passage in the following way, which shows the difficulty of the passage: "Whenever they are summoned to conclude and accept a treaty, they conclude and accept it; when they in turn summon to the like of that, it is for them upon the believers, except whoever wars about religion; for (? = incumbent on) each man is his share from their side which is towards them."[126]

Lecker also notes the complexity of the prose in this passage.[127] He translates (2004, §56, square brackets, parentheses, and question marks in the original): "If they [the Jews] are called [by the other parties to the treaty] to conclude and accept (?) an agreement, they will conclude and accept (?) it; and if they [the Jews] call upon the same, it is incumbent upon the Mu'minūn to give it them, with the exception of those fighting for religion. Everybody should pay their share at their own expense (?)."

Abū 'Ubayd's version (*Kitāb al-Amwāl*, II, 469–470) is somewhat less confused, but it too leaves questions. In addition to the Believers, Abū 'Ubayd's text also mentions the Jews, which is supplied in Lecker's translation in square brackets. The clause indicates, perhaps, that both subgroups, the Gentile Believers and the Jews, can accept treaties with the outgroup, and these treaties apply to the whole of the "one community." The ingroup is allowed to conclude peace treaties with their enemies although the general outlook of the text as a whole is characterized by a wartime mentality. My reading differs from that of Lecker, who states: "Rather than matters of war and peace, this clause refers to the settlement of blood feuds."[128] This is in accordance with Lecker's general tendency to read the document as mostly dealing with cases of homicide and bloodwite. However, I find it unlikely that this clause would be related to blood

125 Lecker 2004, 175.

126 Watt 1956, 225, parentheses in the original.

127 Lecker 2004, 176–177.

128 Lecker 2004, 177.

feuds. Although matters of bloodwite are very important in the "Constitution," so is warfare, and this clause should be understood in that context. After all, the clause itself mentions "those fighting for religion/law" (*man ḥāraba fī al-dīn*).

Curiously, after this, the text mentions *yahūd al-aws* and proclaims that both their clients and they themselves are on a par with other participants in the "Constitution." The mention of "the Jews of al-Aws" is rather surprising since they were already mentioned above (as *yahūd banī al-aws*) and their rights should already be secured. Since the mention of *yahūd al-aws* here is present in both Ibn Hishām and Abū ʿUbayd, it is probable that this passage was part of the original document. Why their rights are repeated is unclear. Perhaps the tribal group of al-Aws was such an important participant in the treaty and perhaps the Jewish component of it so sizeable that "the Jews of al-Aws" were mentioned here again. Earlier commentators have suggested that this clause (§57 in Lecker 2004) is a later interpolation,[129] but I am not sure if that explains the repetition better.

The document now moves to closing statements that aim to make the text firm and binding. The phrase *inna al-birr dūn al-ithm*, "devotion/piety before/without misdeed/sin,"[130] has already occurred in the text and functions as a refrain. Then (Lecker 2004, §59–61), the text states that every person is responsible for her or his deeds and their repercussions (*lā yaksibu kāsib illā ʿalā nafsihi*), adding that God is the most trusted fulfiller of this treaty, who does not intervene to help a wrongdoer or sinner (*wa-innahu lā yaḥūlu hādhā al-kitāb dūna ẓālim aw āthim*). The following clause might have to do with the permissibility to join or leave the treaty[131] or as permissibility to leave or remain in Medina: "Who leaves (*man kharaja*) is safe, and who remains (*man qaʿada*) is safe in Medina, except whoever does wrong and sins." Then comes the very last statement of the document: "God is the protector (*jār*) of those who are pious and fear [God] (*li-man barra wa-ittaqā*), and Muḥammad is the Messenger of God." This is only in Ibn Hishām (*Sīra*, I, 344) but it makes sense as a closing statement. Abū ʿUbayd's version (*Kitāb al-Amwāl*, II, 470) ends differently: "the best partaker/guardian of this document is the pious doer of good" (*inna awlāhum bi-hādhihi al-ṣaḥīfa al-barr al-muḥsin*). In both Ibn

---

129 Lecker 2004, 183–185.

130 This is variously understood by scholars. Watt (1956, 224), for example, translates: "Honourable dealing (comes) before treachery." And Lecker (2004, 151): "The righteous man will restrain the sinner," which, however, I do not find a very likely translation. Prof. Jaakko Hämeen-Anttila has suggested to me (private communication) the following translation, which is rather lucid: "devotion is a matter different from sin." That is to say, in the text, *al-birr* and *al-ithm* are clearly different things and a person chooses between the two.

131 As interpreted by Lecker (2004, 180–181) who also interprets this clause as being addressed to the Jews rather than to the participants in the treaty in general. Why this should be so is not elucidated by him. I do not find this reading likely.

Hishām's (*Sīra*, I, 341) and Abū 'Ubayd's (*Kitāb al-Amwāl*, II, 466) versions the document started by mentioning its source and authority as the Prophet. It would make sense to expect the "Constitution" to end with a mention of Muḥammad as well. So I suggest that Ibn Hishām's version's conclusion has a greater claim to authenticity.

Conclusions on the "Constitution"

To summarize my reading of the "Constitution of Medina," the text aims to recategorize the tribes engaging in the treaty as belonging to the superordinate category that is called "one community to the exclusion of other people," "the people of this document," and "the Believers," although the latter sometimes functions as a subordinate term ("gentile Believers") on a par with "the Jews." The tribal units keep their organization and financial responsibilities intact. Moreover, these subordinate tribal identities are accepted affiliations that the members can still possess while being subsumed under the big-tent identity of the "one community." It is probable that there were tribes in Medina that did not join the treaty: of these we do not know more (since they are not mentioned in the text) without recourse to later Arabic literature.

In addition to tribal identities, the document engages with religious identities. Many members of the tribes that were participants in the "Constitution" were Jewish. Thus, the question of the status of the Jews is of utmost importance in the document. I suggest that the big-tent "one community" mentioned in the treaty consisted of gentile Believers and Jewish Believers as well as what was perhaps a smaller group of Submitters, *al-muslimūn*, whose exact identity remains unclear. However, the exact categorization of the Jews is hard to pinpoint since the two versions of Ibn Hishām and Abū 'Ubayd differ in the crucial part. Abū 'Ubayd's version says that the Jews are "a group from among (*min*) the Believers," while Ibn Hishām has "a group alongside/along with (*ma'a*) the Believers." I would be willing to accept Abū 'Ubayd's text as the more authentic one. However, if Ibn Hishām's version is the original one, then the category of "the Believers" cannot really be said to function as a superordinate category, at least in parts of the document. The Jews and the Believers are, in Ibn Hishām's text, communities on the same conceptual level, and the recategorized superordinate identity is called "one community to the exclusion of other people" and "the people of this document," but not, at least explicitly, "Believers." In any case, the common ingroup model is present in Ibn Hishām's account of the document as well, only with different nomenclature.[132]

Whatever we call this superordinate ingroup, it is clear that the document endeavors to forge solidarity and some shared norms between the subgroups. They share the monotheist credo and acknowledge the Prophet as their leader and arbiter. They fight together against a common foe and help each other in other ways as well, offering sincere advice and counsel. Naming and constructing an outgroup is often an important part of the identity building process. In the document, the outgroup is called Quraysh, although the words *mushrik*, "associator," and *kāfir*, "disbeliever," also appear as attributes of the outgroup members. However, it was argued above that there were associators inside Medina who are told not to collaborate with Quraysh against the Believers but of whom nothing else is said.

If the reading *li-l-yahūd dīnuhum wa-li-l-mu'minīn dīnuhum* (rather than *daynuhum*) is correct, this means that the two religious groups, gentile Believers and Jews, can keep their separate "laws," probably referring to purity regulations, rites, and other such matters.[133] Concerning recategorization, modern social psychologists have noted that outright challenges to existing identities and ways of life are counterproductive for the common ingroup model to take root. In the text of the "Constitution," it appears that the Jews could continue adhering to their traditions and the gentiles to theirs, be it issues such as food laws, circumcision, rites, or other matters. To quote Gaertner and Dovidio's social psychological work on the common ingroup identity model, "when groups have equal status and each group can maintain positive distinctiveness, we can anticipate greater acceptance of a superordinate identity from the members of both groups and more successful intergroup contact."[134]

What unites the "one community to the exclusion of other people" is their shared belief in God and the last day as well as in Muḥammad as God's Prophet and the prototypical group member.[135] All adherents to the common ingroup are

132 See also Rubin 1985, 12–17.

133 Denny 1977, 44 argues in a similar fashion: "Functionally, the Constitution was very much a political-military document of agreement designed to make Yathrib and the peoples connected with it safe. The Jews could be a party to it as a sort of special group, a 'sub-*ummah*' with its own *dīn*."

134 Gaertner and Dovidio 2000, 100.

135 For an analogue in biblical studies, Baker 2011, 201 summarizes his findings on recategorization in the book of Acts: "The superordinate identity offered by Luke in the narrative of Acts is centered upon the belief that Jesus of Nazareth is the resurrected Messiah. This belief is expressed in the two boundary crossing rituals of baptism in Jesus' name and being filled with the Holy Spirit. Ethnic Judeans who embraced this belief remain free to maintain their traditional customs

also required to carry out the costly deeds of spending funds for warfare and of fighting against the enemy. The community is under the protection of God (*dhimmat allāh*), and if a group member is injured or killed in fighting, his blood is avenged by fellow members. The "Constitution" also addresses the community in territorial terms (Rubin 1985, 9), ruling that the inner part of Medina is a sacrosanct area (*ḥaram/ḥarām*) where violence is not permitted.[136] Related to this, the community shall help each other to defend the town against whoever attacks it.

The ingroup members' identities should be conceptualized as hybrid. The members of the treaty affiliated themselves with the following groups, according to the text of the document:

1. Their superordinate identity as "one community."
2. Their ethno-religious identity as Jewish or gentile Believer.
3. Their tribe.
4. Their territorial identity as inhabitants of Medina.

In all likelihood, they also possessed and signaled other identities that are not explicitly addressed in the document, such as gender identity. Their supposed ethnic identity as "Arabs" is, however, nowhere mentioned in the document and, as argued at length by Peter Webb, Arab ethnogenesis could be seen as a post-Islamic phenomenon.[137] Be that as it may, the "Constitution" does not see subgroup identities as a threat to the common ingroup identity of the "one community."

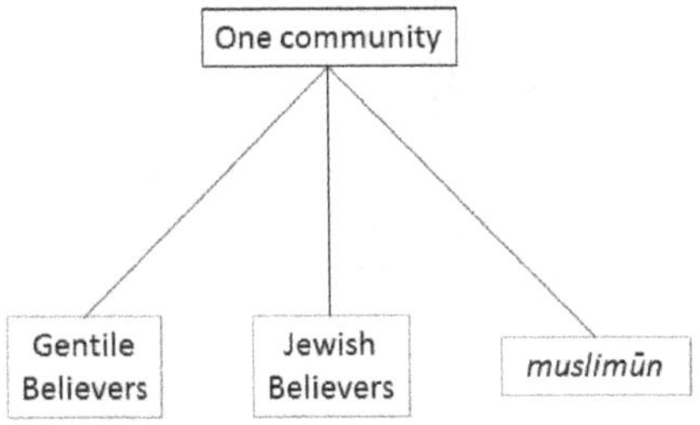

Figure 1: Religious Identities of the Ingroup in the "Constitution".

such as circumcision and Torah observance but non-Judeans who embraced this belief are not required to adhere to ethnic Judean customs. Non-Judean Christ followers are, however, expected to follow minimal guidelines that would allow social interaction between Judean and non-Judean Christ followers." The clause of the "Constitution," *li-l-yahūd dīnuhum wa-li-l-mu'minīn dīnuhum* (if this is the correct reading), endeavors to secure something very similar: the continuation of the traditional customs and law for both subgroups.

136 On the Medinan *ḥaram*, see Munt 2014. Pages 54–64 of the book concern the "Constitution of Medina." He interprets the "Constitution's" declaration of Medina's *jawf* as *ḥaram* to mean that it was considered a sacred space.

137 Webb 2016.

Re- and Decategorization in the Qur'ān

Introduction

A few words about my premises: I approach the Qur'ān as a text contemporary to the Prophet Muḥammad that should be read in the context of late antique religious literature that was current in Arabia and surrounding regions.[138] In addition, I view the Nöldekean chronological division of Qur'anic surahs as basically sound, although only an approximation.[139] The ascription of the surahs to Meccan or Medinan periods does not necessarily mean, in my opinion, that they actually belong to those phases of the Prophet's career. "Meccan" simply means earlier, and "Medinan," later. The Qur'anic texts discussed in section 3 show a somewhat clear development if interpreted according to the Nöldekean chronology, as will be seen. This too, I submit, suggests that there is something to that dating of the Qur'anic passages.

Recently, Marijn van Putten has demonstrated (convincingly, I believe) that early Qur'anic manuscripts go back to a single written archetype, which was codified in the first century AH/seventh century CE.[140] Hence, the Qur'ān (or at least its consonantal skeleton, the *rasm*) was a) canonized rather early; b) transmitted in a written fashion early on. Moreover, since Fred Donner has shown that there is in the Qur'ān, as we now have and read it, very little that could be considered post-Muḥammadan interpolations,[141] I think it is the most probable

138 El-Badawi 2014; Dost 2017.

139 For a defense of at least the basic outlines of Nöldeke's chronology, with suggestions for development, see Sinai 2010 and 2017. The biggest problem of the Nöldekean paradigm was to work with surahs, which is too big a unit (if we exclude the shortest surahs).

140 Van Putten 2019.

141 Notably, Stephen Shoemaker 2011, 153 has questioned this line of argument: "Yet following an identical logic, one could similarly make the argument that the Christian Gospel according to John, which does not assign any predictions to Jesus beyond his own lifespan (or a few days thereafter), must accurately reflect his life and teaching and date to sometime before 60 CE. To my knowledge, however, no serious New Testament scholar has proposed such an argument, and in general John is thought to be perhaps the latest canonical gospel. Accordingly, the mere absence of predictive material in a text cannot be used to date it close to the events that it purports to describe or verify its authenticity." However, Shoemaker's argumentation is strained as regards this point. It is exactly certain aspects and anachronisms in the Gospel of John (the high Christology at the beginning of the text, for instance) that is used to date the text and consider it late, whether or not the text actually assigns predictions to Jesus. Similarly, the Quran can be considered early, because it, for instance, does not attribute Muḥammad the exemplary role he was to receive later in classical Islamic theology.

solution to assume that the bulk of the text can be ascribed, in fact, to the Muḥammadan corpus of revelations.

Although in the above discussion of the "Constitution of the Medina" there are some references to Quranic passages, I have not yet tried to show how well or not the "Constitution" fits with the Qur'ānic evidence. The answer seems to be, quite well, although the Qur'anic social categorizations are somewhat different. Since I have dealt with the classification of the Jews and Christians in the Qur'ān elsewhere,[142] I will discuss here only the Qur'anic passages that have to do with recategorization – constructing a common superordinate identity – in particular.

First of all, it might be remarked that the Qur'anic concept of "the People of the Book" is in itself a recategorized group,[143] including apparently such subgroups as Jews, Christians, and perhaps others, like Sabians. However, the Prophet himself does not, according to the Qur'ān, identify with them. Rather, he is "the gentile Prophet" (*al-nabī al-ummī*, 7:157–158). Indeed, the gentiles (*al-ummiyyūn*) are mentioned alongside with, and in contrast to, the People of the Book in Q 3:20. I have tried to show above that the "Constitution" presents a common identity incorporating both Jewish and gentile Believers. What I am pursuing in this section is looking at Qur'anic passages presenting the recategorization of the People of the Book and Gentiles into a big-tent identity. It will be seen that the Medinan Qur'ān, in contrast to the "Constitution," is especially not keen on allowing subgroup identities. Moreover, while the "Constitution" does not say one bad word about the category of the Jews, the Qur'ān contains numerous criticisms of them. Rather than *recategorization*, we should perhaps speak of *decategorization*, meaning a process where former identities are downplayed or outright rejected and people are treated on an individual basis. The translations of the Qur'anic passages in this article are based on the renderings of Abdel Haleem, although I have occasionally changed the wording to follow my understanding of the text.

The Believers and Recategorization in the Qur'ān

I suggest that we can interpret the Qur'anic category of "the Believers" as a big-tent identity that was easy to affiliate with and did not pose insurmountable

142 Lindstedt, forthcoming a.

143 Or we could call it a grouped term (Ehala 2018, 130–133), since recategorization, as understood in this study, means the expansion and redefinition of the ingroup. The People of the Book, as will be seen below, are not explicitly "in" or "out" but categorized in divergent ways in different phases of the Qur'anic communication.

problems for those Jews and Christians who wanted to partake in it.[144] The Qur'ān is rather explicit in considering some of them Believers (Q 3:110).

The core values and identity signals of the Believer group are rather general. For instance, Q 4:136 characterizes them (as well as the outgroup) as follows: "You who believe, believe in God and His Messenger and in the Book He sent down to His Messenger, as well as what He sent down before. Anyone who does not believe in God, His angels, His Books, His messengers, and the Last Day has gone far, far astray." Other central beliefs are the resurrection of the dead (e.g., Q 2:28) and the fear of God (3:102). In addition to these basic dogmata, the Believers should signal their identity by praying and giving alms (2:2), fasting during Ramadan (2:185), doing good deeds (2:25), performing the pilgrimage (2:196–197), following some regulations concerning, for example, purity and food (Zellentin 2018),[145] and fighting against the outgroup (2:216). Many of the basic tenets of the Qur'anic faith and practice were already embraced by Jews and Christians and accepting new ones (such as fasting during Ramadan) would not, I suggest, have posed a big obstacle to affiliation with the group. The biggest hurdle would probably have been accepting Muḥammad as a Prophet and leader and his revelation as Scripture. The absolute and stringent monotheism and the low Christology of that message could also have been difficult to embrace by some Christians.

My argument is that identity signs marking a difference between Muḥammad's movement and other monotheists are, by and large, absent in the Qur'ān.[146] The Qur'ān makes no mention of the following rituals, practices, and dogma that later became characteristic identity signals of classical Islam: conversion by uttering the testimony of faith or by any other means; circumcision (another, costly, signal of conversion and Muslimness in later Islam); the idea that the Qur'ān abrogates earlier Scriptures; Muḥammad's primacy over earlier Prophets or the perpetual importance of his *sunna* (exemplary way of life); a comprehensive system of law; salvific exclusivity; five daily prayers (though prayer in general is mentioned); or detailed prescriptions of the other so-called five pillars of Islam. The lack of these boundary features show that the identity of the community was still under development at this stage. Scholars working on the question of identity have noted the importance of rites of conversion: "If identities require boundaries, boundaries require boundary-crossing customs for newcomers."[147] Notably, no

144 See Lindstedt, forthcoming a.

145 See Lindstedt, forthcoming a.

146 Such identity signs can also be called "identity descriptors," "boundary features," or "distinctions" (Ehala 2018, 80).

147 Baker 2011, 9.

process of conversion or other boundary-crossing customs are present in the Qur'ān nor in the "Constitution of Medina."

What is more, Qur'anic dietary regulations can be considered rather inclusive because it is stated that the Believers can eat the food of the People of the Book and vice versa (Q 5:5). Since distinctive identity signs are to a large degree absent, it is unlikely that we can talk about a clear-cut religious identity. We have to allow that the boundaries between the Believers, Jews, and Christians were permeable. Rodney Stark has noted that new religious movements are more likely to succeed when they "*retain cultural continuity with conventional faith(s) of the societies in which they seek converts.*"[148] Earlier research stated that Arabia on the eve of Islam was predominantly polytheistic, but more recent scholarship has convincingly showed that Judaism and Christianity had a strong foothold in the region.[149]

Despite these general remarks, let us look more closely at the Qur'anic communication and its development. Especially interesting is the possibility that the Jews and Christians (or the People of the Book) may be part of the Believer group while retaining their Jewish and Christian identities as subordinate groups. This seems to be perfectly possible in the Meccan stratum of the Qur'ān, while the Medinan suras are not so welcoming to sub-identities.

The earliest Qur'anic suras (Mecca I according to Nöldeke's chronology), do not contain statements on the Jews or Christians (or People of the Book). The first mentions of them come in the Mecca II period. These Meccan passages emphasize that the message of the revelation of Muḥammad is similar to or identical with earlier Scriptures. For example, Q 26:192–197 (Mecca II according to Nöldeke 1909–1919, I, 122) remarks: "It is a revelation from the Lord of the World. The trusted Spirit brought it down to your heart that you might bring warning in a clear Arabic tongue. It is [also] in the scriptures (*zubur*) of the ancients. Is it not proof enough for them that the scholars of the Israelites have recognized it?"

This tone continues in the Mecca III phase, to which the following examples belong (Nöldeke 1909–1919, I, 143, 155):

> Q 13:36: Those to whom We have sent the Book rejoice in what has been revealed to you [sing.]; but some factions deny parts of it. Say, "I am commanded to worship God, and not join anything with Him in worship: to Him I call and to Him I shall return."

> Q 28:52–55: Those to whom We gave the Book before believe in it, and, when it is recited to them, say, "We believe in it, it is the truth from our Lord. [Even] before it came we have submitted (*innā kunnā min qablihi muslimīn*)." They will be given their rewards twice over

148 Stark 1996, 136.
149 See, for example, Crone 2015–2016, 2016.

> because they are steadfast, repel evil with good, spend of what We have provided for them (*mimmā razaqnāhum yunfiqūna*), and turn away whenever they hear frivolous talk, saying, "We have our deeds and you have yours. Peace be with you! We do not seek the company of ignorant people."

> Q 29:46–47: And do not argue with the People of the Book except in a way that is best, except for those who commit injustice among them, and say [pl.], "We believe in that which has been revealed to us and revealed to you. Our God and your God is one; and we submit to Him (*wa-naḥnu lahu muslimūn*)." In this way We sent the Book to you [sing.]. Those to whom We had already given the Book believe in it and so do some of these people (*hāʾulāʾ*). No one refuses to acknowledge Our revelations but the defiant.

Not only does the Qur'ān underscore that its message is a continuation of or like the earlier Scripture(s), it also notes quite explicitly that the People of the Book accept its divine status and message. Only "some factions deny parts of it" (13:36). The undertone of these passages is optimistic. There is no intergroup hostility between the People of the Book and "these people" (*hāʾulāʾ*) who also believe (29:47, meaning Believers of gentile background?). If there shall be argument between the groups, it should proceed in the best manner. Indeed, these Qur'anic passages of the Mecca III period recategorize the People of the Book and the gentile Believers as having the same God and believing in the same Scripture. No attempt is made to repudiate the People of the Book as a category or to attach pejorative stereotypes to them. Commenting on 28:52–55 and similar Qur'anic passages, Patricia Crone remarks as follows: "It is notable that the recipients of the earlier book/People of the Book who declare themselves to be believers or Muslims have not abandoned their Jewish or Christian identity."[150] This is to the point (though, I think, the word "Muslims" is an anachronism here). The Meccan Qur'ān, like the "Constitution of Medina," does not present the Believer and the People of the Book identities as clashing.

The rest of the Qur'anic evidence dealt with here is Medinan according to Nöldeke and the classical Islamic exegesis. In this phase, negative depictions of the Jews and Christians arise[151] and the people categorized as such are generally

---

150 Crone 2016:338. It must be noted that the Qur'ān *describes* the People of the Book as declaring themselves to be Believers; we have no independent evidence that they did. Although this is an important caveat, it is less important for my study, which looks at identities, categorizations, and groups in early Islamic texts. Whether or not the People of the Book affiliated themselves with the ingroup in actual fact, the Qur'ān here clearly says that they did and, thus, categorizes them as "one of us."

151 Although, as I have noted in Lindstedt, forthcoming a, there is very little anti-Christian polemic in the whole of the Qur'ān, while anti-Jewish passages are rather numerous in the Medinan phase. The anti-trinitarian and anti-incarnational passages are usually understood in

deemed unreliable because of their group affiliation. The gentile identity of the Prophet and many of his followers was mentioned above. The figure of Abraham is cited as a prototypical gentile Believer who should be emulated (2:135, 139–140):

> They say, 'Become Jews or Christians, and you will be rightly guided.' Say (*qul*), 'Rather the religion of Abraham as Gentile (*ḥanīfan*). He was not an associator.' . . . Say (*qul*), 'How can you argue with us about God when He is our Lord and your Lord? Our deeds belong to us, and yours to you. We devote ourselves entirely to Him. Or are you saying that Abraham, Ishmael, Isaac, Jacob, and the Tribes were Jews or Christians?'

Abraham's belief (and lineage) and gentileness are linked. The point is that one can be a monotheist and submitter to God even if one comes from a gentile background, perhaps also that gentile Believer-ness is better than being Jewish or Christian; it is not obviously clear if these identities are even reconcilable with being a Believer. Nevertheless, God is the Lord of gentile Believers as well as the Lord of Jews and Christians.

The concept of "one community" (*umma wāḥida*),[152] so central (and positive) in the "Constitution," is articulated differently in the Medinan Qur'ān:

> 2:213: Humankind was one community (*umma wāḥida*), and God sent prophets to bring good news and warning, and with them He sent the Book with the truth, to judge between people in their disagreements. It was only those to whom it was given who disagreed about it after clear signs had come to them, because of rivalry between them. So by His leave God guided the Believers to the truth they had differed about: God guides whoever He will to a straight path.

> 5:46–48: We sent Jesus, son of Mary, in their footsteps, to confirm the Torah that had been sent before him. And We gave him the Gospel with guidance, light, and confirmation of the Torah already revealed – a guide and lesson for those who take heed of God. So let the followers of the Gospel judge according to what God has sent down in it. Those who do not judge according to what God has revealed are lawbreakers. We sent to you [sing.] the Book with the truth, confirming the Books that came before it, and with authority over them: so judge between them according to what God has sent down. Do not follow their whims, which deviate from the truth that has come to you. We have assigned a law[153] and a path to each of you. If God had so willed, He would have made you one community (*umma wāḥida*), but He wanted to test you through that which He has given you, so race

---

the context of anti-Christian attacks, but if one looks closely, it can be seen that trinitarian or incarnational views are very rarely ascribed to Christians in the Qur'ān.

152 For the concept of *umma* in the Quran, see Denny 1975. For a polemical (and disorderly) attack against "the Orientalists" and their interpretations of the word *umma*, see Faruqi 2005. The article's discussion on identity (Faruqi 2005, 17–34) is not convincing.

153 In Arabic *shirʿa*, which could simply mean "a path," synonymous with the word *minhāj* that comes after it.

to do good: you will all return to God and He will make clear to you the matters you differed about.

Q 2:213 argues that humankind was one community in some sort of primeval phase. This status was disrupted by people disagreeing with divine Scripture(s). One community is a paradise lost. However, the verse leaves it somewhat open whether this state could be regained: "God guided the Believers to the truth they had differed about: God guides whoever He will to a straight path." Perhaps the idea is that humankind started as one community, then fell into disarray, and now has the opportunity to become one again through the Believer identity (if they are willing to embrace that group affiliation).

Verses 5:46–49 form a long and interesting passage that features the same notion of one community as a lost state but one that can plausibly be regained, at least through resurrection and in the afterlife. However, it is significant in another way too: it proffers a vision of a recategorized community that accepts subordinate identities in a manner very similar to the "Constitution of Medina" and the Meccan Qur'anic suras. According to the passage, God has "assigned a law and a path to each of you." Although the revelation of the Prophet has the final say, the "followers of the Gospel" can retain their own law (which here seems to include the Torah).[154] Hence, the common ingroup identity model is not completely abandoned in the Medinan phase either.

Can we suggest a development, in the Medinan phase, in the concept of *umma wāḥida*?[155] Perhaps, if a) the "Constitution" really hails from the first years of the *hijra* and b) the Nöldekean dating of the Qur'anic suras is anything to go by. If so, it appears that the "one community" expression was used as an ingroup label at the very beginning of the Medinan polity but was abandoned toward the end of the Prophet's life, perhaps because the treaty (that is, the "Constitution") fell apart. After this, the *umma wāḥida* began to be portrayed in the Qur'ān as a past and, possibly, future reality. Humankind was one community but then they fell into disagreement about the revelation (Quran 2:213). However,

---

154 For the possibility that Jewish Christians (that is, followers of Jesus who observed the Jewish law) were present in the Qur'ān and the Qur'anic milieu, see Crone 2015–2016.

155 For this, see at more length Denny 1975, 45–52. The concept also appears in some Meccan passages. Denny's (1975, 49) analysis is similar to mine: "If the Nöldeke chronology is accepted, there is already in M[ecca] II a strong sense of a true *ummah* being a religious community ideally unified in its beliefs. In this period, too, the idea of scripture(s) is prominent, a notion which was very important for Muhammad, scripture being proof of God's having given special guidance for some of his peoples. In M[ecca] II and M[edina] the disunity of mankind as an *ummah* appears as a mystery willed by God and at the same time a consequence of human waywardness."

the redeemed unity of humankind is possible, at least through eschatology and the afterlife (5:48).

Decategorization in the Qur'ān

I argued in the previous section that while the Meccan suras especially engage in recategorization and accept subgroup identities, the Medinan suras are less welcoming to subordinate affiliations. Instead of recategorization, we could speak of decategorization in some instances of the communication of the Medinan suras. That is, although the categories of "Jews," "Christians," and "People of the Book" are somewhat suspect, people affiliated with them can still be approached on an individual basis and accepted as part of the community of the Believers. Group stereotypes, which develop in the Medinan phase of the revelation, are not always transferred to the individuals among the People of the Book.

The decategorized nature of the last judgement and the hereafter is a common message in the Qur'ān. For example, verse 2:123 reads: "Beware of a Day when no soul can stand in for another. No compensation will be accepted from it, nor intercession be of use to it, nor will anyone be helped." This is close to what the "Constitution" also stipulates toward the end of the text, noting that everyone is responsible for their deeds and the possible repercussions of those deeds (*lā yaksibu kāsib illā ʿalā nafsihi*).

As concerns specifically the People of the Book, there are examples in the Medinan suras of a decategorized approach to them. Hence, while the majority of the Jews, Christians, and People of the Book do not wish to join the community of the Believers, some do, and they should be accepted as group members. One can cite for example Q 3:110, 113–115:

> You [the Believers] are the best community singled out for people: you order what is right, forbid what is wrong, and believe in God. If the People of the Book had also believed, it would have been better for them. For although some of them do believe, most of them are lawbreakers . . . But they are not all alike. There is among the People of the Book an upright group (*umma qāʾima*), who recite God's revelations during the night, who bow down in worship, who believe in God and the Last Day, who order what is right and forbid what is wrong, who are quick to do good deeds. These people are among the righteous and they will not be denied [the reward] for whatever good deeds they do: God knows exactly who is conscious of Him.

Thus, while the broader category of the People of the Book consists of mostly transgressors, a subgroup of them is to be counted as Believers. Q 3:199–200, which are the last two verses of the sura, have the same rather positive outlook on *some* among the People of the Book:

> [199] Some of the People of the Book believe in God, in what has been sent down to you and in what was sent down to them: humbling themselves before God, they would never sell God's revelation for a small price. These people will have their rewards with their Lord: God is swift in reckoning. [200] You who believe, be steadfast, more steadfast than others; be ready; always be mindful of God, so that you may prosper.

If these two verses should be read in unison (and not suppose that there is a sort of break in the discourse), then some among the People of the Book are semi-identified as "you who believe," who are the addressed group of verse 200.

It has been argued in section 4 that we can trace a development concerning recategorization in the Qur'ān if we follow the Nöldekean chronology. While the Meccan suras appear to accept Jews and Christians among the Believers and view no tension between the identities, the Medinan stratum categorizes the social situation differently, articulating that the categories "Believer" and "Jew" or "Christian" cannot function in complete harmony. In other words, the recategorization process (such as we can attest in the Meccan Qur'ān and the "Constitution") is mostly abandoned in Medinan suras. However, decategorization or approaching individuals outside their group affiliations still functions, although negative stereotypes are projected to the People of the Book as a category at this stage of Qur'anic communication.[156]

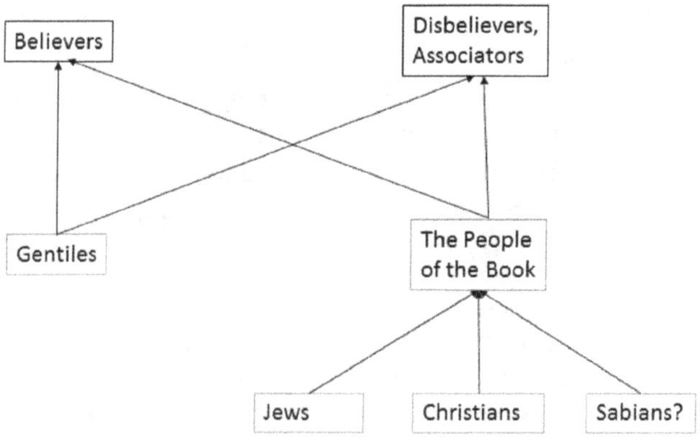

Figure 2: The social categorization into in- and outgroup in the Qur'ān. The People of the Book are not explicitly defined by the Qur'ān, so it is unclear if the Sabians are to be understood as part of that categorization.

156 On Qur'anic polemics from the point of view of the social identity approach, see in more detail Lindstedt, forthcoming a.

Conclusion

I have suggested that the two significant shortcomings in many of the earlier commentaries on the "Constitution of Medina" have been, first, the tendency to read the text in comparison with the biography of the Prophet and other historiographical literature rather than the Qur'ān; if we accept the text as contemporary with the Prophet, then the only other text that goes back to that period is the Qur'ān. Second, most earlier discussions have suffered from simplistic conceptions of social identity. Thus, there has been ample discussion on whether or not the Jews mentioned in the text are "genuine Jews" or "Arab converts."[157] This shows a rather unsophisticated understanding of ethnic and religious identities. To quote Ehala, identities "are not what we are, but what we possess."[158] Identities are socially constituted and structured. Individuals possess many different group affiliations that are switched on and off depending on the social situation. I suspect that, unfortunately, the scholars treating the "Constitution" have often brought their own social categorizations (and biases) into their discussions.

It has been argued in this study that the "Constitution of Medina," which I view as an authentic document of the Prophet Muḥammad, recategorized the Jews and the gentile Believers of Medina as belonging to the common ingroup identity as "one community." The members of the new identity could retain their tribal and religious identities as subordinate ones. What is more, their identity as Medinan is addressed and embraced in the document. What arises from the text is a group that strives for mutual assistance against a common enemy.

Above, it was suggested that "it is by becoming emblematic of a new sense of 'us' that leaders acquire their transformational power" (Haslam, Reicher, and Platow 2011, 89). The Prophet Muḥammad, in drafting the "Constitution," recategorized the gentile and Jewish Believers of Medina as "one community" and depicted himself as its leader. This recategorization act was one of the ways in which he came to power in Medina. Interestingly, although the concept of one community is very positive in the text of the "Constitution," in the Qur'ān it functions as a reference to a sort of paradise lost.

Social categorizations are in a constant state of flux. Hence, the value of recategorization can in some cases be only temporal.[159] The Medinan stratum of

157 See, for example, Lecker 2004, 47–87, for references to earlier scholarly literature.
158 Ehala 2018, 4.
159 Gaertner and Dovidio 2000, 144.

the Qur'ān articulates a sense of a community that is not very accepting of subgroup identities. Individual Jews and Christians, it appears, can be Believers but their identities as Jews and Christians are somewhat suspicious. However, it is hardly the case that the Qur'ān contains a development in which the People of the Book are first embraced and then, toward the end of the Prophet's career, rejected. Passages such as Q 3:110–115 show that we must envision a much more zigzagging trajectory (if we can reconstruct one at all): while 3:110–112 for the most part attack and repudiate the People of the Book, verses 3:113–115 (a later interpolation) embrace and accept them. If we believe in the Nöldekean chronology (still a valid starting point for analysis), the latest strata of the Qur'ān contain both positive and negative depictions of the Jews and Christians. Verses 2:62 and 5:69 promise the salvific reward to them. Perhaps instead of saying that the earlier Qur'anic strata accepted the Jews and Christians while the later ones repudiated them (which is simply untrue), one could say that the earlier Qur'anic passages are more accepting of subgroup identities.

I should make one thing clear. The above-mentioned theorization and reading of the "Constitution" do not mean that I wish to say that the Prophet Muḥammad was aware of modern social psychology.[160] What I intend instead is that we (as modern observers) can conceptualize the discourse and categorization of the "Constitution" and the Qur'ān with the help of social psychology and, more specifically, the social identity approach, which has endeavored to show something universal about the human condition, social categorization, and intergroup behavior.

Moreover, great leaders have always been aware of the need to call for superordinate identities if they wish to join together mutually averse or hostile groups, despite the fact that they were not familiar with or aware of concepts such as "superordinate identity" or "recategorization." Take Nelson Mandela, for instance. He emphasized that the whites have a role to play in post-apartheid South Africa although they had been the oppressor before.[161] This helped undo the systemic white supremacy of apartheid without larger conflicts that might have ensued

160 This is a common criticism that I have heard against employing modern theories or concepts in the analysis of ancient texts or lived realities. But it is criticism that is based on a misconception. The social identity approach is very apt for analyzing the pre-modern world, since basic human cognition has not changed drastically, if at all, in the last few thousand years. Pre-modern people, like us, engaged in social categorization, as is immediately clear from the texts quoted in this study. What is more, in all likelihood people in the late antique Near East saw groups and groupness as more significant to their lives than we do in our modern, more individualistic, times.

161 Haslam, Reicher, and Platow 2011, 32, 89.

otherwise. Martin Luther King represents another example.[162] In his famous "I have a dream" speech, he addresses the particular plight of the African American community but, at the same time, refers to the "destiny" shared by the blacks, whites, and others:

> The marvelous new militancy which has engulfed the Negro community must not lead us to a distrust of all white people, for many of our white brothers, as evidenced by their presence here today, have come to realize that their destiny is tied up with our destiny. And they have come to realize that their freedom is inextricably bound to our freedom. We cannot walk alone.
>
> . . .
>
> And so even though we face the difficulties of today and tomorrow, I still have a dream. It is a dream deeply rooted in the American dream.
> I have a dream that one day this nation will rise up and live out the true meaning of its creed: "We hold these truths to be self-evident, that all men are created equal."
>
> . . .
>
> And when this happens, and when we allow freedom ring, when we let it ring from every village and every hamlet, from every state and every city, we will be able to speed up that day when *all* of God's children, black men and white men, Jews and Gentiles, Protestants and Catholics, will be able to join hands and sing in the words of the old Negro spiritual:
>
> *Free at last! Free at last!*
> *Thank God Almighty, we are free at last!*[163]

In King's speech, although subgroup identities are spelled out and the particular oppression faced by the African Americans is articulated, at the end of the day all people are united in the supercategory of "God's children," created as equals.

162 Haslam, Reicher, and Platow 2011, 57, 131, 162.
163 I quote from https://www.americanrhetoric.com/speeches/mlkihaveadream.htm

Bibliography

Abū ʿUbayd. 1986. *Kitāb al-Amwāl*. Edited by Shākir Dhiʾb Fayyāḍ. 3 vols. Riadh: Markaz al-Malik Fayṣal li-l-Buḥūth wa-l-Dirāsāt al-Islāmiyya.

Al Raffie, Dina. 2013. "Social Identity Theory for Investigating Islamic Extremism in the Diaspora." *Journal of Strategic Security* 6:67–91.

Arjomand, Saïd Amir. 2009. "The Constitution of Medina: A Sociolegal Interpretation of Muhammad's Acts of Foundation of the *Umma*." *International Journal of Middle East Studies* 41/4:555–575.

Assmann, Jan. 1992. *Das kulturelle Gedächtnis: Schrift, Erinnerung und politische Identität in frühen Hochkulturen*. Munich: C.H. Beck.

Al-Azmeh, Aziz. 2014. *The Emergence of Islam in Late Antiquity: Allāh and His People*. Cambridge: Cambridge University Press.

Baker, Coleman A. 2011. *Identity, Memory, and Narrative in Early Christianity: Peter, Paul, and Recategorization in the Book of Acts*. Eugene, OR: Pickwick.

Bashear, Suliman. 1997. *Arabs and Others in Early Islam*. Princeton: Darwin Press.

Barentsen, Jack. 2011. *Emerging Leadership in the Pauline Mission: A Social Identity Perspective on Local Leadership Development in Corinth and Ephesus*. Eugene, OR: Pickwick.

Al-Bayhaqī. 2011. *Al-Sunan al-Kabīr*. Edited by al-Turkī. Cairo, n.p.

Bowersock, Glen W. 2013. *The Throne of Adulis: Red Sea Wars on the Eve of Islam*. Oxford: Oxford University Press.

Bowersock, Glen W. 2017. *The Crucible of Islam*. Cambridge, MA: Harvard University Press.

Burke, Peter J., and Jan E. Stets. 2009. *Identity Theory*. Oxford: Oxford University Press.

Cole, Juan. 2020. "Infidel or Paganus? The Polysemy of *kafara* in the Quran." *Journal of the American Oriental Society* 140/3:615–636.

Crone, Patricia. 1980. *Slaves on Horses: The Evolution of the Islamic Polity*. Cambridge: Cambridge University Press.

Crone, Patricia. 2015–2016. "Jewish Christianity and the Qurʾān (parts I–II)." *Journal of Near Eastern Studies* 74/2:225–253 and 75/1:1–21.

Crone, Patricia. 2016. *The Qurʾānic Pagans and Related Matters*. Leiden: Brill.

Crone, Patricia, and Martin Hinds. 1986. *God's Caliph: Religious Authority in the First Centuries of Islam*. Cambridge: Cambridge University Press.

Denny, Frederick M. 1975. "The Meaning of *Ummah* in the Qurʾān." *History of Religions* 15: 34–70.

Denny, Frederick M. 1977. "*Ummah* in the Constitution of Medina." *Journal of Near Eastern Studies* 36:39–47.

Donner, Fred M. 1998. *Narratives of Islamic Origins: The Beginnings of Islamic Historical Writing*. Princeton: Darwin Press.

Donner, Fred M. 2002–2003. "From Believers to Muslims: Confessional Self-Identity in the Early Islamic Community." *Al-Abhath* 50–51:9–53.

Donner, Fred M. 2010. *Muḥammad and the Believers: At the Origins of Islam*. Cambridge, MA: Harvard University Press.

Donner, Fred M. 2018. "Talking about Islam's Origins." *Bulletin of the School of Oriental and African Studies* 81:1–23.

Dost, Suleyman. 2017. *An Arabian Qur'ān: Towards a Theory of Peninsular Origins*. Dissertation at the University of Chicago.
Ehala, Martin. 2018. *Signs of Identity: The Anatomy of Belonging*. London & New York: Routledge.
El-Badawi, Emran I. 2014. *The Qur'ān and the Aramaic Gospel Traditions*. London & New York: Routledge.
Esler, Philip F. 2003. *Conflict and Identity in Romans: The Social Settings of Paul's Letters*. Minneapolis: Fortress Press.
Faruqi, Maysam J. Al. 2005. "*Umma*: The Orientalists and the Qur'ānic Concept of Identity." *Journal of Islamic Studies* 16:1–34.
Gaertner, Samuel L., and John F. Dovidio. 2000. *Reducing Intergroup Bias: The Common Ingroup Identity Model*. New York: Psychology Press.
Gil, M. "The Constitution of Medina: a reconsideration." *Israel Oriental Studies* 4 (1974): 44–65.
Görke, Andreas, and Gregor Schoeler. 2008. *Die ältesten Berichte über das Leben Muḥammads: Das Korpus ʿUrwa ibn al-Zubair*. Princeton: Darwin Press.
Griffith, Sydney H. 2008. *The Church in the Shadow of the Mosque: Christians and Muslims in the World of Islam*. Princeton: Princeton University Press.
Hakola, Raimo. 2005. *Identity Matters: John, the Jews and Jewishness*. Leiden: Brill.
Hakola, Raimo. 2015. *Reconsidering Johannine Christianity: A Social Identity Approach*. New York: Routledge.
Haslam, S. Alexander. 2004. *Psychology in Organizations: The Social Identity Approach*. London: SAGE Publications.
Haslam, S. Alexander, Steve D. Reicher, and Michael J. Platow. 2011. *The New Psychology of Leadership: Identity, Influence and Power*. New York: Routledge.
Heimola, Minna. 2011. *Christian Identity in the Gospel of Philip*. Helsinki: Finnish Exegetical Society.
Herriot, Peter. 2014. *Religious Fundamentalism and Social Identity*. London: Routledge.
Hoyland, Robert G. 1997. *Seeing Islam as Others Saw It: A Survey and Evaluation of Christian, Jewish and Zoroastrian Writings on Early Islam*. Princeton: Darwin Press.
Humphreys, R. Stephen. 1991. *Islamic History: A Framework for Inquiry*. Princeton: Princeton University Press.
Ibn Hishām. *Al-Sīra al-Nabawiyya*. 1858–1860. Edited by. Ferdinand Wüstenfeld. 2 vols. Göttingen: Dieterichsche Universitäts Buchhandlung.
Ibn Hishām. *Al-Sīra al-Nabawiyya*. 2004. Edited by al-Saqqā. 2 vols. Damascus: Dār al-Khayr.
Jacobson, Jessica. 2006. *Islam in Transition: Religion and Identity among British Pakistani Youth*. London: Routledge.
Johnson, Scott Fitzgerald, ed. 2012. *The Oxford Handbook of Late Antiquity*. Oxford: Oxford University Press.
Jokiranta, Jutta. 2012. *Social Identity and Sectarianism in the Qumran Movement*. Leiden: Brill.
Jones, Edward E., George C. Wood, and George A. Quattrone. 1981. "Perceived Variability of Personal Characteristics in In-Groups and Out-Groups: The Role of Knowledge and Evaluation." *Personality and Social Psychology Bulletin* 7:523–528.
Lane, E. W. 1863–1893. *Arabic-English Lexicon*. Eight volumes with continuous pagination. London: Williams and Norgate.

Lau, Peter H. W. 2011. *Identity and Ethics in the Book of Ruth: A Social Identity Approach*. Berlin: De Gruyter.

Lebedeva, Nadezhda M. and Alexander N. Tatarko. 2008. "Ethnic Identity, Group status and Type of Settlement as Predictors of Ethnic Intolerance." *Psychology in Russia: State of the Art* 1:102–119.

Lecker, Michael. 1995. *Muslims, Jews & Pagans: Studies on Early Islamic Medina*. Leiden: Brill.

Lecker, Michael. 2004. *The "Constitution of Medina."* Princeton: Darwin Press.

Levy-Rubin, Milka. 2011. *Non-Muslims in the Early Islamic Empire: From Surrender to Coexistence*. Cambridge: Cambridge University Press.

Lindstedt, Ilkka. 2015. "*Muhājirūn* as a Name for the First/Seventh Century Muslims." *Journal of Near Eastern Studies* 74:67–73.

Lindstedt, Ilkka. 2019. "Who Is in, Who Is out? Early Muslim Identity through Epigraphy and Theory." *Jerusalem Studies in Arabic and Islam* 46:147–246.

Lindstedt, Ilkka. Forthcoming a. "Religious Groups in the Quran." In *Common Ground and Diversity in Early Christian Thought and Study: Essays in Memory of Heikki Räisänen*, edited by Raimo Hakola, Outi Lehtipuu, and Nina Nikki. Tübingen: Mohr Siebeck.

Lindstedt, Ilkka. Forthcoming b. "Religious Warfare and Martyrdom in Arabic Graffiti (70s–110s AH/690s–730s CE)." In *Scripts and Scripture: Writing and Religion in Arabia, 500–700 CE*, edited by Fred Donner. Chicago: Oriental Institute.

Marohl, Matthew J. 2008. *Faithfulness and the Purpose of Hebrews: A Social Identity Approach*. Eugene, OR: Pickwick.

Marranci, Gabriele. 2009. *Understanding Muslim Identity: Rethinking Fundamentalism*. New York: Palgrave.

Mortensen, Mette B. 2018. *A Contribution to Qur'ānic Studies: Toward a Definition of Piety and Asceticism in the Qur'ān*. PhD diss., Aarhus University.

Moss, Sigrun M. 2017. "Identity Hierarchy within the Sudanese Superordinate Identity: Political Leadership Promoting and Demoting Subordinate Groups." *Political Psychology* 38/6:925–942.

Munt, Harry. 2014. *The Holy City of Medina: Sacred Space in Early Islamic Arabia*. Cambridge: Cambridge University Press.

Nevo, Yehuda D., and Judith Koren. 2003. *Crossroads to Islam: The Origins of the Arab Religion and the Arab State*. Amherst, NY: Prometheus Books.

Nikki, Nina. 2018. *Opponents and Identity in Philippians*. Leiden: Brill.

Nöldeke, Theodor. 1909–1938. *Geschichte des Qorâns*. 2nd ed. 2 vols. Leipzig: Dieterichsche Verlagsbuchhandlung. Translated by W. H. Behn as *The History of the Qur'ān*, with the original pagination in the margins. Leiden: Brill 2013.

Pely, Doron. 2016. *Muslim/Arab Mediation and Conflict Resolution: Understanding Sulha*. London: Routledge.

Penn, Michael P. 2015. *Envisioning Islam: Syriac Christians and the Early Muslim World*. Philadelphia: University of Pennsylvania Press.

Pohl, Walter, Clemens Gantner, and Richard Payne, eds. 2016. *Visions of Community in the Post-Roman World: The West, Byzantium and the Islamic World, 300–1100*. London: Routledge.

Putten, Marijn van. 2019. "'The Grace of God' as Evidence for a Written Uthmanic Archetype: The Importance of Shared Orthographic Idiosyncrasies." *Bulletin of the School of Oriental and African Studies* 82:271–288.

Retsö, Jan. 2003. *The Arabs in Antiquity: Their History from the Assyrians to the Umayyads*. London: Routledge.
Rubin, Uri. 1985. "The 'Constitution of Medina': Some Notes." *Studia Islamica* 62:5–23.
Serjeant, Robert B. 1964. "The Constitution of Medina." *Islamic Quarterly* 8:3–16.
Serjeant, Robert B. 1978. "The *Sunnah Jâmiʿah* Pacts with the Yathrib Jews, and the *Taḥrîm* of Yathrib: Analysis and Translation of the Documents Comprised in the So-Called 'Constitution of Medina.'" *Bulletin of the School of Oriental and African Studies* 41:1–42.
Shaddel, Mehdy. 2016. "Qurʾānic *Ummī*: Genealogy, Ethnicity, and the Foundation of a New Community." *Jerusalem Studies in Arabic and Islam* 43:1–60.
Sherif, Muzafer et al. 1954. *Experimental Study of Positive and Negative Intergroup Attitudes Between Experimentally Produced Groups: Robbers Cave Experiment*. Norman, OK: University of Oklahoma Press.
Sherif, M. et al. 1961. *Intergroup Conflict and Cooperation: The Robbers Cave Experiment*. Norman, OK: University of Oklahoma Press.
Shoemaker, Stephen J. 2011. *The Death of a Prophet: The End of Muhammad's Life and the Beginnings of Islam*. Philadelphia: University of Pennsylvania Press.
Sinai, Nicolai. 2010. "The Qurʾan as Process." In *The Qurʾān in Context: Historical and Literary Investigations into the Qurʾānic Milieu*, edited by Angelika Neuwirth, Nicolai Sinai, and Michael Marx, 407–439. Leiden: Brill.
Sinai, Nicolai. 2017. *The Qur'an: A Historical-Critical Introduction*. Edinburgh: Edinburgh University Press.
Stargel, Linda M. 2018. *The Construction of Exodus Identity in Ancient Israel: A Social Identity Approach*. Eugene, OR: Pickwick.
Stark Rodney. 1996. "Why Religious Movements Succeed or Fail: A Revised General Model." *Journal of Contemporary Religion* 11:133–146.
Stets, Jan E., and Peter J. Burke. 2000. "Identity Theory and Social Identity Theory." *Social Psychology Quarterly* 63/3:224–237.
Tajfel, Henri. 1978. *Differentiation Between Social Groups: Studies in the Social Psychology of Intergroup Relations*. London: Academic Press.
Tajfel, Henri. 1981. *Human Groups and Social Categories: Studies in Social Psychology*. Cambridge: Cambridge University Press.
Turner, John C. 1975. "Social Comparison and Social Identity: Some Prospects for Intergroup Behavior." *European Journal of Social Psychology* 5:5–34.
Turner, John C. 1982. "Towards a Cognitive Redefinition of the Social Group." In *Social Identity and Intergroup Relations*, edited by Henri Tajfel, 15–40. Cambridge: Cambridge University Press.
Verkuyten, Maykel. 2007. "Religious Group Identification and Inter-Religious Relations: A Study Among Turkish-Dutch Muslims." *Group Processes & Intergroup Relations* 10: 341–357.
Watt, W. Montgomery. 1956. *Muhammad at Medina*. Oxford: Oxford University Press.
Webb, Peter. 2016. *Imagining the Arabs: Arab identity and the rise of Islam*. Edinburgh: Edinburgh University Press.
Wellhausen, Julius. 1889. *Skizzen und Vorarbeiten*. Vol. 4. Berlin: Reimer.
Wensinck, Arent J. 1928. *Mohammed en de Joden te Medina*. Leiden: Brill.

Wensinck, Arent J., 1936–1969. *Concordance et indices de la tradition musulmane*. In collaboration with J. P. Mensing and J. Brugman. Leiden: Brill.
Al-Zabīdī, Muḥammad Murtaḍa al-Ḥusaynī. 1975–2001. *Tāj al-ʿArūs*. Edited by ʿAbd al-Sattār Aḥmad Farrāj & al. 40 vols. Kuwait: Maktabat Ḥukūmat al-Kuwayt.
Zellentin, Holger. 2018. "Judeo-Christian Legal Culture and the Qur'an: The Case of Ritual Slaughter and the Consumption of Animal Blood." In *Jewish-Christianity and the Origins of Islam*, edited by Francisco del Río Sánchez, 117–159. Turnhout: Brepols Publishers.

List of Contributors

Mette Bjerregaard Mortensen, Université libre de Bruxelles

Gilles Courtieu, Université Jean Moulin Lyon 3

Julien Decharneux, Université libre de Bruxelles

Guillaume Dye, Université libre de Bruxelles

Valentina A. Grasso, Institute for the Study of the Ancient World

Aaron W. Hughes, University of Rochester

Manfred Kropp, University of Mainz

Ilkka J. Lindstedt, University of Helsinki

Marcus Milwright, University of Victoria

Isaac W. Oliver, Bradley University

Carlos A. Segovia, Saint Louis University – Madrid Campus

Stephen Shoemaker, University of Oregon

Boaz Shoshan, University Ben Gurion of the Negev

Jillian Stinchcomb, Brandeis University

Tommaso Tesei, Duke Kunshan University

Peter von Sivers, University of Utah

https://doi.org/10.1515/9783110675498-015

Printed in the USA
CPSIA information can be obtained
at www.ICGtesting.com
LVHW040815021023
759712LV00007B/211

9 783111 258720